This book is dedicated to the memory of two women who taught me more about election campaigning than anyone else. Phyllis Reeve and Audrey Barker were Conservative Party agents in Norwich South and Norwich North in the 1980s and prior to that had served all over the country. Neither suffered fools gladly. They tolerated candidates merely as 'legal necessities' but had hearts of gold and were always generous with their time and well-meant advice to twenty-something political upstarts like me. I treasure the memories of working with them.

BOOKS BY IAIN DALE

The Honourable Ladies

The Prime Ministers

The Presidents

Kings and Queens

The Dictators

On This Day in Politics

Why Can't We All Just Get Along

BRITISH GENERAL ELECTION CAMPAIGNS
1830–2019

THE 50 GENERAL ELECTION CAMPAIGNS
THAT SHAPED OUR MODERN POLITICS

IAIN DALE

First published in Great Britain in 2024 by
Biteback Publishing Ltd, London
Selection and editorial apparatus copyright © Iain Dale 2024
Copyright in the individual essays resides with the named authors.

Iain Dale has asserted his right under the Copyright, Designs and Patents Act 1988
to be identified as the editor of this work.

All rights reserved. No part of this publication may be reproduced, stored in a retrieval system or transmitted, in any form or by any means, without the publisher's prior permission in writing.

This book is sold subject to the condition that it shall not, by way of trade or otherwise, be lent, resold, hired out or otherwise circulated without the publisher's prior consent in any form of binding or cover other than that in which it is published and without a similar condition, including this condition, being imposed on the subsequent purchaser.

Every reasonable effort has been made to trace copyright holders of material reproduced in this book, but if any have been inadvertently overlooked the publisher would be glad to hear from them.

ISBN 978-1-78590-811-8

10 9 8 7 6 5 4 3 2 1

A CIP catalogue record for this book is available from the British Library.

Set in Adobe Garamond Pro

Printed and bound in Great Britain by
CPI Group (UK) Ltd, Croydon CR0 4YY

CONTENTS

Preface – *Iain Dale*   vii
Seats, Electorate, Candidates and Turnout 1830–2019   xiii
MPs Elected for the Three Main Parties 1830–2019   xv
Vote Share by Party 1830–2019   xvii

1. 1830 – *Gordon Pentland*   1
2. 1831 – *Connor Hand*   9
3. 1832 – *Alun Evans*   21
4. 1835 – *Edward Young*   27
5. 1837 – *Nan Sloane*   39
6. 1841 – *Richard A. Gaunt*   45
7. 1847 – *David Walsh*   55
8. 1852 – *Nigel Fletcher*   61
9. 1857 – *Alex Noonan*   73
10. 1859 – *Matthew Cole*   81
11. 1865 – *Charles Pitt*   91
12. 1868 – *Ian Cawood*   97
13. 1874 – *Robert Buckland*   107
14. 1880 – *Kathryn Rix*   119
15. 1885 – *Luke Blaxill*   133
16. 1886 – *Robert Saunders*   145
17. 1892 – *Leo McKinstry*   159
18. 1895 – *Pippa Catterall*   173
19. 1900 – *Mark Fox*   187
20. 1906 – *Duncan Brack*   197
21. 1910 (January) – *David Laws*   217

22.	1910 (December) – *David Laws*	239
23.	1918 – *Damian Collins*	255
24.	1922 – *Jack Brown*	269
25.	1923 – *Alistair Lexden*	287
26.	1924 – *Robert Waller*	299
27.	1929 – *Rosie Campbell*	315
28.	1931 – *Andrew Thorpe*	323
29.	1935 – *John Barnes*	345
30.	1945 – *Julia Langdon*	365
31.	1950 – *Sue Cameron*	387
32.	1951 – *Vernon Bogdanor*	397
33.	1955 – *Philip Norton*	411
34.	1959 – *Iain Dale*	423
35.	1964 – *Nick Thomas-Symonds*	435
36.	1966 – *Peter Kellner*	443
37.	1970 – *Michael Crick*	457
38.	1974 (February) – *Lewis Baston*	475
39.	1974 (October) – *Michael McManus*	493
40.	1979 – *Simon Heffer*	509
41.	1983 – *Peter Snow*	529
42.	1987 – *Simon Burns*	543
43.	1992 – *Peter Riddell*	553
44.	1997 – *John Curtice*	567
45.	2001 – *Alia Middleton*	591
46.	2005 – *Robert Ford*	601
47.	2010 – *Adam Boulton*	617
48.	2015 – *Philip Cowley*	637
49.	2017 – *Stephen Parkinson*	653
50.	2019 – *Tim Bale*	671

How Candidates Campaign in Modern-Day General Elections 691
– *Sofia Collignon and Wolfgang Rüdig*

PREFACE

Given the title of this book, you might imagine it is a book entirely aimed at political geeks. You'd be wrong. Elections are at the heart of our democracy and to understand the history of Britain over the past two hundred years, you have to understand the electoral politics of the country.

I love elections. I love them so much that I've played most of the roles integral to the running and coverage of elections. I've delivered election leaflets, put up posterboards, canvassed voters, been an election agent, a candidate's aide, a campaign manager, been a (losing) candidate, 'knocked up' voters on polling day, driven voters to the polling station, attended four general election counts, hosted general election debates, interviewed election candidates and hosted four eight-hour general election night shows on LBC Radio. The only thing I haven't done is ever won an election. A minor omission.

General election nights are the equivalent of Christmas Day for lovers of the electoral process. Everyone becomes an armchair expert and thinks they are ideally placed to predict the result. And that's the great thing about democracy: you rarely can. Yes, we have more tools nowadays to enable us to make an educated guess, but in the end, no one can be 100 per cent sure. In 1970, when I was seven years old, Ted Heath defied the pollsters and won the June election with a majority of thirty. Harold Wilson suddenly became 'Yesterday's Man'. I remember being at the count in Norwich North in 1992 when David Amess's victory in Basildon heralded a majority of twenty-one for John Major. I remember this election well, as it was the only election I had put a bet on. I'd never been in a betting shop before, so I asked my friend Tim to put the bet on for me. I bet £20 at 80/1 on a Conservative majority of between twenty and twenty-two. I was set to win £1,600, which was a lot of money in 1992. What a shame Tim forgot to put the bet on.

In that same election, our candidate, the sitting MP for Norwich North Patrick Thompson, took part in an election phone-in on BBC Radio Norfolk. He returned to the campaign office full of beans. 'I think that went really well,' he exclaimed. His entire campaign team fell about laughing, given that every question which made it to air had emanated from our office. Patrick was horrified. In a similar vein, we put out a leaflet on red paper headlined 'A Few Things About Your Labour Candidate You Ought to Know'. It was the sort of thing Liberal Democrat campaigns put out routinely. We felt very naughty, as the leaflet sought to explain the Labour candidate's extreme left-wing past. We put out only fifty of the leaflets as we knew it would be picked up by the local paper. Sure enough, it made the front page of the *Eastern Evening News* two days before polling day. We won by 266 votes. The election agent, Deborah Slattery, and I maintain that the leaflet made all the difference. The Labour candidate later told me that he knew he was toast the moment he saw it. Patrick Thompson, to this day, reckons his majority would have been far bigger had we not indulged in the 'black arts'. We will never know.

Politics, particularly electoral politics, is inevitably very tribal. The joy of canvassing sessions is that talking to voters always results in having funny anecdotes. I remember in 1983 talking to a voter on a council estate in Norwich who said, 'I've half a mind to vote SDP.' I instantly shot back: 'Half a mind is all you need, I suppose.' Cue the door being slammed in my face. The same thing happened a few minutes later when I knocked on another door and the voter bemoaned her lot in life and how it was all Margaret Thatcher's fault. 'I haven't got a penny left at the end of the week,' she said. My fellow canvasser put his head round the door and said, 'Nice new TV and video recorder you've got there.' I put her down as a possible.

My favourite anecdote from the campaign in which I was an actual parliamentary candidate in 2005 will stay with me for ever. We were canvassing on an estate in the North Norfolk village of Trimingham. A lady opened the door, dressed in shorts and a vest, showing off her bare arms replete with Meatloaf tattoos. I started my spiel and mentioned a policy with which she enthusiastically agreed. 'You took the words right out of my mouth,' she roared. I instantly replied: 'It must have been while you were kissing me.' We both broke down in fits of giggles and she said, 'Don't worry, you've got my vote.' If only they were all that easy.

On election night, I turned up at Cromer High School to witness the votes being counted. I knew I was going to lose but initially candidatitis set in and I saw the piles of votes with a X by my name showing me in the lead. It didn't last. I turned a Lib Dem majority of 483 into a Lib Dem majority of 10,600. It was devastating, but it was one of the proudest moments of my life when I delivered a gracious concession speech, which I got through without breaking down in tears. It was only when Norman Lamb, my gracious opponent, put his arm around my shoulders that a few tears slipped out. Perhaps only a fellow candidate who has been through it before could understand. After the count, I had to go to a party at the house of one of our party workers. I got in the passenger seat alongside my partner and spent the short journey howling my eyes out.

The next day's *Eastern Daily Press* had a picture of me at the count watching a portable TV, ostensibly being comforted by a clown, one of the fringe candidates. In this case, a picture did not tell a thousand stories. We had just seen Justine Greening winning the marginal seat of Putney.

And that was my last election, apart from a couple of canvassing sessions in 2010 to help two friends who were standing. Since then, I have covered four election campaigns as a broadcaster, interviewing candidates and co-hosting each election night show on LBC Radio.

I tell you all this to explain why I decided to edit a book on the past fifty general election campaigns going back to 1830. It's the fourth book in this series, which started in 2020 with *The Prime Ministers*, followed by *The Presidents* in 2021 and *Kings and Queens* in 2023. In each book, I have matched a group of contributors with a Prime

Minister, President, monarch or, in this case, general election campaign. I thought this book might be more difficult than the others to find contributors for, especially for the nineteenth-century elections, but I needn't have worried.

Their remit was simple. To explain the background to the election, who the main political personalities were, which issues dominated the campaign, the campaigning methods, the key moments from the campaign and to interpret the results and analyse their short- and long-term implications.

Obviously, some elections were more significant than others. James Callaghan observed in 1979 that there are some times in political history when the tides change and there's nothing anyone can do to hold back the tide of political change. In 1979, Margaret Thatcher was the beneficiary. In 1906, it was Sir Henry Campbell-Bannerman. In 1945, it was Clement Attlee. Of the fifty elections covered in this book, I estimate that there are fewer than ten that would fall into this category. We know quite a lot about all of those, but the delight of this book is that you learn about elections that you didn't realise had even happened. Each election is unique and in even the most obscure election there are delights to behold.

Despite there being fifty essays, most of them are written in a similar style. The exception is the essay for 2017, which is written by Stephen (now Lord) Parkinson, who at the time the election was called was Theresa May's political secretary. I think it is one of the standout essays in the book, even if it is very different from the rest. In these pages, Sir Simon Burns writes about the 1987 election, in which he won his Chelmsford seat for the first time. Harold Wilson's biographer Nick Thomas-Symonds writes about his first victory in 1964, while a former Lib Dem Cabinet minister writes about the two crucial 1910 elections. Historians include Simon Heffer, writing about the Thatcher victory of 1979, Leo McKinstry on 1892, Lord Lexden on 1923, Andrew Thorpe on 1931 (on which he has written an entire book), Sir Vernon Bogdanor on 1951 and Lord Norton on 1955. We have a stellar range of political academics and journalists including

PREFACE

Peter Snow (1983), Sir John Curtice (1997), Sir Peter Riddell (1992), Adam Boulton (2010), Philip Cowley (2015), Julia Langdon (1945), Sue Cameron (1950), Michael Crick (1970) and Tim Bale (2019).

Every effort has been made to ensure that the electoral statistics presented in this book are accurate. This has been done by relying on a number of excellent sources, notably Colin Rallings and Michael Thrasher's 1832–2010 edition of Fred Craig's *British Electoral Facts*, Brian Walker's *Parliamentary Election Results in Ireland, 1918–1992*, the House of Commons Library and House of Commons Information Office along with Election Demon (archived), the Electoral Commission and Wikipedia. In the case of disagreement between sources, where possible this book has sided with the statistics presented by the House of Commons Library, which are often in line with *British Electoral Facts*.

For clarity, for the elections up to 1950, total votes cast and party vote counts have been adjusted, drawing on the work of the Election Demon website, in an attempt to deal with the presence of multi-member constituencies where individual votes voted more than once. Prior to 1885, due to a lack of sources, such adjustments are not possible, meaning that the figures are a true 'total votes cast' number not a 'voted' figure. Beyond 1950, after the abolition of multi-member constituencies, the 'voted' figure simply represents the number of people who voted, meaning that the turnout percentage and the electorate and voted figures largely align, which may not be the case for the elections before 1950.

Equally, there is disagreement within this book's sources on whether the Northern Ireland Labour Party (NI Labour) should be kept as part of the national Labour Party vote. In line with the works of Craig, this book has decided to provide a separate NI Labour total but include it within total Labour figures. For vote share percentages given at the start of each chapter for elections after the 1970s, all percentages provided for Northern Ireland parties relate to vote share in Northern Ireland.

Given the number of electoral statistics presented in this book, it is inevitable that some errors may have crept in. If you notice any, please don't hesitate to get in touch at iain@iaindale.com so they may be corrected in future editions.

I'd like to thank my researcher Alex Puffette for his hard work in compiling the electoral statistics at the beginning of each chapter, and for his wise counsel.

Iain Dale
Tunbridge Wells
January 2024

SEATS, ELECTORATE, CANDIDATES AND TURNOUT 1830-2019

Election	Seats	Electorate	Number of candidates	Turnout
1830*	–	–	–	–
1831*	–	–	–	–
1832	658	812,938	1,037	70.4
1835	658	845,776	945	65
1837	658	1,004,664	994	63.6
1841	658	1,017,379	916	63.4
1847	656	1,106,514	879	53.4
1852	654	1,184,689	953	57.9
1857	654	1,235,530	878	58.9
1859	654	1,271,900	860	63.7
1865	658	1,350,404	922	62.5
1868	658	2,484,713	1,039	68.5
1874	652	2,753,142	1,080	66.4
1880	652	3,040,050	1,103	72.2
1885	670	5,708,030	1,338	81.2
1886	670	5,708,030	1,115	74.2
1892	670	6,160,541	1,303	77.4
1895	670	6,330,519	1,180	78.4
1900	670	6,730,935	1,102	75.1
1906	670	7,264,608	1,273	83.2

* Figures are not available for elections that occurred before the Great Reform Act of 1832.

BRITISH GENERAL ELECTION CAMPAIGNS 1830–2019

1910 (January)	670	7,694,741	1,315	86.8
1910 (December)	670	7,709,981	1,191	81.6
1918	707	21,392,322	1,623	57.2
1922	615	20,874,456	1,441	73
1923	615	21,283,061	1,446	71.1
1924	615	21,730,988	1,428	77
1929	615	28,854,748	1,730	76.3
1931	615	29,952,361	1,292	76.4
1935	615	31,374,449	1,348	71.1
1945	640	33,240,391	1,683	72.8
1950	625	34,412,255	1,868	83.9
1951	625	34,919,331	1,376	82.6
1955	630	34,852,179	1,409	76.8
1959	630	35,397,304	1,536	78.7
1964	630	35,894,054	1,757	77.1
1966	630	35,957,245	1,707	75.8
1970	630	39,342,013	1,837	72
1974 (February)	635	39,753,863	2,135	78.8
1974 (October)	635	40,072,970	2,252	72.8
1979	635	41,095,649	2,576	76
1983	650	42,192,999	2,578	72.7
1987	650	43,180,753	2,325	75.3
1992	651	43,275,316	2,949	77.7
1997	659	43,846,152	3,724	71.4
2001	659	44,403,238	3,319	59.4
2005	646	44,245,939	3,554	61.4
2010	650	45,597,461	4,150	65.1
2015	650	46,354,197	3,971	66.2
2017	650	46,836,533	3,304	68.8
2019	650	47,568,611	3,220	67.3

MPS ELECTED FOR THE THREE MAIN PARTIES 1830-2019

Election	Conservative	Labour	Liberal*
1830†	–	–	–
1831†	–	–	–
1832	175	–	441
1835	273	–	385
1837	314	–	344
1841	367	–	271
1847	325	–	292
1852	330	–	324
1857	264	–	377
1859	298	–	356
1865	289	–	369
1868	271	–	387
1874	350	–	242
1880	237	–	352
1885	247	–	319
1886	393	–	192
1892	314	–	272
1895	411	–	177
1900	402	2	183
1906	157	29	399

* Note that before the 1850s, 'Liberals' were 'Whigs'.
† Figures are not available for elections that occurred before the Great Reform Act of 1832.

xv

1910 (January)	272	40	274
1910 (December)	271	42	272
1918	379	57	127
1922	344	142	62
1923	258	191	158
1924	412	151	40
1929	260	287	59
1931	470	46	35
1935	387	154	33
1945	197	393	12
1950	298	315	9
1951	321	295	6
1955	345	277	6
1959	365	258	6
1964	304	317	9
1966	253	364	12
1970	330	288	6
1974 (February)	297	301	14
1974 (October)	277	319	13
1979	339	269	11
1983	397	209	23*
1987	376	229	22*
1992	336	271	20
1997	165	419	46
2001	166	412	52
2005	198	355	62
2010	306	258	57
2015	330	232	8
2017	317	262	12
2019	365	202	11

* Note in 1983 and 1987, the figure for the Liberals includes the SDP too, as they fought as the SDP–Liberal Alliance.

VOTE SHARE BY PARTY 1830-2019

Election	Conservative	Liberal*	Labour	Green	UKIP/Brexit
1830†	–	–	–	–	–
1831†	–	–	–	–	–
1832	29.2	67	–	–	–
1835	42.7	57.2	–	–	–
1837	47.6	52.4	–	–	–
1841	51.6	46.2	–	–	–
1847	42.6	53.8	–	–	–
1852	41.9	57.9	–	–	–
1857	33.5	64.8	–	–	–
1859	34.2	65.8	–	–	–
1865	40.5	59.5	–	–	–
1868	38.7	61.2	–	–	–
1874	44.3	52	–	–	–
1880	42.5	54.7	–	–	–
1885	43	47.7	–	–	–
1886	51.4	45.1	–	–	–
1892	47	45.4	–	–	–
1895	49.3	45.6	1	–	–
1900	50.2	45.1	1.3	–	–
1906	43.4	48.9	4.8	–	–
1910 (January)	46.8	43.5	7	–	–

* Note that before the 1850s, 'Liberals' were 'Whigs'.
† Figures are not available for elections that occurred before the Great Reform Act of 1832.

1910 (December)	46.6	44.2	6.4	–	–
1918	38.4	12.6	20.8	–	–
1922	38.5	18.9	29.7	–	–
1923	38	29.7	30.7	–	–
1924	46.8	17.8	33.3	–	–
1929	38.1	23.6	37.1	–	–
1931	55	3.7	29.4	–	–
1935	47.8	3.7	38	–	–
1945	36.2	9	47.7	–	–
1950	43.4	9.1	46.1	–	–
1951	48	2.6	48.8	–	–
1955	49.7	2.7	46.4	–	–
1959	49.4	5.9	43.8	–	–
1964	43.4	11.2	44.1	–	–
1966	41.9	8.5	48	–	–
1970	46.4	7.5	43.1	–	–
1974 (February)	37.9	19.3	37.2	–	–
1974 (October)	35.8	18.3	39.2	–	–
1979	43.9	13.8	36.9	–	–
1983	42.4	25.4*	27.6	–	–
1987	42.2	22.6*	30.8	0.3	–
1992	41.9	17.8	34.4	0.5	–
1997	30.7	16.8	43.2	0.2	0.3
2001	31.6	18.3	40.7	0.6	1.5
2005	32.4	22	35.2	1	2.2
2010	36.1	23	29	0.9	3.1
2015	36.8	7.9	30.4	3.8	12.6
2017	42.3	7.4	40	1.6	1.8
2019	43.6	11.6	32.1	2.6	2

* Note in 1983 and 1987, the figure for the Liberals includes the SDP too, as they fought as the SDP–Liberal Alliance.

1

1830

GORDON PENTLAND

Dissolution: 24 July 1830
Polling day: 29 July–1 September 1830
Seats contested: 658
Prime Minister on polling day: Duke of Wellington
Main party leaders: Tory – Duke of Wellington; Whig – Marquess of Lansdowne; Ultra-Tories – Sir Edward Knatchbull

Party performance:

Party	Seats won
Tory	250
Whig	196
Ultra-Tories	60

Result: Hung parliament

The election of 1830 was triggered by the demise of the Crown. This ensured that it had a long prelude. The unofficial starting gun was fired by the death of George IV on 26 June and the formal dissolution followed on 24 July. For months previously, however, ministers and courtiers had been observing the king's rapid and undignified decline in the knowledge that death must be followed swiftly by dissolution and election. By the spring of 1830, spates of debilitating breathlessness and heroic quantities of laudanum had become the norm for a grotesquely obese king surrounded by a bevy of doctors and apothecaries. His Prime Minister, the Duke of Wellington, offered a slightly horrified account of the king's breakfast in April:

> What do you think of His breakfast yesterday morning for an Invalid? A Pigeon and Beek Steak Pie, of which he ate two Pigeons and three Beefsteaks, Three parts of a Bottle of Moselle, a Glass of dry Champagne, two Glasses of Port and a Glass of Brandy! He had taken Laudanum the night before, again before this breakfast, again last night and again this Morning!

With this approach to the most important meal of the day, it is some surprise that the king survived until June.

The 1830 election was not an especially welcome development for the exhausted and somewhat threadbare ministry of the Duke of Wellington. His was the latest manifestation of the broadly Tory governments which had been in power, with only a very brief hiatus, since Pitt the Younger's first government in the 1780s. By 1830, the sorrows for Wellington's ministry were coming in battalions. Most existentially, its constituency of support both inside and outside of Parliament had been ruinously split by the resolution of an explosive issue which had been carefully contained since the beginning of the century. The question of whether Catholics in Great Britain and, more critically, in Ireland should be granted equivalent civil and religious liberties to their Protestant countrymen was a running sore in the Tory Party after the Anglo-Irish Union. It had been resolved by Wellington in favour of the Catholics in 1829 in a series of measures which came to be known collectively as Catholic emancipation. But this was no act of far-seeing and liberal statesmanship. Rather it was a tactical withdrawal, the prudent act of a military commander who diagnosed his own defeat at the hands of the superhuman organisational and electoral efforts of Daniel O'Connell and the Catholic Association. And it was passed in the teeth of fierce and militant opposition from large parts of the populations of England and Scotland, significant sections of both Houses of Parliament and the king himself.

As a result, diehard Tories or 'ultras' – those who viewed emancipation as a sell-out to Rome and European-style absolutism and a betrayal of British liberties – vilified Wellington and his Home Secretary and chief in the Commons, Robert Peel, as 'rats'. The resulting fractures, compounding those which had developed in the instability since the political retirement of Lord Liverpool in 1827 (following a stroke), made for a complex and fluid political situation. Spiteful and passionate recriminations by electors and candidates over Catholic emancipation and urgent cries of the 'Church in Danger' became animating issues of the election in many places. The great moral and political questions involved in Catholic emancipation also rolled the pitch for other liberal causes. The huge and long-running question of the abolition of slavery within the British Empire tracked the Catholic issue and played a prominent role in many constituencies across the UK.

With the bitter feuds birthed by the Catholic question still well and truly live, even if ministers had enjoyed sovereignty over the timing of the election, they almost certainly would not have selected 1830. They were denuded of front-rank debating talent in the House of Commons, where Peel held the floor almost alone. Even in the House of Lords, the Duke of Wellington, an indifferent speaker, faced an increasingly fractious and hostile upper chamber. One of Wellington's close correspondents, Dorothea von Lieven, the wife of the Russian ambassador, was unequivocal before the king's death: 'the position of the government is precarious.'

One of the earliest and most explosive contributions to the election was a short anonymous pamphlet which generated a considerable discussion in the press. In 'The Country without a Government', Henry Brougham and George Agar-Ellis, two prominent sitting Whig MPs, made efforts to fix some of the themes for elections up and down the country. Alongside discussion of distress and foreign instability, slavery and the looming issue of reform, they foregrounded the overriding question of the Duke of Wellington's personality. He was presented as a kind of dictator, the 'sole minister of this great country', lacking support in the country at large or from able politicians and surrounded by the fawning 'parasites of both sexes'.

The character and desirability of the hero of Waterloo as chief minister formed another focal point for electoral contests and a rich vein for satirists. Brougham carried this formidable range of themes and his bruising attacks on Wellington into his own contest, which was in many ways the cause célèbre of the entire general election: the county contest for Yorkshire. In the effort to secure two Whig members for this populous county, a bellwether of popular opinion since the eighteenth century, Brougham's celebrated efforts saw him overcome substantial obstacles to claim a widely reported victory. He became the first non-Yorkshireman elected for the county since the reign of Queen Elizabeth I and the first lawyer since the government of Oliver Cromwell.

In the event, Wellington's character as minister played second fiddle to a much more prominent issue. In both Houses of Parliament, the animating theme that looked forwards from the Catholic question and did most to shape the electoral contest was that of distress. The year 1830 had begun with fierce debates about the nature and scale of economic and social challenges across the United Kingdom. These were clearest in the English countryside, from where a majority of the population still sought to eke a living, in several key manufacturing centres and in Ireland. Debate in Parliament revolved around the severity of distress but particularly around its scale. Ministers' efforts in the King's Speech to present it as localised and partial were met with incredulity by MPs and journalists, who decried the 'all-pervading and intolerable distress' and scoffed at ministers' misrepresentation of it. Such gloomy prognoses were borne out in the aftermath of the election. The autumn of 1830 witnessed the spectacular eruption of the Swing Riots in large swathes of the English countryside.

Consequently, many of the big talking points driving the election revolved around different solutions for this distress. A change of ministry was one potential source of relief. In addressing electors' demands, candidates broached ideas of retrenchment and economy and essayed a range of fiscal and monetary reforms. An increasingly popular solution had been prefigured by the foundation of the

Birmingham Political Union in December 1829 and by an ultra-Tory motion calling for parliamentary reform in February. How, people asked, could governing institutions lacking in legitimacy and riddled with corruption be expected to pass legislation which protected the established church or dealt effectually with vaulting economic and social tensions? From the beginning of the year, then, parliamentary reform was on the political agenda in a more substantial way than it had been for more than a decade, and it played a prominent role in many electoral contests.

Reform as an issue was oxygenated substantially by international developments during the back end of the election. In Paris, the end of July saw the *Trois Glorieuses*, a rapid revolution which overthrew the returned Bourbons and Charles X and installed the House of Orléans in the shape of Louis Philippe as a new constitutional monarchy. Revolution in France – as it had before and would again – acted as an incubator for action elsewhere and set rolling a revolutionary wave across much of Europe over the following year. Its impact was, to the great relief of British ministers, too late in most cases to influence electoral results. It did a great deal, however, to supercharge both the latter stages of the elections in large urban constituencies and the sense of what was at stake in interpreting the election's outcomes.

Overall, the fluidity of the political situation made it challenging to present results. These required a degree of interpretation and rival efforts at political divination came up with widely divergent numbers. The Treasury put a brave face on it and touted an estimated overall gain of twenty seats. A triumphant Brougham, newly minted MP for Yorkshire, went (anonymously) into battle again with another pamphlet, 'The Result of the General Election'. He scoffed at ministers' numbers and reversed them. Wellington had lost *at least* twenty seats following the dissolution, in an electoral context where a new reign and Treasury resources might be expected to boost a sitting government: 'did ever Minister yet sustain such a signal defeat?' Brougham was much closer to the mark. When Wellington, Peel and other ministers faced Parliament in October, in the context of ongoing European revolutions, domestic distress and the eruption of the worst and most prolonged rural violence England had ever seen, they did so with diminished support.

As the penultimate 'unreformed' election, 1830 displayed many of the most prominent features of Hanoverian electoral culture. The corruption exemplified by East India money and memorably satirised in John Galt's novel *The Member* by the figure of Archibald Jobbry, the MP for Frailtown, was fully on show. Indeed, there was widespread belief during the long lead-in to the election that, with the renewal of the East India Company's charter on the table, even more money flooded the race for parliamentary seats and substantially raised their market price in 1830. The carnivalesque, booze-fuelled and frequently violent dimensions immortalised in William Hogarth's *Humours of an Election* series of paintings were alive and kicking. At Bristol, for example, the agitation round the slavery issue coupled with a large itinerant population of sailors and ubiquitous alcohol had predictable outcomes. Rival election mobs sallied forth from the pubs *The Rummer* and *The Bush* and made a no-go zone of the city centre on 22 July, when there were twenty-seven hospitalisations.

There was no straight line between the election of 1830 and the momentous measures of parliamentary reform passed two years later. While reform was *an* issue in the 1830 election, it was far from being *the* issue and jostled for space with many others, most prominently 'bread and butter' questions of material and economic distress. Several aspects of the election, however, did point forwards to the dramatic political context of the next two years. The first was that the election saw a qualified rejection not of a party but of the kind of deferential politics which had marked many electoral contests over the previous century. Men of modest incomes and propertied farmers holding votes used these to reject the traditional electoral authority and influence of the ruling aristocratic elites. Whigs as well as Tories were concerned at this apparent sign of a challenge not to a single party but to the political system *as a whole*. Second, the result presaged what was as close as it was possible to get to an electoral landslide under the Hanoverian electoral system at the last 'unreformed' election in

1831. Finally, the widespread airing of arguments that a whole range of challenges and problems – economic distress, religious disqualifications, inequitable taxation and the holding of other humans as property – were soluble *only* if fundamental changes were made to the way in which MPs were elected foreshadowed the debates that would engross the United Kingdom over the next two years.

Gordon Pentland is professor of history at Monash University in Melbourne. He has published widely on the political and cultural history of Britain since the late eighteenth century. He is currently working on a new book, *The Reform Crisis, 1830–1832*.

2

1831

CONNOR HAND

Dissolution: 23 April 1831
Polling day: 28 April–1 June 1831
Seats contested: 658
Total electorate: Approx. 516,000
Prime Minister on polling day: Earl Grey
Main party leaders: Whig – Earl Grey; Tory – Duke of Wellington

Party performance:

Party	Seats won
Whig	370
Tory	234

Result: Whig majority of 135 seats

The idea of a 'single-issue' election is arguably one of the most overused concepts in our political imagination. All too often, the term proves reductive, ignoring or understating a host of issues at the heart of a campaign. The election of 1831, called a mere 222 days after the conclusion of the 1830 contest, is perhaps an exception. This was, for the Tory Party, an electoral annihilation comparable to the defeats of 1906, 1945 and 1997, where the issue of parliamentary reform dominated proceedings across the country. Yet this chapter will demonstrate that this was a remarkable election which went beyond the size of the Whigs' victory. Fundamentally, it showed that in an age marred by societal change, early industrialisation and upheaval on the Continent, constitutional change could be delivered without revolution. In the process, it also helped to redefine the party political system; local issues, which were typically the chief concern of those eligible to vote, were transcended in a way that had seldom been seen before, laying the ground for the formalised system of political parties we know today.

While the Duke of Wellington had been returned as Prime Minister after the vote of 1830, his victory was, ultimately, pyrrhic. Less than a month after parliament had reconvened, he was ousted, as instability and factionalism within Tory ranks proved insurmountable. The party faced a schism over the decision to grant Catholic emancipation two years prior, which was seen by Ultra-Tories as a betrayal by Wellington and his Home Secretary, Sir Robert Peel. This led to the government collapsing after unexpectedly losing a vote on the civil list on 15 November 1830. Stung by a band of newly elected Tory MPs, seventeen of whom voted in line with the opposition, the Iron Duke was defeated by 233 votes to 207 and tendered his resignation in the days that followed.

Succeeding Wellington was Charles Grey, the 2nd Earl Grey, who had by then been leading the Whigs in opposition for almost a quarter of a century. His ascendancy owed much to the death of King George IV, who never looked favourably upon Grey, and the accession of William IV, whose greater sympathy towards the Whig leader would prove essential to his premiership and eventual electoral success. Though he had long advocated parliamentary reform, it is striking that in the month he became Prime Minister, Grey underestimated the hunger for political change that would propel him to a landslide victory. During the King's Speech, for example, Grey's contemporaries were struck by his 'slight and almost slighting manner' when addressing the question of reform, with John Roebuck arguing that he had presented it 'as a sort of decoration in an opposition speech ... because no one believed it to be of import to party success'.

Towards the end of 1830, however, violent disturbances across Britain ensured reform would be at the kernel of Grey's government's activity. Sparked by agricultural unrest owing to the mechanisation of farming and stagnant wages, the 'Captain Swing' riots saw bands of unemployed labourers smash threshing machines throughout Sussex, Hampshire, Berkshire and Wiltshire. Anarchy was widespread and went beyond the agricultural sector, as textile workers in Lancashire, Staffordshire and the Midlands became increasingly militant under the leadership of John Doherty. By late 1830, his National Association for the Protection of Labour, an early attempt at a national trade union, had amassed 100,000 members in these counties, highlighting the impact of nascent industrialisation and the problems that accompanied it.

This disharmony, along with the aftershocks of the overthrow of Charles X in France, revolution in Belgium and insurrectionary movements in Italy and Spain, crystallised fears among the landed classes about the possibility of revolution in Britain. Attesting to this is an account from December 1830's edition of the *Gentleman's Magazine*, a publication aimed at aristocratic readers, which depicted a scene of near-hysteria in Cambridge following the razing of a local farm, including the sale of '1,500 bludgeons ... within two days'. According to the diarist Charles Greville, widespread disturbances left London resembling the 'capital of a country desolated by cruel war or foreign invasion'. This was unprecedented in his lifetime and Greville was stunned by the atmosphere of 'general agitation' – agitation driven by the issues of reform and economic strife.

Suppressing disturbances dominated the opening weeks of Grey's ministry. A syncretic blend of Whigs and Canningites, which included three future Tory Prime Ministers, Grey's Cabinet swiftly dispensed with violent protests: 200 rioters were initially sentenced to death and around 500 transported to Australia for their involvement. As an unabashed aristocrat, and with a Cabinet that owned more land than any that preceded it, Grey searched desperately for an antidote to revolution. He believed that the answer lay in redistributing political influence to regions that were growing in economic importance.

The First Reform Bill sought to address these iniquities and was introduced to the House of Commons by Lord John Russell on 1 March

1831. Industrialising areas such as Leeds, Manchester, Greenwich and Sheffield were to be allocated two MPs each in a major shake-up of the electoral map. Constituencies with tiny electorates – some with as few as seven voters in the case of Old Sarum in Wiltshire – would be totally disenfranchised to offset this expansion. The 'rotten boroughs', often controlled by a single powerful patron, were targeted ruthlessly, while constituencies with an electorate of between 2,000 and 4,000 would also see their allocations halved from two MPs to one. Though it was to formally disenfranchise women for the first time, the act also advocated extending eligibility to people with property amounting to over £10, granting the vote to a sizeable portion of the urban middle class, whose integration into the political establishment was believed to be an important bulwark against revolutionary currents.

While a number of the prerequisites of a modern democratic system were omitted, such as the secret ballot and universal suffrage, many were struck by the bill's ambition. The Baltic noblewoman Princess Lieven, a confidant of Grey, noted the sense of bemusement in Parliament with the 'Whigs ... astonished, the Radicals delighted [and] the Tories indignant'. The magnitude of the plan, and potential imminence of a general election, was clear to all. Indeed, on the day the bill was unveiled, *The Times* carried an editorial declaring that a 'grand crisis' had been reached, which would culminate in either 'reform or a dissolution within a few days or hours!'

As such, although it would be a number of weeks before an election was actually called, the electoral battlelines had been drawn and the parties sharpened their messaging around the definitive issue of the day. Though Wellington continued to lead the Tories, it was Peel who cautioned against the bill's adoption at the dispatch box, arguing that it would lead to continual constitutional concessions: 'others will outbid you', he said, and would offer 'votes and powers to a million men ... quot[ing] your precedent'. Conscious of parliamentary arithmetic, and the perception of the country at large, the Whigs were at pains to stress the permanence of their proposals – a silver bullet to eradicate electoral evils – a dogged insistence that earned Russell the nickname 'Finality Jack'. Resisting pressures from radicals such as

Henry Hunt to leave the door open to further reform down the line proved critical as the bill passed its second reading by the barest of margins – 302 to 301. In the words of the Whig MP T. B. Macaulay, the moment was equivalent to 'seeing Caesar stabbed in the Senate House … The jaw of Peel fell; and the face of [the anti-reform MP Horace] Twiss was as the face of a damned soul; and [former Tory Chancellor John] Herries looked like Judas taking his neck-cloth off for the last operation.'

With Parliament fractured and tensions evoking biblical comparisons, it is unsurprising that the bill's progress faltered. General Isaac Gascoyne soon introduced a wrecking amendment to preserve the number of seats allocated to England, which was set to fall disproportionately as part of the efforts to uproot rotten boroughs. 'The spoliation of English representation', as Gascoyne described it, raised the spectre of a greater presence of Irish Catholic MPs. Anxieties surrounding the 'enemy within', who would serve to undermine Protestant institutions and the constitution, secured the adoption of the amendment, with bleary-eyed MPs passing it at 4.30 a.m. on 20 April (299 to 291). Parliament was now ungovernable for the Whigs; it was necessary to 'have it the other way', as the First Lord of the Admiralty, Sir James Graham, lamented.

Although Sir James's comments indicate the Whigs' confidence, securing a contest would ultimately require the king's consent. This was by no means guaranteed. Perceived instability in Ireland, augmented by an impending trial for sedition of Daniel O'Connell, the leading light in the campaign for Catholic emancipation, threatened to unravel attempts to call an election. Though O'Connell's trial was cleverly kiboshed by government lawyers, who argued he was being tried under a lapsed statute, the fear of turmoil weighed heavily on the mind of William IV. On top of this, the king was perceptive enough to realise that a contest would essentially be a referendum on a single issue, and therefore mark a significant constitutional departure from previous elections; he agonised over Grey's request for dissolution and, in spite of these reservations, acquiesced after twenty-four hours of deliberation.

As the king prepared to dissolve Parliament on 22 April, the atmosphere inside the chambers was nothing short of febrile. Sensing an election could be imminent, Peel had started to modify his language, indicating he would be potentially open to a version of reform – just not in the immediate future. Now, though, he launched into a stinging attack against both the Whigs and the king. In an invective halted by the Black Rod just as he 'seemed to fall into fit', as the Whig J. C. Hobhouse described it, Peel contended that the Crown had 'ceased to be an object of interest' if it was to be so easily swayed by the government. Unbridled hysteria swept through the Tory benches, with scenes drawing comparisons with the French Revolution's *Serment du Jeu de Paume*; Sir Henry Hardinge, a former Tory minister and ally of Peel, expressed his belief that gunshots would soon ring around the capital. Tory fears were captured most vividly by the eyewitness George Villiers, whose words were recounted by Greville:

> As [I] looked at the King upon the throne with the crown loose upon his head, and the tall grim figure of Lord Grey close beside him with the sword of state in his hand, it was as if the King had got his Executioner by his side and the whole picture was strikingly typical of his and our future destinies.

Less than a week separated these dramatic parliamentary scenes and polls opening. On the face of it, incidents of disorder across the breadth of Britain could have played into the Tories' electoral strategy. Violence, invariably inflicted by groups sympathetic to reform, was reported in areas such as Aberdeenshire, Newcastle-under-Lyme, Pembrokeshire, Wigan and Warwick. Clashes were arguably at their most intense in Lanarkshire and Rye in Sussex, where freemen backing anti-reformers faced a level of physical intimidation which almost resulted in one of them being 'trampled to death'. Elsewhere, aristocratic property was targeted. Upon dissolution, supporters of reform were encouraged to light their houses at night, leaving the unilluminated properties of anti-reformers to be attacked by mobs which, according to accounts from Edinburgh, reached 10,000 in number.

Stones crashed through the Duke of Wellington's London home, the crowd seemingly unconcerned with the personal tragedy that had struck the Tory leader days before, his wife's passing so recent that her body was yet to be removed from the property.

As the ballot commenced, it is perhaps of little wonder that the man who defeated Napoleon was increasingly fatalistic about both his party's electoral chances and the inevitability of revolution. The latter presented a challenge for the Whigs. Given they were still navigating an unreformed system, it was crucial that this perception was not shared by the electorate, namely the landed classes whose approval was essential to secure victory. Consequently, their rhetoric appealed to the restoration of calm throughout the nation. Sentiments such as 'Liberty and Public Order' were deployed in county seats like Norwich, where the notorious anti-reformer Sir Charles Wetherell was defeated. In Liverpool, meanwhile, newspapers favourable to reform consciously highlighted the respectability of the Whigs' hustings and meetings, culminating in the symbolically significant defeat of General Gascoyne, whose wrecking amendment had triggered the election.

The Whigs' ability to communicate this message was aided significantly by the king's presence at the dissolution of Parliament. Initially, William IV was disinclined to attend in person, owing to his concerns over the constitutional precedent the election would set and potential tumult in Ireland. However, Tories in both Houses committed a major tactical error by attempting to move against dissolution. Enraged at this effort to override his prerogative, the king's previous reluctance swiftly dissipated, and he demanded to be taken to Parliament with such urgency that he would settle for a hackney coach if the royal stables were not ready. Undoubtedly, his attendance conferred extra legitimacy on the reform movement, as evidenced by an editorial in *The Times*, which went so far as to call for a monument to King William IV in recognition of his contribution to the cause. The momentum this injected into the Whigs' campaign was encapsulated by Princess Lieven, who observed that 'the moment that the country saw that the King lent himself to the measure ... there was no way of raising a cry against Reform'. This point was not lost on the Tories, with Hardinge conceding a week into polling that 'the reform mania ... is not to be overcome at this crisis when a k[ing] heads the mob or blindly submits to the dictates of his ministers'. Whig candidates across the land urged the public to cast votes in favour of the 'Two Bills' – reform and William – which helped to reassure patrons that their interests were served by backing Grey's party.

That said, while some wealthy landowners offered reform their full-throated support, it was clear to strategists within the party that it would be necessary to be pragmatic in dealing with certain patrons; for this election at least, this meant compromising on their ambition to reduce corruption and ensure electoral integrity. Indeed, this was apparent from the very start of the campaign. Barely twenty-four hours after the election was called, a meeting was arranged at Brooks's Club, a gentleman's establishment in London often frequented by the party's leading lights. In attendance was J. C. Hobhouse, who recalled that over £15,000 – approximately £1.25 million in today's money – had already been collected through donations and subscriptions, a substantial chunk of which was dedicated to 'procuring seats for some good men'. Many patrons sensed a final opportunity to exploit the existing system, for example Lord Yarborough, who demanded a minimum of £4,000 for his seats on the Isle of Wight. As Hobhouse noted, '[though] this appeared somewhat in contradiction to the principles on which we put forward our political pretensions ... we were obliged to fight our opponents with their own weapons, no other mode of warfare would have had the slightest chance of success'.

Other boroughmongers sought not to profiteer as they were implacably opposed to reform and resolved to fight the bill through their nominations. Their resistance, however, was often futile. Many previously powerful patrons – including the Duke of Newcastle in Nottinghamshire, Lord Lonsdale (Cumberland and Westmorland) and the Duke of Beaufort (Gloucestershire) – witnessed the rejection of their anti-reform candidates.

The results for the Tories were therefore shaping up to be about as disastrous as was possible in an unreformed Parliament. Of the English MPs the party returned, 84 per cent represented seats facing disenfranchisement or restructuring, putting them in considerable jeopardy for the 1832 election, following reform's implementation. The vast majority of these individuals also benefited from running unopposed. Where contests emerged, as was the case in roughly a third of the 380 constituencies, the success of the pro-reform movement was overwhelming. Moreover, owing to the ballot taking place over a number of weeks, victorious candidates would also travel to constituencies where the contest was still ongoing and participate in their hustings, as Devon MP Lord Ebrington did when he addressed the voters of Cornwall, providing reformers with further momentum. Consequently, only Shropshire returned two anti-reform candidates when a vote was forced, and pro-reform MPs won seventy-six of the eighty-two county seats overall.

Pockets of resistance occasionally sprouted, perhaps most ironically in university areas. On the Continent, such regions often served as the epicentre for arguments of political reform and even revolution, but these trends were bucked in the Oxford and Cambridge University seats, with the Foreign Secretary and future Prime Minister Lord Palmerston ejected from the latter owing to his support for the bill.

Despite the disappointment of Palmerston's ousting, though, much of the early impetus Grey's party had generated was sustained by the breadth of popular support the bill enjoyed. This found expression through mass gatherings. Even though the proportion of adult males eligible to vote would increase only from 14 per cent to 18 per cent, crowds flocked to counts in unprecedented numbers, particularly in industrialising areas. Dudley and Norwich provide a case in point. Over 20,000 people greeted pro-reform candidates in both these regions, a figure that was still several times the size of their respective electorates even after reform had been achieved, and a procession was organised for the victorious candidates in Bristol.

Nor was such enthusiasm confined to England. Around 50,000 gathered in Glasgow, with the number of contests in Scotland quadrupling and the proportion of pro-reform candidates returned to Parliament soaring to 50 per cent. Even in Breconshire, Wales, where the landed interest was believed to be unconquerable, a contest was forced in the midst of demonstrations in Merthyr which, in the days after the election, culminated in violent clashes in which the red flag was first used as a symbol of working-class resistance.

While the final contest did not conclude until 1 June, it was clear by early May that the Whigs were on course for a resounding victory, with commentators like Greville forecasting a majority of around 140 seats. Although the outcome was inevitable at this point, a crucial development from the 1831 election was best displayed during one of the few ballots that continued until the final days – namely the increasing levels of partisanship across the electorate.

Evidence of this trend had been building through the decline in the number of voters willing to split their ballots between candidates of the two main parties, but the specific circumstances surrounding the contest in Northamptonshire illustrated how local considerations and loyalties were transcended in a way few previously thought possible. Representation in the county had been divided between Grey's Chancellor, Lord Althorp, and the Tory William Cartwright since 1806. Althorp believed it served both men's interests not to force a contest because, irrespective of the national mood around the reform question, 'the two parties in the county were of equal strength'. He assured Cartwright that the Whigs would stand a second candidate only in retaliation to the Tories making the first move. Cries of treachery therefore swept through the constituency when, in spite of Althorp offering his word, the Whigs proposed Lord Milton to run alongside him. Such behaviour was judged to be so egregious that many believed Althorp should step aside to restore his honour. In spite of this controversy, and the conviction in Althorp's camp that 'another Whig candidate could not be proposed with any probability of success', Milton deposed Cartwright after close to two weeks of polling.

In other words, Northamptonshire demonstrated how the election of 1831 challenged the political orthodoxy of the time. Where previously local factors and candidates proved decisive, the electorate had now been polarised over a single issue. This development, alongside the implementation of the Great Reform Act, would have long-term implications. Most notably, it would result in what the historian Jonathan Clark has described as a 'new age of manifestos, platforms and ever-widening appeals' in British politics, a trend reflected in Peel's Tamworth Manifesto three years later and, indeed, in contests throughout this book.

Beyond this, the election had two more enduring consequences. Firstly, it established the precedent that constitutional reform could be achieved through parliamentary means. Far from representing 'finality', as the Whigs argued, this principle helped deliver the reforms of 1867, 1884 and 1918, all of which had significant ramifications for future UK elections. Secondly, this poll showed how parliamentary deadlock on a critical constitutional issue could be unlocked through the calling of a snap poll, an idea with which the 2019 voters will be familiar.

The most immediate implication of the Whigs' victory, though, was the resounding mandate that they now had to implement reform. Though its exact size is disputed, owing to the more informal party structures in the early-to-mid nineteenth century, a reliable indicator of the size of their overall majority was the vote on the Second Reform Bill, which they clinched with a handsome margin of 136 votes. According to this measure, the Whigs gained approximately seventy seats: fifty-one in England, eight in Scotland, seven in Ireland and four in Wales. Wellington's party was crushed. There would still be battles in the Lords, but the Act's eventual passage resulted in an expanded electorate and a host of new constituencies when an election was called the following year – the third in a little over twenty-four months.

Connor Hand is a journalist and senior news-gathering producer at LBC Radio, working across numerous shows, including with Iain Dale in the evening, Nick Ferrari at breakfast and Carol Vorderman on Sundays.

3

1832

ALUN EVANS

Dissolution: 3 December 1832
Polling day: 10 December 1832–8 January 1833
Seats contested: 658
Total electorate / Total votes cast / Turnout: 812,938 (605,518 in contested seats) / 827,776 / 70.4 per cent
Candidates (total 1,037): Whig – 636; Tory – 350; Irish Repeal – 51
Prime Minister on polling day: Earl Grey
Main party leaders: Whig – Earl Grey; Tory – Duke of Wellington; Irish Repeal – Daniel O'Connell

Party performance:

Party	Votes	Percentage share	Seats
Whig	554,719	67	441
Tory	241,284	29.2	175
Irish Repeal	31,773	3.8	42

Result: Whig majority of 225 seats

Anybody today coming out of the Monument Metro Station in Newcastle cannot miss the column at the road junction there. But if they look at whom it commemorates, they may not realise the significance of the politician whose statue is on top of the monument. Grey's Monument was built in 1838 in honour of Earl Grey, the Whig Prime Minister from 1830 to 1834, and the man responsible for the passage of one of the greatest acts of constitutional reform in the United Kingdom – what became known as the Great Reform Act of 1832. The Act was the first to extend the suffrage (albeit only to men) and create a fairer system of parliamentary constituencies. That process of parliamentary reform eventually led to universal suffrage for all men and women over twenty-one in 1928, although that goal was not fully achieved until 1948 with the abolition of plural voting and the universities' seats. In 1969, the voting age was lowered to eighteen, thereby defining the scope of the current United Kingdom electorate.

Earl Grey began that process of electoral reform by steering the Third Reform Bill through the Houses of Parliament and then led his Whig government to victory in the subsequent 1832 general election – the first to be fought under the new and enlarged franchise.

The previous two general elections had been held in 1830 and 1831. The 1830 poll had been indecisive, resulting in what would now be termed a hung parliament, whereas the 1831 poll had produced a Whig landslide of 136 seats over the Tories. It therefore gave Grey a majority in the House of Commons supportive of his reform programme. The outcome of the 1832 general election cannot be fully comprehended without a prior analysis and understanding of the campaign during the spring and summer of 1832 that eventually led to the passage of the Reform Act (it only later acquired the title 'Great').

However, Grey was not in any traditional sense a radical. He came from an aristocratic Northumberland family and had something of a colourful life, fathering a child by Georgiana, the Duchess of Devonshire, when very young, but his family and he supported the child, who was raised by his parents. He went on to have fifteen other children with his wife, Mary.

Grey was aged sixty-six when he finally became Prime Minister. He had first entered Parliament in 1786, at the age of twenty-two, just three years before the French Revolution, the effects of which affected his thinking. He spent most of the next forty years in opposition. His support for electoral reform was not, though, based upon some vision of liberal progress but more as a means of avoiding revolution. As his biographer E. A. Smith commented, Grey supported reform within the context of 'the immediate concern he felt at the dangerous state of the country and the need to preserve the aristocratic system of government ... Reform was merely a part of this major purpose.'

The two aspects that Grey was concerned to change were, firstly, the very narrow size of the electorate and, secondly, the obvious unfairness of the 'rotten boroughs' – those with no or hardly any electors – and the lack of parliamentary representation in other areas. By the early 1830s, there were protests in many of the larger unrepresented new conurbations and demands from the middle classes for change. In 1830 and 1831, there had also been violent uprisings in some rural areas (the so-called Swing Riots) and revolution was once again in the air in Europe when, in 1830, the July Revolution led to the overthrow of the restored French monarchy. Grey was convinced that only reform could reduce or prevent the risk of a similar outcome in Britain.

The death of King George IV in 1830, an implacable opponent of Grey, removed one obstacle to Grey's ambitions and the Whig victory in the 1831 general election provided the springboard for Grey to introduce the bill to reform the franchise. It had two main elements. First, to rationalise the distribution of parliamentary seats by abolishing fifty-six rotten boroughs and creating 130 new parliamentary seats in sixty-seven new constituencies, especially in the growing towns and cities such as Birmingham and Manchester. Second, to expand the franchise, giving the vote to all male householders who paid a yearly rental of £10 or more, as well as to a number of middle-class property owners. However, the bill explicitly excluded women from the electoral register, even though some public commentators such as the philosopher Jeremy Bentham had urged it as long ago as 1819. The reform proposals were, in fact, fairly modest and far from radical – but they were, in Grey's judgement, what could be sufficient to fend off the risk of revolt or worse. There had been further rioting in northern towns and cities in late 1831 and early 1832, with people protesting about the lack of progress in Parliament, and it appeared to Grey that reform was both urgent and essential.

The Third Reform Bill passed easily through the House of

Commons with its massive Whig majority. However, it faced major opposition in the House of Lords. The Tory leader, the Duke of Wellington, was implacably opposed to the reform, arguing that there was nothing wrong with the existing system 'which answered all the good purpose of legislation ... to a greater degree than any legislature ever had answered in any country'. Grey told the new king, William IV, that if the Lords did not pass the bill, he would seek to create fifty or sixty new peers.

When the bill came to its second reading in the House of Lords on 14 April, Grey himself chose to wind up the debate with what observers called one of his finest speeches. He again alluded to the threat that, if the Lords did not pass the bill, he would create many more peers to force its passage through the Upper House. The threat worked and the bill received a majority of just nine in the House of Lords. Two months later, it received royal assent, after many peers had abstained on its third reading and Wellington, though still opposed, did not have enough votes in the House of Lords to block it any longer.

Grey's biographer suggested that 'Britain came nearer to popular revolution during those years [1831 and 1832] than at any others in modern times'. Indeed, it is possible to argue that without the Great Reform Act of 1832, the Chartist movement which emerged a few years later and peaked in the early 1840s might have successfully overthrown the political settlement and even led to some form of revolution, much like those which took place throughout mainland Europe in 1848. That the Great Reform Act had enfranchised a section of the growing middle classes in the new towns and cities of the United Kingdom had helped avert such a possibility and set the pace for future electoral reform, even if it was to be many years until universal suffrage was achieved.

Late in 1832, Grey sought a dissolution of Parliament for the holding of a general election under the new system introduced by the Act. Much was different. The rotten boroughs in places such as Old Sarum, with no or few voters, were gone. The electorate had been expanded by over 50 per cent from some 400,000 voters to 650,000.

Constituencies were of a far more equal size than before the Act. It was during the general election campaign of 1832 that the process of parties seeking votes for their candidate, akin to current political campaigning, first emerged in nearly every constituency.

The election was, though, in some ways, something of a damp squib. The result was never in doubt. Wellington did not campaign to any great extent and, reluctantly, accepted that his argument against the Act had been lost. He had always said that he should feel it his duty to resist reform when proposed by others. In practice, during the election campaign, he backed down from this position. The political classes moved on to focus on the two emerging themes of the election: reform to the laws affecting Irish people (thus building on the Catholic Emancipation Act of 1829) and the great liberal cause of the abolition of slavery. Grey, riding high on the back of the campaign for the Great Reform Act, led his Whig Party to an even greater landslide than had occurred the previous year.

The voting itself took place, unlike nowadays, over several weeks, from 10 December 1832 until 8 January 1833. The Whigs won 441 seats in the House of Commons, compared to the Tories' tally of only 175. The Irish Repeal Party (which existed to campaign against the Act of Union and for Irish independence) won forty-two seats – perhaps an ominous sign for the future. The new Whig government therefore had a massive overall majority of 214. In terms of vote share, the results were even more stark with the Whigs gaining 67 per cent of the popular vote more than double the Tories' 29 per cent. Given the lack of comparable data for 1831, there was no comparison to show how big a two-party swing this represented. Suffice to say, however, that the newly enfranchised regions of the Midlands and the north of England voted heavily for the Whig candidates.

Grey's triumph in 1832, though, was relatively short lived. Less than two years later in 1834, Grey resigned at the age of seventy and returned to his native Northumberland, where he died eleven years later. The 1832 electoral triumph had been the pinnacle of his career, sealing as it did the approval of the expanded electorate for the Great Reform Act.

The 1832 general election was profound both in being the first fought under the extended system, introduced by Grey, but also in that it ushered in the reforming Whig government of 1832–34 whose major achievement was the Slavery Abolition Act of 1833. Its longer-term significance may have been even greater. Grey had begun the process of constitutional change which, by giving more people a political voice, helped avoid the possibility of revolution within Britain, as would later happen throughout much of Europe. Grey's government can take at least some of the credit for that.

The construction of Grey's Monument in Newcastle was therefore a recognition of his achievement of widening participation in the democratic process which continued throughout the nineteenth and twentieth centuries. The project cost some £2,300 (well over £250,000 in today's money) and was funded entirely by public subscriptions in honour of the Prime Minister. By contrast, the most recent electoral legislation in the United Kingdom, the Elections Act of 2022, was designed specifically to restrict the right to vote through measures on photo ID and postal voting. It seems highly unlikely that today members of the public will feel the urge to contribute to fund a statue to commemorate the Prime Minister who oversaw that most recent act of electoral reform.

Dr Alun Evans CBE is a writer and political consultant. He was, for over thirty years, a UK civil servant. He is the author of *The Intimacy of Power: An insight into private office, Whitehall's most sensitive network*, to be published by Biteback in 2024.

4

1835

EDWARD YOUNG

Dissolution: 29 December 1834
Polling day: 6 January–6 February 1835
Seats contested: 658
Total electorate / Total votes cast / Turnout: 845,776 (479,679 in contested seats) / 611,137 / 65 per cent
Candidates (total 945): Whig (including radicals and Irish Nationalists) – 538; Conservative – 407
Prime Minister on polling day: Robert Peel
Main party leaders: Conservative – Robert Peel; Whig – Viscount Melbourne

Party performance:

Party	Votes	Percentage share	Seats
Whig (including radicals and Irish Nationalists)	349,868	57.2	385
Conservative	261,269	42.7	273

Result: Hung parliament, Conservatives continued as minority government

James Hudson had brains but no bounty hunting experience. Nonetheless it was clear in the royal household that he was the man for the job. Hudson had in his youth spent three years in Italy. He yearned to return to the land of the Renaissance and Ancient

Rome. Decades later, Hudson would indeed become a famous diplomat in Italy, commemorated with a plaque on his old home in Turin. But on 16 November 1834, as a junior private secretary aged twenty-four working for William IV, Hudson was firmly based in London. And on that particular Sunday, the king needed someone who knew their way round Italy to track down Sir Robert Peel.

Two years had passed since the immense Tory mauling in the general election of 1832. The Whigs, despite, or perhaps because of, their huge majority, had squabbled over what to reform next. The established Church of Ireland was an obvious target. In an Irish population of almost 8 million, only 800,000 were Anglicans. Yet the resources of the church far outweighed its relevance. The list of grievances was long and complicated, covering everything from the collection of tithes to the number of Irish bishops. But, at its heart, the problem was simple. In the words of the Anglican cleric Sydney Smith: 'On an Irish Sabbath, the bell of a neat parish church often summons to church only the parson and an occasionally conforming clerk; while, two hundred yards off, a thousand Catholics are huddled together in a miserable hovel and pelted by all the storms of heaven.'

One reform in particular had divided the Whigs. What should happen to the surplus income generated by the Church of Ireland? Would it not be fairer to appropriate it for non-ecclesiastical causes? The radicals and Irish Nationalists such as Daniel O'Connell were insistent. But increasingly within the Whigs a conservative group became vocal. In May 1834, the tension bubbled over when Lord Stanley, Secretary of State for War and the Colonies, and a small group of supporters resigned from the government in protest against a policy of appropriation. The schism grew when the then Prime Minister, Earl Grey, himself resigned in July. The king asked Lord Melbourne, the Home Secretary, to form a new government, which he did while continuing half-heartedly to find an Irish compromise.

This new Whig government did not last long. At the start of November, Melbourne proposed Lord John Russell as the new Leader of the House of Commons. Russell was by now well established as a nit-picking reformer and he had already shown his hand as a champion of further changes to the Irish Church. The king meanwhile had grown frustrated at the confusion in government and was genuinely concerned at the prospect of an Irish unwinding of the constitution. He therefore took Melbourne at his word when he informed the king that his government was unstable, and dismissed Melbourne and the Whigs on Friday 14 November 1834.

The flaw in the king's plan was parliamentary mathematics. The Whigs and radicals outnumbered the Tories by more than two to one in the Commons. There was also a separate doubt over who to appoint as Prime Minister. The king sent for the Duke of Wellington on Saturday. But the Iron Duke had by now lost much of his political strength, as well as some of his hearing. The new Prime Minister, he told King William, could only be Sir Robert Peel.

Wellington's decision had profound implications not just for the general election that followed but also for the direction of the Conservative Party. By now Peel and Wellington had worked alongside each other for over a decade. Both shared a strong belief in the constitution and in maintaining the king's government. But politically, Peel was moving step by step away from the Ultras who were loyal to Wellington, and on personal matters the two men were even further apart. In the chaos that autumn, Wellington had as much chance as anyone of forming a Tory government. But what he saw, and what others around him increasingly recognised, was that for the Tories to survive and succeed in future elections, a different approach and new leadership were required.

Unfortunately, this new leadership was on holiday. Sir Robert Peel had decided after the parliamentary session ended to take a trip with his wife and eldest daughter across Europe. No one knew exactly where he had headed, nor indeed how long he would be. Meanwhile in Whitehall, there were concerns about stability. The king had dismissed one government but was unable to appoint a new one. In that era of rioting and reform, this was no endorsement for the continuing power of the Crown. Wellington offered to provide short-term help by forming a caretaker government. To save time, he gave himself every major position – Prime Minister, Foreign Secretary, Home

Secretary as well as Leader of the House of Lords. Under this temporary dictatorship, the hunt began to find Robert Peel.

James Hudson reached Dover late on Sunday evening. Perhaps at the back of his mind was a secret hope that his trip to the Continent would allow him the opportunity to visit those museums and galleries he had admired as a youth. Any such thoughts soon disappeared. The final steamboat to France had already set off. With winter weather setting in, Hudson paid some oarsmen to row him across the Channel. He arrived, freezing, in Boulogne four hours later and began hitchhiking across Europe. At Paris, the embassy told him to go to Italy. Once in Italy, he rattled through the ancient city states – Turin, Milan, Bologna, Florence and Rome – but he had no time for tourism as he wandered in vain round countless hotels. Day after day, the journey became more desperate. He travelled on horseback, rattletraps and oxcarts. At one point the Austrian police confiscated his passport; at another he had to bribe the Papal Guards. He eventually reached Peel's hotel in Rome on 25 November, nine days after his departure – caked in mud, stinking of damp, having abandoned his luggage and wearing huge horse riding boots. It is typical of Peel that before answering the king's summons, he quizzed Hudson on his journey, pointing out it could have been completed in eight rather than nine days. Hudson headed home the next day.

Meanwhile Peel, his wife Julia and their daughter, also Julia, all returned to London. All his life, Peel was a devoted father and husband, and it is telling that rather than leaving his family behind, all three travelled together through the Alpine snows. It took them twelve days to reach Paris, spending four nights in bed and eight in the coach. In Peel's papers in the Surrey History Centre, there is a brown notebook in which he described the final leg of the journey:

> Monday 8 December: [Breakfasted] at Montreuil, reached Calais at 5 o'clock. Sailed that evening at 6, reached Dover at eleven. Julia and Julia staid [*sic*] all night at Dover. I left it in a hack chaise at 20 min to 12, reached London at ½ past 8. Tuesday morning Dec 9. Saw the

King at ½ past ten, accepted the office of First Lord of the Treasury and proceeded forthwith in the formation of the Government.

These were the days of Sir Robert Peel's ascendancy. Gone now was the brittle sense of honour from his time as Home Secretary in the 1820s. Fading, but not forgotten, was his reputation for changing his mind. The snobs still saw Peel as a Staffordshire outsider. The diarist Charles Greville complained that he looked more like a dapper shopkeeper than a Prime Minister. Also he 'eats voraciously and cuts creams and jellies with his knife'. But by now Peel was more at ease with himself than at any point in his career. Aged forty-six, he was in his prime – putting on weight, happy at home in Drayton Manor and growing in stature in Parliament. Thus the same Greville who complained about Peel's eating habits wrote in 1834:

> No matter how unruly the House, how impatient or fatigued, the moment he rises all is silence ... His great merit consists in his judgment, tact and discretion, his facility, promptitude, thorough knowledge of the assembly he addresses, familiarity with the details of every sort of Parliamentary business, and the great command he has over himself.

Peel decided to call a general election immediately. The state of discord in Parliament could be solved only by dissolving it. More to the point, a general election, called by a Tory Prime Minister who had set a new direction, might help the party regain ground lost during the destruction of 1832. A majority was out of the question, but it was possible to imagine a significantly improved minority position, either in power or back in opposition.

But before dissolving Parliament, Peel needed to form a Cabinet capable of agreeing to his plan. His first task was to broaden the appeal of the new government beyond the rump of Ultra-Tories. He therefore wrote to both Lord Stanley and his Whig ally, Sir James Graham. The overture failed, but over the coming days new names and faces agreed to join Peel in government. William Gladstone, still a stern and unbending Tory, entered government for the first time, alongside Lord Lincoln and Lord Wharncliffe. In several Cabinet positions, Peel gave concessions to a few reliable Ultras, but the key roles of Home Secretary, Foreign Secretary and Secretary of State for War went to alumni of the Liberal Tory governments of the late 1820s – Henry Goulburn, the Duke of Wellington and Lord Aberdeen. Peel served as Chancellor of the Exchequer himself.

On 13 December the Cabinet came together over dinner and agreed to a general election. The first step would be a public statement from Peel. Such declarations were not unusual; candidates across the country increasingly published statements setting out their principles. But, in this case, a historical oddity gave Peel's plan an edge. Under the rules of the time, any new minister on taking office would have to fight a by-election in their constituency. This rule, which ten years later would prove a thorn in Peel's side, suddenly gave the Prime Minister an opportunity to move fast and seize the initiative. He would write an address to his own electors in Tamworth which would be published around the country before the general election campaign had even started. By the time the Cabinet met again on 17 December, Peel had finished drafting his Tamworth address. The text was approved by the Cabinet and copied for publication at midnight.

At first glance, the success of the Tamworth manifesto seems a surprise. The language is littered with lofty portents and double negatives. Some of the sentences cover entire paragraphs. All his life, Peel felt the need to justify himself at immense length when taking any decision, and much of the opening is dedicated to explaining why he had agreed to form a government.

But once all this was out the way, Peel's prose sharpened. There were 586 electors in Tamworth, but Peel had other voters in mind:

> I gladly avail myself also of this, a legitimate opportunity, of making a more public appeal – of addressing myself, through you, to that great and intelligent class of society of which you are a portion ... that class which is much less interested in the contentions of party, than in the maintenance of order and the cause of good government.

This was a crucial claim. Peel was in effect making clear that his priority was not simply to protect his core vote and old Tory interests but rather to represent the new voters in boroughs and counties across the country.

Biographers of Peel will point out that none of the pronouncements in the manifesto were new or original. Peel had long ago set out the principles of his approach to the new reformed parliament. He simply repeated and expanded on things he had already declared. The Great Reform Act would, he made clear, be respected not repealed or unpicked by the Tories. Instead, any new Conservative government would find a new, practical, way of approaching reform:

> If, by adopting the spirit of the Reform Bill, it be meant that we are to live in a perpetual vortex of agitation; that public men can only support themselves in public estimation by adopting every popular impression of the day – by promising the instant redress of anything which anybody may call an abuse – by abandoning altogether that great aid of government – more powerful than either law or reason – the respect for ancient rights, and the deference to prescriptive authority; if this be the spirit of the Reform Bill, I will not undertake to adopt it. But if the spirit of the Reform Bill implies merely a careful review of institutions, civil and ecclesiastical, undertaken in a friendly temper combining, with the firm maintenance of established rights, the correction of proved abuses and the redress of real grievances – in that case, I can for myself and colleagues undertake to act in such a spirit and with such intentions.

Then, as now, politicians struggled to gain the trust of the public. Peel found his own way round the problem. Rather than make new promises on key issues, he simply reminded his readers of actions he had already taken. Thus on the inquiry into municipal corporations, Peel wrote that he had already agreed to serve on the inquiry committee so obviously would not interfere with the process. Similarly on Dissenters, he had long ago been clear that they could not attend the universities, but he was keen to help them become lawyers and medics. Finally on the crucial question of church reform,

I cannot give my consent to the alienating of Church property, in any part of the United Kingdom, from strictly ecclesiastical purposes. But I repeat now the opinions that I have already expressed in Parliament in regard to the church Establishment in Ireland – that if, by an improved distribution of the revenues of the Church, its just influence can be extended, and the true interests of the Established religion promoted, all other considerations should be made subordinate.

None of this made the manifesto a marvel. Its power lay not in the content but in the way it was communicated. The innovation was captured by those ten words near the start of the address – 'through you, to that great and intelligent class of society'. On the same night that the Cabinet approved the text of the manifesto, it was copied and couriered round to the national newspapers. The next morning it appeared in print in the *Morning Herald*, the *Morning Post* and *The Times*. Thus came into being the first national manifesto, addressed to local voters and instigated by an ancient quirk of politics.

The plan worked. The manifesto captured the mood of an unsettled electorate. Letters, articles and hustings speeches referred endlessly to its pledges. Greville, a close observer, wrote: 'Nobody talks of anything else.' It spiked Lord Stanley who was planning a mighty speech in Glasgow which later became known as the 'Knowsley creed'. And although Disraeli would later lampoon both Peel and the manifesto ('an attempt to construct a party without principles'), even hardened cynics and reactionaries at the time accepted and repeated Peel's ideas. The Tory *Quarterly Review* published at vast and unnecessary length an essay analysing the manifesto. Having consulted almost every known authority from Burke through to Shakespeare, the essay concluded: 'If Sir Robert Peel fulfils his professions – as no one doubts that he will – by correcting all acknowledged abuses, and operating all salutary reforms, he will leave no man any resting-place between him and Mr O'Connell.'

That indeed was the purpose. But as this book repeatedly shows, manifestos do not win elections alone. The machinery of campaigning was becoming more important. And in 1835, for the first time in history, the Conservative Party entered an election with something resembling a national vote-winning operation.

Part of this was purely technical. One of the results of the Great Reform Act was that all new voters needed to be registered. This requirement added a new dimension to every local campaign. Henceforth, alongside the old Regency practices of bullying, bribery and general brutality which coloured every election, a new political skill became important: voter registration. Any party that wanted to influence elections could now ensure its own supporters were fully signed up and registered appropriately. Lawyers suddenly found themselves at the forefront of party politics.

The focus on registration added to the growing importance of local Conservative associations. Since 1832, the Conservative Party had started to take the need to organise seriously. Richard A. Gaunt in his essay later in this book provides a neat account of the rise of the Carlton Club and growth of local associations. It is significant that this trend was championed overwhelmingly by the Conservatives. No similar effort was made by the Whigs. Even today, a party in power will neglect its own political operations, while opposition obliges any outsiders to organise afresh. The years after 1832 were no exception, and Peel was bolstered by the work of one of the great organisers of British political history.

The career of Francis Bonham, political organiser and erstwhile Member of Parliament, is worth a book in its own right. Despite the solid work of Norman Gash and Robert Blake, we still know exceptionally little about what Bonham actually did for a living. After graduating in 1807, Bonham joined Lincoln's Inn and was called to the bar in 1814. But it does not appear Bonham ever practised law and his career is a mystery until he appears as an MP for Rye in 1830. Silent in Parliament, he was assiduous in other matters, serving as Assistant Whip until he lost his seat the following year. Peel, however, recognised early on Bonham's importance. In December 1834, he found Bonham a minor role in government with a salary of £1,200 a year. 'I never could have accepted office', Peel explained to Bonham, 'without seeking your aid and offering you some appointment or other which might give me the frequent opportunity of communicating with you.'

With Bonham's support and coordination, the Conservative associations got to work. These associations had no say on party policy, nor any direct role in selecting candidates, but they were crucial in registering voters and distributing money. Disraeli later captured the flavour in his novel *Coningsby*: 'a Conservative Association, with a banker for its chairman, and a brewer for its vice-president, and four sharp lawyers knibbing their pens'.

These then were the tools that the Tories took into the general election. Polling began on 6 January and continued for a month. The results fell slightly short of what Peel had hoped for, with just over 270 Conservative MPs elected by the end of January. Overall, the party had gained almost 100 seats from the low base of 175 in 1832 and were now the largest party in Parliament. Many of the most important gains came in the new boroughs, where the Tories gained over fifty new Conservative MPs. Old forces still held sway over large parts of the electorate and the power of the landowner and the mob still shaped many outcomes. But overall, this was positive progress for the party and a strong endorsement of Peel.

Peel and his colleagues continued their work as a minority government. Over the following weeks they toiled where possible to maintain orderly government while also establishing a hugely influential Ecclesiastical Commission. Peel himself designed and drove much of the work of the commission and did so in his promised spirit of thoughtful, considered reform – making changes to the structure and spoils of the Church of England, without overplaying his hand. In the end, around £360,000 a year of church funds were redeployed to more urgent ecclesiastical causes.

It was Ireland which finally brought down the government. In February 1835, Lord John Russell had formed a compact with the Irish radical Daniel O'Connell at Lichfield House with the purpose of voting against the Conservative Party. On 7 April, they defeated the government on an Irish question. This was the end for Peel and his government. They had spent just over 100 days in office but left bolstered by 100 new Conservative MPs.

Every essayist in this book will have an affection for their own election. Even though 1835 does not rank as one of the most important elections in our history, it is undoubtable that the success Peel had in the four months he held office changed the future for the Conservative Party. When Peel finally won an overall majority in 1841, it became the first time a new government came into being directly as a result of a general election. In both practical and political terms, this success was built on Peel's work in 1835. Practical, because Peel gained more new seats in 1835 than at any future election as leader, and more than twice as many as he gained in 1841. And political, because Peel had shown through the manifesto that he and his colleagues would govern as reforming Conservatives, not as Ultra-Tories.

The secret weapon in all this was speed. It had taken the hapless Hudson nine days to track down Peel in Italy; it took Peel a day less to form a government, write the Tamworth Manifesto and prepare for a general election. It was a speed of mobilisation rarely seen in nineteenth-century politics. The Tory machine did its work well during the campaign itself, but the Tamworth Manifesto shone a new light on the Conservatives. Had Lord Stanley taken eight days, rather than eight months, to write his Knowsley creed after resigning from the Whig government in 1834, Peel's Tamworth Manifesto may never have been written.

There is one final reason to celebrate the 1835 campaign. Peel in his manifesto mentioned in passing a characteristic he deplored in politics: public men who 'can only support themselves in public estimation by adopting every popular impression of the day, by promising the instant redress of anything which anybody may call an abuse'. We live in an age where politicians of all parties have been too weak to stand up and make unpopular cases against issues where more detailed investigation is needed. It is one of the reasons why we have seen an avalanche of well-intentioned but ill-thought-out new rules and regulations over many years. An important legacy of Tamworth was not so much any new political idea or strategy but rather Peel's defence of political courage and intellectual integrity. As we look ahead to a new general election, every reader of this book, regardless of political persuasion, should ask themselves whether their candidates locally and nationally truly have the courage to apply the spirit of Tamworth once again.

Edward Young is a partner at Headland Consultancy and the co-author with Douglas Hurd of *Disraeli: or, The Two Lives* (Orion, 2013). This chapter is dedicated to Young's co-author, a lifelong Peelite.

5

1837

NAN SLOANE

Dissolution: 17 July 1837
Polling day: 24 July–18 August 1837
Seats contested: 658
Total electorate / Total votes cast / Turnout: 1,004,664 (647,518 in contested seats) / 798,025 / 63.6 per cent
Candidates (total 994): Whig – 510; Conservative – 484
Prime Minister on polling day: Viscount Melbourne
Main party leaders: Whig – Viscount Melbourne; Conservative – Robert Peel

Party performance:

Party	Votes	Percentage share	Seats
Whig	418,331	52.4	344
Conservative	379,694	47.6	314

Result: Whig majority of twenty-nine seats

The 1837 general election is sometimes described as one of the dullest elections ever. There is some truth in this. It was held less than three years after the previous one and was the fourth in the space of a decade, so even the new electorate called into existence by the 1832 Reform Act was beginning to weary of the polls. It was not the result of any political crisis but merely a constitutional necessity following the accession of a new monarch.

However, the apparent pointlessness of this election obscures a much more interesting story that is usually subsumed into the better-known narrative of the rise of the Conservative Party and its leader, Sir Robert Peel.

In June 1837, William IV died, ushering in the reign of his niece, Victoria. Since 1707, it had been a requirement that a general election should be held on the accession of a monarch, and the one to provide Queen Victoria with a new parliament was duly scheduled for the four-week period between 24 July and 18 August. As usual, each constituency was able to determine its own timetable and polling day, and, despite several attempts to get one, a secret ballot was still decades away. This meant that votes were cast in public and recorded for posterity, a habit which, while handy for historians, led to much trouble at most elections at the time.

The Prime Minister in 1837 was Lord Melbourne, a Whig who had been in office since 1835. Although his government was largely unremarkable, he himself was a controversial figure with a colourful private life. Apart from anything else, he had recently been sued for 'criminal correspondence' (effectively adultery) by the husband of the writer Caroline Norton at a public and highly scandalous trial. Although Melbourne won the case, Caroline Norton was publicly humiliated and Melbourne had to be saved from an ignominious resignation by the support of the king.

Opposed to Melbourne, and leading a Tory (Conservative) Party which was beginning to develop both political coherence and a highly effective grass-roots organisation, was Sir Robert Peel. Peel had been Prime Minister briefly in 1834 and 1835 and would be again following the Tory landslide of 1841. As Home Secretary in the 1820s, he had founded the Metropolitan Police, and during the 1835 general election he produced the Tamworth Manifesto, one of the founding documents of what became the Conservative Party.

Although there was very little enthusiasm for Melbourne's Whigs, there was also very little expectation that the election would result in a change of government. On the other hand, and particularly in the north of England, there was a widespread hope that the polls might at least give the Whigs a bloody nose. The roots of this pugnacity lay in two recent pieces of legislation – the 1832 Reform Act and the 1834 Poor Law Reform Act.

The failure of the 1832 Reform Act to meet the high hopes its supporters had built for it was, by 1837, biting home hard. Working-class people had been persuaded to campaign for it on the promise that their interests would be looked after by the middle classes whom it would enfranchise. The 1834 Poor Law Reform Act, therefore, came as a bitter blow to those hopes. Introduced to correct the deficiencies of Tudor and Stuart Poor Law provision, it seemed to many to be a ferocious attack not only on the poorer classes as a whole but on women and family values in particular. Families forced into the new workhouses would be split up, thus, in many people's eyes, breaching the sacred bond of marriage. Sick children could be removed from their mothers on admission to the workhouse, and all children could be apprenticed, hired out or simply rehomed without their parents' consent or sometimes even knowledge. Women who bore children out of wedlock would no longer be able to claim financial support from the father; instead, all women and girls would be financially responsible for their illegitimate children's upkeep for sixteen years. All this seemed particularly vicious given that destitution in emerging industrial communities was likely to be episodic rather than persistent, and almost all workers, however respectable and independent, were likely to experience periods of unemployment (and therefore intense poverty) at one time or another.

Working-class opposition to the Act was widespread but particularly fierce in the north, where there were large communities dependent on the vagaries of industrial markets for their livings. Many parishes refused to build the new workhouses the Act required. Huge public meetings were held to protest against the legislation – it was estimated that at one, on Hartshead Moor near Huddersfield in May 1837, there were upwards of a quarter of a million people. In some places there was serious rioting. Poor Law inspectors sent out to try to enforce the law were sometimes physically attacked, often by enraged groups of women. The authorities did their best to contain the situation but were unable to prevent the fear and desperation felt in many communities from spiralling out of control. The 1837 general election, therefore, occurred in a political atmosphere in which feelings were already inflamed and hostility to the Whig government and its candidates was widespread.

Whig MPs presenting themselves for re-election were held personally responsible for the passage of the Act, and Tory candidates were consequently supported as they were seen to be likely to either amend or repeal it. There was a widespread industrial depression, which heightened insecurity and focused people's minds on the plight of the unemployed. But most of the people directly affected by the Act could not vote, while the middle-class mill and factory owners who had a direct interest in making the New Poor Law work could. Tories opposed the New Poor Law for various reasons, including ideas about the sacramental nature of marriage and the innate respectability of the British working man, but Whig industrialists took a more pragmatic view based on reducing their rates and dealing with indigent workers during the periodic slumps. Thus, the outcomes of the election did not by any means reflect the strength of popular feeling against those who won.

The West Riding of Yorkshire at this time sent two MPs to Westminster, and in 1837 the Whig candidates, Lord Morpeth and Sir George Strickland, both of whom had been sitting MPs when the legislation was passed, were roundly attacked. The Tory campaign produced a handbill headed 'A Few Plain Questions', which helpfully provides answers as well. 'Who', it demands, 'supported and voted for [the New Poor Law]?' The defiant reply rings clear: 'Morpeth and Strickland!' The question 'Who Voted that the Fathers of Bastard Children should pay NOTHING for their Support in any Case?' elicits the same answer. More in this vein is followed by the demand: 'Who will resist the Introduction of the Poor Law into the West Riding?' a question to which the answer is the Tory candidate 'Mr Wortley!' Finally, it is noted that Lord Morpeth had also voted against holding an inquiry 'into the Cause of the present great Distress of the Hand Loom Weavers. Shame! Shame!'

In Huddersfield, the radical Tory and factory law reformer Richard Oastler, a fierce and uncompromising opponent of the Poor Law Act, stood against the Whig incumbent. Oastler had been a speaker at the Hartshead Moor meeting, describing the Act as 'damnable, infernal, detestable, despotic, unchristian, unconstitutional and unnatural'. Like many other places, Huddersfield saw a fair amount of violence during the election, some of it involving Oastler himself. At Wakefield, two people were killed, while elsewhere election rioting broke out at towns including Salford, Preston, Liverpool, Bolton, Manchester, Birmingham, Stamford and many others. Most of these centred around either the hustings, where candidates presented themselves before an indicative vote as to whether or not to proceed to a poll, or the day of the poll itself. Election rioting was by no means a new phenomenon – indeed, its violence and frequency were sometimes quoted as a reason why voting would be unsuitable for ladies – but in 1837, popular hatred of the New Poor Law gave it added impetus.

In 1835, Morpeth and Strickland had been returned unopposed; in 1837, although they were re-elected, the Tory John Stuart-Wortley came only 403 votes behind Strickland, and little more than a thousand behind Morpeth. In Huddersfield, Richard Oastler lost by only twenty-two votes. Results such as these are usually seen as part of the inexorable rise of Robert Peel's Conservatives, but it is also the case that, in parts of the north at least, a deep suspicion and dislike of the self-interested and authoritarian tendencies of the Whigs was also at play.

The 1837 election had other, less obvious consequences, too. Although the anti-Poor Law cause had made progress, it had not succeeded in getting enough MPs elected to get the Act overturned, and there was some justifiable doubt whether, even if the Tories had won, they would have acted to relieve the miseries of working people during a depression. In 1838, the radical cabinet-maker William Lovett, working with other radicals, produced the People's Charter, which became the basis of the Chartist movement of the 1840s and 1850s. The mass movement for political rights for working-class people had been more or less crushed after the tragedy of Peterloo in 1819, but new generations of working people who felt betrayed by the Whigs and could not entirely trust the Tories were coming to the conclusion that political rights for themselves – or, at any rate, for the men – were the only answer. The 1837 election, in which Whigs like Morpeth and Strickland scraped back in and popular heroes like Oastler were defeated by narrow margins, was a significant thread in the establishment of the early Chartist movement.

By the end of August, when all the votes had been counted, it was clear that Melbourne's Whigs would be returned to government, though with forty-one fewer MPs than before. Resistance to the New Poor Law weakened as gradually workhouses were built and the fear of them came to dominate so many communities, but support for the new Chartist movement, which at times looked almost as though it might succeed, grew over the ensuing years. Melbourne's government stumbled on until 1841, when it was finally brought down by Peel's parliamentary manoeuvring. When, in 1867, the Second Reform Act enfranchised sections of working-class men, it also abolished the necessity for a general election on the accession of a new monarch, so that for many political historians, the 1837 election – if mentioned at all – is worthy of note only because it was the last to be held under the provisions of the old 1707 Act.

Nan Sloane is a Labour historian writing about left-wing and radical movements with particular reference to women's part in them. Her books include *The Women in the Room: Labour's Forgotten History* and *Uncontrollable Women: Radicals, Reformers and Revolutionaries*.

6

1841

RICHARD A. GAUNT

Dissolution: 23 June 1841
Polling day: 29 June–22 July 1841
Seats contested: 658
Total electorate / Total votes cast / Turnout: 1,017,379 (475,233 in contested seats) / 593,445 / 63.4 per cent
Candidates (total 916): Conservative – 498; Whig – 388; Irish Repeal – 22
Prime Minister on polling day: Viscount Melbourne
Main party leaders: Whig – Viscount Melbourne; Conservative – Robert Peel; Irish Repeal – Daniel O'Connell

Party performance:

Party	Votes	Percentage share	Seats
Conservative	306,314	51.6	367
Whig	273,902	46.2	271
Irish Repeal	12,537	2.2	20

Result: Conservative majority of seventy-six seats

The Conservative Party's spectacular victory in the general election of 1841 was the most significant of any which it achieved during the nineteenth century. Although, in retrospect, it came to be overshadowed by the memory of what followed – the rupture of the Conservative Party five years later over the repeal of the Corn Laws – at the time, it was invested with every prospect of success.

The Conservative Party's return to power, with a majority of seventy-six seats in the House of Commons, was once seen as a personal triumph for its leader and incoming Prime Minister. In the words of John Wilson Croker, the long-time editor of the *Quarterly Review*, 'all turned on the name of Sir Robert Peel'. Today, with a more critical perspective on Peel's personality and achievements and a correspondingly wider understanding of the circumstances within which the Conservative Party built and communicated its case to the electorate, that judgement looks far less secure.

It has long been recognised that the Conservative majority was based in the party's traditional strongholds (small towns and county seats), on a platform of constitutional preservation, defence of the Church of England and support for the protectionist Corn Laws. The Conservatives secured some 367 seats in the 1841 election, including the majority of English and Welsh counties (137 out of 159 seats, a gain of twenty-three). However, they achieved a nearly even split in the English and Welsh boroughs (165 seats, including eight gains, to the Whigs' 176). At a post-election dinner at Tamworth, Peel extolled the gains which Conservatives had made in larger, especially urban, borough seats with populations above 2,000, including the City of London, Westminster, Hull, Liverpool and Leeds. However, the Conservative Party only secured a minority of those seats overall, trailing the Whigs by fifteen seats to forty-three. It was in a similar position in Scotland, where the Conservatives secured twenty out of thirty county seats (a gain of two seats) but remained vastly outnumbered in the Scottish burghs, where they returned only two out of twenty-three seats (a gain of one); they were also in a minority in Ireland, returning forty-three out of 105 MPs (a gain of four seats). Perhaps as significantly, the level of split voting – where individual electors cast votes for candidates of different parties in constituencies which returned more than one MP – was the lowest of any general election fought under the terms of the 1832 Reform Act.

The 1841 contest was fought at the height of a financial crisis which had been in force since 1837, with a severe economic depression and high rates of unemployment. The Whig government of Viscount

Melbourne, which had been in power since 1835, was also committed to a series of costly overseas campaigns, including wars in Afghanistan and China. In the midst of these troubles, the Anti-Corn Law League was formed in the winter of 1838 to campaign for the repeal of the Corn Laws. Led by energetic middle-class manufacturers such as Richard Cobden, and powerful, persuasive speakers such as John Bright, the league built a formidable organisational network over the course of the next few years. The Whigs attempted to counter this threat, and meet the immediate budget deficit, by taking up some of the recommendations of a parliamentary Select Committee on Import Duties, which had reported in 1840. In their Budget, unveiled on 30 April 1841, the Whigs proposed major changes in the import duties paid on three staple commodities. On sugar, they proposed to close the gap on duties paid between foreign-grown and colonial-grown sugar, from the existing rates of sixty-three shillings (on foreign-grown) and twenty-four shillings (on colonial-grown) to thirty-six shillings and twenty-four shillings, respectively. On timber, the differential on foreign imports was to be reduced by five shillings. Most alarming of all, insofar as Conservatives (and some Whig protectionists) were concerned, was the proposal to replace the existing sliding scale of duties on imports of foreign corn with a fixed duty of eight shillings.

The government's Budget measures galvanised the Conservative opposition and provided them with the means with which to defeat the ministry in the House of Commons. In June 1840, the Conservatives had lost a motion of no confidence by a margin of 308–287 votes. However, by-election results had continued to run in favour of the Conservatives, with Peel claiming that the government had lost at least a dozen seats between 1837 and 1841. With united Conservative opposition to the government's Budget measures, the party succeeded in defeating the proposed sugar duties by 317–281 votes on 18 May. Buoyed by this success, Peel introduced another motion of no confidence on 27 May 1841. This was put to a division on 4 June; as in March 1979, the Conservative Party won it by a single vote (312–311). Rather than resign, Melbourne's government dissolved

Parliament and went to the country. If they had survived the vote, the Whigs could have continued in office for up to another three years, as the Septennial Act of 1715 (mandating a general election every seven years) was still in force until 1911, and the last election had been in 1837.

As with most elections of this period, the 1841 contest was strongly centred in the constituencies, with the publication of election addresses by candidates circulated as handbills and in the local press, as well as election dinners, canvassing and the traditional ritual of the hustings itself. Because general elections continued to take place at different times in different places, rather than within the confines of a single day, and because voting was conducted in public, rather than by secret ballot, the state of parties was a matter of general knowledge until the final returns were declared.

The Corn Laws featured prominently in the contest, with many Conservatives pledging themselves individually to defend the legislation from the combined threat of Whig free traders and the Anti-Corn Law League. One study of published election addresses calculates that the Corn Laws were mentioned by 60 per cent of all candidates, whether Whig or Conservative. The second most frequently referenced topic in Whig election addresses, mentioned by 30 per cent of their candidates, was the duties on sugar and timber, while 40 per cent of Conservative candidates referenced the defence of the Church of England, in the face of continued campaigns for legislative change from Catholics in Ireland and Nonconformists in England. In his nomination speech at Tamworth, Peel expressed his opposition to the fixed duty on corn, noting that the Corn Laws were one way of relieving the special burdens (such as the poor rate, highway rate, church rate and tithe) which occupiers of land had to endure.

While the principal issue on the hustings had been determined by recent political events, the roots of Conservative electoral success went much deeper. They can be traced back to the dire political situation in which the Conservatives found themselves, following the general election of 1832 – the first to be fought after the 'Great' Reform Act had been passed. Reduced to a rump of some 150 MPs, the newly christened 'Conservative' Party had sought to rally itself in the face of an overwhelming Whig majority.

They did so, in part, as a result of the unintended consequences of the Reform Act. The necessity for electoral registration was one of the novelties of political life that the legislation introduced. There was no formal register of those entitled to vote before this time, but the idiosyncrasies and potential for corruption to which this gave rise meant that electoral registration (for a fee of one shilling) was thought to be a necessary prerequisite for qualification to the franchise after 1832. Pre-election registration offered opportunities for quantifying and sustaining political allegiances which had not existed before. The register was the subject of dispute at annual revising courts. It was in such courts, populated by a host of faithful Conservative-supporting solicitors, that the party proved its adeptness at electoral organisation. By successfully contesting the registration of Whig and radical electors, and overturning challenges to Conservative supporters, the party found an effective mechanism for maintaining constituency strength between elections, patiently laying the foundation for future electoral success. It was a process which took time and was not the only reason for the Conservatives' ultimate success. However, by 1837, when a general election was held upon the accession of Queen Victoria, the gap between the Whigs and the Conservatives in the House of Commons had narrowed to around thirty seats, with the Conservatives returning 313 MPs. Such was the vigilance with which the Conservatives maintained and won the battle of electoral registration in the constituencies that, in 1841, the party secured 113 seats without a contest, more than double the number (fifty-five) they had returned in 1837. Not the least of the reasons behind Peel's election victory in 1841 was the Conservative Party's superior organisation in respect of electoral registration.

The battle for electoral registration was also a catalyst for the formation of Conservative associations, which became a notable feature of political life in constituencies across Britain during the 1830s. The associations tapped into habits of club-life and sociability which had been a hallmark of British politics since the eighteenth century.

Some organisations were borne of local circumstances – notably, electoral defeat during the struggle for the Reform Act and the need to organise a counter-reaction – but were overlaid by wider battles. Conservative associations were given a new focus during Peel's first, minority, government in 1834–35 but were subsequently nourished through a variety of contributory causes: the revival of the traditional cry of 'the Church in Danger'; the defence of local government in light of the reform of municipal corporations by Whig legislation in 1835; opposition to the Poor Law Amendment Act of 1834, with its hated 'workhouse test' and principle of 'less eligibility' to poor relief; and support for the sort of Tory paternalism – including reducing the working hours of factory operatives – which were to influence many local electoral contests in 1837 and 1841.

A distinctive characteristic of Conservative extra-parliamentary organisation in this period was the development of operative Conservative associations, some of which were run alongside their parent associations. The tenor of their values may be inferred from the membership ticket of the Glasgow Conservative Operatives' Association whose legend proclaimed: 'Fear God and honour the king – and meddle not with them that are given to change.' A particularly notable feature of the development of operative Conservative associations was their strength in the industrial north-west of England. The associations were designed to widen the social basis of Conservatism and their success may be judged by the healthy membership figures they achieved – reaching several hundred members in many Lancashire towns. Operative Conservative associations played more than a purely political role, in terms of co-ordinating and organising electoral activity. Educational facilities (lectures, discussion classes and outings), sick and burial clubs, fetes and social events for members demonstrate the extent to which the associations ministered to a wide range of needs, creating an alternative political culture from that offered by reformers. These methods of political incorporation set the Conservatives apart from their Whig opponents, who were correspondingly slower (and less successful) in following suit. At the 1841 election, Peel drew attention to Conservative success in the manufacturing districts of South Lancashire and the West Riding of Yorkshire, not least because of the strength of their operative Conservative associations.

Extra-parliamentary Conservative organisation found its complement in innovations at Westminster. The most famous of these was the formation of the Carlton Club on 17 March 1832 as a central co-ordinating headquarters and sociable environment for Conservative peers and MPs to meet and exchange political intelligence. The unnerving experience of opposition had induced a group of Tory MPs (the 'Charles Street gang') to meet at an address in Charles II Street, off St James's Square, after the general election defeat of May 1831. Ten months later, after a meeting at the Thatched House Tavern on 10 March 1832, a committee was appointed to arrange the new club's premises, which were provided by Lord Kensington at 2 Carlton House Terrace. By the end of March 1832, membership of the Carlton Club already stood above 500. In 1835, the club relocated to Pall Mall, in a building designed for the purpose by Sir Robert Smirke, Peel's favourite architect. A further extension of the club took place in 1846, by which time membership was a prerequisite for aspiring Conservatives, who recognised it as the centre of the party's election machinery.

Much of the day-to-day business of party management during this period was handled by F. R. Bonham, Lord Granville Somerset and Sir George Clerk, with each of whom Peel established close relations. They helped to make the party well-resourced with intelligence and funding and developed whipping-in arrangements for important divisions in the House of Commons. The Conservatives also nurtured their relations with the press. *The Times* could sell up to 40,000 copies daily at this time and supported efforts to educate electors about the virtues of Conservatism. Their frequent reports on the activities of local Conservative associations – their dinners, speeches, toasts, fetes and associated rituals – were crucial in communicating the widespread support attracting to the party during this period.

Peel's personal contribution was significant to these developments and he freely drew upon the popularity of Conservative ideas and the strength of Conservative organisation in leading the party to electoral success. In 1846, as the party broke apart during the repeal of the

Corn Laws, Benjamin Disraeli exclaimed: 'What I cannot endure, is to hear a man come down and say: "I will rule without respect of party, though I rose by party, and I care not for your judgement, for I look to posterity."' It was a charge with more than a little truth within it. Peel's heedlessness of the dictates of party leadership, and his tendency to appeal beyond MPs to his future vindication in history, had, by this time, become endemic characteristics. Conservatives might have recalled the warning which Peel had issued, five years before, on the verge of assuming office: 'If I exercise power, it shall be upon my conception – perhaps imperfect, perhaps mistaken, but my sincere conception – of public duty.'

Peel always viewed the foundation of a strong Conservative Party as a necessary response to the Reform Act. However, the attitudes and conduct displayed by such a party required circumspection. In particular, Peel was concerned that the relationship between the House of Commons and public opinion had become dangerously unbalanced, after 1832, and its much-prized privileges (such as the right to decide election petitions) were in danger of being given up without due consideration. It was necessary for the House of Commons to restore its 'moral authority' and reassert its ability to lead, rather than follow, public opinion by reasserting such rights. However, to do so successfully, in the face of externally generated pressure, it was necessary to demonstrate mature leadership, by avoiding partisan disputes in the interests of good government. This was the origin of Peel's tactic of 'governing in opposition' during the 1830s – working with the Whig governments of Earl Grey and Viscount Melbourne, as far as was practical, to curb the dangerous excesses of the government's more radical supporters, on the one hand, and Peel's Ultra-Tory followers, on the other.

The tension between Peel's status as a party leader and the 'ministerial ethic' he had acquired through prolonged service in the governments of the 2nd Earl of Liverpool and the Duke of Wellington before 1830 has long been a cause of scholarly debate. It is not necessary to judge Peel's actions of the 1830s against the knowledge of what was to come in 1846. There is sufficient evidence, through Peel's widely reported speeches during his 'Hundred Days' ministry of 1834–35 and in his important set-piece statements in opposition – such as his addresses to the City of London (May 1835), his installation as Lord Rector of Glasgow University (January 1837) and his Merchant Taylors Hall speech (May 1838) – to demonstrate his commitment to the creation of a party representing the interests of stability, order and moderate reform.

Most of all, however, it was the legacy of Peel's experience as the head of a minority government, during 1834–35, which set the tone for the subsequent success which the Conservative Party enjoyed. After William IV unexpectedly dismissed the Whigs from office, in November 1834, Peel was summoned from his holiday in Italy to become Prime Minister for the first time. He proceeded to issue what, in retrospect, looked like a remarkably 'modern' initiative – a pre-election letter to his constituents at Tamworth in Staffordshire. The Tamworth manifesto, as this statement quickly came to be known, has assumed canonical status as the founding document of the 'New Conservatism', widely proclaimed as the instigator of a new method of political communication between party leaders and the electorate they hope to win over to a published programme for government. In itself, the proclamation of statements by leading ministers – even First Ministers of the Crown – was nothing new. The urgency for doing so was created by the fact of Peel's unexpected call to office and the stir created by the king's dismissal of the Whig ministry. Though there is nothing to suggest that Peel was innately opposed to the initiative, it was one which was forced upon him by circumstances and reinforced by the prospect of widespread publication in the leading daily newspapers, notably *The Times*, the *Morning Chronicle* and the *Morning Herald*. The draft text was completed within a week of Peel's return to London and issued forty-eight hours later. At Tamworth, where it arrived by stagecoach on 19 December 1834, it was read outside the town hall by Mr Stevens, who reported that it had 'pleased all ranks. Everybody is talking of it. We consider a very high compliment that you should give us the public intimation of the measures of government.'

The manifesto contained Peel's explicit declaration that the Conservatives would not attempt to refight the battle over the Reform Act. Rather, the government committed itself to the reform of 'proven abuses' and 'real grievances' in the institutions of church and state. Peel's statements were thus phrased in terms of a manifesto for his administration rather than as a proclamation on behalf of his party. In one of the more telling phrases, Peel explicitly appealed to those 'less interested in the contentions of party than in the maintenance of order and the cause of good government'.

In spite of doubling its number to some 290 MPs, at the general election of 1835, this policy of moderation was not sufficient to gain the Conservatives a parliamentary majority. Peel's first ministry was out-gunned, politically, by a newly formed combination (the 'Lichfield House Compact', agreed in February 1835) of Whigs and Irish MPs. This proceeded to harry the government at every turn, ensuring that its 'Hundred Days' existence did not outlast the spring. Peel resigned on 8 April 1835 and was succeeded by the Whigs under Melbourne. However, the experience of minority government had a notable consequence, in that Peel's hitherto questionable reputation, as the man who had passed Catholic emancipation into law in 1829 and appeared ambivalent over the party leadership, thereafter, emerged with the status of a latter-day William Pitt the Younger, 'the Pilot that weathered the Storm'. With an enhanced personal reputation and a formidable party apparatus behind him, Peel had helped to establish the foundations for the Conservative Party's subsequent election victory in 1841. When Parliament resumed in the autumn, the Whigs were defeated in the House of Commons by 360–269 votes (a majority of ninety-one). On 30 August 1841, Peel became Prime Minister for the second time, but this time as the head of a majority government.

Dr Richard A. Gaunt is associate professor in history at the University of Nottingham and the co-editor of both the journal *Parliamentary History* and the Royal Historical Society's Camden Series. His *Sir Robert Peel: Contemporary Perspectives* (3 vols) was published in 2022.

7

1847

DAVID WALSH

Dissolution: 23 July 1847
Polling day: 29 July–26 August 1847
Seats contested: 656
Total electorate / Total votes vast / Turnout: 1,106,514 (449,779 in contested seats) / 482,429 / 53.4 per cent
Candidates (total 879): Conservative – 422; Whig – 393; Irish Repeal – 51
Prime Minister on polling day: Lord John Russell
Main party leaders: Whig – Lord John Russell; Conservative – Lord Stanley; Irish Repeal – John O'Connell

Party performance:

Party	Votes	Percentage share	Seats
Whig	259,311	53.8	292
Conservative	205,481	42.6	325
Irish Repeal	14,128	43.6	36

Result: Hung parliament, Liberal minority government due to Conservative division

Inasmuch as Lord John Russell was Prime Minister leading a weak minority government both before and after the general election of 1847, the election itself was not a landmark one. It was, as Russell's first biographer Spencer Walpole noted, a government maintained in office not by its own strength but by division among its adversaries.

And yet, the political fragmentation in the United Kingdom, starkly illustrated by the 1847 general election, would not lead to revolution as it did across Europe in 1848.

To understand 1847, it is necessary to look back to the events of the previous year. The then Prime Minister, Robert Peel, had what appeared, at least on paper, to be an unassailable position. His Conservative Party had been elected five years earlier with a majority of seventy-six, the Commons being divided between his 367 Tories on the government benches and the opposition benches occupied by 271 Whigs and twenty members of Daniel O'Connell's Irish Repeal Party. In reality, however, Peel's party was riven by disagreement over free trade. The repeal of the Corn Laws, a tariff on the import of corn, had divided the Conservatives. Peel favoured repeal. The protectionists, led by Benjamin Disraeli and Lord George Bentinck, were violently against it. Peel, with the support of Lord John Russell's Whigs, had the votes to carry repeal but not to keep his party together. In the early hours of Friday 26 June 1846, while two weary parliamentary clerks announced to the Commons that repeal had passed through the House of Lords, Disraeli and Bentinck had corralled enough parliamentary support to defeat Peel on a bill designed to quell growing crime and disorder in Ireland. The *Northampton Mercury* noted that 'there are some victories which are necessarily fatal to the conqueror'.

In an era when a lost vote could lead to the fall of a government, and with Peel's great enterprise of repeal accomplished and with no hope of reuniting his party, Peel tendered his resignation to the queen. Victoria was left with few good options to replace him. Disraeli, she thought (at least at this stage), was 'dreadful' and Bentinck and his protectionist ilk she described as 'abominable, short-sighted and unpatriotic'. That left 'poor Lord John', depicted by *Punch* as diminutive in stature but with a big head and an even bigger top hat, to take the premiership.

Russell belonged to the Whig aristocracy. A man who was neither liked nor disliked but had proved himself to be a competent politician. As one of a committee of four, he had drafted the bill which became the Great Reform Act of 1832. As Home Secretary, he achieved considerable reforms, including the Marriages Act of 1836, which introduced civil marriages to England and Wales and allowed Catholics and Protestant Dissenters to marry in their own churches. He steered seven Acts through Parliament that reduced the number of criminal offences carrying the death penalty and also secured the pardon of the Tolpuddle Martyrs.

As Prime Minister, however, Russell was considerably less successful. Queen Victoria thought him 'torn in pieces by the number of people he (very unwisely) consults'. His nasal voice made for few occasions of oratorical brilliance in the Commons. Indeed, even his closest supporters seemed relieved when he managed to deliver a rare half-decent speech. In reality, though, it was not any personal failings on the part of Russell which caused the failure of his first administration but rather simple parliamentary arithmetic.

The exit of Peel from the Conservative Party with his free trade supporters, nominally around 110 MPs in the Commons, left a rump of about 260 protectionist Tories. Russell's 270 or so MPs were, therefore, the largest party but were very far from holding a majority. Second-rate though Peel might have thought Russell's administration to be, his main concern was to preserve free trade. As such, the Peelites chose to prop up the government rather than risk letting the protectionists back in.

With legislative success eluding him, Russell's only tangible impact was to worsen the situation in Ireland. In the previous year, a devastating potato blight had struck Europe. Nowhere was the impact greater than in Ireland, where the poorest strata of society was particularly reliant on potatoes as a source of food. By 1847, the numbers that had died of malnutrition and starvation were likely already in the hundreds of thousands. Peel's government had some success in mitigating the worst effects through the introduction of soup kitchens. This government intervention was stopped, however, by Russell's incoming administration which, in the mistaken belief that the worst of the famine was over, closed the kitchens and directed the handling of famine relief to the already badly funded Poor Law unions. The consequence was an unexampled demographic shock as around a million died and a similar number fled abroad.

One might have expected the Irish Famine to feature heavily in the general election of 1847 but, even in the Irish constituencies, the famine was conspicuous in its absence from the hustings. In part, this can be explained by the lull in the famine during the summer of 1847. In July of that year, the newspapers carried stories reporting a good season for the potato crop. But that overlooked the fact that only small numbers had been planted and severe shortages would return later in the year. With the election taking place in late July/early August 1847, however, the usual themes of Irish politics, rather than the famine, were at the fore of voters' minds. Conservatives in Ireland were just as split over free trade as their colleagues in England. The Repealers, those who favoured repeal of the Union between the United Kingdom and Ireland, were in a considerable state of flux and division, with a breakaway group called the Confederates rejecting O'Connell's insistence on non-violence.

On the eve of the 1847 general election, therefore, the political situation was fractious. Whigs against Tories, free traders against protectionists, Unionists against Repealers and Repealers against Confederates. In County Clare, the protectionist candidate resorted to personally handing out food rations to bribe his electorate. After his victory, when these rations stopped, the police had to be called out to prevent rioting. In Drogheda, the police were too late, with the local press reporting that 'there is scarcely a whole pane of glass in the windows fronting the streets'. In England, too, contests were marked by violence. In Marlow, it was reported that 'a set of blood-thirsty ruffians' had been 'assaulting any respectable person who was not favourable to the [protectionist] cause'. In other constituencies, a desire to avoid violence led to uncontested elections. As *The Times* noted of Berkshire, 'a compact at present exists amongst the influential portion of the constituency to retain the recent sitting member, professedly with a view of not disturbing the peace of the county'.

There was no hope of a strong government emerging from such an election (not least because so few seats – around 44 per cent – were contested), and so it proved. *The Times*, the *Morning Herald* and the *Morning Post* all gave slightly different results, reflecting the difficulty of assigning a particular MP to a particular party in an age before the professionalisation of politics. Broadly speaking, however, Russell's Whigs gained around twenty-one seats, rising to 292 seats, but still fell short of a majority. The position of the Peelites improved, perhaps rising by about six seats up to 116. The Irish Repealers returned thirty-four seats (and the Confederates two) and, interestingly, the Chartists succeeded with their one (and only) election victory at Nottingham. It was the protectionist Tories who lost out, dropping to around 209 seats. One protectionist MP, perhaps frustrated with the lack of support across the country, berated his Essex North constituents: 'we have endeavoured,' he said, 'with no slight difficulty to ourselves, to penetrate some of your thick heads, lest you return home as ignorant as you came!'

Without a majority, Russell's government limped on much as it had done before the election. It seems scarcely credible then that Britain, under such ostensibly weak leadership, would almost completely avoid the turmoil that struck Europe in 1848. Britain, like most of Europe in that year, had a large proportion of its population under very high levels of social and economic stress. But where short-term shortages of food pushed millions on the Continent into a genuine state of emergency which brought them out on the streets, Britain, which faced the same shortages (particularly in Ireland), was calm. The political fragmentation in Britain offers at least a partial explanation for this. On the one hand, the victory of free trade over protectionism, even while it split the Tories, at least promised cheaper, more-certain food supplies for the masses. On the other hand, opposition to the government was too divided to generate anything like the revolutionary forces that emerged first in Italy and later across much of Europe. In Ireland, where the famine could have created fertile ground for revolution, the split between the Repealers and the Confederates meant that nascent Irish nationalism did not evolve into full-blown revolution.

Russell's government may have been politically weak, but in terms of its powers of law and order, few European countries could compare. Britain had the advantage of being able to deport its most troublesome citizens to the colonies. It was also the most policed state in Europe by a considerable margin. As a result, when the new Chartist MP for Nottingham organised a Chartist rally at Kennington in April 1848, attended by around 150,000 Chartists, the government could call upon 80,000 special constables (all volunteers – including Gladstone and the future Emperor of France, Napoleon III). This, probably more than anything else, explains why the minority government elected in 1847 and the country as a whole passed through 1848 unscathed.

David Walsh is a historian and solicitor working in the Lloyd's market in London. He has contributed to history books including *Kings and Queens* and *Prime Minister Priti ... and other things that never happened*.

8

1852

NIGEL FLETCHER

Dissolution: 1 July 1852
Polling day: 7–31 July 1852
Seats contested: 654
Total electorate / Total votes cast / Turnout: 1,184,689 (652,821 in contested seats) / 743,904 / 57.9 per cent
Candidates (total 953): Conservative – 461; Whig – 488
Prime Minister on polling day: Earl of Derby
Main party leaders: Conservative – Earl of Derby; Whig – Lord John Russell

Party performance:

Party	Votes	Percentage share	Seats
Conservative (including Peelite Conservative)	311,481	41.9	330
Whig	430,882	57.9	324

Result: Notional Conservative majority of seven seats, but the Peelites held the balance of power

Ahead of the 1852 general election, a well-informed political commentator put pen to paper to sketch out their analysis of the prospects for British politics:

One thing is pretty certain – that out of the present state of confusion and discordance, a sound state of parties will be obtained, and two parties, as of old, will again exist, without which it is impossible to have a strong Government. How these parties will be formed it is impossible to say at present.

This insightful forecast came not from a newspaper pundit or a politician but from a rather more elevated vantage point. Its author was Queen Victoria, surveying the political scene in a letter to her uncle, the King of the Belgians, in March 1852.

Certainly it was true that there had been much 'confusion' in the politics of her kingdom in the preceding years. The Conservative split over the Corn Laws had driven Sir Robert Peel from office in 1846 and ushered in a Whig government under Lord John Russell. The general election of the following year had resulted in a diverse spread of party factions, with the Conservatives divided between the protectionist grouping under Lord Stanley (soon the 14th Earl of Derby) and around 100 Peelite free trade Conservatives. Against this backdrop, Russell's minority government was able to continue in office for the next five years.

In December 1851, the dismissal of the Foreign Secretary, Viscount Palmerston, weakened Russell's administration, which was then defeated in the Commons in February and resigned. The Earl of Derby was called upon to form a minority Conservative government, in which Benjamin Disraeli was made Chancellor of the Exchequer and Leader of the House of Commons.

This government has become known to history as the 'Who? Who?' ministry, after the infamous response given by the elderly Duke of Wellington when Derby read him a list of the inexperienced figures who had accepted office. It was a striking demonstration of the weakness of the new Cabinet, in which more established figures had declined to serve. Even the new Chancellor's rise to high office was more a matter of necessity than a recognition of his inherent talents.

Having been a leading figure in the protectionist cause, Disraeli had now concluded that six years after the repeal of the Corn Laws, any return to such tariffs was unlikely to occur. The popular mood in the country, particularly in the industrial towns and cities, was now firmly in favour of free trade. With a characteristic sense of pragmatic populism, he set about trying to move the Conservatives to accept the new settlement, despite resistance from Derby himself.

This was also a matter of parliamentary arithmetic. The Peelites held the balance of power and had undertaken to support the new government only on condition that a general election was held in the summer and that, if returned to office, it brought forward its next Budget before the end of the year. Disraeli had thus delivered a placeholder Budget in April in which he made no changes to tax policies and spent a portion of his speech extolling the virtues of the previous year's free trade Budget.

As Prime Minister, Derby was concerned by the rhetoric being employed by his colleague in the Lower House. This was particularly so given his own commitment in his first speech after taking office to press for the restoration of some form of duty on corn. He wrote a letter to Disraeli protesting at the tone of the Budget speech and recording his 'great anxiety' that by moving away from protectionism so markedly, they risked losing the support of their colleagues.

Given its minority status, the government was essentially a caretaker administration, and it spent the few months ahead of the promised election passing pieces of legislation that had been inherited from its predecessor and were relatively uncontentious. Despite this, Lord John Russell as Leader of the Opposition sought to cause difficulties by attacking them over the Militia Bill, the very legislation on which his own government had fallen. This approach was seen by many in his party as unnecessarily combative, and to his frustration, his MPs failed to back him in the division lobbies. Disquiet among the Whigs about his leadership increased.

The general election was set for July, with Parliament dissolved at the start of the month. In anticipation of this, *The Times* published a lyrical paean of praise for the whole British electoral system. While other countries, it said, satisfied their national instinct for freedom by electing a President or dictator, or 'by an occasional revolution', in Britain, by contrast:

> We have several hundred little revolutions instead of one, and many of those revolutions counteract one another; so that the aggregate is not much of a revolution at all. In this way do we glide from one Parliament to another by no very violent transition; and the nation grants a renewal of the lease to what is substantially the old firm of lawgivers. Hence it is that a general election, though a great national act, is not a great national change, and is often no change at all.

This evocation of stability was not without a political point. The column then moved on to predict that the forthcoming election would result in a new mandate for the established policy of free trade. No one worth listening to would ever propose reversing the policy of the past seven years, it stated. As the matter was therefore settled, it appealed to the politicians to 'let bygones be bygones' and move on from the issue. The election provided the opportunity for the 'old feud' to be buried, while also 'releasing from their oaths the adherents of an obsolete cause'.

The authors of this appeal would have been somewhat encouraged by Disraeli's election address, published earlier that month as an appeal to his electors in Buckinghamshire. In this, he spent a good few paragraphs reiterating the damage that he believed had been done to the agricultural interest by the repeal of the Corn Laws, but he conceded that the time had passed when those measures could simply be reversed. 'The spirit of the age tends to free intercourse,' he wrote, 'and no statesman can disregard with impunity the genius of the epoch in which he lives.'

Having apparently ditched a return to protectionism, the most he was prepared to offer to the landed interest was the intention of ministers to propose unspecified measures to 'diminish, certainly not to increase, the cost of production'. The rest of the manifesto rattled through some other issues, before dealing with another controversy of the age which would play a role in the election – the treatment of the Roman Catholic Church in England.

As Disraeli put it, the government had been 'anxious to subdue the heat of religious controversy', by dealing impartially with all people,

Protestant or Catholic. However, he warned that ministers could not 'sanction an opinion now in vogue, that since the [Catholic Emancipation] Act of 1829 the constitution of this country has ceased to be Protestant'. The British constitution was that of a Protestant monarchy, he stated, and it was the belief of the Conservatives that the people wanted to maintain that 'not only in form, but in spirit'.

This was a reference to a potent political issue that had been simmering since September 1850, when Pope Pius IX issued a papal decree unilaterally reintroducing Catholic bishops to England and Wales for the first time since the Reformation. This sparked an outbreak of anti-Catholic feeling in the country, to which politicians had responded. For the Whigs, Lord John Russell condemned the move and stated that 'no foreign prince or potentate will be permitted to fasten his fetters upon a nation which has so long and so nobly vindicated its right to freedom of opinion'. The following year, with Tory support, he had passed the Ecclesiastical Titles Act, making the adoption of territorial titles by anyone outside the Church of England a criminal offence. This won him support in England but rather predictably caused him difficulties with his Irish MPs.

Not to be outflanked, the Conservatives had also sought to capitalise on anti-Catholic sentiment, as Disraeli's election address had suggested. Other Conservative candidates went further, with some stating their opposition to any measures for the tolerance of Catholics. Then, on 15 June, just weeks before voting began in the election, the government issued a proclamation forbidding Catholics from marching in processions in the streets with the symbols of their religion. This provocative populist move would result in a violent start to the election.

On 27 June, Roman Catholics in Stockport took part in their traditional annual procession through the streets of the town. In deference to the proclamation, they carried no banners or religious emblems and even the priests wore ordinary clothes. The event passed off without incident and the evening was also peaceful. This did not last. The next day the local Protestant Association paraded an effigy of a priest through the streets and that night a fight broke out in a pub between Irish and English labourers.

The next evening the violence escalated, with large crowds gathering armed with sticks and stones. The homes of Irish residents were ransacked and their furniture smashed in the streets. A young Irish labourer was struck on the head and died of his injuries. As full-scale rioting took hold, local Irishmen retaliated by attacking a Protestant church, prompting the English mob to smash up and desecrate the Catholic church. The ugly scenes led to over a hundred arrests and prompted questions in the House of Commons to the Home Secretary, Spencer Walpole. Those were not the only questions he received. Queen Victoria also wrote to him asking for more information, saying she was 'much distressed at the account she has read in the papers of the dreadful riot at Stockport, alas! Caused by that most baneful of all Party feelings, *religious* hatred.'

The link between the violence and the election was made explicit in the days afterwards, with anonymous posters appearing addressed 'to the Protestant electors of the Borough of Stockport' expressing approval of the attacks against Catholics and urging voters to reject candidates who had voted against anti-Catholic legislation in Parliament. The *Manchester Guardian* pointed the finger of blame for the Stockport disturbances directly at the government, stating in an editorial comment: 'The riot appears the direct offspring of Lord Derby's proclamation against Roman catholic processions and costumes ... Had not the tory government, by a popularity-hunting attack upon Roman catholic ceremonials, cast about to stimulate the sectarian passions of the electors, we should have been free from the shame and danger.'

But anti-Catholic prejudice was not the only 'popularity-hunting attack' being exploited for electoral purposes. As the election proceeded, the Conservatives' ambiguous stance on protectionism allowed their opponents to stoke fears that they would in fact seek to reintroduce the Corn Laws. In his speech accepting nomination in his constituency of Tiverton, Lord Palmerston declared that protection involved taxing the food of the many for the benefit of the few. The election, he said, would determine the issue of 'protection or no protection' once and for all. Conservative candidates, meanwhile, differed markedly in their attitude to the issue on the hustings, with the accusation being made that Tories were protectionist in the shires, free traders in the big boroughs and somewhere in between in the smaller boroughs.

Another issue that floated around the margins of the campaign was the prospect of further political reform. With the Great Reform Act twenty years earlier, the franchise had been widened and the worst 'rotten boroughs' abolished. But the system was by no means free of abuse and corruption. The electorate remained comparatively small and there was no secret ballot, with electors instead required to record their votes publicly. Under these conditions, undue influence could continue to be exerted.

In 1851, an inquiry was launched after reports of systematic bribery in a parliamentary by-election in St Albans. The borough constituency had around 7,000 residents at the time, of whom fewer than 500 were entitled to vote. The successful candidate, Jacob Bell, was found to have spent £2,500 on his campaign (over £250,000 in today's prices), much of it used to buy votes. The inquiry found that over 300 voters had taken bribes at an average rate of £5 per vote (worth over £500 today). The system was so routine and well known that locals jokingly referred to the bribes as 'Bell-metal'.

As a result of this scandal, St Albans was disenfranchised by Act of Parliament, losing its right to return an MP until 1885. But it was certainly not the only place in which such practices occurred. During the 1852 general election, police acting on a tip-off apprehended a man in a backroom of the County Tavern in Derby who was found to have bags of gold and bank notes about his person. On the table in front of him was a list of electors with sums of money written alongside them. Police also found a note giving him instructions on where to go and how to advertise his presence. This smoking gun was signed 'W. B.' and was soon recognised to be in the handwriting of none other than the government Chief Whip and Secretary at War, the Rt Hon. William Beresford MP.

Beresford was later investigated and ultimately censured by the House of Commons for 'reckless indifference to systematic bribery'.

He was sacked from government but escaped criminal sanction. Action to investigate and punish corrupt electoral practices had become an increasingly common preoccupation of the Commons prior to the 1852 election, but action to root it out seems to have had a limited effect. According to Samuel Warren, author of the 1852 edition of a legal textbook on parliamentary election law, 'bribery is seen perhaps in fuller action at this moment than ever before, as is testified on all hands'.

Whatever influences might have been at play during the campaign, the results at the end of July showed that the electorate had not delivered a particularly decisive result. The Conservatives under Derby and Disraeli had around 290 seats, a significant increase on their previous strength, while the Peelites were now down to around forty MPs. Between them they would have a slim majority in the Commons. The Whigs, meanwhile, had around 270, with another forty Irish members likely to side with them. A return to clear two-party politics it was not. The only thing that was totally clear was that free traders were once again in the majority.

Once the results were in, it was some months before the Commons assembled for the new session at the start of November. During the intervening period, Lord John Russell began plotting a return to office, sounding out leading Peelites to join a coalition under him. Palmerston, meanwhile, had set aside his own ambitions for the top job and was seeking to persuade the Whig Lord Lansdowne to step forward as a potential Prime Minister instead. During these discussions, it soon became clear to Russell that he had lost support for his own claim, so he eventually made clear he would also be willing to serve under Lansdowne.

Derby and Disraeli, meanwhile, were disappointed not to have achieved the majority that at one point during the election they thought might be possible. Without it, the government's hold on power remained fragile. But at least the issue of free trade versus protectionism was now firmly settled. When Parliament met, Derby confirmed in his speech on the Loyal Address that the Conservatives would now 'bow to the decision of the country' and seek to carry forward free trade 'as if we ourselves had been the authors of that policy'.

The Peelites remained to be convinced that this conversion was heartfelt, but at least in theory it removed the fundamental obstacle to a reunification of the Conservative Party. Derby had a private conversation at the end of November with one of the leading Peelites, William Gladstone, to explore the possibility, and he was encouraged by the response. At around the same time, Disraeli had a meeting with Palmerston to see if he might possibly accept an offer to join Derby's Cabinet. While he declined, he did so mainly because he did not wish to come in alone. Derby believed there was now a path to winning over both.

The crucial issue was now Disraeli's Budget, due in December. Having firmly buried protectionism, he intended to use it to set out a distinctive Conservative fiscal policy that would appeal across the parties and win over their former critics. To cut a long story short, it didn't work. While his four-hour Budget speech was well received on the night, in the days afterwards the proposals unravelled, as Budgets often do. By the time it came to the last night of the Budget debate on 16 December, leading Peelites were actively hostile. Disraeli's final speech was made against the dramatic backdrop of a loud thunderstorm outside, which was perhaps a bad omen. Nevertheless, he put in a powerful performance and was loudly cheered as the Commons headed towards the vote. Then William Gladstone stood up. He used a procedural device to deny Disraeli the last word and instead launched into a furious attack on the Budget. It was devastating in its effect.

When the vote was called, Disraeli's Budget was defeated by 305 votes to 286 – an opposition majority of nineteen. Watching from the peer's gallery, Lord Derby was heard to say, 'Now we are properly smashed.' The following day he chaired a final meeting of the Cabinet then set off for Osborne House to tender his resignation to Queen Victoria. His government was replaced by a coalition of those who had brought him down, headed by the Peelite Earl of Aberdeen, in which Palmerston became Home Secretary and William Gladstone replaced Disraeli as Chancellor of the Exchequer.

Sometimes a general election is more significant for what did not happen, rather than what did. Politics is a game of luck and chance at least as much as it is one of skill and talent, and relatively small differences can have a big impact. Had Derby's Conservatives achieved the overall majority they sought in the 1852 election, Victorian politics could have taken a rather different turn. For a start, it would have meant that the defeat of Disraeli's December Budget would almost certainly not have occurred. The government could thus have continued and entrenched its move away from protectionism and consolidated support by attracting more of the remaining Peelites to rejoin the party. There was also a strong likelihood that Palmerston could then have been persuaded to join them in government, overcoming his reticence about changing parties. The 1850s and '60s, instead of being wilderness years for the Conservatives, could then have been ones of renewed hegemony for them as a reunited force.

In this scenario, the 1852 Aberdeen coalition of Peelites and Whigs would not have been formed, and William Gladstone would not that year have become Chancellor of the Exchequer, the position that first made his name. What might he have done instead? Like the other Peelites, he was still nominally a Conservative, and while his hostility to Disraeli and uncompromising free trade credentials presented barriers to him being reconciled with Derby's Conservatives, it is certainly not out of the question. During the campaign, Disraeli had predicted that if their overtures to Palmerston were successful, Gladstone and other prominent Peelites would follow.

The idea of Gladstone and Disraeli competing for power not from opposite sides of the Commons but from within the same Cabinet is a delicious prospect. Would Gladstone have displaced his rival as Chancellor? Which of them (if either) would have ended up as Prime Minister, and when? If Palmerston had also taken office with them at the same time, things would have become even more interesting. Fiercely ambitious himself, he would certainly have wished to press his claim to the premiership eventually, but in the meantime his presence would have hugely strengthened the government and further weakened the Liberal opposition. The formation of the modern Liberal Party in 1859 would not have occurred in quite the same way.

As the triumphant head of a victorious government, the Earl of Derby would have been in a very powerful position, and his reputation would today be very different. As it is, he is little-remembered as a Prime Minister, despite returning to the office twice more for brief periods in the years that followed. He still holds the record for being the longest-serving Conservative leader, but his 22-year tenure in that job was overwhelmingly spent in opposition. Had he succeeded in 1852 in winning that elusive majority, we might now be looking back at Derby as one of the dominant figures of nineteenth-century politics and a significantly long-serving Prime Minister.

I am always being told that such counterfactuals are just amusing parlour games that serious historians should avoid. We cannot know where the path not travelled might have led, so to try to map it out is ahistorical speculation. I understand this argument, but I reject it. In my view, examining critical junctures (or *Sliding Doors* moments) helps to reinforce how particularly sensitive political events are to small changes in conditions. General elections are not the only such decision points, but they are particularly intriguing ones. A few votes (or even bribes…) here or there in market towns and rural villages can lead to massive historical ramifications.

As it was, the 1852 election can be said to have finally settled the free trade question and to have laid the foundations for the epic rivalry between Gladstone and Disraeli that would last for the next twenty-eight years. The events surrounding it did indeed also point the way towards the (eventual) restoration of more stable two-party politics, just as Queen Victoria had predicted. But it was in determining 'how these parties will be formed', as she put it, that made the outcome of this particular election so crucial.

Dr Nigel Fletcher is a political historian at King's College London and the author of *The Not Quite Prime Ministers: Leaders of the Opposition 1783–2020*.

9

1857

ALEX NOONAN

Dissolution: 21 March 1857
Polling day: 27 March–24 April 1857
Seats contested: 654
Total electorate / Total votes cast / Turnout: 1,235,530 (616,929 in contested seats) / 716,552 / 58.9 per cent
Candidates (total 878): Whig – 507; Conservative – 351; Independent Irish – 19
Prime Minister on polling day: Lord Palmerston
Main party leaders: Whig – Lord Palmerston; Conservative – Earl of Derby

Party performance:

Party	Votes	Percentage share	Seats
Whig	464,127	64.8	377
Conservative	239,712	33.5	264
Independent Irish	12,099	8.6	13

Result: Whig majority of 100 seats

A Parliament divided. A Prime Minister thwarted by parliamentary opponents over a key plank of government foreign policy. A single-issue election campaign to settle the matter, with the Prime Minister being rewarded with a handsome parliamentary majority by the electorate and some of his key opponents unseated. You might very well believe this to be a description of the election of 2019, when Boris Johnson prevailed where his predecessor had failed in successfully running a single-issue campaign to 'get Brexit done'. However, it is an equally apt summary of the events of the British general election of 1857. Lord Palmerston bestrode and dominated the stage of mid-nineteenth-century British politics, a populist distrusted by many of his fellow politicians but adored by the masses of mid-Victorian Britain. Going to the country in early 1857 over his government's conduct in the *Arrow* affair of the Second Opium War, Palmerston led his Whigs to a resounding victory over the opposition Conservatives, with the election also having some unexpected longer-term consequences for the future of British democracy.

Despite the implications of Lord Palmerston's title, which he had inherited from his father in 1802, the holders of Irish peerages were ineligible to take a seat in the House of Lords, so it was into the Commons as a Tory MP that Palmerston launched his political career in 1807, at the age of twenty-three. Within two years he had been appointed to the Cabinet as Secretary at War, a post responsible for army administration, which he held for nearly twenty years until 1828. He defected to the Whigs in 1830 and held the position of Foreign Secretary for three successive periods, from 1830 to 1834, 1835 to 1841 and 1846 to 1851. It was in this position that Palmerston did much to formulate the essentials of British foreign policy at a time when Britain was at the peak of its global power, with his abrasive style earning him the sobriquet 'Lord Pumice Stone' and his emphasis on military intimidation being often described as 'gunboat diplomacy'. Perhaps the most infamous example of this was his role in the Don Pacifico affair of 1847, when a British subject in Greece was unaided by local police after being attacked by an antisemitic mob. Palmerston responded by having the British fleet blockade a Greek port, declaring that every British subject the world over should be able to call upon protection from their government in the same way the Romans had done at the height of their empire.

Lord Palmerston would never return to the Foreign Office after 1851, when he had resigned as Foreign Secretary after being accused by Queen Victoria of failing to request official royal sanction in conducting his policy. While he was therefore unable to influence the events that led to the outbreak of war in the Crimea in the early 1850s, such was his perceived popularity and importance in forming a government that he was made Home Secretary in 1852. One biographer of Palmerston's recounts an anecdote to suggest, however, that his heart still truly lay in the sphere of foreign affairs. Summoned to the palace to update the queen on a wave of strikes breaking across the north of England, Palmerston is alleged to have responded: 'There is no definite news, Madam, but it seems certain that the Turks have crossed the Danube!' With the fall of the Earl of Aberdeen's Whig–Peelite ministry in 1855 over the conduct of the Crimean War, and with all other plausible candidates either unwilling or unable to form a government, it was with great reluctance that Queen Victoria sent for Lord Palmerston to become Prime Minister in February 1855. At the age of seventy, he remains to date the oldest individual in British history to assume the premiership for the first time. In this era, the linkage between ministries and party composition in the Commons was not as obvious as it is today. While the 1852 election had seen the Conservatives secure a nominal parliamentary majority, the party was in fact irreconcilably divided between Peelite supporters of free trade, such as William Gladstone, and protectionists such as Benjamin Disraeli, allowing the Whigs to form governments with Peelite support.

A determination to bring about a swift resolution to the hostilities in the Crimea occupied Palmerston's first twelve months in office, convincing the French Emperor Napoleon III to back away from peace negotiations with Russia until Britain and France had captured the port of Sevastopol. This stronger negotiating position forced Russia to make terms unequivocally, and a peace treaty signed in March 1856 saw the final resolution of conflict around the Black Sea. It was, however, controversy around Palmerston's actions much farther to the east, in China, that was to precipitate and dominate the election campaign of early 1857. As Foreign Secretary, Palmerston had been instrumental in the First Opium War of 1839–42, when the British had bombarded Chinese ports in response to the ruling Qing dynasty's attempts to ban the opium trade, which was extremely financially lucrative for British merchants. Much as the following century saw how the humiliating terms of the First World War contributed directly to the outbreak of the Second, so the Treaty of Nanking which the British imposed upon China in 1842 directly contributed to the start of the Second Opium War in 1856. The treaty had mandated the Chinese to open five ports to Britain for their permanent use in the opium trade, as well as transferring control of Hong Kong to the British Empire. These were humiliations which the Chinese found hard to stomach.

The immediate spark for a renewal of hostilities was the so-called *Arrow* affair, when in October 1856 a Chinese-owned and Chinese-manned ship, the *Arrow*, sailed into the port of Canton. Upon making shore, a member of the *Arrow*'s crew was recognised by the owner of another Chinese cargo ship as being one of a gang of pirates who had previously raided one of his other vessels, and the *Arrow* was seized by the Chinese authorities as a result. What brought the British into all of this was the fact that the owner of the *Arrow* had registered the ship in Hong Kong, allowing it to fly the British flag and thus expect British protection. As previously described, Palmerston had made it a cornerstone of British imperial policy that British subjects and supplicants could expect to have their interests robustly defended wherever they were across the globe. Thus, a British diplomat stationed in Canton, Harry Parkes, demanded an immediate apology from the local commissioner. When this commissioner, Ye Mingchen, refused, his compound was shelled by British naval forces, unleashing a chain of events in which Ye called upon the locals of Canton to rise up against their British oppressors, offering a $100 bounty for the head of any British subject. The Second Opium War had begun, and at the height of the hostilities, shells were being unleashed on Canton by the British every ten minutes, with the full support of Lord Palmerston's ministry back in London.

There was immediate parliamentary opposition to the government's support for the hostilities in China, with many 'Peelite' Conservatives, most prominently William Gladstone, upon whom

Palmerston's Whig ministry depended for support, being appalled at the Prime Minister's jingoistic drum-beating for war, which they believed to be a betrayal of liberal principles. There was a hope that this might lead to a rapprochement between Peelite free traders and protectionist Conservatives. The protectionist Conservative leader in the Commons, Benjamin Disraeli, could sense the opportunity to inflict a humiliating defeat upon Palmerston's Whig ministry, and a motion of censure against the government was tabled in the House of Commons in early 1857.

Palmerston did not take this lying down, taking to his feet at the dispatch box to decry his opponents, who he argued had displayed 'an anti-English feeling, an abnegation of those ties which bind men to their country and to their fellow countrymen', with their mindset being that 'everything that was English was wrong, and everything that was hostile to England was right'. Voting to censure the government for its role in the outbreak of the war would, argued the Prime Minister, demonstrate that the House of Commons had chosen to 'abandon a large community of British subjects at the extreme end of the globe to a set of barbarians, a set of kidnapping, murdering, poisoning barbarians'. Opponents of the action, and thus of Palmerston, were quick to point out that the *Arrow*'s British registration had actually expired a month before it was seized. They doubted the claims of any direct insult to Britain and argued it was legitimate for China to try to prosecute the activities of organised pirates. In the event, Palmerston lost the vote of censure by a majority of sixteen votes, to which the Cabinet agreed the only correct response would be to request a dissolution of Parliament from the queen and to fight a general election to settle the matter.

The campaign that followed the dissolution of Parliament in early 1857 hinged almost solely around support or opposition for the Prime Minister's policy in China. Collating the early results in late March 1857, *The Times* announced that 'the country having been appealed to by Lord Palmerston to decide between him and the late House of Commons upon the question of the Chinese hostilities, we have distinguished the members returned as Ministerial and Oppositional according to their declared opinions upon that subject', with two columns sorting MPs by this category rather than by party political allegiance. As the celebrated historian A. J. P. Taylor wrote, 'in 1857 there was no issue before the electorate except whether Palmerston should be Prime Minister, and no one could pretend Palmerston had any policy except to be himself'. This was certainly recognised by his opponents; in his election address to his Buckingham constituency, Disraeli accused Palmerston of ensuring that 'his external system is turbulent and aggressive that his rule at home may be tranquil and unassailed', or, in other words, that he had engineered a belligerent foreign policy to distract from having to do much in the way of domestic policy or social reform. While many of the Prime Minister's earnest and high-minded opponents took exception to his foreign policy and style, the electors of Britain turned out to have quite a different opinion. The election took place over a period of a month, with results trickling in from 27 March to 24 April 1857. When the final results were tallied, Lord Palmerston's Whigs had secured a parliamentary majority of 100 seats, with 377 Whig MPs to 264 Conservatives and thirteen MPs for the Independent Irish Party. The Whigs had secured 64.8 per cent of the vote, to 33.5 per cent for the Conservatives, on a turnout of 58.9 per cent. The result represented a resounding success for Palmerston's policy, approach and style. Two of the leading supporters of the vote of censure, Richard Cobden and John Bright, even lost their seats. While Disraeli grumbled that the result was *actually* due to voters' disgust at the Conservatives' failure to form an administration back in 1855, few found this a convincing explanation, including Cobden himself, who complained that the Prime Minister had 'made greater use of that means of creating an artificial public opinion than any minister since the time of Bolingbroke'.

A caveat must be added at this juncture for readers, as elections held before our own democratic era differed considerably from their contemporary counterparts. First and foremost, most of the population in Britain simply had no right to vote in the 1857 election. The total of those entitled to vote in 1857 stood at 1.23 million, out of an estimated population of 27.36 million, meaning just under 4.5

per cent of the total population were permitted to take part in the election. In addition, the political parties were not the cohesive, coherent organisations of today, being instead parliamentary groupings in which temperament and background often mattered as much as any ideological conviction or belief. It was only in the following decades, with the rise of Gladstone and Disraeli, that the Conservative and Liberal parties emerged in a form recognisable to us today. The election was held before the introduction of the secret ballot in 1872, with public voting used to tally results. While the passage in 1854 of the Corrupt Practices Prevention Act had been an attempt to limit the use of bribery and intimidation in election contests, via the use of small levies for miscreants, a lack of provision in the Act for any legal enforcement of its provisions meant it had little effect. Finally, 328 seats out of 654 were uncontested in 1857; this meant that just over half of all seats, 50.2 per cent, featured a single candidate who was elected unopposed as a result. This was one of the four times since the passage of the 1832 Reform Act that a majority of seats had returned MPs unopposed, alongside 1841, 1847 and 1859. This not only serves as a useful reminder of just how different the conduct of general elections was in the nineteenth century but also perhaps gives us an indication that the dominating issue of the *Arrow* affair was not quite as divisive in the country at large as it had been in the House of Commons.

Nevertheless, in the immediate aftermath of the election, it appeared that Lord Palmerston was the master of all he surveyed. As Earl Granville had written in a letter to Earl Canning on 8 April 1857, 'the elections have turned entirely on Palmerston personally', and they cemented his place as the dominating figure of British politics. The 1857 election was the last where it makes sense to speak of Whigs, with Palmerston being able to unite Whigs and Peelite Conservatives to form a new party, the Liberals, which William Gladstone would come to dominate for the rest of the nineteenth century. There was, however, to be an unexpected long-term consequence of the fact that the election had so singularly focused on support for, or opposition to, the Prime Minister's policy in China. Lord Palmerston was highly ambiguous on the question of who should be able to exercise the right to vote. This is perhaps not surprising, given his overwhelming interest and preoccupation in the field of foreign affairs, and he neither supported nor dismissed the idea of widening the electoral franchise in his public pronouncements on the subject. There had been no enlargement of the franchise since the 'Great' Reform Act of 1832, which had produced a uniform national qualification for the vote for the first time. As a consequence of Palmerston's ambiguity on the issue, and as the historian Robert Saunders has argued, candidates at the 1857 election 'could wrap themselves in Palmerston's mantle while declaring for household and even manhood suffrage'. The parliament elected in 1857 was to prove more radical than might have been expected, with a higher number of MPs in favour of reform after the election than had been the case before it. With the result of the election causing the resolution of the intense disagreements over foreign policy that had dominated the previous parliament, a space opened up in British politics which the question of franchise reform was to fill, with three consecutive governments between 1857 and 1860 promising legislation on the subject. The 1867 Reform Act was to follow just ten years later, putting Britain firmly on the road towards becoming a full democracy. Above all else, perhaps the most enduring lesson of 1857 is that 'single-issue' elections, in so clearly resolving a particularly contentious issue of the day, can open up the political agenda to unexpected and unanticipated avenues of debate. It is a lesson that perhaps our present-day politicians would do well to heed.

Dr Alex Noonan is a political and socio-cultural historian of modern Britain. He recently completed his doctoral thesis, 'Spectators or Citizens?', a study of British political culture from 1974 to 1994, at the University of Sheffield.

10

1859

MATTHEW COLE

Dissolution: 23 April 1859
Polling day: 28 April–18 May 1859
Seats contested: 654
Total electorate / Total votes cast / Turnout: 1,271,900 (471,302 in contested seats) / 565,500 / 63.7 per cent
Candidates (total 860): Liberal – 465; Conservative – 394
Prime Minister on polling day: Earl of Derby
Main party leaders: Liberal – Lord Palmerston; Conservative – Earl of Derby

Party performance:

Party	Votes	Percentage share	Seats
Liberal	372,117	65.8	356
Conservative	193,232	34.2	298

Result: Liberal majority of fifty-nine seats

Like points in the course of a river, some elections mark continuity, others change. Contests such as 2001, 1983 or 1935 mark continued public approval of a clear decision made at the previous election about government personnel and policy. The elections of 1997, 1945 or 1906, on the other hand, are examples of a watershed – a decisive change in direction. The general election of 1859 is a hybrid, even different, type: superficially it gives the impression that nothing much had changed – the two main parties continued to jockey uneasily for power, led by the same four key figures as at the previous election; candidate and voter activity was lower than at any time since before the Great Reform Act or subsequently; and neither party's vote moved by more than 1 per cent. Yet British politics was significantly changed by the way in which this result was achieved, and its impact on the next government, the party system and the political agenda. Looked at in terms of seats, votes and ministers, 1859 is something of a non-event; but it marks an unseen breaking point in parliamentary relationships which made change on the ground possible. The election of 1859 is characterised by neither simple change nor continuity – it was, if the geographical analogy applies, a hidden watershed.

Following the clear battle lines drawn between Tories and Whigs over the Reform Act in 1832, the party system had fragmented by the 1850s to the point that one of its veterans, Lord John Russell, complained that it was 'as unstable as water'. Starting with the resignation of the Prime Minister responsible for the Act, Earl Grey, there were ten changes of premier in the quarter century leading up to 1859 – an average term of office of two and a half years, which rivals post-Brexit Britain. The corresponding figures in the previous and subsequent quarter centuries were seven new Prime Ministers lasting a more respectable three and a half years at a time.

Part of the cause of this was party splits over both policies and personalities. Some Tories were uneasy about Peel's modernisation of the party with the Tamworth Manifesto of 1834, which accepted Whig reforms, and his adoption of the party title 'Conservative'. This strategy won back some supporters who had defected to the Whigs but did not save Peel at the next year's election. More damaging was the split over Peel's abandonment of the Corn Laws ten years later, following which his own MPs removed him as leader and Prime Minister, and his supporters (including Gladstone) walked out to form a distinct parliamentary group. Irish Catholic MPs, who until the potato famine of the late 1840s had mostly supported the Whigs, had begun to form an independent group in the Commons campaigning on questions of land and education, only to split into three factions.

It was the support of Peelites which sustained the Whig government led by Lord John Russell after Peel's fall, but bitter arguments between Russell and his Foreign Secretary Palmerston led to a coalition under Lord Aberdeen, then a Whig administration led by Palmerston who lost a vote of confidence and was replaced by a short-lived minority government under Tory leader Lord Derby. Constitutional observer Walter Bagehot wrote a decade later that multi-factional, transactional intrigue had brought British politics to a chaotic standstill:

> The events of 1858, though not a perfect illustration of what I mean, are a sufficient illustration. The Radical party, acting apart from the moderate Liberal party, kept Lord Derby in power. The ultra-movement party thought it expedient to combine with the non-movement party. As one of them coarsely but clearly put it, 'we get more of our way under these men than under the other men'; he meant that, in his judgment, the Tories would be more obedient to the Radicals than the Whigs.

'It is obvious', Bagehot concluded, 'that a union of opposites so marked could not be durable.' It was the defeat in the Commons of Derby's attempt at electoral reform on 31 March which triggered the 1859 election in circumstances of suspicion and division among parliamentary leaders on all sides.

It is worth examining the key personalities involved in the 1859 campaign. Lord Derby is the longest-serving Conservative leader in the party's history and the second-richest person to be Prime Minister after Rishi Sunak. Notoriously lugubrious in outlook, Derby wrote to his Chancellor Disraeli before the election that the Conservatives, 'if not an actual corpse', were at best 'in a state of suspended animation'; he had persuaded Queen Victoria to extend the prorogation of Parliament by three weeks in January to secure Cabinet agreement on his Reform Bill but suffered two resignations anyway. Disraeli's character contrasted dramatically with Derby's: flamboyant, ambitious and outspoken in criticism of others, the future Prime Minister complained to supporters about Derby that 'we never see him. His house is always closed; he subscribes to nothing, though his fortune is very large, and expects, nevertheless, everything to be done.'

The Whig opposition had two rival leaders: Lords Palmerston and John Russell. Both former Prime Ministers, they both keenly anticipated a return to No. 10 Downing Street. Though both opposed the Tories, they disagreed fiercely over some key issues of mid-Victorian policy – notably foreign policy, where Palmerston had made his name as an imperialist Foreign Secretary given to gunboat diplomacy; and voting reform, where Russell was ready to go further in extending the franchise. Palmerston's erstwhile Chancellor George Lewis wrote that 'the personal jealousies and alienations among the liberal party are such as to deprive it of all compact strength' and another of Palmerston's Cabinet, Sidney Herbert, despaired at the start of 1859 at the prospects 'of the formation of an efficient party, let alone government, out of the chaos on the opposition benches'.

Caught between the two main parties, Peelite Gladstone bewildered the House with a speech insisting that though he would vote with the government, MPs should not draw the conclusion that he supported it. Even members of Gladstone's own family confided privately that they had no idea of his attitude to the state of party politics, and they were unsure of whether he had either.

Despite their misgivings and the uncertainty of political relationships, Russell and Palmerston jointly promoted a resolution on reform in March 1859 opposing that of Lord Derby, which carried in the Commons causing the latter to call a general election. Parliament was dissolved the following month, and the campaign ran from 28 April until 18 May.

To describe the 1859 campaign as a damp squib would be a gross understatement. Two historians of the Conservative Party, Robert Blake and John Ramsden, have dismissed the contest's atmosphere as 'apathetic'. In modern terms, it barely happened. In most of the country, no election took place at all: nearly three-fifths of constituencies, containing nearly two-thirds of all entitled voters, saw no contest – a figure higher than any other election after 1832. In county seats, this figure rose to three-quarters, and only eight Scottish and four Welsh seats held polls. Some significant figures were missing in action: radical free trade advocate Richard Cobden was in the United States, and Gladstone spent the campaign in London, reading *Adam Bede* and continuing his 'rescue' mission with sex workers. Palmerston spoke in his constituency of Tiverton; Derby at the Mansion House; and Russell to the electors in the City – but the contents of their speeches were aimed at parliamentary colleagues more than voters. Especially on controversies in foreign policy, notably Britain's response to the conflict between Austria and Italy, party leaders edged closer towards potential allies: Palmerston, in particular, redrafted his constituency speech at short notice to seek conciliation with Russell and Gladstone.

The Conservatives built up a campaign war chest of £50,000 (larger than their opponents') but devoted it entirely to forty seats. Other Conservative candidates had to fend for themselves. Overall, total spending by candidates fell between 1857 and 1859, before shooting up by a factor of four at the next election in 1865. Expenditure per contest similarly dipped compared with 1857, then almost doubled from just over £400 to nearly £800 in 1865. Unsurprisingly, despite the usual clutch of constituency controversies, there were fewer petitions to challenge election outcomes in 1859 than at either of the surrounding general elections.

The key figures in the campaign were mostly of a generation or more's familiarity to the public: Palmerston, Russell and Derby – 'the pre-'32 statesmen', as Bagehot called them – had all been in the Commons for a decade or more when the Great Reform Act passed a quarter of a century earlier; they and Disraeli had all held at least one of the great offices of state. Between them, these four had fifty-eight years of Cabinet service, and with an average age of sixty-three, they hardly represented a break with the past; but according to Bagehot, they 'retained great power'.

There was little in the way of electoral swing or rebalancing of the Commons, either: the outcome undershot both the hopes and fears of those in all parties. Although with party labels and loyalties in such flux it is difficult comprehensively to measure changes in support, there was a change of less than 1 per cent in the share of the votes given to candidates identified as Conservatives to those regarded as Whigs, the latter retaining almost two-thirds of the votes cast. The Tories gained ground in smaller borough seats, winning fourteen seats with populations under 10,000, but failed to break through in bigger towns and cities; in Ireland, on the other hand, they gained more seats than the Liberals for the first and only time. Disraeli told colleagues that he thought the Conservatives would gain between forty and sixty seats overall depending on luck. In the end they gained thirty-four, and the Liberal majority in the Commons fell from the 1857 peak of 113 to a still-workable fifty-eight. Nor did the exclusive social background of MPs change: while it is unsurprising that the Tories remained overwhelmingly from an aristocratic and landed background, the same remained true of nearly two-thirds of Liberal MPs elected in 1859.

However, despite the appearance of stagnation in the personnel of high politics, 1859 showed evidence of a public keen to voice its opinions, particularly in urban England. Where they had a choice, voters turned out in larger numbers than at the previous and following general elections. In a context in which polls were open for nearly three weeks – candidates sometimes withdrew halfway through polling or employed lawyers to dispute the right of their opponents' supporters to vote in the run-up to the election – it is harder than today to make meaningful statements about turnout. However, F. W. S. Craig reckoned that, where a contest took place, 63.7 per cent of electors used their vote in 1859, above the corresponding figures for 1857 (58.9 per cent) and 1865 (62.5). Of the seventy-two constituencies contested in 1857, 1859 and 1865, fifty-nine had a higher raw turnout in 1859 than two years earlier, when the electorate nationally was less than 3 per cent smaller. In fourteen of these seats, the number of voters in 1859 was higher than in 1865 as well, despite a rise of over 6 per cent in the number of Britons entitled to vote.

A study of campaigning in the cities of Yorkshire in 1859 by W. L. Guttsman found widespread activity by 'Household Franchise and

Ballot Associations', non-electors' committees and other working-class radical organisations, helped by the press being recently freed from stamp duty:

> What is more, there is clear evidence of strong and vocal participation of working men in the meetings urging electoral reforms which preceded and followed the government bill. Their presence on the platform of such meetings presents a comparatively novel feature and was regarded by one working-class speaker as an indication of the political emancipation of his class.

Another historian of urban life, Asa Briggs, remarked that 'the populous districts were never completely quiet in the mid-Victorian period even when they appeared to be quiescent'. Politicians were not as active in 1859 as their constituents – a signal from the people that the tired elite could not ignore.

It was political sociologist Moisei Ostrogorski who noted a generation later in 1902 that the turbulence in Parliament ultimately reflected a disjuncture from the changing social order of industrial Britain. Even though only one man in six – and no women – could vote, and those that did voted in view of candidates, employers and landlords, it was impossible for the Commons to isolate itself from the demands of the excluded:

> Parliament ceased to exhibit its old consistency because society had lost it. The constant multiplication of degrees in the social scale, the variety of new aspirations, the change of social relations from the concrete to a generalised standard, all found their way into the House, narrow as the entrance to it was at that time.

The outcomes of the 1859 campaign were much more significant than its arithmetical results, its effects more dramatic than its campaign. Firstly, the party system in Parliament took on its modern, consolidated form: the independent Irish MPs and the Peelites disappeared or merged into the two main parties. The Chartists – the independent vehicle for working-class representation since the Reform Act – had already lost their only seat and fought their last election in 1859. The MPs of the main parties then began to consolidate and develop a national political brand: in the 1850s, nearly a third of non-Conservative MPs used designations such as 'Whig' or 'Reformer' to describe themselves – in the 1859 parliament, over 90 per cent of them used the label 'Liberal'.

The clearest demonstration of this strengthening of party organisation came with the meeting at Willis's Rooms in St James's Street, London, on 6 June 1859 of 274 Whig, Peelite and radical MPs who agreed to support a government under Palmerston, drawing supporters of all three groups into its ranks. This is generally regarded as the foundation of the modern Liberal Party, the forerunners of the Liberal Democrats.

Palmerston kept his word, including in his government a new generation of radical free traders such as Thomas Milner Gibson, an ardent supporter of Richard Cobden, and giving former Peelite Gladstone the role of Chancellor of the Exchequer in which his reforms earned him the sobriquet 'the People's William'. Palmerston's rival Russell accepted the position of Foreign Secretary in a not-so-tacit deal similar to those struck by Anthony Eden and Gordon Brown, awaiting their turn to be premier (and ultimately with similarly frustrating rewards). Cobden did not take up office, but he and John Bright gave their broad support to Palmerston, who wrote to reassure Cobden about his new administration that 'I have endeavoured so to form it that it should contain representatives of all sections of the Liberal party, convinced as I am that no government constructed upon any other basis could have sufficient prospect of duration, or would be sufficiently satisfactory to the country'.

A. J. P. Taylor's assessment nearly a century later confirmed the significance of these developments:

> The government which Palmerston organised in June 1859 was a coalition of a different kind: not a coalition of groups which looked back to the past, but a coalition which anticipated the future. Had it not

been for Palmerston himself – too individual, too full of personality to be fitted into a party-pattern – it would have been the first Liberal government in our history. Everything that was important in it was Liberal – finance, administrative reform, its very composition.

Thus, high politics was required to react, however imperfectly, to social change; but it was the judgement and foresight of figures such as Russell, Gladstone and Palmerston which determined the timing and nature of that change. Though driven by a mixture of necessity and personal ambition, Palmerston was unusual as a statesman of such seniority in being ready to embrace change in the last stages of his career in a way that Gladstone, Churchill and Thatcher after him struggled to do.

Fabian historians G. D. H. Cole and Raymond Postgate commented bitterly in the 1930s that 'it was a mark of the new passivity of the working class that the great majority of it was willing to believe that the victory of Gladstone and Palmerston at this election would mean a great instalment of reform'; but this was to ignore the changing course of the historical river below the very highest levels of politics. In 1860, Liberal MPs founded their party's Registration Association to co-ordinate themselves more closely and to register and recruit voters in the way parties have done ever since. In the same year, Lord John Russell presented a Reform Bill aiming to extend the franchise, and this demand was supported before the next election from outside Parliament by the activities of the Reform League and the Reform Union. After another Liberal victory in 1865, Russell's bill was put before the House and even Disraeli felt obliged to take up reform as Prime Minister, passing the Second Reform Act of 1867 which nearly doubled the electorate by granting the vote to more prosperous working men in towns and cities. They duly thanked Gladstone's Liberals with another election triumph only nine years after the 'apathy' of 1859.

Looked at in terms of its background and conduct, the election campaign of 1859 represents the death throes of a dysfunctional, closed political system unable to govern a changing Britain. Yet it ushered in a new political generation and a new agenda of social and political reform which came to be known as the 'spirit of the '60s'. It is more than coincidence that 1859 is the publication date of Charles Darwin's *On the Origin of Species*, John Stuart Mill's *On Liberty* and *Self-Help* by Samuel Smiles – in their different ways, three texts symbolising the individualist, rationalist and secular world emerging through demands for education, the free press and representation for workers and later women. The river which emerged from the hidden watershed of 1859 had an increasingly deep, fast-flowing and turbulent course which Gladstone, Disraeli and their contemporaries had to navigate. The lesson of 1859 is that the swing in votes and seats is not always a barometer of the significance of an election.

Dr Matthew Cole teaches history at the University of Birmingham.

11

1865

CHARLES PITT

Dissolution: 6 July 1865
Polling day: 11–24 July 1865
Seats contested: 658
Total electorate / Total votes cast / Turnout: 1,350,404 (695,235 in contested seats) / 854,856 / 62.5 per cent
Candidates (total 922): Liberal – 516; Conservative – 406
Prime Minister on polling day: Lord Palmerston
Main party leaders: Liberal – Lord Palmerston; Conservative – Earl of Derby

Party performance:

Party	Votes	Percentage share	Seats
Liberal	508,821	59.5	369
Conservative	346,035	40.5	289

Result: Liberal majority of eighty-one seats

The 1865 election was a contest between two highly experienced politicians leading fractious political coalitions. The Liberal Prime Minister, Viscount Palmerston, was a political colossus, popular in the country and renowned for his skills in foreign affairs. He had been in office for a decade and had skilfully balanced the factions for reaction and reform in his party – though the tensions were never far below the surface. The Conservatives under Lord Derby were still haunted by the Corn Laws of 1846 and the seismic splits in the party which followed.

The election was the last act of Palmerston's long career – he would die before the House of Commons returned after the election. It was also the last election to take place before the 1867 Reform Act, which would end many of the corrupt practices that characterised the campaign. The government increased its majority, and the campaign was widely seen as uneventful – 1865 is not one of our more memorable elections. But it has a fine cast of characters, a worrying level of bribery and corruption and the defenestration of a political giant – William Gladstone lost his seat. It tells a story of political class right at the end of a period of profound change in British politics and raises the curtain for the coming age of Gladstone and Disraeli.

The timing of the election was not caused by a political crisis – unlike many others in the nineteenth century. In 1852, the Budget introduced by Chancellor of the Exchequer Disraeli – and ongoing rows over the Corn Laws – forced an election. The 1857 election followed a vote of censure on Palmerston's government over the *Arrow* affair and the Second Opium War in China. The 1865 election, however, was held because the parliament had run its term – the 1715 Septennial Act extended the maximum length of a parliament from three to seven years, and it remained in place until 1911. The *Illustrated London News* noted that 'a Dissolution of Parliament, when it is effected by mere lapse of time, calls public attention to the general principles on which the policy of the country has proceeded'. Unlike recent elections, in 1865 the electorate were not voting on an issue or a person but on the 'whole field of politics'.

Unusually for an election held at the last possible moment, the consensus was that the government had done a reasonably good job. Since 1859, the country had enjoyed 'profound peace, unusual contentment and singular prosperity', and while the *London News* recognised that much of this could not be attributed to Parliament, the people are 'ready enough to connect together a progressively satisfactory condition of public affairs with wise and beneficial legislation'.

Palmerston remained hugely popular. His administration had

passed important legislation. The 1861 Offences Against the Person Act brought together and codified statutes around violent crime and remains the basis for prosecution for personal injury today. The basis of 21st-century company law lies in the 1862 Companies Act. Having legislated to make divorce easier, Palmerston found himself named as a co-respondent in 1863, and while it was a false claim, his reputation as an adulterer did not harm to his popularity.

Palmerston's flair for diplomacy and his mastery of foreign affairs had also been evident since the last election. When the American Civil War broke out in 1861, he was sympathetic to the breakaway Confederate states – even though he was an opponent of slavery. Self-interestedly, he felt a divided United States would mean more trading opportunities for Britain. Despite the impact of the war on cotton supplies, and support among the people for both the Union and the Confederacy, Palmerston's official position was aloof neutrality. The other foreign affairs crisis over Schleswig-Holstein was famously so complicated it prompted Palmerston's line: 'Only three men in Europe have ever understood it. One was Prince Albert, who is dead. The second was a German professor who became mad. I am the third and have forgotten all about it.' He deftly avoided a vote of censure for failing to intervene when Bismarck annexed two duchies of Denmark to Prussia in 1864.

The Leader of the Opposition was Edward Smith-Stanley, 14th Earl of Derby. He had served as Prime Minister briefly from February to December 1852, displacing Lord John Russell's Whig government and winning more seats than him in the June election. In December that year, his Chancellor Disraeli could not get a Budget through the House of Commons and the queen sent for Lord Aberdeen. When that administration fell in 1855, Derby declined to form a government, to the frustration of Disraeli. He returned to Downing Street in February 1858 for sixteen months and successfully formalised British rule in India following the Indian Rebellion of 1857 but was again undone by a coalition of Whigs and radicals, who united behind Palmerston in July 1859.

Derby's brief premierships, sandwiched between bigger political beasts, have made him famously forgettable – his most recent biography was subtitled *The Forgotten Prime Minister*. When he accepted the Garter in 1859, it was thought his career was ending, but he stayed on as Leader of the Opposition, with his protégé Disraeli leading in the House of Commons.

As well as time in government, Derby knew the business of opposition, making famous the Whig George Tierney's quote: 'The duty of an opposition [is] very simple ... to oppose everything, and propose nothing.' But in opposing Palmerston's government, Derby was restrained, relying more on masterly inactivity than on tribal attacks. His aim was to build up his reputation as a statesman acting not in his party's but in the nation's interest – something reinforced by the popularity of Palmerston's approach to foreign policy on all sides of the House. He described his approach as 'armed neutrality' and wanted to give the government the space to cause their own ruin: 'Wait, don't attack ministers, that will only bind them together – if left alone they must fall to pieces by their own disunion.'

When first in opposition, he attempted to heal the rifts in the Tory Party caused by the row over the Corn Laws, but hopes of unifying his party faded through the parliament. Instead, his best hope was to try to effect a split in the Liberals. Palmerston's old age and infirmity were also a reason in Derby's mind to bide his time and the Prime Minister had several health scares in the early 1860s. Another tactic was to expose splits between Palmerston and his Chancellor Gladstone – who occasionally threatened to resign. However, after the 1862 Budget, which included popular tax cuts, Gladstone was less vulnerable to attack. Queen Victoria's deep mourning for Prince Albert, who died in 1861, and her wish that politics be calm and uncontroversial also gave Derby grounds (or an excuse) to support Palmerston individually and a private undertaking not to undermine him by joining forces with his opponents in government.

When Parliament was dissolved by Queen Victoria on 6 July 1865, most commentators expected Palmerston and the Liberals to remain in power. According to *The Economist*, 'the next parliament will wholly resemble the late parliament in its most conspicuous bias – in its utter indisposition to organic change.'

There was one big name casualty of the election, William Gladstone, who lost his seat for the University of Oxford. In 1864, he had set out his views on reform during a debate on a bill to lower the franchise qualification from £10 to £6, in effect extending voting rights. He said that every man 'who is not presumably incapacitated by some consideration of personal unfitness or of political danger is morally entitled to come within the pale of the constitution'. The bill was defeated, but Gladstone had put on record his support of the moral right of all men to have the vote. Liberals welcomed his comments, but his constituents were appalled, and he lost; a large number of Oxford graduates were Anglican clergymen opposed to further reform. Palmerston himself campaigned for Gladstone, hoping it would constrain him: 'Keep him in Oxford and he is partially muzzled; but send him elsewhere and he will run wild.' Gladstone quickly returned to Parliament as one of the MPs for South Lancashire and seemed to revel in his newfound freedom as a reformer – 'At last, my friends, I am come among you; and I am come – to use an expression which has become very famous and is not likely to be forgotten – I am come "unmuzzled".' The 1865 election did not change political history by providing a defeated candidate with a period of reflection, as happened to Michael Portillo in 1997, but it did accelerate Gladstone's zeal for reform.

The election was noted for its corruption and violence, something *The Spectator* ascribed to the fact that the election was fought not on policy but on party lines: 'such violence and frauds seem to be connected with the absence of any except a party issue in the elections. A keen feeling about a cause would probably bring out too much earnest feeling to admit of dishonour, as a strong wind clears away the mists.' *The Times* wrote that 'the testimony is unanimous that in the general election of 1865 there was more profuse and corrupt expenditure than was ever known before'. Bribery was widespread. Research has shown that 64 per cent of Lancaster's electorate took or gave a bribe and that in Totnes votes were sold for as much as £200. As a result, these seats, along with Great Yarmouth and Reigate, would be singled out for disenfranchising in the 1867 Reform Act. Following the election, fifty petitions were lodged to challenge results and thirty-five of these resulted in trials. Thirteen elected MPs were unseated in this process and the government appointed a Royal Commission into corrupt practices – supporting the case for further electoral reform.

Once all the votes had been counted, the Liberals gained thirteen seats taking their total to 369, and the Conservative lost nine seats, leaving them with 289. The Liberals had increased their overall majority.

Palmerston would not live to see the fruits of his victory and he died in October 1865. Despite his wishes to be buried near his home in Romsey Abbey, the Cabinet insisted he have a state funeral and he was buried in Westminster Abbey. He was succeeded by Lord John Russell and the House of Commons returned in January 1866. It was to be a short and frustrating ministry as Russell tried to introduce a new Reform Bill and, in the process, split his party. The disunity that Derby knew was bubbling under the surface revealed itself in Palmerston's absence and helped Derby return to Downing Street for the third time, with his protégé Benjamin Disraeli back in the Treasury and effective leader of the party in the House of Commons. Between them, they steered the 1867 Reform Act through Parliament, meaning that the 1865 election was the last time the infamous rotten boroughs would return MPs.

The 1865 election marked the end of Palmerston's long and colourful career. Though Lord Derby did not win the election, its aftermath returned him to office for the third and final time before ill health ended his record twenty-two years as party leader. The election itself was not a watershed moment, indeed it seemed not to change a thing as the commentators had predicted. Rather it set the stage for a period of further reform and the towering ministries of Gladstone and Disraeli that would dominate politics until the eve of the twentieth century.

Charles Pitt is corporate affairs director at Sovereign Network Group, a housing association. He was formerly a parliamentary researcher. He read modern history at Oxford University.

12

1868

IAN CAWOOD

Dissolution: 11 November 1868
Polling day: 17 November–7 December 1868
Seats contested: 658
Total electorate / Total votes cast / Turnout: 2,484,713 (1,870,549 in contested seats) / 2,333,251 / 68.5 per cent
Candidates (total 1,039): Liberal – 600; Conservative – 436
Prime Minister on polling day: Benjamin Disraeli
Main party leaders: Liberal – William Gladstone; Conservative – Benjamin Disraeli

Party performance:

Party	Votes	Percentage share	Seats
Liberal	1,428,776	61.2	387
Conservative	903,318	38.7	271

Result: Liberal majority of 115 seats

At first glance, the general election which took place in the United Kingdom between 17 November and 7 December 1868 seems insignificant compared to others. The election was still fought under the traditional public hustings model of nomination and election, which left employees, retailers and tenants open to intimidation, bribery and blackmail. On introducing the second franchise Reform Bill, which the Conservatives subsequently successfully navigated through Parliament despite being in a minority administration, Disraeli had promised to tackle this problem and just before Parliament was prorogued in July 1868, the Election Petitions and Corrupt Practices at Elections Act was passed. In the election which immediately followed, however, there was, if anything, more corruption than in 1865, with candidates spending, on average, between £1,000 and £3,000 in order to win a seat, and the results of twenty-two constituency elections were declared void on petition.

The election of 1868 also failed to have a significantly different outcome to the previous election in 1865. In that year, Lord Palmerston delivered 369 seats for the Liberals, three months before his death in office, against the 289 seats won by Lord Derby's Conservatives. In 1868, the Liberals under William Gladstone won only eighteen more seats from Benjamin Disraeli's Conservatives – hardly a landslide reversal of fortunes to compare with the elections of 1831, 1895, 1906, 1945 or 1997.

So why is the election of 1868 so significant in the political history of Britain?

While Gertrude Himmelfarb probably exaggerated when she claimed that it was the Reform Act of 1867 'that transformed England into a democracy', it is certainly true that the effects of the Act turned Britain into a more truly representative political system. Gladstone and many Liberals believed that the working class had demonstrated political maturity in their quietist, mutually supportive response to the 'Cotton Famine', caused by the US Civil War in the early 1860s, and had therefore supported amendment clauses to Disraeli's Reform Bill which had effectively enfranchised most heads of urban households. In this way, while those wholly economically dependent on others – such as agricultural labourers, wives, children and the poorest workers who were, therefore, still vulnerable to intimidation and bribery – were denied the vote for themselves, they could still exert moral influence on the voter through engagement with the public sphere and within the privacy of the home.

The fact that candidates who supported measures such as universal elementary education, the abolition of purchase of commissions in the armed forces and the introduction of recruitment to public service by open examination, as well as a host of other radical ideas, were elected as Liberals across the country demonstrated that the priorities of the new voters lay principally in domestic issues and not in the foreign adventures so beloved by Palmerston as a distraction from franchise reform.

The growing power of Prussia, which had defeated the Austrian Army in 1866, sharpened demands for education reform, the reduction of aristocratic patronage and the introduction of meritocracy in the civil service and the army. To give one example, when he stood against the whisky merchant John Ramsay in the Stirling Burghs by-election of April 1868, the young radical Henry Campbell lost by seventy-one from 1,059 votes cast. In the general election in November, however, Campbell won a majority of 519 over Ramsay, with 3,883 votes cast. The wealth which Ramsay could bring to bear on a small electorate was no longer capable of surmounting the desire for radical change that Campbell personified and which he continued to do under his newly adopted surname, Campbell-Bannerman, going on to represent Stirling for the next forty years until his death at No. 10 Downing Street in 1908.

While Parliament was prorogued in July 1868, the election itself did not commence until 11 November, which, in many ways, makes the campaign of 1868 the first modern one, in that it lasted months, rather than weeks. This was not, however, deliberate. Given the massive increase in the size of the electorate from approximately 1.4 million to almost 2.5 million, it took months for the new electoral registers to be prepared before Parliament could be formally dissolved. Disraeli's hope was that the newly enfranchised urban workers would thank him for steering the Reform Act through Parliament, that the middle-class voters of the new suburban constituencies would be repelled by the radicals among the Liberal alliance and that the traditional Conservative hold over the rural seats could prevent a calamitous defeat. The Conservatives, therefore, put forward 436 candidates, meaning that there were far fewer uncontested seats than in previous elections, which became the norm thereafter.

It was also an election fought largely on a single issue – that of the disestablishment of the Irish Church, an issue to which Gladstone had committed himself. The Conservatives hoped to benefit from traditional anti-Catholic attitudes among the working classes, as had been demonstrated in the riots that followed the speeches given by the Protestant orator William Murphy in Lancashire and the west Midlands in 1867 and early 1868. Some Conservative candidates were tempted to play the Protestant card and warned darkly that the Liberal leaders were subject to the 'shackles of Rome', but they received little support from their party leadership and were mocked in the pages of *Punch*, while the Liberals responded that disestablishment was a necessary measure to reduce support for the Fenians, whose campaign of violence had spread to England in 1867. The Anglican Church of Ireland, although funded by the state, comprised only 12 per cent of the population of Ireland. Although the Anglican Church was usually the most ornate building in an Irish community, Anglicans were not a majority in a single county of the thirty-two counties of Ireland. Attempts to convert the Catholics of Ireland since the Act of Union of 1800 had failed, yet the Anglican establishment refused to contemplate a compromise to share their financial and political privileges with other denominations, so Gladstone persuaded Whig landlords in Ireland to support the cause and rallied the nascent radical and Nonconformist alliance in his call to eliminate the unjustifiable privilege of the Church of Ireland. Some Welsh and English radicals even hoped that the disestablishment of the Irish Church would lead to similar treatment of the Anglican Church in their countries (though Gladstone was careful that neither he nor his parliamentary colleagues gave any such undertaking).

Finally, 1868 was also a campaign in which the personality of the party leaders was given greater importance than ever before. Gladstone's reputation as a high-minded, efficient and principled leader was cited by Liberal candidates across the country, who described themselves primarily as 'supporters of Mr Gladstone' rather than Liberals. Gladstone's reputation for financial orthodoxy, nurtured during his long period as Chancellor under Aberdeen, Palmerston and

Russell, reassured those aristocratic Whigs who feared the social upheaval that radicalism seemed to threaten, which was heightened by the riots in Hyde Park during the reform debate in 1866. Gladstone's appeal across the Liberal alliance and his increasing sympathy with the lives of working people meant that his name engendered mass support. As he had written to A. H. Gordon in 1864, 'I am become for the first time a popular character' and his name and face appeared on banners, posters, memorabilia and pamphlets distributed by the Liberal associations.

In another respect, the election paved the way for the emergence of modern political campaigning, as it saw the emergence of the 'caucus' in urban politics. In 1865, inspired by the oratory of George Dixon and R. W. Dale, the Birmingham Liberal Association was founded to push for municipal reform, but it failed to make an impact until after the passage of the Second Reform Act. Then, with a key policy, the expansion of elementary education, the architect William Harris, together with Dixon, George and Philip Muntz and the young Joseph Chamberlain, set about organising their voters. Under the so-called minority clause of the reformed political system, although Birmingham now had three MPs, the electors still had only two votes each. Thus there was a danger that all the Liberal voters would cast their ballot for the most popular candidate (John Bright) and reduce the chances of enough votes being cast for each of the two remaining candidates (Dixon and Philip Muntz) to prevent the Conservatives from being able to elect one of their candidates (Sampson Lloyd or Sebastian Evans). The strategy of directing every voter in particular wards to vote for a particular pair of candidates worked magnificently and the three Liberal candidates were returned with only 500 votes to separate them and with the lowest polling Liberal still scoring over 5,900 more votes than the highest placed Conservative. Similar organisation in Glasgow resulted in the lowest polling Liberal candidate there gaining nearly a majority of 7,000 over the Conservative candidate. The new electorate required a new level of party organisation and demonstrated that party managers and party leaders, both local and national, would rise to a new level of dominance in the politics of mass electorates.

In fact, the 'minority clause' had been specifically added to the 1867 Reform Act by Disraeli, for precisely the reason that the Birmingham Liberal Association's leaders had feared, and in some cases it did pay off. In Manchester, the heartland of Liberalism, the Liberal vote went to the most well-known candidates, Thomas Bazley and Jacob Bright, allowing the Conservatives to concentrate their votes on Hugh Birley and thus top the poll (and come within 470 votes of winning a second seat). Likewise, in Leeds, the failure to organise the vote left the third Liberal candidate, Andrew Fairbairn, near 10,000 votes behind his fellow Liberals and let William Wheelhouse win a seat for the Conservatives. The strategy of what some term the 'limited vote' had little long-term effect, however, as Gladstone abolished three- and four-seat constituencies in the Redistribution of Seats Act of 1885 which followed the Third Reform Act. But the message was clear. The Conservatives needed to step up their organisation and so in 1870, John Gorst was appointed as Conservative agent and tasked with turning Disraeli's idea of 'Tory democracy' into a marketable message to the voters. The effective network he established via the National Union of Conservative and Constitutional Associations gave the Conservatives the instrument with which to strike back when the 'volcanoes' of Liberal reform became 'exhausted' after 1873. Disraeli's true achievement in 1868, which was possibly the apogee of Gladstone's personal popularity, was to keep the fall in the Conservative share of the popular vote down to a mere 1.4 per cent, which was a sufficient base from which the party was able to gain its first majority for nearly thirty years in 1874.

The new mass electorate led to the emergence of a new electoral culture in Britain which could be discerned in some aspects of the 1868 campaign, although it was by no means fully formed at this stage. The size of the electorate led to a significant increase in the use of campaign literature, now that it was no longer possible for a candidate to address any significant proportion of the voters in a constituency in person. While copies of election addresses were still the most common context for the election pamphlets, the limited literacy of many of the new urban voters meant that visual materials became widely used for the first time outside the pages of satirical periodicals. As Matthew Roberts has demonstrated in his study of electoral literature in Derbyshire and South Yorkshire, the election cartoon began to play a huge role in campaigns from 1868 and be commercially exploited by the press, even though, at this stage, the majority of these were locally produced, rather than nationally circulated, as was the case by the mid-1880s.

A mass electorate could best be reached through the media therefore and Gladstone was lucky to inherit the support of the most influential elements of the political press from Palmerston, an arch-manipulator of newspapers. *The Times* and the relatively new (and astonishingly cheap) *Daily Telegraph* were both Liberal in attitude, if not as closely linked to the party as the *Daily News*. *Punch*, then at the height of its popularity, consistently depicted Disraeli in unflattering guises, such as that of Richard III shortly before polling opened, while Gladstone was shown as far more positive characters such as William Tell and even with Mr Punch alongside him in 'Before the Tournament' on 21 November 1868. Although he was approached to invest in a number of new publications in the years leading up to the 1868 election, Gladstone refused to do so, determined to win the support of the press for his policies rather than by paying them to print stories supportive of his party. In the face of the Liberal press phalanx, the Conservative message, propagated by the *Standard* and a few provincial papers, failed to get the same level of traction with the reading public. Disraeli was determined to improve his party's coverage in the press and courted Palmerston's chief organ, the *Morning Post*, as well as later establishing *The Sun*, to spread the Conservative message to rural constituencies. While Gladstone hoped to win support of the quality press with his message, Disraeli began the assiduous recruitment of the popular press, a strategy which culminated with the Unionists' near monopoly of the newspapers by the late 1880s.

The debate on the levels of violence seen in 1868 and whether mass electorates reduced or encouraged more confrontation between supporters of rival candidates has been protracted and, until recently, largely unresolved. Cornelius O'Leary highlights the violence provoked by supposedly respectable figures such as solicitors, clergymen and tradesmen once the scale of the Liberal victory in 1868 was clear, as well as sectarian conflict in Manchester and widespread intimidation of Methodist voters by Anglican landlords in Wales. Jon Lawrence cites the disorder in Bristol in 1868 and theorises that 'radical enthusiasm' lay at the heart of riotous behaviour in elections under the new franchise. On the other hand, Angus Hawkins believes that 'the traditional public rituals and rowdy ceremonies that had characterized electoral contests prior to 1868 were gradually suppressed'. The latest quantitative research by a group of Swiss historians suggests that Hawkins was right and that 1868 saw a significant reduction in levels of electoral violence, particularly between different denominational or ethnic groups, which went hand in hand with a stimulus to economic activity among newly enfranchised voters which further promoted what the authors term 'social peace'. It seems that 1868 was more of a turning point than has previously been accepted.

Despite Disraeli's efforts, the election result demonstrated that Gladstone had not only managed to keep the Liberal alliance intact after Palmerston's death and the expansion of the electorate – he had succeeded in expanding it, with the Liberals achieving over 60 per cent of the national vote, the first political party to win more than a million votes across the nations of Britain and Ireland in a general election. Disraeli was the first Prime Minister to resign immediately once the final result was known, rather than waiting for Parliament to reassemble. Gladstone now had a mandate with which he proceeded to disestablish the Irish Church and set about attacking the privileges of the aristocratic classes which had survived the reforms earlier in the century. Although it would be wrong to claim that political power passed into the hands of the middle classes in 1868, as the Cabinet which Gladstone formed was largely made up of aristocrats, the progressive agenda was clearly established and pursued relentlessly by the Liberal Party from this point until the outbreak of the First World War with varying degrees of success. Holding the party's electoral base together proved a far from easy task, however, which is an issue that has bedevilled all progressive parties in the modern age of mass electorates.

In the shorter term, the success of the Liberals in 1868 led firstly to the introduction of state-run (and remarkably democratic) elementary education, which began the transformation of the life chances of working-class boys and girls, even though it was designed largely to allay the fears among right-wing Liberals of an ignorant electorate prone to manipulation by unscrupulous demagogues. It also led directly to the introduction of the secret ballot in 1872, which was probably catalysed by the high levels of corruption found in the 1868 contest. This significantly reduced the traditional methods of influencing voters' decisions, even though it failed to prevent venality and 'treating', which peaked at the 1880 election and required further legislation in 1883. The secret ballot also inadvertently led to the emergence of the Irish Nationalist Party whose clear mandate from the Irish electorate eventually led Gladstone to commit to granting some measure of Home Rule to the island of Ireland. And it was this issue which, after 1886, finally broke up the progressive alliance which Gladstone and the Liberal Party had forged in 1868 and brought the age of Liberal hegemony to an end.

Dr Ian Cawood is associate professor of modern British political and religious history at the University of Stirling. He is the author of *The Liberal Unionist Party: A History* (2012) and co-editor of *Joseph Chamberlain: International Statesman, National Leader, Local Icon* (2016), *Print, Politics and the Provincial Press in Modern Britain* (2019) and *The Many Lives of Corruption: The Reform of Public Life in Modern Britain, c.1750–1950* (2022).

13

1874

ROBERT BUCKLAND

Dissolution: 26 January 1874
Polling day: 31 January–17 February 1874
Seats contested: 652
Total electorate / Total votes cast / Turnout: 2,753,142 (2,088,636 in contested seats) / 2,466,037 / 66.4 per cent
Candidates (total 1,080): Conservative – 507; Liberal – 489; Home Rule – 80
Prime Minister on polling day: William Gladstone
Main party leaders: Liberal – William Gladstone; Conservative – Benjamin Disraeli; Home Rule – Isaac Butt

Party performance:

Party	Votes	Percentage share	Seats
Liberal	1,281,159	52	242
Conservative	1,091,708	44.3	350
Home Rule	90,234	39.6	60

Result: Conservative majority of forty-nine seats

For much of the thirty years prior to 1874, the Tory Party had lain in the doldrums. Apart from the occasional minority Tory administrations – such as the 'Who? Who?' ministry of 1852, the 1858 minority and then, most famously, the 1867–68 minority where Disraeli 'dished the Whigs' with his own Reform Act – the Whig/Liberal/

Peelite faction had dominated politics. The Liberal Prime Minister Gladstone had himself been a direct participant in the schisms that had torn the Tories apart in the aftermath of the abolition of the Corn Laws by Peel. Gladstone and Disraeli had once sat on the same side of the Commons, but after the rupture caused by fundamental disagreements over free trade, their political and personality differences could not have been deeper.

The 1868 Liberal election triumph saw the end of Disraeli's first ministry and the creation of Gladstone's first administration as Prime Minister, with a strong Cabinet including Lord Granville, Lord Ripon, Lord Aberdare and Robert Lowe. Its first task was the disestablishment of the Irish Church, which had been central to the campaign and an issue around which the party united after the controversies over the Reform Act in 1866–67. This coalescence, however, was not typical, as the government was caught between the Whigs and the radicals on many other issues.

The 1868–74 government was, to begin with, an energetic one. It was responsible for significant and widespread reform. The army and the civil service were opened to promotion on merit. The War Office was reformed by Edward Cardwell, with the purchase of military commissions being outlawed. Most civil service posts were thrown open to entrance by examination. In 1873, the administration of justice was reformed and legislation establishing local sanitary authorities was passed. This is the effective beginning of what became local government later under Lord Salisbury's administrations.

A key reform was the introduction of the secret ballot in 1872. Now, voters could exercise their franchise in private, without the risk of bribery or undue influence. William Forster's Education Act of 1870 is the best remembered of this government's achievements, and it was the culmination of a series of reforms. At the end of 1868, the governing bodies of Britain's best known public schools were reorganised and in 1869, it was the turn of the grammar schools. In 1871, Nonconformists were enabled to receive scholarships and hold teaching posts at the ancient universities.

Church primary schools were well established, but there were insufficient places to meet demand and Anglican faith teaching did not find favour with the growing Nonconformist movement. The Forster Act established elected and ratepayer-funded local school boards and prohibited religious education, but this was not free; fees were charged to all but the poorest, but the path to free universal state education was opened. Within the details of the Liberal government's greatest achievement lie the reasons for the government's ultimate failure.

The Act was only passed with the support of the Conservatives, however, with 132 Liberals voting against and 133 abstaining. The legislative compromises that were necessary to carry the Act disappointed the radicals who sought the elimination of church education. In particular, the provision of public funds for the poorest children, to be used in existing, mainly church schools, antagonised them greatly. It was the Cowper-Temple clause, which made provision for non-denominational religious education in the new board schools, that led to the schisms between Chamberlain and the radicals who wanted no hint of Anglican instruction in the new schools and Forster and others who had forged the 1870 compromise. This, in some places, led to splits in the Liberal/radical movement, with radicals via the National Education League opposing Liberal candidates at the 1874 election who accepted the continuance of church schools.

At the other end of the uneasy Liberal coalition, there were senior Whigs who feared the spread of Irish land reform to Great Britain. Working-class Liberal reformers felt that trade union reforms were too limited when it came to strike action and the need for protection from legal action. Neither the growing temperance movement nor the brewery industry were satisfied with reforms to alcohol licensing. The hostility of brewers to the government manifested itself in active support for the Tory opposition at the 1874 election.

In foreign affairs, the Liberal government was cautious when it came to imperial expansion and anxious to avoid embroilment in the affairs of Continental Europe, particularly in the wake of the Franco-Prussian War of 1870, save for updating the 1839 treaty on Belgian neutrality. Britain agreed with the new German Empire and with France that if one of those two countries invaded Belgium, Britain would assist the other in its defence. Forty-four years later, this agreement would be of pivotal importance when it came to Britain's involvement in a world war. In 1872, Gladstone also resolved the *Alabama* dispute with the United States, which had been rumbling since the Civil War, when compensation was finally paid to the US government for war damage caused by a marauding Confederate vessel that had been launched in Liverpool in 1862 and allowed to sail to America as a warship stocked with armaments and supplies.

By 1872, things were turning sour for Gladstone. After four years of government activism and reform, a sense of fatigue had set in. Disraeli's famous description of the Treasury bench as 'a row of exhausted volcanoes' in his lengthy speech at Free Trade Hall in Manchester in 1872 was an apt one. Added to this was a sense that Gladstone could be somewhat high-handed when it came to public appointments, attracting opprobrium and questions about his judgement.

It was Gladstone's 1873 proposal to reform university education in Ireland that brought matters to a head. Although the Prime Minister had long been considering reform, he failed to adequately roll the pitch for the creation of a central authority over the various religious denominations of colleges in Ireland. The proposal managed to displease both the varying factions of English Liberalism and the Irish MPs who wanted to see an endowed, Catholic Irish university in Dublin. When the bill was defeated, Gladstone resigned, but unlike previous occasions, Disraeli resisted Queen Victoria's invitation to form a minority government, believing that the longer that Gladstone staggered on, the greater the prospects for an outright Tory victory at the next election.

Gladstone resumed office, and after a controversy about irregularities in the telegraph service accounting system, he took on the Exchequer himself, moving the anti-1867 Reform Act protagonist Robert Lowe, who cut taxes but increased public spending and who Gladstone famously described as 'wretchedly deficient', to the Home Office. As Chancellor, Gladstone proceeded to cut public spending with the aim of accumulating a surplus, while his tired ministry soldiered on. Another controversy centred upon Gladstone's failure to resign his Greenwich seat and submit himself for re-election, as was then the requirement for those appointed to ministerial office. Seven by-elections were lost to the Conservatives in 1873, and despite a win at Bath, a by-election in Stroud was lost to the Conservatives as 1874 dawned.

In early 1874, with the Greenwich issue playing on his mind as Parliament was due to resume in February, Gladstone played his last card and surprised colleagues with a snap election called after a Cabinet meeting on 23 January, with a manifesto offering the prospect of the abolition of income tax. Gladstone hoped that a cry for sound finance would be the banner under which squabbling factions of Liberalism could all campaign, and he promptly issued a lengthy address to his electors at Greenwich, followed by three public rallies. Within his Cabinet, there were, however, concerns about the income tax proposal, particularly from ministers representing the British Army and the Royal Navy, as any call on military resources would necessitate further taxes or a draw upon reserves. Although Gladstone's timing now looks extremely rash, his calculation that things would have only got even worse for the government if an election had been held later was probably the right one.

The big defeat of the Conservatives in 1868 had resulted in much soul-searching, and it was the Tory Chief Whip, Gerard Noel, who proposed to Disraeli that the party's principal agent, in succession to the solicitor Markham Spofforth, should be John Gorst. Gorst, a practising barrister who had experienced a colourful few years as an administrator in New Zealand in the early 1860s and who had already briefly been a Conservative MP, was given two main tasks: to find Tory candidates for every constituency in the country and to find a new London office for the party organisation. The very first Conservative Central Office was set up at 53 Parliament Street and introduced the approved list of candidates from which local Conservative associations could select. Gorst worked hard to improve the party's organisation in the towns and boroughs, where elections after 1867 were won and lost.

Under the joint leadership of Gorst and his fellow party secretary Major Keith-Falconer, Central Office became the hub of organisational and political information to be used by local associations and started to generate national literature promoting the party. Gorst's work paid off; the number of local associations rose from 289 in 1871 to 472 by 1874. In particular, the growth of Conservative working men's associations contributed to the growth of what became known as the National Union. Crucially, Disraeli did not view the reformed party machine as being subject to the authority of the Chief Whip, meaning that it operated with the leader's direct authority, giving it more strength. Fundraising efforts were redoubled, with great success.

Gorst was extremely keen to see Disraeli make speeches directly to members in places outside Westminster, so the famous 1872 tour of Lancashire by the Tory leader, including that marathon speech at Free Trade Hall, followed by the huge rally at Crystal Palace later in that year, were all products of the new mass-membership Tory Party. Conservative success in the 1873 local elections provided an early indicator of a shift in public opinion against the Liberals, and the very first handbook for Conservative candidates was produced in that year, later to be called the 'Campaign Guide', becoming a hallmark of efficient Conservative research and presentation at general elections right up until the early twenty-first century.

When the election was called, Disraeli, who, having come up to London from Hughenden for a meeting of the trustees of the British Museum, was shocked on the morning of Friday 24 January to read about the dissolution of Parliament and Gladstone's manifesto in *The Times*. He summoned Gorst to Edwards's Hotel and gave him the direction he needed, which was to use his own initiative and to run a unified national campaign. Disraeli hurried over that weekend to prepare a campaign on several themes: firstly, to end the uncertainty he claimed was caused by Gladstone's reformist activism; secondly, more positive support for Britain's empire and thirdly, social welfare. By Monday, he had fired his first shot in the election campaign with a letter to his constituents in Buckinghamshire, which was a riposte to

Gladstone's 'prolix document', as the Tory leader described it. Apart from a major rally for Gladstone at Greenwich and a speech at Aylesbury by Disraeli, the national campaign was brutally short.

The clearest part of the Liberal election platform was Gladstone's pledge to abolish income tax, which would be funded by a continued reduction in public spending and the accumulation of a surplus of over £5 million within several months of the election. There was also the promise of further electoral reform to include rural areas, local government finance reform and changes to government in London. Disraeli sought to assure electors that he would avoid more domestic upheaval and the problems that would be caused to representation in the urban boroughs if there was yet more electoral reform. He also chose to attack Gladstone on his imperial policy, asserting that British interests in Malaya and Singapore had been threatened by the government's accommodation with the Dutch there. In general, Disraeli advocated more activism abroad and less activism at home.

Increasing doubts over the soundness of Gladstone's income tax pledge were exploited by Disraeli in his campaign speeches, to the extent that abolition in his view risked a reversion to consumption tax and other direct measures that risked covering more than just the most well-off. As most of the new working-class urban electorate did not pay income tax anyway, these messages resonated. The borough electorate had expanded by 15 per cent since 1868, largely as a result of a legislative change made by the Liberals in 1869 that in essence allowed household occupiers to vote irrespective of whether or not they had personally paid the rate due on the dwelling. This particularly enfranchised more tenants and is an often-overlooked coda to the 1867 reform debate.

Constituency voting began on 31 January, only a week after the election had been declared. Results came in over the ensuing eighteen days; elections before 1918 were rolling events, with individual constituency results being declared at varying stages over that period. The number of seats not contested by a Conservative shrank from 120 in 1868 to only fifty-nine. The number of seats not contested by the Liberals rose, however, from ninety to 127. In 1868, the Conservatives had not contested 213 seats, but this shrank to 150 while the Liberals, who had not contested 116 seats in 1868, saw their figure rise to 178. This gave the Conservatives an immediate advantage on close of nominations. Gorst's pre-election estimate of a Tory majority of fifty was met with derision at the Carlton Club, which dubbed it a 'champagne estimate'. In the event, Gorst was right.

The early results showed a shift in seat gains towards the Conservatives, which became more and more apparent. Although Gladstone was re-elected in the two-member Greenwich constituency, he came second to the Conservative, in a snub that led him to seek election elsewhere in 1880. The schisms within Liberalism burst into the open. At Bradford, the Education Act's author, Forster, beat a radical candidate and at Sheffield, the radical Joe Chamberlain similarly lost to the veteran contrarian John Arthur Roebuck in a bitter campaign fought on the issue of religious education. A week into polling, the Conservatives were gaining seats in central London and the adjoining Home Counties. By the last week of polling, they scored three gains in Wales and nine in Scotland. In Ireland, although most Ulster seats were won by Liberals, fifty-seven Irish seats were lost by them to Home Rulers, predominantly in the south. This was the beginning of the end of Liberal hegemony in Ireland, with the era of Parnellite nationalism and the rise of Unionism just around the corner.

By the time Disraeli topped the poll in his Buckinghamshire seat, the extent of the Tory victory was clear. Although the Conservatives won only 1.09 million votes to 1.28 million Liberal votes, they gained twenty-three Liberal seats with a total of 350 to the Liberals' 242. The Tory focus on the boroughs paid off handsomely, with the 1867 franchise extension now bringing electoral benefit to Disraeli, as opposed to short-term political gain. Of the seventy-four Tory gains in England and Wales, sixty-five were achieved with the help of active local associations, as opposed to previous ad hoc arrangements. Party reform had played a key role in securing this victory.

The election of 1874 marked a further stage in the strengthening of Tory representation in Britain's towns and cities. Prior to this, the Tories had been predominantly a party of rural representation, but 1874 saw a distinct shift towards urban areas, which increased and was magnified by further electoral reform in the 1880s. What Salisbury later coined as 'villa Toryism' had its roots in the late 1860s and early 1870s.

The Liberal Party, on the other hand, had not updated their methods. The government Chief Whip, Arthur Wellesley Peel, who was later to become Speaker of the Commons, oversaw the party organisation and was assisted in Scotland by the Lord Advocate and Scottish Whip and in Ireland by the Chief Secretary and the Irish Whip. With no party manager or election agent to help, Peel was solely responsible for the campaign, in sharp contrast to the improved Tory machine.

As Britain made the transition from a limited electorate towards universal suffrage and as literacy and mass communication improved, the role of national newspapers and their regional daily counterparts became ever more significant. Both leaders' speeches were published in full in the newspapers, and satirical weeklies like *Punch* also gave great prominence to the ongoing electoral tussle. Although we tend to think of general elections as being fought on national issues, there is no doubt that in 1874, the issues affecting the different nations of the UK loomed large in the consciousness of electors, as did truly local and other issues in each of the four home nations.

In a letter to his brother after the loss of both Liberal seats at Brighton on 6 February, a shocked Gladstone wrote 'we have been borne down in a torrent of gin and beer', as the Tories took advantage of the brewing industry's dissatisfaction with the government. The true reasons for his big defeat in 1874, however, lay in the fundamental divisions that beset the Liberal Party in Parliament and in the country, and the organisational and political readiness of the Tory Party to take the reins of government with a Commons majority.

The election result sealed the 1868 precedent of the incumbent resigning on behalf of himself and his ministers before Parliament met, and it was on 17 February 1874 that Gladstone did just that, following Disraeli's 1868 example. Gladstone stepped back from leadership, giving way to the Marquess of Hartington in the Commons and spending more time with his library and trees at Hawarden.

Disraeli formed a small but broad-based Cabinet, placing Sir Stafford Northcote at the Treasury, Lord Derby at the Foreign Office, Richard Cross at the Home Office and bringing Salisbury and Lord Carnarvon back after their split over the 1867 Reform Act to India and the Colonial Office, respectively. Gathorne Hardy went to the War Office and Sir Michael Hicks Beach went to Ireland. The major social reforms to housing, employment and public health that Cross championed over the next six years and for which the Disraeli/Beaconsfield ministry is chiefly remembered for now were not part of the 1874 campaign but were undoubtedly part of Disraeli's ambition to 'elevate the condition of the people', heralded in his Crystal Palace speech of 1872.

It is still fashionable to dismiss Disraeli as a politician devoid of ideas or principle, but I think that this is greatly overdone and almost entirely based on the 1867 'leap in the dark' being characterised as a purely short-term Tory tactic, when it most certainly was much more than that. Mid-Victorians could see the contrast between the traditionalism and growing imperialism of the Tory Party laced with a strong social conscience and the laissez-faire and small government approach of Gladstone, accompanied by the forces of nonconformity, and seeking an accommodation with the rising power of organised labour. It is no accident that the fictional Mr Gradgrind of Dickens's mid-1850s masterpiece *Hard Times*, with his obsession with facts and his Utilitarian views, becomes a Liberal MP, rather than a Tory one.

The election of 1874 was Disraeli's last as leader from the Commons. In 1876, he went to the Lords as Earl of Beaconsfield, in the same year as the government legislated to make Queen Victoria Empress of India. His foreign policy triumph at the Congress of Berlin in 1878 was followed by military failure in Afghanistan and South Africa and Gladstone's return to front-line politics through his Midlothian campaign. This led to the end of the Tory government in 1880 and also to Beaconsfield's time in power, as he died the following year on what loyal Tories remembered for years afterward as Primrose Day, in memory of his favourite flower.

The year of 1874 was an important inflexion point in the politics of the nineteenth century, when, for the first time in a generation, an overall Conservative majority was won, heralding thirty years of Tory electoral dominance under Beaconsfield and Salisbury. The deep schisms in the Liberal movement caused by the Irish Home Rule question were yet to come, but at the 1874 election, the scene was most definitely set.

Rt Hon. Sir Robert Buckland KBE KC MP is Conservative MP for South Swindon. He was Solicitor General from 2014 to 2019, Lord Chancellor and Secretary of State for Justice from 2019 to 2021 and Secretary of State for Wales in 2022. He is chair of the Commons Northern Ireland Affairs Select Committee.

14

1880

KATHRYN RIX

Dissolution: 24 March 1880
Polling day: 30 March–27 April 1880
Seats contested: 652
Total electorate / Total votes cast / Turnout: 3,040,050 (2,596,776 in contested seats) / 3,359,416 / 72.2 per cent
Candidates (total 1,103): Conservative – 521; Liberal – 499; Home Rule – 81
Prime Minister on polling day: Benjamin Disraeli
Main party leaders: Liberal – Spencer Cavendish, Marquess of Hartington (Commons) and Earl Granville (Lords); Conservative – Benjamin Disraeli; Home Rule – William Shaw

Party performance:

Party	Votes	Percentage share	Seats
Liberal	1,836,423	54.7	352
Conservative	1,426,349	42.5	237
Home Rule	95,535	37.5	63

Result: Liberal majority of fifty-one seats

In January 1875, in the wake of his party's defeat at the 1874 general election, the former Prime Minister William Gladstone stepped down from the Liberal leadership, intending to shift his focus away from Westminster politics. The man whose popularity among the working classes had earned him the nickname 'the People's William' was succeeded as leader by two aristocratic figures from the Whig section of the party. The former Foreign Secretary Earl Granville led in the Lords and his cousin Spencer Cavendish, Marquess of Hartington, in the Commons. They were still at the helm when the 1880 general election produced an unexpectedly strong showing for the Liberals, winning an outright majority over the Conservatives. It was, however, neither Granville nor Hartington but Gladstone who, to Queen Victoria's reluctance, replaced Benjamin Disraeli as Prime Minister.

The Conservatives' victory in 1874 had seen Disraeli take the premiership for the second time. The social reforms of his 1874–80 ministry, tackling issues such as factory working hours, public health and working-class housing, have been much scrutinised by historians. One interpretation is that they represented a commitment by Disraeli to 'Tory democracy', with his party endeavouring to cultivate support from the urban working-class men it had enfranchised in 1867. Against this must be set the fact that these reforms were piecemeal rather than programmatic, with several of them limited in scope and permissive in nature, giving local authorities discretionary powers.

Disraeli, who went to the Lords as the Earl of Beaconsfield in August 1876, paid greater attention to foreign policy. He scored an early success with the purchase of Suez Canal shares in 1875, facilitating a shorter route to India. More fraught with complications were events in south-eastern Europe. Revolts against Ottoman rule had spread in May 1876 to Bulgaria, where the harsh Turkish response included the massacre of 12,000 Christians. While Disraeli took a pro-Turkish approach when it came to the 'eastern question', Gladstone joined those agitating on behalf of the Bulgarians. His September 1876 pamphlet, 'The Bulgarian Horrors and the Question of the East', sold 200,000 copies within a month. Although public interest soon died down, this episode was significant in marking Gladstone's return to the political fray in a popular campaign based on a moral cause.

Concerns about Russia's advance towards Constantinople (which would enable access to the Mediterranean) following the outbreak of the Russo-Turkish War saw the Royal Navy ordered to the area in January 1878, despite Cabinet divisions about whether to intervene. The patriotic response provoked by the Russian threat was famously encapsulated in a music hall song which gave rise to the term 'jingoism'. Fortunately, war with Russia was averted. After protracted negotiations over peace terms between Turkey and Russia, Disraeli returned in July 1878 from the Congress of Berlin claiming to have achieved 'peace with honour'. This success boosted the government's prestige, prompting suggestions of an early dissolution. The Chief Whip Sir William Hart Dyke advised against this, fearing it would anger loyal MPs. He was also concerned that 'the pressure of taxation' – income tax had risen from 2d in the pound in 1874 to 5d in 1878 – would provide easy political capital for the Liberals, but he believed that future Budgets would produce 'such a Balance Sheet in 1880 as can command the support of the Country' and anticipated that matters would similarly improve when it came to the state of trade. Contrary to his hopes, the government faced an increasingly difficult economic situation, with growing signs of both industrial and agricultural depression. A run of bad harvests was capped off by the century's wettest summer in 1879. In addition, the government's reputation was tarnished by humiliating, costly and mismanaged events in 1879 in Afghanistan and South Africa, with Britain's defeat by Zulu troops at Isandlwana a particular low point.

Having decided to contest the Scottish county of Midlothian instead of Greenwich at the next election, Gladstone introduced himself to its voters in November 1879. MPs commonly used the recess to visit their constituencies and address meetings, but Gladstone's first 'Midlothian campaign' was on a different level, both in scale and in impact. Travelling by train from Liverpool to Scotland, he drew crowds of thousands as he stopped to speak en route. His charismatic appeal as a popular statesman was such that 'even at wayside spots hundreds assembled, merely to catch a glimpse of the express as it dashed through', according to his biographer John Morley.

Gladstone followed this with a series of speeches in Midlothian and the Scottish Lowlands in which he built a moral critique of the evils of 'Beaconsfieldism', centred on Conservative mishandling of foreign policy and mismanagement of the nation's finances. As Gladstone put it: 'What we are disputing about is the whole system of government.' He wanted to base foreign policy on six 'right principles': good domestic government; peace; maintaining the European balance of power; avoiding 'needless and entangling engagements'; equal rights for all nations; and 'love of freedom'. Gladstone calculated that 86,930 people heard his speeches, but far more significant was the wider audience they reached through the national and provincial press. Reporting was aided by the favourable transmission rates given to news agencies such as the Press Association under the 1868 Telegraph Act.

The Conservatives, meanwhile, had yet to decide when to call the election. Hart Dyke felt an early dissolution – possibly in January 1880 – was preferable, advising Disraeli in July 1879 that the government was more popular in most of England than at any point during the past three years, although he predicted some losses in northern England due to 'bad trade', together with a few in Scotland. Hart Dyke's reassurances about Conservative prospects contrasted with the Liberal Chief Whip William Adam's anticipated Liberal majority of fifty. Adam's predictions became even more optimistic after Gladstone's first Midlothian campaign, to the extent that Granville refused to believe them.

Wishing to pass legislation such as relief measures for Ireland and to present Sir Stafford Northcote's Budget, ministers met Parliament for the 1880 session. On 14 February, Disraeli told Queen Victoria that his Cabinet had unanimously agreed that only 'a very critical state of affairs' would prompt a dissolution, noting his concerns about the obstruction of Commons business by Irish MPs. While the 1879 municipal contests had gone well for the Liberals, parliamentary by-elections seemed to offer the Conservatives more hope. The Liberals only narrowly won at Sheffield in December 1879 and the Conservatives held a seat at Liverpool on 6 February 1880, before winning what the Conservative minister Lord Cranbrook described as 'a great triumph' at Southwark on 14 February. Two days later, in conversation with Disraeli's private secretary, the chief party agent William Baillie Skene cited the latter results as evidence of moderate Liberal support for Conservative foreign policy, one reason for recommending an early dissolution. With parliament having lasted longer than average, Skene warned against appearing afraid to appeal to the country and noted that the increasing difficulty of managing the Commons made any major legislation 'impossible'. He forecast Conservative losses of sixteen to eighteen seats, leaving them with a working majority.

The catalyst for the dissolution – decided on by the Cabinet on 6 March and announced to general surprise two days later – was the prospect of a Commons defeat over the Metropolis Waterworks Purchase Bill. This measure, consolidating London's private water companies into a municipal monopoly, faced criticism for its over-generous compensation of shareholders. The session's premature ending was backed by Conservative Central Office and the party whips. The Colonial Secretary Sir Michael Hicks Beach was the only Commons minister who spoke out against it, although the Lord Chancellor Lord Cairns would have preferred an autumn dissolution, hoping for 'a good harvest & revived trade'.

By the time Parliament met for the last time on 24 March, campaigning was already underway. Disraeli's elevation to the Lords meant he had to comply with the traditional abstention of peers from electioneering, although he did publish an open letter to the Duke of Marlborough, Lord Lieutenant of Ireland, on 8 March. His choice of correspondent reflected Disraeli's desire to present Irish affairs as a key election issue, warning against the 'destructive doctrine' of Home Rule, but this gained little traction. He also highlighted the importance of Britain's 'ascendency ... in the councils of Europe' in preserving peace, a position he implied the Liberals would endanger, but was silent on domestic matters. Other leading Conservatives, including Cairns, Cranbrook and Lord Salisbury (who was recuperating from illness in Biarritz) were similarly debarred from campaigning, putting them at a disadvantage in comparison with the Liberals. Granville, still Liberal leader in the Lords, played a minimal role at the election but was criticised for making a political speech when he opened a working men's club at Hanley on 20 March.

Unaffected by such concerns, Gladstone had left London on 16 March for his second Midlothian campaign, speaking en route at Grantham, York, Newcastle and Berwick, all of which subsequently saw Liberal victories. He spoke up to three times a day in Midlothian, but, again, his real audience was not his future constituents but the wider British public through the press. *The Times* alone published 250,000 words of Gladstonian oratory during 1879–80. He continued his attacks on the profligacy, immorality and opportunism of the Conservatives' foreign and financial policy, concluding his final campaign speech by protesting that Britain had 'found its interests mismanaged, its honour tarnished, its strength burdened and weakened, by needless, mischievous, unauthorised, unprofitable engagements'.

Gladstone's presentation of a clear-cut choice between opposing political approaches, his 'whistle-stop' campaigning and the widespread press attention this generated has led the historian Martin Pugh to argue that 1880 was in some respects 'the first modern election'. Although Disraeli was absent from the platform, the sense of him and Gladstone as political rivals was reinforced in political cartoons. Another factor making 1880 more of a national event than previous elections was the reduced number of uncontested seats, the lowest since 1832: 109 MPs were elected unopposed, compared with 187 in 1874. Yet although more constituencies saw contests, polling was still spread over four weeks, rather than taking place on the same day. The franchise remained restricted, varying between boroughs and counties and between England, Ireland, Scotland and Wales. The electorate totalled just over 3 million voters and less than half (194) of the 416 constituencies were single-member seats, the last general election where this was the case.

Although the Midlothian campaign attracted considerable interest, Gladstone was not the only Liberal to make an impact from the platform beyond his constituency. Indeed Hartington, whose stature as leader had grown during the latter stages of the 1874–80 parliament, made twenty-four major election speeches to Gladstone's fifteen.

Opening his campaign for North East Lancashire on 13 March, he rebutted Disraeli's attempts to associate the Liberals with the obstructionist Home Rulers. He also developed his own critique of Tory incompetence in foreign, domestic and financial policy. The Conservative Home Secretary Richard Cross, contesting another Lancashire seat, made a particular effort in his speeches to challenge points made by Hartington. Cross's Cabinet colleagues Northcote and William Henry Smith each made six major election speeches, as did Sir William Harcourt and John Bright for the Liberals. An easy Liberal target was the £8 million budget deficit accumulated by the Conservative ministry, in contrast with the £5.5 million surplus they had inherited from Gladstone's 1868–74 ministry. The Liberals' campaign focused more on criticism of their opponents than their own future legislative programme, although there were references to intended measures such as extending the county franchise and reforming local government.

This was the first general election for the National Liberal Federation (NLF), established in 1877 to improve Liberal organisation after the 1874 defeat. The driving force behind the NLF, pejoratively referred to by detractors as the 'caucus', was Birmingham's radical MP, Joseph Chamberlain. It aimed to encourage the formation of Liberal associations based on the model of popular representation used by the Birmingham Liberal Association. While it later became a key part of the central party organisation, moving in 1886 to offices alongside the Liberal Central Association in London, at this stage the NLF was based in Birmingham, where in May 1877 Gladstone addressed its inaugural conference. After the 1880 election, Chamberlain highlighted the fact that the Liberals had gained or retained seats in sixty of the sixty-seven boroughs and all ten of the county constituencies with local party associations 'on the Birmingham model'. These figures pointed to both the NLF's embryonic nature and its future potential. The Liberal whips offered some financial support to candidates, but their fund of around £39,000, largely distributed as grants to thirty-four constituencies, represented only a fraction of total election spending.

Expenditure by Conservative Party headquarters was similarly limited, with an estimated £24,000 available for distribution to candidates from the Carlton Fund. Hart Dyke's illness during the contest contributed to a lack of direction at the centre when it came to election preparations. Skene, the Scottish landowner who had been chief agent since 1877, has generally been regarded as less proficient than his predecessor, John Gorst, admitting himself shortly before the election that he was 'an idiot' to have taken the role. The NLF's Conservative equivalent, the National Union of Conservative and Constitutional Associations, was created in 1867 to encourage local constituency associations to mobilise newly enfranchised urban voters. Its limited reach was shown by the fact that in 1878, less than a third of the 950 local Conservative organisations were affiliated to it. It provided some election literature to the constituencies in 1880, sending out 1.6 million copies of its 'Election Handy Sheets' of statistics and information and selling around 750,000 placards and handbills. But on the whole, commercial publishers and local printers remained a more important source of election literature for candidates than central party organisations, and electioneering continued to have a predominantly local focus.

One change in electioneering resulted from a measure which Disraeli's ministry rushed through a near-empty House at the end of the 1880 session. Since 1867, payments for conveying voters to the poll, such as providing railway tickets or hiring cabs, had been illegal in borough constituencies, but this law was widely evaded and the penalties rarely enforced. The Conservatives, therefore, repealed it (for England and Wales) in March 1880, to the disgust of many Liberals, with Gladstone condemning this measure 'for the promotion and revival of corrupt practices'. Candidates spent a total of £273,000 on conveyances in 1880.

This was only the tip of the iceberg in what was one of the nineteenth century's most expensive and corrupt elections. Eighteen MPs, including the recently appointed Liberal Cabinet minister John Dodson, were unseated after the election for corrupt practices and a further four following by-elections later that year. Eight royal commissions, the highest ever number, went on to investigate the worst constituencies, including Oxford, where Harcourt's failed attempt to secure re-election following his appointment by Gladstone as Home Secretary was also found to have been tainted with corruption. The proven venality of voters was at odds with the rational rhetoric underpinning Gladstone's Midlothian campaign. Moreover, there were strong suspicions that the successful election petitions had not revealed the true extent of bribery, treating and other misdemeanours. There were also significant concerns about the ever-increasing sums spent by candidates, whose declared election expenditure of £1.7 million was approximately £750,000 more than in 1874. Actual spending was reckoned to be higher still, at between £2 million and £3 million. The new Liberal Attorney-General, Sir Henry James, described this lavish expenditure as 'so near akin to corruption that it was almost the very father of corruption'. Prompted by the excesses of 1880, he oversaw the passing of the 1883 Corrupt and Illegal Practices Prevention Act, a landmark reform which, for the first time, placed strict limits on candidates' election spending.

Before the polls opened, predictions regarding the result varied. The *Manchester Guardian* reported that leading Conservatives had foreseen a majority of twenty to thirty the week before the dissolution, but their expectations had since dwindled to twelve or fifteen. The latter was also Granville's forecast, but many Liberals were more optimistic: few expected the Conservatives to gain a workable majority and some hoped for a Liberal majority of fifteen. The election began on 30 March, when MPs were returned without contests in some boroughs. Overall, fifty-eight Conservatives, forty-one Liberals and ten Home Rulers would be elected unopposed. Voting took place in sixty-nine boroughs on 31 March, producing a Conservative loss of fifteen seats. By 3 April, the Tories were fifty seats down, sealing their fate. Polling in England's counties did not improve matters. In a major blow, the Conservatives suffered a net loss of twenty-eight English county seats, although they still held 116 to the Liberals' fifty-four. Most of these Liberal gains came in more industrialised counties.

By 15 April, Orkney and Shetland was the only constituency outside Ireland yet to poll. Its declaration – a Liberal victory – on 27 April concluded the election. The Conservatives were reduced to seven seats in Scotland, compared with nineteen in 1874, while the Liberals now held fifty-three. In Wales, the Liberals won twenty-nine out of thirty-three seats, ten more than in 1874. Slightly improving its position, the Home Rule Party remained the major force in Ireland, winning sixty-three seats, with twenty-five for the Conservatives (down eight seats from 1874) and fifteen for the Liberals. Although they were bolstered by their strong performance in the 'Celtic fringe', the Liberals also enjoyed a majority over their opponents in England, winning 255 seats against 201. They performed best in the Midlands, Yorkshire and Lancashire, where the defection of Disraeli's former Foreign Secretary Lord Derby to the Liberals boosted morale. The Conservatives did well in the Home Counties, where his family name proved of little service to Herbert Gladstone, defeated in Middlesex. However, the Tory gains of 1874 in large English boroughs were mainly overturned, although they performed well in smaller boroughs and rural areas. The overall result saw the Liberal and Conservative positions in the Commons almost exactly reversed, with 352 Liberals and 237 Conservatives, plus sixty-three Home Rulers.

The scale of this Liberal victory was a surprise. Gladstone declared it 'such a smash', outstripping his expectations, while Cranbrook likened it to 'thunder ... from a clear sky'. When interpreting the result, however, it is important to realise that the Liberal triumph was less of a landslide than it appeared. If just 4,054 voters had polled the other way, the Liberals would have been defeated in the seventy-two most marginal seats. Given the narrowness of many Liberal victories, it was unsurprising that some looked to Conservative organisational failings. Northcote put 'want of suitable organisation' at the top of his explanations for defeat, while Lady Salisbury observed that 'by all accounts the organisation has been deplorable. We must have "Caucuses".' Gorst was more measured, arguing at that year's National Union conference that it was unfair to blame 'faulty organisation' for their defeat but agreeing that they had been 'left far behind' by their opponents. His return as chief agent in July 1880 was part of efforts to reinvigorate Conservative organisation.

With the Liberals benefiting from a greater number of active frontbench speakers to outline Conservative failings in government, Lady Salisbury did 'not think that our side has talked enough'. Although Gladstone's charismatic oratory helped to engage party activists and voters, and the NLF's efforts strengthened Liberal organisation, credit should also be given to Hartington. The improved Liberal performance in the counties was aided by the support of his fellow landed Whigs. For some voters, specific issues struck a chord. The Irish vote in England went against the Conservatives after the Irish Home Rule Confederation, in response to Disraeli's letter to Marlborough, urged electors to vote against Disraeli as 'the mortal enemy of your country and your race'. Some Nonconformists had abstained from voting Liberal in 1874 because they disliked the Liberal ministry's 1870 Education Act. Gladstone's moral crusade against Beaconsfieldism, resonating with the party's long-standing commitment to 'Peace, Retrenchment and Reform', encouraged them to poll in 1880, as did concerns about the Tories' renewal in 1875 of legislation on the contentious subject of endowed schools. In contrast, the Anglican vote was less whole-heartedly pro-Conservative than usual, with some 'High Church' Anglicans upset by the 1874 Public Worship Regulation Act's efforts to tackle ritualism (the introduction of Roman Catholic practices) in the Church of England. However, for many leading Conservatives, the economic situation was the key explanatory factor. Writing to Salisbury as the borough results came in, Disraeli pointed to 'Hard Times' as 'our foe, and certainly the alleged cause of our downfall'. Salisbury concurred that 'bad harvests & bad trade have done the most'.

Following the precedent of 1868 and 1874, Disraeli did not attempt to form a government, accepting the electorate's verdict. He had already informed Queen Victoria, who was visiting Baden-Baden, of his ministry's impending defeat on 2 April, which she considered 'a great calamity for the country and the peace of Europe'. She was particularly alarmed by the prospect that Disraeli, her great favourite, might be followed as Prime Minister by Gladstone, telling her private secretary Henry Ponsonby that she would 'sooner abdicate than send for ... that half-mad firebrand who would soon ruin everything and be a Dictator'. Given that Hartington was Liberal leader in the Commons and that Gladstone had previously voiced his reluctance to take the premiership again, even the Liberal press was initially doubtful about whether Gladstone, aged seventy to Hartington's forty-six, would become Prime Minister. Writing to Bright in November 1879, Gladstone listed his age, the 'formidable' work, his loyalty to Hartington and Granville, likely hostility and the queen's dislike of him as reasons against resuming the leadership. However, his role in the election and his belief that 'skilled and strong hands' were required to tackle the situation left by the Conservatives changed his mind.

Having met Disraeli on 18 April after returning from Germany, Queen Victoria followed his advice that 'the right and constitutional course' was to send for Hartington. When she asked Hartington on 22 April to form a government, he told her that neither he nor Granville considered this possible without Gladstone, who they did not think would serve other than as Prime Minister. Having, at the queen's behest, confirmed with Gladstone that he would not take a subordinate post, Hartington returned to Windsor the following day, when both he and Granville advised the queen to appoint Gladstone. That evening, Gladstone kissed hands at Windsor as Prime Minister.

Queen Victoria was unimpressed by Gladstone's new Cabinet, finding 'all these Radicals ... a great trial'. In practice, they were only a small element, with the Cabinet including many members of Gladstone's 1868–74 ministry. Chamberlain had made a pact with Charles Dilke that one of them should be in the Cabinet, but as Dilke's earlier republican views made him unpalatable to the queen, Gladstone gave him a non-Cabinet post at the Foreign Office. Chamberlain, an MP since only 1876, joined the Cabinet as its least experienced member, serving as president of the Board of Trade, while the veteran radical Bright returned to the chancellorship of the Duchy of Lancaster. Another radical, Henry Fawcett, the first completely blind MP, received ministerial office as Postmaster General but was not in the Cabinet.

Ten of Gladstone's fourteen-strong Cabinet had previous Cabinet experience. Harcourt became Home Secretary, while Hartington was appointed Secretary of State for India. Six Cabinet ministers sat in the Lords, including the leading Whigs Earl Spencer (Lord President of the Council), the Earl of Kimberley (Colonial Secretary) and Granville (Foreign Secretary).

Gladstone himself initially combined the premiership with the chancellorship of the Exchequer, a dual role he had also performed in 1873–74. However, his second ministry has generally been regarded as less successful than his first. Although the government succeeded in carrying out a major reconstruction of the electoral system in 1884–85, Irish affairs occupied a considerable amount of parliamentary time and began to cause divisions within the Liberal Party. Ironically, given that his attack on Disraeli's foreign policy failings helped to bring Gladstone into office in 1880, it was foreign policy difficulties, notably the death of General Gordon in the Sudan, which were a major factor in the demise of Gladstone's second ministry in June 1885.

Dr Kathryn Rix is assistant editor of the House of Commons 1832–1945 project at the History of Parliament Trust. Her publications on parliamentary and electoral history include *Parties, Agents and Electoral Culture in England, 1880–1910* (2016).

15

1885

LUKE BLAXILL

Note: After this point, including this election, results have been adjusted to take into account multi-member constituencies

Dissolution: 18 November 1885
Polling day: 24 November–18 December 1885
Seats contested: 670
Total electorate / Total votes cast / Turnout: 5,708,030 (5,429,708 in contested seats) / 4,347,984 / 81.2 per cent
Candidates (total 1,338): Liberal – 572; Conservative – 602; Irish Parliamentary – 94; Independent Liberal – 35; Independent Conservative – 8; Crofters – 6
Prime Minister on polling day: Marquess of Salisbury
Main party leaders: Liberal – William Gladstone; Conservative – Marquess of Salisbury; Irish Parliamentary – Charles Stewart Parnell

Party performance:

Party	Votes	Percentage share	Seats
Liberal	2,071,868	47.7	319
Conservative	1,869,560	43	247
Irish Parliamentary	307,119	67.8	86
Independent Liberal	55,652	1.3	11
Crofters	16,551	0.4	4
Independent Conservative	12,599	0.3	2

Result: Hung parliament, Liberals were the largest party

The general election of December 1885 was one of numerous 'firsts'. Thanks to Gladstone's Third Reform Act of 1884, it was the first to feature an electorate which included the majority of adult men. Secondly, it was the first to be fought overwhelmingly in arithmetically equivalent single-member constituencies on account of the Redistribution of Seats Act passed earlier in 1885. Thirdly, it was the first generally 'clean' election where the direct bribery of voters played a comparatively insignificant role following the harsh crackdown of the Corrupt and Illegal Practices Act of 1883, which had been passed off the back of widespread dismay at the scale of bribery seen in the previous election of 1880.

Finally, 1885 was the first election to feature a national manifesto, with Joseph Chamberlain's 'Unauthorised Programme' setting the campaign agenda to a polarising set of proposals: radical land reform, Church of England disestablishment and free education. Like its predecessor, the 1885 election also saw significant developments in party organisation, with the Conservatives having founded the Primrose League to fight back against their opponents' National Liberal Federation (NLF). Central parties became more involved in constituency campaigning through distributing literature, providing workers and volunteers and parachuting in an unprecedented number of 'carpetbagger' candidates into the new redrawn constituencies.

While some way short of its final transformation to nationalised twentieth-century mass democracy, it certainly *felt* like the political system had undergone a profound and irrevocable metamorphosis. The electorate, constituencies and tools of electioneering had all been drastically altered. The new system of 1885 was described by Sir Henry Maine as 'unmoderated democracy', leading to the election of a government that Lord Acton declared to be 'the first of our democratic constitution'. The sharp fall in uncontested returns (numbering forty-three, down from 109 in 1880) and increased volume of platform speech reporting in newspapers further pointed to enormous popular excitement. The *Manchester Guardian* forecast 'great uncertainty as to the result of the coming election, on the grounds (1) of the vast number of new electors [and] … (2) in consequence of the large number of new constituencies created'. Similarly, *The Times* described 'the uncertainty as to the result of the struggle' stemming from 'the unknown effect of the extension of the franchise'.

In 1880, Gladstone (despite not being the official Liberal leader) had been propelled into office on the back of his Midlothian campaign, where he had denounced Disraeli's profligate finance and unethical foreign policy in the Balkans. The 'Grand Old Man' (GOM) had supposedly retired from front-line politics six years earlier in 1874, but he returned for a full premiership in what came to be known as his 'ministry of troubles'. Despite an impressive record of domestic reforms (especially the 1883–85 electoral reforms we have mentioned), the ministry blundered on foreign policy. Gladstone was forced to abandon his non-interventionist principles and sent troops to quell disorder in Egypt following the revolt of Egyptian nationalists against Ottoman control. More politically serious was his refusal to rescue the enormously popular General Gordon from Khartoum who had disobeyed instructions to evacuate. The death of Gordon, in January 1885, led to an outcry of indignation in the press and the reversal, by critics, of 'GOM' to 'MOG' ('Murderer of Gordon'). Gladstone's policy on Ireland was also the subject of sharp Cabinet disagreement over land purchase, coercion and the issue that was shortly going to shake politics to its very foundations six months hence: Irish Home Rule.

By mid-1885, an election was in any case firmly in the offing. Firstly, simply because it had already been five and a half years since the previous contest. Secondly, because the present House of Commons had been delivered by a now-defunct electoral system. The moment Gladstone's ministry fell, however, was largely a consequence of lax whipping and parliamentary skullduggery. At a late-night sitting on 8 June, Chancellor Hugh Childers's income-tax-raising Budget was unexpectedly defeated by twelve votes. Around seventy radical Liberals – unhappy with the Budget and Gladstone's leadership – had abstained, and the sixty-three Irish Nationalists, led by Charles Stewart Parnell, had struck a secret agreement with the Conservative leader Lord Salisbury to vote with the opposition. As the government regarded the Budget as a confidence vote, a night of Commons intrigue brought Gladstone's second ministry to an abrupt end. Salisbury then began a nominal caretaker minority government which did little more than prepare for the election, and Parliament was dissolved in mid-November.

The Liberals, still riding their wave of mid-Victorian dominance, were a formidable electoral force. Gladstone was in no mood to retire and remained a titanic figure at the height of his seemingly inexhaustible powers. He planned to embark on a second Midlothian campaign which would feature a series of hugely attended (and widely reported) public speeches to galvanise three important groups in the electorate behind the Liberals: middle-class moralists, Dissenters and the skilled working classes. He also hoped that agricultural labourers and miners in county constituencies – the two principal groups enfranchised by his Third Reform Act the previous year – would also succumb to the oratorical magic of 'Gladstonisation'. Liberal electoral intelligence was optimistic that the party would be returned with a handsome majority, and perhaps make gains from 1880. Despite Conservative attempts to catch up, the Liberals still held the organisational advantage, especially in urban constituencies in the Midlands and north on account of the Birmingham-based NLF. Still, more promisingly, the Conservative strongholds in rural England – where Liberals often had no history of organisation – had been dramatically transformed by the 1885 redistribution and seen the largest increases in their electorates. While it was the subject of speculation on how the agricultural labourer – or 'Hodge', as he was popularly known – would vote, his enfranchisement had served to shake up rural electoral politics, giving the Liberals a chance of making gains in previously impregnable landed electoral monopolies.

While such omens were auspicious, all was not well at the top of the party. Despite Gladstone's stature, the 1885 election represented the greatest challenge to his leadership in his seven-decade political career in the shape of Chamberlain. While best remembered today as a Unionist statesman (and cited as a political hero by Theresa May) the Chamberlain of 1885 was on the hard left of the Liberal Party. The former screw manufacturer and mayor of Birmingham had seen his star rise dramatically since his appointment to Gladstone's Cabinet in April 1880, and by 1885, he could reasonably claim to be Britain's best-known radical. The transformation of the electoral system emboldened him to propose his controversial 'Unauthorised Programme' which included free education, land reform, Church of England disestablishment, graduated taxation, death duties, manhood suffrage and payment of MPs. These proposals were regarded across the spectrum as an audacious attempt to start a debate on state intervention, the condition of the poor and the legitimacy of wealth and property. Chamberlain presented his programme explosively as heralding a new 'radical millennium', 'reign of democracy' and 'ransom of private property'. Unsurprisingly, these pyrotechnics alarmed traditional 'Whig' Liberals on the right of the party, who looked to Gladstone to calm their nerves by proposing a counter-manifesto. However, he offered only uninspiring promises on streamlining parliamentary procedure, reforming registration and modestly empowering local government. Despite having been treated with kid gloves by his leader, Chamberlain was furious and regarded Gladstone's reluctance to embrace his programme as 'a slap in the face'. He then turned his fire on the Whigs, regarding George Goschen and Lord Hartington as 'whipping boys' to be attacked in speeches.

Conservative auguries on the election result – and indeed their party's future in the looming age of mass democracy – were gloomy. Salisbury privately predicted the extinction of 'true Conservatism of the kind our ancestors knew' and believed the party's likely future role was as a brake to Liberal overzealotry from the opposition benches.

The marquess had big shoes to fill after Disraeli died in 1881, and he was of an extremely different background, status and temperament to the party's flamboyant former chief. A great landowner, Salisbury disliked speaking before public audiences and strongly disapproved of recent governments' addiction to passing legislation. While his outspoken opposition to enfranchisement of the working classes also marked him out as a politician of a former age, he was a master tactician and worked hand-in-glove with his chief agent, the electioneering genius Captain Richard Middleton. Moreover, Salisbury's tone – outlined in a rare public speech at Newport in October – vowed to mix a new 'liberal Conservatism' with a more traditional Tory message of 'Church in Danger'. The plan was on one hand to appeal to Whigs and moderate liberals frightened by the spectre of Chamberlainite radicalism and Anglicans of all stripes alarmed by disestablishment. On the other, the Conservatives – especially through the oratory of Randolph Churchill – planned to appeal to urban working men by emphasising 'manly' patriotic independence from radical Liberal statism and to champion their right to a quiet pint unmolested by puritanical temperance reformers. The Tories were pessimistic that they could manage more than 250 seats but believed they stood a chance of depriving the Liberals of an overall majority in the new House.

The 1885 campaign saw an explosion of what *The Times* called 'political oratorical pandemonium'. Due to the unpredictability of the new electoral system, predictions of which seats were safe and which were marginal were vague at best. The new voters – especially agricultural labourers – were widely regarded to be slow-witted and only partially literate and thus could not be counted on to read lengthy newspaper reports or densely argued handbills. Not for nothing was Conservative candidate William Tyssen-Amherst warned by an agent that his Norfolk seat 'would not be worth a dog's purchase' unless he 'took talk to the labourers in their own language'. The *East Anglian Daily Times* declared that the election was to be 'fought amid a blaze of publicity. Electors are no longer boxed up all night in a public house and taken to the poll in an omnibus, but are brought to attend public meetings, where the fiercest light is shed on the questions of the day.'

Parliamentary candidates across the country thus mounted the platform at mass meetings, open to all, and held them on most nights. Even in villages, overflow gatherings were common as the population embraced what was popularly seen as thrilling political drama. The provincial press was at the height of its historic influence, and long (often verbatim) reports of public speeches by local candidates alongside national leaders filled each newspaper with a word count equivalent to a short novel. Candidates would read what their opponents said and then reply, so a constituency campaign was analogous to an interactive debate featuring blasts and counter-blasts from rival platforms. An estimated half-billion words of speech were reported in newspapers up and down the country during the campaign.

It has been an enduring challenge for historians of Victorian elections to analyse this unreadably vast textual corpus and summarise what these grass-roots campaigns in the constituencies were actually about. Election addresses (manifestos of candidates) give us an indication of what they *thought* it should be about before the oratorical pandemonium began, but a more reliable measure can be derived from computerised text mining of millions of words of actual speeches themselves. My published analysis of the 1885 campaign reveals that Chamberlain's bid to set the agenda through his Unauthorised Programme was a resounding success, with disestablishment, land reform and free education being the first, second and fifth most-mentioned issue respectively by both parties. Radicalism itself was placed second, with finance, foreign policy and Irish Home Rule occupying fourth, sixth and seventh positions, respectively.

Radical Liberals extolled Chamberlain's proposals. Peter Falk at East Norfolk proclaimed that 'a man who had more landed property than he knew what to do with should be compelled to sell part of it ... to be given out to the agricultural labourer'. Meanwhile, the campaigning slogan 'three acres and a cow' gained wide publicity in agricultural divisions as labourers were promised a stake in the soil. At Woodbridge, the Liberal candidate Robert Lacey Everett described the state church as a 'yoke' which he would 'rejoice to see broken into pieces and destroyed'. A Leeds Liberal beseeched his audience to 'grant free education to the toiling millions' to break Church of England schools' hold over the minds of children which caused them to become 'saturated with reaction and toryism'. Jesse Collings, a Birmingham radical, described Chamberlain as the working classes' 'greatest and most powerful friend, the man of the future ... where the hopes of democracy lie'. Whiggish Liberals, meanwhile, were rather more reserved in their praise of Chamberlain, such as Charles

Alan Fyffe (Oxford) who 'appreciated Mr Chamberlain's great power and abilities ... but did not admit that either he or any other single man whatever could be the Pope and the infallible mouthpiece of the Liberal party'. However, it was not for nothing that William Tuckwell, a Warwickshire clergyman and Christian socialist, recalled that in 1885, '[Chamberlain's] influence with the democracy had for some time past exceeded Gladstone's; I found of late that if audiences cheered Gladstone's name for two minutes, they cheered Chamberlain's for five.'

Chamberlain's programme – and the Liberal divisions it exposed – were naturally a prime target for Conservative attack. Thomas Weller-Polley (Sudbury) claimed the Liberals wanted to 'seize the land altogether, an act on par with highway robbery', while Robert Bourke (King's Lynn) complained of the 'revolutionary doctrines ... Free Education ... land compulsorily taken ... compulsion was the Alpha and Omega'. The proposal to disestablish the Church of England aroused particular fury, and James Agg-Gardner (Cheltenham) urged his audience to 'do their utmost to stem the tide of Infidelity and Atheism, which was sure and rapid conveyance to national disaster and national ruin'. Meanwhile, William Charley (Ipswich) complained of the 'legislative straightjacket' composed of 'compulsory, communistic and socialistic ideas'. H. J. Tollemache (Eddisbury) complained that 'Mr Chamberlain's agents were working about the country districts in labourers' cottages and were beguiling and befooling them with "three acres and a cow"'. Mocking the division in the Liberal Party, the chairman of a Derby meeting chastised the moderates for their impotence in standing up to the radical menace, remarking that 'Whiggism has had among its ranks men who have graced the history of England ... but it has now assumed the functions of a dead fish ... The old Liberalism is dying by the hands of its own offspring.'

Organisationally, the 1885 election witnessed some important developments. The first was the sporadic appearance of paid agents to help candidates run campaigns, such as Herbert Nash in Ipswich who had been imported from Birmingham after having been handpicked by chief NLF organiser Francis Schnadhorst. Next there was evidence that a number of national or regional electioneering bodies – including the NLF, the Primrose League, the National Union of Conservative and Constitutional Associations and the London and Home Counties Liberal Union – had supplied campaigning materials such as posters and handbills to a range of constituencies. Third was the dramatic increase of 'carpetbagger' candidates who did not have local ties to the constituencies they fought. All three developments represented a growth of influences from outside constituencies' political micro-climates that suggested the beginning of a slow move towards the nationalisation of electoral culture. It is also worth remarking that while the Corrupt Practices Act enjoyed striking success in curbing direct bribery, the 1885 election saw considerable violence instigated by hired roughs, especially in the countryside, with meetings broken up and candidates sometimes suffering physical assault. In a sense, the shady electioneering economy had adapted: it had become risky and expensive to bribe enlarged electorates, but disruption of large meetings of politically undecided voters represented a much more tempting target. Finally, the Primrose League saw the Conservatives make the first widespread use of women to act as election volunteers, and the 'dames' formed an indispensable staple of the party's future electioneering efforts until well into the twentieth century.

The Liberals won 319 seats, a net loss of thirty-three from 1880, leaving them seventeen shy of an overall Commons majority. While a disappointing result compared to expectations, they remained comfortably ahead of the Conservatives, who gained eight seats to finish with 247. Perhaps the clearest winners of 1885 were the Parnellites, who managed twenty-three gains and a nigh-clean sweep of Ireland outside of Ulster, finishing with eighty-six seats. This not only was the best British general election result by an Irish Nationalist party but also placed Parnell – as he had hoped – in the role of kingmaker, thus seemingly vindicating his instruction to Irish voters living in England, Scotland and Wales to tactically vote Conservative.

The headline tallies tell only a partial story, however, and contemporaries observed some fascinating psephological subtrends. The first was that the Conservatives had performed remarkably well – and the Liberals remarkably badly – in English boroughs. The Conservatives had picked up seats in Manchester, including unseating prominent cotton magnate Jacob Bright, and won three of the five Leeds seats. London was the brightest spot, and the Tories won victories even in heavily working-class divisions including in Finsbury, Newington, Southwark and Tower Hamlets. In the newly created suburban constituencies, the party did so well that some historians have claimed 1885 birthed a new class of 'villa Tory' voters who underpinned the party's late Victorian revival. Added to this were impressive performances in provincial towns – especially the kind that had retained their second member. In Norwich and Ipswich, for example, local Conservatives exploited the obvious division where a Whig and a Chamberlainite were awkwardly paired together on a joint Liberal ticket.

These results were declared first and – for a time – raised Tory hopes of a truly momentous national upset. However, these hopes were dashed when the Scottish and Welsh boroughs declared solidly for the Liberals. Results from the Birmingham conurbation – under the spell of Chamberlain – were similarly disappointing, symbolised by the failure of Randolph Churchill's audacious bid to win the central division. However, when the counties declared, it was evident that the Liberals' quiet optimism on the political inclinations of the new agricultural labourer voters had been well founded. The party won seventeen of the nineteen Welsh counties and thirty-two of the thirty-nine Scottish, and in England, broke the backbone of historic Tory gentry support, winning 134 of the 239 county seats (a result they bettered only in 1906). Liberal candidates – often unknown carpetbaggers – achieved hitherto unimaginable victories across true-blue rural England, including in Buckinghamshire, Somerset, Wiltshire and Suffolk. No fewer than seventy Tory country gentlemen and sons of peers failed to return to the House of Commons, including Viscount Weymouth, Sir Henry Hoare, Viscount Newport, Lord Henry Bentinck, Sir Ailwyn Fellowes and Lord Elcho. As the *Eastern Daily Press* remarked: 'Liberal candidates have won victories in counties where Liberalism has been at a discount for generations ... it is impossible not to read its lesson: the labourers are Liberal.' Results from the expanded mining county divisions were similarly one-sided, with the Liberals winning all twelve seats in Durham and Northumberland and dominating South Yorkshire.

The 1885 election saw an enormous changing of the political guard from the previous House of Commons. Only 234 MPs who had sat in the old House at the time of its dissolution were returned, and the vast majority of the 436 new members had no prior parliamentary experience. While it was to be expected that the 1885 redistribution would lead to more than the usual number of political retirements on account of old seats being abolished, the fact that both parties made gains in each other's heartlands greatly exacerbated the churn. The new Commons Liberal Party was less aristocratic, less commercial and more Nonconformist. Significantly, around 160 to 180 of the new MPs could be classed as Chamberlainite radicals. The Conservatives, too, counted less landed gentry among their numbers and more industrial and commercial professionals. Indeed, no fewer than 38 per cent of MPs overall were from the newer middle-class professions: bankers, merchants and manufacturers.

The parliament that emerged after the election had tremendous potential to push Britain towards radical government, especially after Parnell withdrew support for Salisbury and gave Gladstone the keys to Downing Street for his third premiership. The election had been dominated by Chamberlain's proposals, and the schism in the Liberal Party between the Whigs and radicals was exactly what he wanted. The irony was that he misunderstood his power base. Like most British radicals (then and now), Chamberlain had been thinking primarily of urban areas when he proposed his programme and had little interest in the rural backwaters. As it transpired, the fact that the Liberals imploded in the boroughs and stormed the counties confused him, making him gun-shy of claiming the mandate to succeed Gladstone as Liberal leader. However, he might have come to realise that his intervention had placed him at the heart of a new and emerging political divide with an increasingly radical Liberal Party on one side and a more self-consciously progressive Conservative Party on the other. However, the final twist in the drama of 1885 was that its result ended up counting for almost nothing because Gladstone surprised the country with his sudden announcement of Irish Home Rule just a few months later. Historians are undecided as to whether he did this to spike Chamberlain's guns, but the resultant crisis detonated a party realignment of a still larger scale. It also served to upend the new parliament and deprive this most dramatic election of what might have been a definitive political legacy.

Dr Luke Blaxill is lecturer in British history at Hertford College, University of Oxford. He has published widely on nineteenth- and twentieth-century British electoral politics, including psephological studies and especially on campaign language. His *The War of Words: The Language of British Elections, 1880–1914* was published in 2020 by the Royal Historical Society.

16

1886

ROBERT SAUNDERS

Dissolution: 26 June 1886
Polling day: 1–27 July 1886
Seats up for election: 670
Total electorate / Total votes cast / Turnout: 5,708,030 (3,734,832 in contested seats) / 2,758,151 / 74.2 per cent
Candidates (total 1,115): Conservative and Liberal Unionist – 563; Liberal – 449; Irish Parliamentary – 100
Prime Minister on polling day: William Gladstone
Main party leaders: Conservative – Marquess of Salisbury; Liberal – William Gladstone; Liberal Unionist – Lord Hartington; Irish Parliamentary – Charles Stewart Parnell

Party performance:

Party	Votes	Percentage share	Seats
Conservative and Liberal Unionist	1,417,627	51.4	393
Liberal	1,244,683	45.1	192
Irish Parliamentary	91,083	46.7	85

Result: Hung parliament, Conservatives were the largest party

The 1886 election was among the most dramatic, divisive and consequential in modern British history. Like its nearest rivals – the 'reform' election of 1831 or 'the peers versus the people' in 1910 – it centred on a single, tempestuous issue: 'Home Rule for Ireland', a question that struck British politics like a lightning bolt. Home Rule electrified public debate, broke the party system and rewrote the map of British politics. It shattered the once-dominant Liberal Party, made the Conservatives the largest party for only the second time in four decades and created a new political alliance, 'Unionism', that would govern for sixteen of the next twenty years. It established for the first time the dominance of the Conservative Party in both the media and the House of Lords, and it ended the best chance of self-government for Ireland within the Union. There are few elections of which it can be said with confidence that the shape of British politics – and of the United Kingdom itself – would have been different had the result gone the other way. The election of 1886, indubitably, is one.

Home Rule was the latest attempt to solve the 'Irish question', which had bedevilled UK politics since the Act of Union in 1800. It offered Ireland self-government within the United Kingdom, with a parliament and executive sitting in Dublin. Westminster would remain sovereign, with control over trade, security and foreign relations, but the Irish parliament would have law-making powers over most domestic questions. That seemingly modest proposal triggered one of the great crises of the nineteenth century, and in the years before 1914 would bring the country close to civil war.

Home Rule was so divisive because it spoke to all the most important questions of the nineteenth century. It was an imperial question, a religious question and a matter of national security. It ignited fundamental constitutional dilemmas – what made a people 'fit' for self-government? What constituted a 'nation'? When was it appropriate to coerce a population? And it doused these dilemmas in the petrol of race and religion. Opponents feared that Home Rule would rupture the Union, break up the empire and place the Protestant minority under the heel of the Catholic priesthood. Lord Salisbury, the Conservative leader, likened the Irish to the 'Hottentots' of Southern Africa and told supporters that self-government was suited only to those 'of Teutonic race'. Conservative journals conjured a nightmare vision of 'plunder', 'oppression' and 'extermination', while

Lord Randolph Churchill (father of Winston) predicted that 'Ulster will fight and Ulster will be right'. Supporters, by contrast, saw in Home Rule a new 'treaty of peace'. Home Rule, they believed, would be a great act of justice, establishing a 'union of hearts' in place of what Gladstone called 'a paper union, obtained by force and fraud'. It would secure Irish loyalty in time of war and prevent the British from destroying their own liberties in the attempt to coerce their neighbour. Cecil Rhodes, the most celebrated imperialist of his day, donated £10,000 to the cause, in the belief that it offered a model for the reorganisation of the empire.

Outside Ireland, Home Rule had not been a central issue in the 1885 election. But within days of the polls closing, a bombshell exploded in the press: William Gladstone, the 'Grand Old Man' of Liberal politics, was revealed to be a convert to the policy. For his critics, this was a naked power-grab. The elections had produced a hung parliament in which the eighty-six Irish Nationalists held the balance of power, so embracing Home Rule allowed Gladstone to evict the Conservatives from office and return to No. 10. In fact, Gladstone had hoped that the Conservatives would take up the issue, allowing it to be settled on a cross-party basis. The election *was* an influence on his thinking but not in quite the way his critics proposed.

Only a year earlier, at Gladstone's insistence, the 1884 Reform Act had more than tripled the Irish electorate, extending to Ireland the same electoral rights enjoyed by the rest of the United Kingdom. The result had been a landslide: Home Rule candidates had won eighty-five of Ireland's 103 seats, sweeping every constituency outside Ulster and more than half the seats in the north. On a practical level, that threatened to make stable government at Westminster impossible: a disciplined phalanx of Home Rule MPs, operating in hung parliaments, could bring government to a standstill, while attempts to neutralise them risked subverting Britain's own system of parliamentary government. Morally, the result challenged MPs to accept the verdict of the constituencies they themselves had created. The 'voice of Ireland', thought Gladstone, had been 'clearly and constitutionally spoken'. Parliament must either recognise that demand or use the power of the other three nations to overrule it. One route led to Home Rule; the other, to a new, more fearsome coercion.

Gladstone's decision to take up Home Rule struck the political system like a tsunami. It shipwrecked the Liberal Party and sent new alliances floating tentatively onto the political main. Radicals and Whigs alike found themselves swept overboard, only to wash up together on the shores of a new 'Liberal Unionist' party. Within a decade, Joe Chamberlain and Lord Hartington – old rivals who had fought to shape the destinies of Liberalism – would be Cabinet colleagues in a government dominated by the Conservatives. The Liberal press defected en masse: papers like the *Daily Telegraph*, *The Economist*, *The Spectator*, the *Daily Chronicle* and *The Scotsman*, once the flagships of the Liberal armada, now turned their guns on their own fleet, giving the Conservatives a dominance in the media they have enjoyed ever since. It was not just parties that splintered under the strain but churches, friendships and family relationships. The emerging women's suffrage movement first buckled and then fractured, broken by an issue that even the *Women's Suffrage Journal* thought 'dwarfs ... every other question that Parliament has had to settle in the whole course of its existence'.

Even the monarch was drawn into the controversy. For the first time since the death of her beloved Disraeli, Queen Victoria opened Parliament in January in person, telling MPs that she was 'resolutely opposed' to any change in the 'fundamental law' of the Union. She fired off a volley of letters designed to stiffen the sinews of prospective rebels, presenting the unusual spectacle of a monarch agitating against her own government.

The decisive battle in Parliament came in the early hours of 8 June, when the bill went down by 341 votes to 311. Ninety-three Liberals had broken with Gladstone, more than a quarter of the entire parliamentary party. Seventy-eight of those subsequently crossed the floor and sat as a separate block, known as either 'Liberal Unionists' or 'Union Liberals'. Rebels included a former party leader, Lord Hartington, the veteran radical John Bright and the man who had been widely regarded as the Liberals' leader-in-waiting, Joe Chamberlain. They were joined by 120 of the 183 Liberal peers, stripping the party of much of its wealth and social influence. That left the party fatally weakened in agricultural constituencies, where the influence of the peerage remained crucial, and made the House of Lords for the first time an overwhelmingly anti-Liberal body.

In his closing speech before the vote, Gladstone had issued a challenge to his opponents: 'You have power, you have wealth, you have rank, you have station ... What have we? We think that we have the people's heart; we believe and we know we have the promise of the harvest of the future.'

Two days later, he would put that claim to the test, dissolving Parliament and appealing directly to the voters. That carried the struggle out of Westminster and into the country, in a contest that *The Times* predicted would 'profoundly influence the future of the Empire'.

The Liberals could hardly have been in worse shape for an election. Their party was hopelessly divided, its major donors had defected and the Liberal press had gone over en masse to the opposition. The split in Parliament was replayed in constituency associations across the country, as Home Rulers and Liberal Unionists wrestled for control of their local organisations. In more than a hundred seats, the party proved unable even to put up a candidate. Across England, Scotland and Wales, more than a quarter of all MPs (155) were elected unopposed, of whom all but forty were Unionists. Including the Irish seats, 224 MPs were elected unopposed, up from just forty-three the previous year.

By contrast, Conservatives and Liberal Unionists could sink their differences in defence of the Union. The two parties quickly agreed a pact: the Conservatives would not run a candidate in the seventy-eight seats held by Liberal Unionists and would give them a free run against the Liberal in sixty-seven more. Elsewhere, Unionists of all stripes would be encouraged to vote Conservative. That avoided a split in the Unionist vote and encouraged men like Hartington, Chamberlain and Bright to concentrate their fire on their former colleagues. In at least 114 constituencies, voters had to choose between rival Liberal candidates, splintering local associations, confusing allegiances and sending turnout plummeting.

Local divisions could be intensely damaging. At Frome, in Somerset, the Liberal Association lost both its president and its serving MP – the former, because he opposed Home Rule; the latter, because he had voted for it with insufficient enthusiasm. The party was still scrabbling around for a candidate only weeks before the vote, and duly lost a seat it had held for eighteen of the past twenty years. At Edinburgh West, Thomas Buchanan was deselected at a turbulent party meeting but maintained the support of a third of those voting. He promptly ran as a Liberal Unionist and retained the seat. At Carlisle, Robert Ferguson was deselected after a hostile speech by Gladstone at the railway station, prompting complaints that he had been struck down by 'an oratorical rotten egg'.

Such incidents exposed a new phenomenon at a British election: the willingness of a party leader to intervene publicly in local candidate selections. Home Rule had been defeated by a majority of thirty, so if Gladstone could hold his existing seats and replace just sixteen of the Liberal rebels with Home Rulers, a bill would pass through the next parliament. At Leith, Gladstone even stood for election himself – despite an unopposed return at Midlothian – to block the re-election of William Jacks, who had voted against Home Rule but hoped to remain in the Gladstonian party. That raised questions about the right of conscience for MPs to disagree with party leaders. Even among Home Rulers, there was some unease at the expulsion or deselection of MPs for voting against a policy that had never been put to the country and which the party as a whole had opposed only months earlier. Critics warned that Liberalism was becoming a personality cult, in thrall to 'the Papacy of Mr Gladstone'. Liberals were said to 'worship Mr Gladstone, as a fetish is worshipped', in an atavistic manifestation of a primitive cult. That, for some, was reason in itself to keep the Liberals from power: *The Economist* warned that Gladstone, if re-elected, would be a 'dictator' with a control over the House that was 'without precedent' – a menace 'more urgent even than the danger of Home Rule'.

Liberal rhetoric gave some support to that allegation. Electors at Ipswich were told that 'it was the bounden duty of England to follow in the footsteps of Mr Gladstone', while at Norwich, voting Liberal became a way of 'showing our gratitude to the Greatest Statesman of the Age'. Voters were offered a choice between two visions of the future: the Conservative policy of 'coercion and conspiracies' and the Liberal offer of 'Gladstone and gladness'.

As a study by Luke Blaxill has shown, the warring parties not only promised different policies; they spoke a different language. Unionist rhetoric was emotive and apocalyptic, centring on words like 'rebellion', 'separation', 'Catholics' and 'control'. Home Rule would plunge the country into 'civil war' and reduce Ireland to 'a savage wilderness', 'infested with foreign dynamitards'. It would see the 'flag torn down and Empire dismembered', while placing 'the Loyalists of Ulster under the heel of the Catholic priesthood'. Liberals preferred to speak of 'justice', 'conciliation' and the prospect of *real* union: a union of hearts', not 'that sham union which has existed for the last eighty-six years'. Home Rulers insisted that they were 'as much Unionists as were the Conservative Party': they were seeking to *rebuild* a Union for which consent had broken down. Emotive appeals to 'justice for Ireland' jostled with a more hard-nosed plea to get the issue settled, so that Parliament could get Irish politics out of its collective hair. Unionists made the obvious riposte: if, as the mustard-magnate Jeremiah Colman insisted, Home Rule 'blocks the way', was not the best remedy simply to vote against it?

Given the stakes, it is perhaps surprising that the election was not more violent. There were, of course, some hair-raising moments. A meeting was attacked at Aston Manor, windows were smashed at Pontefract and shots were fired at Tyldesley. A Conservative newspaper office was besieged at Cardiff, voters at Colchester had powdered dye thrown in their faces and there was 'violent rowdyism' at Leigh, apparently in the mistaken belief that there was 'no law on election day'. The Unionist press blamed 'Irish' electoral tactics, intended 'to coerce and bully the advocates of union', while *The Times* accused 'Separatists' of 'violence and disorder on a scale hitherto unknown'.

Yet this was tame stuff by the standards of Victorian elections, and far below the levels experienced a year earlier. The 1886 contest in fact saw a steep and enduring *decline* in election violence, while the use of 'hired roughs' – paid for from party funds – all but disappeared. Riots were few and far between and only three people were killed, the lowest figure since 1859.

Violence was more likely to be rhetorical or figurative than physical. The Colchester Liberal Club portrayed Joe Chamberlain, once a hero to many Liberals, as

> a hound attacking Mr Gladstone, as a masked conspirator dripping his dagger in blood, as an assassin waiting outside Mr Gladstone's bedchamber to kill him, as a 'Birmingham Macbeth', as a snake writhing on the ground and spitting fiercely in Mr Gladstone's face, as a criminal handcuffed in the dock, and found 'guilty of the Wilful Murder of a Treaty of Peace and Conciliation', as a person crowning a villainous statue of Coercion, and as a clown with a fools' cap and long asses' ears.

When a former Liberal minister, George Goschen, lost his seat at Edinburgh, Gladstone sent a telegram of congratulation to his former constituents, rejoicing that 'the capital of dear old Scotland has shaken off her chains'. Gladstone himself was denounced by Unionists as a 'false prophet' and 'the English Jefferson Davis'; a man whose 'vulgar and tortuous tactics' and 'perverted ingenuity' made him more fit for an asylum than for Downing Street. When Lawrence Baker, a Liberal who had reluctantly voted for Home Rule, popped into the Stock Exchange after its defeat, he was assailed with a 'volley of hisses and groans' – a performance that briefly interrupted the singing of 'God Save the Queen'. That animus was heartily reciprocated: a Liberal Unionist complained that his former colleagues 'talked about the Tories in the way that Christians talked about Jews in the middle ages'.

Gladstone had hoped that 'the people's heart' would swell to the cause of 'justice for Ireland', overruling the power of 'wealth', 'rank' and 'station'; but the result, he acknowledged, was 'a smash'. Out of

670 seats, Gladstone's supporters won 196 at most: fewer than the Conservatives in 1945 or Labour in 2019. Even with the eighty-five Irish Nationalists, the Home Rule forces could muster barely 280 seats in total. Liberal Unionists won between seventy-two and seventy-eight seats (a few candidates proved reluctant to pick sides), while the Conservatives returned 316. That gave the Unionist forces a majority over the Home Rule parties of at least 107.

The slaughter had been particularly severe in England, where 283 Conservatives and fifty-six Liberal Unionists confronted 125 Gladstonians and a solitary Irish Nationalist. The Gladstonians lost thirty-five county seats and twenty-eight boroughs, shedding almost all the gains they had made among agricultural labourers in 1885. It did not help that most of the great landed families had gone over to the Unionists, or that the election happened during the hay harvest, when agricultural labourers had other things on their minds. Nor had the heady promises of a year earlier ('three acres and a cow!') been delivered. In consequence, the party returned no MPs at all in the county divisions of Middlesex, Surrey, Kent, Hertfordshire, Buckinghamshire, Berkshire, Hampshire, Huntingdonshire, Rutland, Worcestershire, Shropshire and Herefordshire. In London, the Liberals slumped from twenty-five seats to eleven, while the Conservatives won forty-nine seats (up from thirty-seven) and the Liberal Unionists two.

The damage was less severe outside England – but damage it remained. In Scotland, where the Liberals had won sixty-two out of seventy-two seats in 1885, they held just forty-three a year later, compared to twelve Conservatives and seventeen Liberal Unionists. In Wales, the Liberals had won twenty-seven of the thirty seats in 1885; in 1886 that fell to twenty-three. Ireland, ironically, saw the least movement. Only thirty-three seats were contested at all, down from seventy-nine a year earlier, and just seven of those were outside Ulster. The Nationalists won eighty-four seats in total (plus one in Liverpool), including every seat in the south except Dublin University. In Ulster, the balance tipped fractionally back to the Unionists, who won seventeen seats (fifteen Conservative, two Liberal Unionist) to sixteen for the Nationalists.

Yet the scale of the defeat was in some respects misleading. The story of the election was not a surge in support for Unionism but a collapse in the numbers voting. In 1885, around 4.3 million people in Britain had cast their ballots. Seven months later, less than 2.8 million did so: a staggering drop, even allowing for the number of uncontested seats. Compared to 1885, the Conservatives gained nearly ninety additional MPs while winning 800,000 fewer votes. The Liberals haemorrhaged seats with a loss of 700,000 ballots. The Liberals won only 76,000 fewer votes in Great Britain than the two Unionist parties combined, but the distribution of those votes produced a defeat of landslide proportions.

Across the country, Liberal defeats were closely linked to turnout. In Norwich, where Jacob Tillett was defeated by just thirty-seven votes, turnout dropped by 1,230. Joseph Arch was beaten by twenty votes in Norfolk North-West, where turnout fell by 640. In Mid-Norfolk, only 5,657 registered a vote at all – barely higher than the 5,275 who had backed the Liberal a year earlier. Constituencies where Liberals fought one another saw particularly steep drops in turnout: 11 per cent in Barnstaple, 15.6 per cent in South Molton, 17.7 per cent in Tavistock and 20.2 per cent in Totnes.

There were grounds for Liberal optimism here. The high level of abstentions suggested, to Gladstone, that much of the electorate had suspended judgement on Home Rule. Unable to reach a verdict on a question of which they knew little, and confused by rival Liberal candidates, voters had stayed at home and hoped things would blow over. By the next election, however, Home Rule would no longer be an unfamiliar idea; on the contrary, a subject that had once been 'as foreign to the British mind as the differential calculus' would be 'among the chief lessons of ... Liberal teaching'.

Liberals could also take comfort from their performance outside England. By Gladstone's calculations, Scots had voted for Home Rule candidates by a ratio of 3:2, Ireland by 4.5:1 and 'gallant Wales' by 5:1. For Gladstone, the disparity of size between the different parts of the Union helped to explain their different attitudes to Home Rule. With its 'vast preponderance in strength', England could 'overbear' the votes of the other nations and 'reverse their combined judgement'; that gave it 'a favourable view' of 'incorporating unions', in which decision-making was concentrated at Westminster. By contrast, Wales and Scotland were more reluctant to concentrate power in 'a body, English in such overwhelming proportion as the present Parliament is, and must probably always be'. The 'spirit of nationality', Gladstone predicted, would continue to bind Scotland and Wales to Ireland, and where they led, the 'slower acknowledgement' of England would surely follow.

Within Parliament, too, the Conservatives' position was more fragile than at first appeared. With Conservatives returning just 316 of the 670 seats, Salisbury had no independent majority. He was dependent on the Liberal rebels, who continued to sit on the opposition benches. Many were radicals on every subject but Ireland; and if the survival of a Conservative government rested on the votes of Joe Chamberlain and his followers, it was not at all clear how long it could endure. Any attempt to coerce Ireland was likely to drive some, at least, of the 'dissentient Liberals' back into the main body of the party. With the Nationalists now firmly in Gladstone's corner, even a modest defection by the Liberal Unionists would imperil the Conservatives' hold on power.

Underpinning all this was a deep scepticism – shared across all parties – about the Conservatives' long-term electoral prospects, once the peculiar circumstances of 1886 had passed. Since the Great Reform Act in 1832, the Conservatives had won a majority in the Commons only twice. Even in 1886, when the Liberal Party was on its knees, the Conservatives had fallen twenty seats short of a majority. For half a century, Liberal defeats had proven only temporary interruptions to the Liberal monopoly on power. From the abolition of church rates to reform of the franchise, it was hard to think of a single issue on which the Liberal Party had set its mind that had not, after a struggle of some kind, been carried into law – in some cases, by their opponents.

Like many other Liberals (and, indeed, Lord Salisbury), Gladstone found it hard to conceive that a mass electorate of the kind inaugurated in the Third Reform Act would be more favourable to the

Conservatives than the one it displaced. Voters might, in the confused conditions of 1886, stay away from the polls, but they would not, in the long term, support reaction. If Conservatism could not win a majority in 1886, there seemed little reason to believe that its hold on power would endure. 'Toryism', thought Gladstone, 'can never by its own resources win ... a majority of the House of Commons, unless and until the tendencies and temper of the British nation shall have undergone some novel and considerable change.'

In consequence, Gladstone led his 'small but crack army' back to Westminster in bullish mood. The 'cause of Irish self-government', he proclaimed, 'lives and moves ... It will arise, as a wounded warrior sometimes arises on the field of battle, and stabs to the heart some soldier of the victorious army, who has been exulting over him.' Given time, the Conservative coalition would surely crumble; and if the government would not retrace its steps in office, the next election would seal its fate. In that spirit of optimism, Gladstone did not wait to meet Parliament before resigning, on the grounds that 'if there is to be an anti-Irish Government the sooner it begins the sooner it will end'.

With the next election in mind, he launched a six-year campaign designed to educate the public on Home Rule. His model was the campaign against the Corn Laws, which had been 'neither ... cared about nor understood till Cobden illuminated it with his admirable intellect'. The result was a rare effort, over the duration of a parliament, to persuade the public of a new policy departure – and perhaps the first example of the 'permanent campaign'.

The by-election record over the following years suggested it was bearing fruit. The Liberals gained twenty-two seats over the course of the parliament – nine from Liberal Unionists and thirteen from Conservatives – with just two going the other way. Victories in Burnley, Coventry, Southampton, Kennington, Rochester, Buckingham, St Pancras North and the Hartlepools suggested that Home Rule was picking up strength in England, while gains in Edinburgh West, Govan and Caernarvon Boroughs (where a young David Lloyd George emerged blinking from the political womb) tightened its hold on Scotland and Wales. By 1887, Chamberlain was at his 'wit's end' to know how 'to prevent the disappearance of our followers in the country'. The 'Liberal cry', he told Hartington, 'is too strong for us'; 'the Liberal Unionists of 1886 have largely become Gladstonian.'

As early as 1887, Gladstone was confidently predicting a return to power. Addressing a meeting of the National Liberal Federation, he told them that 'we have stood by one another in darkness and in storm'; now 'the morning has dawned upon us and … the sun is mounting in the sky'. Yet his opponents, too, were in bullish mood. For the Conservatives, the spectacular defeat of a radical policy – so soon after the expansion of the electorate in 1884 – was immensely cheering. It suggested that the new electorate could be trusted with the defence of empire, the Union and established institutions, a discovery that eased the party's embrace of democracy.

For the Liberal Unionists, the future was less clear. So long as the Union remained the biggest issue in British politics, Conservatives and Liberal Unionists would almost certainly hold together. But if a more normal politics began to reassert itself, or if political debate began to polarise around questions of domestic or imperial reform, the alliance might become more precarious. That dynamic would exert a powerful effect over the politics of the coming years.

Dr Robert Saunders is reader in British history at Queen Mary University of London. He specialises in the history of British democracy, and his books include *Democracy and the Vote in British Politics* (2011) and *Yes to Europe! The 1975 Referendum and Seventies Britain* (2018).

17

1892

LEO MCKINSTRY

Dissolution: 28 June 1892
Polling day: 4–26 July 1892
Seats contested: 670
Total electorate / Total votes cast / Turnout: 6,160,541 (5,614,202 in contested seats) / 4,317,312 / 77.4 per cent
Candidates (total 1,303): Conservative and Liberal Unionist – 606; Liberal – 535; Irish National Federation – 85; Irish National League – 44; Independent Labour – 9; Independent Liberal – 6; Independent Conservative – 4
Prime Minister on polling day: Marquess of Salisbury
Main party leaders: Conservative and Liberal Unionist – Marquess of Salisbury; Liberal – William Gladstone; Irish National Federation – Justin McCarthy; Irish National League – John Redmond

Party performance:

Party	Votes	Percentage share	Seats
Conservative and Liberal Unionist	2,028,586	47	314
Liberal	1,958,598	45.4	271
Irish National Federation	227,007	57.7	72
Irish National League	70,251	17.9	9
Independent Labour	22,198	0.5	3
Independent Conservative	5,556	0.1	0
Independent Liberal	3,572	0.1	1

Result: Hung parliament, Liberals form a minority government with support from Irish Nationalists

William Gladstone, the titan of nineteenth-century Liberal politics, was the oldest party leader in British history when he fought the 1892 general election at the age of eighty-two. He was also bidding to become the first politician to win a fourth term as Prime Minister, though in private he was uncertain that he would be up to the task because of his growing infirmities, particularly his deafness. In a conversation in mid-June that year with Sir Edward Hamilton, his former Downing Street aide and now a senior Treasury official, he asked how he could conduct the business of Cabinet when he 'could hear no talk around the table?'

Yet Gladstone had a remarkable spirit of resilience which could be enhanced by the pressures of his position. Just as he drew energy from his epic speeches in the Commons or on public platforms, so he was galvanised by the demands of campaigning. Indeed, from the late 1870s, he had famously pioneered in his Midlothian constituency near Edinburgh a new, more dramatic style of electioneering that featured torchlit parades, firework displays, banners, bonfires and vast, adoring crowds at his rallies.

Now in the summer of 1892, he was ready to enter the fray once again as the Marquess of Salisbury's second Tory-led administration came to a close after six years in office. On Friday 24 June, Hamilton recorded in his diary: 'Went to see Mr G. this morning to say goodbye and bid him God-speed on his last campaign. There is something rather touching about the old political warrior, buckling on his armour for the last fight.' Hamilton added that he found Gladstone 'very sanguine' about his party's prospects and even believed 'a Liberal majority was unavoidable'.

This optimism contained a large element of wishful thinking, for the British political scene in the last decades of the nineteenth century was too fluid, too unsettled to allow such forecasts to be made with confidence. The primary reason for the upheaval was Gladstone's attempt from 1885 to give Ireland Home Rule, which caused a large group of MPs, led by the urbane aristocrat Lord Hartington and the charismatic radical Joseph Chamberlain, to break away from the Gladstonian party and form their own group, the Liberal Unionists. With seventy-seven MPs elected in the 1886 general election, the Liberal Unionists held the balance of power in Parliament and they used their influence to keep Lord Salisbury in Downing Street and Gladstone in opposition, though they did not build a formal ruling coalition with the Tories.

In the run-up to the 1892 election, there was another crucial ingredient of the Irish question which made predictions of the outcome all the harder. This was the explosive scandal that had engulfed the Irish Nationalist Leader Charles Stewart Parnell after revelations of his long affair with his lover Kitty O'Shea, with whom he fathered three children. His relationship was exposed in public when her husband, Captain William O'Shea, sued for divorce, citing Parnell as correspondent. Parnell died in the arms of his beloved Kitty in October 1891 from pneumonia, but the legacy of his downfall continued to be felt across the political landscape of the British Isles. In Ireland, the cause of Irish nationalism was badly split after the Catholic Church came out against Parnell, while in Britain, support for Home Rule diminished within the Nonconformist hierarchy, one of the pillars of Liberalism.

Other factors that contributed to the sense of political instability were the growing importance of the labour movement, the radicalisation of the trade unions, the rise of Welsh nationalism, agitation over the House of Lords, demands for more state intervention and concerns about the threat to Britain's place as the world's leading imperial and economic superpower. Amid anxiety about the traditional order breaking down, this backdrop made the election highly unpredictable. The *Manchester Guardian* referred to 'the difficulty of forming any trustworthy judgment as to election prospects', which meant that 'even the most skilled political meteorologist' would struggle to pick the winner. Nor were there any opinion polls then to serve as a guide. According to one of his biographers, Joseph Chamberlain himself found that 'never in his experience had the electoral tide been so hard to gauge as in the spring of 1892. It might turn in either direction.'

But it could not be denied that recent by-election results had gone the Liberals' way. As well as successfully defending all their own seats over the past year, they had also taken Wisbech off the Tories on a swing of over 9 per cent, and two seats off the Liberal Unionists, at South Molton in Devon and Rossendale in Lancashire, caused by the elevation of Lord Hartington to the House of Lords as the Duke of Devonshire. Privately, Chamberlain, having expected a narrow win, confessed to a colleague that the Rossendale result was 'a great blow'. Moreover, the Liberals had in their favour the continuing lustre of Gladstone's name and a far greater sense of unity than had existed in the previous election of 1886. That cohesion stemmed partly from the near universal support for Irish Home Rule within their ranks, following the departure of the Liberal Unionists. Their solidarity was reinforced by the Liberals' excellent organisation, headed by the Birmingham draper Francis Schnadhorst, the secretary of the party's ruling body, the National Liberal Federation, though he paid a heavy price for his workaholic tendencies. Forced to resign all his positions in the party in 1893 at the age of just fifty-three because of ill health, he suffered a nervous breakdown the following year and died in a 'lunatic asylum' in 1900.

But his organisational skill had been essential in rebuilding the party after the electoral disaster of 1886. Just as importantly, in October 1891, the National Liberal Federation had adopted at its annual meeting in Newcastle-upon-Tyne a bold manifesto that both enhanced its appeal and provided a clear agenda for government. Known as the 'Newcastle Programme', this list of pledges included, in addition to Home Rule, 'better provision for the housing of the working-class', limits on factory hours, the disestablishment of the church in Wales and Scotland, leasehold reform, greater support for state schools and technical training, the equalisation of death duties, payment of MPs and 'popular control of liquor traffic'. Chamberlain argued that the real aim of the Newcastle Programme was to make Irish Home Rule acceptable to English voters. 'Gladstonians have now lost confidence in the attractions of Home Rule as an election cry and they acknowledge that it will only pass if sandwiched between more alluring proposals,' he said. The culinary metaphor was taken up by other Unionists. Salisbury likened the Newcastle Programme to a series 'of capsules made of gelatine in which some very nasty stuffs are enclosed', while the Duke of Devonshire claimed that Home Rule would 'only be swallowed if accompanied by a great quantity of more palatable jam'.

But some Liberals felt that the Newcastle Programme, far from serving as an electoral asset, just illustrated the party's descent in 'faddism' and surrender to single-issue pressure groups. 'It begins by offering everything to everybody and will end by giving nothing to nobody,' said Lord Rosebery, the wealthy Liberal peer and former Foreign Secretary. Widely regarded as a future party leader despite his erratic temperament, Rosebery was to act as Gladstone's host at his grand home of Dalmeny by the Firth of Forth during this final Midlothian campaign. The more discerning Liberals also recognised that they were up against a formidable opponent in the Conservative–Liberal Unionist alliance. Chamberlain was a master organiser, a dynamic force on the stump and had played an important role in pushing the Tory government to adopt an impressive catalogue of social legislation in the 1886–92 parliament, such as the introduction of compulsory education and the creation of county councils. Despite his air of gloomy pessimism, Salisbury had proved to be a Prime Minister of towering authority, skilful in international diplomacy and the maintenance of British interests without resorting to bellicosity. His government had also upheld the principle of sound money and had quelled disorder in Ireland through the dual approach of addressing agrarian grievances while dealing ruthlessly with militants. His ministry's success in pacifying Ireland led Salisbury to argue that the case for Home Rule had been effectively demolished. The verdict of the distinguished historian Élie Halévy was that this administration was 'perhaps one of the best that England has ever known', and Hamilton, despite his devotion to Gladstone, conceded that Salisbury's 'had been a good Government. It has held together well. It has got into few scrapes. It has avoided war abroad and passed some very useful liberal measures at home.'

It was on 28 June that Parliament was dissolved and the short campaign formally began. That day, Salisbury had a letter published in *The Times*, which essentially set out his manifesto. Referring to his record over the past six years, he wrote that 'a sound system of finance, based on a pacific policy, has enabled us to mitigate taxation, to deal effectively with difficult social questions and to provide for the fleet and the armaments of this country a strength which it has never possessed before'. James Bryce, the Liberal MP for Aberdeen South, sneered that Salisbury's manifesto was almost devoid of content: 'The Tory programme might be dismissed in a few words. It consists of appealing to the past for confidence in the future.' But Salisbury believed that he should concentrate on his dire warnings of the consequences for the Union if the Liberals were to regain power.

> There is one interest to which this election is above all others vital. It is the interest of a large portion of the Irish people who are in effect threatened with separation from Great Britain. To them, this election is of terrible importance. On your votes in the next two or three weeks will depend whether it will be to send them a message of hope or a sentence of servitude and ruin. For the loyal minority of Ireland the crisis is supreme. A wrong decision now means the certainty of a bitter and protracted struggle, culminating probably in civil war.

Apart from the apocalyptic language, which Gladstone privately described as 'wicked', there was controversy over Salisbury electioneering at all, given the convention that peers did not take part in such contests. In 1880, the incumbent Prime Minister the Earl of Beaconsfield, as Disraeli had become four years earlier, had scrupulously avoided any involvement, just as Gladstone embarked on his greatest Midlothian crusade on his way back to Downing Street. But Salisbury had shown no intention of abiding by that tradition in 1886; nor did he do so in 1892. *The Times* thought he was fully justified in his approach: 'The humblest individual in the country can issue a manifesto to the electors of the United Kingdom whenever he thinks fit. It would be strange if the head of the government might not embrace the same privilege when his own policy and conduct are the subject of unusual contest.'

The intensity of the brief campaign had one severe physical consequence for Gladstone. Travelling from London to Scotland on 25 June, he stopped in Chester to make a speech on behalf of the Liberal candidate Hugh Halkett. As he was driven in a carriage towards the arena, where over 6,000 people had gathered to hear him, a woman came forward and with surprising vehemence threw a missile directly at his face. The object, which turned out to be a hardened piece of gingerbread, struck him in his left eye and caused him to reel back in his seat. Despite his pain and bleeding, which entailed a visit to the local infirmary, he returned to the campaign venue and bravely delivered his speech, opening with a reference to the incident: 'Our opponents have apparently found it rather hard to keep the field in argument and consequently they have unnaturally resorted to other weapons.' But behind this brave front, the injury left him badly shaken. By the time he reached Dalmeny, he was in a sour mood – his despondency compounded by dental problems, the heavy drizzle that hung over Scotland, the mixed, often disappointing, reports from the constituencies and the prickly disengagement of Rosebery, whose wife Hannah had died recently, prompting him to claim that he would refuse office if the Liberals won the election. The darkened atmosphere was further worsened by the macabre pair of thick black goggles that Gladstone had to wear in private to protect his damaged eyesight, which gave him the appearance of a pantomime grotesque. In his diary, the Liberal politician and intellectual John Morley, perhaps Gladstone's most devoted follower, left this description of his visit to Dalmeny towards the end of the campaign as the first results came through:

> My host could not contain his weariness. They had passed a horrid week of rejection and dismay, the telegrams coming to the house all day long and smashing the illusions of many months; Mr Gladstone, in his dark goggle glasses, slightly mad and rambling about the Scottish church. I laugh at it today but at the moment, like Rosebery, I felt something horrible and gruesome about it.

In the Midlothian constituency itself, the campaign was a pale shadow of the previous spectacular crusades. No proper canvassing was carried out by local members; nor was there any of the excitement of the past generated by parades and firework displays. The flames of Gladstone's oratory now flickered low as his voice grew weaker on the platform.

As the campaign unfolded, it was inevitable that Home Rule should dominate, not least because both the main parties felt that the issue worked in their own interests. Research by the historian Naomi Lloyd-Jones reveals that two-thirds of Liberal candidates in 1892 put Irish self-government at the head of their constituency addresses. Furthermore, the Liberal Party tied the demand for political justice in Ireland to the quest for wider constitutional reforms, such as strengthened parish councils and a more democratic Lords'. In a meeting in his Derby constituency, the Liberal heavyweight Sir William Harcourt maintained that the party had got the balance of policies right and was in tune with public opinion. He said:

> The Liberal party, after a long march, had reached the field on which the battle was to be fought ... There was a confident expectation of victory and he [Harcourt] believed they were about to strike a famous blow for the good old cause of Liberalism and to bring joy and pride to the heart of their glorious chief.

For their part, Unionists inverted arguments about priorities by asserting that, despite the Newcastle Programme, the Liberals' obsession with Home Rule would limit the scope of Gladstone's government to introduce other, badly needed legislation, such as employers' liability, old-age pensions and modernisation of the Poor Law. In contrast the Unionists, unencumbered by the Irish question, would be free 'to attend to England's wants'. But their main accusation was still the threat to the United Kingdom from Home Rule, described by Arthur Balfour as 'an act of national dishonour' from which 'could spring in the future nothing but disaster'. Both the Conservatives and Liberal Unionists seized on the position of Ulster, where the majority in several counties were opposed to Home Rule, as a means of trying to torpedo the Liberals' case. Gladstone told Hamilton that any pressure for an Ulster exemption would be 'preposterous', given that overall the province returned as many Nationalists as Unionists. The former Liberal Cabinet Minister James Stansfeld, defending his seat in Halifax, presciently warned against the appeasement of Ulster Protestant prejudice: 'Belfast merchants have been accustomed to sit in pride of place and keep their foot on the great majority of Catholic Irishmen. What they were troubled with was the pride of ascendancy and the bigotry of religion.' Yet the importance of Ulster Unionism could not be airily dismissed. Its strength was illustrated by a huge convention called in Belfast on 17 June, attended by 12,000 delegates. The atmosphere was captured by the *Pall Mall Gazette* which recorded how 'a formidable array of conventionists gathered in the public thoroughfares and special and almost startling badges, supplied with great generosity, were everywhere to be seen'. In a portent of the future, this was the first election in which the Irish Unionist Alliance, led by Colonel Edward James Saunderson, put up candidates, winning impressive support, especially in Ulster.

The closeness of the contest generated a level of disorder and violence which would become unthinkable in the twentieth century. No fewer than three riots took place, one of them in Peterborough where 'stones, broken glass and iron were thrown at a detachment of the police, who charged the mob'. Three officers were injured and eight people were charged with offences, including assault and damage to property. At Headington in Oxfordshire, a 'rough element in the crowd hurled insults at the Unionist candidate and his wife', then targeted the police, 'showering them with sharp flints' which led to several injuries. At Exmouth in Devon, a gang of Liberals 'attacked Conservative supporters, smashed windows and threw stones at the police' before they were dispersed. The catalogue of incidents covered the entire country, from Rugby, where the Tory candidate and his supporters were assaulted with stones, horseshoes and 'brickbats', to Wellingborough, where a meeting held by the Liberal candidate was broken up by Tory supporters hurling chairs at the platform. Even in refined Tunbridge Wells, rotten eggs were thrown at the carriage of the Tory candidate, while in Chelmsford several Conservatives brawled with each other. Yet for all such discord, much of the public did not seem gripped by the election at all, showing more interest in the London Season or the county championship in cricket, then cementing its place as England's national sport. In his diary for 1 July, the Tory grandee the Earl of Derby recorded:

> It is a sign of the division that began long ago between the social and political world that although the elections are on and all concerned in them are engaged in canvassing, balls and parties in London are as much frequented as ever. Formerly the season would have closed with the session. Now they seem to have nothing to do with one another.

Unlike in modern elections, there was no single, national polling day in the late nineteenth century, so the results came in on a staggered basis over several weeks, which heightened the speculation about the outcome. After the initial declarations, it looked like Gladstone's hopes of a majority might be fulfilled, as the *Manchester Guardian* reported on 6 July: 'the first day opened brilliantly and, it seemed, decisively for the Liberal cause', with the party gaining fourteen seats. Lady Knightley of Fawsley, the Tory hostess whose husband had been an MP, was sunk in gloom by the news from the constituencies. 'The first returns came in and were not encouraging. It is a bad lookout,' she noted in her diary on 5 July. But then the Unionists began to hold on more stubbornly to their own territory and even encroach on Liberal ground. 'For hours together the crowds that watched the fronts of the newspapers were kept in a state of by no means subdued excitement by the way in which a gain on one side was promptly counterbalanced by a gain on the other.' The fluctuating fortunes meant that neither of the main parties felt satisfied. Still based in Dalmeny, Gladstone and his allies could sense the prospect of a strong Liberal government evaporating. 'The outlook is certainly not good,' wrote Hamilton. But the Unionists were not doing well enough to retain power, much to Salisbury's dismay; their retreat was symbolised by the defeat of his own son Viscount Cranborne by 214 votes in Darwen, Lancashire, by his Liberal challenger Sir Charles Huntington. When the report of this loss reached Salisbury's home of Hatfield House, he retired disconsolately to his room to brood on 'the ingratitude of the country', while Lady Salisbury burst into tears as she blamed Lancastrians, Liberals and the Church of Rome. 'Damn the Catholics! Damn the Catholics!' she cried. One guest at Hatfield described the atmosphere there 'as gloomy as possible'.

Once all the results were in, both parties were almost evenly balanced. The Unionists won slightly more votes, 2.02 million or 47 per cent of the national share, compared to the Liberals' 1.9 million or 45.4 per cent of the national share. However, the Liberals won marginally more seats. This meant that Gladstone was destined to return to Downing Street because the eighty-one MPs of the Irish Parliamentary Party, whose vote had held up remarkably well despite the Parnellite split, gave him an overall majority of forty, the Liberal Unionist group having performed disappointingly and slumped to forty-seven MPs, though Chamberlain was as dominant as ever in the west Midlands. No fewer than thirty out of thirty-nine seats in his bailiwick of the west Midlands returned Unionists. 'You have done gloriously,' the Liberal Unionist peer Lord Woolmer told Chamberlain.

Gladstone could not have been said to have done gloriously in Midlothian, where his vote fell heavily from 7,879 in 1886 to just 5,845, only narrowly ahead of the 5,155 votes for his Conservative rival, the army officer Colonel Andrew Wauchope. Clearly in physical decline, Gladstone put the blame for the setback on local opposition to the disestablishment of the Scottish Church. Even so, he had retained his membership of the Commons, where he now had a sufficiently large following to become Prime Minister for a record fourth time, having first been elected an MP in 1832. Sixty years later, the 1892 general election had two notable firsts, both of them with huge implications for Britain's political future. One was the contest at Finsbury Central, which saw the Liberal candidate Dadabhai Naoroji elected as the Liberal Party's first ethnic minority MP. A distinguished scholar, writer and Indian politician, he moved to Britain in the 1880s and created a keen impression with his intellect and ease of manner. Of his victory, the *Manchester Guardian* commented:

> That a native Indian should find a place in the Imperial Assembly and have taken part in the legislation and administration of the Empire would have been considered too wild to be ever realized ... It is an honour for England and we acquiesce when we are told it is an honour for India.

The other first was the election of the Scottish former miner and ship-worker Keir Hardie for West Ham as the first independent Labour MP, presaging the formation of the first Labour government within little more than thirty years. 'A strong teetotaller, an inveterate smoker, a plain-spoken, plain-looking man, he won the hearts of a London constituency by advocating a Labour programme,' said the *Pall Mall Gazette*.

Hardie, a rugged individualist, caused a stir by wearing a cloth cap when he was sworn in as an MP on the return of Parliament after the election. It was this return of Parliament that brought the immediate defeat of the Unionist government at the hands of the Liberals and the Irish, resulting in Salisbury's resignation, much to Queen Victoria's regret. In her old age, she had become a fierce anti-Liberal partisan, with her antipathy focused on the party's 'wild and incomprehensible' leader who represented a 'very great danger to the country, to Europe and to her vast Empire'. Nevertheless, the constitutional nature of Britain's monarchy meant that she had no alternative but to send for him after the election. Unable to cajole or flatter his sovereign, Gladstone felt she was 'enough to kill any man' and the coldness of their relationship was a further burden in his final administration, which lasted less than two years and was dominated by the forlorn quest to pass Home Rule. Succeeded by Rosebery, Gladstone finally retired in March 1894, bringing a close to the most remarkable political career of the nineteenth century.

Born in Belfast, **Leo McKinstry** has been a political commentator and historian since 1995. A twice-weekly columnist in the *Daily*

Express, he also writes regularly for the *Daily Mail*, *The Sun* and *The Spectator*. He is the author of thirteen books, including a quartet on the wartime RAF, a life of the cricketer Sir Geoffrey Boycott and a study of Winston Churchill's relationship with Clement Attlee. His biography of the Victorian Liberal Prime Minister Lord Rosebery won the award of the Channel 4 Political Book of the Year in 2006.

18

1895

PIPPA CATTERALL

Dissolution: 8 July 1895
Polling day: 13 July–7 August 1895
Seats contested: 670
Total electorate / Total votes cast / Turnout: 6,330,519 (4,597,886 in contested seats) / 3,575,868 / 78.4 per cent
Candidates (total 1,180): Conservative and Liberal Unionist – 588; Liberal – 447; Irish National Federation – 77; Independent Labour Party – 28; Irish National League – 26; Social Democratic Foundation – 4; Independent Liberal – 3
Prime Minister on polling day: Marquess of Salisbury
Main party leaders: Conservative – Marquess of Salisbury; Liberal – Earl of Rosebery; Independent Labour Party – Keir Hardie; Irish National Federation – John Dillon; Irish National League – John Redmond; Social Democratic Foundation – Henry Hyndman

Party performance:

Party	Votes	Percentage share	Seats
Conservative and Liberal Unionist	1,759,484	49.3	411
Liberal	1,628,405	45.6	177
Irish National Federation	92,556	≈ 45	70
Irish National League	47,698	≈ 25	12
Independent Labour Party	34,433	1	0
Independent Liberal	3,733	0.1	0
Social Democratic Foundation	3,122	0.1	0

Result: Conservative majority of 153 seats

On 29 May 1895, Lord Rosebery's racehorse Sir Visto won the Derby, the second year running that his stable had pulled off this feat. The veteran Tory statesman Lord Cranbrook noted in his diary that Rosebery's 'luck is on the course'. However, the then Liberal Prime Minister was certainly not having much luck within the walls of Parliament. Within a month, he was out of office. Within two, it was clear that his party had lost the ensuing general election by a landslide.

Rosebery had not sought what turned out to be the poisoned chalice of the premiership. Nor had he angled for the position of Foreign Secretary, to which he was appointed by Gladstone when he formed his fourth administration, a minority government maintained in office primarily by Irish support, in 1892. The foreign secretaryship, however, ensured that Rosebery was a frontrunner to succeed Gladstone as Prime Minister two years later.

Gladstone later referred to his last ministry as the 'blubbering Cabinet', because of the lachrymose encomiums showered on the elder statesman as he left office. It was certainly not a lucky one. The ministry was blown off course by the immovable obstacle the Lords presented to Gladstone's attempts to pass Home Rule for Ireland, rejecting it by 419 to forty-one on 8 September 1893. Yet naval policy also crucially shaped the fate of the Liberal governments of 1892–95. Naval expansion in face of a build-up of the French and Russian fleets had begun under the Conservatives in 1889. When these powers responded, the Admiralty Board demanded additional expenditure of £3 million in 1893, backed by a threat to resign en masse. The self-appointed 'Member for the Unemployed', Keir Hardie, the independent Labour MP for West Ham South, pressed for one of the new cruisers to be built in his constituency. The extravagant valedictories that Sir William Harcourt, the Chancellor of the Exchequer, and others heaped on Gladstone reflected awareness that the Prime Minister alone in the Cabinet strongly opposed such spending.

To resolve the impasse, Gladstone suggested a dissolution to the

Cabinet on 5 February 1894. He regarded this a good opportunity to go to the country on a 'Peers versus People' platform. However, his Cabinet were unanimously opposed. Their party was unprepared for an election, though that was also true of their Unionist opponents. Tensions between Conservatives and Liberal Unionists were visible at the local level. Pursuing radical measures that Joseph Chamberlain, the Liberal Unionist leader in the Commons, felt compelled to support, such as Harcourt's death duties in 1894 or Welsh disestablishment, could also drive wedges into the Unionist alliance as late as April 1895. Nonetheless, the opportunity, if such it was, passed. The 84-year-old Gladstone resigned instead, ostensibly on grounds of ill health. The retirement of their long-time leader created a vacuum at the top of the party. The difficulties of filling that satisfactorily in a manner to galvanise the party explain why the Liberals did so little to resolve their electoral deficiencies during the ensuing fifteen months.

Lord Kimberley, the Liberal leader in the Lords, noted that the succession to the premiership was fraught with difficulties. If Queen Victoria had consulted him, Gladstone would have advised her to send for Earl Spencer. Despite Spencer's role as First Lord of the Admiralty in the proposals that led to Gladstone leaving office, the old man still felt that Spencer's thirty years of political experience fitted him best for the premiership and party leadership. In contrast, if Liberal MPs had been consulted, they would have gone for Harcourt, the leader in the Commons. Those on the radical wing would certainly have preferred not to have a Prime Minister in the Lords, such as Spencer or Rosebery, foisted upon them. Harcourt's talent for witty and waspish speeches endeared him to his parliamentary followers. As Rosebery sourly noted, only those who had endured Harcourt as a colleague could understand his deficiencies. This certainly told against Harcourt among the Cabinet and with the queen. Even as he was appointed on 3 March 1894, Rosebery was aware of having become a very reluctant Prime Minister on the negative grounds that he was not his main rival for the post.

The day before, Rosebery wrote to the queen's private secretary, Sir Henry Ponsonby: 'I am altogether unfitted for the post, as regards capacity and knowledge.' Arguably this was even more true of his other new role, that of leader of the Liberal Party. As the Scottish Liberal MP Richard Haldane observed, Rosebery aspired to be William Pitt, whose biography he published in 1893, but his was more like the failed premiership of Viscount Goderich. In any circumstances, the overly sensitive Rosebery would have been temperamentally ill-suited for his position. The situation was exacerbated by his difficulties with the disappointed Harcourt. As Rosebery complained to the queen on 7 April 1894: 'The Cabinet is perfectly harmonious, indeed unanimous, with one exception, but the voice of that exception never ceases during the sitting of the Cabinet.'

Among Conservatives rumours swirled that Rosebery would seek to broaden the base of his government by appealing to Liberal Unionists. Instead, Rosebery attempted a different political narrative, telling a great meeting in Bradford on 27 September 1894 that the next election would be fought not on Welsh disestablishment – the main measure in that parliamentary session – or liquor control but on the House of Lords. Rosebery had his own personal reasons for wishing to deal with the Lords. He was horribly conscious of the lonely ordeal of trying to carry the Liberal cause against the massed ranks of Unionists in the Upper House. Yet the Cabinet indignation at this speech indicates that he was unable to impose this agenda on his party.

Meanwhile, Chamberlain aimed to occupy the reforming ground that the Liberals appeared to have vacated. The programme he put to the Conservative leader, Lord Salisbury, in October 1894 envisaged support for artisans' housing, industrial arbitration courts, labour exchanges, workmen's compensation, technical education and restrictions on immigration. Chamberlain thus attempted to seize the political initiative against a background of widespread economic distress. Unionists portrayed the Liberal government as focused on constitutional issues at the expense of economic ones. Little was done to tackle the rural distress – driven by increasing cheap imports of food and a series of bad harvests – that the Liberals had majored on in 1892. Their one significant measure, the introduction of parish councils through the Local Government Act of 1894, had been rendered largely toothless by Unionist amendments in the Lords. Meanwhile, Unionists argued that Harcourt's death duties hit investment on landed estates. Apart from the naval programme, little was done on unemployment. By the start of 1895, over 1 million people were out of work, according to Hardie.

When Hardie put forward an amendment to the Queen's Speech about unemployment in 1893, backed by the Conservative protectionist Howard Vincent, Harcourt told him that this was a matter for local rather than central government. Hardie retorted that Harcourt's party would suffer at the polls if they did not support him. In late 1894, the Liberals indeed lost a string of by-elections. Their notional majority in the Commons fell below twenty. In February 1895, the Unionists joined with Hardie on an amendment to the Queen's Speech lamenting the state of agriculture, textiles and other industries and 'the consequent increase in the number of the unemployed'. Disgruntled radicals led by Sir Charles Dilke and Henry Labouchère joined in attacking the government. Defeat on the amendment was warded off only by promises of a select committee on unemployment. A petulant and insomniac Rosebery nonetheless complained in Cabinet on 19 February 1895 of a lack of support from ministerial colleagues in the Commons. Although Rosebery was persuaded not to resign, Lord Kimberley noted that 'he has considerably shaken confidence in his judgement'. Kimberley's opinion of Harcourt was still worse: 'What can one think of a Minister who ostentatiously and publicly expresses his delight at the prospects of the Government being beaten and coming to an end?' To such personal difficulties were added Cabinet divisions between those Liberal Imperialists like Rosebery and Kimberley who favoured a forward policy in Africa, and those who did not, like Harcourt and the Chief Secretary for Ireland, John Morley: another petulant character who threatened to resign six times over the exclusion of Irish Home Rule from the 1895 Queen's Speech.

Harcourt concluded that his main chance of gaining the party leadership was if the Liberals were beaten at the coming election.

Not that he was able to do much to stave off such an eventuality. Labouchère wrote to Harcourt's son Lewis that 'if some fine democratic bribe is paid, and a general election follows, we might have a chance of winning'. However, boxed in by a further £2 million on the naval programme, Harcourt's 1895 Budget was a dull affair. Furthermore, in cutting spirit duty to please Irish allies, while increasing beer duty, he fuelled Unionist jibes that the Liberals were benefiting Ireland at the expense of the produce and pleasures of English labourers.

The Unionists, in contrast, were increasingly well prepared for the coming election. Chamberlain established a harmonious relationship with A. J. Balfour, the Conservative leader in the Commons. Balfour's determined coercion of local Conservative associations to accept Liberal Unionist candidates was exemplified by his handling of the local dispute at Warwick and Leamington when the Speaker, Viscount Peel, retired. Warwick and Leamington duly became one of several Unionist by-election victories in May 1895. Cranbrook noted that, buoyed by such developments, Chamberlain and the Liberal Unionist leader in the Lords, the Duke of Devonshire, were making increasingly frequent speeches 'forecasting a Unionist Government, in which Liberal Unionists are to have responsibility as well as authority'.

Nevertheless, the government did not lose a vote in the Commons until 21 June 1895. The Conservative MP for Evesham, Sir Richard Temple, claimed in his posthumously published memoirs that this was carefully engineered. On a motion censuring the Secretary of State for War, Henry Campbell-Bannerman, over military supplies of cordite, the government lost by 132 to 125. Dilke was the only Liberal to vote against the government, but six ministers were absent unpaired.

On 22 June, Tom Ellis, the Chief Whip, advised the Cabinet that Robert Hudson, the secretary of Liberal Central Office, had said that sudden resignation 'with no comprehensible election cry and half the work of the session uncompleted would be suicidal'. An affronted Campbell-Bannerman, however, refused to ask for the cordite vote to be rescinded. A weary and fractious Cabinet fell to debating the invidious choice between resigning as a government or asking for a dissolution. Kimberley urged Rosebery: 'If you dissolve ... we shall go as a "united" body to the country. If not, will not our dissensions become apparent when the Tories dissolve, to the great injury of the party?' Morley advised that the Irish also favoured dissolution. On the back benches, it seems it was the same. The veteran temperance campaigner and Liberal MP for Cockermouth, Sir Wilfrid Lawson, noted: 'I suppose that most people were rather glad when this session collapsed, for ... working away at measures which one knows the Lords will not pass, is a kind of political treadmill.'

However, in a rare moment of agreement – though for different reasons – Rosebery and Harcourt were both for resigning and carried the day. This was despite Ellis's warning that an incoming Unionist government would likely immediately ask for a dissolution themselves. After Salisbury had formed a government on 24 June, that is exactly what happened. After some remaining business was dispatched, Parliament was dissolved on 8 July 1895.

Lord Tweedmouth, the Liberal Chief Whip in the Lords, wrote to Gladstone on 12 July that 'our weak spot is the want of one leader and one policy'. For instance, Morley spoke of nothing but Irish Home Rule, while Harcourt concentrated on liquor control. A month earlier, Labouchère noted to Lewis Harcourt the deficiencies of the Liberal programme: 'The Lords will not "fight". Liquor will lose us votes. Home Rule is dead. By the Welsh Church we certainly do not gain votes in England, and Scotland seems to be going against us.'

In contrast, the Unionists went into the election campaign united and confident, if vague about their programme. Salisbury had merely called for 'the restoration of prosperity and the decrease of suffering among the poorer classes of the population', indicating that his government would boost business confidence through tax relief, tackle agriculture through promoting smallholdings and somehow reform the Poor Law. This vagueness was successfully picked up by Campbell-Bannerman and the outgoing Home Secretary, H. H. Asquith, who were among the few Liberals to increase their majorities in 1895. With both the respective party leaders in the Lords and thereby by convention disbarred from electioneering, they were also the leading Liberal spokesmen in 1895, while Balfour and Chamberlain played a similar role for the Conservatives and Liberal Unionists.

Chamberlain majored on economic measures ranging from reduced rail rates for farmers through to imperial development. His lead was widely picked up, from the Scottish National Union to the 52 per cent of Unionist candidates who highlighted pensions. Few Liberals joined David Lloyd George in supporting this idea – which both Morley and Asquith dismissed – and under 10 per cent of them mentioned unemployment. Liberal candidates generally concentrated on old Gladstonian staples such as Home Rule, while Balfour focused on exposing 'the merits and demerits of the ... Liberal Government', particularly on the economy.

The anti-Liberal tide was apparent from the moment the first results came in on 13 July 1895. Cranbrook crowed in his diary: 'Harcourt out by 1,000. What a victory!' The ex-Chancellor lost on a 10.8 per cent swing in Derby. Lawson had claimed a week before that it was the Midlands capital for temperance sentiment. It was on this that Harcourt, who had introduced a Local Option Bill in April, seemingly relied. Yet its provisions for local referendums on the closure of 25 per cent of local licensed premises raised unresolved problems concerning which premises to close and also hit businesses by threatening no compensation. Not surprisingly, the Licensed Victuallers Association in Derby was particularly active in campaigning against Harcourt.

Chamberlain later argued that these bodies were not much use electorally, except 'when they are really excited and alarmed, as they were in 1895'. Temperance campaigners like W. S. Caine certainly blamed the concerted efforts of the 'Drink Trade' for the Liberal defeats, including his own, in Bradford. Trade money flowed into local campaigns, including in West Ham where the *Daily Chronicle* partially attributed Hardie's defeat to his teetotalism. In Southampton, the Unionist campaign slogan was 'Vote for Chamberlayne and beer'.

Yet there was more to the 1895 election than beer-barrel politics. Harcourt had neglected his seat. His main Tory opponent, Henry

Bemrose, in contrast, had an exemplary record as a local philanthropist and funded food and fuel supplies for local people during the difficult winter of 1894–95. This was significant considering since 1893 there had been short-time working at the Midland Railway Works, which employed 40 per cent of the electorate. In comparison, the temperance vote was probably worth only around 1,000 to 1,500 votes in Derby because so many supporters were disenfranchised women. Or compare the situation in Cockermouth, where Lawson held on but the second Liberal candidate, who opposed the trade union and socialist campaign for an eight-hour day, lost to the Tories. Harcourt himself recognised that 'bad trade' scuppered his chances in Derby, before scuttling off to the ultra-safe Liberal seat of West Monmouthshire.

The *Review of Reviews* in August noted that Liberal defeat was widely expected before the campaign started, but Harcourt's in Derby indicated its likely scale: 'Probably no single incident waked the electorate to a consciousness of the fact that the Liberals were smashed … When he was toppled over in the first day's fighting the whole stage shook.' Harcourt's defeat presaged the same fate for three other former Cabinet ministers. One of them, John Morley, reflected: 'In attention to Ireland I had been negligent of Newcastle; the eight-hour day men had their turn, and the running political currents helped them to bring me down.'

Morley's adamant opposition to the eight-hour day pushed George Lansbury out of the Liberal Party and into the Marxian Social Democratic Federation (SDF) in 1892. In 1895, he was one of only four SDF candidates, running in the south London constituency of Walworth. The seat had just been won by the Tories at a by-election. In the general election, Lansbury's vote halved to a mere 3.8 per cent of the poll. The more readily familiar Unionist panaceas were preferred to Lansbury's claims that only socialism could solve the problems of the unemployed, the aged and the sick. None of his comrades fared much better in the 1895 election.

Lansbury had recently attacked John Burns for alleging that the SDF were helping the Conservatives against him in his Battersea constituency. Burns won that seat as an independent Labour candidate in 1892 but had since moved towards the Liberals. In the event, Burns narrowly held the seat despite a 7 per cent swing. Genuinely independent Labour candidates, however, all went down to defeat. Even where they had enjoyed promising by-election polls, such as Halifax, Leicester, West Bradford and East Bristol, they saw their vote share fall in July 1895.

Of these, twenty-eight stood for the Independent Labour Party (ILP), founded in Bradford in 1893 to bring together various local Labour organisations. By 1895, the party claimed 35,000 members. At its conference that Easter, a motion to support only ILP or SDF candidates was defeated by the vehement opposition of Hardie, who was trying to build a more broadly based working-class party. Yet many local ILP organisations still urged their supporters to abstain in 1895, including Derby where this was estimated to cost Harcourt up to 600 votes. Nor did the trade unions encourage their members to vote for the Liberals, though they were still often unwilling to endorse ILP candidates, too.

These abstentions and interventions hurt the Liberals in close contests, such as those in Leeds, Southampton and Bradford. Yet Hardie and his party were also hit by the pro-Unionist tide. None came close to winning. Poor trade, which affected the party's finances, did not help. Beatrice Webb, whose Fabian Society stood aloof from the contest, waspishly observed that 'the ILP has completed its suicide'. Hardie himself was unseated by an unusually large 11 per cent swing. His support for nationalisation of the drink trade alienated voters, without winning temperance supporters to his cause. He had also necessarily spent much time speaking elsewhere. The Tory victor, G. E. Banes, was a local philanthropist and eminent member of the local school board who won back the seat he had held from 1886 to 1892. Education seems to have bulked large in this constituency, with the sizeable Irish electorate won over by the emphasis placed both locally and nationally by the Conservatives on religious education. With Home Rule a dormant political issue, the Catholic hierarchy urged their flocks to vote Tory on education grounds. This issue, alongside noisy opposition to Indian cotton duties, helped the Unionists win thirteen net gains in Lancashire.

There was a relatively small swing of 1.5 per cent in the Lancashire constituency of Burnley. The SDF leader Henry Hyndman stood there, gaining a respectable 12.4 per cent of the vote. He later alleged that the radical MP Philip Stanhope held on thanks to the fortune of his wife, Countess Tolstoy: 'I therefore declared that the election had been won by Russian roubles and Radical resurrectionists ... [and] the graveyards of Burnley were brought to the poll with assiduity and success.'

Whatever the truth of this, local factors clearly counted in individual constituencies. These included Colchester, a rare by-election won from the Tories in February 1895 which the businessman and local philanthropist Sir Weetman Pearson retained in July. The outcome was a patchwork of results: for instance, the Liberals registered five gains and thirteen losses in Scotland.

Nonetheless, the general pattern across most regions was clear. Liberal problems in Scotland reflected dismay at the inadequacy of proposed crofting legislation as opposed to promises from Unionist candidates to extend Irish land purchase legislation to Scotland. Yet the swing there was only 2.5 per cent, as opposed to 7 per cent in Wales. The Liberals did particularly badly in urban Wales, resulting from a combination of revived Anglicanism and opposition to the provisions for disendowment of the Welsh Church. In London, the party fell back to eight out of sixty-two seats. Liberal attempts at reform there, such as the Equalisation of Rates Act of 1894, proved inadequate. It provided subsidies for landlords at the expense of tenants, while failing to redistribute the burden of the Poor Law effectively across the capital. The party also did poorly in smaller semi-industrial towns in the north and the Midlands and was heavily hit in rural England.

The exception to these trends was Ireland. There the political situation was complicated by the feud between the pro- and anti-Parnell factions that the Home Rule Party had split into at the start of the decade. The larger anti-Parnellites were nonetheless short of money. Indeed, the Liberals registered two gains in Ulster by paying them to stand aside. Despite the opposition of the Catholic hierarchy, the

Parnellites gained a net three seats, mostly around Dublin where clerical influence was less intense. The Unionists meanwhile lost two seats in Ireland but consolidated their position in Ulster.

Most constituencies had declared by 19 July 1895, even though the last result did not come in until 7 August, with the new parliament assembling five days later. The election resulted, Kimberley lamented, in the 'complete smash of our party'. The Liberals had a net loss of ninety-four seats, falling to 177, their worst result since the 1832 Reform Act. Successful Unionist co-operation, in contrast, enabled the Liberal Unionists to gain a net twenty-three seats, several in long-standing Tory strongholds. The outcome was a Unionist majority of 152, the largest recorded since 1832.

Richard Middleton, the Conservatives' national agent, attributed this success largely 'to the utter unpreparedness of the other side, whose organisation, for lack of candidates, had been very much neglected'. This also led to deficiencies in voter registration processes, helping the Unionists to win many of the most marginal seats. The consequence of this lack of Liberal candidates was apparent in the number of Unionist unopposed returns – 132, including in all nine university seats – compared to eleven Liberals and forty-six Irish Nationalists. The UK-wide vote shares of 49.1 per cent for the Unionists and 45.7 per cent for the Liberals were therefore deceptive. Nonetheless, the Liberals' 26 per cent share of the seats in the new parliament almost certainly meant that they were under-represented. However, this did not prompt them to revisit the issue of electoral reform, much debated ten years earlier, though one of the measures they called for in 1895 was curtailment of the plural vote.

Lawson attributed the results to a combination of drink and Liberal disorganisation. The prominence Liberals gave to the former enabled the Tories to portray them as bent on coercion, while depicting themselves as the defenders both of property and of the working-man's liberty, leisure and pleasure. To the gains they made among the wealthy and suburbanites in the 1880s, they added a growing working-class Toryism, based on a patchwork of anti-immigration, promises of social reform and Unionism. Their emphasis on restoring economic confidence was, meanwhile, more vehement than before, enabling them to capture growing business support. Unionists thus aligned themselves successfully with the salient issues in the 1895 election and adeptly positioned themselves to claim competence to address them.

In contrast, by precipitously resigning, an unprepared and divided Liberal Party maximised its chances of defeat. Liberals had to defend a poor record in government in an election which was partly a referendum on their competence in office. They were also vulnerable to Unionist charges that they prioritised constitutional issues over those that mattered to ordinary people. The *Derby Mercury* thundered three days before polling that the Liberals 'seem to fancy that the working man can live on Newcastle Programmes, they have apparently no idea that the first question is the great one of Bread and Cheese'. The 1891 Newcastle Programme proved a blind alley. Rosebery felt it offended every interest but himself failed to offer an alternative lead.

The result was that the Liberals entered the election tied to a disparate series of causes associated with individual party figures, none of which offered an overall narrative. Moreover, these causes were related to the era of constitutional reform associated with their former leader, rather than solutions to present discontents. Permanently filling that vacuum was to be a challenge, particularly with a would-be rival in the field. Hardie's threats to the future of the Liberals may have proved premature in 1895. Rosebery indeed rejoiced in the 'defeat of Socialism of the rabid kind', while musing that 'it is always possible that that may happen which has happened in Belgium – the elimination of Liberalism, leaving the two forces of Socialism and Reaction face to face'. For the present, however, the local pact that Ramsay MacDonald arranged with the Liberals following his defeat as the ILP candidate in Southampton signified the shape of things to come.

Pippa Catterall is professor of history and policy at the University of Westminster, chair of the George Lansbury Memorial Trust and co-editor of the journal *National Identities*. She has published widely on modern British political and constitutional history and her current research focuses on Prime Ministers and their political strategies.

19

1900

MARK FOX

Dissolution: 25 September 1900
Polling day: 26 September–24 October 1900
Seats contested: 670
Total electorate / Total votes cast / Turnout: 6,730,935 (4,369,284 in contested seats) / 3,262,696 / 75.1 per cent
Candidates (total 1,102): Conservative and Liberal Unionist – 569; Liberal – 402; Irish Parliamentary – 83; Independent Nationalist – 18; Labour – 15; Independent Conservative – 7; Independent Liberal – 3; Scottish Workers' – 1
Prime Minister on polling day: Marquess of Salisbury
Main party leaders: Conservative – Marquess of Salisbury; Liberal – Henry Campbell-Bannerman; Labour – Keir Hardie; Irish Parliamentary – John Redmond; Scottish Workers' – Robert Allan

Party performance:

Party	Votes	Percentage share	Seats
Conservative and Liberal Unionist	1,637,683	50.2	402
Liberal	1,469,500	45.1	183
Irish Parliamentary	57,576	≈ 43	76
Labour	41,900	1.3	2
Independent Nationalist	23,706	≈ 18	6
Independent Conservative	13,713	0.4	0
Independent Liberal	6,423	0.2	1
Scottish Workers'	3,107	0.1	0

Result: Conservative majority of 135 seats

The 1900 general election was a watershed moment in British politics. It resulted in a surprise landslide victory for the incumbent Conservative government. The government had been in office since 1895 and the single great issue that dominated British politics was the conduct and progress of the war in South Africa. Even though its imperial reach was at its height, Britain was already wearying of the unceasing responsibilities of running its empire. There was a seemingly never-ending number of military engagements, with the South African War being the most domestically politically polarising and the methods employed to try to defeat the Boers becoming ever more demanding. Indeed, the Liberal leader, Henry Campbell-Bannerman, would criticise the use of concentration camps and accuse the government of employing 'methods of barbarism'. It was widely felt, too, that the Prime Minister, the Marquess of Salisbury, had for too long spent too much of his time focused on foreign affairs at the expense of concentrating on much-needed and long-overdue domestic reform. It was no surprise, therefore, that the election swiftly became and remained a single-issue vote on the conduct of the South African War, the so-called khaki election.

Parliament was dissolved on 25 September and voting took place between 26 September and 24 October. It was a bitter campaign, fought on the conduct of the war and the false belief that it had to all intents and purposes already been won. In fact, it would last for a further two years. It was an election won and lost on the pride of empire and Britain's role as an imperial power. So strong were such feelings that they sufficiently outstripped concerns about pressing matters at home.

The principal protagonists were both highly experienced and long-serving politicians. Robert Gascoyne-Cecil, 3rd Marquess of Salisbury, was at the end of a long and varied political career. He would retire in 1902, from both being an elected member of the House of Commons and, having succeeded his father to the family titles, sitting in the House of Lords. Salisbury's Conservatives were staunchly against change and pessimistic about anything improving.

It was by instinct and practice, as well as by name, a conservative party.

Sir Henry Campbell-Bannerman, who in 1906 would lead his party to a landslide victory over the Conservatives and in the process win the last ever outright victory the Liberals would attain in a general election, led a party eager to embrace reform and improvement. Campbell-Bannerman would die in 1908 at 10 Downing Street, but before that he had had a long and varied career as a parliamentarian. He led what was an increasingly fractured and fractious party. The Liberal Party was fully aware of the strength of pro-empire feeling in the country at large but contained within it many forceful anti-imperial figures and many who were concerned about the state of Britain at home.

The Conservative Party's huge victory was all the more remarkable in the context of it winning only 5.6 per cent more of the vote than the Liberals, due in no small part to the fact that, unaccountably, in 163 seats the Conservative candidate was returned unopposed.

Salisbury's Conservatives were deeply unpopular because of the seemingly endless foreign wars Britain became embroiled in. The Boer War of this time was in fact the second of the Boer Wars. At the end of the nineteenth century, Britain was a country in the middle of swift economic and social change and support for foreign adventuring had seemed to come a poor second in many people's views than to the state of Britain at home. The rapid pace of industrialisation was having a huge impact on the political face of the country, as people moved from the countryside into the towns and cities. The move was driven by the massive expansion in job opportunities brought about by the new factories, expanding railways and the development of a new urban way of living. At the same time as the growth in manufacturing and the increasing ease of transport was taking place, so too did the need for power to drive them. The demand for coal to power the new industrial base led to a huge increase in jobs in mining and commercial transport. The growing railway network enabled people to travel for pleasure, not just for work.

Rapid industrialisation brought about not only new jobs and increased mobility but also huge new social challenges. Wages were low, housing was poor and employee rights were limited to non-existent. Working hours were long and conditions unsafe and poor. Tensions between employees and employers increased and occasionally became violent. Women and children often endured even tougher working conditions than men did. There were all too few legislative or regulatory protections.

In the midst of all this change and upheaval sprang the emergent force of political workers, tentative at first but gaining members and momentum as time moved on. The Liberal Party desperately tried to harness this growing part of the electorate as their own by championing greater rights, more protection and reform of the electoral franchise. Most, if not practically all, of which Lord Salisbury's Conservatives implacably opposed. In turn, this resistance led to the establishment of trade unions, followed by the establishment of the Labour Party itself. The 1900 general election was notable for seeing the election of the first two Labour politicians.

In government, the Liberal Party had tried to address these issues by introducing measures on pensions, health, housing and education. In opposition to Lord Salisbury's government, the Liberals continued to press for reform in these areas and all the indications were that there was much popular support for this approach. The Liberals were fatally and bitterly split, however, in their approach to the Boer War, and this undermined their whole campaign and credibility.

The defining issue of the time and the determining factor of the election was the Second Boer War. Britain was at the height of its imperial power. The empire had brought the mother country huge wealth, military dominance and vast political control of a huge swathe of the world. At home, the empire was not only the source of huge wealth but also an increasingly divisive political debate about how it was managed and its future.

The Boer War lasted from 1899 to 1902 and was predominantly a conflict over who should control the vast diamond and mineral resources in South Africa. The vastly expensive and seemingly never-ending nature of the war caused a particularly polarising political debate to emerge in British politics. The debate raged about not only the morality and ethics of Britain maintaining its empire, and the manner in which it sought to do so, but also the country's ability to sustain such a military campaign at such a long range. The terrain and the demands of the campaign also forced a huge revision in how the military conducted its operations. For Campbell-Bannerman's Liberals, the polarisation of opinions and approach proved too much for the party to be able to contain the disparate views in one coherent campaign.

The Liberals went into the 1900 general election confident of the popularity of their domestic reform agenda. The party's approach was characterised by its belief that government had an important part to play in supporting those who were in need, unemployed, vulnerable and disadvantaged. As a result, they proposed a bold policy package that included establishing basic unemployment benefit aimed at supporting people while they looked for work, healthcare reform to ensure everyone had access to basic healthcare and the introduction of a universal minimum pension for the elderly. All these measures were aimed at keeping people out of the extreme poverty and hardship that increasingly stalked the country's fast-growing towns and cities.

As well as the social reforms they proposed, the Liberals also understood the growing demands for workers' rights and protections. The party sought to establish itself as the champion of urban and industrial workers, a fast-growing and as yet unrepresented part of the population.

Not only did the party propose better wages and safer working environments but it also suggested the establishment of labour unions to campaign for workers' rights, thereby sowing the seeds for the party's own future destruction as a significant political force at the hands of the unions' own political party, the soon-to-be-formed Labour Party.

The challenge for the Liberal Party and the nascent trade unions and workers' party was the limited nature of the electoral franchise. It was restricted to roughly half the male population over twenty-one years of age and no women. This meant that the people whose policies the Liberals were trying to help the most were mainly excluded from voting.

Lord Salisbury and the Conservative Party understood the nature of the electorate well and what was needed to secure its continuing support. The campaign, therefore, focused on stability and security, placing at its heart the importance of maintaining and increasing the size of the empire. With the increase in trade competition from France, Germany and the emerging United States, the campaign stressed the need for an experienced hand on the national tiller. There was also a heavy emphasis on the importance of maintaining the established order at home as well as abroad. These messages resonated strongly with the limited nature of the franchise then in operation.

Lord Salisbury personified the call for experience and steadiness. A long-familiar and respected figure in national politics known for his balanced and cautious decision-making, he was able to point to the government's track record of maintaining law and order, promoting economic growth and expanding the empire. Any deviation from these policies, it was argued, would cause upset and instability at home and abroad. The Conservatives warned against the radical and untested policies of their opponents.

In addition, they portrayed themselves as the guardians of the nation's institutions – the monarchy, the Church of England, the 'British way of life'. In short, they portrayed themselves as the only safe bet against an increasingly competitive and dangerous world.

Although he had fallen out of political favour and then died some years before the 1900 general election, Lord Randolph Churchill had done much to prepare his party for the fast-changing nature of the electorate with his championing of Tory democracy and the establishment of the National Union of Conservative Associations. He inspired a generation of Conservative agents and campaign managers and prepared the party for the changes that were to come. His impatience in championing the need for change and to appeal to wider society led him to a disastrous falling out with Lord Salisbury. His early death in 1895 robbed him of the chance to see his ideas come to fruition, but it is arguable that Lord Salisbury greatly benefited politically from his adversary's work.

The Irish Parliamentary Party was focused on Home Rule for Ireland. Established in the aftermath of the 1874 general election, it would be dissolved in 1922. Over that period it played a significant, if secondary, role in the politics of the House of Commons. Essentially, it helped divide the Liberals between those who were staunch Unionists, who supported Lord Salisbury and the Conservatives, and those who would entertain discussion about measures for self-government for Ireland. This split would in the end help destroy the Liberal Party and it is notable just how many Liberal Unionists there were, helping Lord Salisbury to his huge majority.

The Labour Representation Committee (LRC) fielded fifteen candidates in the 1900 general election and succeeded in winning two seats. This may seem a modest slate of candidates and an even more modest success rate, but in fact the achievement was remarkable. With the Liberal Party proposing many of the policies working people might well have been expected to support, and bearing in mind the restricted nature of the franchise, the LRC's achievement was notable. It was even more so due to the fact that the LRC had been established only earlier in the same year as the election itself. The formation of the committee was proposed by members of the trade unions dissatisfied with the speed of social and welfare reform and as an expression of frustration with the prevailing political settlement.

A special conference of the Trades Union Congress (TUC) was held at the Memorial Hall in Farringdon Street on 26 and 27 February 1900 and brought together in alliance all the working and left-of-centre organisations to form a single political entity. Keir Hardie, the future Labour Party leader and first Labour Prime Minister, took the lead in proposing the formation of 'a distinct Labour group in Parliament, who shall have their own whips, and agree upon their policy, which must embrace a readiness to cooperate with any party which for the time being may be engaged in promoting legislation in the direct interests of labour'.

From such modest beginnings, the Labour Party was born, and the seeds of the destruction of the Liberal Party were sown.

The themes, if not the principal protagonists, may feel in many ways all too familiar. So too was the campaign. Campaigns at this time were highly energised and personal. Vast numbers of posters bearing pictures and slogans were posted and reposted as the messages changed throughout the campaign. Pamphlets and leaflets were written and delivered in their tens of thousands. These efforts required a large number of enthusiastic volunteers to deliver and to meet the voters.

Above all else, this was the era of the large public meeting as senior political figures and their local candidates addressed and directly engaged with the public – most of whom, it must be remembered, could not actually vote. Nevertheless, all the parties thought it was important to connect with the people as a whole.

On the face of it, the triumphant return of the Conservative Party to government and Lord Salisbury to the premiership looked like an overwhelming victory for the status quo. In reality, the election was the last hurrah of an order of things that would change rapidly thereafter. The Conservatives had been forced to embrace the need for social, welfare and educational reform. They would champion a slow and incremental approach to such change and provision, but they had been forced to recognise the need for it and there would be no going back. From here on, the British state would provide ever-increasing amounts of support to its citizens.

Although it would take until 1928 before all adults over the age of twenty-one could vote, the scene had been set for the coming of the universal franchise, driven by the need for fairness and equity. This, in turn, had been driven by the swiftly changing nature of Britain away from being predominantly a rural to an industrial economy. With increasing wealth came the demands for increased equality of representation and democracy.

The 1901 general election may well be the high-water mark of High Toryism, but it was a fleeting illusion. Within a year and a half of the election, Lord Salisbury had retired, handing the premiership to his nephew, Arthur Balfour. Campbell-Bannerman would defeat Balfour and become Prime Minister in 1905 but die in office just three years after his victory. His party would never win a majority in the House of Commons again.

The election themes of 1900 would set the terms of political debate for the next century – welfare, employment, safety at work, education and care of the poor, elderly and vulnerable. Britain's role in the world and its place in global affairs, the dominant focus of the 1900 election, would hang over British politics like a cloud up to the current day. Barely fifty years after Lord Salisbury had wooed and won an electorate with a patriotic, pro-imperial, steady-as-you-go message, that same empire had dissolved, the country had opted for a radical nationalising Labour government and Britain, having prevailed in two bitter World Wars, had been brought financially to its knees.

The 1900 campaign was notable for one further defining characteristic in that it set the tone for every Conservative general election campaign up to the rise of Ted Heath and then, more successfully, Margaret Thatcher.

The 1900 general election was the last of the nineteenth century, the last of the Victorian era and the last where a peer (hereditary or otherwise) sitting in the House of Lords led their party into an election. (In 1963, Sir Alec Douglas-Home would have to renounce his hereditary peerage as Earl of Home to succeed Harold Macmillan as Prime Minister mid-parliament. He would go on to lead his government to defeat in the 1964 general election.)

The general election of 1900 was also one of firsts. Another future Prime Minister was also elected for the first time: Winston Churchill. It was also the first to be dubbed a khaki election, a name given to a number of subsequent general elections.

Finally, it was the first election to see a small number of Labour Party candidates elected as MPs, among them the future first Labour leader Keir Hardie. Indeed, the 1900 general election saw the birth of Labour as a parliamentary political force that would go on to grow ever stronger over the following decades and with it the beginning of the long slow decline of the Liberal Party.

Mark Fox is chief executive of the Business Services Association and a former Conservative parliamentary candidate.

20

1906

DUNCAN BRACK

Dissolution: 21 December 1905
Polling day: 12 January–8 February 1906
Seats contested: 670
Total electorate / Total votes cast / Turnout: 7,264,608 (6,347,660 in contested seats) / 5,246,672 / 83.2 per cent
Candidates (total 1,273): Conservative and Liberal Unionist – 557; Liberal – 528; Irish Parliamentary – 84; Labour – 50; Social Democratic Federation – 8; Free trader – 5; Scottish Workers' – 5
Prime Minister on polling day: Henry Campbell-Bannerman
Main party leaders: Liberal – Henry Campbell-Bannerman; Conservative – Arthur Balfour; Liberal Unionist – Joseph Chamberlain; Labour – Keir Hardie; Irish Parliamentary – John Redmond; Social Democratic Federation – Henry Hyndman; Scottish Workers' – George Carson; Free trader – John Eldon Gorst

Party performance:

Party	Votes	Percentage share	Seats
Liberal	2,565,644	48.9	399
Conservative and Liberal Unionist	2,278,076	43.4	157
Labour	254,202	4.8	29
Irish Parliamentary	28,292	21.5	81
Social Democratic Federation	18,446	0.4	0
Scottish Workers'	14,877	0.3	0
Free trader	8,974	0.2	0

Result: Liberal majority of 132 seats

The general election of 1906 ranks as one of the most consequential elections of twentieth-century British politics, on a par with 1945, 1979 and 1997. It saw the biggest Liberal landslide victory since 1832 and remains the most crushing Conservative defeat of any included in this book. It ushered in a period of radical social and constitutional reform, in which Liberal governments, in the eight years before the outbreak of the Great War, laid the foundations of the welfare state, broke the power of the House of Lords and – almost – resolved the problem of Ireland. Yet it was also the last election in which the Liberal Party was to gain a majority, and the first in which the new Labour Party was to win a sizeable number of seats. Just sixteen years later, Labour was to drive the Liberals into third place in the House of Commons, a prison from which they have never since escaped.

After the previous election, in 1900, no one would have predicted such an outcome. Held in the middle of the Second Boer War, the Conservative–Liberal Unionist alliance had repeated its landslide election victory first won in 1895, with only a tiny reduction in its massive overall majority. The Liberal Party was riven by disputes over the war and more fundamentally over the post-Gladstonian direction of the party, and the new leader, Sir Henry Campbell-Bannerman, seemed weak and ineffectual.

Yet it was not a good guide to the future. The combination of the 'khaki' wartime election and the absence of Liberal candidates in many seats (the Liberals fought only 406 out of 670) – circumstances which seemed unlikely to be repeated – together with the workings of the first-past-the-post election system gave the Unionist coalition an exaggerated appearance of strength. Despite their evident weaknesses, the Liberals had still won 45 per cent of the vote. As Winston Churchill, newly elected as a Unionist MP, wrote: 'I think this election fought by the Liberals as a soldiers' battle, without plan or leaders or enthusiasm, has shown so far the strength, not the weakness, of Liberalism in the country.'

As the Boer War ground on, the country's enthusiasm for it began to wane, especially after the revelations of the British Army's response to guerrilla warfare after the Boer armies had been defeated in the field: building networks of blockhouses and wire fences, burning the Boer farmsteads and imprisoning Boer women and children in conditions of hardship in concentration camps. Campbell-Bannerman stepped up his criticisms of government policy, and, in June 1901, after hearing first-hand evidence of the disease and starvation in the camps, delivered what became his most well-known speech, denouncing the 'methods of barbarism' used in South Africa.

In the short term, this apparent tilt towards the 'pro-Boer' wing of the party caused virtual civil war. The Liberal Imperialists in the party set up their own organisation, the Liberal League, and begged the former leader Lord Rosebery to return; but although Rosebery frequently hinted at the possibility, he was too indecisive and too self-obsessed ever to make a real move. The Liberal Imperialist challenge collapsed after Campbell-Bannerman demanded and received a vote of confidence in his leadership from the Liberal MPs.

The ending of the war in May 1902 helped to heal the divisions within the party. Public opinion began to swing towards the Liberals, as awareness grew of the costs of the war and of the government's role in provoking it and its inefficiency in managing it. In fact, Campbell-Bannerman was frequently underestimated as Leader of the Opposition (and was to be even more so as Prime Minister). Though neither particularly energetic nor a great speaker, he was courageous, shrewd and tenacious, as well as generous and kind; he was most frequently admired for his common sense. Above all, he was a great party manager.

At the same time as the Liberal Party was reviving, the Unionist government was coming under strain. Lord Salisbury finally retired in July 1902, worn out after twenty-one years at the head of his party, almost fourteen of them as Prime Minister. His record, in legislative terms, was entirely negative; he had avoided action and postponed problems where he could. In foreign policy, he sought to maintain Britain's position in the world by avoiding entangling alliances, an increasingly unrealistic stance. By postponing change, as Vernon Bogdanor put it in his magisterial survey of British politics between 1895 and 1914 (*The Strange Survival of Liberal Britain*), 'Salisbury ensured that pent-up forces, when they eventually came to the surface, proved even more disruptive than they might otherwise have been.'

Salisbury's successor, Arthur Balfour, was not equal to the task of suppressing or managing those forces. His appearance as languid, lackadaisical and cynical was in fact deliberately misleading; he was intelligent and well read and could be ruthless when needed. But he had no understanding of the conditions of life of the British people and no ability to read the popular mood or to take the pulse of the Commons; he made little effort to cultivate his backbenchers. A respected author of philosophical tracts, he tended to see all sides of an argument too clearly, with the result that he could be indecisive; and he so hedged his own positions with qualifications that it was often difficult to determine exactly what they were.

The Education Act of 1902 accelerated the undermining of the Unionist government. Introduced to the Commons by Balfour in March 1902, in many ways it was an admirable effort to rationalise the provision of elementary education, split, after legislation in 1870, into voluntary schools run by churches (most commonly the Church of England), with some central government support, and board schools, funded from local rates and managed by locally elected school boards. The Balfour Act abolished the school boards in England and Wales and placed elementary schools in the hands of local education authorities under the control of the county and county borough councils. The Act also, for the first time, made significant provision for secondary and technical education.

The political debate focused mainly on the provision of religious education, a critical dimension of the religious divides that were at the time more politically salient than class divisions. The 1870 Act had determined that while voluntary schools could teach religion in any manner they liked, board schools were to provide only nondenominational religious teaching (which meant in practice learning the Bible and a few hymns), to avoid Nonconformist ratepayers subsidising Anglican education. By bringing voluntary schools under the control of – and in receipt of funding from – local ratepayers, Balfour's proposals largely reversed this principle. The 'Nonconformist conscience' was outraged. The Free Churches established a National Passive Resistance Committee to coordinate non-payment of rates; by 1905, there had been over 65,000 prosecutions and 170 individuals had been sent to prison.

The provision, one historian wrote, was welcomed by the still-disunited Liberal Party 'as a shipwrecked boat's crew would welcome the sight of land'. Liberal MPs almost universally opposed the legislation, and David Lloyd George's speeches in particular strengthened his reputation. And while the controversy did not in fact engender all that much popular opposition, except in Wales, it helped to revive the Nonconformist churches' alignment with Liberalism and ensured that they became highly effective recruiting agents for the party at the 1906 election. The 1904 Licensing Act, which was widely held to have been excessively influenced by the brewers and pub owners, reinforced Nonconformists' and temperance campaigners' (often the same people) dislike of the government.

Government support was further weakened by its response to the *Taff Vale* judgment of 1901. This was the outcome of a case brought by the Taff Vale Railway Company against a trade union, the Amalgamated Society of Railway Servants, for organising a strike to protest against the company's treatment of a signalman who had been unfairly treated after repeatedly requesting higher pay. Underneath the specific circumstances of the case lay a festering grievance against the company for refusing to award more than modest pay increases during a period of rapidly rising prices. In the end, the strike was resolved, but the company decided to sue the union for the loss of profits caused by the strike, and it won. The court's judgment sent a shock wave through the growing trade union movement; previously it had been understood that unions could not be sued because they were unincorporated entities. Two weeks later, another court found that a trade union boycotting a butcher's shop to enforce a closed shop (an agreement to employ only union labour) was unlawful. To many trade unionists, the rights of organised labour seemed to be being systematically dismantled.

This combination of judgments gave a significant boost to the Labour Representation Committee (LRC), which had been formed in 1900 by the Independent Labour Party (which had succeeded in electing two MPs in the 1900 election), the Trades Union Congress and the Social Democratic Federation (Britain's first socialist party, which in fact disaffiliated the following year). The aim of the new organisation, to seek greater representation of working men in Parliament, seemed distinctly more important after the two judgments, and between February 1900 and February 1903, its affiliated trade union membership grew from 350,000 to nearly 850,000.

The LRC's political positions were virtually indistinguishable from those of advanced Liberals. Many trade unionists continued to support the Liberals as the more likely party to deliver social and labour reforms, and a sizeable number of Liberal MPs were themselves trade union members – the so-called 'Lib-Labs', drawn particularly from mining constituencies. So, in 1903, it was not difficult for Herbert Gladstone, the Liberal Chief Whip, and Ramsay MacDonald, secretary of the LRC, to agree an electoral pact. This was a limited agreement designed to avoid splitting the anti-Unionist vote in certain constituencies. In some single-member seats, either Labour or the Liberals gave the other a free run, and in several two-member seats, including Newcastle, Blackburn, Bolton, Preston, Derby and Leicester, each party ran one candidate against two Unionists.

In retrospect, it became clear that the Liberals would have won in 1906 without the Gladstone–MacDonald pact, and as twenty-four of Labour's twenty-nine members were to be elected in the absence of a Liberal, it was easy to argue that the party had made an unforced error in helping its rival to its first real foothold in Parliament. However, this was not foreseen at the time, and the fear of splitting the progressive vote was a real one (and was to become more necessary in the 1910 elections, when Liberal and Unionist support was much more evenly balanced). In addition, the pact enabled both parties to save money by reducing the number of candidates standing; shortage of funds had contributed to the Liberals failing to contest many Unionist seats in recent elections, and the LRC was similarly short of resources.

In addition to restoring Liberal morale, the Education Act also undermined Joseph Chamberlain's position as leader of the Liberal Unionists, a party much more reliant on Nonconformist support than its Conservative coalition partner. In the face of the growing number of defections from his party, Chamberlain needed a new cause. Defence of the Union with Ireland – the origins of the Liberal Unionist split from the Liberals in 1886 – would not do, though the Unionists attempted to raise the spectre as the election drew closer. While Campbell-Bannerman, in most of his views a traditional Gladstonian, continued to support Home Rule for Ireland, along with a majority of the Liberal rank and file, very few wished to make it an election issue, after the disastrous elections of 1886 and 1895 and the evident lack of public support for it in England. The Liberal manifesto in 1900 had not mentioned it at all, and in November 1905, Campbell-Bannerman made it clear, in a speech at Stirling, that while the 'opportunity of making a great advance on the question of Irish Government will not be long delayed', it would not be an immediate priority in the face of more pressing social problems. Liberal MPs were happy with this position, and even John Redmond, the leader of the Irish Parliamentary Party, accepted it given the circumstances. It largely neutralised Unionist attacks.

Accordingly, Chamberlain chose instead to revive an old dispute over free trade. The topic was to dominate politics from 1903 to 1906 and to destroy the Unionist government.

By the beginning of 1903, Chamberlain was increasingly frustrated with his own government. He was the strongest and most popular figure in the Cabinet, as Colonial Secretary, but had little to show for his time there: Salisbury's negativism had prevented him from introducing any of the ambitious social reforms for which he had once campaigned, such as old-age pensions. Salisbury's replacement by Balfour, and the government's evident need for a new agenda following the end of the Boer War, seemed to offer an opportunity, but government finances were struggling under the costs of the conflict, his Conservative allies would not support increases in income tax, and higher indirect taxes would be electorally unpopular.

The solution Chamberlain found was to propose raising import duties, a measure which he linked to his other great passion, for imperial unity. Strengthening the empire, he believed, was the only way in which a small island like Britain could hope to compete with other great powers such as Russia, Germany or the United States. His ideal solution was a federation, or possibly a customs union, but both proposals proved too great a surrender of political or fiscal autonomy for the colonies to swallow. But they would, it seemed, accept tariff preferences for imports from Britain – Canada had introduced one unilaterally in 1897 – so a scheme of 'imperial preference', through which Britain and its colonies traded between themselves at lower rates of duty than with the rest of the world, seemed to offer both encouragement for imperial unity and higher revenue for the Treasury.

In October 1902, the Cabinet agreed to the Canadian proposal to scrap the import duty on corn (introduced earlier in the year to help meet the costs of the war) but only for imports from the colonies. However, the Chancellor, Charles Ritchie, a free trader, had not agreed and in 1903 threatened to resign if he were not allowed to include the complete abolition of the corn duty in his Budget; the fiscal position was improving and he wanted to avoid confining tax reductions to only income tax (then paid only by the well off). Balfour drew back from confrontation and gave in. In response, in a speech in May, Chamberlain called for an inquiry into the fiscal system. His allies in the Conservative Party established the Tariff Reform League (which by 1905 had 250 branches); in June his Unionist opponents set up the Unionist Free Food League.

'Wonderful news today,' declared the Liberal frontbencher Asquith, the day after Chamberlain's speech, 'and it is only a question of time before we sweep this country.' He was right. Chamberlain's proposal united the Liberals and divided the Unionists. Balfour, typically, had no strong views on the issue but could see the electoral dangers of food taxes and attempted to find a compromise position to hold his party together. He proposed to allow for retaliation against countries which raised import duties against British exports but not a general protective tariff. (His approach was caricatured by the Liberal MP Sir Wilfrid Lawson in a verse which began: 'I'm not for Free Trade, and I'm not for Protection; I approve of them both, and to both have objections. In going through life I continually find; It's a terrible business to make up one's mind.') Balfour so badly mishandled the subsequent discussions in Cabinet that both the free trade ministers (Ritchie and two others) and Chamberlain resigned, followed later by the Duke of Devonshire, the former Liberal Unionist leader, who remained faithful to his Liberal free trade inheritance.

Chamberlain then launched a campaign to convert the party organisations, both Liberal Unionists and Conservatives, to his cause. Some Unionist free trade MPs were deselected; in 1904 and 1905, twelve of them crossed the floor to join the Liberal Party. This included, most notably, Winston Churchill, who, as an indefatigable platform speaker and an innovative minister, proved to be a huge asset to his new party. Legislation ground to a halt, as the Unionists repeatedly split over fiscal debates in the Commons.

All of this was of course a gift to the Liberals. They were the inheritors of the Anti-Corn Law League of the 1840s; later in the century, they had championed the 'free breakfast table', which meant levying no duties on the staple food items of working families. This was not a particularly useful message when free trade was not under threat, but suddenly they had the opportunity to defend cheap food for ordinary people. Most employers, too, appreciated that dearer food would expose them to higher costs in the form of increased wages; and major industries such as cotton relied heavily on free trade to allow them to buy their raw material cheaply and to export their finished products. Asquith cemented his reputation as an effective campaigner by chasing Chamberlain round the country to refute his protectionist propaganda. Liberal candidates appeared on public platforms with two loaves of bread, contrasting the Liberal 'big loaf' with the Tory 'little loaf' that would follow the imposition of food taxes. Between 1904 and the election in 1906, the Liberals won no fewer than fourteen by-elections from the Unionists, some in hitherto solidly Tory seats.

In November 1905, after the annual conferences of both Unionist parties passed resolutions in support of tariff reform, Balfour finally gave up the struggle. On 4 December, the government resigned – the last occasion on which a government was to resign without calling an election. Resignation was preferable to a dissolution, Balfour believed, because an immediate election campaign would simply expose Unionist divisions, and forcing the Liberals to form a government would reveal their own divisions, still not fully healed, over imperial issues, social reform, Home Rule and the leadership. On both counts he was completely wrong.

On 5 December 1905, Campbell-Bannerman accepted the king's commission to form a government. The need to construct a new administration dispelled any remaining opposition to his leadership. Although Asquith and two of his Liberal Imperialist colleagues, Grey and Haldane, had previously agreed (in the 'Relugas compact', named after the location of Grey's fishing lodge) not to serve under Campbell-Bannerman unless he agreed to go to the Lords, the Liberal leader had already defused the plot by offering Asquith the chancellorship and, by implication, the leader's position after he stepped down. Personal ambition, coupled with the need to show Liberal unity, persuaded all three of the plotters to accept office. The government he formed was one of the most talented of the century, containing three future Prime Ministers: Asquith, Lloyd George and Churchill.

On 21 December, the Commons was dissolved and the Prime Minister launched the election campaign with a speech at the Albert Hall. Neither his speech nor his election address set out much hint of what the new government proposed to do. They stuck mainly to excoriating the Unionists for financial mismanagement, for the South African settlement and for supporting vested interests rather than the good of the country. Campbell-Bannerman's most positive point was a defence of free trade, not just for keeping food costs down but for avoiding favouring vested interests at the expense of the common good. His election address concluded by promising to uphold the 'time-honoured principles of Liberalism – the principles of peace, economy, self-government, and civil and religious liberty' and, 'by a course of strenuous legislation and administration, to secure those social and economic reforms which have been too long delayed'. Balfour's election address showed the strains he was under by failing to mention tariffs or imperial preference at all. He reminded voters of Campbell-Bannerman's attack on the army and implied that the Liberals would bring in Home Rule, banish religion from elementary education and weaken the empire. It contained almost nothing at all about his own government's record or his plans for the future.

This was many decades, of course, before the publication of detailed election manifestos. But it would be wrong to think that policy issues played no part in the election campaign. The *Morning Post* estimated, on 3 January 1906, that the Unionists were issuing election leaflets at the rate of 2.5 million a day (for a total UK population of 38 million, of whom about 7 million possessed the right to vote). In the campaign period alone, Liberal HQ issued 22 million leaflets and 3 million booklets.

On top of that, most of the candidates issued their own personal election addresses, which helped to identify the main themes of the campaign. Liberal candidates' addresses were characterised by near-unanimous support for free trade (98 per cent of them included it) together with a wide range of social and other topics, including amendment of the Education Act (86 per cent); reform of Irish government (78 per cent); licensing reform (78 per cent); 'Chinese labour' (75 per cent) (see below); Poor Law reform and pensions (69 per cent); land reform (68 per cent); and reform of trade union law (59 per cent).

The defence of free trade formed the core of the Liberal campaign. Its central appeal was to consumers and their interest in cheap food. 'You know how difficult it is to provide for your families,' said one Liberal leaflet, directed mainly at women:

> If [Mr Chamberlain] succeeds, you will find it more difficult to pay for the food for your families and the clothes that they wear ... If you

want to stave off HARD TIMES, have nothing to do with Mr Chamberlain or Protection ... but urge your husbands and sons to vote for Liberals and Free Traders.

As half a million copies of another leaflet more succinctly put it, 'If you want your loaf, you must shut up Joe.' More broadly, the Liberals portrayed tariff reform as an attempt to turn the clock back to a narrow and harmful protective system which might help a few specialist companies but would hit consumers and damage the economy as a whole, as well as quite possibly triggering a global trade war.

While there is no doubt that the main issues of Liberal candidates' campaigns were traditional Gladstonian topics – free trade, freedom of religion, land reform, Ireland (though not, in the next parliament, Home Rule) – there was a notable increase in support for social and labour reform. This was true in particular of younger candidates, many of whom were not satisfied to remain merely passive free traders. As the Liberal candidate for Stepney explained, 'as an imperial race ... [their] first and finest imperial effort' was to raise standards of living and housing, to charge themselves 'with the proper education and well-being of the children and ... by a system of Old age Pensions to wipe away the lasting reproach to a great country, that one third of its aged citizens [were] paupers'. Pensions was the social reform most commonly mentioned, but schemes to alleviate unemployment, deliver housing, workers' compensation and – especially – reform of trade union law in the wake of the *Taff Vale* judgment were frequently included. Candidates also drew attention to the appointment of John Burns as president of the Local Government Board (the second working man ever to serve as a government minister) to reinforce Liberal determination in these fields.

The LRC's manifesto was even shorter than the other parties' leaders' election addresses. 'This election is to decide whether or not Labour is to be fairly represented in Parliament,' it started, and then set out the reasons why this was needed; there was no other party programme as such. In other respects, LRC candidates' election addresses were not very different from Liberals', stressing almost exactly the same topics but with slightly more priority given to labour and social issues. Hardly any of the LRC candidates' addresses contained any reference to socialism; they were not even remotely revolutionary.

Unionist candidates tended to focus on a much narrower range of issues. Only five were mentioned in more than 50 per cent of candidates' addresses: tariff reform (98 per cent); Home Rule (89 per cent); defence of the Education Act (67 per cent); foreign policy (62 per cent); and a strong army and navy (61 per cent). Given that the Liberals had ruled out Home Rule in the short term, and had explicitly pledged themselves to continuity with the previous government in foreign policy, this did not look like a winning platform.

A few Unionist free traders remained, but Chamberlain's campaigns had driven most of them out of the party, or at least out of candidacies; their number was reduced from forty to fifty MPs in 1903 (10 per cent of the parliamentary party) to about fifteen to twenty candidates (3 per cent of the total) in 1906, most of whom were opposed by Unionist tariff reformers. However, while almost all of the Unionist candidates were convinced tariff reformers, there was far less agreement over how far they wished to go: more than half were notably evasive on the extent of the tariffs they advocated and very few explicitly argued for a general tariff and imperial preference for corn. Leaflets issued by the Tariff Reform League were full of statistics attempting to prove that prices overall would not rise; but their simultaneous promise of tax reductions to offset increases in the prices of some foodstuffs fed rather than allayed voters' suspicions. The main thrust of the Unionist campaign was thus compromised from the outset.

The Unionists in effect started the campaign even before the Commons was dissolved, trying to exploit internal Liberal differences by attacking them over Home Rule. But if Home Rule was such a danger, why should the Unionist government not have stayed in office? As the Liberal journalist J. A. Spender observed, it was absurd for the Unionists to claim that they had resigned only to 'find out what the Radicals intended to do with regard to Ireland'. In the New Year, the Foreign Secretary, Sir Edward Grey, stated explicitly that there would be no legislation for Home Rule without a new mandate. On 1 January, the former Liberal Unionist leader the Duke of Devonshire drove a stake through the Unionist argument by publishing a manifesto in which he declared that while the declarations of leading members of the Liberal government made it 'in the highest degree improbable' that they would introduce a Home Rule Bill, there was real danger to free trade.

'Chinese slavery' played an unexpectedly high-profile role in the campaign. After a general boom in the South African economy after the war had led to shortages of workers for the gold mines of the Rand, the mine owners and the Transvaal government had turned to China, a large source of surplus cheap labour; by February 1905, 27,000 Chinese labourers had arrived in South Africa. Most of them were recruited to serve three- to four-year contracts with no possibility of early exit; the work was hard, their living conditions and food often substandard and in their free time they were restricted to specially built compounds adjacent to the mines. When these conditions became known, British public opinion was outraged – not just, or even probably mainly, for humanitarian reasons but because the mine owners were undercutting more skilled (white) labour (racism undoubtedly also played a part). This was not what British lives had been sacrificed for in the war.

Lloyd George summoned up the spectacle of 'introducing Chinamen at 1 shilling a day into the Welsh quarries ... Slavery on the hills of Wales!', and strings of pigtailed and manacled 'Chinamen' became as familiar at Liberal election meetings as big and little loaves. Balfour seriously miscalculated the public mood by seeking to justify the measure on economic grounds and by querying the use of the word 'slavery' – technically, the Chinese workers were indentured labourers, not slaves, but this rather missed the point. As the *Daily News* observed, Balfour was not the first Conservative leader to have come to grief 'through a wrong estimate of the moral conscience of the nation'. Unionist candidates who attempted to defend the policy were mercilessly heckled; those few who admitted it had been a mistake had a much quieter reception.

On the Unionist side, Chamberlain was a more effective speaker than Balfour, and in speeches in early January, he made the case for protection, arguing that the £30 million worth of foreign manufactures imported each year into the colonies would be better made in the UK. He attacked the Liberals for having no real social policy and contrasted levels of unemployment in free trade England and protectionist Germany. Chamberlain was criticised in turn by Liberals – including his own brother Arthur – and Unionist free traders.

Campbell-Bannerman's opening speech at the Albert Hall on 21 December was met with wild excitement; one eye-witness recorded that 'the vast hall was filled in every seat, while enthusiasm reigned almost to a frenzy ... [the] gathering went almost beside itself when Campbell-Bannerman announced that the importation of Chinese labour into South Africa had already been brought to an end'. When constituency campaigns began in earnest after the Christmas break, Liberal leaders and candidates stressed time and time again the need for free trade, a fair deal for the poor and the ending of Chinese slavery.

In an era before widespread popular media, this was the great age of the political meeting. As the novelist Joyce Cary had one of his characters say in his 1952 novel *Prisoner of Grace*, 'no one who has not fought in one of those ... elections at the beginning of this century ... can ever imagine the excitement of them or how one could be carried away by enthusiasm for one side and scorn and hatred for the other'. Halls were decorated with big and little loaves for the Liberals, maps of the empire and Union Jacks for the Unionists. Processions were enlivened with banners and mock 'Chinamen'; party songs were sung with gusto (the Liberals had much better ones). Hecklers were common – directed especially against Unionist speakers – and candidates had sometimes to defend themselves against bricks and bottles, and a symbolic 'red herring', which was thrown at Balfour in Manchester. The suffragettes of the Women's Social and Political Union disrupted many meetings, particularly those of the Liberal leaders. The *News of the World* observed on 7 January that 'disorderly meetings, if not the order of the day, were at any rate very frequent'.

Motorcars, while still rare, were used to a greater extent than at any previous election, to transport candidates and supporting speakers to meetings and voters to the polls, and sometimes to play phonograph records of speeches to passers-by. The *Daily Mail* estimated that as much as half of the total of 36,000 private vehicles were called into service, either hired or lent by their owners.

The election took place over almost four weeks, from 12 January to 8 February. There was little doubt in anyone's mind that the Liberals would win, but the scale of the victory took almost everyone aback. Of the fifty-four seats declared in the first two days, 12 and 13 January, twenty-three of them were gains from the Unionists by Liberal or LRC candidates. In Manchester and Salford, the Unionists lost not merely the four or five seats predicted by the *Manchester Guardian* but all eight they had won in 1900, six to the Liberals and two to the LRC. The defeated Unionists included Balfour (he was elected later in the election for the City of London); Winston Churchill was one of the victorious Liberals.

Liberal excitement was tremendous. As the results came in, diners danced on the tables of the National Liberal Club. 'Can the oldest of you remember anything like it?' asked Campbell-Bannerman at Glasgow. 'Not a single seat lost to the government and more than a score of seats won, and this not by small chance haphazard majorities, but by resounding numbers. Everywhere – east, north, south, west – the same story is told.'

For the 400 or so seats declaring during the following week, mostly in cities and towns, the story was the same. Everywhere the scale of the victory exceeded the most optimistic Liberal hopes. In London, the Unionists lost thirty-four of the fifty-three seats they were defending. In Leeds and Bradford, the Liberals won every single seat. Only Liverpool, Birmingham (Chamberlain's stronghold), the City of London and a few residential suburbs resisted the Liberal tide. The results were repeated in the counties, which began polling on 19 January. Liberals won seats they had never held before; in Sleaford, the Liberal agent could only describe the result as 'an act of God'. All the Unionist candidates in Wales were defeated, and in Scotland only ten held on, compared to thirty-six in 1900. Only the regaining of some of their by-election losses gave the Unionists any comfort.

The last four seats declared on 8 February. It was a Liberal landslide, on the back of a swing of 12 per cent, a larger swing than was to be achieved by Attlee in 1945 or Blair in 1997. The Liberals gained 224 seats and lost only eight (mostly by-election wins in the previous parliament), to end on 399 (some studies give 400 – party allegiances at the time being more fluid than subsequently). The LRC (renamed the Labour Party soon after the election) jumped from two to twenty-nine, all but five elected with Liberal co-operation. The Gladstone–MacDonald pact had worked: almost all the LRC candidates who fought three-cornered contests, against Liberals as well as Unionists, came bottom of the poll, and several of the seats the LRC won would probably not have been gained by the Liberals.

The Unionist result was the worst of any election in this book. A mere 157 (156 in some studies), including twenty-four Liberal Unionists, survived the rout. They lost 250 seats, almost two-thirds of the number elected in 1900, and gained only five. Only three Unionist Cabinet ministers out of seventeen retained their seats. The result in Ireland was rather less exciting; the Irish Party retained their dominance, with eighty-one MPs, seventy-three of whom were elected unopposed. Together with their Labour and Irish allies, the Liberal government had an effective majority of 356 in the new House of Commons; the Liberals alone enjoyed a majority of 132. No wonder the president of the Royal Statistical Society described the result as 'the most surprising of any that has taken place since 1832'.

The election also marked a new era in the makeup of the Commons, now dominated by men from middle- or working-class backgrounds, including more Nonconformists than ever before. It was the end of aristocratic government. In the Balfour Cabinet of 1905, just four of the seventeen members had not belonged to the aristocracy or landed classes. The new Liberal Cabinet contained only six out of nineteen who did; the rest came instead from the professional classes – mainly lawyers, journalists and academics – and one working man, John Burns.

What explains the magnitude of the Liberal victory? Herbert Gladstone, the Liberal Chief Whip, attributed it to: '(1) The Liberal–Labour pact. (2) Free trade. (3) CB's South African policy. (4) Conservative outstay of Welcome, (a) inducing a wish for change and (b) arrears of industrial and social legislation. (5) Education.'

Of all these, free trade was the most important. As the *Manchester Guardian* commented on the election results in Lancashire:

> A candidate had only to be a Free Trader to get in, whether he was known or unknown, semi-Unionist or thorough Home Ruler, Protestant or Roman Catholic, entertaining or dull. He had only to be a Protectionist to lose all chance of getting in, though he spoke with the tongues of men and angels, though he was a good employer to many electors, or had led the House of Commons, or fought in the Crimea.

It was not just the threat to cheap food that turned a certain defeat into a rout – it reinforced the image of the Unionists as caring more for vested interests than the common welfare, coupled with Unionist divisions over the issue and the evasiveness of most of their candidates over their precise proposals.

'Chinese slavery' was almost as important; Chamberlain believed that 'for one seat lost by tariff reform, ten have been lost by libels and baseless stories about Chinese labour'. While most observers did not rate it that strongly, as Campbell-Bannerman observed, 'it has helped sicken the country of the record of the government'. It fortified the feeling that a new start was needed, a government that would introduce social reform in the interests of the working classes.

To Gladstone's list could be added the state of party organisation. On becoming Chief Whip in 1899, Gladstone had overhauled the party organisation, expanded the employment of professional agents, used funding to put good candidates in place and introduced targeting of resources on the most winnable seats, especially in London. Party membership grew substantially; the National League of Young Liberals had 300 branches by 1906 and the Women's Liberal Federation

100,000 members, many of whom were active during elections even though they could not vote.

In contrast, the Unionists struggled with the combined effects of apathy, inexperience and division. In many areas of the country, elections had been won – or not even contested – for years; local party organisations had in many places effectively ceased to exist. Staff at Conservative Central Office were ineffective and coordination between the Conservatives and Liberal Unionists was poor. But the real damage was done by Chamberlain's campaign for imperial preference, as the Tariff Reform League concentrated its efforts on taking over local and national Unionist organisations. The defections and deselections which followed demoralised party activists.

The efforts of various social and religious groups also helped the Liberals. The voice of the Nonconformist churches, the National Free Church Council, established a special department for electoral work and circulated millions of leaflets attacking Unionist policy, including in particular Chinese labour, education and licensing reform; its manifesto proclaimed that the Liberal government 'represented the people as no other has before'. Nonconformist ministers canvassed voters, chaired Liberal and LRC election meetings and provided venues for headquarters and committee rooms.

The Irish vote was just as important; the United Irish League, the main supporters of the Irish Parliamentary Party, had organisations in 192 constituencies throughout Britain and paid agents and branches in all the major cities. Given Liberal reassurances over the position of Catholic education in schools, and Home Rule (however long term), the league strongly advocated support for the Liberals. Gladstone identified ninety-seven seats that the Liberals had held in the 1886 and/or 1892 elections in which the Irish vote was significant; in 1906 the Liberals won ninety-two of them.

Together, all these factors created the landslide. More than any other issue, the threat to free trade brought Liberals together and united them with employers and the workers they employed, with miners, dockers, transport workers, agricultural labourers and their mothers, sisters and daughters; the split in the Unionist ranks made it easier for traditional Unionist voters to desert them. Chinese labour, education and licensing ignited the consciences of the Nonconformists. *Taff Vale*, and Chinese labour, again, provided a cause behind which working men could unite for the Liberals, and the LRC, and the pact, ensured that their votes were not wasted. Coupled with the general revulsion at the Unionists, a stale and out-of-touch government which had no positive agenda and which treated politics as a game in which the business of the nation got attended to only incidentally, it should be no surprise that the outcome of the 1906 election was a Liberal landslide.

Duncan Brack is the editor of the *Journal of Liberal History* and has co-edited all of the Liberal Democrat History Group's books and booklets. He has also co-edited, with Iain Dale, a series of collections of political counterfactuals, the most recent of which is *Prime Minister Priti … and other things that never happened* (Biteback, 2021). Professionally, he is an independent environmental policy analyst and adviser; in 2010–12, he was special adviser to the Secretary of State for Energy and Climate Change in the Liberal Democrat–Conservative coalition government.

21

1910 (JANUARY)

DAVID LAWS

Dissolution: 10 January 1910
Polling day: 15 January–10 February 1910
Seats contested: 670
Total electorate / Total votes cast / Turnout: 7,694,741 (7,201,029 in contested seats) / 6,234,435 / 86.8 per cent
Candidates (total 1,315): Conservative and Liberal Unionist – 594; Liberal – 511; Irish Parliamentary – 85; Labour – 78; All-for-Ireland – 10; Independent Nationalist – 10; Social Democratic Federation – 9; Free trader – 4
Prime Minister on polling day: H. H. Asquith
Main party leaders: Conservative – Arthur Balfour; Liberal – H. H. Asquith; Labour – Arthur Henderson; Irish Parliamentary – John Redmond; All-for-Ireland – William O'Brien; Social Democratic Federation – Henry Hyndman; Free trader – John Eldon Gorst

Party performance:

Party	Votes	Percentage share	Seats
Conservative and Liberal Unionist	2,919,236	46.8	272
Liberal	2,712,511	43.5	274
Labour	435,770	7	40
Irish Parliamentary	74,047	35.1	71
All-for-Ireland	23,605	11.2	8
Independent Nationalist	16,533	7.8	3
Social Democratic Federation	13,479	0.2	0

| Free trader | 11,553 | 0.2 | 0 |

Result: Hung parliament, Liberal minority government

The year of 1910 was the first in which there were two general elections – both held in the depths of winter, in January and December.

Unusually, these two elections weren't necessitated by either division in the government or inability to command a Commons majority. Instead, they were required to break a constitutional logjam. They were essentially referenda – in January, on the Budget of 1909; and in December, on curbing the powers of the House of Lords. They resolved who ran the UK – the elected Commons or the unelected and Unionist-dominated Lords.

In 1906, the Liberals had won 399 seats out of 670. But in the Lords, there were 461 Unionist peers and only ninety-eight Liberals. Rosebery, the former Liberal Prime Minister, had once told Queen Victoria that the Lords was 'a permanent barrier raised against the Liberal Party'. That is what the elections of 1910 were about – and what they resolved.

The elections also represent a watershed moment in British politics. It was the moment when the politics of the nineteenth century gave way to the politics of the twentieth. Modern democracy. The birth of big government. And a new party line-up. After 1910, nothing was the same. It was one of the biggest turning points in British politics.

Few people would have guessed in 1906 that they were living under the last majority Liberal government.

The Conservative–Unionist hegemony of 1886–1906 was over and the party was bitterly split over tariff reform. In his book on the 1910 elections, Neal Blewett wrote: 'Consumed by ideological passion, the Unionist Party, the great exemplar of political pragmatism, degenerated into a set of squabbling factions venting their invective on each other rather than on the Liberals.'

The 1906 parliament had a greater domination of Liberals than at any time since the high-water mark of Gladstone. Their majority was a thumping 132. Even this understates their strength. The Unionist opposition had a miserable total of 157 MPs – 132 Conservative and twenty-five Liberal Unionist. The Liberals could generally rely on the support of eighty-three Irish and thirty Labour MPs. So, the effective majority in the Commons was around 356 – a stronger Liberal position than since 1832. On the face of it, they could do what they liked.

Liberal Leader Henry Campbell-Bannerman was still Prime Minister in 1906. Not all his colleagues felt he should be. But he deftly saw off rivals, sending Asquith to the Treasury, Sir Edward Grey to the Foreign Office and Lord Haldane to the War Office. Lloyd George continued as president of the Board of Trade. Meanwhile, an ambitious defector from the Conservative Party – Winston Churchill – secured his first ministerial post, as Under-Secretary of State for the Colonial Office.

Campbell-Bannerman sought to bridge the gap between the nineteenth-century Liberalism of Gladstone and the new and more 'active' Liberalism of the twentieth century. His government enacted a modest but progressive set of social reforms: enabling free school meals, strengthening the powers of trade unions and improving workplace compensation for accidents. But his political instincts were those of the Victorian era.

It was Campbell-Bannerman's Chancellor, Asquith ('a financier of a respectable and more or less conservative type', as he would later describe himself), who signalled the beginnings of a more radical approach to finance and social policy, in his second Budget, of 1907. Asquith introduced a differentiation between the rates of tax on earned and unearned incomes. He also made provision for the major social reform of 1908 – the introduction of state pensions. These were modest in scope but radical in potential. 'Old-school' Liberals were appalled. An over-excitable Lord Rosebery even suggested they were 'so prodigal of expenditure as likely to undermine the whole fabric of the Empire'.

Fortunately, Asquith's brilliance lay in introducing radical policy measures in a soothing and consensual way. But, soothing or not, it was impossible to ignore the threat to the government's wider legislative programme from the Lords.

In January 1906, the Unionist leader Balfour had warned that 'the great Unionist Party should still control, whether in power or whether in opposition, the destinies of this great Empire'. Both Campbell-Bannerman and Asquith had understood the threat. After the Lords' defeat of the Education Bill, in December 1906, Campbell-Bannerman toyed with calling a general election, to assert the primacy of the Commons. But the Cabinet was strongly opposed – feeling this was the wrong issue and fearing the expense and risk.

In 1907, Campbell-Bannerman toyed with a different strategy. He advocated limiting the powers of the Lords and removing their veto. His government had by now seen its key legislation on plural voting, education, land and licensing reform scuppered in the second chamber.

Beyond the disputes over domestic policy, Campbell-Bannerman was determined to avoid entanglement in overseas wars. His government granted the Boer states self-government within the British Empire, just years after that conflict. But he also approved a secret plan devised by Sir Edward Grey to send an army of a hundred thousand men to France in the event of a Franco-German war. It was to be a decision with huge implications.

In 1906, Campbell-Bannerman had turned seventy. He was the oldest first-time PM. In 1907, he established another record – the first and only Prime Minister to simultaneously be Father of the House (the MP having the longest service). It was a notable achievement. But not a good omen. Soon after, he suffered a series of heart attacks. In February 1908, he spoke in the Commons for the last time. That night, he suffered a further heart attack and never again left his room. Weeks later, on 3 April, he finally resigned. He died just under three weeks later – the only Prime Minister to do so in 10 Downing Street.

Campbell-Bannerman had not the time in office nor the boldness of vision to rank as a great PM. But he was a man of principle, courage and humanity. He had kept his party broadly united and there was a talented team from which to choose a successor.

By general acclaim, that person was Asquith, the 55-year-old Chancellor. Asquith travelled alone by boat and train to south-west France, and on 8 April kissed hands with King Edward VII in the Hôtel du Palais in Biarritz. By early May, he and his wife, Margot, had moved into 10 Downing Street. She complained that it was 'an inconvenient house, with three poor staircases', and grumbled that few taxi-drivers knew where it was. Some people are not easily pleased.

Asquith appointed Lloyd George to the key role of Chancellor. He wanted to ensure political balance at the top of his party and felt that the promotion of a 'man of the left' would help.

The 33-year-old Winston Churchill was promoted to the Cabinet. With typical modesty, he had written to Asquith a month earlier, setting out his order of preference for Cabinet posts: Colonial Office, Admiralty and (finally) local government. Asquith appointed him president of the Board of Trade. Overall, it was a formidable team, led by an impressive Prime Minister, who dealt with his responsibilities with speed and efficiency.

Asquith was astute and skilful in managing Cabinet disagreements, as he demonstrated in 1909, when senior ministers were divided over the rate of naval shipbuilding needed to meet an emerging challenge from Germany. He also had the soothing and reassuring demeanour needed to lead and unite what was increasingly a quite radical government, breaking from the small-state, laissez-faire, Liberal approach of the last century. Asquith was the Blair of his day – with Lloyd George the more radical Gordon Brown figure.

By the winter of 1908–09, Asquith's political skills were sorely needed. The landslide of 1906 was a distant memory. The Lords had mutilated a large portion of the legislative agenda.

These political problems might have passed electors by. What did not were the bleak economic conditions. Unemployment was 3 per cent in spring 1907. By early 1908, it had doubled to 6 per cent. A by-election in Mid-Devon in January 1908 signalled that the electoral rot had set in. A Liberal majority of 1,289 became a Unionist majority of 559. This 10 per cent swing was large enough to set Liberal knees wobbling. The local Liberals made excuses – claiming the Unionists had 'inundated the constituency with lying placards'. But this was not some aberration. Over the remainder of 1908, a further six government by-election defeats occurred, with the same average swing of 10 per cent. The economic downturn continued, with unemployment rising to a peak of over 9 per cent in late 1908.

Early 1909 saw further by-election losses. Senior Liberals were privately forecasting an electoral rout in 1910 or 1911, complaining 'we are knee deep in pledges we cannot keep and promises we must abandon'.

Liberal frustration now focused on the Lords. In 1906, it had scuppered the Liberal Education Bill and the Plural Voting Bill. In 1907, it sank a series of land bills. In 1908, two Scottish Reform Bills and the Licensing Bill were blocked. To these attacks on the Liberal programme there had been little real response.

But, at last, Asquith and Lloyd George were plotting a 1909 comeback that would put social reform and economic assistance centre stage. The clue was there in the 1909 King's Speech: 'the provision necessary for the services of the state ... will require very serious consideration, and, in consequence, less time than usual will ... be available for the consideration of other legislative measures.' The government was clearing the ground for the most famous Budget Statement in British history.

The strategy was to use the Budget to force through bold economic and social reforms, which (being financial measures) might provoke the Lords but which could not – by long-established practice – be blocked by them. It was hoped that this populist Budget, along with a recovery in the economy, might provide for a political comeback and a general election in late 1910.

But the faltering economy had created a challenging backdrop. There was a budget deficit and large spending pressures from naval commitments and pensions. All this would mean one of the largest peacetime increases in taxation. Could Lloyd George really turn a budget deficit into a political windfall?

Budgets are nowadays prepared in great secrecy. In 1909, it was very different. Hours of deliberation in Cabinet followed. Between mid-March and Budget Day (29 April), fourteen Cabinet meetings discussed the Budget.

On 29 April, the product of all this work was unveiled. The Commons was packed. Ominously, the Peers' Gallery was particularly full. At 3 p.m., Lloyd George rose. He was normally a formidable speaker. But not on this occasion. His throat was sore, his voice weak. There were shouts of 'speak up'. And it was a long speech. By 5 p.m., the Chancellor was struggling so badly that there was an adjournment of thirty minutes. In a rare moment of cross-party co-operation, Balfour supplied him with a mug of beef tea.

It was 8 p.m. before the Chancellor closed his speech – declaring his statement a 'war Budget' – an attack on 'poverty and squalidness'. But the Unionists saw the Budget as class war – and a 'bribe to the poorer part of the electorate'. There were seven new taxes, including a super-tax on the highest incomes and four new land taxes. With the exception of taxes on tobacco and alcohol, the changes were targeted on those with high incomes and significant wealth. The super-tax proposals affected just 12,000 individuals. This was a Budget designed to target the rich.

In the Liberal Party, there was excitement tinged with foreboding. Churchill told his wife that 'this Budget will kill or cure'. But what would the public think? By July, evidence was available, in four by-elections. The results were encouraging. The average swing to the Unionists was 4.6 per cent – less than half that experienced in 1908. Perhaps this reflected an improved economy. But Conservative agents reported that the High Peak constituency 'would have been captured ... but for the Budget'.

The Budget now made its way slowly – very slowly – through the Commons. Labour was, unsurprisingly, supportive. The Irish were less enthusiastic – disliking the increase in spirits duty and land taxes. There were an astonishing 550 divisions. Many sittings continued throughout the night.

Throughout the summer of 1909, the Budget had been the subject of bitter political debate. The Northcliffe press (*The Times* and the *Daily Mail*) urged rejection. Would the Lords now respect the tradition which dictated that Finance Bills were never blocked? No Money Bill had been vetoed for fifty years. The Unionists leaders could see that an election was coming. The more astute were determined to avoid this becoming 'Peers versus the People'. They wished to frame the battle as 'Peers protecting the People' from policies which did not have a specific public mandate.

Tariff-supporting Unionists sensed an opportunity. They would argue that import duties on goods and food could generate the revenue needed to scrap the planned tax rises. One set of bold fiscal policies might be swapped for another, with very different winners and losers. The political debate was polarising between the free trade, radical supporters of the Budget and the tariff-backing, small-state lobby. In the Unionist Party, those in the centre ground were marginalised.

Prior to 1906, the Unionist Party had been seriously split over tariff reform. There was still then a strong contingent of free trade supporters, bitterly opposed to tariffs. Balfour had achieved party unity through a position of carefully constructed ambiguity. He feared to leap either way, in case this precipitated a deeper split. His general attitude to his opposition duties was to make hay from government problems, rather than presenting an alternative programme.

Balfour's fence-straddling had left the field free for those who were most passionate and organised. These were the so-called 'whole hoggers', who wanted to end the policy fudge and make tariff reform the central plank of the Unionist programme. The position of the whole hoggers had been reinforced by the slump, which seemed to demand a change of course.

Balfour was slowly forced to harden up his position. The whole hoggers took greater control of the party. In 1909, one leading 'free fooder' complained that 'the extreme section of the Tariff Reformers are in possession of the local machinery of the Unionist Party'. By January 1909, Conservative Central Office was requiring all future candidates to accept the pro-tariff position. A secret society of extremist whole hoggers, known as the Confederacy, was established and gradually worked to impose the tariff policy across the party. Free food MPs and candidates were forced out.

In summer 1909, Asquith privately approached the king and asked him to consider appointing more Liberal peers, to ensure passage of the Budget. It was not an approach that would commend itself to a conservative institution and to a monarch who had some sympathy with the Unionist cause. Edward VII resisted giving any guarantees. He made clear he would not consider this unless the Liberals won an election, and the Lords still refused to concede. But, fearful of the heightened political tensions in the country which seemed to threaten class war, the king privately urged the Unionist leaders, Balfour and Lord Lansdowne, to pass the Budget.

But opposition in the Lords was hardening, among Unionists and some of the more conservative Liberals. The ever-helpful Rosebery described the Budget as 'inquisitorial, tyrannical and Socialistic'. Warming to his theme, he claimed it marked 'the end of all, the negation of faith, of family, of property, of monarchy, of Empire'.

On 4 November, the Budget finally, and decisively, passed in the Commons. Would the Lords blink? On 30 November, not long before midnight, the Lords voted. The 'not content' division lobby was so full that it took peers twenty minutes to vote. Just after 11.30 p.m., the result came: decisive rejection, by 350 votes to seventy-five. The majority against the Budget had been exceeded only once in the past 100 years. When the Lord Chancellor announced the result, there were hisses from the seats reserved for MPs. Outside Parliament, two red rockets were shot into the air from the *Daily News* offices, informing the public that the 'evil deed' had been done.

The Unionists claimed their rejection was based on the need for explicit public approval of the Budget – 'this House is not justified in giving its consent ... until it has been submitted to the judgement of the country.'

On 2 December, the Finance Bill returned to the Commons. Asquith was in fine form. He condemned this 'new-fangled Caesarism which converts the House of Lords into a kind of plebiscitary organ' designed to protect the people from their own representatives. The Lords, he correctly discerned, 'rejected the Finance Bill ... not because they love the people but because they hate the Budget'. A sick Balfour replied in terms that convinced none of his political opponents and not all of his political friends.

On 3 December, Asquith had Parliament prorogued. The real fight had begun.

This was a twentieth-century election, but it had a distinctly nineteenth-century feel. Those entitled to vote were a minority. No women. Only about 60 per cent of men – and 550,000 of these had two or more votes. Joseph Chamberlain is thought to have possessed six votes and claimed to know someone who had entitlement to twenty-three.

The excluded men were in multiple categories – those living in short-term accommodation, lodgers in lower-value properties, bachelors living with parents, resident domestic servants, soldiers in barracks, paupers, 'aliens', criminals, 'lunatics', peers and those who had failed to navigate the complexities of registration. By excluding these groups, but including those with multiple properties, the system was almost certainly biased against both Liberal and Labour parties.

Parliamentary seats were of unequal size, with huge variations. Romford had 58,984 voters, Kilkenny just 1,742. Ireland was seriously over-represented – with perhaps double its fair quota. Unionists felt they were the losers, with one campaigner undiplomatically claiming that 'Liberalism flourishes on the over-representation of the most backward parts of the country'. In fact, there is little evidence that the Liberals gained overall from this issue. Many of their votes piled up in Liberal seats in areas of rapid population growth. Overall, the Unionists were net gainers in Britain, but the anti-Unionists negated that advantage when Ireland was included.

Electoral corruption was relatively modest but not unknown. In Liverpool, the Labour candidate noted that many men 'from the cemetery' voted against him. In some areas, candidates found other ways of buying influence – the Unionist MP in Wakefield had apparently given every local child a savings account with a shilling in it.

There were more candidates (1,315) in the election than for twenty-five years, with almost every seat outside Ireland being contested. The social, occupational and age characteristics of Liberal and Unionist candidates seemed quite similar. Around 50 per cent of Liberal and Unionist candidates had attended higher education. Only 3 per cent had left school at the elementary level. By contrast, over 80 per cent of Labour candidates were educated to elementary level and only 6 per cent had gone into higher education. A total of 1 per cent of Unionist candidates and 2 per cent of Liberals had been manual workers. For Labour, it was 84 per cent.

Looking more closely, we can see that the Unionist Party was selecting an elite within the elite: an astonishing 206 of the Unionist candidates had attended just two of the top public schools – Eton (153, thereby one in four Unionist candidates!) and Harrow (fifty-three). Only fifty-nine Liberal candidates had attended these schools. In higher education, Oxford was particularly significant for the Unionists, accounting for two-thirds of those with a higher education. Three times more Unionists than Liberals came from a landed or military background. The Liberals had more candidates from business backgrounds and the professions. The religious differences were even more striking: 90 per cent of Unionists were Anglicans, but only 3 per cent Nonconformists. For the Liberals, it was 56 per cent and 35 per cent, respectively.

What of the party machines? Unionist organisation had gradually been deteriorating in quality. Responsibility was also split between the National Union (responsible for constituency associations) and the Central Office. The only things they had in common were their location, the low quality of their staff and their mutual animosity. The party's principal agent, Percival Hughes, had a laid-back attitude and went on holiday halfway through the campaign. The contrast with Liberal organisation was notable. This was led by Sir Robert Hudson, a skilful and energetic individual, who had been a key driver of the Liberal election machine since 1893. Hudson worked across the National Liberal Federation, the Liberal Central Association, the Liberal Publication Department and the Free Trade Union – ensuring a consistency of approach.

Money is always important in elections. Traditionally, the Unionists had the edge, and the Budget risked driving rich donors away from the Liberals. The election would be the most expensive for thirty years. But the party election expense returns would show little difference between the main parties, with Conservative and Unionists spending a combined £652,000, versus £550,000 for the Liberals and £68,000 for Labour.

One area of new technology was beginning to tell in the elections of the twentieth century – the motor car. In some areas, the major car companies supplied vehicles to help the Unionist cause. Liberals and Labour could not match Unionist access to this expensive new item. Instead, they urged their voters to 'ride to the polls in Unionist motor cars'.

Election tactics were as important in 1910 as they are today. Much thought was given to the day on which polls would open and maximising the turnout of supportive voters. Many Liberals favoured starting the elections on a Saturday, but they had to overcome the objections of the Liberal Chief Whip, who was worried about the effects of cup-tie football matches on working-class turnout. After contrary advice from Lloyd George, the first polling day was finally set for Saturday 15 January.

What now commenced was the longest general election campaign in modern British history – starting on 3 December and continuing until the last ballots were cast on 10 February.

There was an unprecedented volume of propaganda. The Liberal Publications Department produced a tidal wave of paper – 42 million leaflets, pamphlets and posters. This was 50 per cent more than in 1906. The Unionists produced over 50 million items of literature. Even Labour managed over 5 million leaflets and a remarkable 800,000 copies of its manifesto.

But these were not the days of long-winded election manifestos. Asquith's pithy address, running to barely a side of A4, focused heavily on the Lords' veto of the Budget – 'a proceeding without precedent in our history, a wanton breach of the settled practice of the Constitution ... The House of Lords has violated the Constitution in order to save from a mortal blow the cause of Tariff reform.' For Asquith, the election was about the Budget, the primacy of Commons over the Lords and the cause of free trade – which was particularly electorally significant in the constituencies of the north and the Midlands.

Asquith made clear that if the Liberals prevailed, the 'limitation of the veto is the first and most urgent step'. Liberal candidates took his lead – Lords reform was the main priority in 82 per cent of their addresses. Most (75 per cent) mentioned tariff reform, which they argued would raise prices, and the Budget. Moreover, 75 per cent also mentioned pensions. They were much less keen to make an issue of Home Rule – only 39 per cent referred to this, and one quarter of these opposed it!

By contrast, while the election addresses of most Unionist candidates (94 per cent) mentioned the Lords issue, only 15 per cent placed this first. Overall, 100 per cent mentioned tariff reform and 75 per cent gave this pride of place among their priorities. Candidates primarily linked tariff reform to higher wages and more jobs. Almost all mentioned defence (the navy scare), Home Rule and the Budget (particularly the taxes on tobacco and booze).

Unionist election propaganda cast up the spectre of the unscrupulous German exporter 'Herr Dumper', who would undercut British manufacturers, destroying jobs and incomes. The three nationalistic themes (tariffs, defence and Ireland) were again used to wrap the Unionist Party in the Union Jack – a variation on the tune of 1900.

There was also an unprecedented degree of campaigning by pressure groups – formally separate from the parties but often closely aligned. The Tariff Reform League played a vital role in selecting and supporting Unionist candidates. It issued over 53 million leaflets and posters in the year before the election – most of which were circulated during the election period. Its competitor, the Free Trade Union, was small in comparison. The brewing industry – no friend of the Liberal Party – also campaigned actively, and pubs often became rallying points for anti-government activities. In general, the Unionists benefited more than the Liberals from pressure group campaigning. Many of those with power and wealth saw the Liberals as a threat to their economic interests.

The suffragettes were also active. They were keen to disrupt the elections, to highlight their cause. Much of this was targeted on government ministers – Asquith had to duck to avoid being hit by a ginger-beer bottle while visiting Liverpool. This disruption caused women to be excluded from many large public meetings.

In these pre-television days, speeches by leading politicians were regarded as hugely important. Meetings were often packed. The press baron Lord Northcliffe complained about the naivety of many politicians. His four 'top tips' included:

> If making an important speech, only do so in locations with ample telegraph services; decline to speak later than 7.30 p.m. [newspaper trains left London at 1.45 a.m., so early copy was essential]; send *The Times* a short speech precis beforehand to help the Leader writers; let *The Times* know in advance if the speech is going to be important.

As owner of *The Times*, Northcliffe might be viewed as biased. But his warning that in general elections 'the modern newspaper ... has entirely superseded the meeting' needed to be taken seriously.

From 3 December to the end of January, around one-third of column inches were election focused. Papers were overwhelmingly behind the Unionist cause. No quality London morning paper supported the Liberals, and no major papers supported Labour. *The Times*, the *Daily Telegraph*, the *Morning Post*, *The Standard*, the *Daily Express*, the *Daily Mail* and four evening papers were all solidly Unionist – with a combined circulation of around 2.3 million. The Liberals were backed by the *Daily Chronicle*, the *Daily News*, the *Morning Leader* and two evening papers – accounting perhaps for 1.3 million papers. Among the provincial dailies – important in an era where distribution outside London was challenging – Liberal and Unionist papers were more evenly balanced.

One newspaper campaign was particularly salient. From 13 to 24 December, the *Daily Mail* ran a highly inflammatory campaign about the risk of Germany destroying the British Empire and the need for more military spending. Published as a pamphlet, 1.3 million copies were sold by the end of January and 250,000 were given away free. The Liberals were slow to respond, fearing to give it the oxygen of more publicity. Balfour, sniffing an opportunity, joined the fight in early January, warning that a war with Germany was inevitable and 'we are predestined to succumb'.

The Liberals helped neutralise their newspaper disadvantage by deploying more well-known and effective speakers, and by making greater efforts to get their speeches covered. During his tour of Lancashire constituencies, Churchill deposited all of his speeches in advance with the Press Association, complete with insertions indicating where the crowds would be applauding.

While Balfour struggled with poor health, Asquith opened the Liberal campaign with a speech at the Albert Hall, on 10 December. The Prime Minister addressed an audience of 10,000 – all men, due to fears that the suffragettes might disrupt the meeting. He spoke from a platform on which almost all the Cabinet were seated, under a huge banner reading 'Shall the People be Ruled by the Peers?' It was a masterful and wide-ranging performance, perhaps the best of his career.

Asquith spoke of 'three capital issues' – the supremacy of the House of Commons over Finance Bills, the continuation of free trade and the limitation of the powers of the Lords. His commitment that 'in the new House of Commons the hands of a Liberal Government and a Liberal majority will [on Irish Home Rule] be entirely free' cleared the way for an arrangement between Irish MPs and the Liberal Party, should the latter lose its majority. The Irish leader, Redmond, had two weeks earlier sent a private ultimatum, warning that unless the Liberals came out firmly for Home Rule, they would lose the support of both Irish voters and Irish MPs.

Asquith set out his views on the role of the state in delivering social reform, speaking about the state lending 'a helping hand'. He argued that social reform would require extra finance which could come from either tariff reform – taxation of 'the necessities of life' – or the Budget measures, which would raise money from 'the superfluities of one class, the luxuries of another, the monopoly values of a third'.

Crucially, Asquith pledged to establish the primacy of the Commons, with an Act of Parliament to guarantee that the Lords would not be able to interfere with 'our national finance' and which would 'prevent the indiscriminate destruction of our legislation'. But he wisely shunned any detailed policy commitments on the future shape of the Lords.

The Times described the speech, hysterically, as 'that orgy of promises made to all the fanatical and disruptive forces in political life'. It was far from that. The speech was the most significant and memorable of a divisive campaign.

Lloyd George and Churchill were the other leading Liberal speakers. Lloyd George energised supporters and outraged opponents. At Caernarvon, he claimed that 'neither Ireland nor Wales can ever obtain its rights except by marching over the ruins of the House of Lords'. His appeal to the Nonconformist vote was described by the Archbishop of Canterbury as 'in the most literal sense, the work of the Devil'. Some Liberals thought that Lloyd George was too inflammatory. Margot Asquith considered his speeches 'a disgrace: vulgar, silly, and infinitely bad for us'. While Lloyd George provoked, Asquith providing the balm – preferring to gently tease and rubbish his political opponents, rather than inflaming class tensions. Meanwhile, Churchill maintained a middle course – more partisan than Asquith but less provocative than the Chancellor.

Labour's manifesto shared the brevity of Asquith's address. Its central pitch was along Liberal lines – 'The great question you are to decide is whether the Peers or the people are to rule this country ... The Lords must go.' The manifesto, while strikingly short by modern standards, would be more recognisable to our current generation than the discursive efforts of the Liberal and Conservative leaders. There was a list of delivered 'pledges' and of four or five promises for the parliament to come. The manifesto finished with a snappy list of slogans: 'The land for the people. The wealth for the wealth producers. Down with privilege. Up with the people.'

But Labour's campaign was limited. It was standing candidates in only seventy-eight of the 670 seats – largely in the industrial north of England. That was down from 110 in 1906. Labour essentially acted as a radical offshoot of the Liberal political family. The Liberals were content to leave Labour unchallenged in the seats they had won in

1906. But they were not keen to see Labour expand further – fearing that growth would come at their expense. Labour's leadership had to satisfy vociferous critics on both left and right. The left saw co-operation as a sell-out of socialist principles. The right, including in mining areas, wanted to see more local deals with the Liberals. On the whole, the party favoured the latter strategy.

Of the seventy-eight seats Labour fought, fifty-one had no Liberal opposition. Of the seats Labour had won in the past, only three fielded Liberal candidates. Of the other twenty-seven seats that Labour sought to gain, twenty-four of these also had Liberal candidates – indeed twenty of these seats were held by Liberal MPs and six were Unionist/Liberal marginals. Perhaps unsurprisingly, Labour would fail to break through in every one of these seats. In twenty-three, Labour finished last.

In two-member seats there was explicit tactical voting, often with Liberal candidates signalling that the second vote should go to the Labour candidate, or vice versa. In most seats, over 90 per cent of Liberal and Labour voters gave the other party their second vote. But Lib-Lab co-operation was not universal – it depended on the decisions made in individual seats. And sometimes, narrow party interest prevailed over anti-Unionist pacts.

What of the opposition? The Unionists had fewer first-rank campaigners than the Liberals. Balfour was also ill for much of the campaign.

The Unionist leader issued his election address on 10 December. It was considerably longer than Asquith's and focused primarily on the need for the Lords to provide 'constitutional safeguards' to protect the people and give them a 'right to be consulted'. It argued that the Liberals were plotting to destroy the Lords and move to a single-chamber parliament. There was a brief section on the case for tariff reform but not as much as many Unionists would want to see.

The period from 3 December to Christmas was the busiest phase of the campaign, with public speeches and copious leaflets. The Christmas period itself would normally see a one-week truce. But such was the feverish nature of the campaign that calm lasted just four days.

The Liberals had the better of the first part of the campaign. A party which had written off its prospects twelve months before felt that victory was now within its grasp.

It is difficult to know how public opinion changed during the campaign. In 1910, there were no carefully sampled and frequently occurring national opinion polls. But the extreme length of the campaign meant that maintaining Liberal momentum into the New Year was a challenge. Churchill noted a flagging of efforts, including by Asquith, who appeared to tire. As the campaign continued, it also became more divisive. Tariff reform shops were damaged. Speeches were interrupted. A Unionist MP had a fist fight with a heckler. Lloyd George fled an angry mob.

Meanwhile, Balfour – recovering from his recent illness – was able to adopt a higher profile, with a string of speeches from Ipswich to Aberdeen.

Unionist candidates were increasingly keen to turn the spotlight away from the Lords and on to tariff reform, which had particular resonance in the agricultural districts. Unionists also sought to avoid being painted as old-fashioned defenders of an unreformed Lords – indeed, half of the Unionist election addresses argued for reform of the composition of the second chamber. The constitutional issue was a 'shield' issue that had to be downplayed. Their 'sword' was tariff reform – the argument that this could both secure the revenue to fund social reform and protect the British economy from overseas competition.

These were still difficult economic times, and for many voters the economy was a greater concern than esoteric arguments about the constitution. A joint pledge on tariff reform and the cost of living from Balfour and Joseph Chamberlain underlined the extent to which the Unionist Party had now decided to back this political horse. Even the cautious Balfour felt obliged to push the policy boat out. In mid-January, he pledged to impose 'import duties over a wide fiscal field', including taxes on foreign wheat.

The Liberals sought to respond to this 'bread and butter' politics with speeches on pensions, social reform and the impact of tariffs on the costs of food.

So, in these final stages of the campaign, the long-rehearsed arguments on the Budget and the Lords gave way to wider questions of economic and social policy.

Home Rule ultimately played little part in the election. Liberal candidates were worried it would cost votes. Unionists felt that voters saw it as a second-order issue.

On the Sunday before first polls, one national newspaper published six supposedly reputable forecasts, which ranged from a Unionist majority of ninety to an anti-Unionist majority of 200. On both sides of politics, a divisive election which aroused strong passions had produced a conviction that success was guaranteed. Unionists and Liberals looked forward with optimism to the first results. They could not both be right.

Those of more measured opinion had long seen which way the wind was blowing. Asquith had told the king as far back as October that the election would produce a minority Liberal government, reliant on the Irish. And more sensible Unionists guessed that the landslide of 1906 was so huge as to require two elections to win back power.

On 15 January, the polls finally opened in sixty-six English boroughs. Rain fell heavily in the north, less heavily down south. In the Hartlepool seats, an 'intimidating' invasion of hired miners sought to deter Liberal voters from attending the polling station. Lloyd George broke election day convention by speaking in Grimsby – provoking a hostile demonstration against him.

But neither the rain nor the football matches nor the demonstrations prevented voters turning out in record numbers. Turnout was just under 87 per cent – a stunningly high figure and the highest in any election before or since. Compared with 1906, there were over 1 million additional votes – a 19 per cent increase.

In London, crowds gathered in the Strand, Fleet Street and Trafalgar Square, and giant screens were erected to display the results. The Manchester area was first to declare – a Liberal hold at 9.21 p.m., followed by a Liberal gain at 9.27 p.m. Then the first Unionist win in a three-way competition in Southwest Manchester. By early morning, the picture was clearer – an average swing to the Unionists of 4.4 per cent. A Unionist majority was no longer in prospect. But could the Liberals hold on to their outright majority?

What made predictions tricky was strong regional variation. In Lancashire and the north, the Liberal vote was holding up. But in the Midlands, the Unionists were making solid gains. In the south and west, the Liberals were suffering big defeats. The abstainers of 1906 were returning home. Where turnout rose most, so typically did the Unionist vote.

On 19 January, the first of the English counties went to the polls. The results here would be crucial. Votes were counted on 20 January, and this was the day on which Liberal hopes of a majority free of Irish dependence were dashed. They suffered sweeping losses, not least in the Home Counties. On 24 January, they suffered their worst results yet – losing nine out of the seventeen seats. Only in Scotland, Wales and the industrial north was the Liberal vote holding up. In the south-east, outside London, Liberal support and Liberal seats were melting away. Losses continued to pile up across the south-west, East Anglia and into the Midlands. The few Liberal and Labour gains arose largely in the north.

When the results were all in, the scale of the regional variation was clear. The north, Scotland and Wales was still heavily Liberal–Labour. In these areas, the anti-Unionists held 201 seats, or 80 per cent of the total. This was similar to 1906 but dramatically up from around 56 per cent on average from 1885 to 1900.

But in the south, there was a collapse. In 1906, Liberals had secured 70 per cent of the seats in the southern half of England (including the Midlands and East Anglia). This plummeted to 37 per cent. Never had the performance gap between the two halves of England been so wide.

Across Great Britain, there were outcrops of strength and weakness for both parties, and London was highly contested. But there was no doubt that the country was not responding uniformly to the political battle. In the north, Wales and Scotland, there was very little swing to the Unionists. But in the south, particularly the south-east, there was a mammoth swing to the Unionists. This reached 8 per cent in the Home Counties and 10 per cent in Surrey, Hampshire and Sussex. It was this dramatic southern swing which wiped away the Liberal majority. Over half of Unionist gains were in their southern heartlands.

By late January, it was clear that there would be a hung parliament. The question was which party would emerge largest. With the results all in, the Liberals had just squeaked through. They had 274 seats to the Unionist 272. Liberal losses (against 1906) were 123, and Unionist gains 116. Labour was down from forty-five seats in December 1909 (but up from twenty-nine in 1906) to forty.

The Liberal vote share had fallen from 48.9 per cent (1906) to 43.5 per cent, almost a mirror image of the Unionist rise from 43.4 per cent to 46.8 per cent. This was the lowest Liberal share on record, while Labour's 7 per cent was the highest. The first signs that the Liberal–Conservative hegemony was about to crumble could just be discerned.

The balance of MPs meant that with Irish and Labour support, the government still had a working majority of 112. But a government which previously had an outright majority was now at the mercy of both Labour allies and less dependable Irish MPs.

Some Liberals thought the outcome a disaster. Others were more composed. 'Our victory – though substantial – is clearly Wagram not Austerlitz,' wrote Churchill.

David Laws was Liberal Democrat MP for Yeovil Constituency (2001–15) and was a minister in the 2010 coalition government.

22

1910 (DECEMBER)

DAVID LAWS

Dissolution: 28 November 1910
Polling day: 3–19 December 1910
Seats contested: 670
Total electorate / Total votes cast / Turnout: 7,709,981 (6,011,004 in contested seats) / 4,876,409 / 81.6 per cent
Candidates (total 1,191): Conservative and Liberal Unionist – 548; Liberal – 467; Labour – 56; Irish Parliamentary – 81; All-for-Ireland – 21; Independent Conservative – 4; Independent Labour – 4; Social Democratic Federation – 2
Prime Minister on polling day: H. H. Asquith
Main party leaders: Conservative and Liberal Unionist – Arthur Balfour; Liberal – H. H. Asquith; Labour – George Barnes; Social Democratic Federation – Henry Hyndman; Irish Parliamentary – John Redmond; All-for-Ireland – William O'Brien

Party performance:

Party	Votes	Percentage share	Seats
Conservative and Liberal Unionist	2,270,753	46.6	271
Liberal	2,157,256	44.2	272
Labour	309,963	6.4	42
Irish Parliamentary	90,416	43.6	74
All-for-Ireland	30,322	14.6	8
Social Democratic Federation	5,733	0.1	0
Independent Conservative	4,647	0.1	1
Independent Labour	3,492	0.1	0

Result: Hung parliament, Liberal minority government

The January election had delivered a hung parliament – a disappointment for Liberal leaders, but their continuation in office was not in doubt. The Labour Party and the Irish would clearly prefer the Liberals over the Unionists, who could be confident of securing a majority on most issues.

The Unionists, though out of power, were more content with the results. Their opponents had lost their majority. For the 'whole hoggers', tariff reform was now centre stage. Balfour relished the opportunity to make opposition to Home Rule a major political issue. He had established his reputation on this and knew it would unite his party.

For Asquith, the big problem was what to do about the Lords. The Irish wanted its veto removed, to pave the way for Home Rule. The Liberals and Labour had to ensure the Lords would no longer be a block on 'progressive' legislation.

As soon as the election was over, Asquith rushed off to the south of France to relax in the winter sun. He was so desperate to get away that he forgot that he had a commitment to dine with the king at Windsor Castle. The monarch was not amused. He and his Prime Minister had much to discuss. The monarch and his advisers had been cheered by the election result. They felt that Asquith was now in a weaker position to press for a mass creation of peers. The Unionists also concluded that the Liberals had no mandate to neuter the second chamber. They would concede on the Budget but not on this. They were convinced that the king would insist on a further election if the Liberals wanted to press the point. New MPs had barely been sworn in before informed Westminster opinion was turning to the inevitability of a second election.

There was now a major debate in government. Should the Lords be significantly reformed or even abolished? Or should the government focus narrowly on the issue of the veto? Looking to the likelihood of a second election, many senior Liberals such as Grey and Churchill began to feel that the Unionists would more easily be defeated by a plan to turn the second chamber into a reformed and democratic body, rather than limiting its powers and allowing the Unionists to rail against 'single-chamber government'. For a while, Asquith seemed unsure. But he plumped for the less radical objective of curtailing powers of veto – he judged that it would be easier to secure an electoral mandate for this, than for a new policy of elected peers. He was right. Over a hundred years would pass without democracy intruding into the second chamber.

As with the Budget, however, these were days in which the Cabinet expected to have a serious and extensive debate before decisions were made. Between Asquith returning from his holiday in Cannes to the reopening of Parliament in late February, the Cabinet met an astonishing seven times in nine days.

Many Liberals assumed that before the election Asquith had extracted a commitment from the king to create new peers, but he shocked and disappointed supporters by now announcing in the Commons 'I have received no such guarantee and that I have asked for no such guarantee.' The Chief Whip described the speech as 'the very worst I have ever heard him make'.

Some in Cabinet wondered if the government could survive. But Asquith seemed to gain new energy and purpose. He also faced down the Irish Nationalists, who had been demanding the axing of Budget plans to raise spirits duty. For Redmond and the Irish, removing the power of veto of the Lords was more important than cheap spirits. But the Irish wanted the Lords' veto dealt with before they would give their backing to the Budget.

Asquith gradually shifted a wavering Cabinet towards the curtailed veto option. He united his divided colleagues with another masterly compromise, which emphasised early action on the veto, without jettisoning reform.

The Cabinet finally agreed its position on 13 April. A Parliament Bill would end the ability of the Lords to veto or amend a Money Bill and would limit the Lords' blocking power over other bills to a period of two years. The maximum term of parliaments would be cut from seven years to five years. The bill vaguely referenced further Lords reform – enough to quieten those for whom this was a key principle. The Cabinet also agreed to request from the king clear guarantees of additional peers if the Lords should seek to block these changes, after a further election.

On 27 April, the Budget again passed in the Commons with a healthy majority of almost 100, with most Irish MPs in support. On 28 April, the Budget also cleared its Lords stages, without divisions, and in just a few hours. The battle of the Budget was over.

Balfour had publicly acknowledged that the election had decided the Budget issue, but his strategy was to deny that it had determined anything on the powers of the Lords or on Home Rule. He intended to paint the Liberals as being held to ransom by the Irish and threatening the unity of the kingdom.

Meanwhile, some Unionists felt that their party should also contemplate a reformed Lords. The proponents of tariff reform, in particular, believed that this was a winning electoral card. They did not wish for its impact to be diluted by being on the wrong side of a row over the second chamber. But Balfour was more cautious and recognised that his party could easily split. To deliver unity, he needed the same cunning that Asquith had already displayed. A multiplicity of options for Lords reform were now suggested in Unionist circles and among other interested peers, including Rosebery. All the proposals had one thing in common – a majority of peers was against them. No magic formula could be found to unite the clashing principles of selection by crown, birth, office or public vote.

While Balfour was seeking a tactical solution to his conundrum, Asquith now felt that he was close to persuading the king. On the evening the Budget passed, he went to Buckingham Palace to see Edward VII and 'found him most reasonable'. After dinner at the Savoy Hotel, the PM headed for Portsmouth and embarked on the Admiralty yacht *Enchantress* for another ten days of sun and warmth – this time in Spain and Portugal.

Asquith's political strategy now seemed clear. The Budget was passed. The veto must go. If the Lords continued to obstruct, they would face another election and this time the king would accept the case for a mass creation of peers. This would ultimately lead to primacy of the Commons.

There was only one flaw in this strategy: Asquith had seen the king for the last time.

On 7 May, Asquith received a surprise message. It was from the new king, George V. Edward VII was dead. The yacht was turned around and sailed back to Plymouth, escorted by two fast cruisers. Asquith must rerun his discussions with a new and less experienced monarch.

In the Lords, the resolutions which had passed the Commons, to curtail the veto, proved too much to stomach. The Unionist-dominated chamber would not give way. Asquith determined to force the new king to give him the guarantees he was so close to securing from his father. But George V was far from persuaded.

A constitutional crisis threatened, and a summer general election seemed inevitable. Neither party was sure what the outcome would be. The Liberals feared asking the public to vote twice in barely six months. The Unionists feared that many of their voters – the comfortably off middle classes – might be off on holiday if the election was held in August.

Instead, a constitutional conference was held. The king was hopeful that a solution might be found. He did not relish being at the centre of a political crisis. But there was no way through. The Unionists had no agreed plan for Lords reform and were certainly not going to agree to drop their veto over Irish Home Rule.

The Liberal leaders now considered their options. A by-election in Walthamstow in early November saw a small swing in their favour. Some favoured an immediate election. Others wanted to wait for the new register in January.

On 9 November, the Liberal Chief Whip made a careful tally of the electoral position in every key seat in England and Wales. His view was that his party was set for a net gain of twenty-nine seats.

Buoyed by this assessment, and frustrated by continued Unionist obstruction, the Cabinet now determined to act. On 10 November, they decided on a pre-Christmas election. Asquith asked the king to dissolve Parliament. The Prime Minister made clear to the king that he must guarantee that if the government was returned and Lords reform was blocked, there must be a mass creation of new peers. Refusal to grant this request would lead to the Liberals leaving office.

The king remained unenthusiastic. His advisers were divided. But eventually he realised he had no choice – if the will of the people was ignored, this would pose a threat to the whole constitutional edifice. It would not just be the Lords in the dock but the monarchy, too.

On 14 November, Asquith had an audience with the king. It was 'the most important occasion of my life'. He left a happy man. The reluctant monarch had finally conceded to his Prime Minister's demand. In his diary that night, George V recorded:

> I agreed most reluctantly to give the Cabinet a secret understanding that in the event of the government being returned ... I should use my Prerogative to make Peers if asked for. I disliked having to do this very much, but agreed that this was the only alternative to the Cabinet resigning, which at this moment would be disastrous.

Before Parliament was prorogued, the Lords debated their future. Unionist peers suddenly switched to backing a reformed Lords. Some even supported a future 'democratic element', though it was unclear what entirely this meant. On 21 November, the 'Lansdowne resolutions' were announced. There were to be 'joint sittings' of both houses, to resolve disputes. There might be a referendum on chosen major issues of substance that had not been settled in a general election. And Money Bills could be exempted from interference.

These resolutions raised a hundred or more questions of both substance and detail. But clarity was not the point. The Unionists did not wish to concede an election on which they would be painted into a corner again by Asquith, Lloyd George and Churchill. But they knew they were too divided to offer anything more than a vague sense of policy direction. To what extent the voters noticed or cared about all this is an interesting question. One Unionist complained that 'amid all the tumult the House of Lords debates were not read at all, even by people of the shopkeeping class ... We shall have to simplify somewhat, so incredibly crude are the minds of the multitude.'

The one issue that seemed sufficiently simple was the idea of a referendum. Who could disagree with that? It might seem odd that a conservative party could promote such a directly democratic instrument. But Unionists saw in this device an opportunity to shield themselves from electoral attack, to paper over internal divisions and to appeal to an essentially conservative electorate to block radical reforms. Lord Cromer argued that a referendum would avert the dangers from 'a coalition of discordant elements ... Home Rulers, Socialists, Suffragists and I know not what besides'. The referendum was essentially an extension of the Unionist tactic which led to the January 1910 poll.

While these Lords debates continued, on 18 November, Asquith announced a dissolution for 28 November. First polls would take place on 3 December. After the long election campaign of January, this was to be the shortest ever between the formal notice of election and the first polls. The starting gun was fired.

Fewer candidates (1,191) stood in this election than in January (1,313). Labour cut its number back dramatically again from seventy-eight to fifty-six. It had learned its lesson in January and had concluded that it would fight only in those seats where party organisation, finances and the Lib-Lab relationship meant that success was likely. Only in south Wales was there a notable deterioration in Lib-Lab relations, after the aggressive manner in which the coalfield riots in early November at Tonypandy had been tackled by the government. Keir Hardie spoke bitterly against the Liberals, who came close to fielding a candidate against him in Merthyr Tydfil.

Liberal and Unionist candidate numbers fell by around fifty each. The parties had run down their election coffers and decided to concentrate their resources.

In this election, candidates of all parties put Lords reform as top priority. Liberal focus on ending the Lords' veto was so great that social reform was mentioned more by Unionists than Liberals. In total, 95 per cent of Unionist candidates pledged themselves to Lords reform – a dramatic change since January.

Tariff reform and free trade ranked second in importance, but 30 per cent of Liberals still ignored the issue, and only 17 per cent of Unionist candidates ranked the issue first (notably down from 74 per cent in January). Defence and the danger of Home Rule remained firm Unionist favourites, being mentioned in almost 90 per cent of addresses. For Labour, the Lords, the *Osborne* judgment (on trade union funding of politics), Home Rule and social reform were the top issues. The Budget and old-age pensions now received little attention from any party.

The campaign was not merely shorter. It was less heated. The arguments had all been rehearsed. The public was bored. But this did not mean they were disengaged. They were determined to settle the arguments. Nothing had happened since January to change minds.

For the Liberals, Asquith was dominant throughout, with Lloyd George and Churchill again playing important but secondary roles. Avoiding the inflammatory rhetoric of Lloyd George, which again so irritated the king (the Chancellor claimed that some peers owed their place to 'indiscretions of kings'), Asquith teased his Unionist opponents for their alleged conversion to the cause of Lords reform – 'with a coat, however thin, of democratic varnish'. He dismissed the Unionist referendum proposal as a 'trick … to gain time to load the dice again' and a 'deadly blow at the very foundation of representative government'.

Asquith's election address was even shorter than that of January. The election was about 'a single issue … Are the people, through their freely chosen representatives, to have control, not only over finance and administrative policy, but of the making of their laws?' He asked the public 'to repeat, with still greater emphasis, the approval which only eleven months ago you gave'.

Meanwhile, Lloyd George and other Liberals decided to call the Unionists' bluff on a referendum. Why not, they suggested, use one to resolve the tariff issue, too?

Balfour played as dominant a role for his party, as did Asquith. Balfour had already set out his election case in a swashbuckling speech in Nottingham on 17 November. He put tariff reform centre stage and tried to play down the Lords issue, with a nod towards possible future reform. He produced a much shorter address than in January. After complaining that the government had selected a time of year when the election register was outdated, and 'most inconvenient to trade', he claimed there was a 'Single-Chamber conspiracy', behind which lurked 'Socialism and Home Rule'. The Unionist policies which he gave primacy to were 'Tariff Reform, National Defence ... and other social reforms'.

The Unionists were gifted an opportunity of marrying their traditional themes of nationalism and opposition to Home Rule when the Irish leader, Redmond, returned in November from a highly successful fundraising trip to the USA. Unionists who had previously portrayed him as the 'Irish Dictator' now dubbed him the 'Dollar Dictator'. They even issued a mocked-up dollar bill with the slogan: 'Will you be ruled by the dollar or the sovereign?' The Unionists were never short of loyal rottweilers in the national press, and they merrily took up this theme.

Labour's manifesto remained short – a few hundred words. It, too, led on the Lords. But it listed other issues: legal protections for the trade unions, the payment of MPs and a range of social reforms and employment protection. As in January, it finished with a flourish: 'Now is the time to unite. The poverty of one is the poverty of all. Let those who suffer join to remove their suffering.'

Early in the campaign, in an attempt to highlight the issue of tariff reform, Andrew Bonar Law dramatically gave up his London constituency and announced that he would contest the Liberal seat of North-West Manchester. It was one of the few exciting moments of a dreary election. It was also a gamble. But the Unionists thought that Lancashire might be the key to No. 10. Unless they could win seats in the north, they could not win power. And the 'whole hoggers' feared the consequences of losing three successive elections on a tariff reform agenda.

With the upturn in the economy, the tariff reform pledge seemed to be winning the Unionists no new converts. The advocates of free trade could point to renewed growth and further falls in unemployment.

The Unionist wobble on Lords policy had become, by early November, a wobble on food taxes, too. Poor Balfour was now battered by both wings of his party. Balfour was told by a number of key supporters that he could not win unless he dumped food taxes. Even some whole hoggers agreed. J. L. Garvin, editor of the Unionist-backing *Observer*, suggested a new slogan: 'tax the foreigner but not your food.' Industrial protection would be kept but without the imperial element of the programme. But most tariff reformers were against compromise. And election agents warned of lost votes in rural seats if the agricultural tariffs were dropped.

Balfour had been a late convert to the tariffs cause, and having changed his position once, he had neither the stomach nor the credibility to change it twice. Fortunately for Balfour, an alternative and less immediately risky proposal now arose – to concede the Liberal call to put tariff reform to a referendum. Bonar Law, struggling in his Lancashire fight, put this idea to Balfour in a letter of 27 November. He argued that a referendum would 'destroy' the Liberal attack on tariffs. Lord Lansdowne made the same case. Balfour was now persuaded that he had found the silver bullet that would shoot the Liberal fox, without splitting his own supporters. He decided to use his Albert Hall speech on 29 November to announce the policy shift.

Not everyone agreed. Austen Chamberlain, leader of the tariff reformers, wrote urgently to warn about the change. His telegram reached London at 9 a.m. on the day of the speech. A detailed letter followed but did not arrive until 7 p.m., an hour before Balfour was due on stage. The letter contained a somewhat daft suggestion that the Unionists should offer to trade a referendum on tariffs for the Liberals promising to drop their attempt to axe the Lords' veto. It was too late and far too eccentric.

Meanwhile, poor Balfour was receiving more advice. This was from Bonar Law, who was now getting cold feet over his own idea. It might lose votes, he feared, and cause longer-term problems. His new proposal was as daft as Chamberlain's: offer the Liberals a referendum on tariff reform, in exchange for one on Home Rule. This was the land of short-term election gimmickry. The referenda were all being proposed as tactical devices. It would be hard to think of three issues – Home Rule, Lords reform and tariffs – that were less fit to be treated in this simplistic way.

Balfour ignored the late advice. He had found a fence to sit on, and he was not moving.

That evening, looking understandably rather tired, he arrived at the Albert Hall. A crowd of around 10,000 awaited him. He started and finished with Home Rule. But the meat in the sandwich was his new pledge. Days from the start of voting, and without further consultation with senior colleagues, he announced a pledge for a referendum on tariff reform. 'That's won the election!' an over-excited supporter shouted, and the audience 'rose to its feet in a tumult of cheering'.

On the whole, the Unionist press was supportive. Most whole hoggers bit their lips. The election agents awaited the public verdict. But the pledge was perhaps of more interest to the political cognoscenti than to the man in the street. It buttered few parsnips in Lancashire. But it irritated many of those in the Unionist Party who were most wedded to tariffs, who felt that Balfour could never be trusted again. And Liberals unsurprisingly claimed that the pledge showed: 'We have got them on the run.' Asquith mercilessly teased his opponent for 'a bewildering series of twists, gyrations and somersaults'.

The pledge had little impact on the election campaign, but in the longer term it would prove divisive and damaging in Unionist ranks. A referendum pledge made for short-term electoral gain was to have profound long-term consequences.

The public was essentially being asked to rerun the election of January. This is exactly what they did.

But turnout was down from 86.8 per cent in January to 81.6 per cent. In the January election, 6.2 million votes were cast. In December, this had fallen to just 4.8 million. Some have suggested this reflected voter apathy. It didn't. The decline is largely explained by the ageing of the electoral register (the new register was due on 1 January 1911) and the decline from 571 to 485 in the number of contested seats.

By holding the election on the old register, the government had denied the vote to up to 250,000 voters. In England, a stale resister saw turnout fall by 5.8 per cent. In Wales, it fell 6.7 per cent. In Scotland, which used a new register, the fall was just 3.4 per cent in fought seats. In December, there were ninety-three uncontested seats in England, Wales and Scotland, against just six in January. Indeed, 22 per cent of the entire electorate found themselves in uncontested seats.

In constituencies fought in both elections, the vote was only 350,000 down. And 80,000 of these voters had died. So, the 'real' decline in turnout, as a result of apathy or abstention, was quite small. Despite December 1910 being one of the wettest Decembers on record, turnout was impressive.

Because the campaign was considerably shorter than that of January, it cost less, too. In January, candidates spent in total £1,068,225 – the highest figure yet recorded. In December, that figure had fallen to £790,960. Leaflet printing costs were almost 30 per cent lower.

On 2 December, there were declarations in unopposed seats. And 3 December was the first key day, on which voters in sixty-nine parliamentary seats would go to the polls. The weather in London was miserable. Heavy rain limited crowds.

Few expected a big change in the balance of power. There had been ten contested by-elections in 1910 – four saw swings to the Liberals, five swung to the Unionists and the last was a Liberal–Labour clash. In late November, the Stock Exchange odds were 5/1 against a Unionist victory. A small gain of twenty seats for the government was expected – similar to the internal Liberal forecasts of mid-November.

The first results, from Lancashire, were surprisingly poor for the Liberals. In Ashton-under-Lyne, the Liberal member was toppled by a young and unknown Canadian Unionist – Max Aitken, who had only been in the constituency for five days. But the good news was the defeat of Bonar Law in North-West Manchester.

And when the London results came in, Liberal fears turned into joy and relief. London had turned away from Unionism, and it was now clear that Unionist chances of winning a majority were remote.

Across Britain, there were small swings to one party or the other. The Unionists were doing a little better in the north, the Liberals in

London and the Home Counties. In Wales and Scotland, there was little change. The *Daily Mail* described it as 'a very slight and infinitesimal oscillation of the pendulum'.

The two elections of 1910 had been highly partisan events which had entrenched and strengthened existing divisions. They polarised the parties and the country. The south, the rural counties, suburbia, market towns and the middle classes were consolidating around Unionism. The north, the industrial areas, the working classes, Scotland and Wales were increasingly loyal to the Liberal (and Labour) parties.

The Liberals and Unionists both started the campaign with 274 seats. The Liberals finished with 272. The Unionists with 271. No general election had ever resulted in a smaller change.

Labour increased its seats by just two, from forty to forty-two. It was still hugely dependent on co-operation with the Liberals. It failed to win a single three-way battle. Its victories occurred in two member seats in partnership with the Liberals (eleven), in straight fights with Unionists (twenty-six) or in unopposed seats (three). In only two seats did it win straight fights with a Liberal.

Party vote share hardly budged. The Unionist vote was 46.6 per cent, versus 46.8 per cent in January. The Liberal were up slightly from 43.5 per cent to 44.2 per cent. Labour had fallen back from 7 per cent to 6.4 per cent.

Never has a UK election appeared to make less difference. But the election of December 1910 was decisive in a way that its January carbon copy could not be.

The Liberals had won three general elections in a row, for the first time since the 1830s. The country had in one year faced two elections presented as referenda – on the Budget and the Lords. Both had been resolved in favour of the Liberals and their allies. Soon, the Lords would for ever lose its powers to veto and block the elected chamber.

In the Unionist Party, there was despair over the results and a bitter internal review of the referendum pledge on tariffs, which many whole hoggers now declared had lost them the election. One man was blamed for this – Balfour, who had led his party to three election defeats.

These outcomes meant that the elections of 1910 were seen at the time as of unusual significance. But few people recognised in December 1910 the momentous watershed moment that they were witnessing.

Up to 1910, elections were a straight fight between the Conservative/Unionist and Liberal parties, which shared 90 per cent of the vote. Labour was an electoral minnow. After 1910, Liberal splits and Labour's growth ushered in a new politics. Labour would never again poll under 20 per cent in a general election.

Up to 1910, elections were dominated by divisions over constitutional, religious and foreign policy matters. After 1910, the huge expansion of state spending, prompted by the First World War and by greater expectations of social protection, meant that elections were increasingly about economic and social policy. Before 1910, governments rarely allocated more than 10 per cent of national income to public spending. After 1910, the government share would fluctuate between 25 per cent and 60 per cent.

The elections of 1910 were fought on what was essentially an evolution of the nineteenth-century voting system. While the turnouts were high by both contemporary and modern standards, this was because around four in ten adult males were excluded from the electoral register. In 1910, there were no female voters and no female MPs. There was a property qualification for voting. Parliamentary seats were not all elected on the same day. These were the last elections to be fought under the increasingly discredited system of 1884–85 – which permitted at least half a million of the most affluent citizens to cast more than one vote.

The year of 1910 was to prove the end of a political era. It was the end of qualified democracy. The end of the politics of small government. The end of the Liberal–Unionist hegemony.

The new dividing lines between left and right, Liberal/Labour and Unionist would echo down the next 100 years. Social reform and progressive taxation versus incremental change. Devolution versus Westminster rule. International co-operation versus nationalism. Open borders versus trade barriers.

Many in the Liberal Party felt that these new political tides were running in their favour. But 1910 was to mark the end of Liberal electoral success.

The politics of the nineteenth century were finished. The parliament to come would usher in the politics of the twentieth.

David Laws was Liberal Democrat MP for Yeovil Constituency (2001–15) and was a minister in the 2010 coalition government.

23

1918

DAMIAN COLLINS

Dissolution: 25 November 1918
Polling day: 14 December 1918
Seats contested: 707
Total electorate / Total votes cast / Turnout: 21,392,322 (18,310,666 in contested seats) / 10,434,700 / 57.2 per cent
Candidates (total 1,623): Coalition government: Conservative – 445; National Liberal – 145; Coalition National Democratic – 18; Coalition Labour – 5. Non-coalition parties: Labour – 361; Liberal – 277; Sinn Féin – 102; Irish Parliamentary – 57; Independent NFDDSS – 30; Independent Labour – 29; National – 26; Independent Conservative – 17; Co-operative – 10; Independent Liberal – 8; Agriculturalist – 7; Labour Unionist – 3
Prime Minister on polling day: David Lloyd George
Main party leaders: National Liberal – David Lloyd George; Conservative – Bonar Law; Labour – William Adamson; Liberal – H. H. Asquith; Sinn Féin – Éamon de Valera; Irish Parliamentary – John Dillon; National – Henry Page Croft; Independent NFDDSS – James Hogge; Co-op – William Henry Watkins; Labour Unionist – Edward Carson; Agriculturalist – Edward Mials Nunneley

Party performance:

Party	Votes	Percentage share	Seats
Coalition government	5,529,441	53	520

Conservative (including Irish Unionist)	4,003,848 (257,314)	38.4 (25.3)	379 (22)
National Liberal	1,318,844	12.6	127
Coalition National Democratic	156,834	1.5	9
Coalition Labour	40,641	0.4	4
Non-coalition parties			
Labour	2,171,230	20.8	57
Liberal	1,355,398	13	36
Sinn Féin	476,087	46.9	73
Irish Parliamentary	220,837	21.7	7
Independent Labour	116,322	1.1	2
National	94,389	0.9	2
Independent NFDDSS	58,164	0.6	0
Co-operative	57,785	0.6	1
Independent Conservative	44,637	0.4	1
Labour Unionist	30,304	3	3
Independent Liberal	24,985	0.2	1
Agriculturalist	19,412	0.2	0

Result: Conservative–Liberal coalition majority of 238 seats

On 11 November 1918, bells tolled to mark the end of the Great War and an enormous crowd gathered around Westminster. Some having heard the news made their way early to Downing Street, others poured out into the streets from nearby offices as soon as it was confirmed. From a window the Prime Minister David Lloyd George declared that they'd won such 'a victory for freedom as the world has never seen. You have all had a share in it.' The *Evening Mail* reported that 'a rousing cheer, which will long be remembered by those who heard it, greeted the speech, and then the crowd ... surged into Whitehall to begin a day of rejoicing unequalled within the memory of man'.

At 3 p.m. Lloyd George arrived in Parliament to receive the judgement of his peers. Six months before when the German offensive threatened to break the Allied armies on the western front, he'd fought in the House of Commons for his political life. Now when Lloyd George entered the packed chamber he was, according to *The*

Times, greeted by 'loud cheers, members rising in their places and waving their order papers'. When the Prime Minister stood at the dispatch box, he memorably announced, 'This morning came to an end the cruellest and most terrible war that has ever scourged mankind. I hope we may say that thus, this fateful morning, came to an end all wars.' According to the press, he was 'the man who won the war', and even the Conservative Party leader Andrew Bonar Law believed he could be 'Prime Minister for life if he likes'.

Lloyd George held an immense position in the hearts and minds of the British people, just as Winston Churchill would do at the end of the Second World War in 1945. However, unlike Churchill, Lloyd George was able to secure a landslide victory in the general election of 1918. He believed it was a watershed moment for British politics in the twentieth century, reflecting the attitudes of a country changed forever by war, that politicians should work together across the old party divides in the national interest. Lloyd George was correct that the 1918 election would define the parameters for politics in the inter-war years but just not in the way that he hoped.

In November 1918, Lloyd George's hold on power was far more precarious that it seemed in his moment of triumph. Under a presidential system of government where the leader is directly elected by the people, he would have swept all before him. However, in a parliamentary democracy, like all Prime Ministers, he relied on the support of a majority of the MPs in the House of Commons. In his case, this was unusually complicated as Lloyd George was the first Prime Minister in modern times not to be the leader of a major political party. The Liberals, whom he'd supported since entering Parliament in 1890, were still led by Herbert Asquith, the man Lloyd George deposed as Prime Minister in December 1916. Then, as Secretary of State for War, Lloyd George believed that Britain was losing the war and without more dynamic leadership would be defeated. At that moment, Britain's allies France and Russia were exhausted and the Americans were yet to enter the conflict. In the Atlantic, German U-boat submarine attacks on British shipping threatened to starve the nation of essential resources. On the western front, British forces sustained heavy causalities in the Battle of the Somme but had been unable to break through against the Germans.

Asquith's style of leadership was seen as too laid back for the stresses of war time. He presided at Cabinet like a judge in a court room, considering the cases brought by others but not leading the debate himself. No minutes were taken of meetings and important decisions were allowed to drift. The contrast between Asquith and Lloyd George was summed by the *Daily Mail* as 'wait and see' versus 'do it now'. With the support of Bonar Law, leading Unionist politicians like Sir Edward Carson and Lord Northcliffe, the greatest of the press barons who owned both *The Times* and the *Daily Mail*, Lloyd George gave Asquith an ultimatum. He could either resign as Prime Minister or hand over control of the war effort to a small committee that Lloyd George would lead. Asquith chose to relinquish his office, wrongly believing that no alternative government could be formed, but he remained leader of a rump Liberal Party. Lloyd George became Prime Minister with the support of only 126 MPs from his own party and was forced to rely on old rivals and opponents in the Conservative and Labour parties to sustain a majority in the House of Commons.

Lloyd George revolutionised the government, creating a small Cabinet of five members supported by the first Downing Street secretariat of experts and officials, to co-ordinate the direction of the war effort. Under his leadership, the naval convoy system was adopted to protect merchant shipping, conscription into the armed forces was extended and, against the wishes of the British generals, unified command for the Allied armies was established on the western front under the French General Ferdinand Foch. In 1918, the superiority of British war equipment and supplies, as a consequence of decisions made by Lloyd George when he established the Ministry of Munitions in 1915, helped it to withstand the great German offensive that spring, and a series of crushing British victories in August turned the tide in favour of the Allies. Shortly before the war ended, Lloyd George told his friend, the newspaper proprietor George Riddell:

Bonar Law said to me, 'Do you want to go down to history as the greatest of all Englishmen.' I replied, well, I don't know that I do ... But tell me your prescription! Do you mean retire into private life now that the war has been won? Bonar Law said, 'Yes!' He is right.

Nevertheless, three days after the Armistice was proclaimed, the government announced that Parliament would be dissolved on 25 November for a general election, the first for eight years, which would be held on 14 December.

This was not a snap decision but one that had been long in the planning. On 6 February that year, new legislation which would nearly triple the size of the electorate had come into effect. Now all men over the age of twenty-one would have the vote, regardless of income or ownership of property. For the first time women over the age of thirty would be enfranchised and they would account for nearly 40 per cent of the electorate. Lloyd George has always supported votes for women, and this decision delivered on the promise he'd made to the leading suffragette Christabel Pankhurst. In 1915, she'd agreed to support the call for women to work in factories for military production, on the understanding that the vote would come after the war. The new voter registers took effect from 1 October, making an election under the new franchise possible from that date. In the summer of 1918, in anticipation of this reform and with the situation on the western front improving, Lloyd George brought together his political advisers to start planning for an autumn general election, whether or not the war had been won.

The finances for the campaign were being organised by Lloyd George's political fixer, William 'Bronco Bill' Sutherland. On 15 August, Riddell met with Sutherland at the Carlton Club in Pall Mall, where he found him

> an amusing cynical dog. He was engaged as usual in supping and wining, being entertained to dinner by a Tory magnate who is coming over to LG. A few days ago Sutherland dined with Lord Charles Beresford, who has £100,000 for party purposes and proposes to utilise it for LG's campaign. Sutherland says they want cash. I gave him some

likely names, including Sir Howard Spicer, who came to me the other night to say that he and nineteen friends of his can put up £250,000. The Asquithians are busy hunting for cash and the Tories are doing the same, so not withstanding all the pious protestations against the party system, it is still in reality as strongly entrenched as before.

The Cabinet Secretary, Maurice Hankey, also believed that the only reason Lloyd George had made the press baron Lord Beaverbrook a government minister was 'in order to induce him to finance the new party machine, which he tells me he is about to found. A shady business.'

The key question for Lloyd George was whether to make an appeal to the nation, seeking the election of candidates standing on his personal manifesto, or for the wartime coalition to stand together with the Lloyd George Liberals and the Conservatives forming an electoral pact. His close adviser Thomas Jones believed that Lloyd George 'underrated his unique power to sway the country, of which his wife and some of his secretaries sought in vain to convince him: he could not ignore the mechanics of party warfare, he had to provide a programme and to endorse candidates'. So, by the summer of 1918, he'd come to the conclusion that the best prospect for success was to seek the re-election of the coalition government with the broadest possible base of support. His plan, though, was that this would be an interim step towards the fusing of the coalition Liberals into a new centre party, with moderate Conservative and Labour MPs. Such a combination would reflect Lloyd George's own beliefs which did not fit neatly into the traditions of any one party. He was a Liberal who'd championed illiberal methods, like conscription, in order to win the war. Lloyd George had been a pioneer of the welfare state, introducing state pensions and national insurance when he was Chancellor of the Exchequer, but he was not a socialist and certainly had no sympathy for the leading Labour Party pacifists like Ramsay MacDonald. As he would tell Riddell, Lloyd George thought of himself

> incongruous as it may appear, as a Nationalist-Socialist. I was and am

a strong believer in nationality, and I believe in the intervention of the State to secure that everyone has a fair chance and that there is no unnecessary want and poverty ... Every member of the community who behaves properly and does his best should be secured a fair chance.

Bonar Law's political secretary J. C. C. Davidson 'was convinced' from the early days of the wartime coalition 'that Ll.G had made up his mind that somehow or other he would create a united Centre Party ... of which he would be the head'. He even thought that should Bonar Law choose to retire, Lloyd George had

> set himself out to lead the Tory Party, and integrate his Liberals into the government to win the war, and convert the non-party into a party which would have been a national party after the war. That might have had an appeal to a Conservative, because there is one repetitive sentence which you will find in all Conservative leaders' speeches, namely that the Conservative Party is not a party of factions; it is a national party ... Lloyd George was clever enough to make that appeal in order to get the leadership of the Tory Party.

Yet Lloyd George was understandably cautious about placing his future prospects in the hands of a Conservative Party that had before the war been his principal opponent. In August 1917, Geoffrey Dawson, editor of *The Times*, wrote in his diary after meeting with Lloyd George:

> He didn't want either to relapse into the old Liberal Party ... or to be left entirely with the old Unionists. He kept recurring to the fate of [Joseph] Chamberlain, who (according to LG) had placed himself in a false position when he joined the Conservatives and abandoned his old nonconformist backing.

In early November 1918, Lloyd George and Bonar Law agreed the text of a letter which would be the basis of their co-operation in a future government. This set out the need for a 'fresh Parliament' where candidates could be returned to support the coalition government 'not only to prosecute the War to its final end and negotiate the peace, but to deal with the problems of reconstruction which must immediately arise directly an armistice is signed'. The commitment was made to 'the imperative need for improving the physical conditions of the citizens of this country through better housing, better wages, and better working conditions', without going into details as to how this would be funded. On Home Rule for Ireland, there was a commitment not to support any 'settlement which would involve the forcible coercion of Ulster'. It was also recognised that any future decision 'must be postponed until the condition of Ireland make it possible'. Again, what that would mean in practice was open to wide interpretation. A compromise was also reached on the single issue that had caused the greatest division in the previous decades between the Liberals and the Conservatives, that of free trade. Lloyd George agreed that protectionist measures could be introduced to protect vital industries that were essential for the war effort. In return, Bonar Law agreed that there would be no new taxes or tariffs on food. Overall, the Conservatives believed the continued political pact with Lloyd George would help ensure support from working people, and returning soldiers, under the new expanded franchise. Together they also represented a united front against what was seen as the emerging threat in European politics, that of revolutionary socialism.

On 12 November, at a private meeting of the coalition Liberal MPs at Downing Street, Lloyd George challenged them:

> Are we to lapse back into the old national rivalries and animosities and competitive armaments, or are we to initiate the reign on earth of the Prince of Peace? ... We must not allow any sense of revenge, any spirit of greed, any grasping desire to override the fundamental principles of righteousness ... I was reared in Liberalism ... I am too old to change. I cannot leave Liberalism ... Now is the great opportunity of Liberalism! Let it rise to it! Don't let it sulk. If there are personal differences, in God's name what do they count compared with the vast issues and problems before us? Let us help to regenerate the people, the great

people who have done more to save the world in this great crisis than any other nation.

Overtures were also made to Asquith to join the coalition government as Lord Chancellor, an offer that had also been made in 1917. Once again it was rejected, and Lloyd George believed Asquith was 'too proud' to serve in government under him. Instead, he and his supporters would stand for election as independent Liberals. On 14 November, the Labour Party also voted to leave the wartime coalition and to stand as an opposition party at the general election. As the meeting closed, George Bernard Shaw famously remarked, 'Go back to Lloyd George and say, "Nothing doing."' It was an important step for Labour as they would from that moment work to establish themselves as a national party of government, rather than seek to influence policy as a junior partner in a progressive alliance. Their manifesto, distinct from that of their former coalition partners, would call for the permanent nationalisation of the coal mines, shipping and railways.

The coalition Liberal and Conservative candidates each received a letter of endorsement from Lloyd George and Bonar Law, along with a guarantee that neither party would challenge the other's representatives in their constituencies. Asquith derisively referred to this as a process where 'seats are bartered and candidates ticketed and political coupons distributed'. For this reason, the 1918 campaign is often referred to as the 'coupon' election. However, the distribution of coupons greatly favoured the Conservatives, who had 364 candidates compared to 159 for the coalition Liberals.

In public, the election campaign was a triumphal procession for Lloyd George, starting in Wolverhampton on Saturday 23 November, where he was given the freedom of the borough and in a famous speech at the Grand Theatre told his audience, 'What is our task? To make Britain a fit country for heroes to live in (cheers). There is no time to lose. I want us to take advantage of this new spirit. Don't let us waste this victory merely in ringing joy bells.' However, in the background, there was a great dispute raging between Lloyd George and Lord Northcliffe over the position the government would adopt in the peace negotiations with Germany. At a meeting at 10 Downing Street shortly after the Armistice, Lloyd George claimed that Northcliffe insisted on being among official delegates from the British government to attend the Paris Peace Conference. The Prime Minister also informed him that George Riddell would be in charge of news and information during the negotiations. The meeting, according to Lloyd George, left Northcliffe 'visibly astonished and upset at my declining to accede to his request', and ended with him telling the great press baron to 'Go to Hell.' The two men never met again. When the election was announced on 14 November, Northcliffe arrived at the offices of *The Times* where, according to Dawson's diary, he told his editors that 'he'd served notice on LG that he could no longer support him'. Of his meeting with Northcliffe, Lloyd George would later tell Tom Clarke, the news editor of the *Daily Mail*:

> I broke with Northcliffe. I refused absolutely to have him at the Peace Conference. I put up with him for four years. The break had to come – when he wanted to dictate to me. As Prime Minister I could not have it. Northcliffe thought he could run the country. I could not allow that.

The Times would adopt a more critical tone of Lloyd George and the coalition campaign, based on Northcliffe's concern that the coupon system would give too much authority to the 'old gang' Conservative politicians. On 4 December, the paper declared: 'Nobody, we imagine, has any doubt that Mr Lloyd George would have been wiser if he had frankly gone to the country on his own great war record and his own views on social reform without any attempt at securing pledges or making bargains over candidates.' *The Times* also observed that the Conservative Party 'is anxious for a true Coalition, and is bent on doing all it can to prevent the revival of party politics. It has seen a definite reassertion of the old party position by the Asquith Liberals, and frankly it does not like the spectacle.' Although, it would certainly seem that they gave as good as they got. The former Home Secretary, John Simon, complained that, during the election,

'Liberal candidates, who regarded Asquith as their leader, were effectively proscribed, as though they had not supported the prosecution of the war.' Asquith himself recalled in his memoirs that 'as I drove round the voting stations in Fife on the polling day, I saw, amongst other specimens of the electioneering appeals of my Conservative opponent, huge placards with the inscription "Asquith nearly lost you the War. Are you going to let him spoil the Peace?"'

Despite Lloyd George's hope when he addressed the coalition Liberal MPs in Downing Street on 12 November that Britain should avoid imposing a peace motivated by 'revenge' against Germany, the mood in the country was that they must be made to pay. Although personal relations had broken down between the two men, on 7 December Northcliffe sent the Prime Minister a telegram stating:

> The public are expecting you to say definitely [the] amount of cash we are to get from Germany. They are very dissatisfied with [the phrase] 'limit of her capacity' which [may] mean anything or nothing. They are aware France has an amount. I am apprehensive of serious trouble in the country on the matter.

Two days later, the First Lord of the Admiralty Eric Geddes, a coalition Liberal who was close to Lloyd George, told an election audience in Cambridge that as far as extracting reparations from Germany was concerned, 'I will squeeze until you can hear the pips squeak.' On 11 December, Lloyd George gave a speech in Bristol where he asked rhetorically about the costs of the war: 'Who is to foot the bill?' to which someone in the crowd responded 'Germany' and another 'in full'. The Prime Minister replied, 'Certainly in full, if they have got it.' Again, Lloyd George's statement could have meant everything or nothing, but the inference was reported as a commitment to make Germany pay. In the same speech, he also suggested that the government-appointed committee of experts had calculated that the total cost of the war to the Allies had been £24 billion.

In 1918, for the first time in a British general election, all the votes were cast on the same day, 14 December. However, they weren't counted until 28 December, to allow time for the ballots of soldiers serving overseas to be returned. That evening King George V wrote in his diary: 'The results of the General Election are coming in fast. Lloyd George & his coalition party have got a great majority.' In total, 379 Conservatives and 127 Lloyd George Liberals were elected, giving them a total of 506 MPs out of a House of Commons of 707 seats. In reality, their advantage within the parliament was even greater as the old Irish Parliamentary Party had been reduced to just seven members, their places having been taken by the seventy-three MPs elected for the republican party Sinn Féin, who refused to take their seats and swear allegiance to the king. These also included Constance Markievicz, the first woman to be elected to the House of Commons. Herbert Asquith was defeated in his constituency and in total only thirty-six of his Liberals were returned. For the first time, the Labour Party would lead the official opposition with fifty-nine MPs, an increase of fifteen.

Lloyd George had the mandate he needed to negotiate the peace and begin the task of reconstructing Britain after the war. However, the coupon election had made the Conservatives the dominant party in the House of Commons. In the absence of the Sinn Féin members, on their own they had a majority of 124 over all of the other parties combined. At any moment they could force Lloyd George and his coalition Liberals out of power and govern by themselves. There was no question that the Prime Minister's personal standing in the eyes of the nation had never been greater, but in his moment of electoral triumph, he had also placed his fate in the hands of his rivals. He would survive for only as long as they thought they needed him to win.

Sinn Féin's success in Ireland marked a permanent change in the politics of that island following the proclamation of the Irish Republic during the Easter Rising in 1916. Now, Home Rule was not to be achieved through pressure in Westminster but by the assertion of their claim in Ireland. Sinn Féin established a revolutionary parliament in Dublin, the Dáil Éireann, in January 1919, and so began a war of independence, which would end in 1921 with the signing of the treaty which established the Irish Free State.

For Lloyd George, the immediate aftermath of the 1918 election was dominated by the Paris peace negotiations and the signing of the Treaty of Versailles on 28 June 1919. However, that summer he again turned his attention towards the creation of a new national party. With the encouragement of the Prime Minister, a parliamentary body called the Centre Coalition Group was created by Winston Churchill, the War Secretary, and Lord Birkenhead, the Lord Chancellor, advocating for this reform. At a dinner in London in July, Churchill told the group that 'party organisation must in these serious times be definitely subordinated to national spirit, national interests, and national organisation. At the present time it would be a folly and a crime to revert to the ordinary party basis. That would be a crazy game to play.' In December that year, Lloyd George would tell a dinner at the Manchester Reform Club, to mark his third anniversary as Prime Minister:

> What was the alternative to the Coalition ... The alternative was confusion. If there was a dissolution, was there anyone who would pretend that there was a single party which could get a majority. There was no reason why the best elements of the Liberal and Unionist parties should not work together where there was ground for agreement.

In March 1920, Lloyd George would put the question of closer co-operation with the Conservatives to the coalition Liberals but was rebuffed. The Conservative leaders would have accepted the proposal at that time in return for the merger of Lloyd George's political fund with their own resources. However, the moment was lost, and there began growing opposition to the coalition from the next generation of Conservative leaders, men like Stanley Baldwin, Neville Chamberlain and Samuel Hoare. Without the fusion of the coalition parties, the 1918 general election had merely established the Conservative Party as the dominant political force in the land. The Liberals were divided and after Lloyd George resigned in 1922, following the withdrawal of Conservative support from the coalition, they would never lead a government again. From 1918 until 1945, the Conservative

Party would be in government either on their own or in coalition for all but three years.

Damian Collins OBE MP is the Member of Parliament for Folkestone and Hythe. He is the author of a new biography of David Lloyd George, *Rivals in the Storm: How Lloyd George seized power, won the war and lost his government*.

24

1922

JACK BROWN

Dissolution: 26 October 1922
Polling day: 15 November 1922
Seats contested: 615
Total electorate / Total votes cast / Turnout: 20,874,456 (18,927,762 in contested seats) / 13,748,300 / 73 per cent
Candidates (total 1,441): Conservative – 482; Labour – 414; Liberal – 334; National Liberal – 151; Independent Conservative – 20; Agriculturalist – 4; Communist – 4; Independent Labour – 4; Nationalist – 4; Constitutionalist – 1; Scottish Prohibition – 1
Prime Minister on polling day: Bonar Law
Main party leaders: Conservative – Bonar Law; Labour – J. R. Clynes; Liberal – H. H. Asquith; National Liberal – David Lloyd George; Nationalist – Joseph Devlin; Communist – Albert Inkpin; Agriculturalist – Harry German; Scottish Prohibition – Edwin Scrymgeour

Party performance:

Party	Votes	Percentage share	Seats
Conservative (including UUP)	5,294,465 (107,972)	38.5 (51.9)	344 (11)
Labour	4,076,665	29.7	142
Liberal	2,601,486	18.9	62
National Liberal	1,355,366	9.9	53
Independent Conservative	116,861	0.9	3
Nationalist	90,053	43.3	2
Communist	30,684	0.2	1

Agriculturalist	21,510	0.2	0
Independent Labour	18,419	0.1	1
Constitutionalist	16,662	0.1	1
Scottish Prohibition	16,289	0.1	1

Result: Conservative majority of seventy-four seats

All elections are of interest, but some are more interesting than others. The general election of 1922 was simultaneously one of the dullest and the most significant of the modern era.

Even the dullness was intriguing. The election took place in a potentially radical moment. Overseas, the Russian Revolution raged on, radiating radical energy and generating fear of similar uprisings elsewhere. At home, a difficult economic situation was colliding with rising working-class power, increasing trade unionism and the Labour Party emerging as an electoral force in British politics. Yet much of the election's conduct and its overall result were both firmly conservative, and the eventual winner led a campaign that pledged to do little or nothing much at all if elected.

It was also a particularly impactful election, and the reasons for this are threefold. Firstly, it was the first properly contested election under the newly expanded franchise established in the aftermath of the First World War. While suffrage was not yet universal, voting expanded from an elite to a mass activity. It can therefore be argued to be the first proper election of the modern era. Secondly, it was brought about by the dissolution of the wartime coalition government, which had outlasted the conflict itself. In this sense, it marked the end of the extended wartime era and the transition into peacetime.

And thirdly, it was significant in its consequences. The 1922 election saw the political party system in the United Kingdom realign, and political giants emerge and crumble. The once-mighty Liberal leader David Lloyd George's grip on power finally collapsed and the Liberal Party split into two competing factions. The Liberals were then usurped by a still relatively young Labour Party as the main party of opposition.

In one sense, the 1922 election result would prove short-lived, with the Prime Minister it elected dying within a year of polling day, and another election called the following year, producing a very different result. But in the longer term, its impact was long-lasting, heralding the stuttered beginning of a new era of Conservative-dominated electoral politics in Britain.

The context to the 1922 general election is important. The previous election of 1918 took place in the immediate aftermath of the First World War. It was the first such election for eight years. A Liberal government first elected in 1910 had become a wartime coalition under the leadership of H. H. Asquith in 1915. David Lloyd George seized control of the coalition in December 1916 and managed to hold it together for the long-overdue post-war election of 1918, providing letters of endorsement (or 'the coupon') to coalition-friendly Liberal and Conservative candidates.

This election was significantly influenced by the war. The British electorate had shot up from 7.7 million in 1910 to 21.3 million in 1918, with over three-quarters of voters never having registered their votes before. The Representation of the People Act of 1918 created almost universal male suffrage and for the first time gave some women over the age of thirty the right to vote in parliamentary elections, although it is important to note that universal adult suffrage would not arrive until 1928.

But the 'coupon' meant that this dramatically expanded new franchise was asked in 1918 to choose between candidates aligned to the dynamic Lloyd George's war-winning coalition and their opponents, rather than from a full menu of political options. The collapse of the coalition in 1922, therefore, arguably gave this recently expanded electorate a real choice for the first time. In addition, 1922 was the first election not to include constituencies in Southern Ireland, following the signing of the Anglo-Irish Treaty in December 1921, reducing the number of seats by nearly 100. A case can therefore be made that the 1922 election was the first proper test of Britain's new post-war democracy.

The election took place in the context of rising unemployment. A post-war boom had proved short lived, and the nation's economic prospects were looking increasingly grim, with war debt high and intense debate over Germany's ability to pay reparations. This placed government spending under great pressure. In 1921, newspaper proprietor Lord Rothermere established the Anti-Waste League. The league attacked what it perceived as wasteful government spending and excessive levels of income tax, having some success in a series of by-elections that year. In response, Lloyd George appointed a commission under Sir Eric Geddes to explore savings in national expenditure. This led to the famous 'Geddes Axe', a package of drastic spending cuts decided by the Cabinet in early 1922 in response to the commission's report.

In addition, the First World War had seen the state mobilised to a previously unprecedented extent. Trade union membership had been actively encouraged by the wartime government to avoid wildcat strikes, and membership doubled between 1914 and 1920. Strikes followed the war in 1919, 1920 and 1921. The coalition government had calmed potentially revolutionary moments in the immediate aftermath of the war, and by 1921 the perceived threat of communism was reducing at home and the argument for coalition was weakening. But the economic situation remained highly challenging, and both the Conservative and Liberal parties still feared the electoral threat represented by the rising Labour Party.

Overseas events were equally concerning. The previous administration had nearly taken a war-weary nation back into conflict in what was then referred to as the 'Near East', with Prime Minister Lloyd George bringing the nation close to war with Turkey in the 'Chanak Crisis'. While this crisis was avoided, it added to growing discontent with the Prime Minister's peacetime leadership. Andrew Bonar Law, leader of the Conservative Party until March 1921 when he had been forced to step down due to ill health, attacked the government's Chanak policy in the press, asserting that 'we cannot alone act as the policeman of the world'.

Facing difficulties both at home and abroad, the coalition began to fragment.

The collapse of the coalition was formally brought about at a famous meeting of Conservative MPs at the Carlton Club in London on 19 October. The meeting was called by Conservative leader Austen Chamberlain, Bonar Law's successor and a pro-coalitionist. Chamberlain had proposed to fight the next election under the coalition banner, but there was clear discontent emerging within his party. He hoped the Carlton Club meeting could assuage these sentiments. Chamberlain planned to offer anti-coalition Conservatives the possibility of producing a separate manifesto from the Liberals, and he hoped that an expected Labour victory in the Newport by-election of 18 October would bolster his arguments for coalition as the best means of defeating socialism. However, an Independent Conservative won in Newport, beating Labour and Liberal candidates and strengthening the Conservative case for acting outside of coalition.

The Conservatives had become increasingly divided over the quality of Lloyd George's leadership. Some began to believe that the party's electoral prospects were in fact brighter outside of coalition. Figures such as Andrew Bonar Law and future leader Stanley Baldwin emerged as leading anti-coalition voices. The Carlton Club meeting saw Baldwin respond to praise of Lloyd George as 'a dynamic force' with the observation that 'a dynamic force is a terrible thing; it may crush you, but it is not necessarily right'. Bonar Law then delivered a devastating if unspectacular speech against Chamberlain's policy. Chamberlain was decisively defeated. He resigned the Conservative leadership, and Lloyd George immediately resigned as Prime Minister, triggering the election.

Contrary to popular myth, the 1922 committee of Conservative backbenchers is not named after this meeting or decision. Rather, the committee came about in the aftermath of the general election itself.

The events of the Carlton Club did, however, mean that Chamberlain's replacement as Conservative leader Bonar Law was unable to draw on the full range of talents across his party when appointing his Cabinet. Around forty MPs remained pro-coalitionists and would not serve. The shadow of the coalition, therefore, loomed over the 1922 election, complicating the party system and leading to huge local and individual variation across the country.

The election saw pro-coalition and anti-coalition Conservatives, Lloyd George-supporting 'National Liberals' and Asquithian 'Liberals' all take on the Labour Party, alongside the usual range of independents, smaller and single-issue parties. In some parts of the country, the coalition endured in practice regardless of national policy, with National Liberal and Conservative candidates agreeing not to run against one another to avoid splitting the anti-Labour vote. In some constituencies, co-operation between Lloyd Georgian and Asquithian Liberals endured. Elsewhere, almost limitless numbers of local variations and particular circumstances made for a disjointed if intriguing election.

Bonar Law became leader of the Conservative Party, and therefore Prime Minister, on 23 October 1922. Parliament was dissolved by 26 October. A *Times* leader celebrated 'A Welcome Dissolution', attacking the coalition's 'miserable record of disappointment and failure' and opining that 'nothing became it so much as its ending'. A general election was fixed for 15 November, with post-war elections now taking place on a single day nationally rather than being staggered across multiple days.

Andrew Bonar Law was a significant political figure in the history of the Conservative Party, but his personal style was restrained and his 1922 policy platform pledged inaction and non-intervention wherever possible. His premiership was not to be a radical one. One probably apocryphal anecdote describes Liberal Leader Asquith remarking at Bonar Law's funeral at Westminster Abbey that they were burying the Unknown Prime Minister next to the Unknown Soldier. Yet Bonar Law's actively 'negative' campaign message was consistent, simple and effective.

Launching his election campaign on 27 October in his home seat in Glasgow, the Prime Minister asserted that 'the crying need of the nation is tranquillity and stability at home and abroad'. Overseas, this meant honouring Britain's treaties and commitments to its allies and its empire but no more. At home, it meant government intervening and legislating as little as possible, enabling free enterprise to help the struggling British economy recover. Public expenditure needed to be lowered, alongside some limited emergency measures to mitigate unemployment, and an imperial conference was considered as a method of devising a way to improve trade.

Bonar Law's platform also featured an economy drive within government, including dramatically scaling back the size of the Cabinet Secretariat. This machinery of government innovation had been introduced during the First World War, alongside the role of Cabinet Secretary itself, to help Lloyd George manage the challenge of total war. Latterly, it had come to be seen as an instrument of an overmighty Prime Minister. Bonar Law also pledged to abolish the Ministry of Pensions (but not its function) to save money. The Prime Minister also promised not to reopen the Irish question and to hold an election before any new food taxes were introduced, thus attempting to kill the two most potentially divisive issues for the Conservatives and provide further stability. In the event, the latter pledge would eventually lead to another general election being called the following year, by Bonar Law's successor.

If Bonar Law's campaign promised stability for the nation, it was also stable and consistent in its delivery. His opening address of the campaign accepted that while his manifesto could be labelled 'purely negative ... it is intended to be so. My strongest belief is that at this moment what the country needs ... is to leave the people of this country unhampered by a Government to their own initiative, and let them work out their salvation in that way.' By his final pre-election address, back in Glasgow on 14 November, the Prime Minister summarised his 'main appeal' to the country as ensuring that it 'was to be free from interference from harassing legislation, that it should be left to its own energy and its own initiative to struggle through the difficult morass in which they were placed'. *The Times* recorded that this rather bland statement of non-intervention was cheered vociferously by the crowd – a perhaps surprising foreshadowing of things to come.

Former Prime Minister David Lloyd George's 'National Liberals' offered little substantial difference from the Conservatives in terms of policy. Lloyd George had been a dynamic and effective wartime leader and his strong personality was crucial to sustaining the coalition after the war. Once the Conservatives collapsed the coalition, he proclaimed his National Liberals the party of the 'middle course' between Conservative and Labour extremes. But differences with his former coalition partners were primarily about personality, with Lloyd George's personal dynamism contrasted with Bonar Law's calm non-interventionism. Bonar Law's opening address in the election campaign praised Lloyd George's abilities as a war leader but claimed that 'for different diseases, different specialists are wanted ... We have differences in temperament.' These differences in temperament were famously described by Violet Bonham Carter, Asquith's daughter, as being 'asked to choose between one man [Bonar Law] suffering from sleeping sickness and another suffering from St Vitus's Dance [Lloyd George].'

In terms of domestic policy, a slightly more interventionist tone was struck: a programme of 'stern economy' was to be balanced by industrial co-operation and 'generous encouragement of agriculture'. But the similarity between the National Liberal and Conservative policy platforms was perhaps best demonstrated when discussing foreign policy. Launching his electoral programme on 26 October, the former Prime Minister contrasted Bonar Law's 'tranquillity' with what he was calling 'peace', a word Lloyd George felt less pretentious: 'I should not have thought it was worth breaking up a great national combination [the coalition] for the sake of using a more euphonious word to describe exactly the same thing.' However, the difference was to be found in personality: Lloyd George claimed that the 'will for peace' also required the 'skill for peace', something that he was uniquely talented in.

Asquith's Liberals presented a manifesto arguably more distinctly Liberal and closer to that of the Labour Party. There were points of consensus: like both the Conservatives and the National Liberals, Asquith's position was broadly pro-League of Nations, advocating for swift reparations for the war and stating the need for drastic economies in public spending. He endorsed assistance for the unemployed and called for co-operation between capital and labour. He underlined the traditional Liberal commitment to 'unqualified free trade' but also demanded that government commit to essential social services and called for an end to British military adventures abroad.

However, more radically, Asquith's Liberals advocated for reform of the land system (including a land value tax), reform of the licensing system, the establishment of total political and legal equality between the sexes and the introduction of proportional representation. Asquith acknowledged that the Labour Party had 'borrowed' some of their policies but highlighted a fundamental difference over the extent of state ownership and intervention.

J. R. Clynes was widely seen as a relatively moderate leader of the Labour Party, and the Labour manifesto had moderate elements. It too expressed support for the League of Nations, an acceptance of the Irish Free State and the importance of paying down the national debt. However, there was much that distinguished Labour's platform from the rest. Labour's proposed methods for raising the funds were seen as radical at the time. The notion of a 'capital levy' caused especial controversy. A land value tax and an increase in death duties were also proposed, alongside reductions of income tax for the lowest paid. At home, mining and the railways were to be nationalised, 'work or maintenance' promised to the unemployed, agriculture reorganised in favour of workers over landlords, and rates equalised between poorer and richer districts. Overseas, Labour proposed independence for Egypt and self-governance for India.

On 11 November, *The Times* summarised the positions of the main parties so far:

> Socialism, as represented by such items in the Labour policy as the capital levy and nationalisation of mines and railways, is the only clear-cut issue ... What the electors who reject Socialism are called upon to do is choose the men and the parties best fitted to pursue and make a success of a more or less common policy.

The national campaign was an exhausting endeavour. Party leaders and senior figures across all parties travelled the country relentlessly for the duration of the three-week campaign, regularly addressing audiences of several thousand. Print media dominated the era, with major political speeches reproduced in full for wider public consumption the following day. A great number of words in these speeches were dedicated to responding to the previous night's attacks from the opposition, regardless of the location. Sore throats and colds were rife as the campaign progressed. By 11 November, *The Times* was reporting that Bonar Law had been forced to cancel engagements in Manchester and Sheffield, suffering from a severe cold. Lloyd George was also resting that day, following medical advice. Elsewhere, Asquith missed a meeting, rushing between Paisley and across parts of England.

Polling day for the 1922 general election took place the day after the birth of the British Broadcasting Corporation. The corporation's first news and weather broadcast took place on 14 November, with chairman Sir William Noble promising news, concerts and perhaps 'speeches written by popular people' to come in future broadcasts. However, the BBC was concerned to be seen as providing a complementary rather than competing function to existing media. The chairman went as far as to state that even if the BBC had begun its operations two weeks prior to the election, it would not have broadcast major election speeches, as 'that would have been usurping the legitimate functions of the Press. We do not want to do that.' On 30 October, the Prime Minister's election address had been broadcast on the wireless across the United States and Canada but not at home. The role of radio, and later television, in British election campaigns was just around the corner but not yet clear in 1922.

The Carlton Club meeting may have formally ended the coalition, but the degree to which Conservative–National Liberal co-operation might endure beyond it was initially uncertain. As early as 20 March, *The Times* opined that 'the stoniest heart must feel a twinge of pity for the plight of the Coalition Liberals. They seem destined to become the waifs and strays of politics. No Barnardo Home offers them unconditional refuge or training for emigration.' This proved an astute observation.

Lloyd George initially attacked those Conservatives who collapsed the coalition as unpatriotic opportunists seeking credit for the government's successes. Equally, the decision of the Asquithian Liberals to operate independently was 'a folly, but it is their folly'. But despite all this, he claimed to hold no 'personal resentments'; while his party would fight 'diehard' Conservatives, they would be open to co-operation with others.

Unsurprisingly, this confrontational style did not win many allies. By 31 October, *The Times* reported that Lloyd George was losing what was a 'battle of life and death' for his party. A meeting the previous day, organised by pro-coalition former Conservative leader and Prime Minister Lord Balfour, had revealed only mutual frustration and resulted in no electoral pact. Conservative Party chairman Sir George Younger wrote to all Conservative constituency associations effectively granting a 'charter of freedom' to co-operate or otherwise with National Liberals locally as they saw fit. This killed hope of a national policy of co-operation between the parties.

Elsewhere, Liberal support was drifting to Asquith in Manchester, Leeds and parts of Scotland, and local Conservative associations had decided to oppose Lloyd George's candidates in a quarter of all seats they were contesting so far. The National Liberals were by then running around 160 candidates nationally. Lloyd George claimed to have a similar number in 'reserve', which he threatened to call to action should the Conservatives not stand down. The Asquithian Liberals were by then running twice as many candidates; the Conservatives nearly three times as many. By 1 November, Lloyd George was said to be having second thoughts about his threat. While there was some local co-operation between National Liberal and Conservative associations, as in Winston Churchill's seat in Dundee, many National Liberals went on to become political orphans, as predicted.

Elsewhere, Labour's 'socialist' manifesto caused great controversy throughout the campaign. Its commitment to a capital levy especially united the party's opponents against it. At the start of November, former coalition Chancellor of the Exchequer and Conservative Sir Robert Horne called for moderates to co-operate against Labour 'who held views which were subversive to all the great principles upon which the country's prosperity had been built up'. Clynes wrote to *The Times* to clarify that Labour was 'not wedded to the idea of a levy on capital' but simply committed to the essential work of balancing the nation's books. The following day, it was reported that Labour candidates across the country appeared to have been instructed to discuss the policy with more ambiguity – although the manifesto commitment was not dropped.

On 6 November, Bonar Law attacked the idea: 'I condemn it utterly, not because it is necessarily confiscation, but because in the present condition of this country it is absolutely mad.' Another Clynes letter to *The Times*, observing that Bonar Law had expressed support for a capital levy during wartime, did not stop the attacks. On 10 November, Lloyd George branded Labour's policies anti-trade; on 13 November, Chancellor of the Exchequer and future Conservative leader Stanley Baldwin attacked Labour as dominated by intellectuals: 'men of no practical experience, not one of whom probably possessed the qualification for running a pawnshop'. On 15 November, Lloyd George compared the capital levy to the outdated medical practice of 'bleeding' a sick patient. The country was short on capital as it was, the former Prime Minister claimed, and 'even the doctors never bled a patient who was suffering from anaemia, yet that was what the Labour Party proposed. It was the stupidest programme ever put before the electorate.' However, this 'stupid' programme would ultimately receive three times as many votes as Lloyd George's.

The disintegration of the coalition, alongside the similarity in policy platforms between its former constituent parts, meant that issues of personality rose to the fore as the campaign progressed. On 1 November, Asquith told an audience in Paisley that whatever new government was elected could not be as bad as the previous administration, going on to claim that there were only two fixed points in the whole political landscape: one held by the Liberal Party, the other by Labour. 'All the rest was vague and chaos.' Amid that chaos swirled several personal attacks.

Lloyd George attacked the new Cabinet, shorn of pro-coalition members, as inherently intellectually inferior. This was reinforced by

Lord Birkenhead, who famously stated that first-class problems could not be dealt with by second-class brains. The Conservative Lord Robert Cecil retaliated by observing that a second-class brain was preferable to second-class character. Minister for Health Arthur Griffith-Boscawen defended Bonar Law's government by claiming that 'I think the country attaches more importance to character and honesty of purpose than it does to the most dazzling brilliance', going on to observe that the 'dazzling brilliance' of 'certain persons' had recently brought the nation close to war in Turkey.

On 6 November, Bonar Law claimed that 'a good clear head' was the most important quality for a successful minister. The Prime Minister noted that Lloyd George had accused him of having no policy, rather a 'yawn'; Asquith had said that to stand still was to go backwards. 'Well, that is a metaphor which is not physically accurate.' Instead, Bonar Law compared his 'go-slowly' policy to that of Disraeli's hugely successful 1874 campaign and quoted from Ecclesiastes: 'To everything there is a season and a time for every purpose under heaven.' Meanwhile, at Kingsway, Lloyd George was attacking Bonar Law: 'Avoid the extremists and Socialists, but do let us avoid the extreme of "standstillism".'

On 8 November, Bonar Law responded to further criticism at Old Kent Road Baths. Winston Churchill had accused the government of containing so many peers and relatives of peers that it took the nation back to the Middle Ages. The Prime Minister pointed out that the current government had only one more peer than its predecessor and noted that Churchill himself was the grandson of a duke. He also offered further defence of his platform, which had been accused of being 'a policy of going to sleep', by comparing his approach to that of a steam turbine, providing gradual but consistent energy. By way of contrast, Lloyd George was a motor engine, operating by way of a series of explosions. A slower, more stable approach was necessary. As the Prime Minister moved to discussing unemployment, protesters sung 'The Red Flag' outside the venue.

Away from the national back and forth between party leaders, a hugely diverse local campaign took place across the country. In

Manchester, for example, Liberal co-operation was the norm, with a single Liberal candidate 'without prefix and without suffix' contesting most seats. This meant three-way fights between Labour, Conservative and Liberal candidates in most seats. This included Labour leader J. R. Clynes's seat of Manchester Platting, which he went on to win by 869 votes, despite early uncertainty.

The other party leaders encountered varying local circumstances. Asquith did not face Conservative opposition in Paisley, leaving a straight fight with Labour which he won by just 316 votes, or 1 per cent of the total. Bonar Law faced both Liberal and Labour candidates in Central Glasgow, going on to beat Labour by 2,514 votes or 8 per cent. Lloyd George was elected unopposed in Caernarfon.

Elsewhere, local races differed hugely. In the Sutton division of Plymouth, Conservative candidate Lady Astor, an American-born Brit and the first female MP to take her seat in the UK, competed against an 'Independent Conservative' and a Labour candidate. Licensing was an important local issue, and Astor was portrayed as a prohibitionist, forced to publicly state: 'I am not trying to take away anyone's beer.' Astor went on to win the seat, with Labour finishing second. In Dover, the Conservative candidate was the unrelated but also American-born John Jacob Astor. He faced an Independent Liberal candidate as well as incumbent Thomas Polson, who had won a by-election as an Independent in 1921 before joining the Anti-Waste League. Astor ultimately emerged victorious.

Near-infinite combinations of parties competed across the country. South Paddington saw a straight battle between pro- and anti-coalition Conservatives. In Leicester East, the incumbent Labour MP George Banton faced a National Liberal candidate endorsed by the local Conservative candidate, who stood down. In Edinburgh, National Liberal candidate for Berwick and Haddington and sitting MP John Hope was presumed to have Conservative support. However, local opposition to his candidature emerged among both parties, which eventually disowned him, although not before Lord Balfour had written a public and ultimately embarrassing letter of support.

Hope then ran as an 'Independent Liberal', finishing fourth behind National Liberal, Labour and Liberal candidates.

The 1922 election also saw one significant future party leader elected to Parliament and another deposed. In Limehouse, east London, National Liberal MP William Pearce faced Labour's Major Clement Attlee. Pearce had been Limehouse's MP since 1906, winning four elections in a row. *The Times* derided the Labour challenger as an 'all-outer' and highlighted his position as lecturer in economics rather than his wartime service. The newspaper claimed Attlee 'belongs to a type of politician which is becoming more familiar at this election – the type that would construct a new heaven and earth on violently geometrical principles. The fight, however, is conducted on earthly lines.' Attlee went on to beat Pearce by nearly 2,000 votes, or 10 per cent of the total.

In Dundee, Winston Churchill defended his seat, with an equally surprising result. Then a Liberal and one of two Dundee MPs, Churchill publicly pledged his allegiance to Lloyd George, claiming that 'I was his friend before he was famous'. His calls for Liberal–Conservative unity against Labour saw Communist candidate William Gallacher claim of Churchill that 'no greater enemy to the working class could be found'. Churchill went on to contest the election unopposed by Conservatives but was bedridden for most of the campaign with appendicitis. He lost his seat, finishing fourth; Gallacher finished sixth. A 'Scottish Prohibition' candidate and a Labour candidate won Dundee's two seats, surely the future Prime Minister's least favoured possible outcome. He would later write that the campaign had left him 'without an office, without a seat, without a party and without an appendix'.

On 13 November, *The Times* stated that its reporting across the country suggested a Conservative victory seemed likely. However, 'there have been more baffling factors in the present contest than in any in living memory'. A Conservative majority of thirty to eighty seats was predicted, but there was great uncertainty, with fifty-one seats deemed impossible to call. The Conservatives had forty-two of the fifty-seven MPs being re-elected unopposed, as well as commanding 'several fat blocks' of seats across the country, including the universities. This amounted to over 100 seats where Conservative victory was almost certain. Labour, by way of contrast, had 'little patches' of strong support, especially in mining areas. The Asquithian Liberals had strong support in east Scotland, while the National Liberals found support in parts of Wales. But these were comparative 'drops in the bucket'.

On election day, 15 November 1922, the polls opened and the war era closed. The post-war government had been elected by a recently expanded electorate, who voted to continue the coalition under the man who had won them the war; the country now chose a government to lead the peace. The morning's *Times* hoped for stable majority government, and that this majority would be Conservative, given the paper of record's opposition to socialism, and the Liberals' division. At first glance, the electorate appear to have broadly agreed.

The Conservative Party won a decisive victory with 334 MPs, with 308 seats needed for a majority. However, this majority was brought about primarily by the division of their opponents: the Conservatives lost around thirty-five seats from 1918 but benefited from an opposition split three ways. The general election of 1923 would see a hung parliament result from the Conservatives garnering roughly the same percentage of the national vote as in 1922. The result was more notable for Labour, which became the official opposition, winning 142 seats. Asquith's Liberals won sixty-two seats, only slightly more than the National Liberals' fifty-three, meaning that the two Liberal factions still managed fewer seats than the rising Labour Party.

The coalition had decidedly ended, and Bonar Law had a clear mandate for his programme of non-intervention. His party suffered very few significant casualties. But the striking point about the results was Labour's performance, and the Liberal collapse. Elsewhere in this intensely local general election, an overtly Communist candidate won a seat in Motherwell. The election also saw the first MP of British Indian descent elected, as the Communist-aligned Shapurji Saklatvala won in Battersea North under the Labour Party banner.

Conservative Party historian John Ramsden later observed that the 1922 election victory occurred

> in uniquely favourable circumstances: Labour was on the rise, but not yet ready to challenge for a Parliamentary majority, the Liberals were split and fighting among themselves, and the electorate was all too ready to accept as premier an honest man of limited communicative powers after six exciting years shaped by Lloyd George's flashier talents.

But Bonar Law also made a series of conscious decisions that took his party to victory. His policy decisions around tariffs and Ireland killed or temporarily froze potentially divisive issues for the Conservatives, and his calm non-interventionism contrasted positively with Lloyd George's dynamism.

The 1922 election was also impactful in its consequences. Its results were decisive, if only in terms of seats won, and it begun a new era of two-party politics. It struck the first of three rapid electoral blows that signalled the relatively sudden and 'strange death' of a divided Liberal Party, with the Labour Party then cementing its place as the main party of opposition over the course of three elections in as many years.

This was not immediately obvious. The 1922 government would prove extremely short-lived. Andrew Bonar Law was forced to resign due to ill health after 209 days, dying shortly afterwards of throat cancer. Stanley Baldwin took over the Tory leadership. Becoming convinced of the need for a more protectionist trade policy, he followed his predecessor's commitment to an election before any such policy was introduced, and the government was dissolved after just over a year.

However, despite the shorter-term effects, the 1922 election brought about the beginning of an era of Conservative domination, with relatively brief interludes of Labour control. Baldwin would go on to be a successful leader. When Bonar Law took the leadership of the Conservative Party, he became the first Conservative Prime Minister in seventeen years. The era that followed was one of relative

Conservative dominance that has arguably continued ever since. Therefore, in both its electorate and its results, 1922 can be argued to be the first real election of the modern era.

Dr Jack Brown is a lecturer at the Strand Group, King's College London. He studies London-wide and national government. He is author of *No. 10: The Geography of Power at Downing Street* and *The London Problem*.

25

1923

ALISTAIR LEXDEN

Dissolution: 16 November 1923
Polling day: 6 December 1923
Seats contested: 615
Total electorate / Total votes cast / Turnout: 21,283,061 (19,621,367 in contested seats) / 13,909,017 / 71.1 per cent
Candidates (total 1,446): Conservative – 536; Liberal – 457; Labour – 427; Communist – 4; Nationalist – 2; Constitutionalist – 1; Scottish Prohibition – 1
Prime Minister on polling day: Stanley Baldwin
Main party leaders: Conservative – Stanley Baldwin; Labour – Ramsay MacDonald; Liberal – H. H. Asquith; Communist – Albert Inkpin; Nationalist – Joseph Devlin; Scottish Prohibition – Edwin Scrymgeour

Party performance:

Party	Votes	Percentage share	Seats
Conservative (including UUP)	5,286,159 (117,161)	38 (48.4)	258 (11)
Labour	4,267,831	30.7	191
Liberal	4,129,922	29.7	158
Nationalist	87,671	36.2	2
Communist	34,258	0.2	0
Constitutionalist	15,500	0.1	0
Scottish Prohibition	12,877	0.1	1

Result: Hung parliament, Labour formed a minority government with Liberal support

A snap general election, which destroyed a secure Conservative government and brought the Labour Party to power for the first time, took place on 6 December 1923. Although the existing parliament elected in November 1922 had four more years to run, it was dissolved by the king on 16 November 1923 at the request of Stanley Baldwin, who had become Prime Minister less than six months earlier, inheriting a Commons majority of seventy-five. A fiercely contested three-week campaign ensued, the last to be held so late in the year until 2019. Business organisations protested strongly about the disruption of their Christmas trade.

Like most snap elections, it was called to resolve a single issue, which, in the Prime Minister's view, had to be settled urgently in the national interest. Baldwin hoped to secure a clear mandate for a fundamental change in economic policy in order to tackle high and rising unemployment.

There was a general expectation in the summer of 1923 that the number of people without a job would increase over the coming twelve months from 1.5 million to 2 million, 15 per cent of the working population. In June, the Minister of Labour, Sir Anderson Montague-Barlow, wrote despairingly that 'the next will be the fourth winter of grave unemployment ... Fewer trades unions can continue unemployment benefit, and the deterioration and hopelessness of the workers increases.' At a Cabinet meeting on 23 October 1923, it was agreed that 'unemployment is the outstanding problem in the political life of the country. Failure to deal with it might wreck the Government.' Unresolved, the unemployment problem could obviously be expected to draw ever-increasing numbers of working-class voters into the arms of the Labour Party, assisting its further advance after the dramatic increase in the number of its MPs from sixty-three to 142 at the 1922 election.

After careful thought during his long summer holiday at Aix-les-Bains, followed by private consultations with various Cabinet ministers, Baldwin came to the conclusion that there was only one answer to unemployment: the introduction of tariffs on imports, ending Britain's long commitment to free trade. In an aide-mémoire composed at Chequers on 7 October, he wrote that 'every attempt to relieve unemployment is only applying palliatives: the only way to safeguard the future is to protect our own industries and develop our own Empire'. The latter was already under discussion with the Prime Ministers of the dominions.

'But Bonar's pledge stands in the way,' Baldwin added in his note of 7 October. This was the commitment, given by his predecessor Andrew Bonar Law at the November 1922 election, that 'this Parliament will not make any fundamental change in the fiscal system of this country'. It was only through a further election, the Cabinet agreed, that the pledge could be set aside and the way cleared for the introduction of economic protection.

Baldwin took his constituency associations and the wider public totally by surprise when he announced his dramatic shift in policy in his leader's speech to the annual Conservative Party conference in Plymouth on 25 October. But the unexpected démarche was not accompanied by any indication that an election was imminent. Baldwin made clear 'that he had no desire to rush the country into an election, but wished to give the electorate time to examine the Government's economic policy before they were called on to vote on it'.

The intense pre-election atmosphere which the Plymouth speech unleashed quickly altered the calculations. Several Cabinet members expressed impatience at the delay; others had serious misgivings about protection itself, which seemed likely to grow if no election were to be held until 1924.

The most skilful and least scrupulous politician of the day helped hasten the election. Rumours abounded that Lloyd George intended to seize the initiative by launching his own crusade for protection in the company of two formidable disaffected leading Conservatives, Austen Chamberlain and F. E. Smith (Lord Birkenhead), who were outside the government and openly contemptuous of Baldwin. Stanley Jackson, the Conservative Party chairman, warned that 'LG and

FE with the Rothermere press were going strongly for protection'. Could they use the issue to recreate the Tory–Liberal coalition under Lloyd George which had been overthrown at the famous Carlton Club meeting in October 1922, and in the process destroy Baldwin?

These factors settled the matter. Overriding considerable scepticism in his divided Cabinet, while simultaneously flirting with Chamberlain and Birkenhead in an attempt to curb their troublemaking, Baldwin suddenly announced on 12 November that Parliament would be dissolved. There was by this point a growing belief that the government had lost the tactical advantage and that the new protection policy could be saved only by going to the country in the hope of snatching victory before the opposition parties could mobilise fully. At this early stage of his long period as Tory leader, Baldwin never looked like a man who was firmly in control of events.

That impression was not diminished by Baldwin's conduct during the election campaign. He failed to explain the case for protection with the force and passion needed to banish scepticism and doubt. Though Conservative Central Office had assured him that victory was certain, its literature was inevitably prepared in great haste and lacked effective slogans to galvanise enthusiasm and electoral support. Within the party itself, protection failed to conquer every heart. A number of MPs who had planned to stand again withdrew from the contest rather than repudiate free trade, while thirteen actually stood as free traders with the support of their constituency associations.

There were insistent demands for a clear indication of the implications of the government's plans. The Conservative manifesto was little help, providing only a general outline of the government's intentions. It said that action would be taken to 'impose duties on imported manufactured goods' in order 'to raise revenue' and 'give special assistance' to industries facing 'unfair foreign competition', while negotiating for 'a reduction of foreign tariffs' to help British exports and giving 'substantial preference to the Empire'.

In his campaign speeches, Baldwin confined himself to vague promises that great benefits would be forthcoming, or at the very least that no harm would be done. Asked in Liverpool at the end of the campaign how shipping would be affected, he replied that its prosperity had long preceded the arrival of free trade 'and to imagine that it would decline on a return to protection, or indeed that any responsible statesman could support measures that would put it in peril, was absurd'.

This inevitably created much frustration. *The Times* noted on 22 November: 'The statement is constantly heard that what is wanted is a plain, straightforward explanation of the Government's scheme.' The trouble was that no proper scheme had been prepared in the run-up to this snap election.

The Times, like most of the other leading dailies, was unwilling to give the Tories strong backing. Never before, it was said at the time, had a Conservative campaign suffered more from lack of press support. The mass circulation newspapers caused much tribulation among Tory Party officials. The leading press barons of the right, Lords Rothermere and Beaverbrook, whose papers had a combined daily circulation of 4.5 million, did not allow a good word to be said about Baldwin throughout the campaign. They yielded to no one in their enthusiasm for protection but were unimpressed by Baldwin's rapid conversion, and above all wanted a definite scheme to assist goods coming from the empire, which Baldwin failed to bring forward.

For the first time in electoral history, money was a problem for the Tories. The party treasurer, Viscount Younger of Leckie, told Baldwin that £150,000 to £160,000 would be needed, but 'money is really very scarce, and subscriptions come in very badly'. He had to dip into the party's capital reserves. The demands on the party's resources were considerably greater than at the previous election. More seats were contested. In 1922, when many of Lloyd George's supporters were given a clear run by the Tories (despite the collapse of the coalition), there were 483 candidates; the number rose to 540 in 1923. As a result, the total Conservative vote went up in an election that was lost.

This was the last election in which broadcasting played no part. The BBC, under John Reith's dynamic direction, had just been set up. Conservative Central Office, buffeted by the press, saw the potential of this new powerful medium. Reith's diary contains the following entry for 20 October 1923: 'Met Sir Reginald Hall, chief agent for the Unionist party [as the Conservatives were at this point generally known]. He hoped we should be able to broadcast the prime minister from Plymouth, but I am sure this will not come off.' It didn't and no broadcasts were made during the election campaign, but this early Tory interest in the BBC put it far ahead of the other parties, which worked greatly to its advantage at future interwar elections.

In 1923, however, very little worked to the Conservatives' advantage. Unsettling reports from constituencies across the land reached Central Office as the campaign wore on. It took no notice. On 4 December, two days before polling, it told Baldwin to expect a majority of eighty-seven (which it increased on polling day itself to ninety-seven), giving no indication how it had arrived at its figures. The Prime Minister had just returned from the last of his election tours by rail, conforming to the tradition set in the late nineteenth century. He was 'very cheerful', his confidant, Thomas Jones, recorded in his diary, having received 'very favourable reports of the progress of the campaign in the North', where the case for protection had seemed unlikely to be well received. As he departed for his Bewdley constituency, Baldwin said: 'I don't want any bands when I come back!' That was just as well, since they could have played only a lament.

Labour and the Liberals could hardly believe their luck. Their support for free trade had never wavered over the generations. When the Tories had first proposed tariffs twenty years earlier, they had profited enormously in electoral terms. Now they hoped that history would repeat itself. They were not to be disappointed.

Their gains in 1923, though substantial, would have been spectacular if they had fought the election as allies, dividing up constituencies between them, as they had when Labour had been the Liberals' very junior partner before the First World War. But now they were deadly rivals. While united in condemning Baldwin for violating a sacrosanct element of national life, they also fought each other unyieldingly for electoral supremacy. In the astute hands of Ramsay MacDonald who had been reinstalled in the party leadership after the 1922 election (having been forgiven for his pacificism during the First World War), Labour looked to a future in which the Liberals barely existed (an objective which, as it happened, it shared with Baldwin).

In 1923, however, the Liberals had particular cause to thank Baldwin. Nothing, it had seemed, would ever end the deep animosity between Asquith and Lloyd George, which had torn the Liberals asunder at the end of 1916 when Lloyd George formed his coalition with the Conservatives. The two men had hardly spoken to each other since then. At the 1922 election, the two Liberal parties had fought each other venomously. Baldwin achieved what had been regarded as impossible: his election campaign for protection united the warring Liberals. Abandoning his pro-protection intrigues with dissident-leading Conservatives, Lloyd George travelled to Asquith's Paisley constituency where, as he put it, 'the rites of Liberal reunion were celebrated at an enthusiastic meeting in the town hall'.

This meant not just a united campaign fought on a common programme but a well-financed one, too. Asquith's faction had hardly any money; Lloyd George had plenty, thanks to the personal political fund he had built up while he was Prime Minister. The Welsh wizard put some £90,000 into the party's election account, helping to take the total to around £150,000, so matching Tory expenditure. This large sum met the costs of effective campaign literature and assisted many candidates with their expenses. A committee was established to fuse the two Liberal organisations at constituency level and stop rival Liberal candidates fighting each other. It did a good job; the Liberal vote was split in only two seats. The reunited party contested 453 constituencies, husbanding its strength a little after the 490 contests that the two divided parties had mounted in 1922.

The predominant theme of the Liberal campaign was that Britain had been forced into a cost-of-living election by Baldwin's irresponsible new tariff policy. Cartoons were produced portraying 'Baldwin and Co. high price tailors', with shop windows displaying signs such as 'All prices raised by 20 per cent' and 'You pay – we prosper'. A circular issued in the name of Asquith's daughter denounced protection as 'an attack on the standard of life of the poorest homes in the country'.

This Liberal theme was given strong backing by several newspapers, including the *Glasgow Herald* which stated on 1 December that 'this is a cost-of-living election. More and more candidates are being pressed to talk about the effect of protection on the cost of living. It is a subject of absorbing interest to all the electors.' The Liberals were mining a rich electoral seam. Few could complain about the vigour with which the two leaders of the reunited party went about it. They undertook long railway journeys across the country to address meetings on the iniquity of protection. Asquith's travels were especially protracted as a result of a rather poorly planned programme of speaking engagements.

Throughout the campaign, Lloyd George insisted that it was not enough simply to denounce protection and its effects on the cost of living. The Liberal manifesto contained the first draft of his radical interventionist initiatives for economic revival and much fuller employment that he was to develop dramatically during the rest of the decade. There were proposals for the 'bold and courageous' use of 'national credit' to provide cheap power for industry and homes, along with road and water transport, afforestation and land reclamation. There was a ringing call for a welfare state: 'Liberal policy concentrates upon lifting from the homes of the poor those burdens and anxieties of the old, the sick, the widow with young children, which the community has the power and duty to relieve.' Lloyd George challenged the Labour Party on its strongest ground.

Ramsay MacDonald struck back. The Labour manifesto matched the Liberals' point for point under the heading 'practical idealism'. The party's 'national schemes of productive work' included all the interventionist initiatives that Lloyd George had put in the Liberal manifesto, with the addition of town planning and housing. On the latter, there was no lack of ambition. Labour promised to 'abolish the slums [and] build an adequate supply of decent homes'. Socialism made a brief appearance in a short section of the manifesto attractively entitled 'The Commonwealth of Co-operative Service'. Just three industries would be nationalised: the mines, railways and power stations.

It was a left-wing taxation reform which became the most

controversial element of Labour's programme. What was described as 'a non-recurring, graduated war debt redemption levy' was announced for 'all individual fortunes in excess of £5,000'. This capital levy came under strong attack from other parties in the closing stages of the campaign. MacDonald insisted that the proceeds of the levy would be used to reduce debt, not to finance left-wing hobby-horses. The measure was a 'symbol of financial straightforwardness'. He did not allow it to throw Labour seriously on the defensive.

Overall, MacDonald offered a reformist agenda with a dash of socialism to tackle unemployment as a constructive alternative to Baldwin's protectionist policy, which he attacked as vigorously as the Liberals. Labour fielded 427 candidates, up slightly on 1922. With pardonable exaggeration, a senior Labour official described it as 'an effort which may be regarded as almost unique in the history of British politics'. As usual, Labour's funds were much more modest than those of the other two parties. The party had to make do with £23,565 provided by the trade unions.

Not much was heard about MacDonald's colleagues during the campaign. The Labour leader, eloquent and masterful on the platform, commanded almost all the attention. While his rivals in the other parties followed tradition and campaigned by rail, he took to the road. The press gave lavish coverage to his progress by car from London to his Aberavon constituency in south Wales in this novel form of electioneering. Crowds gathered in large numbers at his meetings in the cities and towns through which he passed. In Newport, the car was towed through the streets. In Port Talbot, 'the crowd bore down on the car like an avalanche'. No other party leader evoked so much enthusiasm in 1923. A relatively new form of transport had moved to the centre of British elections.

This was the first election at which results were broadcast. The newly established BBC announced constituency poll declarations between 9.45 p.m. on 6 December and 1 a.m. the following day without commentary (music from two bands at the Savoy Hotel filled the gaps). Two million people were estimated to have gathered around wireless sets across the country.

Manchester Exchange, a Conservative seat, was the first to be declared. It was lost to the Liberals on an 11.8 per cent swing. It was the harbinger of Tory disaster in Lancashire, a bastion of the party since Disraeli's day, and elsewhere in the north-west with its deep attachment to free trade in the interests of the cotton industry. The Liberals won five of the ten Manchester seats, their first victories in the city since 1910.

Thomas Jones, faithful friend of Baldwin (despite being a Labour voter), listened to the results in the Cabinet room at No. 10. 'As the Liberal and Labour gains continued in an unbroken stream,' his diary for 6 December recorded, 'our faces grew longer [and] we saw less and less chance of the home counties putting things right. Bath and Nottingham were a great shock. If Nottingham would not vote for a tariff after all the trouble about foreign competition in the lace trade, who was going to support Baldwin?' (Jones added that he listened to 'the growing tale of Labour victories with undisguised joy'.)

The Liberals won Bath on a 10.7 per cent swing. The *Manchester Guardian* noted on 8 December that 'it is indeed curious how many Liberal successes there have been in places which have cathedrals, racecourses, and esplanades'. The party had victories in a number of seats which had been safe Tory strongholds since at least 1885, including Basingstoke, Blackpool, Chelmsford, Chichester and Shrewsbury. Asquith asked: 'What is the explanation of these unexpected, and in some cases un-hoped for, victories?' The victors themselves were often utterly astonished. In Chichester, they 'only knew twelve Liberals' and were without a candidate until the last minute.

Twenty-three Tory urban constituencies fell to the Liberals, who did better still in Tory county seats, where they made forty-four gains, most notably in the south Midlands and the south-west. This was the only election between 1918 and 1966 in which the Conservatives did not win a majority of agricultural seats. Farm prices had fallen sharply, and farmers were furious since they had been promised in the 1920 Agriculture Act that, with government support, prices would be maintained at a high level. Tariffs offered nothing to them since food was to be exempted from Baldwin's scheme.

Overwhelmingly, however, in both rural and urban seats, Liberal victories came with insubstantial or very small majorities, which were destined to be overturned when the tariff controversy faded in 1924. Some Liberal successes were due to the absence of a Labour candidate in seats where the Labour vote would have been large enough to hand victory to the Tories; a marked increase in Labour candidates in 1924 had just that effect. Furthermore, the Liberals did not in 1923 recover lost ground in some former strongholds, such as the industrial regions of Scotland, south Wales and parts of Yorkshire. The election of 1923 was one in which the Liberals did very well in non-industrial seats, a development which foreshadowed the Liberal revivals of the 1960s and 1970s.

Labour advanced less spectacularly in terms of seats than the Liberals in 1923, emerging with 191 seats – an increase of forty-nine – as against the Liberal increase of seventy-two, which took its total representation, no longer split between two warring parties, to 159. In some constituencies, Labour organisation displayed notable efficiency: in Leicester West, the party showed its detailed canvass returns to journalists, who were impressed by the accuracy with which they indicated the majority by which Winston Churchill, fighting his last election as a Liberal, would be defeated. Labour gained eighteen seats where, as in Leicester West, a Liberal supporter of the Lloyd George faction had been elected in 1922.

In 1923, Labour consolidated its position in many northern industrial constituencies and made some useful gains in a variety of urban seats elsewhere, such as Coventry, Ipswich and Cardiff. Its most conspicuous advance occurred in the greater London area, where it more than doubled its MPs from sixteen to thirty-seven, chiefly at the expense of the Conservatives.

Baldwin and the Conservatives paid a heavy price for their sudden, unexpected tariff election. They were defeated in 108 seats, with the overall loss being reduced to eighty-eight by the gain of twenty seats, chiefly from the Liberals in eastern Scotland and elsewhere. Northern Ireland sent eleven Ulster Unionists, most of them unopposed, to give their loyal support to Baldwin after an election in which tariffs played little part. The contest there had been dominated by the threat to Northern Ireland posed by a Boundary Commission that had been set up to consider the redistribution of territory between the two parts of Ireland. 'Not an inch,' said the Unionists. Baldwin would display much skill in protecting their interests in the next two years.

With their MPs down from 345 to 258, the Conservatives had lost their substantial majority and become the largest party in a hung parliament. It was clear where the blame lay. Summing up the election on 8 December, *The Times* stated: 'The general opinion in Unionist circles yesterday was that Mr Baldwin's policy had been defeated on the "dear food" cry', even though Baldwin had said that tariffs would not apply to the main foodstuffs. His assurances seemed to carry little conviction, particularly among those who at that time did most of the shopping. *The Times* added: 'In the main the women's vote was cast against the Government.' Baldwin told Thomas Jones: 'The people of this country can't be shaken out of their fear of high prices.'

Resignation passed fleetingly through Baldwin's mind, but he came under no serious pressure from his party to depart. It yearned for stability after the turmoil of the coalition years with Lloyd George, and Baldwin seemed best placed to provide it, despite his rash tariff election. The Liberals sought no deal with either him or Ramsay MacDonald, but Asquith made plain in mid-December that his party would support Labour in the hung parliament which met on 15 January 1924. Baldwin was defeated on the address six days later, and Ramsay MacDonald formed the first Labour government.

Alistair Lexden is a Conservative peer who writes and lectures on modern political history. Much of his recent work has been on the history of the Conservative Party. Full details of his publications can be found on his website, www.alistairlexden.org.uk.

26

1924

ROBERT WALLER

Dissolution: 9 October 1924
Polling day: 29 October 1924
Seats contested: 615
Total electorate / Total votes cast / Turnout: 21,730,988 (20,654,552 in contested seats) / 15,856,215 / 77 per cent
Candidates (total 1,428): Conservative – 534; Labour – 514; Liberal – 339; Constitutionalist – 12; Communist – 8; Sinn Féin – 8
Prime Minister on polling day: Ramsay MacDonald
Main party leaders: Labour – Ramsay MacDonald; Conservative – Stanley Baldwin; Liberal – H. H. Asquith; Communist – Albert Inkpin; Sinn Féin – Éamon de Valera

Party performance:

Party	Votes	Percentage share	Seats
Conservative (including UUP)	7,418,983 (451,278)	46.8 (86.9)	412 (13)
Labour	5,281,626	33.3	151
Liberal	2,818,717	17.8	40
Constitutionalist	185,075	1.2	7
Communist	51,176	0.2	1
Sinn Féin	46,457	8.9	0

Result: Conservative majority of 209 seats

Apart from 1830–32, the only other time in the scope of this book that there were three general elections in successive years culminated in the October 1924 contest. If an observer were to interpret this as an indication of a period of political instability, they would be correct. This was a time of fluid three-party politics. The years 1922–24 witnessed the last ever Liberal Party Prime Minister and the first belonging to the Labour Party. Although at first sight the heavy Conservative victory in the 1924 election may be seen as a negative response to the inaugural Labour government, in fact the greatest losers were the Liberals. Britain was now well on the way to replacing a Conservative–Liberal duopoly with the Labour–Conservative pattern of cleavage that has become so familiar over the 100 years since that 1924 general election campaign.

The previous contest, a mere nine months earlier on 6 December 1923, had been caused by an outbreak of principle in politics. In the November 1922 general election, the Conservatives under Andrew Bonar Law had won a comfortable overall majority, following their withdrawal from Lloyd George's continuation of the First World War coalition. But Stanley Baldwin, who had taken over as party leader and Prime Minister from the terminally ill Law in May 1923, decided he needed to seek a new mandate on making the very significant (at that time, as on other occasions) policy change from free trade to protectionism. This notion of 'tariff reform' had proved disastrous for the Conservatives in the 1906 election, and in December 1923 they were again defeated. This time no party had an overall majority, but the Liberals allowed Labour and Ramsay MacDonald to form their first ever government, secure in the knowledge that it was very much in a minority, with only 191 MPs out of a House of Commons complement of 615. Thus, the next general election was bound to be seen largely as a judgement on the performance of Labour's stewardship.

The 'long campaign' in 1924 really started during the summer months. In July, just before the parliamentary recess, discussions ongoing since the early weeks of the Labour administration concerning regularising Britain's position with regard to the Soviet Union began to crystallise. Two treaties were being negotiated – a trade agreement which also improved the position of British bondholders whose claims on the pre-revolutionary government had been repudiated by the Bolsheviks after 1917, and in return a British loan of £30 million to the USSR. These suggestions were immediately strongly opposed, by both the Liberals and the Conservatives, on anti-communist grounds. By September, it was becoming clear that if the opposition stood in the way of the government on the Russian treaties, that would be grounds for a dissolution of Parliament. This then became folded into another issue relating to MacDonald's administration and communism.

The actual trigger of the October 1924 election campaign was, in essence, the Campbell case. This revolved around the August 1924 decision of the Attorney General, Sir Patrick Hastings, to advise the prosecution of John Campbell, the editor of the Communist Party newspaper *Workers' Weekly*, under the 1797 Incitement to Mutiny Act. It had published an article calling on men in the armed services to refuse to use their guns against fellow workers, either in war or in the suppression of industrial action. A week later, the government forced the charges to be withdrawn.

But the real damage to MacDonald was done as autumn replaced summer. The issues were whether the Cabinet had instructed the Attorney General to withdraw the prosecution (which it was not entitled to do), and MacDonald's own role in the decision. On 20 September, the Conservative MP Sir Kingsley Wood gave notice that he would ask parliamentary questions on these matters. In reply, MacDonald claimed he had had no notice or knowledge of the prosecution. This opened him to the very serious charge of misleading the House of Commons. At the beginning of October, both the Liberals and Conservatives supported a motion of censure against the Prime Minister. MacDonald decided that this was to be treated as a matter of 'no confidence' in his government. The time had now come for the opposition parties to combine and bring the first ever Labour administration to an end.

The debate came on 8 October 1924, and both Liberal and Conservative motions were passed by around 360 votes to 198. Asquith's speech proposing the former turned out to be the last of his thirty-eight years in Parliament, as well as leading to the end of the eight months of the first Labour government. MacDonald went to Buckingham Palace the next morning to seek a dissolution of Parliament and a new election. Undoubtedly, he had made a massive blunder in his responses to Wood. Lying to the House was, at least at that time, in effect a resignation matter. On the other hand, the first Labour government was always at the mercy of the opposition majority, and it had no long-term future in any case. The 1924 general election was set for 29 October. Thus, the election campaign itself was very short, lasting just twenty days.

Not surprisingly, the key personnel at the heads of the main competing parties remained unchanged from the previous general election less than a year previously. Ramsay MacDonald was the incumbent Labour Prime Minister. There had been no challenge to Stanley Baldwin from within his Conservative and Unionist Party, despite the loss of power following his decision to dissolve Parliament in 1923. As for the Liberals, Herbert Henry Asquith remained the leader of a party that had been relatively recently reunited. This was following the split initiated when David Lloyd George had ousted him as Prime Minister in 1916, subsequently extending his wartime coalition through the 1918 general election, until the Tories ended it in 1922. Asquith and Lloyd George had finally reached an agreement in November 1923, united behind a free trade manifesto during Baldwin's 'tariff reform' election. This was not to prove a permanent solution to the 'Lloyd George problem', but it largely held for the October 1924 campaign.

It would be wrong to characterise the 1924 campaign as being the first 'radio election'. However, it was the first in which there were party political broadcasts on the 'wireless': one each for the main party leaders. The year of 1924 was an important one for the new medium. The first broadcast by a monarch had been by King George V, on opening the British Empire Exhibition on 23 April 1924, and Winston Churchill's first ever use of radio had been in June 1924; the year had also seen the first shipping forecast, Greenwich time signal and radio play. There was not much drama in Stanley Baldwin's address on BBC radio on 16 October. His approach was low key but effective. Baldwin was to be the first Prime Minister to master the technique of the microphone, and he spoke quietly and in simple terms but with authority. He was conciliatory: 'No gospel of hate will be the gospel of our people.' On 16 October, Baldwin used the director-general's private office as a studio, in the BBC headquarters at Savoy Hill.

MacDonald, on the other hand, had his opening speech of the campaign at a Glasgow meeting hall on 13 October broadcast too, but the effect was that it sounded overblown and hectoring. The Labour leader's main point was that his government had been unfairly cut short by a conspiracy between Conservatives and Liberals not because he had 'made a mess of things' but because it had been successful. Three days later, by contrast, Baldwin appealed to the political centre by promising a 'sane, commonsense Government, not carried away by revolutionary theories or harebrained schemes ... We cannot afford the luxury of academic socialists or revolutionary agitation.' Thus, despite his honeyed tones and down-to-earth manner, he was associating MacDonald's far from radical administration with left-wing extremism of the kind that had produced the Soviet Communist government, which fitted in with the two main themes of the early campaign, the Campbell case and the Russian treaties.

The three weeks of the campaign were marked by distinctly different styles between the protagonists. MacDonald's preference for a campaigning style based on large meetings continued throughout the 1924 election. He completed two major speaking tours, each consisting of a series of major set-piece speeches. According to his friend and confidante Molly Hamilton, MacDonald was incapable of delivering five-minute 'whistle-stop' speeches. It was an exhausting approach. The Labour leader ranged from London on 13 October to Edinburgh, then through the north-east and Yorkshire to Birmingham on the 16th; to his constituency at Aberavon the next day speaking at Worcester, Gloucester, Newport and Cardiff. It was said that 15,000 had attended at Birmingham and 20,000 at Huddersfield. Another aspect that was extremely different from modern campaigns was the Prime Minister's lack of support staff. For the first seven days, he was not even accompanied by a secretary. Baldwin had the advantage of being unopposed in his own seat of Bewdley in Worcestershire, but he still travelled less than MacDonald, though he did tour the west Midlands and Lancashire, and in a speech at Southend, he did make a rare descent to the prevailing tone of anti-communism in the Conservative campaign by declaring: 'I think it's time someone said to Russia: "Hands off England."'

The Conservative and Unionist Party's official manifesto, personalised as Stanley Baldwin's election address, led with the two 'immediate issues' that they said had precipitated the general election: the Campbell case and the Russian treaties. It clearly suggested malpractice by the Labour government as far as the former was concerned: 'The admissions already extorted from Ministers in Parliament are sufficient to convince any reasonable person that it was as a result of undue political pressure that the Attorney-General withdrew a prosecution instituted on the grave charge of inciting the troops to sedition and mutiny.' They also connected this with the 'indefensible' agreement with the Soviets by claiming that that had been brought about by the same 'extremist section' of the Labour Party which had applied the pressure in the Campbell case. The result was that the British public would have to foot the bill if the Bolsheviks failed to repay a Labour government loan to the Bolsheviks – as they would 'in accordance with their principles and their practice'. On more general policy, the Conservative manifesto criticised MacDonald's administration for raising unemployment. It promised to protect agriculture 'from Socialistic and bureaucratic tyranny', lower the cost of foodstuffs (still an issue a century later) and increase the rate of new-build housing. There was a strong tone of appealing to 'imperial' sentiment, in specific terms of 'preference, unity, foreign policy and defence'. Finally, Baldwin's manifesto warned of the dangers of a Labour government untrammelled by a minority status, which would be open to the influence of that 'extremist section'. Only a solid and stable 'Unionist' majority could avert such an alarming possibility.

Labour's manifesto, by contrast, opened on the theme of 'Peace', looking back to the aftermath of the First World War and the 'embittered relations between France and Germany' left by the 'disastrous tangles of preceding Governments' – thus taking aim at both Liberals and Conservatives in Lloyd George's continuing coalition up to 1922, and stressing MacDonald's work in European diplomacy. This was linked to their unashamed refusal 'to exclude from this general pacification the Russian people, with whom it is essential to resume our trade in the interests of our unemployed and the country as a whole', specifically opportunities in fishing and as an export market. The second topic to be highlighted was housing, followed by education, unemployment and a list of measures 'the Liberals and Tories have combined to stop'. This was clearly a plea for a majority in the next House of Commons. Also, the order of the two parties mentioned may suggest an attempt to monopolise more of the anti-Tory vote – perhaps in modern terms trying for tactical voting by Liberals now it was clearer that only Labour could form an alternative to a Conservative government. The Labour manifesto closed with a moral appeal to the public with almost a religious tone, headed 'The spirit that giveth life', ending with a plea for an 'opportunity for Good Will to conquer Hate and Strife, and for Brotherhood, if not to supersede Greed, at least to set due bounds to that competition which leads only to loss and death'.

The Liberal manifesto did to an extent reflect this middle position between the other two major parties, giving a prominent position to 'the Russian blunder' and mentioning communism twice before two paragraphs were completed, but also claiming they had assisted MacDonald's government in its moves towards 'sound social reform'. However, it did take the party's distinctive particular lines towards free trade and temperance (looking to the past) and reform of the voting system (to the future). In the end, its final paragraph headed 'Sane Progress' left the impression that the Liberals were indeed now struggling to escape from a squeeze between Labour and Conservative, the only parties that would lead governments over the next 100 years at least.

In 1924, before the days of television, never mind the internet and 24-hour news coverage, the manifestos and election addresses played a much larger role in determining the key issues and approaches of the parties to the campaign. Initially, the campaign was dominated by two issues, the Campbell case and MacDonald's Russian treaties, which were vigorously opposed by both Conservative and Liberal parties. The Unionist candidate for the Abbey division of Westminster said that 'a vote for the Socialists is a vote for the Communists'. Conservative election posters showed villainous-looking Russians in rags and fur hats saying, 'I wantski £49 million', a clear reference to MacDonald's planned loan. *The Times* headlines on 23 October thundered at 'A Bankrupt Party' and 'Red Designs on Britain ... Striking Through India and Egypt'. This was a clear reference to the alleged closeness between MacDonald's government and the Soviet Union, though so far they were based on no more sinister revelations than a pamphlet issued by the Russian National Students Association in exile in Paris. *Punch* offered a cartoon of the USSR, represented as a shabby sandwich-man carrying a placard: 'Vote for MacDonald and Me'. There were also catchy little songs, like

> Bolshevik, Bolshevik, where have you been?
> 'Over to England where the Reds are still green.'

As the campaign went on, it became more intense in tone and style. There were complaints of Labour rowdyism at meetings and the Conservative-dominated press became more strident. For example, *The Times* commented about a Labour plan for a national system of electric generating stations that 'some such project was dear to Lenin'. A Conservative leaflet to female voters under the leading 'Communism destroys marriage' claimed that 'children will be taken from their mothers and made the property of the State'.

However, the 'Communist connection' was to become even more controversial as the 1924 election campaign came to a climax, with the one major development that had not been anticipated when the election had first been called and in the manifestos. This was truly what the Americans would call an 'October surprise'.

The 'Zinoviev letter' was purportedly 'a secret letter of instruction from Moscow to the British Communist Party', as splashed by the right-wing *Daily Mail* on 20 October, five days before election day. The headlines read 'MOSCOW ORDERS TO OUR REDS – GREAT PLOT DISCLOSED YESTERDAY' and continued (still in large type) 'PARALYSE THE ARMY AND NAVY – AND MR MACDONALD WOULD LEND RUSSIA OUR MONEY'. Over the signature of the president of the Communist International, Grigory Zinoviev, the 'English translation' included a suggestion that communists should infiltrate the British armed services. The reason that it damaged the Labour Party, and MacDonald as Prime Minister, was the government's response, which appeared to accept the letter's authenticity. It did protest at the apparent interference in British affairs but seemed to have been only stimulated by the publication of the letter. Given the context of the Russian treaty negotiations that were already a contentious issue in the election, the government's response did not clearly suggest that relations between the two countries should be broken off.

The negative impact of the Zinoviev letter was compounded by two more factors. Its publication on 25 October was accompanied by an official letter of protest, signed by J. D. Gregory of the Foreign Office (himself an active anti-Bolshevik), to the Russian *chargé d'affaires* in London, Rakovsky, protesting at the letter as outside interference in British domestic matters, which added to the impression that the letter was authentic. Secondly, MacDonald himself delayed making any comment until the afternoon of 27 October, despite having known about the letter since the 15th. He did not commit himself to claiming it was a forgery. It is difficult to see what he could have done further at this stage – he would be damned either if it were genuine or if he claimed it were not.

We know now – and MacDonald himself strongly suspected at the time – that the Zinoviev letter was a forgery. The latest and most thorough scholarship, by the former FCO chief historian Gill Bennett in her 2018 book *The Zinoviev Letter: The Conspiracy That Never Dies*, suggests that in fact it was probably concocted in Riga (Latvia) as black propaganda by Ivan Pokrovsky, a former Tsarist officer and a member of a group of White (anti-Communist) Russians. This was perhaps with the knowledge if not the assistance of some members of the British intelligence services, although possibly in the shape of rogue officers, who played a role in making it available to right-wing elements in Britain opposed to the re-election of the Labour government, such as the *Daily Mail*.

It is probably impossible to prove exactly what happened, but to a large extent it does not matter who wrote and circulated it and why; it was the effects that were important. It suited the opposition parties to regard the Zinoviev letter as genuine, and MacDonald did not handle the issue as well as he could. For example, he did try to shift some of the blame for the inadequate response to the Foreign Office and the civil service – the permanent and non-political arm of his own government. In any case, the timing meant it was yet another negative influence for his party's election result. As the votes were counted after election day, 29 October, it soon became apparent that Labour had lost and MacDonald was out of office.

Analysing the detailed results, the Conservatives (or Unionists, as they were still widely known in 1924) were clearly the winners. They emerged with 154 net gains, reaching a commanding total of 412 MPs, an overall majority of 209. Their share of the votes cast increased by 8.8 per cent to 46.8 per cent. This established a very solid basis for Baldwin's government, which lasted for the next five years, until May 1929.

Despite the ousting of MacDonald's government, Labour went down by only forty net losses, from 191 seats to 151. These figures are somewhat deceptive. In terms of raw votes, Labour actually increased compared with the previous year – up from 4.3 million to 5.3 million, and also improved from 30.7 per cent of the votes cast to 33.3 per cent: their highest ever number of votes and percentage, and higher than their share more recently in 2015 and 2019, for example. Only one Cabinet Minister was defeated, F. W. Jowett at Bradford East, though half a dozen junior ministers whose careers were on the up were forced to take a break from Parliament, including Margaret Bondfield, Emanuel Shinwell and Herbert Morrison. A key outcome of the 1924 campaign was that Labour were now by a very clear margin the second largest party in the country, and without doubt formed the principal opposition and the only serious candidates to form an alternative government. This set the pattern for the predominantly two-party pattern of contest that has pertained ever since in Westminster governmental politics.

What is more, Labour's main anti-Conservative rivals, the Liberals, suffered great losses, going down from 158 seats to forty, and from 30 per cent of the vote to 19 per cent. They lost 106 seats to the Conservatives and also eight net to Labour. The Liberal share dropped from 29.7 per cent just a year before to 17.8 per cent, and the first-past-the-post system, so bemoaned by third parties in times since, ensured that they were rewarded only with 6.5 per cent of the 615 seats in the House of Commons. Their reduction in share was heavily influenced by their offering only 339 candidates, contesting scarcely more than half the constituencies, compared with 457 in 1923 – but this was in itself partly a reflection of their lack of financial strength, another indicator of their decline as a major party. The 72-year-old Asquith (even though not opposed by a Conservative) was beaten in his own seat at Paisley by over 2,000 votes in an aggressive campaign by the charismatic ILP activist Rosslyn Mitchell. Asquith never fought another election, accepting the title of Earl of Oxford and Asquith in 1925 and resigning the Liberal Party leadership in October 1926, after further disputes with Lloyd George over the latter's more sympathetic attitude to the general strike of that year. Asquith died in February 1928. Although there was some Liberal revival in the next general election in 1929, their time as contenders to lead a government was over.

Outside the three main parties, there were some interesting returns in the results of the 1924 general election. There were two victorious Independents, Ernest Graham-Little representing London University (at that time graduates of certain universities had a second parliamentary vote) and Austin Hopkinson of Mossley, who had been opposed by Labour and the Liberals but not the Conservatives. There was one Communist, an unusual story: Shapurji Saklatvala of Battersea North was the first person of Indian heritage to be elected as a Labour MP, having been born in Bombay and moved to Manchester to run Tata's Manchester office in 1905. Saklatvala had been a committed left-wing socialist since 1909 and was first elected at Battersea North in 1922 and defeated in 1923, under the Labour Party label on each occasion, but in October 1924 he stood again and won, this time as a Communist without formal Labour endorsement (though not opposed by them).

There was even an Irish Nationalist elected in England, T. P. O'Connor in the Liverpool Scotland division, which despite its name was the heartland of Irish immigration to the west coast seaport. 'Tay Pay', as he was known from how he pronounced the initials by which he was usually known, was born in Athlone in County Westmeath and retained Liverpool Scotland for the twelfth time since his first win there in 1885 – and he was unopposed, as he had been in every general election since December 1906. He was to win once more in the 1929 general election, and then died in possession of the seat later that year at the age of eighty-one.

In Dundee, one of the two seats was retained by the individualistic Prohibitionist Edwin Scrymgeour – who had first been victorious in the 1922 general election in the jute-manufacturing town, when Winston Churchill had lost his seat there. Churchill himself, in some ways the Flying Dutchman of British party politics and of constituencies, returned to Parliament in the 1924 general election, but now under the unusual label of Constitutionalist – which he had also done in his previous attempt in the March 1924 by-election in the Westminster Abbey constituency, when he lost to the official Unionist by just forty-three votes.

In the October general election, Churchill was one of seven successful Constitutionalist candidates, himself now standing at Epping in Essex, this time not opposed by a Conservative/Unionist. His migration through the parties completed its full circle as he rejoined the Conservative Party on being appointed Chancellor of the Exchequer in Baldwin's government on 6 November 1924. The other successful Constitutionalists in October were also all former Liberals who had supported Lloyd George's continuing coalition after 1918. There was no formal party organisation and they did not work together as a group after the 1924 election. Although two of the seven joined Churchill in almost immediately taking the Conservative whip after being elected (Sir Hamar Greenwood, Walthamstow East, and Algernon Moreing of Camborne), the others took the Liberal whip. The Constitutionalists were a brief and ill-fated attempt to broaden the British political choice of parties, though they were firmly anti-socialist.

Overall, the turnout in the 1924 general election was 77 per cent, very high by modern standards – each one since 1992 has been lower than that figure, and the participation rate has been less than 70 per cent every time since 1997 (although it reached 72 per cent in the 2016 Brexit referendum). The 1924 figure was also the highest of any of the seven general elections between the two world wars and was not exceeded until the extraordinary high of 84 per cent in 1950. Why were so many electors persuaded to exercise their democratic franchise in 1924? It is understandable that the turnout was higher than in elections severely disrupted by the end of great conflicts, such as 1918 and 1945, or than in landslides when the outcome was certain, such as 1931 and 1935. But the interest generated by the 1924 campaign requires explanation, not least because as the third general election in a mere two years, theories of 'voter fatigue' would suggest that the turnout should have dropped compared with 1922 and 1923, rather than topping them. Nor was there as full a party candidature pattern as, say, the year before in December 1923, when the Liberals fielded 118 more candidates.

Clearly one factor was the response to the first ever Labour government, which galvanised both of what were rapidly becoming the two main parties. As noted, not only did the Conservative position strengthen substantially; but Labour itself increased both its actual vote, by a million, and its share as well. More clearly than in the previous elections, there was now a clear choice between these two parties. The issues of the campaign, such as the Campbell case, the Russian treaties and towards the end, of course, the Zinoviev letter, also caught the imagination of the voting public and sharply divided them. This all added to the higher level of 'civic responsibility', the feeling that it was a citizen's duty to vote, that was so much more widespread a century ago than it is today; and it should not be forgotten that for most of the electorate, not only women but up to 40 per cent of adult men, they had been able to exercise that right only since 1918, a mere six years previously. There had already been an increase in interest in parliamentary politics, as measured by the fact that the weekly sales of Hansard's parliamentary debates had nearly doubled during the brief term of Labour government compared with 1922.

To sum up the 1924 campaign: although MacDonald had made tactical mistakes over the Campbell case and the Zinoviev letter, Labour did not lose *because* of these factors. They were also vulnerable as the incumbent government on the issue of unemployment, for example. More than a million people were jobless, and the unemployment rate had fluctuated between 9 per cent and 12 per cent from January to October 1924, dipping in the summer but rising again to 10.6 per cent in September and 10.9 per cent in October. Though not the leading issue in the campaign, this was not a happy context for an administration to be re-elected. The Wheatley Housing Act and MacDonald's work for peace in Europe – however worthy – could not be converted in the short term into votes. The Conservatives' temporary abandonment of tariff reform helped them secure the free trade Liberal vote. The Liberals were in general hopelessly squeezed, with no distinctive policy appeal or united or dynamic leadership. Whether their decline was the result of long-term factors such as the rise of class as the key cleavage in British politics, or more contingent short-term circumstances, will continue to be debated. However, the existence of a Labour government had made people decide between two viable choices: a continuation or Baldwin's Conservatives.

Baldwin's new government, his second administration, contained many familiar and established names – indeed, compared with MacDonald's Cabinet, it strongly represented a return to the establishment. There were six members of the House of Lords among the twenty-one Cabinet members, along with Lord Eustace Percy, a son of the Duke of Northumberland who, with his courtesy title, was allowed to represent Hastings in the Commons. There were also eight knights of the realm, and only four men apart from Baldwin himself without a title. These did include the Cabinet's most interesting appointments and members, though. Despite his election for Epping under the label Constitutionalist, Winston Churchill was immediately invited by Baldwin to take the senior position of Chancellor of the Exchequer. Also in the Cabinet list were two men who were to vie with Churchill for prominence in the great crisis Britain was to face in 1940. Neville Chamberlain, whom Churchill was to replace as Prime Minister in that fateful year, was Baldwin's choice for Minister of Health (ironically having been Chancellor of the Exchequer himself immediately before the end of Baldwin's previous government, a year previously). Edward Wood was appointed Minister of Agriculture – as Lord Halifax, he was to be the main alternative to Churchill as Prime Minister sixteen years later.

All that, though, was in the future. For the time being, the main challenges facing Baldwin's renewed period in office were in economic and labour matters, leading up to Britain's one and only (so far) general strike in 1926, and eventually the return of MacDonald and Labour to form their second government in 1929. Despite a modest recovery by the Liberals in that year, this alternation – Conservative and Labour, Baldwin and MacDonald – emphasises and encapsulates the main implications of the 1924 election campaign for its winners and losers. In a way, both the Conservative Party and the Labour Party were winners.

Although Baldwin returned to office with a very comfortable majority in the short term, Labour had proved themselves to be credible enough contenders for government to be returned with far more seats at the next election. They were now the clear alternative, as that alternation was the precursor in all usual circumstances of the pattern over the full century ever since. It was the Liberals who were the principal losers in 1924, which marked a further critical step in the end of their status as a major party contending for government. Labour may have lost the election after their first taste of office; but they would be back for more.

Dr Robert Waller is a historian and psephologist. He wrote the 'Ramsay MacDonald' chapter in Iain Dale's *The Prime Ministers* and *The Almanac of British Politics*, which is now fully updated online at https://vote-2012.proboards.com/board/186/vote-almanac-british-politics-boundaries.

27

1929

ROSIE CAMPBELL

Dissolution: 10 May 1929
Polling day: 30 May 1929
Seats contested: 615
Total electorate / Total votes cast / Turnout: 28,854,748 (28,521,997 in contested seats) / 21,685,779 / 76.3 per cent
Candidates (total 1,730): Conservative – 590; Labour – 569; Liberal – 513; Communist – 25; Independent Conservative – 9; Independent Labour – 4; Nationalist – 3; Scottish Prohibition – 1
Prime Minister on polling day: Stanley Baldwin
Main party leaders: Conservative – Stanley Baldwin; Labour – Ramsay MacDonald; Liberal – David Lloyd George; Communist – Harry Pollitt; Scottish Prohibition – Edwin Scrymgeour; Nationalist – Joseph Devlin

Party performance:

Party	Votes	Percentage share	Seats
Conservative (including UUP)	8,252,527 (354,657)	38.1 (69.5)	260 (11)
Labour	8,048,968	37.1	287
Liberal	5,104,638	23.6	59
Communist	47,554	0.2	0
Independent Conservative	46,278	0.2	0
Scottish Prohibition	25,037	0.1	1
Nationalist	24,177	4.7	2
Independent Labour	20,825	0.1	1

Result: Hung parliament, Labour minority government

The 1929 general election was a momentous occasion, the first under universal suffrage, yet there is surprisingly little written about it. Perhaps because Lord Rothermere's so-called 'flapper danger' failed to materialise or because the campaign itself was a little boring. Nonetheless, it represents a fascinating moment in British electoral history.

The Representation of the People (Equal Franchise) Act of 1928 extended the right to vote to women aged over twenty-one, rather than thirty, and removed all property restrictions. The Act added approximately 5 million women to the electorate and meant that, for the first time, women made up the majority of potential voters. The Act was brought in by the Conservative government, with support of all three main parties. Despite being the handmaiden of this historic legislation, Prime Minister Stanley Baldwin was at best a reluctant supporter of extending the franchise, viewing it as an inevitable evil that must be contained and controlled by sensible, conservative leadership.

Baldwin called the election as soon as the new voting rights were in place, to take advantage of the Conservatives' local readiness for the election, and used the opportunity to appeal to voters to make a considered choice at the ballot box and 'return the trust' the government had shown in the new voters.

A restrained approach typified both the Conservative and the Labour campaigns. The Conservative government had a strong midterm performance and was perceived to have handled the general strike well. However, the party was losing popularity, unemployment was an average of 11 per cent in the year prior to the election and Baldwin had developed a reputation for indecision. Baldwin tried to exploit his cautious image by running on a 'safety-first' ticket, stressing his personal character and moderation against the radical threat he perceived from the Liberals, Labour and the extension of the franchise. He feared the consequences of unleashing a politically unschooled electorate and adopted a paternalistic approach designed to 'educate' the uninformed masses and to inspire their trust. The term 'safety first' was coined to stand for both Baldwin's personal leadership style and the industrial policy from which the name was derived. In his Plymouth speech in 1923, Baldwin had advocated safeguarding British industry by using protectionist strategies as a remedy for unemployment, contrasting the Conservatives with the Liberal commitment to free trade.

Ramsay MacDonald, the leader of the Labour Party, also ran a cautious campaign. Labour was still recovering its reputation from the impact of the Zinoviev letter, discussed in a previous chapter, and did not make radical promises, instead insisting that Labour would lead to no 'monkeying' policies. His goal was to position Labour as ready for competent government and de-emphasise trade unionism and nationalisation. Labour's attempts to present itself as moderate is illustrated by the fact that only 8 per cent of Labour candidate statements mentioned socialism.

Although the campaign itself was somewhat lacklustre, its scale was not. The election was fiercely fought, with the parties fielding candidates in more seats than in the previous elections. In 1929, 1,730 candidates stood compared with approximately 1,400 in each of the three elections between 1922 and 1924. The reason for this intensity was that the Liberals were spending much more on the contest, as David Lloyd George opened his personal war chest for the first time freely to Liberal candidates. Baldwin's desire to drive out the Liberals was driven by a personal animosity towards Lloyd George and a belief that Labour would appeal to only a minority of the electorate, and as such was not such a significant long-term threat to the Conservatives as the Liberals, who could challenge Tory candidates outside of the industrial heartlands. Churchill was one of the few Conservatives who feared Labour gains; he met with Baldwin to see if the number of three-way marginals could be reduced, but his argument did not cut through. MacDonald, too, was determined to eliminate the three-party system and to contest as many seats as possible to drive down the Liberal vote.

The result was a large number of three-way marginals with the Conservatives and Labour standing 'wrecking' candidates in seats they did not expect to win, with the intention of squeezing out the Liberals. For both Baldwin and MacDonald, seeing off Lloyd George and pushing the Liberals to the margins of British politics were key strategic goals of the election. In this they were enormously successful. The 1929 election was the moment when the Labour Party became firmly established as one of the two main parties, in a two-party system.

Most Conservatives viewed the Liberals as their main threat in 1928 and early 1929 and feared that they would split the anti-Labour vote. The Conservative policy platform and campaign strategy largely had the Liberals and not Labour as their target. A pivotal moment in the run up to the election was Lloyd George's promise, made on 1 March 1929, to 'cure' unemployment within two years. The Conservatives thought this unachievable, yet they feared it sounded impressive and could lose them votes. Lloyd George set out his strategy in his 'Yellow Book', entitled *We can conquer unemployment*, published in early 1929. He advocated a massive programme of public spending on key infrastructure, including roads and housing. Lloyd George ridiculed Baldwin's claim that increased broccoli sales in Cornwall were evidence of a recovering economy; Baldwin responded by wearing a sprig of broccoli in his lapel. According to several accounts, Lloyd George dominated the campaign.

Baldwin's approach was to attempt to harness the risk of electing the radical-sounding Lloyd George by portraying the Conservatives as the 'party of performance not promises'. Another significant feature of the Conservative campaign was a commitment to derating. After initially rejecting Winston Churchill's plan to derate (reduce taxation) and therefore reduce costs for agriculture and industry with the aim of stimulating production and thereby reducing unemployment, Baldwin later adopted derating as one of the key policy commitments of the Conservative campaign, alongside Neville Chamberlain's Poor Law reform plan and safeguarding British industry.

Labour policy commitments focused on tackling unemployment and affordable housing. They also made specific attempts to attract rural voters highlighting the low pay and precarious housing tenure of farm labourers, many of whom lived in tied housing belonging to their employer. In an attempt to appeal to small family-run businesses, such as shopkeepers, Labour criticised the Conservative plan for derating as a gift to agricultural landholders and big business, excluding small businesses. Labour's attention was on the north of England, which received the majority of visits from MacDonald and other leading Labour figures. MacDonald also visited Scotland, Birmingham and Bristol. Key Labour figures did not speak in marginal London seats and resources were focused where the party was strongest.

This was an election where, unsurprisingly, female voters were the subject of considerable attention from the parties and the media alike. Lord Rothermere had run a none-too-subtle campaign through the *Daily Mail* against removing the remaining limits on women's suffrage. 'Stop the Flapper Folly' was the title of the initial article that criticised changing gender roles, declining birthrates and racial and cultural decay. The younger women who would be entering the electorate were portrayed as superficial party-goers, ill prepared to make an informed choice at the ballot box. Lord Rothermere feared that young women would support Labour in their droves. In hindsight, he need not have been so afraid. Analysis of quality survey data, available only after the Second World War, shows that among the generations that came of age in the interwar period, women were more likely to support the Conservative Party than men, and this habit is likely to have developed when they first voted in 1929.

However, some analysis from the time came to different conclusions, but erroneously, because it made the mistake of falling into the ecological fallacy – that is, attempting to draw conclusions about individuals using group-level data. For example, American political scientist James Pollock claimed that Labour's advances in industrial areas resulted from securing a disproportionate share of younger women's votes: 'It is evident from the results that the Labor Party secured more than its share of the new "flapper" vote. The young women workers in the industrial areas swelled the Labor poll, but the effect of the woman vote has been less obvious in the residential areas.' But it is equally possible that men in these areas, who had previously voted Conservative, switched to Labour.

Arguably one reason why Lord Rothermere's fear that new female voters would support Labour en masse was unfounded is that the Conservative Party electoral machine was led by women at the local level. By the late 1920s, the Women's Unionist Organisation (WUO – the Conservative women's section) claimed to have approximately 1 million members, compared with peak membership of the Women's National Liberal Federation of around 88,000 members in 1926 and Labour women's sections consisting of circa 250,000 members in 1929. The WUO was already the most important Conservative election organisation on the ground and was ideally situated to target newly enfranchised female voters. The WUO distributed millions of copies of *Women of Today and Tomorrow*, a publication that focused on women's issues and featured a column where 'Mrs Maggs', an older and sensible charlady, gave advice to 'Betty', a politically apathetic maid. After the 1928 Act was passed, the Conservative women's advisory committee was given more power and oversight of the WUO, and as a result local Conservative associations hired female organisers to reach the newly enfranchised women in their constituencies. The WUO ran a campaign targeted at some 60,000 registered nurses: each received a letter with information about the government's work for women and children and an invitation to join the party. Nurses were thought to be strategically important given the volume of contact they had with women in their communities.

Labour did not have anything like this scale of women's organisation, but attempts to attract female voters were a feature of their campaign. The overwhelming majority of Labour candidates made reference to female voters in their campaign material and stressed Labour's support for votes for women. Labour leaflets described the party as being the party for women because of their emphasis on children and peace as well as championing better medical care for expectant mothers and the need for open-air nurseries. Labour also drew attention to taxes placed on household items such as pots and pans by the Conservative government in an attempt to attract female voters. However, given how important face-to-face contact is to mobilising voters, it is likely that the Conservatives had an advantage in 1929 when it came to recruiting women to the party.

The BBC ran eight radio election broadcasts prior to the start of the campaign, and four were allocated to the Conservative government. During the campaign itself, six broadcasts were allocated, with two to the Conservatives. Three of the broadcasts were made by women. At this time, about a quarter of households had a radio and most likely these were wealthier families; thus, broadcasts were unlikely to have been critical to Labour's advances in the election. MacDonald himself stressed the importance of his speaking tours and claimed to have addressed a quarter of a million people.

Despite three by-election losses in March 1929 – two to the Liberals and one to Labour – many Conservatives, including Baldwin, anticipated a Conservative victory; they viewed the Liberal advances as resulting from their increased spend rather than evidence of a groundswell of support. While the Conservatives might have been right about the Liberals, they underestimated Labour.

The strategy of squeezing out the Liberals was highly effective, half the seats in the election were won on minority votes and although the Liberal vote share increased to over 5 million (23.6 per cent of the vote), their representation in Parliament went up only from forty to fifty-nine. Lloyd George's last hurrah had failed. The Conservative Party won the most votes (gaining 38.1 per cent of the vote compared to Labour's 37.1 per cent) but won 260 seats, twenty-seven fewer than Labour (287). Baldwin resigned immediately; having made his personal appeal a core part of the campaign, he felt it was impossible to carry on.

The 1929 election saw the consolidation of the Labour Party as the main rival to the Conservatives. Industrial England had been moving towards Labour since 1918; after the 1929 election, this process was complete. The Conservative losses were mostly in the urban and mining districts, especially in the north of England where Labour gained more than seventy seats. The Conservatives lost fifteen seats in London, sixteen seats in Scotland and Conservative representation in Wales went down from nine to one. Labour's advance also continued to change the House of Commons, according to Professor H. Laski, writing at the time that there were 'fewer businessmen, lawyers, rentiers and soldiers and sailors' and 'more Trade Unionists than ever before'. While women were now the majority of voters, female candidates made up a mere 4 per cent of the total. The attention paid to female voters in 1929 was forgotten in most subsequent elections, to the extent that it is now sometimes necessary to remind commentators and party strategists that the majority of voters are women.

Rosie Campbell is a professor of politics at King's College London. Her publications cover the subjects of voting behaviour, public opinion, the politics of diversity and political recruitment. She has presented eight episodes of Radio 4's *Analysis*, most recently on 'does it matter who our MPs are?'

28

1931

ANDREW THORPE

Dissolution: 7 October 1931
Polling day: 27 October 1931
Seats contested: 615
Total electorate / Total votes cast / Turnout: 29,952,361 (27,130,119 in contested seats) / 20,693,475 / 76.4 per cent
Candidates (total 1,292): National government: Conservative – 518; Liberal – 112; National Liberal – 41; National Labour – 20. Opposition: Labour – 490; Communist – 26; New – 24; Independent Labour – 19; Independent Liberal – 6; Nationalist – 3
Prime Minister on polling day: Ramsay MacDonald
Main party leaders: National government: Conservative – Stanley Baldwin; Liberal – Herbert Samuel; Liberal National – John Simon; National Labour – Ramsay MacDonald. Opposition: Labour – Arthur Henderson; Independent Labour Party – James Maxton; Independent Liberals – David Lloyd George; Nationalist – Joseph Devlin; Communist – Harry Pollitt; New – Oswald Mosley

Party performance:

Party	Votes	Percentage share	Seats
National government	13,902,232	67.2	554
Conservative (including UUP)	11,377,022 (149,566)	55 (56.1)	470 (11)
Liberal	1,346,571	6.5	32
Liberal National	761,705	3.7	35
National Labour	316,741	1.5	13

Opposition			
Labour	6,081,826	29.4	46
Independent Labour Party	239,280	1.2	3
Nationalist	123,053	38.9	2
Independent Liberal	106,106	0.5	4
Communist	69,692	0.3	0
New	36,377	0.2	0

Result: National government majority of 492 seats

There have been close-call elections, safe majorities and sweeping victories, but no election before or since has resulted in such a massive landslide as the National government's victory over the Labour Party in October 1931. With 554 seats to Labour's forty-six, the government achieved a victory that dwarfed even the results in 1906, 1945, 1983, 1997 and 2019. A coalition of unequals comprising the Conservatives and Liberals but led by the erstwhile Labour Prime Minister Ramsay MacDonald, with the support of a dozen or so 'National Labour' MPs, the National government had been formed that August as a temporary expedient to deal with a major financial crisis. But things had moved on quickly, and an election had been called to stabilise the situation conclusively. Now, its victory would lead to a decade in power under first MacDonald (to 1935), and then Baldwin (1935–37) and Neville Chamberlain (1937–40). For good or ill, the National government would dominate British politics in the 1930s; only after Chamberlain's wartime fall from power in May 1940 would Labour return to office, as part of the Churchill coalition.

British political life in the 1920s was characterised, above all else, by a three-way competition for the electoral middle ground. Baldwin's particular brand of 'one-nation' Conservatism appealed strongly to many people. Labour, for its part, played down its trade union and socialist roots, instead emphasising its image as a party of moderate progress. In between, the Liberals worked, at some times more effectively than others, to shore up their crumbling support and make a wider appeal based on their supposedly new approach to the most pressing questions of the day. This three-way competition peaked at the May 1929 general election, but the results were somewhat inconclusive. Although the Conservatives won more votes, Labour took more seats but not an overall majority. Labour thus formed its second minority government, sustained initially with rather grudging Liberal tolerance and then, from mid-1930 onwards, in a more orderly arrangement of broad support. In opposition, the Conservatives struggled for some considerable time, with Baldwin coming under strong attack amid demands for a more strident, partisan form of Conservatism.

The second Labour government made a positive start. MacDonald, described by a German journalist around this time as 'the focus for the mute hopes of a whole class', was a political star, widely seen as a major electoral asset for the party. Moreover, he was respected and trusted by much of the political and government establishment. His Chancellor, Philip Snowden, was disliked by the more radical people in Labour's ranks but was seen by many in financial and business circles as offering at least some assurance of fiscal rectitude. Arthur Henderson, in many ways the founding figure of the post-1918 Labour Party, took over as Foreign Secretary, with a determination to bring Britain right to the centre of the League of Nations and use its influence in the direction of pacification and disarmament.

The underlying economic situation was not favourable, however. Unemployment had soared with the end of the post-war boom and had stood at more than a million since early 1921. Labour had fought the 1929 election as the party that could solve the problem, but the worsening conditions, symbolised and exacerbated by the Wall Street Crash of October 1929, led to a massive increase in the jobless total, which was to rise from 1.1 million to 2.8 million over the government's life (May 1929–August 1931). Even so, the government proved surprisingly resilient. First, despite noise and the breaking away of small splinter groups (Oswald Mosley's New Party, and also a group of left-wing members of the Independent Labour Party) in early 1931, the parliamentary party as a whole remained remarkably cohesive and loyal. Second, the Liberals, many of whom were viscerally opposed to Labour and would have liked to see the government fall, were initially reluctant to join forces with the Conservatives to overthrow it because they feared a further election, especially given the refusal of their leader, David Lloyd George, to continue the heavy levels of funding he had provided from his political fund in the run-up to 1929.

The government survived, but it did not thrive. The economic depression was bad in itself; it also inhibited new public expenditure, thwarting any prospect of meaningful social reform. Foreign affairs seemed brighter, with Henderson restoring Britain's reputation at the League of Nations, and MacDonald leading efforts to bring Anglo-American relations out of the deep freeze into which they had fallen under the Baldwin government. But, for the most part, things were quite grim. Indeed, the financial position began to deteriorate as tax revenues fell and expenditure – on unemployment benefits, among other things – rose. By early 1931, there were fears of a looming budgetary crisis. In February 1931, a Liberal motion in the House of Commons led to the establishment of a committee under the businessman Sir George May to look into the position.

When the May Committee reported in July 1931, it suggested that the budget deficit would be around £120 million, at the time an unconscionable amount. This frightening verdict actually suited the Chancellor, Snowden, who had long wanted a weapon to force through the spending cuts that he believed were necessary to balance the Budget, and so begin the restoration of 'sound finance': his Cabinet colleagues, instinctively spenders rather than savers, had thus far been able to thwart him. There was a problem, however, in that the financial markets took fright. They had always been nervous about Labour's ability to govern, and nothing that had happened in the past two years had disabused them of that view. Worse still, a recent and ongoing banking crisis in central Europe was continuing to damage both confidence and liquidity. In retrospect, the result was predictable – a run on the pound, a sense of crisis and a perceived need for rapid action.

In mid-August, key ministers were called back to London from their holidays to try to agree the details of spending cuts that would balance the Budget and restore confidence. Between 19 and 24 August, the whole Cabinet met daily and sometimes twice a day to hammer out a package. There was quite early agreement about £56 million of cuts, which mainly involved cutting the pay of government employees and other public servants. But attempts to save more on unemployment benefits by transferring responsibility to local authorities came to nothing.

This mattered: any package would have to pacify, if not satisfy, the financial markets, while Labour's minority position meant that the opposition parties would have to be prepared to co-operate in its passage through Parliament. Now, the bankers told MacDonald and Snowden that the agreed economies would not be enough to satisfy the markets. The Conservative leaders said the same. Crucially, the Liberals sided with the Conservatives, and also demanded greater cuts, thus marking the end of their period of co-operation with Labour, and removing any realistic prospect of an alternative, Lib-Lab approach. But attempts to make larger spending cuts came up against the adamantine opposition of the TUC general council, led by Ernest Bevin and Walter Citrine. Both men had been thoroughly unimpressed by Labour's record in government, which they saw as having done very little for the unions, or the working class more broadly. Far from agreeing to larger economies, the general council stated its opposition to all cuts (except, perhaps, in the salaries of Cabinet ministers, as Bevin put it), and proposed raising new revenues instead.

While some of the TUC's suggestions had support in respectable economic circles, no one close to government believed that the crisis could be solved without making any economies whatsoever. The result was that on the weekend of 22–23 August, the Cabinet agreed to ask bankers in New York whether they would be prepared to lend money to cover the Bank of England's immediate crisis, if a cut of 10 per cent was made in unemployment benefit as an earnest indication of the government's good intentions regarding fiscal prudence. In essence, their response was positive. But there was no Cabinet agreement on making the 10 per cent cut. Instead, ministers divided eleven to nine in favour of the cut, with the minority, led by Henderson, making clear that they would resign rather than accept it.

MacDonald was incandescent with his colleagues. As he saw it, he had been working for thirty years to establish Labour's 'fitness to govern'. Now, faced with a supreme test, the party had failed and chosen to run away from its responsibilities. It was a humiliation, not just for the party but for him personally. Increasingly tired of, and indeed bored with, some of his senior colleagues, his original thought was to resign and sit on the back benches as an independent MP giving broad support to a Conservative–Liberal coalition under Baldwin. The Conservative leaders, however, could see merit in MacDonald remaining premier to push through spending cuts that might prove unpopular, and which could be inflammatory in a 'class war' sense. This was a point that King George V also saw very clearly. When MacDonald went to Buckingham Palace on the morning of Monday 24 August to tender his government's resignation, the king made it clear that he would like him to remain as Prime Minister. He 'trusted that there was no question of the Prime Minister's resignation'; and he 'assured the Prime Minister that, remaining at his post, his position and reputation would be much more enhanced than if he surrendered the government of the country at such a crisis'. While not the vain, preening, self-obsessed character of post-1931 Labour legend, MacDonald was susceptible to flattery and came to believe that he would be able to make a real difference.

Thus it was that, when MacDonald returned to Downing Street from Buckingham Palace, he told his shocked Labour Cabinet colleagues that he had agreed to the king's request to form a National government 'to deal with the national emergency that now exists'. It would 'not be a Coalition Government in the usual sense of the term, but a Government of Co-operation for this one purpose', and '[w]hen that purpose is achieved, the political parties will resume their respective positions'. Parliament would meet on 8 September to approve a new Budget and pass legislation to put the planned economies into effect. Reporting back to the Cabinet, MacDonald added that at the end of the emergency period there would be a general election, at which there would be 'no "coupons", pacts or other arrangements'. MacDonald was joined in the ten-strong emergency Cabinet by Snowden, J. H. Thomas and the Labour Lord Chancellor, Lord Sankey; four Conservatives, namely Baldwin, Chamberlain, Sir Samuel Hoare and Sir Philip Cunliffe-Lister; and two Liberals, the acting leader Sir Herbert Samuel and Lord Reading, who became Foreign Secretary.

MacDonald also seems to have been playing with the idea of the possibility of engineering a significant breakaway from Labour, which would be the basis of a new Labour Party beyond the control of the unions. In this, he would prove much less successful. He did hold a meeting for the Labour government's junior ministers in the Cabinet room on the afternoon of the new government's formation. But he did not impress: 'Christ crucified speaks from the cross,' noted Hugh Dalton, who had been Henderson's number two at the Foreign Office. Those present were unclear whether he wanted them to follow him or not. In the event, only about a dozen Labour MPs went on to support the National government. Most were insignificant, but they did include Snowden and the senior minister Jimmy Thomas, the railway union leader. It was enough to give the government a 'National' veneer. But the National Labour Organisation that resulted would never make anything other than a few brief, localised challenges to Labour.

Labour in opposition elected a somewhat reluctant Henderson as its leader, but initially, at least, its policy shifted strongly towards the line of the TUC general council, which as we have seen, rejected the need for any cuts at all. This was, to say the least, uncomfortable for Henderson and the other ex-ministers. They had all, after all, agreed to the £56 million package which had included significant pay cuts for groups such as civil servants, teachers, armed forces personnel and the police. It was even worse for the six ex-ministers who had voted for the 10 per cent cut but not followed MacDonald. Henderson and his colleagues responded by employing sophistry: any agreement had been only 'provisional'; no decisions had finally been reached; and so on. It is not often that such sophistry convinces voters. It would not do so in 1931.

The problem with the 'emergency government' formulation was that it would never be easy to define when the 'emergency' period was over. This was especially so because, once in opposition, Labour swung sharply to the left, despite Henderson's best efforts to keep it on the moderate path. Talk of a 'bankers' ramp' – a financiers' conspiracy to destroy the Labour government and do down the working class – became more and more prevalent. Labour policy moved towards a much more stridently socialist position, which would culminate in Harold Laski's election manifesto slogan, 'We Must Plan or Perish'. Meanwhile, the National government warmed to its task and began to look like business as usual. When Parliament met on 8 September, it won a vote of confidence by a majority of sixty. Snowden, who remained Chancellor, introduced a Budget which cleverly limited its spending cuts to the £56 million to which the whole Labour Cabinet had agreed ('provisionally' or not), plus the 10 per cent unemployment benefit cut that had been supported by six ex-ministers who had not followed MacDonald. Thereafter, despite Labour's efforts, the government majority held, and the Budget passed.

Increasingly, therefore, the question became not 'why have an election as a National government' but 'why not?' The main resistance within the government came from Sir Herbert Samuel. He was instinctively anti-Conservative and broadly in sympathy with much of moderate Labour. He had led for the Liberals in the relationship with Labour in 1930–31. He was now acting in place of Lloyd George, who was out of action following a major prostate operation in the summer. Lloyd George was even more opposed to an election than Samuel. They both realised that an early election was likely to lead to a Conservative majority and the end of free trade. They argued against an election, but their position was weak. The Conservatives had been electorally confident even before the August crisis, regularly gaining seats at by-elections and showing every sign of having overcome their divisions, with Baldwin once more secure in the leadership. They had also decided their policy in favour of national economy, protection, help to agriculture and a bi-partisan policy on India. This, they believed, was a compelling package of proposals that would convince the electorate to back them. Voters were tired of equivocation and wanted clarity; soaring unemployment had seriously diminished faith in free trade. The election results would prove them right.

Even by mid-September, therefore, pressure was growing for an election, and increasingly there was support for fighting the election as a National government. The Invergordon Mutiny and the departure from the gold standard on 21 September offered nothing more than a brief hiatus in such pressure. A split in the Liberal Parliamentary Party, with the formation of a group under Sir John Simon, meant that there would be a credibly Liberal presence in the government, even if Samuel and his followers left. And the question of continuing tensions over trade policy was overcome, for the time being at any rate, by MacDonald's suggestion of a 'doctor's mandate': that the government would not rule out any expedient if it was in the interests of economic security and prosperity. All of this meant that, although the Liberal split went ahead (hence the 'Samuelite' and 'Simonite' Liberals), Samuel and his colleagues did eventually fight the election as supporters of the National government.

Labour's period in opposition had started with some optimism. The party's newly elected joint deputy leader Willie Graham had published an article in the *Daily Express* on 31 August claiming that it had a great opportunity, because voters would soon forget its disappointing record in office and would, instead, soon come to blame the National government for all the country's ills. It was an utterly ill-judged intervention. In fact, Labour's leaders struggled to show the basis of their resistance to the proposals that had brought the government down, while also trying to explain away their (now withdrawn) support for cuts to their supporters. Henderson cut an equivocal figure, often seeming to pull his punches in relation to MacDonald, perhaps through grief at the end of a long relationship, perhaps because he still hoped for some kind of reconciliation – when Britain went off gold he even seems to have believed, briefly, that he was about to be asked to join the government and bring the party with him. The unions, after their early assertiveness, began to realise that the party was heading towards electoral defeat and, although they backed the party financially and in other ways during the campaign, Bevin and Citrine were realistic enough to know that they needed to start preparing to work with the National government after the election. Thus, they were largely observers as the party swung sharply leftwards, partly through a Marxian-influenced analysis of the crisis, and partly as catharsis. They, and the more moderate Labour modernisers, such as Dalton, would get their chance to reform the party after the now-expected electoral setback.

When the Labour Party conference convened in Scarborough on 5 October, therefore, it was in a rather gloomy state. There was talk from some delegates of a coming struggle for power, but there was also a lot of pessimism. This mood was captured in a model election address, drafted around this time in Labour's Transport House headquarters, which spoke in one voice about the forthcoming Labour government and an implied socialist millennium but in another about the way in which every vote for Labour was a vote against reaction, and an insurance against further cuts, which hardly suggested optimism.

Meanwhile, MacDonald, riled by his formal expulsion from the Labour Party on 28 September, had become reconciled to the idea of an election. He continued to have doubts as to how credible he would be as Prime Minister leading a National appeal, given the small size of his Labour following, but Baldwin was happy to play second fiddle, and George V continued to buoy up his premier. When MacDonald told the king, towards the end of September, that he was 'beginning to feel that he had failed and had better clear out', he was greeted with a gruff response to the effect that he must 'brace himself up to realise that he was the only person to tackle the present chaotic state of affairs', and that even if MacDonald offered his resignation, the king 'would refuse to accept it'. On 5 October, George V agreed with alacrity to the request for a dissolution of Parliament on 7 October, with polling on Tuesday 27 October.

The parties' election manifestos were produced quickly. They were, of course, much shorter than their modern counterparts. Labour, which had played down its socialism to the extent of promising the nationalisation of only one industry (coal) in 1929, now pledged to bring large swathes of industry and finance into public ownership, on the grounds that capitalism had failed. The Bank of England, bête noire of the party following the financial crisis, would be included. There was a promise to plan the economy, although no one had much more than a rudimentary idea as to what that might involve. At the back of it all, though, were some rather more old-fashioned pledges, including a strong commitment to the maintenance of free trade and opposition to tariffs, even though it was known that some Labour leaders had, in the final days of the late government, been prepared to stomach a revenue tariff as an alternative to an unemployment benefit cut. Whatever else could be said about it, the manifesto was certainly radical and placed the party's socialist and trade union identities very much to the fore.

Each of the National government parties issued its own manifesto. The most coherent was that of the Conservatives. It repeated the four key pillars of policy that had been hammered out earlier in 1931: economy in public expenditure; protection and imperial preference; help for agriculture; and support for a bi-partisan policy on India. It appeared to be what it was – a coherent set of policies aimed squarely at trying to set the economy back on a positive track, while maintaining the empire as it evolved. The Samuelite Liberals favoured the government, obviously, but also defended free trade strongly, arguing that there was no presumption that the Conservatives' policies on trade would be followed. The whole National appeal was couched within the context of MacDonald's own appeal, which contrasted the cowardice of the Labour ex-ministers with his own courage, and which argued strongly for a 'free hand' or 'doctor's mandate':

> These are times of exceptional urgency and exceptional conditions, which demand exceptional treatment. As it is impossible to foresee in the changing circumstances of to-day what may arise, no one can set out a programme of detail on which specific pledges can be given. The Government must therefore be free to consider every proposal likely to help, such as tariffs, expansion of exports, and contraction of imports,

commercial treaties, and mutual economic arrangements with the Dominions. It must also watch how the devaluation of money and the economies which had to be made ... affect the lives of our people, and take every step which can be made effective to protect them against exploitation.

This formula was designed to allow people of all parties to support the government. Some, though, saw it as dishonest. Snowden, still Chancellor, although not standing for re-election, claimed that it would offer no mandate for protection: a further election would be needed for that. But he was slapped down by Chamberlain (soon to replace him at the Treasury); and it is clear from analysis of their constituency election addresses that the overwhelming majority of Conservative candidates were only too glad to boast of their protectionism. The truth of the matter was that free trade was now a diminishing electoral asset: it might have done down the Conservatives in 1906 and 1923, but the changing terms of electoral trade meant that increasing numbers of people blamed it for the country's economic woes and were ready for a change.

The party leaders ran very different campaigns. Baldwin had inherited his seat at Bewdley, in Worcestershire, from his father in 1908, and was so secure that he was re-elected unopposed in 1931, leaving him free to campaign across the country with impunity. Chamberlain was scarcely less secure. In 1924, he had retained his seat at Birmingham Ladywood by only seventy-seven votes against the youthful Labourite Oswald Mosley, but he had transferred to the leafier Edgbaston constituency in 1929 and secured a majority of over 14,000 (which would almost double, to 27,000, in 1931). MacDonald was worried about retaining his seat in the County Durham coalmining constituency of Seaham, but in the event, he was able to retain it against Labour and Communist opponents by a majority of almost 6,000. Henderson, on the other hand, had long feared that he would lose his seat at Burnley, where support for Labour had been collapsing, in part because of the abysmal condition of the cotton textiles industry that dominated the town. He had held it in 1929 in part because of a split opposition vote, taking 46 per cent to the Conservatives' 33 per cent and the Liberals' 21 per cent; but now, he had a single, 'National' opponent, Vice-Admiral Gordon Campbell VC, who had been a hero of the Q-ships during the Great War. So concerned was Henderson about losing his seat that he barely ventured outside east Lancashire and west Yorkshire during the campaign. The fact that he was also secretary and treasurer of the party meant that he had a massive workload, too. He would, in the event, lose the seat conclusively, with Campbell taking 56 per cent of the vote to his own 43 per cent. By then, Henderson was so ill and exhausted that he was bed-ridden and unable to attend the declaration of the poll.

One of the key players during the election campaign was not even running for election. Snowden, partially disabled from a young age and having had a serious operation earlier in the year, had announced that he would not stand for re-election in his west Yorkshire constituency of Colne Valley. However, he remained Chancellor for the time being and stayed at 11 Downing Street throughout the campaign, covering for MacDonald on government business. He had never been an admirer of the post-1918 Labour Party, which had been largely created by Henderson in his role as party secretary, with a heavy emphasis on the trade union link. Instead, he looked back to the days of the 'old' ILP, when ethical socialists had come together to dream about, and plan for, a socialist future. It may well be that he had hopes of re-creating such a body from the ashes of the August crisis, but, as with MacDonald, any hopes in that direction came to very little. Nonetheless, he was determined to bring down the people who had betrayed the government during that crisis. In a series of media interventions, he exposed the extent to which the Labour ex-ministers had agreed to spending cuts in Cabinet, and also the fact that many of them had voted in favour of a revenue tariff (which he had vetoed).

Snowden's crucial intervention, though, would come via a relatively novel medium. The first radio election broadcasts had come in 1924 but had been very rudimentary: the three party leaders (MacDonald, Baldwin and Asquith) had each been broadcast once, addressing public meetings. In 1929, a series of talks were broadcast from the

BBC studios, but they had been largely unremarkable in content and impact. This time it was different. Perhaps recognising the potential of radio more fully (and as the ownership of radio sets continued to expand, with an estimated 16.3 million people capable of listening, as opposed to 11.8 million in 1929), the parties had been keen to press the BBC for more broadcasts. In the end, it was agreed that there would be ten, with Sir John Reith deciding that there should be two for the Conservatives (both delivered by Baldwin, who was widely regarded, not least by himself, as something of a master of the art); three for the Liberals (each to the leader of a separate faction – Lloyd George, Samuel and Simon); two for National Labour (Snowden and MacDonald); and three for Labour (J. R. Clynes, Graham and Henderson). Reith claimed that this was an equal split between Labour and the rest, but of course this was nonsense – the battle was between the government and opposition, and there the split was 6:4 (given that Lloyd George had now come out in opposition to the government).

Of the ten broadcasts, it was Snowden's that was the most sensational. Delivered just after 9 p.m. on Saturday 17 October, it came just ten days before polling. In a twenty-minute diatribe, he attacked his former party and colleagues in no uncertain terms. They had shown a lack of 'courage' in the face of the threat of 'national bankruptcy'. The National government, by contrast, had defended the value of money, so that 'the purchasing power of the pound at home is still worth twenty shillings'. He denied that Labour was a free trade party: its policies of state subsidies to agriculture and industry were the very negation of free trade, and a month earlier Henderson had been prepared to countenance a 20 per cent revenue tariff in preference to a 10 per cent benefit cut. Warming to his task, he went on:

> I hope you have read the election programme of the Labour Party. It is the most fantastic and impracticable programme ever put before the electors. All the derelict industries are to be taken over by the State, and the taxpayer is to shoulder the losses. The banks and financial houses are to be placed under national ownership and control, which

means, I suppose, that they are to be run by a joint committee of the Labour party and the Trade Union Council. Your investments are to be ordered by some board, and your foreign investments are to be mobilised to finance this madcap policy. This is not Socialism. It is Bolshevism run mad.

This was, he said, very different from the 'sane and evolutionary Socialism' that he still supported. Labour's plans would 'destroy every vestige of confidence and plunge the country into irretrievable ruin'. In supporting the National government, he concluded, he was doing his best to serve 'the best interests of the working classes and safeguarding their future progress'.

This was incendiary stuff. The phrase 'Bolshevism run mad' was perfect for newspaper editors to use as a headline, in both the Sunday and the Monday papers. The *Daily Mirror*, at the time a right-wing pictorial paper owned by Lord Rothermere, headed its Monday edition with the phrase, accompanied by a large photograph of Bolsheviks opening fire on a crowd in Petrograd in 1917. It would repeat the headline on the eve of polling a week later, this time using a photograph of starving children in the Volga region from 1922. This was unfair, perhaps even slanderous, but it was effective. Snowden followed up with further charges against his former colleagues. In an article in the *Daily Mail* on 20 October, he attacked 'Labour's Little Lenins', and when Graham tried to answer his charges in a broadcast that same day, he responded swiftly in print.

This was not the end of the fierce attacks on Labour. On 23 October, Henderson defended the nationalisation of the banks on the grounds that the Post Office Savings Bank was state owned and run, with no concern about the security of people's deposits there. But the following day, Walter Runciman, the Liberal National MP (who, after the election, would become president of the Board of Trade), argued that such deposits had, in fact, been rendered vulnerable because the Labour government had allowed the unemployment insurance fund to borrow so much from it. It was true that the fund's borrowing powers were underwritten by the funds in the bank, and that the borrowing powers allowed by legislation had increased significantly as the fund's position had deteriorated due to increased unemployment. However, the bank had been far from insolvent (the debt stood at £75 million at the end of 1931, as against overall assets of almost £300 million). Henderson dismissed the claims as a scare, but Snowden (inevitably) supported them, and the 10 million or so Post Office Savings Bank account holders must have paid some attention. When these stories and claims were added to by gimmicks such as MacDonald waving around German banknotes from the period of hyperinflation in 1923, it was not surprising that Labour called 'foul'. In fairness, though, Labour itself was happy to impugn the motives of ministers, and to claim that there was an intention to 'starve' workers via benefit and wage cuts that did not, ultimately, eventuate.

Labour was also up against it when it came to the press. The party had always been opposed by most national and local newspapers. But the position was even worse in 1931, in two ways. Papers that might have been even slightly sympathetic, particularly a Liberal paper like the *News Chronicle*, came out firmly for the National government. And, secondly, the tone of pretty much every national and regional daily paper was stridently anti-Labour and pro-National. Apart from the *Daily Herald*, which was jointly owned by the TUC and Odhams Press but over which the TUC had full editorial control, every national daily was strongly pro-National. The *Herald* had a circulation of 1.1 million – the other eight papers totalled 7.4 million. Out of eleven Sunday papers, meanwhile, only the Co-operative movement's *Reynolds's Illustrated News*, with a circulation of 400,000, stood up for Labour, with the other ten – totalling nearly 12.5 million sales – coming out for the government.

The conduct of the campaign itself was reckoned to be fairly quiet. This remained an age when electioneering largely took place in person, either at public meetings or via canvassing. National figures could command audiences of thousands in major venues, but the typical public meeting was likely to be held in a school room, or similar, and candidates might address four or more such meetings most evenings throughout the three weeks of the campaign (although attitudes towards Sunday campaigning varied for religious reasons). Election addresses were posted out free to households in each constituency, with every candidate having the chance to get their message across in that way. Typically a folded sheet (thus comprising four pages of text and illustrations), these varied considerably according to party and candidate. They repay close analysis: for example, detailed study shows, among other things, that most Conservative candidates were very open about their support for tariffs. The Labour claim that the doctor's mandate was a protectionist 'ramp' thus had little basis in reality. All parties produced a plethora of leaflets and pamphlets, although in Labour's case this was complicated by the fact that MacDonald's defection meant its 'stock' literature was rendered unusable, given that his picture featured on it prominently. There was only limited public disorder during the campaign. Much of it surrounded the campaigns of the twenty-six Communist candidates: in Edinburgh Central, for example, an effigy of Willie Graham was burnt in the street by some of his Communist opponents. But these were fairly isolated incidents. The Communist Party, like Mosley's New Party, which ran a similar number of candidates, was unable to make any kind of breakthrough whatsoever.

More significant, by far, was the fact that the unemployment figures began to fall once Britain left the gold standard. Weekly figures, published in the press, showed a downward trend that was so interesting to the government that it ensured that the figures for the final week of the election were published early, in time for polling day. We now know, of course, that the trend did not last: indeed, unemployment would rise even higher in 1932 than it had been in 1931. But, for a time, the National government looked like a prosperity government, and ministers made great oratorical play of the fact that the chimneys were beginning to smoke again, a sure sign, they believed, of happier times ahead.

For all the apparent melodrama, turnout in 1931, at 76.4 per cent, was only 0.1 per cent higher than in 1929, and marginally lower than in 1924 (77 per cent). Tuesday 27 October was unremarkable weather wise, with some fog in the south and rain in the north, but nothing out of the ordinary for the time of year. There were no opinion polls, of course, but the most popular stock market predictions of the outcome started at a 150 majority for the government, and by polling day this had risen to 205.

As it transpired, the margin would be much larger. When the results began to be declared late that evening, it became clear that Labour had been not just defeated but pretty well annihilated. The National government polled 14.5 million votes (67.2 per cent) and won 554 of the 615 seats in Parliament. Labour, by contrast, won only forty-six seats on the back of 6.3 million votes (29.4 per cent). Of course, the result in seats was disproportionately favourable to the National government, which won 90 per cent of the seats on two-thirds of the vote. But even had the seats been proportionally aligned, it would still have been a heavy defeat for Labour. Its poll share had dropped by around a quarter, from 37.1 per cent in 1929. More notably still, given the essential realignment from a truly three-party system into two opposing blocs, Labour was a long way off the kind of poll share that it would need if it was to form a government in future.

The bulk of the National government's MPs (470 out of 554) were Conservatives. Even before the summer of 1931, the party had been well prepared for the next election and had had a settled slate of candidates in place. A few of them were prepared to stand down in the interests of a National candidate from the Liberals or Labour, but most were not; and where such candidates faced Conservative opposition, they almost invariably lost. The Liberals were now split three ways: the Simonites, now styled Liberal Nationals, who would stick with the government come what may, took thirty-five seats, while the official Liberals, or Samuelites, won thirty-three. That left the Lloyd George family group, who had opposed the government, with four MPs (Lloyd George himself, his son Gwilym, his daughter Megan and Gwilym's wife's sister's husband, Goronwy Owen). The high hopes of National Labour had not come to much. Despite raising a significant amount of money from wealthy backers, MacDonald's group numbered just thirteen. But MacDonald had held Seaham, while Thomas had easily retained his seat at Derby.

The brooding MacDonald, as ever able to pluck gloom from joy, reflected privately that 'it was all too terrible' and said in public that 'the very emphasis of the response [was] embarrassing'. Embarrassing or not, it gave a huge mandate to the National government. The scale of the victory was astounding, not least to some Conservative candidates who had agreed to stand for hopeless seats because they were safe in the knowledge that they would not win, only to find themselves stuck in Parliament until the next general election. MacDonald was to remain Prime Minister until June 1935, when, after George V's Silver Jubilee, he swapped offices with Baldwin, to become Lord President of the Council. Chamberlain took over from Snowden as Chancellor and served at the Treasury for five and a half years until, following the coronation of George VI in May 1937, he succeeded Baldwin as Prime Minister. The government was quick, in early 1932, to impose tariffs on imports, a major development in British trade policy and one that reflected the increasing international economic tensions of the time. The free traders – the Samuelites and Snowden (now Lord Privy Seal) remained in the government for the time being but resigned that September when the conclusion of the Ottawa agreements on inter-imperial trade indicated the permanent nature of protectionism. Simon (now Foreign Secretary) and his followers remained, however. At the November 1935 general election, the National government under Baldwin won another conclusive, if not quite so spectacular, victory; and there is little evidence to suggest that Labour would have ousted it at a general election in 1938 or 1939.

Labour's woes were certainly not over. The scale of its defeat had been spectacular. It had not gained a single seat, and the Conservatives had not lost any. The movement was all in one direction – away from Labour. Not only had it lost all the marginals that had helped to carry it to office in 1929: it had lost seats which had been safely Labour for years. These included constituencies such as Manchester Platting, the seat that Clynes had held since 1906. Seats that the party had won with huge majorities in 1929 – such as Rotherhithe (1929 Labour majority 42.3 per cent), Sheffield Attercliffe (40.8 per cent) and Morpeth (39.2 per cent) – now went National. It was a bitter defeat.

Out of the members of the late Labour Cabinet, only one held their seat – George Lansbury, in the East End of London. Only two of the former junior ministers hung on – Clement Attlee, also in the East End, and Sir Stafford Cripps, in Bristol East. Henderson retained the leadership but, no longer an MP, could not lead in Parliament, and that task fell to Lansbury. During 1932, Henderson became increasingly preoccupied with chairing the World Disarmament Conference at Geneva, and when his moderate speech at the October 1932 party conference saw him shouted down by party members on the conference floor, he resigned the leadership and was replaced by Lansbury. Attlee's survival in 1931 catapulted him into the deputy leadership in a way that no one would have predicted prior to the events described above, and when Lansbury was forced out of the leadership in 1935, it was Attlee who was on hand to take over, at first temporarily, and then on an ongoing basis, only finally retiring in 1955 after a five-year stint in the Churchill coalition (1940–45) and six years as Prime Minister of the first majority Labour government (1945–51). During the 1930s, Labour would seek to remodel itself, and indeed it did make some progress in terms of policy development, leadership and organisation. But it would take the events of the Second World War to propel it once more to the centre of power in British politics.

The 1931 election, then, was one of the most sensational in British history. It saw the culmination of trends that had been in place since the end of the Great War – Conservative hegemony, Liberal decline and a check to the rather headlong Labour progress of the 1920s. It showed how much Labour struggled when it tried to make a broad appeal with its trade union and socialist bases prominently on display – something that would also prove to be the case in 1983 and 2019. As far as the Conservatives were concerned, the 1931 election demonstrated the value of having a clear set of policies in a context where many voters were keen to support anything that looked like a credible and practicable solution to the current crisis. But what it perhaps demonstrated, above all else, was the ability of the British political system to provide democratic, parliamentary solutions to even the most extreme of political, financial and economic crises. In that sense, it marked an important moment not just in the development of the twentieth-century party system but also in the development and survival of liberal democracy in Britain at a time when it was under fierce, and increasingly fatal, attacks elsewhere.

Andrew Thorpe is professor of modern history and executive dean of arts, humanities and cultures at the University of Leeds. His publications include *The British General Election of 1931* (1991), *Parties at War: Political Organization in Second World War Britain* (2009) and *A History of the British Labour Party* (4th edition, 2014).

29

1935

JOHN BARNES

Dissolution: 25 October 1935
Polling day: 14 November 1935
Seats contested: 615
Total electorate / Total votes cast / Turnout: 31,374,449 (29,556,328 in contested seats) / 20,991,488 / 71.1 per cent
Candidates (total 1,348): National government (total 583): Conservative – 515; National Liberal – 44; National Labour – 20; National – 4. Opposition: Labour – 552; Liberal – 161; Independent Labour – 17; SNP – 8; Independent Liberals – 5; Independent Republican – 3; Nationalist – 2
Prime Minister on polling day: Stanley Baldwin
Main party leaders: National government: Conservative – Stanley Baldwin; National Liberal – John Simon; National Labour – Ramsay MacDonald. Opposition: Labour – Clement Attlee; Liberal – Herbert Samuel; Independent Labour Party – James Maxton; Independent Liberals – David Lloyd George; Nationalist – T. J. Campbell; SNP – Alexander MacEwen

Party performance:

Party	Votes	Percentage share	Seats
National government	11,183,908	51.8	429
Conservative (including UUP)	10,025,083 (292,840)	47.8 (64.9)	387 (11)
National Liberal	866,354	3.7	33
National Labour	339,811	1.5	8

National	53,189	0.3	1
Opposition			
Labour	7,984,988	38	154
Liberal	1,414,010	6.7	21
Independent Labour Party	136,208	0.7	4
Nationalist	101,494	22.4	2
Independent Liberals	67,653	0.3	4
Independent Republican	56,833	12.6	0
SNP	29,517	0.2	0

Result: National government majority of 242 seats

The importance of the National government's victory in the 1935 election can scarcely be overstated in that it ensured Britain's survival in 1940. Its overwhelming majority was won in unusual circumstances. The government was dealing with an international crisis when Baldwin told his constituents on 19 October that he had decided to go to the country. Mussolini had invaded Abyssinia on 3 October and the League of Nations had branded him an aggressor on the 7th. The Cabinet had agreed to the gradual imposition of economic sanctions on the 8th and the league had imposed limited sanctions on Italy between the 11th and the 19th. While claiming the election to be unnecessary, the Labour opposition looked beyond the current crisis, campaigning for significantly different defence and foreign policies from those pursued by the government. They were agreed only on their support for the League of Nations, but Labour demanded 'speedy action, through the League, to bring the war in Africa to an end, to be followed by an immediate resumption of negotiations for all-round disarmament'. While pledged to maintain 'such defence forces as are necessary and consistent with our membership of the League', it claimed that

> the best defence is not huge competitive national armaments, but the organisation of collective security against any aggressor and the agreed reduction of national armaments everywhere. Labour will propose to other nations the complete abolition of all national air forces,

the effective international control of civil aviation and the creation of an international air police force; large reductions by international agreement in naval and military forces; and the abolition of the private manufacture of, and trade in, arms.

At the very least, a Labour victory would have led to an immediate halt to British rearmament and a long delay while it sought to bring about World Disarmament and Economic Conferences. A year's delay might well have proved fatal when war came. Giving a stronger lead to the League of Nations, particularly in seeking an oil sanction against Italy and attempting to deny Italians the use of the Suez Canal, was feasible, but its consequences were uncertain. Such moves would not have had French support, a major problem had Mussolini responded with force.

Historians underrate the significance of the 1935 election because they deem Baldwin's victory inevitable; and it is true that the Labour Party had a mountain to climb. To be sure of victory, it would need to increase its vote by a fifth. However, a fall in the government vote of only 12 per cent was likely to produce a hung parliament. Those advising Baldwin did not see that as an unlikely outcome. Between East Fulham (25 October 1933) and Dumfries in September 1935, twenty-seven by-elections took place. In all but three, the results could be meaningfully compared. While there were three in which the government lost less than 10 per cent of its 1931 vote, in the remaining twenty-one, the fall was never less than 16 per cent. In eight, it was more than 22 per cent. If we exclude Liverpool Wavertree and Norwood – where Winston Churchill's son, Randolph, ran independent Conservative candidates, splitting the government vote – the largest fall in the Conservative share was at Putney on 28 November 1934. A fall of 26.6 per cent suggests that continuing concerns expressed by Conservative Central Office about the success of Labour's 'Peace and Disarmament' campaign were well founded. Hence, when Baldwin sought advice in July 1935 on whether to hold the election in November or the spring of 1936, the Central Office official concerned added a rider to his argument in favour of delay:

> Even if the Socialist party did not obtain the support of a largely increased section of the electorate, we could still lose the next election or at any rate arrive at a stale-mate position if the bulk of the Liberal vote went over to them. From that point of view the Liberal vote is vital and no political issue is likely to influence them more than the question of peace and war and the future of the League of Nations.

Baldwin became Prime Minister on 7 June 1935 largely because the Conservatives, as the dominant party in the coalition, were unwilling to fight on a national platform unless its leader headed the government. He was also seen to be accorded an unusual degree of confidence by the country. He faced an increasingly difficult international situation, but at home the economy had been growing and unemployment falling since 1932–33, which was why the Labour Party since the summer of 1933 had made 'Peace and Disarmament' the major theme of their by-election campaigns. The spectre of German rearmament was the major international problem faced by the government in the early months of 1935, but with the summer, Mussolini's intention to absorb Abyssinia into the Italian Empire came to the fore. Every effort by Britain and France to find a solution that would preserve the country's independence while giving Italy control over its economic resources was rejected. Mussolini wanted his war.

The British government faced an almost impossible choice. It had reached an agreement with France and Italy in April about the way in which they would handle Hitler's demand to be freed from the shackles of Versailles, the treaty imposed on Germany in 1919. While there remained a significant body of opinion on the right, backed by the newspapers owned by Lords Beaverbrook and Rothermere, which wanted to stand aside from European conflicts and build up Britain's defences, a very much larger part of the nation shared Sir Edward Grey's belief that 'great armaments lead inevitably to war' and agreed with Baldwin that the next war would wipe out European civilisation. They put their trust in the League of Nations.

The extent of that support is evident from the replies to the ballot organised by the all-party League of Nations Union in 1934–35. They were made known to a National Convention on 28 June and put to the Prime Minister by a deputation headed by the league's principal architect, Lord Cecil, on 23 July. In total, 11.6 million votes had been cast, well over a third of the total electorate. Asked whether Britain should stay in the league, nearly 11.2 million said 'yes' and only around 358,000 'no'. The continued pursuit of disarmament by international agreement was favoured by 10.3 million to 868,000, and the abolition of naval and military aircraft by 9.6 million to 1.7 million. The prohibition of the manufacture and sale of armaments for private profit also got a strong 'yes' vote of 10.5 million with 780,000 against. The final question had been split into two parts, allowing those favouring the use of economic sanctions against an aggressor to decide whether they also favoured taking military measures should those prove necessary. Overall, 10 million voted for economic sanctions, 639,000 against and 863,000 giving no answer. The figures were strikingly different when it came to military measures, with 6.8 million in favour, 2.4 million against and 2.4 million making no answer. While publicly critical of the assumption that questions three to five could be answered by a simple 'yes' or 'no' and still more of publicity that represented the choice as that between peace and war, Baldwin knew that many of the bodies backing the ballot had no intention of criticising the government. He chose to treat the results as support for the government's commitment to the League of Nations.

While the greater part of the Labour Party would have given an affirmative answer to these questions, a significant minority agreed with Cripps and the Socialist League in seeing the League of Nations as an instrument of the imperialist powers. Nor was the party's leader, George Lansbury, alone in his outright pacifism. Notwithstanding these differences, the questions were used to harass government candidates as part of Labour's highly effective by-election strategy. The party indicted the government for its 'failure' to support the league over the Japanese seizure of Manchuria, for 'wrecking' the World Disarmament Conference and for embarking on an arms race when it decided to add forty-one squadrons to the RAF in July 1934. That Germany was rearming, and that the British government's purpose was to induce it to return to the negotiating table and to secure an arms limitation agreement based on parity which would bind Britain, France and Germany, was brushed aside. The increase was 'calculated to lead to a renewal of international rivalry and to hinder the establishment of durable peace through the League of Nations'. Moving a vote of censure, Attlee argued that Britain had no need to seek parity with any other nation since military activity would be undertaken only at the behest of the league and Britain could rely on powers with more powerful air forces to be part of a joint enterprise. Instead, Britain should propose the abolition of military aviation, international control of civil aviation and the creation of an international air force.

In the face of Churchill's claims that the Luftwaffe was already rapidly approaching equality with the RAF and would be its equal, if not its superior, in 1935, the government felt compelled to make public its knowledge that Germany was rearming and to accelerate its expansion of the RAF. On 4 March 1935, it published a White Paper defending its decision and the modernisation of the other armed services. Hitler's response to the White Paper – introducing conscription, increasing the size of the army and announcing the existence of the Luftwaffe – was seen by the Parliamentary Labour Party (PLP) as confirmation that the White Paper marked a disastrous change of policy: 'we are back in the system of alliances and rivalries and an armaments race.' The party offered the only sure road to salvation, a move forward 'to a new world – a world of law, the abolition of national armaments with a world force and a world economic system'. The Liberal Party backed them.

Hitler's spurious claim that the Luftwaffe was already the equal of the RAF prompted the British government to embark in May 1935 on a much larger expansion of the RAF, to be completed by 1937. The decision won reluctant backing from the Liberal Party and exposed something of a rift within the Labour movement. A majority of the TUC general council thought that the PLP ought to refrain from opposing the measures, and they found some support in the party's national executive. But Hitler's emollient broadcast on 21 May was sufficient reassurance for the PLP. Attlee and Cripps responded by calling for an immediate halt to the government's programme, coupled with the calling of a World Disarmament Conference to consider Hitler's proposals. There could be no defence against aerial attack, hence the government should press for the abolition of military aircraft and the internationalisation of civil aviation. While there were faint signs in Scotland that, as reported by the secretary of the Scottish Labour Party, 'the positive passion for Peace which gave us such a powerful plea in earlier elections was not so effective under the shadow of Hitler's threats', the government took little comfort from its victories, its vote falling by 18.1 per cent in Edinburgh West and 17.7 per cent at Aberdeen South.

West Toxteth (16 July 1935), Conservative until 1924, and now Labour again, confirmed that the party's electoral prospects in England remained bleak. The Labour majority was double that in 1929, the Conservative vote down by 18.8 per cent. As *The Times*'s correspondent observed, the outcome was believed to rest with the Liberals locally, and they had not voted Conservative. Chamberlain was urging that, since Labour 'obviously intend to fasten upon our backs the accusation of being warmongers', they should appeal to the country on their defence programme, but Conservative Central Office doubted that scare tactics would work. Baldwin told Chamberlain that he would leave his decision until his return from a summer break in France, but in his mind the choice lay between November and the spring of 1936. Central Office favoured the latter, convinced that the Conservatives should make the continuing economic recovery their major theme. Chamberlain's Budget in April had completed the reversal of the austerity cuts made in 1931 and increased tax allowances. It was a substantial boost to the standing of the government. Even more important was the rise in the standard of living. The fall in prices since the early 1920s had left almost all but the rich a good deal better off. National income might remain slightly below its 1929 total, but wage rates were well on their way back to their 1924 level, with prices less than two-thirds of where they had then been. In terms of purchasing power, therefore, the employed were some 20 per cent better off, but even an unemployed man with a family had gained.

Although there were still 2 million out of work, the number was falling month on month: since the measure referred to insured workers, the actual figures were higher and the percentage of those out of work lower than the figures usually quoted. More relevant in terms of its political consequences were the regional variations, with the percentage out of work less than 7 per cent in the south-east, below 8 per cent in the Midlands and the south-west, but 14 per cent in the north, almost 16 per cent in Scotland and more than 23 per cent in Wales. The figures in some of the former staple industries were even higher: 25 per cent in coal and 30 per cent in shipbuilding and steel. However, for more than three-quarters of the population – not least because a house could be built for £300, a Ford Ten bought for £100 and two out of three homes were now fully wired for electricity – there was a marked shift towards a consumer economy. Economic recovery and housebuilding should be major planks in Baldwin's election platform, hence the strong case for leaving the election to the later date.

It is time to turn to the Liberals and their erstwhile supporters, since those were the votes Baldwin needed to target. A rough estimate would suggest that his victory in 1924 had been founded on taking three votes from the Liberal Party for every one taken by Labour. The Liberal revival in the late 1920s had cost Baldwin the 1929 general election. The leaders of Liberal Party had left the National government in September 1932 and crossed the floor into opposition in November 1933. The party was well on the road to disintegration, lacking in distinctive policies and short of the cash necessary to fight by-elections. Where it did fight, its vote collapsed. Its erstwhile leader, Lloyd George, refused to link his fortunes with it and pursued his own agenda. Where there was no Liberal standing in a by-election, he had given public support to the Labour candidate, giving disarmament as his reason. On 18 October 1933, the East Fulham Liberal Association, 'regarding the question of disarmament as of vital importance', gave its support to the Labour candidate and he won an unexpected victory in a seat which Labour had never won. That became the norm and where there was a Liberal intervention, as at Rushcliffe, it enabled the Conservatives to retain the seat.

What determined the timing of the election and made Baldwin's victory a certainty was Mussolini's determination to incorporate Abyssinia in the Italian Empire. The details of the dispute that came to the League of Nations need not concern us, as it was merely a pretext for the Italian invasion. The tripartite agreement reached with Italy and France in April would be at risk if Italy went ahead. The league would have no choice but to impose sanctions and the government would have to support the league. It is tempting but wrong to accept the view that Britain's policy was determined by electoral considerations. Although public opinion was a major factor in the government's decision to back the league, it had become a valued actor in international efforts to maintain peace. Both the Chancellor and the Foreign Secretary thought it must be tried out in the hope that both France and Italy, with more than one eye on Germany, would see the sense of vindicating the league's authority, and Baldwin concurred. They were far from confident about a successful outcome, but if the league were to fail, it was best for everyone to recognise the fact and for its Covenant to be revised. When consulted, virtually every political leader who mattered agreed that the government had no option but to back the league, provided that the other members, and in particular France, were prepared to take the same action. They included the leaders of the Labour and Liberal parties, Austen Chamberlain, Lloyd George, Churchill and Lord Cecil. No doubt that influenced the inner Cabinet, and its decision that the only safe course was to honour their obligations to the league was ratified by the Cabinet on 22 August. Were the system of collective security damaged or destroyed, Britain's leaders were certain that it would weaken their ability to cope with Germany and foster the growth of isolationism in Britain. When Hoare stated British policy at the League of Nations Assembly on 11 September, his speech unexpectedly captured the attention of both the world and the British public. The reception of the speech transformed the political climate. With the notable exception of the Rothermere newspapers, the British press enthused – although Beaverbrook anticipated that collective action would not follow and that the government would then become isolationist.

Baldwin recognised the opportunity to gain support for rearmament by deploying the argument that effective support for the league required Britain to bring its armed forces up to date. What he may not have anticipated was the impact of the crisis on the Labour Party. The three executives that made up its collective leadership had met prior to the Trades Union Congress and agreed a joint declaration supporting any league action to enforce peace. Since the Socialist League saw the League of Nations as an imperialist and capitalist institution, Stafford Cripps opposed the move. The Labour leadership in the Lords also dissented. The leader of the Labour Party, George Lansbury, was a committed pacifist. In his fraternal address, while not questioning his party's support for the league, he concentrated on calling for a World Economic Conference to internationalise the supply of raw materials. While Cripps and Lord Ponsonby resigned from the party's national executive, Lansbury was content to publicise his dissent, pending a meeting of the PLP when the Labour Party conference assembled at Brighton on 28 September. The debate on the national executive's resolution on 1 October, which called for a World Economic Conference but endorsed the full range of league sanctions, became notorious for Ernest Bevin's brutal denunciation of Lansbury for 'hawking your conscience round from body to body'. Because of the unions' block vote, the outcome was never in doubt, but a hundred constituency parties were in the minority, and many Labour MPs held that law-action against should not lead to war-action. Lansbury had to force his resignation on a reluctant PLP, and they chose Clement Attlee as a temporary leader to take them into the election. It was for Attlee, therefore, to define the party's position: while the league needed to be backed and strengthened, 'this occasion should be taken for a great leap forward towards disarmament and not towards increased armaments'.

By the time Baldwin spoke to the rally at the conclusion of the Conservative conference on 3 October, the Italian invasion of Abyssinia was underway. Emphasising that the government's support for the League of Nations did not involve hostility to the Italian people, he brought that support and Britain's need to rearm together in a skilfully framed argument that they were the best hope of avoiding war. An admiring friend noted that he had 'a great ovation. Denounced the isolationists, reconciled the party to the League by supporting rearmament and reconciled the pacifists to rearmament by supporting the Covenant. Spoke strongly in favour of Trade Unions. All with an eye to the election, on the date of which he was inscrutable.' A fortnight later, he decided to go for 14 November, almost certainly because he feared that, when faced with Mussolini's intransigence and French hesitations, the league would not be able to live up to public expectations. If Mussolini doubted that the British people were behind their government, an election would demonstrate that the nation was united in its support for the league. On 14 October, Chamberlain, speaking to Scottish Conservatives in Glasgow, suggested that with a long period of uncertainty ahead, it would be best to get the election out of the way. Bluntly stating that the country needed more arms, he noted that the rearmament programme would bring increased employment in the depressed areas. Cabinet on 16 October put the drafting of the manifesto in train: the final version would be signed by Baldwin and MacDonald. Baldwin alerted his constituents on the 19th but left it to the closing stages of the Commons debate on the international situation on 23 October before indicating that he had sought and obtained a dissolution. Speaking with 'unusual force', he made it clear that he was seeking a mandate to strengthen Britain's defences in order to provide effective collective security in Europe. The dissolution took place on the 25th and Baldwin delivered the first election broadcast that evening.

Lloyd George had already staked out his position. He had been campaigning for a British equivalent of Roosevelt's New Deal since January but had been outmanoeuvred by Chamberlain. Drawn into lengthy discussions with the inner Cabinet, with the bait that he might join the Cabinet, it became clear that his programme was poorly thought through and offered no more than the government already had in mind. Frustrated, he published his proposals in June and created a Council of Action. The government's rejoinder was hard-hitting. Lloyd George's free church allies made it clear that they were not prepared to see the council used to criticise the government. Instead of running candidates, therefore, it was reduced to endorsing those from other parties with similar ideas. When he published pamphlets on 'Peace' and 'Reconstruction' a few days before the dissolution, the press gave them a cool reception. The Liberal manifesto, published on the 24th, fared no better. It was not even reported in the *Daily Mail* or the *Daily Herald* and had nothing new to offer. The Labour manifesto published on the following day was overshadowed by reports of Baldwin's broadcast – even the *Daily Herald* choosing to give greater space to its critique than it did to setting out Labour's policy. The party's international stance was familiar, and it had long been advocating a massive programme of nationalisation: banking, coal, transport, electricity, iron and steel, cotton and land were to be publicly owned. Surprisingly, its ambitions for welfare differed little from those to which the government subscribed in its own manifesto, but the household means test would go, trade union legislation be reversed and the problem of the distressed areas attacked. The House of Lords would be abolished and Parliament reformed, although as with much else in the manifesto there was no detail as to what that entailed.

The Conservative manifesto was long and detailed, but its essence was distilled into a highly effective message delivered by Baldwin on cinema newsreels:

> There are a million good reasons why you should support the National government. They are to be found in the homes where owing to the trade revival a million breadwinners are now drawing a regular wage instead of searching for work. The government's first aim is to keep that trade revival in being. But I warn you that the opposite will happen if confidence is shattered by political upheaval. Our second aim is social improvement. Our housing and slum clearance campaigns are already far beyond anything that has ever been attempted before. We must push ahead with them, and in addition we want to build up a fitter nation by expanding our health and educational services. Above all, we desire to go on working to maintain world peace and strengthen

the League of Nations. But it is clear from recent events that both our own influence in the world and that of the league itself will be weakened unless we make good the gaps in our defence. I will never stand for a policy of great armaments and give you my word – and I think that you can trust me by now – that our defence programme will be no more than sufficient to make our country safe and enable us to fulfil our obligations. That much we must have.

The electoral importance of the cinema newsreels has probably been underestimated. There were more than 4,300 cinemas and some two-thirds of the electorate visited them at least once a week. Most of the regulars unsurprisingly were from the working class. The film offering was accompanied by a newsreel, two versions being shown in the course of a week. Although the rival leaders all featured in the newsreels, Attlee's staccato remarks, delivered from the arm of a sofa, were no match for Baldwin's statesmanlike presentation, nor did any of the other featured leaders come close to equalling his ability to blend authority and sincerity.

The opposition parties had been arguing since early October that there was no need for an election and that the Conservative Party was exploiting the international crisis to serve its own ends. There is no evidence that the charge worked with any but committed voters. By the time the election was actually called, it had lost much of its force. Nor did Sir Herbert Samuel's predictions that MacDonald would be dropped from the new government and Churchill included carry any more credence than Labour assertions that Baldwin's reassuring personality was a screen for warmongers like Chamberlain and Churchill. Samuel could not deny that some measure of rearmament was needed, although he advised that where there was no Liberal candidate, his supporters should vote for a candidate endorsed by the Council of Action. However, when Lloyd George revealed the names of those who had pledged themselves to his programme on 4 November, there were only 365, and the press made much of this meagre total. They had even more fun when some of those named denied that they had signed. Lloyd George's speeches offered little but wit.

Denunciation of the government for pursuing economic sanctions that were too little and too late, and for embarking on an armaments race, did not amount to a policy, and his broadcast on 1 November with its call for public works and a disarmament conference seemed over-emphatic and lacked substance.

It had been agreed that there should be a dozen radio broadcasts. Baldwin gave the first and the last and his mastery of the 'fireside chat' was never more evident. Simon, MacDonald and Chamberlain gave the remaining broadcasts on behalf of the coalition, but only Chamberlain's response to Lord Snowden's vitriolic attack on his former colleagues came close to matching the effectiveness of his leader's final broadcast. Snowden and Lloyd George had been allotted broadcasts by Samuel, a decision that angered the Conservatives. The director-general of the BBC refused to intervene, and Snowden made good, if destructive, use of his time to suggest that the Conservatives had pursued their traditional policies under the cover of the National label. There had been a row over who should speak for Labour apart from Attlee. Greenwood and Clynes could not be excluded, although the latter had been notably ineffectual in 1931. The fourth place went to Morrison, and he proved the most effective of the four. Nevertheless, it was widely thought a mistake to make no use of Lansbury's warmth and sincerity.

The candidates' platform speeches, the thousands of leaflets delivered and door-to-door canvassing shaped 575 individual campaigns, but until the last week, even in local newspapers, these were somewhat overshadowed by the election broadcasts made every weekday evening from 28 October until 8 November. There were some 7.5 million radio licences in 1935 and a rush to buy radio sets before the election. Some two-thirds of households had a licence, although less than half that number anticipated listening to the broadcasts. Press reports of platform speeches were therefore important and the local press carried reports of what leading politicians had said. Baldwin's four campaign speeches, delivered to mass rallies in Wolverhampton (28 October), Liverpool (4 November), Leeds (7 November) and Newcastle (12 November), were extensively covered. No other speaker seems to have been given as much space. What mattered was less the coverage in *The Times*, whose circulation was only 195,000 and its readership largely confined to households with an annual income of more than £500, or even the *Daily Telegraph* (500,000) which, like the *Morning Post*, reached some households with whose income totalled £250 per annum, than that in the mass dailies. The political content in the Sundays, apart from *The Observer*, was low. That presented Baldwin with some problems. The Beaverbrook and Rothermere press empires, although seemingly destined to come down on the government's side as the lesser of two evils, were less than enthusiastic about his leadership and took their time to do so. The *Daily Mail*, in particular, advertised that it was giving a platform to all the party leaders and to Lloyd George and his New Deal. The Berry brothers, who owned the *Telegraph* and *Sunday Times*, had been encouraged by Baldwin supporters to buy up much of the local press. Together with some of the larger provincial papers like the *Yorkshire Post* and *Leeds Mercury*, they gave Baldwin unquestioning support, as did the Rothermere-owned *Mirror*, yet to move to the left. But the Labour Party enjoyed the unqualified support of only the *Daily Herald* and *Reynolds's News*, while the Liberal Party among the mass circulation papers could count on only the *News Chronicle*.

What became evident as the campaign developed was the Labour Party's reluctance to say much about its nationalisation programme and the stress it laid on the government's pursuit of 'swollen armaments'. In this context, Baldwin's address to the Peace Society on 31 October, which had been arranged long before the campaign and was not really intended to be part of it, took on unusual significance. Gaumont British News filmed it. Much of his speech was devoted to the importance of collective security, but he also gave his word that 'there will be no great armaments'. Historians miss the conscious reference to Grey's words and as a result fail to realise that he was denying that Britain was embarking on an arms race. As he had already said in his initial broadcast, the purpose of the rearmament programme was defensive and if an arms limitation agreement was on offer, Britain would take it. More striking still is academics' failure to realise that he was engaged in another argument: the *Edinburgh Evening News* gave it a headline, 'NO GREAT ARMAMENTS REPLY TO ISOLATIONISTS'. Nor is the assumption that Chamberlain and Churchill must have been dismayed at Baldwin's words correct. The former thought it 'one of the finest things he had ever done' and recognised that 'if I supply the policy and the drive SB does also supply something that is even perhaps more valuable in retaining the floating vote'. And Churchill, whatever he thought subsequently, was certain at the time that the election had been fought, and largely won, on rearmament.

The candidates' individual election manifestos reached every household and were likely to have been read by the great majority of those who bothered to vote. Unusually, foreign affairs and defence loomed larger than domestic issues. Only 2 per cent made no mention of foreign affairs. Few urban candidates mentioned agriculture, and unemployment went unmentioned in 16 per cent of the addresses, mostly where it was not a problem but also where it was all too significant.

Major issues covered (per cent)

Subject	National	Labour	Liberal
League of Nations	90	90	93
Italian/Abyssinian war	41	50	38
Rearmament	86	29	38
Fear of massive rearmament	–	85	38
Prosperity	89	20	18
Tariffs and trade	77	49	93
Employment/unemployment	86	82	83
Nationalisation	–	69	8
Socialism	52	54	40
Means test/public assistance	27	84	63
Education/school leaving age	61/47	76/62	33/23
Housing	72	67	35
Health	44	60	18
Pensions	53	61	33
Agriculture	43	53	65

The results of the municipal elections held on 1 November were a clear indication that the Conservative Party was on the road to victory, and the campaign lost much of its intensity. Only the mining areas, balloting for a strike, saw a lively campaign continue. When all the results were in, 432 National government supporters had been elected, three as independents, joining the twenty-six whose re-election had not been contested. The government made a clean sweep of twenty-four English counties: Bedfordshire, Berkshire, Buckinghamshire, Cambridgeshire, Cheshire, Dorset, Hampshire, Hereford, Hertfordshire, Huntingdonshire, Kent, Leicestershire, Middlesex, Norfolk, Northamptonshire, Oxford, Shropshire, Somerset, Suffolk, Surrey, Sussex, Westmorland, Wiltshire and Worcestershire, as well as the East and North Ridings of Yorkshire. Rather more surprising was their 100 per cent hold on Belfast, Birmingham, Blackburn, Bolton, Brighton, Cardiff, Croydon, Derby, Leicester, Newcastle-upon-Tyne, Norwich, Oldham, Plymouth, Portsmouth, Preston, Rochester, Salford, Southampton, Stockport and Sunderland. In Scotland, National candidates had carried forty-four of the seventy-one seats and only in Wales was it well behind its Labour opponents. In the 450 constituencies where a direct comparison is possible, Professor Tom Stannage calculated that the average swing to Labour was 9.4 per cent, but where there was a straight fight between Conservative and Labour in both 1931 and 1935 (230 seats), the swing was 9.9 per cent. There were considerable regional variations, particularly the west Midlands, where the swing was half the national average, and in Liverpool (13.25 per cent), London (12 per cent) and Nottingham (12.7 per cent), Labour fared rather better against National Liberal candidates (12.4 per cent) while National Labour candidates fared disastrously (the average swing to Labour was 16.8 per cent). In Scotland, the National Liberals held the swing to Labour to 9.3 per cent. Where Liberals turned the fight into a three-cornered contest, the Conservatives benefited (5 per cent swing to Labour).

The Liberal Party was the most obvious casualty. With 6.7 per cent of the vote and twenty-one seats, it was relegated to the political margins. Its leader lost his seat. It had a modest success in agricultural constituencies, gaining North Cumberland and Berwick, but one of its six urban victories was won because the Conservatives did not stand. Even in the seats it contested, the Liberal Party averaged less than a quarter of the vote. As significant, if not more so, Labour had won 134 seats fewer than the 288 it had won in 1929 and only twelve seats more than their total in 1922. In thirteen years, Labour had lost ground in Central Scotland and on Tyneside and gained in east London, Liverpool and West Yorkshire. Central Scotland was the only area where it failed to regain mining seats. In percentage terms, Labour's overall vote was marginally higher than in 1929, but it had regained only ninety-seven seats and lost three to the Conservatives. Even in London, regarded by Morrison as a success, the Labour Party held only twenty-two seats, well short of its 1929 total (thirty-six). Although the transfer of votes will have been more complex, the Conservatives had clearly managed to rally the bulk of the votes lost by the Liberals behind the National government.

There can be no certainty about the reasons underlying Baldwin's victory, although the 'feel-good' factor must rank high, with the expectation that the economic recovery would continue not far behind it. Fear of Labour's nationalisation programme, and more particularly of the nationalisation of the banks, was clearly a significant factor and may have inspired more general apprehension that the radicalism of Labour's economic policy would damage confidence. Although the party had distanced itself from Cripps and the Socialist League, government candidates were able to point to his anticipation that Labour's policies would head to an economic and constitutional crisis when they claimed the National government represented an oasis of stability in an uncertain world. Nor was it unhelpful that in the course of the campaign, the government announced a new programme of road construction, that new naval construction would go to areas with high unemployment, that the Ebbw Vale Steelworks was to reopen and that Palmers shipyard in Jarrow would reopen to break up the *Olympic*. Labour had done its best to highlight the blank cheque the government was seeking for rearmament, claiming that Baldwin was not the real leader of his party but served as a front to warmongers like Churchill and Chamberlain, but their lack of success was evidenced by the greater stress that government speakers put on economic recovery as the campaign neared its conclusion.

The argument that 1935 confirmed the emergence of a class-based two-party system, which remained in being until 1974, underestimates Baldwin's achievement. The Conservatives had become the dominant party, and the evidence suggests that but for the war, they might well have remained so. Dr Tom Nossiter calculated that half of the working-class vote had gone to the Conservative Party and its allies. What needs explanation therefore is not why so large a part of the working class voted Tory (even after the war, a third of the working class continued to do so) but what enabled working-class Labour voters to insulate themselves from the dominant political culture. There is a powerful argument that this was in large part the result of powerful trade union movement, still more perhaps the existence of communities which were made up entirely of workers, the mining villages being the most obvious example. Here a different value system could emerge. Baldwin and his allies had created a party which embodied the values dominant in England but was ready to make the policy changes necessary to meet the current needs of the society within which they operated. The election of 1935 consolidated the hold that 'Baldwinism' had on his party and on future leaders like Eden, and that made it likely that the party would be in government far more often than not.

Baldwin's timing of the election had been impeccable. Although he would have denied any change in policy, the emphatic support given to the League of Nations nullified the advantage that the Labour Party had enjoyed on that subject for the previous two and a half years. He had obtained his mandate for rearmament, and the programme that emerged in the following spring was rather more extensive than even the government had envisaged. But for his victory, it is unlikely that Britain would have been in any position to fight in 1939 or survive in 1940. It is telling not only that the Labour Party continued to oppose rearmament but that Attlee in August 1937 could still claim:

to say what the government is doing is necessary for the defence of the country is to beg the whole question. I do not believe that then entry into a competition in arms will give security. On the contrary ... it is leading straight to the disaster of another world war.

No doubt there is much that Baldwin, and still more Chamberlain, got wrong in the ensuing years, but it should stand to their credit that by 1939, Britain was out-performing Germany in the production of military aircraft and possessed a navy with modern aircraft carriers and battleships. That was the legacy of Baldwin's victory, and it was crucial for Britain's fate.

John Barnes taught history at Cambridge before moving to a lectureship in the government department at LSE. He is the co-author (with Keith Middlemas) of *Baldwin: A Biography* and co-editor of the *Leo Amery Diaries*.

30

1945

JULIA LANGDON

Dissolution: 15 June 1945
Polling day: 5 July 1945
Seats contested: 640
Total electorate / Total votes cast / Turnout: 33,240,391 (33,110,662 in contested seats) / 24,073,025 / 72.8 per cent
Candidates (total 1,683): Labour – 603; Conservative – 559; Liberal – 306; National Liberal – 49; Common Wealth – 23; Communist – 21; National – 10; SNP – 8; Plaid Cymru – 7; Nationalist – 3
Prime Minister on polling day: Winston Churchill
Main party leaders: Conservative – Winston Churchill; Labour – Clement Attlee; Liberal – Archibald Sinclair; National Liberal – Ernest Brown; Common Wealth – C. A. Smith; Communist – Harry Pollitt; Nationalist – James McSparran; SNP – Douglas Young; Plaid Cymru – Abi Williams

Party performance:

Party	Votes	Percentage share	Seats
Labour (including NI Labour)	11,967,746 (66,223)	47.7 (9.2)	393 (0)
Conservative (including UUP)	8,716,211 (394,373)	36.2 (54.5)	197 (9)
Liberal	2,177,938	9	12
National Liberal	686,652	2.9	11
Nationalist	148,078	20.5	2
National	130,513	0.5	2
Common Wealth	110,634	0.5	1

Communist	97,945	0.4	2
SNP	26,707	0.1	0
Plaid Cymru	16,017	0.1	0

Result: Labour majority of 146 seats

They called it the 'People's War'. The historian A. J. P. Taylor was partly responsible for that. He used the phrase in the final volume (1914–45) of the Oxford History of England, suggesting that the British people came of age in the Second World War and that the remarkable election which followed was thus a reflection of this. He wrote: 'Imperial greatness was on the way out; the welfare state was on the way in. The British Empire declined; the condition of the people improved. Few now sang "Land of Hope and Glory". Few even sang "England Arise".'

Memorably, he concluded: 'England had risen all the same.'

In order to understand that rising, the context of the 1945 election held on 5 July and the sensational outcome which took the world by surprise when the results of the poll were revealed three weeks later on 26 July, it is necessary to look at what life was like in the United Kingdom in that momentous year: one which saw the end of the Second World War, the explosion of the atom bomb and the election of the first majority Labour government in history, with the largest national swing from the governing party since William Pitt the Younger. And it is vital also to look at the politics of the previous decade, since the last election in 1935, and the way in which the apparent national unity of the wartime administration established an agreed political framework for post-war policy.

During the election campaign, it had, of course, seemed predictable that the justly celebrated and now victorious Winston Churchill, Prime Minister of the wartime coalition since May 1940, would cruise to a comfortable election triumph, trailing clouds of powerful rhetoric and pillowed by personal popularity. He who had so famously promised his own blood, toil, tears and sweat in his inaugural speech in that post to the House of Commons certainly expected no less from a suitably grateful electorate. The newspapers thought the same. 'That Mr Churchill and his party will be returned is practically taken for granted,' declared the *Financial Times*. 'The point of uncertainty is the sum of the majority.' The view of the British public, as articulated in the press and studied in the nascent science of opinion polling, appeared to confirm this outcome. But while those 'many, many long months of struggle and suffering' after the war that Churchill had foreseen had, indeed, brought about a national unity to prosecute the war with Germany, reflecting the views of the coalition government, there would be a difference – as the world found out – between the people's war and what the people thought of the prospects for peace.

The arrival of Clement Attlee at Buckingham Palace that historic evening in late July to accept the invitation of King George VI to head the new peacetime government startled everybody, including the victor himself. 'The poor little man had only heard a couple of hours before that he was to be called upon to fill Winston's place,' wrote the king's private secretary, Alan Lascelles, with staggering condescension after Attlee had kissed hands on appointment. King George himself noted in his own diary that his new Prime Minister 'was very surprised his party had won'.

And so he was. Attlee had been leader of the Labour Party for ten years, had been in the war Cabinet since the coalition was formed in 1940 and had occupied the post of Deputy Prime Minister for the past three years. In government, he had proved powerful and effective. While Churchill ran the war, concentrating on the military struggle, Attlee was organising the policy areas on the home front, mobilising the resources necessary to run the country *and* the war. Churchill was the figurehead of the government, a magnificent personification of what it meant to be British. Attlee was the very opposite; yet while characteristically unobtrusive, he still kept his own party and the wartime coalition together. He could take decisions; he didn't grandstand or make a fuss; he was a brilliant manager. He kept meetings short and summed them up succinctly, even though not an impressive speaker. His public profile was perhaps best summed up by a 1942 opinion poll on potential successors to Churchill in which he had scored a derisory 2 per cent. No, he didn't expect to win the election either.

What perhaps proved crucial was that while Churchill was winning the war, he had effectively handed to the Labour Party an authority over domestic policy which enabled them throughout the coalition to dictate the direction of post-war policy. The coalition had ended the Conservative hegemony that had been in place since 1918 (Labour having governed for a total of only three years, in 1924 and from 1929 to 1931, and then in minority) and the collectivism of the coalition would now lead to a managed economy and the birth of the welfare state; this as a result of an election in which both major parties apparently agreed on the outlines of the way forward.

Both recognised the importance of housing and employment in the years to come; both offered a comprehensive system of national insurance; both proposed to set up a new national health service and to expand the provisions of the 1944 'Butler' Education Act, introduced by R. A. Butler, to establish free secondary education; both recognised the need for greater efficiency in British industry. The main political difference between the two parties was their respective beliefs in private enterprise and public ownership; but what would matter much more was the public's perception of the difference between them – and that was which of them could more be trusted?

This degree of consensus about the way forward had largely come about as a result of the publication of the now-famous and celebrated report by the Liberal economist Sir William Beveridge, in the winter of 1942. The 'People's William' – as he was affectionately dubbed – was then a civil servant and had been commissioned the previous year to report on the country's welfare needs, particularly post-war. His report identified the five 'giant evils' of want, disease, ignorance, squalor and idleness and proposed a universal plan of insurance against old age, sickness and unemployment. It was powerfully argued – Beveridge's own wife, the mathematician Janet Philip, deserves credit as part of the team behind its production and promotion – and, not surprisingly, coming in the middle of the war's darkest days, it sounded to the British public as if it might represent a sort of national reward for the sacrifices everyone had made in wartime. It was published shortly after the Allied victory at the Second Battle of El Alamein, which marked the beginning of the end of the war in North Africa and had boosted morale about the possibility of a turning point in the war. The report had a less-than-compelling title ('Social Insurance and Allied Services') but was an immediate hit and sold 630,000 copies. Beveridge compared his popularity to that of someone who found himself riding an elephant through a cheering mob.

The report was debated in the Commons in February 1943, but the government's suggestion that its recommendations could not be implemented until the end of the war provoked a huge rebellion: 119 MPs refused to accept the government line, including all but two of the Labour backbenchers. The Prime Minister, of course, saw the writing on the wall and in a broadcast that March from Chequers, Churchill promised that after the war there would be 'a system of national comprehensive insurance for all classes for all purposes from cradle to grave'. This was his 'Four Years' Plan' which would evolve later into the Conservative election address, 'Mr Churchill's Declaration of Policy to the Electors'. From this point onwards, the Labour Party was able to propel the Conservatives towards mutually agreed plans for widespread social and welfare reforms, including education, employment, health and social security, some of which was already in progress of implementation during the war years. As Quintin Hogg (Lord Hailsham) wrote in his analysis of the 1945 election in *The Case for Conservatism*, published in 1947: 'Over 80 per cent of the field of politics the great mass of decent opinion of all parties was agreed as to the best practicable course to take. Never before perhaps at a great General Election did the intentions of the principal protagonists more closely resemble one another.' Or, as Labour's Ellen Wilkinson would put it to the party national executive in October 1944: 'What were we going to fight about?'

The answer was to be a simple one: politics. In May 1945, Churchill had a personal popularity rating of 83 per cent. Throughout the election, he would be – mostly – cheered. But the cheers were for the great wartime leader, the extraordinary rhetorician whose language had galvanised the nation, for all that he had done, for the defeat of Adolf Hitler; not for being the leader of the Conservative Party. Attlee did not have a comparable standing and completely lacked charisma (indeed, arguably he had a political condition once dubbed 'amsirach' – which is 'charisma' sort of spelled backwards), yet what mattered when the election got underway was that nevertheless he was the leader of a party which had been 18 per cent ahead in the polls for at least three months.

Victory in Europe was declared on 8 May 1945, following Hitler's suicide on 30 April and the unconditional surrender of Germany on 7 May. There was predictable relief and jubilation on the streets of the United Kingdom and the celebration of VE Day was duly embroidered into the fabric of our history. A public holiday was declared. Church bells were rung. Churchill, trademark cigar clamped between his lips, waved to the ecstatic crowds from the balcony of the old Ministry of Health building in Whitehall and later appeared again at Buckingham Palace, heroic with the royal Family. The king and queen would make eight appearances on their balcony that day, but by the evening the young princesses had been excused waving duty and allowed to disappear incognito into the happy crowds. Sailors rolled up their bellbottoms and danced with their darlings in the fountains of Trafalgar Square. The king, still in his uniform as an admiral of the fleet, spoke to the nation at 9 p.m. It was, at thirteen minutes, his longest ever broadcast – which given his speech impediment was itself heroic. The nation listened, glued to their wireless sets – if, that is, they weren't doing the conga – as George VI warned that 'much hard work awaits us'.

The politicians knew that. It had been understood for at least the last year of the war that there would be a general election as soon as it was over. The coalition had rubbed along well enough until late in 1944, by which time victory for the Allies in Europe was already becoming a matter of time, and it was not until this point that political strains began to emerge. A significant aspect of the coalition was that the parties had agreed an electoral truce for its duration. This meant that if a parliamentary by-election arose, the parties would not nominate a candidate to stand against the party that had previously held the seat. This would prove a severe test for Labour, however, which could not improve its parliamentary standing and put up candidates in former Tory-held seats – and the Conservatives, of course, still had a huge Commons' majority – and had instead to watch when the Common Wealth left-wing party (which was not bound by the truce) took eleven seats from the Conservatives.

Equally significant, however, was that there was no agreement about a political truce, and this would prove crucial. The Labour Party continued its party operation, as well as it could in wartime, and held annual conferences. The Labour left wing behaved as if it was in formal opposition to the government. Meanwhile, the Conservatives had disbanded their party organisations, did not meet in conference and their agents and organisers were less likely than Labour activists to be in 'reserved' occupations, like heavy industry, and thus more likely to have joined the services. There was plenty of Labour Party propaganda about the post-war world and much of it would remind people about what the pre-war world had been like – the one that had been run almost continuously by the Conservatives, the one that had led to the slump of the 1930s.

So it was in late 1944, during the passage of the annual legislation that year which suspended the democratic process, the Prolongation of Parliament Bill, that Churchill gave the first indication of his political thinking for the post-war period. Churchill liked the coalition and he could see that the public did, too. It was at this point, during the debate on prolongation, that he floated the possibility that the coalition should therefore continue once peace in Europe had been secured, until the less predictable date of peace in the Far East.

It seemed possible, then, that this might even be two or three years away. Would the United States invade Japan? Would the Soviet Union enter the war in the east? There was no public inkling, of course, of the coming decision to drop an atomic bomb. Churchill and President Franklin D. Roosevelt had agreed in principle in September 1944 that an atomic weapon could be used against Japan, when developed. What happened in reality was that President Harry

Truman, who assumed the presidency on FDR's death in April 1945, would on 21 July – five days before the outcome of the British general election – approve the use of the bomb on a date after 3 August. Hiroshima was bombed at 8.15 a.m. on a clear day on 6 August and Nagasaki three days later. Japan surrendered on 15 August. The B-29, named *Bockscar*, which dropped the Nagasaki bomb, is on display in a US Air Force museum in Dayton, Ohio, with the caption 'the aircraft that ended World War Two'.

But whatever was to happen in the east, it had already become clear that the British parties would fight independently whenever the election came and, moreover, that it would not be a 'coupon election', such as had occurred in 1918 endorsing Lloyd George's governing coalition. Now Churchill suggested that the election would go ahead after the defeat of Germany – unless it was agreed to maintain the coalition until the Japanese were defeated.

Churchill's proposition was not pursued, nor taken up. At Labour conferences in 1942 and 1943, there had been unsuccessful moves to end the coalition. In October 1944, the Labour national executive issued a statement that agreed to its continuation – but only as long as was necessary in the national interest. Nevertheless, at the Conservative conference in March 1945, the first the party had held since the coalition had been formed, Churchill now explicitly proposed that should the Tories be successful in the coming election and he thus be invited to form an administration, he would again seek the co-operation of other parties to form what would have been a National government. This idea did not go down well with the audience beyond the Conservative Party and, indeed, provoked an outbreak of political hostility from Labour, such as raised doubts about whether the coalition could last even until the coming peace in Europe.

In the event, public attention was gripped by the drama of military events in Europe and the coalition held. The impact of victory then led to a curious suspension of politics for ten days until 18 May, two days before the Labour conference was to be held in Blackpool. This setting had been expected to provide the backcloth for future political developments, but it turned out to be Churchill who instead took the initiative. He wrote identical letters to Attlee, Sir Archibald Sinclair, the Liberal leader, and Ernest Brown, leader of the National Liberals, the group which had broken away from the rest of the Liberals in the 1931 government. What he proposed was a simple choice: that the coalition should be retained and the election postponed until a resolution of the war in the Far East or that it should be ended immediately and an election held in July. Recognising, however, that the first option rather contradicted the widespread impression that there would be an election and that the government should seek an 'expression of the nation's will', he suggested some sort of public referendum on whether the government should continue.

It was a canny move by Churchill, but it wasn't going to wash. The Labour Party conference rejected the idea out of hand in a private session and Attlee replied suggesting that there had to be an election but that it should be in the autumn. A more accurate electoral register could be effective by then; members of the services needed more time to consider the issues and their votes and people in the services who wanted to stand as candidates would find such a swift timetable a great disadvantage. Labour would continue to help support the war against Japan, but a referendum was an unacceptable, alien concept and out of the question. He suggested, moreover, that Churchill was trying to rush things in order to secure party advantage at the expense of the national interest – a suggestion at which Churchill predictably took great offence. Sinclair wanted an autumn election but was slightly more amenable to perhaps maintaining the coalition. Brown promised to support Churchill.

Churchill, of course, did his own thing. Just two weeks after the nation woke with its VE Day hangover, on 23 May, he went to Buckingham Palace and resigned as Prime Minister. Four hours later, he returned to the palace, accepted the king's offer to become Prime Minister of a caretaker government and asked for the dissolution of Parliament on 15 June. The election would be held on 5 July, except in some northern towns where, because of 'wakes weeks' (traditional holiday periods that were still observed at the time), voting would be on 12 or 19 July. Counting would be delayed until 26 July to allow for this and for service votes to be flown home. An Italian journalist observed that it said something for Britain that it was prepared to trust its government with the secrecy of its vote for three whole weeks without fearing that its trust might somehow be abused.

There had been no boundary reviews since 1918 (1922 in Northern Ireland) and the size of some constituencies had become distorted. Twenty-five new seats were created and distributed among the larger constituencies, increasing the number of MPs elected to 640. There were 1,683 candidates for these seats: Labour put up 603 and the Conservatives 559 – but their total was boosted by a number of Ulster Unionists, National candidates and Liberal Nationals, making a total of 624. The Liberal Party wanted to contest 500 seats but had only 306 candidates. On the independent wing of the left, there were twenty-one candidates for the Communist Party, twenty-three for the Common Wealth, five for Independent Labour, five for the Democratic Party and three Irish Nationalists. Both Wales and Scotland fielded eight Nationalist candidates each. The one Scottish National Party MP, Robert McIntyre, who had won his Motherwell seat at a by-election in the spring lost in the general election. The deposit was £150 and each candidate required ten nominations. Most candidates were middle-aged: the mean age of those standing for both Labour and the Conservatives was forty-six. There were eighty-seven female candidates, of whom twenty-four were elected: twenty-one Labour out of forty-one; one Conservative out of thirteen; one Liberal out of twenty; one Independent out of four and nine unsuccessful others.

There were three classes of voters: civilians, those with business premises and service voters who were also offered the opportunity to appoint a proxy. The electorate was just over 33 million and with a turnout of 72.8 per cent the total number of votes cast was 24,073,025. Nearly 3 million service voters registered and about two-thirds of them registered proxies. The Home Office would report in November that 59.4 per cent of service voters cast their votes.

The campaign got under way in a bad humour, largely as a result of Labour's resentment about the rush to the polls, but it was the Labour Party that was better prepared. The election manifesto 'Let

Us Face the Future' was drafted by a 29-year-old research officer at Labour's headquarters, Michael Young – better known later as Lord Young of Dartington who coined the word 'meritocracy' among many other claims to fame – and was very much under the aegis of Herbert Morrison. It had been thought through and it was thorough. It would sell 1.5 million copies.

'Mr Churchill's Declaration of Policy to the Electors' was more buoyant than any of the other manifestos, but also more vague. His Four Years' Plan had not moved on much and the emphasis was all on the moment, the problems of the world as seen through the eyes of a great statesman. 'Even when all foreign enemies are utterly defeated, that will not be the end of our task. It will be the beginning of our further opportunity ... to save the world from tyranny.'

The Liberal manifesto was high-minded. They had 'clean hands' and 'no axe to grind'. They were, besides, blameless for the inter-war years, but as events would prove, they would now also become politically irrelevant. Lady Violet Bonham Carter, who would fail to win the seat she contested in Wells in 1945 but would become president of the Liberal Party thereafter, described the election 'as a choice between two rotten apples'.

The most telling difference between the parties' campaigns is best summed up by two visual images. One was a cartoon by Philip Zec which showed a couple – he in a three-piece suit; she in a hat and coat – angrily confronting a complacent shopkeeper, who is wearing the apron of the 'Tory Peace Stores (Very Limited)'. Beneath his counter are 'decent schools', 'good homes', 'jobs' and 'proper medical attention'. There is also a label on 'the fruits of victory – reserved for the rich and privileged'. The male customer is saying: 'What do you mean – you're out of stock – I've paid twice for those goods – once in 1914 and again in 1939!' The other is a picture of the Winston Churchill who won the war, looking directly at the camera with a slight furrow in his brow but a confident smile on his lips. 'HELP HIM finish the Job. VOTE NATIONAL,' it says.

It wouldn't be enough, and Churchill made matters considerably worse for himself with an ill-judged broadcast on 4 June, when he unwisely suggested that Labour would need back-up from 'some sort of Gestapo' if they wanted to impose socialism on Britain. It enabled Attlee the next evening to retort in a subsequent broadcast that he was grateful to his opponent for reminding people of the difference between Churchill, the great wartime leader, and Churchill, the peacetime politician.

It was Labour's policy of winning the peace that was going to count in favour of change. And it was the Conservatives' record from between the wars that was now going to count against them. The problem was that at the beginning of the war, the Conservatives' failure to fulfil the promised 'land fit for heroes' was still very much in evidence. The wartime coalition had been a success, yes, but it had not eradicated the memory of what had happened since 1918 and the relevance of that would be demonstrated in this election.

The Churchill war ministry had come into existence on 10 May 1940. War had been declared on 3 September the previous year under the troubled premiership of Neville Chamberlain, whose appeasement policy and signing of the Munich Agreement in 1938 had proved so mistaken – dividing political opinion, not least within the Conservative Party. Chamberlain's government had enjoyed a stunning overall majority of more than 200, which he had inherited with the Conservative Party leadership, after Stanley Baldwin's 1937 resignation in the wake of Edward VIII's abdication. The Labour Party vote (as opposed to that of National Labour) had meanwhile begun to recover under the leadership of Attlee, who had been deputy leader and succeeded the 76-year-old pacifist, George Lansbury, on his resignation just before the 1935 election and had then been confirmed in that post after the general election.

Herbert Morrison, who would become deputy Labour leader after the 1945 election, was out of the House of Commons between 1931 and 1935 and was defeated by Attlee for the leadership at this point – and subsequently consistently thwarted in his pursuit of the post. As leader of the London County Council, however, he had recognised the domestic political damage the Conservatives were suffering as a result of the mass unemployment, deprivation and poverty experienced by so many in the 1930s slump. He had been responsible for rebuilding Labour's electoral base after the disaster of Ramsay MacDonald splitting the party and leading his rump of supporters into the 1931 National government – which had cost Morrison his parliamentary seat – and Morrison also saw that in order to be credible, the party had to reach beyond the manual working class. His local government experience had also taught him the value of advertising agencies and the skilful deployment of election posters using cheering images, preferably featuring happy children and new blocks of flats.

Had there been a general election in 1939, the opinion polls suggest there would have been another Conservative victory. The first ever Gallup poll had been published in 1937 and at the beginning of 1939, the Tories had 50 per cent support and a 6 per cent lead over Labour. After the declaration of war, that lead had increased to 14 per cent and by February 1940 it was 24 per cent (Conservative 51 per cent, Labour 27 per cent and 'don't know' 22 per cent). This state of play steadily reversed throughout the years of the war, however, as Labour's role in the coalition led to a steady growth in its public support. By 1943, it was on 44 per cent, with the Conservatives on 36 per cent and the Liberals on 10 per cent. By the last year of the war, Labour was regularly polling between 45 per cent and 47 per cent, while the Conservatives were between ten and twenty points below and the Liberals on 12 per cent. These were all polls by Gallup, published in the *News Chronicle*, but in June 1945, with the election under way, a new poll by the Centre of Public Opinion appeared in the mass-selling *Daily Express* suggesting a dead heat between the two major parties claiming 45 per cent support each. In the event, little attention was given to Gallup's election day poll which gave Labour 48 per cent, the Conservatives 39.6 per cent and the Liberals 9 per cent. When the actual result became known, that result was spot on: the new governing party polled 47.7 per cent of the popular vote and scorched its name into the history books.

Another opinion poll of significance in the first winter of the war – the 'phoney war' during which Chamberlain remained impervious to criticism – was the growing public popularity of the new First Lord of the Admiralty. Winston Churchill had accepted this post in Chamberlain's war Cabinet, although he had been out of public office – what were known as his 'wilderness years' – since 1929. A British Institute of Public Opinion poll in December 1939 showed Chamberlain could still count on 52 per cent public support, but 30 per cent of those questioned would prefer the polymath Churchill as Prime Minister. Tellingly, the Prime Minister commanded loyalty from women, the well off and the elderly; Churchill won the endorsement of men, young adults, those on lower incomes and the majority of Labour supporters. And he also got the biggest applause in the newsreels at the cinema. Mass Observation, the influential social research project which recorded what everyday life was like at the time, suggested in a report that Churchill was the popular favourite to succeed Chamberlain. Paul Addison in his brilliant account of the politics of the time, *The Road to 1945*, records that a Conservative MP, Somerset de Chair, consulted his party officers in the ninety polling districts of his South West Norfolk constituency and discovered that Churchill had a 10 per cent popularity lead over the PM. (De Chair had cause for anxiety: he would lose his seat by fifty-three votes in the election.)

It was against this background that on 7 May 1940, the House of Commons began the historic two-day Norway Debate about the role of the British expeditionary force in Norway and their failure to prevent invasion by Germany but which was to become, in effect, a discussion on the need for a coalition government. Labour forced a division which became a vote of confidence in the government's conduct of the war and Chamberlain's majority of 213 was reduced to a humiliating eighty-one. He tried subsequently then to form a coalition, but after a telephone call from Attlee reporting that Labour was not prepared to accept office with him remaining in charge – the view of the Labour National Executive Committee meeting at the party conference in Bournemouth – his resignation became inevitable. Labour *was* prepared to accept another Conservative, however, and the only two candidates in the running were Churchill and the Foreign Secretary, Viscount Halifax, who effectively ruled himself out on the grounds that his membership of the Lords would be inappropriate for a wartime Prime Minister. He continued briefly at King Charles Street in the coalition and subsequently served as ambassador in Washington.

Thus, it was on 10 May, as German troops swept into the Netherlands, Belgium and Luxembourg – the desperate precursor to Dunkirk and the fall of France the following month – that Winston Churchill became Prime Minister of a coalition government and the head of a five-man war Cabinet. Clement Attlee resigned as Leader of the Opposition and became Lord Privy Seal; the deputy Labour leader, Arthur Greenwood, was made Minister without Portfolio; Halifax was at the FCO and Chamberlain was Lord President of the Council. The Labour Party had just over a third of the other ministerial appointments. The Liberal Party had twenty-one MPs at this time but secured only three ministerial seats: the party leader Sir Archibald Sinclair became Secretary for Air and his close friend, Sir Harcourt Johnstone, who largely financed the party, was made Secretary for Overseas Trade. Dingle Foot (later a Labour MP and older brother of Michael) was a junior minister at Economic Warfare.

The war Cabinet would quickly expand; only Churchill and Attlee were members throughout. By the end of 1940, it had eight members. Chamberlain was discovered to have terminal bowel cancer in July 1940 and died four months later. He was replaced by John Anderson (later Chancellor of the Exchequer from 1943); Kingsley Wood was Chancellor until his death in 1943; Anthony Eden became Foreign Secretary in succession to Halifax; Lord Beaverbrook, the Minister of Aircraft Production, was an early addition and Ernest Bevin became Minister of Labour and National Service. Churchill was greatly impressed by the transport union leader – by 'far the most distinguished man that the Labour Party have thrown up in my time' – and Bevin's awkward lack of a parliamentary seat was quickly resolved with an unopposed by-election in June 1940.

The country was no longer in the mood for unopposed elections or National governments by the time the war ended. It was in the mood for change and that was what was delivered on 26 July. It was astonishing. The new House of Commons had 393 Labour MPs and 197 Conservatives. Labour had an overall majority of 146, a net gain of 239 seats and had won 47.7 per cent of the popular vote. The Conservatives had a net loss of 190 seats, on 36.2 per cent of the popular vote. The Liberals had a net loss of nine seats, including that of Sir Archibald in Caithness and Sutherland, on 9 per cent and the Liberal Nationals a disastrous net loss of twenty-two seats, including Mr Brown in Leith, on 2.9 per cent of the popular vote. The Liberal Nationals merged with the Conservatives in 1947. Among those elected for the first time were Harold Wilson, James Callaghan, Barbara Castle, Hugh Gaitskell and Michael Foot. Harold Macmillan lost his seat in Stockton but returned to the Commons in a November by-election in Bromley. It was altogether a remarkable result and it was one achieved despite the extraordinary assumption of the whole of Fleet Street – and of Lord Beaverbrook's *Daily Express*, in particular, that quite the opposite would occur. The press paid insufficient attention to public opinion.

The United Kingdom may have been in good heart as a result of the victory of the Second World War, but it was nevertheless in a sorry state. There was a record national debt of £3.5 billion and a quarter of the country's national wealth had been spent on the war effort. There were shortages of everything – except the black market spivs who had come into their own during the 1940s, trading over the odds and under the counter. Two-thirds of the ships of the Royal Navy had been lost in the war and enemy action had also sunk 177 merchant vessels with an inevitable impact on supplies. Digging for victory was more than a slogan; it was a necessity. Petrol, clothing, shoes and soap were rationed and so, most importantly, was food. Coupons for weekly allowances provided one egg, two ounces each of tea and butter, one ounce of cheese, eight ounces of sugar and four ounces each of bacon and margarine per person – if available. Fresh fruit and vegetables were not rationed during the war but were often difficult to come by. And yes! There were no bananas; it was not until the very last day of the year that the first bananas since the outbreak of war would at last arrive in the docks. The war was over but still austerity persevered. Goods subject to rationing even increased in the coming years.

Everyone was a bit hungry and in the winter months quite a lot of people were cold. Chilblains were a common nuisance – but not fatal; tuberculosis was the biggest killer and carried off 19,200 people that year. Penicillin had been first administered in the UK in 1941, but it was not generally available and only in February 1945 was the means developed for it to be given orally. Until then 'M&B pills' were the thing, a pharmaceutical manufactured by May & Baker of Dagenham; Winston Churchill name-checked 'M&B' for saving his life from pneumonia in 1943. Middle-aged women (aged forty-five to forty-nine) were most at risk of dying from breast cancer and men over fifty-five from coronary problems. Most people couldn't afford to go to the doctors and a child leaving primary school during the war had a 98 per cent chance of tooth decay. A somewhat bizarre new statistic in 1945 was that boys aged five to fourteen were more at risk of dying in a motor vehicle accident – dashing across the road, as boys will – than for any other reason. The necessity for driving tests had been suspended on the outbreak of war and the examiners sent off to supervise fuel rationing. The consequences, although obviously not entirely due to incompetent drivers, were dire: there were fewer than 2 million cars on British roads but 5,256 fatalities in 1945, a figure which included one new Labour MP, Alfred Dobbs, the day after he captured Smethwick from the Conservatives on a stunning 18.4 per cent swing. (In September 2023, there were 41.3 million cars licensed in the UK and 1,633 people were killed in road accidents during that year.)

Life was bleak, dull and colourless, like the television if there had been any in most people's homes. TV broadcasting was suspended throughout the war for fear that the signals would be of use to German bombers. There were no supermarkets, no consumer goods, no motorways, few fridges. Tea bags and sliced bread had yet to be popularised. The first ballpoint pen went on sale in October – in the United States. Even cultural life seemed largely gloomy: Benjamin Britten's *Peter Grimes* opened at Sadler's Wells in June. George Orwell's satire against Stalin, *Animal Farm*, appeared in August, after some difficulty because criticism of our then Soviet ally seemed inappropriate to several publishers. In May, the Rev. Wilbert Vere Awdry published the first *Thomas the Tank Engine* stories and in creating the character of the Fat Controller, the very epitome of capitalism, clearly had little intimation of railway nationalisation. Meanwhile, the tear-inducing *Brief Encounter*, starring Celia Johnson, Trevor Howard and Rachmaninoff, was showing in the cinemas by November. When 'God Save the King' was played at the end of every evening at 'the flicks', most people stood up and some even sang.

The country was tired of war, exhausted by its privations and still coming to terms with five years of a devastating conflict that had cost so many lives (70 million to 85 million worldwide; equivalent to 3 per cent of the pre-war global population) including 384,000 UK service personnel and 70,000 UK civilians. This last figure was itself shocking, given that 2,000 civilians died in the 1914–18 war.

Britain was ready for change.

It was, of course, the German bombing raids which were primarily responsible for the domestic death toll, more than half of whom had died in the seven months of the Blitz between September 1940 and May 1941 and more than half of *those* in London. But the bombing was countrywide and more than 750,000 houses had been destroyed or damaged by enemy action: 95 per cent of houses in Kingston-upon-Hull were hit and one-third of housing in Coventry (*and* the cathedral) were destroyed. Similarly, 70,000 houses on Merseyside, 40,000 in Plymouth and 35,000 on Clydeside had been lost. Manchester, Sheffield, Belfast, Portsmouth and Birmingham all suffered devastating air raids, taking out homes, industry and innocent lives. There was thus an acute housing crisis – and there were 7 million houses with no hot water, 6 million without an inside lavatory and 5 million without a fixed bath. Two million homes had no gas or electricity. It was housing, hardship and health which dictated the outcome of the election and put Clement Attlee into Downing Street.

The word 'modest' is customarily attached to Attlee's name – often unkindly with Churchill's jibe that he had 'much to be modest about'. Yet he *was* modest and in the best sense. Years after retirement, when he was travelling in a third-class railway carriage, a fellow passenger would laughingly observe that she hoped he didn't mind her saying how closely he resembled the former Prime Minister. He politely assured her that he did not. But Attlee was a committed socialist and indeed modest about everything except his political ambition. He wrote poetry; his childhood ambition was to be a poet. 'No, I had not much idea about destiny,' he said once.

Latterly, Attlee has come to be lauded, certainly in Labour Party circles, as among the great Prime Ministers, heading a historic government. Yet he had become party leader in 1935 – 'a little mouse shall lead them' noted Hugh Dalton at the time – originally as a stop-gap in the run-up to the election of that year. Beatrice Webb, who, with her husband Sidney, had been responsible for writing the seminal Clause IV of Labour's constitution on public ownership, dubbed him 'this little nonentity' – an irony she herself would not live to observe, as she died in 1943. By the time of his premiership, he had already faced a number of attempts to topple him. At the very beginning of the 1945 campaign, the party chairman, Harold Laski, had written suggesting that he stood down in favour of Herbert Morrison (defeated by Attlee in 1935). Characteristically, Attlee replied with one famous laconic sentence: 'Dear Laski, Thank you for your letter, contents of which have been noted.' Now, at the eleventh hour, he still only just made it to the palace to accept the king's invitation to form a government. This time, even while Churchill was handing his resignation to George VI at 7 p.m., Morrison attempted a last-ditch manoeuvre to displace Attlee, claiming erroneously that the rules of the Parliamentary Labour Party demanded a leadership election. He then left the room in Transport House to take a telephone call. 'Clem, you go to the palace straight away,' Ernest Bevin counselled, while Morrison was absent. Attlee did just that. His wife, Violet, was waiting outside in their Hillman Minx and she drove him directly to his 7.30 p.m. appointment with the king. Both men were poor public speakers, as well as being shy. History records that Attlee spoke first when he was shown in. 'I've won the election,' he said. The king replied: 'I know. I heard it on the six o'clock news.'

And so with glorious understatement began the celebrated Attlee government which would change the face of the United Kingdom and usher in what came to be known as the post-war consensus. The father of macroeconomics, John Maynard Keynes, was given his own room in the Treasury and what came to be called 'Keynesianism' – that demand management could be used to regulate the economy and increased government spending would lead to increased output if other factors remained constant – became the accepted economic doctrine. It meant that the country would see the introduction of the welfare state, unemployment benefit, sickness pay and retirement pensions, through implementation of the Beveridge report. It brought about the nationalisation of 20 per cent of the country's economy, including the coal industry, the railways, road transport, the Bank of England, civil aviation, electricity, gas and steel. It led to the building of over a million new homes, mostly council housing, in six years. And most famously of all, it created a National Health Service, with nationalised hospitals and free universal healthcare.

Countless books have been written and learned historical analyses published on this period and that which followed. The historians have disagreed among themselves about that post-war consensus, about whether wartime unity led to the agreement about post-war domestic policy; Paul Addison, author of *The Road to 1945* (first published thirty years later in 1975) even disagreed with himself. He acknowledged in the edition published in 1994 that he was wrong to have imagined that the brave new world of Attlee, Beveridge and Keynes was an enduring structure. When he originally wrote the book, he explained, he did not imagine that any government had the power to repeal the post-war settlement. Yet society changed. Margaret Thatcher was a student at Somerville College, Oxford, at the time and had already read Friedrich Hayek's *The Road to Serfdom*, published the previous year, and from it she had taken her own view of the way forward. What had been constructed in the years between 1945 and 1951 was, rather, wrote Addison, 'more like a Ministry of Works prefab, intended for some deserving young couple at the end of the war.' He concluded: 'But finally it was bulldozed away in spite of many pleas to preserve it as a memorial to a more civilised era: and with it there departed the essential wartime vision of a society in which the state maintained a framework of social justice and citizenship for all.'

Julia Langdon is a political journalist, author and broadcaster. Her next book is *Tales from the Ancient Onion Wood: A Celebration of Friendship and Wild Garlic*.

31

1950

SUE CAMERON

Dissolution: 3 February 1950
Polling day: 23 February 1950
Seats contested: 625
Total electorate / Total votes cast / Turnout: 34,412,255 (34,271,754 in contested seats) / 28,771,124 / 83.9 per cent
Candidates (total 1,868): Conservative (including UUP) – 619; Labour (including NI Labour) – 617; Liberal – 475; Communist – 100; Independent Labour – 6; Independent Conservative – 3; Irish Labour – 2; Nationalist – 2
Prime Minister on polling day: Clement Attlee
Main party leaders: Labour – Clement Attlee; Conservative – Winston Churchill; Liberal – Clement Davies; Communist – Harry Pollitt; Nationalist – James McSparran; Irish Labour – William Norton

Party performance:

Party	Votes	Percentage share	Seats
Labour (including NI Labour)	13,266,176 (67,816)	46.1 (12.1)	315 (10)
Conservative (including UUP)	12,492,404 (352,334)	43.4 (62.8)	298 (10)
Liberal	2,621,487	9.1	9
Communist	91,765	0.3	0
Nationalist	65,211	11.6	2
Irish Labour	52,715	9.4	0
Independent Labour	26,395	0.1	0
Independent Conservative	24,732	0.1	0

Result: Labour majority of five seats

London had a ball on election night in 1950. The mood was more festive than at almost any time since the end of the Second World War. Describing the scene, a study of the election by Nuffield College, Oxford, reported that hotels and restaurants were full of convivial election night parties, while a holiday atmosphere prevailed among the crowds outside. As the first results were flashed up on screens in Piccadilly Circus and Trafalgar Square, they were greeted by good-humoured cheers and counter cheers with people revelling in the 'suspense and thrill of the occasion'.

At first, Labour looked to be well in the lead, but then the combined totals of Conservative and Liberal seats drew level. For a while it was neck and neck, but the final results showed that Labour Prime Minister Clement Attlee's great reforming government had been returned – but only just with its Commons majority crashing from 146 to a mere five.

Despite the dramatic result, the 1950 contest has become the forgotten election. People remember that of 1945 which brought the shock defeat of the Conservatives, and the 1951 election is memorable for the Tory revival and the return of Winston Churchill as Prime Minister. Yet the outcome of the 1950 race was sensational and politically significant, with the once-powerful Labour Party reduced to a pyrrhic victory and the Liberals humiliated. This was also the election that paved the way for three decades of what many describe as consensus politics. It also heralded the start of great political divisions that are still with us more than seventy years on.

The 1950 result was certainly dramatic. Turnout was 83.9 per cent, an all-time record. Labour won the biggest share with 13.2 million votes (46.1 per cent) as against the Tories' 12.5 million (43.4 per cent) and the Liberals' 2.6 million votes (9.1 per cent). Labour finished with 315 seats, the Tories with 298, the Liberals with nine and others two.

The national swing to the Tories was 2.8 per cent and they gained ninety seats. So how could Labour win more votes yet fewer seats? The key factor was a redrawing of constituency boundaries in 1948 to take account of major population shifts into the suburbs. It was laudable of Attlee to bring in the changes, but it meant that Labour piled up votes in its safe seats and lost in the more marginal, mainly suburban ones. The Nuffield study reckons that between a quarter and a half of Labour's loss of seventy-nine seats was down to boundary changes. Had the election been fought on the old boundaries, Labour would have had an estimated majority of around sixty. Attlee himself later admitted: 'We suffered from being too moral over that.'

If Labour's results were disappointing, the Liberals' showing was disastrous. The Liberals, led by Clement Davies, fielded 475 candidates – more than at any time in the previous twenty years. Davies, in what must have seemed an astute move, took out insurance from Lloyd's against more than fifty candidates losing their deposits. In the event, a record 319 lost their deposits, more than at any time until 2015. Despite rumours that Liberals and Conservatives had informal pacts either to run joint candidates or for one to stand down and give the other a clear run, the Liberals had to face three-cornered fights almost everywhere. Both main parties insisted that a vote for the Liberals was a wasted vote, but it seems that in practice Liberal voters in key seats switched to the Conservatives. The Liberals ended up with only nine seats – down from the twelve they had had previously. It was a humiliation from which the Liberal Party never recovered.

The Labour government fought on its record in 1950 and few would gainsay its achievements. It had created the National Health Service, established the modern welfare state with a comprehensive social security system and nationalised around 20 per cent of the economy, including railways, electricity and coal. Abroad, it had given independence to India and played a key role in founding NATO as a western bulwark against Soviet expansionism. What it had not been able to do was to control the crisis in living standards or even hold out real hope of an end to austerity.

The Second World War had bankrupted Britain. Only a week after the Japanese surrender, and without warning, the US ended Lend-Lease, under which America gave Britain and other allies the financial support needed to win the war. The abrupt ending of

Lend-Lease left Britain without enough dollars to buy all the food the country needed. The Attlee government sent the distinguished economist John Maynard Keynes to the US to secure an interest free loan, but the Americans offered a much smaller sum than was wanted and with stringent conditions. One was that pounds should be freely exchangeable for dollars. In 1947, this caused a drain on the UK's dollar reserves and a convertibility crisis. Two years later, the pound was devalued from $4.04 to $2.80. These financial shocks increased pressure on living standards and forced the Labour government to intensify austerity measures rather than reduce them as it had hoped. This alienated the public. In 1948, further help did come from America in the form of the Marshall Plan, providing much-needed aid to help Europe's recovery. Britain received by far the largest share, but much of the money went on defence.

The economic pain was intensified by appalling weather. The winter of 1947 was one of the coldest ever. Heavy snowfalls blocked roads and railways, coal deliveries couldn't reach the power stations, electricity supplies were severely disrupted and factories had to close. Cattle and sheep froze to death in the fields or died of starvation. When the thaw finally came, there were floods. If there was a turning point in public attitudes prior to the 1950 election, this was it. Significantly, coal had just been nationalised. Manny Shinwell, Labour's Minister of Fuel and Power, who had overseen the nationalisation, received death threats.

The public had, of course, become used to power cuts and shortages during the war and immediately afterwards, but they had accepted privation as the price of victory. They had tolerated the drabness of post-war Britain, the gaps left by bomb sites in city streets, the hurriedly built prefabs which bore witness to a crisis in homelessness, the scarcity of food and the strict regulation imposed by ration books – buff coloured for adults and green for children.

Yet by 1950, the war had been over for nearly five years and the public were looking to an easing of austerity. Instead, they were squeezed even harder. Bread, which had never been rationed during the war, went on the ration in 1946. Butter and meat rations were reduced and there was growing discontent over petrol rationing. Women, in particular, were resentful – they had had to run households, feed families and endure endless queues in shops. Small wonder if many voters felt they had put up with it all for long enough and were starting to think that Labour's central economic planning didn't work.

Building schemes across the country were beset by supply bottlenecks caused by responsibility being split between dozens of different bodies from ministries to local authorities. The result was bricks with nobody to lay them, and bricklayers with no bricks to lay. Coal nationalisation was another example. Within the first year, output per man-shift was well below pre-war rates, absenteeism had more than doubled and the number of unofficial strikes had risen from 1,329 to 1,635. One problem was that the motive for nationalisation was too ideological. As Andrew Marr says in his *History of Modern Britain*: 'Labour had the ultimate Fat Controller world view. It wanted everything from lorries and ships to trains and barges under one giant thumb.'

Public sentiment was reflected in the local elections in November 1947 when Labour lost 652 seats. By late 1949, amid feverish press speculation about the timing of the election, polls such as Gallup were showing the Tories with a lead over Labour of up to ten points. Attlee and his deputy, Herbert Morrison, wanted to delay the election until May 1950, hoping that by then they could end petrol rationing. They were stymied by the Chancellor, the puritanical Sir Stafford Cripps, who felt it would be wrong to produce a Budget just before an election and threatened to resign over the issue. Attlee said Cripps was 'no judge of politics' but felt he must go along with his Chancellor. Besides, he still believed he could win. Indeed, Labour leaders were so confident of victory that at the end of 1949, Attlee and a group of fourteen senior ministers took bets on the size of their majority, with most expecting it to be at least seventy. On 10 January, Attlee announced that the election would be on 23 February 1950.

In truth, the economic situation was improving and opinion polls showed the gap between Tory and Labour steadily narrowing. The last poll before the vote, published in the *News Chronicle*, showed Labour on 45 per cent, the Tories on 43.5, the Liberals on 10.5 and others on 1. The race was too close to call. The Nuffield study noted that all parties continued to focus on constituency canvass returns but added that 'in 1950 for the first time polling analysis became one of the recognised adjuncts of political planning'.

There were other election 'firsts' in 1950. It was the first election to take place after the 1948 Representation of the People Act which concluded 'the progress of the British people towards a full and complete democracy begun by the Great Reform Bill of 1832. From now on every citizen will have a vote and only one vote.' Plural voting and the university vote were abolished.

Another election 'first' in 1950 was the televising of the election results. The programme was presented by Richard Dimbleby and a young David Butler. Sadly, no recordings have survived, but we know it started at 10.45 p.m. and ran until 1 a.m. Not many watched – only 350,000 TV licences were held. There was footage of the crowds in Trafalgar Square but nothing on the election campaigns because of the BBC's fear of breaching impartiality rules.

Professor Herbert Nicholas, main author of the Nuffield study, wrote that the BBC 'kept aloof from the election as if it had been occurring on another planet' but added that 'the decision to carry neutrality to the lengths of castration was the only right one'. He noted, however, that the potential for education and discussion on radio was 'deliberately and completely suppressed' and said this could hardly stand as 'the last word in the collective wisdom and courage of a mature democracy'. A 'first' perhaps for Beeb bashing? Audiences for election broadcasts – all done on radio – were down on 1945. Not a worry for Attlee, who believed that 'the preparation of a broadcast is not so important as even a trivial committee'.

The election campaign proper started after the dissolution of Parliament on 3 February, almost three weeks before polling day. A record-breaking number of 1,868 candidates stood for 625 seats, slightly reduced under the new Act from 640 in 1945. Only 126 candidates were women. The main themes were housing, employment, the cost of living and rationing – this last was probably the most vexed question of all and it was underlined when news came in January that

Germany, the defeated enemy, was ending food rationing. The Conservatives seized on this. Their manifesto – 'This is the Road' – said: 'Almost all our neighbours in Europe have ended food and indeed petroleum rationing. As soon as we have been able to ensure that the price of the necessities of life are within the reach of every family we shall abolish the existing rationing system.' Labour's manifesto – 'Let Us Win Through Together' – pledged to continue rationing, saying: 'Only by price control and rationing can fair shares of scarce goods be ensured.'

Out on the campaign trail, Churchill told an audience in Plymouth: 'We realise the deprivation and often hardship involved in the strict rationing of petrol which the Socialist government have enforced, and we are determined to put an end to it at the earliest opportunity.' Attlee responded: 'Petrol costs dollars and if you have only a limited amount of dollars, more petrol means less food or less raw materials.' Yet as the Nuffield report noted, Churchill's objective had not been to win the motorists' vote, which was comparatively small, but to present Labour as the 'niggardly, unimaginative upholder of austerity for austerity's sake'.

The electioneering styles of the two party leaders contrasted sharply. Attlee refused an official car on the grounds that he would be on party political not national business, and he was driven round the country by his wife, Violet. During a 1,000-mile 'seven-towns-a-day' tour of the country, he sat in the front of their battered family car with a briefcase on his knee while in the back was a single detective and a journalist from the Labour-supporting *Daily Herald*. Backseat passengers often kept their eyes shut – Vi was a notoriously bad driver. If the Attlees arrived early and had time in hand, Vi would get out her knitting while her husband did *The Times* crossword. A US newspaper, the *Baltimore Sun*, marvelled at Attlee being a 'soft spoken, mild mannered man who looks more like a schoolmaster or a bank clerk than the executive of the British Empire'.

Meanwhile, Churchill travelled by chauffeur-driven limousine. He had cut short a holiday in Madeira and arrived home by flying boat on 12 January, saying he'd heard there was going to be an election and thought he'd better come back in case he was wanted. He had found time in the post-war years for painting, writing and swanning off to exotic locations like the Côte d'Azur, where he stayed at La Capponcina, the villa owned by the press baron Lord Beaverbrook.

Inevitably, the campaign was dominated by Churchill, war leader, orator and wordsmith – the latest volume of his memoirs came out only weeks before polling day and its serialisation in the *Daily Telegraph* was advertised by posters picturing the great man. Far fewer column inches were devoted to Attlee even by Labour-supporting papers. Historian Peter Hennessy says being out of office enabled Churchill to become a 'freelance statesman extraordinaire'. In 1946, in Fulton, Missouri, Churchill had spoken of an iron curtain descending across Europe. Hugely controversial at the time, the speech helped relaunch him. He was proved right when in 1948 Stalin blockaded Berlin. During the 1950 election campaign, Churchill returned to the theme, using a speech in Edinburgh to call for a 'summit' with Soviet Russia 'to bridge the gap between two worlds'. It was the first time the phrase had been used in a diplomatic context and the speech attracted worldwide press coverage, enhancing the Tory leader's stature and raising him above the knockabout party fray.

The years out of office enabled the Tories as a whole to recharge batteries, build up the party's grass roots and rethink their policy approach. The reboot was largely down to two individuals: Frederick Marquis, later Lord Woolton, and Rab Butler. Woolton, a Lancashire businessman with a talent for public relations as well as administration, had been the wartime Minister of Food. He joined the Tory Party the day after they lost the 1945 election and set about modernising it. He raised over £1 million and spent it on training and paying hundreds of new agents, he reformed the selection of candidates so that they couldn't 'buy' seats and he set up a nationwide on-the-stump campaign glorying in the title of Operation Knocker.

R. A. Butler, known as Rab from his initials, was a former academic and civil servant who had been the minister responsible for the progressive 1944 Education Act. In 1946, he became chairman of the Conservative Research Department, which was able to attract a whole cadre of bright young men including leading figures of the future such as Reginald Maudling, Iain Macleod and Enoch Powell. Butler, a moderate 'one-nation' Tory, believed in full employment and acceptance of the welfare state. Crucially, this was an approach that was incorporated into the Conservative Party's election manifesto. The manifesto pledged that full employment 'would be the first aim of a Conservative government', and it promised to 'maintain and improve the NHS' and 'to provide a solid base of social security below which none shall fall'. This was hugely significant because it marked a fundamental change from pre-war Toryism and helped undermine Labour attempts to label the Tories as reactionary.

The Tories' new vigour in both organisational and intellectual terms was in contrast to Labour. By 1950, Labour leaders had lost much of their dynamism. They were tired and ill. Most had been in power for a decade, first as members of the wartime coalition and then, without a break, they had set to work trying to build a 'new Jerusalem' in Britain. It left them exhausted and with few new ideas. As Robert Crowcroft and Kevin Theakston put it in their paper on the end of the Attlee government: 'The crusading army of 1945 was reduced to a host of walking wounded.'

Attlee had been Deputy Prime Minister during the war. Once in No. 10 himself, he became the great ringmaster holding together a diverse and talented but increasingly fractious Cabinet. Democracy, he once said, meant government by discussion – but it worked only if you could stop people talking. The effort took its toll on his health and in 1948 he was hospitalised with an ulcer. His deputy, Herbert Morrison, was also ill – in 1947 he almost died of a thrombosis. Ernest Bevin, the Foreign Secretary, who had played a major role in the creation of NATO in 1949, had heart problems. The Chancellor, Sir Stafford Cripps, a God-fearing, teetotal vegetarian, was dying of cancer. His Marxist sympathies had led Churchill to make him ambassador to Russia during the war though the two men did not get on. Told by a Commons official that Cripps wanted to speak to him urgently, Churchill, who was in the gents, replied: 'Tell Sir Stafford I am on the lavatory and I can only deal with one shit at a time.'

Following the election, Attlee had a reshuffle and made one of Labour's rising stars, Hugh Gaitskell, Minister for Economic Affairs. Gaitskell, a future leader of the party, became de facto deputy Chancellor before taking over officially from the ailing Cripps in October. Despite the infusion of new blood, with a majority of only five, the Labour government was in its dying phase – and under pressure as never before. Already, the NHS was costing far more than expected, but in June 1950, the outbreak of the Korean War brought huge new demands on the public purse. Gaitskell demanded the introduction of charges for dentistry and spectacles, a move fiercely opposed by Aneurin Bevan, creator of the NHS, who resigned from the Cabinet. So too did the future Prime Minister Harold Wilson, who had been president of the Board of Trade. In the longer term, the divisions between Bevanites and Gaitskellites marked the start of a split between left and right that was to become a critical feature of Labour politics.

There had already been arguments over French Foreign Minister Robert Schuman's proposal in May 1950 for the establishment of a 'supra-national community' in Europe, precursor of the EU. This too would be a source of internal disagreement in the Labour Party for years – and in British politics generally.

From the moment the result of the 1950 election was known, everyone was certain there would be another one soon. It was duly called in September 1951 and saw Labour defeated. Yet, by then, the pattern for future decades had already been set. The 1950 election forged political agreement on major areas such as social policy and the NHS, setting the seal on some of Labour's greatest achievements. It confirmed the reform and reshaping of the Conservative Party, creating a new electoral machine that set it on the path to thirteen years in power. And it marked another step in the collapse of the Liberal Party as an independent political force. It may have become a largely forgotten election, but it was pivotal.

Sue Cameron is a writer and broadcaster. A former presenter of BBC's *Newsnight* and of *Channel 4 News*, she has also been a columnist on the *Financial Times* and the *Daily Telegraph*.

32

1951

VERNON BOGDANOR

Dissolution: 5 October 1951
Polling day: 25 October 1951
Seats contested: 625
Total electorate / Voted / Turnout: 34,919,331 (34,627,060 in contested seats) / 28,596,594 / 82.6 per cent
Candidates (total 1,376): Conservative (including UUP) – 617; Labour (including NI Labour) – 617; Liberal – 109; Communist – 10; Independent Nationalist – 1; Independent Republican – 1; Irish Labour – 1; Nationalist – 1
Prime Minister on polling day: Clement Attlee
Main party leaders: Conservative – Winston Churchill; Labour – Clement Attlee; Liberal – Clement Davies; Irish Labour – William Norton; Communist – Harry Pollitt; Plaid Cymru – Gwynfor Evans; SNP – Robert McIntyre; Nationalist – James McSparran; UUP – Basil Brooke

Party performance:

Party	Votes	Percentage share	Seats
Labour (including NI Labour)	13,948,883 (62,324)	48.8 (13.5)	295 (0)
Conservative (including UUP)	13,717,850 (274,928)	48 (59.4)	321 (9)
Liberal	730,546	2.6	6
Irish Labour	33,174	7.2	1
Independent Nationalist	33,094	7.1	1
Nationalist	32,717	7.1	1

| Independent Republican | 26,976 | 5.8 | 0 |
| Communist | 21,640 | 0.1 | 0 |

Result: Conservative majority of seventeen seats

Few were surprised when, on 20 September 1951, Prime Minister Clement Attlee announced on the radio that he would ask George VI for a dissolution of Parliament on 5 October so that a general election could be held on 25 October, the first time a dissolution had been announced on that medium. Although the Labour government was only nineteen months into its five-year term, the February 1950 election which had reduced Labour's 1945 majority from 144 to five had resulted in a parliament that was barely viable and a severely weakened government.

The government had in addition been undermined by the loss of its leading ministers. In 1950, apart from Attlee, there were four big figures in government widely known to the public – Herbert Morrison, Lord President of the Council, Leader of the House of Commons and in effect Deputy Prime Minister; Ernest Bevin, the Foreign Secretary; Sir Stafford Cripps, Chancellor of the Exchequer; and Aneurin Bevan, Minister of Health and Housing. However, by the time of the 1951 election, all but Morrison had gone. Cripps had resigned because of ill health in October 1950, Bevin had died in April 1951, the same month in which Bevan, together with Harold Wilson, president of the Board of Trade, had resigned from the government. The reputation of Morrison, the sole survivor of the quartet, had been seriously diminished after he had replaced Bevin at the Foreign Office in March 1951, a role for which he was little suited.

Nevertheless, the 1950 government lasted longer than many had expected. That was partly because it abstained from controversial legislation, apart from a bill to nationalise iron and steel. Otherwise, it was, so Morrison declared, a time not for eating but for digestion.

Even so, Attlee's announcement of the election dismayed his leading colleagues, though Morrison and Hugh Gaitskell, Cripps's replacement as Chancellor of the Exchequer, had been informed in

May that Attlee's mind was moving towards an October election. The main considerations influencing Attlee were the Bevanite split and the problems of governing with a wafer-thin majority – Labour MPs were being harried mercilessly by the opposition, with sick MPs required to attend every division. Attlee may also have been influenced by the king, who was proposing a five- or six-month tour of Australia, New Zealand and Ceylon (now Sri Lanka) in 1952 and felt unwilling to go without some resolution of the political uncertainty. The tour had already been postponed from 1951, owing to the Festival of Britain, and it would, the king believed, offend the three countries were it to be postponed again. Offence would also be caused if the tour had to be interrupted because of a general election in Britain. This consideration was not decisive, but it did confirm the Prime Minister's inclinations. In the event, however, ill health was to prevent the king going on the tour, although this could not be foreseen until after the election date had been announced.

Even though the election had been expected for some time, few advance preparations had been made. The Conservatives, in place of a manifesto, reverted to an older practice of a personal statement by the leader of the party, Winston Churchill, followed by a longer document entitled 'Britain Strong and Free'. Churchill's personal statement proposed building 300,000 houses a year, a commitment resulting from a motion carried, against the advice of the platform at the 1950 party conference, but one that was to be achieved in 1953. Policies which might have proved divisive such as trade union reform – banning the closed shop and contracting in to pay the political levy to the Labour Party instead of contracting out – were omitted. Instead, there would be a Workers Charter, designed to show that a Conservative government would work with rather than against organised labour. Surprisingly, the Conservatives proposed to introduce an excess profits levy to help finance rearmament, something upon which Churchill had insisted. Churchill also promised to restore the university constituencies, but nothing came of this idea. Nor did anything result from the proposal for all-party meetings to consider House of Lords reform – *plus ça change*!

Labour's slogan was 'Forward with Labour or Backward with the Tories'. The tone of its manifesto was largely defensive, taking pride in what had been achieved, rather than offering a clear sense of direction for the future.

The Liberals, who put up just 109 candidates, could no longer claim, as they had been able to do in 1950, when they had fielded 475, that they could form a government. Their manifesto argued that a strong Liberal representation at Westminster was essential to combat the class and sectional interests of Labour and the Conservatives. The main proposal in the Liberal manifesto was for Scottish and Welsh Home Rule. Surprisingly, there was no mention of proportional representation, which had been a staple of Liberal manifestos since 1922. This was ironic as 1951 was to be, together with February 1974, the only post-war election in which the party with the greatest number of votes did not win the greatest number of seats. In 1950, the Liberals had been opposed to conscription, but that opposition was now dropped in the more dangerous international circumstances of 1951.

None of the manifestos had much to say on the economic problems facing the country, in particular inflation, a result of the rising costs of commodities and wage claims. The economy was also under strain as a result of the commitment to a heavy rearmament programme.

The 1950–51 parliament had been dominated by issues of foreign policy, on most of which there was bipartisan agreement. In June 1950, North Korea had attacked the south. Led by the United States, the United Nations had committed itself to the defence of South Korea, with Britain, as America's closest ally, playing a leading part. The government's policy was supported by the Conservatives and Liberals and there was little opposition from Labour's left wing, committed as it was to collective security. On domestic policy, too, there was a broad consensus. All three parties accepted the mixed economy, the welfare state and the commitment to full employment. The main areas on which they diverged were nationalisation and the need for rationing and food subsidies, but on controls the differences were more of emphasis than of principle. Labour's manifesto contained no new proposals for nationalisation, the policy with which the party had been so strongly identified in 1945 – only a vague declaration to 'take over concerns which fail the nation and start new public enterprises wherever this will serve the national interest'. And the government had already begun to remove wartime restrictions and clothes rationing in the bonfire of controls by the president of the Board of Trade, Harold Wilson, in 1948 and 1949. The Conservative government elected in 1951 was to do little that Labour would not have done apart from abandoning the policy of low interest rates, de-nationalising road transport and iron and steel, and removing rationing and such wartime controls as remained slightly more rapidly than Labour. The 1951 election was less about which new policies should be adopted than about which party could best implement policies which were broadly agreed.

The Korean War had necessitated a heavy rearmament programme, which, in the words of the government's 'Economic Survey for 1951', was now 'the first objective' of its economic policy. The programme, announced in January 1951, would cost £4.7 million over three years. To finance it, Hugh Gaitskell, the Chancellor, had proposed user charges on false teeth and spectacles, precipitating the resignation of Bevan and Wilson, who believed, rightly as it turned out, that the rearmament programme was beyond the capacity of the British economy to sustain. Bevan's resignation inaugurated a battle between left and right in the Labour Party which was not to be resolved until Tony Blair became Labour leader in 1994; but perhaps it has not been resolved even today. After his resignation, Bevan and the left proposed a further programme of nationalisation for which the party leaders had little enthusiasm, believing that it would alienate the floating voter. The party leadership, however, seemed bereft of any other radical new ideas. As a future Labour minister, Anthony Crosland, was later to claim, Labour was divided between those who were radical but not contemporary, and those who were contemporary but not radical.

The Bevanites were comparatively restrained during the 1951 election campaign, but the split offered the Conservatives an easy target. In a radio election broadcast, one Conservative spokesman called Bevan the 'Tito of Tonypandy' and declared that 'a team can't do its stuff with two captains, one trying to kick the other when the crowd isn't looking'. The Liberal leader, Clement Davies, absurdly predicted that, if Labour won, Attlee would be displaced by Bevan as Prime Minister and relegated to the Ministry of Health! Both the Conservative and Labour campaigns were essentially based on fear. The Conservatives suggested that a future Labour government would fall into the hands of the Bevanites. Labour suggested that a Conservative government would make war more likely, as well as putting in danger the achievements of full employment and the welfare state. It is not clear whether Labour's leaders really believed what they were saying. Hugh Gaitskell confided presciently to his diary that 'intelligent Tories' would say to the voters, 'No war, no unemployment, no cuts in social service, just good government.' Still, the fears aroused by Labour were more potent than those aroused by the Conservatives. It was difficult for anyone to be frightened by Attlee, and difficult to believe that a government led by Attlee, Morrison and Gaitskell wouldn't be too weak to resist left-wing extremism.

Ill luck continued to dog Labour even during the election campaign. In March 1951, the Iranian government had nationalised the Anglo-Iranian Oil Company (now British Petroleum), costing Britain much-needed dollars, since the country would now have to pay for oil in dollars rather than sterling. The ensuing crisis seemed to prefigure Suez in 1956. Herbert Morrison, the Foreign Secretary, backed by the Minister for Defence, wanted to respond with force, but the Cabinet, with the Americans being opposed to military action, preferred to negotiate, keeping force as a possible later option. Since Britain and the United States were fighting in Korea on a United Nations mandate, it would have been difficult to defend military action in Iran which did not enjoy such a mandate. The crisis in Iran intensified just after the election campaign began, when, on 27 September, Iran peremptorily ordered the final expulsion of British employees from the oil refinery at Abadan. Egypt then tweaked the lion's tail. On 8 October, it abrogated the 1936 Anglo-Egyptian Treaty, which provided for British forces to remain in the Suez Canal zone, and threatened to annex Sudan, currently ruled, in theory jointly, by Britain and Egypt, but in practice by Britain alone. It was easy for the Conservatives to lambast British weakness. Churchill said that the Labour government was confronted by three disasters – Bev*an*, Abad*an* and Sud*an*. But perhaps Churchill's attack backfired, arousing fears that war would be more likely under a Conservative government. 'The Tory', Labour's manifesto declared, 'still thinks in terms of Victorian imperialism and Colonial exploitation. His reaction is to threaten force – he would have denied freedom to India, Pakistan, Ceylon and Burma.' One Labour leaflet asked: 'Will your boy die in Persia?'

Fear of war had been increased by events in Korea. In October 1950, Chinese 'volunteers' had intervened in the war, and there were widespread fears that it could escalate into a third world war involving the Soviet Union. Careful diplomacy was needed to ensure that it did not. Labour could suggest that Churchill's sabre-rattling and gunboat approach was dangerous. Suddenly, so it seemed, foreign policy came to the forefront of the election. In May 1951, Hugh Dalton, a former Labour Chancellor, had predicted that 'if we get Churchill and the Tory Party back at the next election we shall be at war with Russia within twelve months'. And, during the election campaign, Bevan declared, 'If you send back a Conservative administration, you will be declaring to the rest of the world that the people in this crowded island are prepared to run the risk of a third world war, and this time an atom war.' Labour election leaflets contained messages such as 'Vote Tory and reach for a rifle. Vote Labour and reach old age', 'A Third Labour Government or a Third World War', 'Your X can save a million crosses' and 'Welfare with Labour or Warfare with the Tories'. On 20 and 22 October, the Labour-supporting *Daily Mirror* asked 'Whose finger on the trigger?' On election day, it published a cartoon of a hand holding a gun with the slogan 'Today YOUR Finger is on the Trigger?' counterposing a war-mongering Churchill with a peaceable Attlee. This slogan led to a libel action by Churchill, which was settled in the Conservative leader's favour after the election. The 1951 election has been labelled the war-monger election.

Even so, the campaign was not dominated by stunts but seems to have been marked by considerable seriousness. Overall, 52 per cent of electors claimed to have read at least one election address while 30 per cent claimed to have been to at least one election meeting, even if the meetings seem to have attracted primarily the party faithful, rather than undecided voters. Every party with over fifty candidates was entitled to at least one radio broadcast. The Communist Party, which put up just ten candidates as compared to 100 in 1950, did not qualify. No fewer than 82 per cent claimed to have listened to at least one party election broadcast on radio. Each broadcast was heard by between 20 per cent and 50 per cent of the adult population. There was also an important innovation. For the first time, there were three television election broadcasts, one by each of the major parties. The very first was delivered by the Liberal veteran Lord Samuel. It was not a success, as he read a prepared document in a dry unvarying monotone, more suited to radio than to this new medium. Television, however, provided one of the few lively exchanges in an otherwise dull campaign, when Labour accused the Conservatives of exaggerating the rise in the cost of living by displaying a graph in which one axis was illegitimately broadened and the other illegitimately narrowed. 'Crippen', the Labour spokesman declared, 'was the first criminal to be caught by wireless; the Conservative Central Office are the first criminals to be caught by television.' But television probably had a negligible influence on the outcome, since only around 10 per cent of the population owned a set capable of receiving the broadcasts. In his book on the election, the psephologist David Butler declared that the advent of television in 1951 was not an influence but a portent.

The BBC enjoyed at the time a broadcasting monopoly. There were no commercial channels. And, at the insistence of the parties, the BBC was not allowed to broadcast any election material other than party political broadcasts, except for the announcement of the date of dissolution and the arrangements made for polling day. Such debates as there were between the parties, therefore, would take place in constituency election meetings, not on the broadcast media. Campaigning was determinedly traditional, consisting primarily of local election meetings. Prime Minister Attlee campaigned with his wife – a notoriously bad driver, who was in charge of the small family car

– speaking at nearly seventy meetings in his standard low-key and unrhetorical style. The *Manchester Guardian*, as *The Guardian* was then called, commented ironically that the Prime Minister 'looked like the sort of man who might be suspected of harbouring an intention of voting against Mr Attlee'.

Turnout in 1951 was 82.6 per cent, exceeded only by the post-war record of 84 per cent in 1950. In no other election since 1910 has turnout been over 80 per cent, and since 2001, it has always been under 70 per cent. One reason why it was slightly lower in 1951 than in 1950 was because of the longer period between the composition of the electoral register and the election. But in many marginal seats, turnout was higher than in 1950, and in general, the drop in turnout was greatest in the safer seats.

The 1950 election had resulted in a swing against Labour of 3.3 per cent. The 1951 election resulted in a further small swing of 1.1 per cent, just sufficient to topple the government. Only twenty-seven out of 650 seats changed hands. Labour remained the largest party in terms of votes, but the Conservatives, with 231,000 fewer votes, enjoyed a net gain of twenty-three seats, twenty-one of them from Labour, and they secured a majority of seventeen, just sufficient to last a full parliament.

The Conservatives benefited from the liberalisation of postal voting in the 1948 Representation of the People Act. The psephologist David Butler has calculated that their greater efficiency in marshalling the postal vote was worth twelve seats to them in 1950 and ten in 1951. With twenty-two fewer seats in 1951, the Conservatives would not have enjoyed a majority.

Part of the reason for the discrepancy between seats and votes in 1951 was that there were four uncontested Ulster Unionist seats in Northern Ireland, at a time when the Unionists sat with the Conservatives. Had they been contested, the Conservative vote would obviously have been larger. But there was also a bias in the electoral system worth around 500,000 votes to the Conservatives. Labour was piling up votes in safe working-class constituencies – indeed its vote in many of these constituencies was higher than in 1945 – but it was losing the suburban middle-class marginals in London and the west Midlands which had given it so large a majority in 1945. Both parties secured their largest ever vote up to that time. The Conservative vote was not to be surpassed until John Major's victory in 1992, and Labour's not until the Blair landslide in 1997.

The only other election since the war in which the winning party secured fewer votes than its main rival was that of February 1974. But that election was followed by a minority government. The outcome of the 1951 election, by contrast, allowed the Conservatives to control the Commons for a full term.

For the Liberals, the election was a disaster, reducing their representation from nine to six MPs. Sixty-six of the 109 candidates they fielded lost their deposit by failing to secure one-eighth of the vote. Only one of their MPs, Jo Grimond, in the remote constituency of Orkney and Shetland, had faced Conservative opposition and a three-cornered contest. All other Liberals in three-cornered contests were defeated. Lady Megan Lloyd George, daughter of the last Liberal Prime Minister, was defeated in the Anglesey constituency which she had represented for twenty-two years. She and the other Liberal MPs who lost their seats, together with Frank Byers in Dorset North, were the only defeated candidates who came within 5,000 votes of the winner. There seemed some doubt as to whether the party could survive. After the election, Churchill offered the Ministry of Education to Clement Davies, the Liberal leader. Davies, supported by Lady Violet Bonham Carter, wanted to accept, but the party refused to countenance it. Had Davies accepted, the Liberals would probably have been absorbed into the Conservative Party as the National Liberals were to be.

Of the thirty-three candidates of the minor parties and independents, twenty-six, including the ten Communist candidates, lost their deposits. The election, then, marked the apogee of the two-party system, in which local factors, the ability of the local candidate and the strength of local party organisations seemed hardly to affect the outcome. In that era, the two-party system was able to yield decisive results from relatively narrow majorities of the vote. Had either party won a further 5 per cent of the vote, it would have enjoyed a landslide. Labour would have had a majority of 156, the Conservatives 200. But as the 1950s wore on, the two-party system was gradually to be undermined, though at a glacially slow pace, until in 2019 there were to be as many as eighty-two out of 650 MPs not owing allegiance to the two major parties.

The key to the outcome of the 1951 election would depend, in Attlee's words, on 'which way the Liberal cat jumps'. How would those who had voted Liberal in 1950, but were without a Liberal candidate in 1951, cast their votes? In 1951, the Liberals were more friendly to the Conservatives and more hostile to Labour than they were later to become. The Conservatives did all that they could to secure Liberal allegiance, stressing that the two parties shared a common hostility to 'socialism'. There were local electoral pacts between the Conservatives and the Liberals in the two Bolton seats and the two Huddersfield seats. Two at least of these four seats would have been won by Labour had the anti-Labour vote been split. The Conservatives opposed just one Liberal incumbent, Jo Grimond, and he proved to be the only one of the six Liberals to be returned against Conservative opposition. Nor did the Conservatives put up candidates in Dundee West or Colne Valley, where the Liberal candidate was Lady Violet Bonham Carter, daughter of Asquith and a long-standing friend of Churchill's. The first list of prospective Conservative candidates even included Liberals in seats not being contested by the Conservatives! It seems indeed that Churchill regarded the Liberals as really Conservatives in disguise! He himself spoke for Lady Violet Bonham Carter in Colne Valley, even though she was standing for another party, declaring that he found 'comfort in the broad harmony of thought which prevails between the modern Tory democracy and the doctrines of the famous Liberal leaders of the past'. Churchill was after all himself an ex-Liberal, while Clement Davies, the Liberal leader, had, as a National Liberal, been a supporter of the Conservative-dominated National government in the 1930s. Nevertheless, despite Churchill's advocacy, Colne Valley as well Dundee West were won by Labour which, by contrast with the Conservatives, did little to win over Liberal support.

The swing to the Conservatives was greater in constituencies which the Liberals had fought in 1950, but not in 1951, than in other constituencies. It was believed indeed that the 1950 Liberal vote divided between seven to three and six to four in favour of the Conservatives. A 6/4 split would account for eight of the twenty-one Conservative gains from Labour, a 7/3 split for eighteen out of the twenty-one gains. Paradoxically, the Liberals had more influence in the 1951 election when they put up so few candidates than in 1950 when they had fought on a broad front.

British general elections may be divided into contests where the outcome is largely predetermined before the campaign begins – notably, 1906, 1931, 1945, 1983, 1997 and 2019 – and those where the outcome is contingent and could have been different. The 1951 election lies firmly in the latter category. The outcome might indeed have been very different without the resignation of Bevan and Wilson, or if an alternative election date had been chosen. The result surprised many not because Labour lost but because the margin was so narrow. At the beginning of the campaign, the Conservatives had enjoyed a 10 per cent lead in the opinion polls, and a large Conservative victory was widely expected. The Chancellor, Hugh Gaitskell, had felt that 'we should be badly beaten'. The reason why this did not occur is probably due to the campaign, quiet as it was. Two issues seemed to resonate with the electorate. The first was defence of the welfare state and full employment which, some thought, would be threatened by a Conservative victory. The second was fear that a Conservative government would increase the danger of war.

The narrow Conservative victory rendered many Labour supporters falsely optimistic. The party had been narrowly defeated but not routed. Attlee called Labour's performance 'an extraordinary achievement. Our vote has not only kept up; it has increased.' Hugh Dalton wrote in his diary, 'The election results are wonderful. We are out just at the right moment, and our casualties are wonderfully light.' Few Labour MPs appreciated the significance of what had happened. 'What is really significant', declared backbench Labour MP Richard Crossman in his diary, 'is the cheerfulness and morale of the

Party, compared with its state of semi-disintegration just before the election.' But then he added, presciently, 'Personally I am inclined to regard this sort of optimism as extremely complacent. We are an Opposition without any idea of a constructive Socialist policy, and it may be a great deal more difficult to unseat the Conservatives than many of my colleagues imagine.'

In office, the Conservatives did the opposite to what Labour feared. They succeeded in maintaining full employment and avoided any tampering with the welfare state. Fulfilling the commitment to build 300,000 houses made the career of Harold Macmillan, the Housing Minister. Churchill, instead of war-mongering, devoted his declining years to a brave if unsuccessful attempt to secure a summit with the Soviet Union to alleviate Cold War tensions. With Anthony Eden as Foreign Secretary, the Conservatives continued Labour's policy of withdrawal from empire. Churchill had set the tone in a post-election speech in which he called for 'a lull in our party strife which will enable us to understand what is good in our opponents, and not to be so very clever at all their shortcomings'. And the Conservatives had a great stroke of luck when commodity prices fell in 1952, cheapening imports and yielding a windfall increase in the standard of living. Had Labour been able to hold on until 1952, it might well have been returned to power, in which case it would probably have been able to continue governing through the rising prosperity of the 1950s. And, although there seemed in 1951 so little difference between the parties, it is just possible that Labour would slowly but surely have established in Britain a Scandinavian style of socialism based less on nationalisation than on redistributive taxation. Instead, it was the Conservatives who were to administer the mixed economy cum welfare state established by the wartime coalition and the 1945 Labour government. Labour could claim to have lost the election but won the argument. But winning the argument was of little use. The 1945 government had appeared to many in the Labour Party as a beginning on the road to socialism. The election of 1951 showed that the road was now blocked and would not be reopened for many years, if it ever has been.

In his diary, Harold Macmillan summed up the message of the election for the Conservatives.

> The truth is that the Socialists have fought the election (very astutely) not on Socialism but on Fear. Fear of unemployment, fear of reduced wages, fear of reduced social benefits, fear of war. These four fears have been brilliantly, if unscrupulously, exploited. If, before the next election, none of these fears have proved reasonable, we may be able to force the Opposition to fight on Socialism. Then we can win.

And so it proved to be.

As for Labour, it seemed to have little new to offer. Attlee remained as leader until a second election defeat in 1955, primarily to prevent Morrison succeeding him. New thinking would have to await the election of Gaitskell as leader in 1955, though even that did not prevent a third defeat in 1959.

The 1951 election yielded a knife-edge and in a sense freak victory for the Conservatives, and yet it was to determine the course of British politics for the next thirteen years. Only three members of the outgoing Labour Cabinet were ever to hold office again. The Conservatives became, as they had been between the wars, the natural party of government, a position from which, over the next seventy years, only Harold Wilson and Tony Blair were able to displace them. So, contrary to appearances, the quiet and demure election of 1951 turned out to be decisive for the future of Britain.

Sir Vernon Bogdanor is professor of government at King's College London and was for many years professor of government at Oxford. His books include *The Strange Survival of Liberal Britain* and *Making the Weather: Six who Changed Post War Britain*, to be published by Haus in autumn 2024.

33

1955

PHILIP NORTON

Dissolution: 6 May 1955
Polling day: 26 May 1955
Seats contested: 630
Total electorate / Voted / Turnout: 34,852,179 / 26,759,729 / 76.8 per cent
Candidates (total 1,409): Conservative (including UUP) – 624; Labour (including NI Labour) – 620; Liberal – 110; Communist – 17; Sinn Féin – 12; Plaid Cymru – 11
Prime Minister on polling day: Anthony Eden
Main party leaders: Conservative – Anthony Eden; Labour – Clement Attlee; Liberal – Clement Davies; Communist – Harry Pollitt; Plaid Cymru – Gwynfor Evans; Sinn Féin – Paddy McLogan; UUP – Basil Brooke

Party performance:

Party	Votes	Percentage share	Seats
Conservative (including UUP)	13,310,891 (442,647)	49.7 (68.5)	345 (10)
Labour (including NI Labour)	12,405,254 (35,614)	46.4 (5.5)	277 (0)
Liberal	722,402	2.7	6
Sinn Féin	152,310	23.6	2
Plaid Cymru	45,119	0.2	0
Communist	33,144	0.1	0

Result: Conservative majority of sixty seats

The general election of 1955 was unremarkable in terms of the campaign waged by the parties. It resembled a traditional election campaign of the twentieth century. Both main party leaders, the new Conservative Prime Minister Sir Anthony Eden and Labour leader Clement Attlee made extensive tours throughout the country, Attlee being driven in his own car by Mrs Attlee. Eden was also driven to engagements, with his assistant, Peter Tapsell, sat in the back seat with a typewriter. 'On the whole,' recalled Sir John Smyth VC, defending the marginal Conservative seat of Norwood, 'it was a quiet election as elections go.' How quiet, we shall explore. However, it was distinctive in three respects.

First, it was notable in that it followed the appointment of a new Prime Minister and resulted in the incumbent party not only winning the election but also increasing its majority, something not seen for almost a century. The Conservatives had won a majority of seats in the 1951 election but with fewer votes than the Labour Party. This time, they not only got more seats but also got more votes than Labour. Winston Churchill resigned as Prime Minister on 5 April and his long-time heir apparent, Foreign Secretary Sir Anthony Eden, was summoned the following day to Buckingham Palace to kiss hands as his successor. Nine days later, Eden announced that there would be an election, with polling day on 26 May. David Butler, in *The British General Election of 1955*, conjectured that there were various reasons why Eden chose to seek an election so soon – a worsening economic situation in the autumn, the prospect of being enmeshed in strikes, the need to strengthen his hand for international negotiations – but whatever the motivation, 'the Prime Minister showed courage and, as it proved, good judgement'. The Conservatives won almost 50 per cent of the vote (49.7 per cent) and 345 seats (including the Speaker), against 277 for Labour. The overall majority rose from seventeen to sixty.

Second, the election constituted a transition from one type of election campaigning to another. There was still a notable emphasis on old-style campaigning: leaders delivering campaign speeches around the country; Eden, for example, spoke at forty meetings. At the same time, a new type of campaign medium was starting to appear. 'The leading figures on each side', noted *The Times Guide to the House of Commons*, 'often drew good audiences, but there was a tendency to hold fewer election meetings, probably because of the impact of television.' Television created a new opportunity for the parties, as well as a challenge. Speaking to camera required a different style of delivery to the oration on the public platform, though, perhaps reflecting the nature of the campaign, there were no outstanding performances. Eden in his last broadcast of the campaign was deemed to have done well. In his memoirs, he admitted that he was not someone who enjoyed elections but rather endured them. He did, though, recognise the importance of the new medium of television. It was, he said, something to which 'I attached first importance'.

Third, the change in the nature of politics was also reflected in the fact that this was the first election in modern political history (and possibly in the history of Parliament) in which not a single seat was uncontested. All 630 seats (up from 625 as a result of Boundary Commission recommendations) saw two or more candidates battle it out. (The five new seats were in England.) However, the election itself was very much a two-party contest, the overwhelming majority of seats witnessing a battle solely between a Conservative and a Labour candidate. Three- or four-way contests were rare. The Liberals put up 110 candidates. That was only one more than in 1951 and they were defending only six seats. There were also seventeen Communist and thirteen Nationalist candidates, along with twenty-five who stood under other, usually independent, labels. The presence of Nationalist candidates meant that four-way contests were more notable in Wales and Northern Ireland than in England. Of the Nationalist candidates, one of the Welsh Nationalist candidates and eight of the Sinn Féin candidates in Northern Ireland were serving prison sentences.

Winston Churchill had returned to Downing Street following the 1951 election victory. As the author and journalist Robin Harris put it, the incoming government was faced with a choice between holding power and using power. Churchill, who had largely been an absentee leader in opposition and had no great interest in domestic policy, 'chose simply to hold it'. He was also variously absent by virtue of ill health, leaving other senior ministers to run government. He was aided by some effective senior ministers, including Rab Butler at the Treasury, Anthony Eden at the Foreign Office and Harold Macmillan in the Ministry of Housing. The party was also aided in terms of organisation by a skilled chairman, Lord Woolton, the wartime Minister of Food and former chairman of Lewis's department store. The principal skill of the government was in conveying that the Tory Party was a party of governance and could be trusted with the affairs of the nation. Both Churchill and Eden had major international recognition.

The Conservative performance was contrasted with a Labour Party that had been noted for internal divisions, with a socialist group, dubbed 'Bevanites', though not led or controlled by Aneurin Bevan, committed to state ownership, and estimated to be about three dozen strong in the parliamentary party, clashing with the party leadership and the Gaitskellites, social democratic followers of shadow Chancellor Hugh Gaitskell. Attlee had continued as leader following the 1951 defeat, despite some Labour MPs believing he should step down. Bevan called for him to do so in 1954, but Attlee persisted, not least to thwart the leadership ambitions of his deputy, Herbert Morrison. When Churchill retired in 1955, at the age of eighty, Attlee was seventy-two. The Liberal Party also had a 72-year-old leader in Clement Davies.

Anthony Eden was relatively young upon taking office – at fifty-seven notably younger than Churchill and Attlee – and had a good war record. He was the youngest adjutant in the British Army in the First World War and had been awarded the Military Cross. He had a good Second World War as Foreign Secretary, returning to the post in 1951. He achieved various successes while at the Foreign Office, brokering a compromise on Indochina and Korea in 1954 in Geneva and in London on European security. He also came across as a dashing figure, seen as a poster boy of British politics. Selwyn Lloyd referred to 'Eden's brilliant diplomatic skills, his intuition, charm and ability to command affectionate loyalty'.

In reality, Eden was not in good health when he succeeded Churchill. A gall bladder operation in 1953 had been botched – it left irreparable damage – and he suffered from a tendency to overreact at times of stress. The intuition ascribed to him by Lloyd was notably lacking when faced with a crisis shortly after entering Downing Street. He was also bad at delegating. However, none of this was apparent to electors during the election campaign. Rather, he came across as representing a new and vibrant brand of Conservatism and someone who could provide leadership for Britain on the world stage. He also led a government that had not been mired in controversy or pursued any policies that had been notable failures. There had been some industrial unrest, but the economy was not a cause for major concern and rationing had been abolished.

The election campaign failed to generate any significant conflict or incite intense public interest. One commentator described the beginning of the campaign as 'the lull before the lull'. The campaign got under way shortly after a newspaper strike had ended, but there was nothing for the press to report that generated notable public interest, let alone excitement. The campaign also took place against a backdrop of a general expectation of a Conservative victory. The party had a lead in the opinion polls and a Gallup poll revealed that 52 per cent of those questioned expected a Conservative victory, against 22 per cent expecting a Labour win. Even Labour supporters were pessimistic, fewer than half (49 per cent) believing that Labour would emerge the winner. Even a well-known Labour figure, Sir Hartley Shawcross, was sufficiently injudicious to tell journalists that the odds were on a Conservative victory.

The campaign was preceded by the Budget, in which Butler was able to give out £150 million in tax relief, both reducing the basic rate of income tax and increasing allowances. As journalist Anthony Howard noted, 'For the time being ... Rab's fourth budget bore all the marks of being a political success.' It was also measured, not being overly generous, but rather, as Howard put it, more of 'a political aperitif'. The following week, the government announced another tax cut, with purchase tax on non-woollen goods being abolished.

Once Parliament was dissolved, the campaign got under way but with neither side managing to raise issues that gained significant traction with the media or electors. Party leaders largely stuck to the party's policies rather than engage directly with their opponents. The most prominent speakers for the Conservatives were Eden and his predecessor and for Labour Clement Attlee and in practice Aneurin Bevan. Eden and Attlee – allies in the wartime government – stuck to their parties' positions and avoided trading insults. Eden variously referred to Labour as 'our Socialist friends' and his election address devoted only three lines to his opponents, it being, as he later recorded, 'my conviction that the British people soon wearies of strictures upon the other party'. Attlee was not prone to making fierce personal attacks, focusing instead on the issues of the day or Labour's policies. The leaders themselves were promoted by their own side for their virtues. As David Butler recorded, 'however much such quiet virtues might commend themselves to the voter, the press hankered after more spectacular speakers'. The problem was in finding any. Churchill was past his glory days – he was the oldest Conservative to stand in the election – and was not utilised in any of his party's broadcasts. Bevan, who had narrowly avoided losing the Labour whip just before the election, similarly was largely confined to the public platform. He made various attacks on the Conservative Party, attracting media attention, not least in claiming that 'Toryism and Christianity are inconsistent' and that it was 'a party of political gigolos kept by the Americans'. However, his attacks were blunted by the failure of Tory leaders to rise to the challenge. Churchill, when he spoke in his constituency, did attack him as a threat and a careerist (and even Eden protested against his claims about the party and Christianity), but the leadership focused instead on divisions within Labour's ranks. It was left to Conservative candidates to use Bevan as a bogeyman: he was mentioned by name in 10 per cent of Conservative candidates' election addresses. Bevan was also limited by his own leadership. He was not deployed in either the sound or the television broadcasts during the campaign. Labour relied on the more establishment figures of Attlee, Hugh Gaitskell and Herbert Morrison. For television broadcasts, they also utilised James Callaghan and former Liberal MP Lady Megan Lloyd George (youngest daughter of David Lloyd George), who had defected to Labour.

Labour tried to make issues out of the cost of living and monopolies, as well as the plight of old-age pensioners, but the state of the economy was not such as to cause public panic. The Conservatives were able to argue that they had twice increased old-age pensions. An attempt by Labour to suggest that industrial relations would worsen and that the Conservatives may threaten the right to strike did not gain significant coverage. In any event, traditional Conservative voters may not have been that averse to some constraints on strike action, given recent strikes.

The failure of any particular issue to make a notable impact during the campaign meant that the press tended to look to other stories to cover. The election at times became almost incidental. Despite the polls at one point suggesting the parties were neck and neck, for most of the campaign the Conservatives maintained a lead in the polls and Labour was not able to do anything to dent it. The economy was not in obvious trouble and earnings were higher; Macmillan had delivered on the promise, made at the 1950 party conference, to build 300,000 houses a year, a target achieved at the end of 1953, a year ahead of schedule. The party was also led by someone who had obvious standing on the international stage. Eden's field was very much foreign affairs. There was a perception that Labour was struggling. All the Conservatives had to do was avoid any slip. They were aided by an efficient party organisation. 'Central Office', recalled Eden, 'was well organized and staffed. Lord Woolton was a wise and urbane chairman who did not make the mistake of interfering too much in detail himself.' The Conservatives had more constituency agents than Labour and spent more on average in the constituencies. In many constituencies, Labour organisation was largely unprepared. The Tories also benefited, or at least did not suffer, from the use of the new media.

The use of television became significant for the first time as an election tool. When Robert McKenzie began the BBC's coverage on election night, he quizzed Lord Woolton as to whether this was, as was variously claimed, the first 'television election'. Radio listening figures remained significant, but the audience was about a third of what it had been in 1951. The growth in ownership of television sets meant that television now matched radio in terms of audience. The audience for each sound or television broadcast was between 4 million and 8 million. Politicians recognised the significance of the media, being able to reach a mass of voters in their homes without the need for extensive and essentially inefficient door-knocking or holding of public meetings. The parties were able to use allocated party political broadcasts prior to the election, though both the main parties used radio broadcasts (only the Liberals used television), and during the campaign itself each was allocated, in addition to radio slots, three television broadcasts and the Liberals one.

For the radio broadcasts, Eden gave the first for the Conservatives, stressing what had been achieved and, in his own area of strength, addressed the international situation. The other broadcasts were given by a new MP, Edith Pitt, the Member for Birmingham Edgbaston (she had been elected in a by-election in 1953) and by the Defence Secretary (Selwyn Lloyd) and Chancellor (Butler). They emphasised the government's achievements and usually the threat posed by a divided Labour Party. The attacks were hardly vitriolic. 'I am not going to suggest that the Socialists do not want peace,' declared Lloyd. 'No doubt they would do their best.' For Labour, the reliance was on senior figures in the party: James Griffiths, Herbert Morrison, Margaret Herbison and Attlee. They stressed what the party stood for, though Morrison had an effective dig at his opponents and what the government would be like without Churchill.

The broadcasts, though, were more dutiful than exciting. As David Butler summarised them:

> It is hard to escape the feeling that a general lack of enterprise was shown. Nothing was attempted which had a fraction of the originality or the impact of Dr Charles Hill's broadcast in 1950. The anecdotes, the analogy, and the fable were all eschewed. Not one good joke was ventured.

The television broadcasts represented the most important development, but the need for different skills when before the cameras to those needed for speaking into a microphone created challenges for what were mostly broadcasting novices. The first broadcast for the Conservatives was given by the new Foreign Secretary, Harold Macmillan, shown standing before his own fireplace. His rehearsed script, emphasising the government's successes and talking about the meeting of foreign ministers from which he had just returned, came across as rather wooden and he was described as appearing ill at ease. The second broadcast was a novel departure, entailing ten newspaper editors quizzing five ministers, led by Eden. Macmillan, one of the five, recalled: 'It was a curious and not altogether satisfactory experiment. Ten newspaper editors asked questions and five Ministers sat in a row like schoolboys to answer them.' The editors took it in turn to ask a question and Eden acted essentially as chair of the panel, answering the question or directing it to one of his colleagues. The exercise may have been a little stilted, not least with the editors making use of their opportunity to develop questions, but it enabled those questioned to come across as in command of their ministerial brief. The third broadcast was given by Eden and it was regarded as the best of all the broadcasts. He spoke directly and fluently to the camera for fifteen minutes. There was nothing new in what he said, and he avoided controversy – there was no attack on his opponents – but rather a sense of competence in governing.

For Labour, the opening broadcast was not dissimilar in effect to Macmillan's, with Attlee and his wife being interviewed in a mock-up of their home, with Attlee, who was not an orator or prone to histrionics, not saying anything particularly memorable. It was followed by one by Harold Wilson and Dr Edith Summerskill, focusing on the price of food, and the final broadcast took the form of four senior parliamentarians – Herbert Morrison, Hugh Gaitskell, James Callaghan and Lady Megan Lloyd George – forming a panel to answer questions from a question master, Wilfred Pickles. The members of the panel were criticised for each being a little too eager to be the one to answer the question, but that fact may also have added some appeal to it as a television performance.

The Liberals used their slot to have two married voters put questions to former party chairman Frank Byers and an established broadcaster (and Liberal candidate) John Arlott. The programme perhaps typified the party's somewhat disorganised approach, with Lord Samuel being squeezed into having a minute at the end to summarise what the party stood for.

The television broadcasts appear to have made little difference to a lacklustre campaign, but they reflected the parties' recognition of the growing importance of television and the need to adapt to it. The broadcasts were of variable quality and impact but were perhaps most important as experiments in seeing how best to utilise the medium. The Conservative broadcast appears to have been more well received than Labour's. A Gallup poll gave Macmillan forty-one marks out of 100 as a performer, whereas Attlee got only twenty-eight. Conservative candidates also appeared more adept than Labour candidates at putting the new medium to use in their constituencies, some candidates having large screens erected to show the party's election broadcasts. The more traditionalist local Labour associations failed to follow suit.

Polls closed at 9 p.m. and at 9.30 the BBC began broadcasting its seventeen-hour election special, fronted by Richard Dimbleby, assisted by a young Oxford don, David Butler. The spokespersons for Labour and the Liberals put a brave face on the poll, both claiming a high turnout and optimism as to the outcome, but the results, when they began to be announced from about 10 p.m., did not come as a great surprise. The first result to be announced, in Cheltenham, produced a swing of just over 2 per cent to the Conservatives. A similar result followed in Salford. In both, turnout was down. It was soon clear, as other results began to flow in, that the Conservatives would be remaining in office.

The share of the vote achieved by the parties was largely in line with the opinion polls, although the polls slightly inflated the Conservative share. The swing from Labour to the Conservatives (of 1.6 per cent) was fairly uniform, though Labour managed to buck the trend slightly in East Anglia, with a tiny swing of 0.1 per cent in their favour.

The principal victims on the Conservative side fell foul of the boundary changes. Two MPs lost out as a result. There were no major scalps taken by Conservative candidates. One former minister, Maurice Webb, lost, as did the left-wing journalist Michael Foot in Plymouth Devonport, both seats affected by boundary changes. The independent-minded Labour MP Woodrow Wyatt had failed to be reselected in the redrawn seat of Birmingham All Saints and ended up standing as a candidate in the Conservative-held seat of Grantham, losing to the sitting Member. Anthony Crosland, a rising figure on the Gaitskellite wing of the party, who had sat since 1950 for South Gloucestershire, also found a new berth, contesting, but losing, Southampton Test. His influential tract, *The Future of Socialism*, appeared the following year.

The Liberals held on to their six seats, aided by the fact that the Conservatives did not contest five of them, a result of local agreements to prevent Labour taking the seats. The only seat won by a Liberal with Labour and Conservative opponents was the most northerly, Orkney and Shetland, represented by the party's Chief Whip, Jo Grimond, the Member since 1950. Anticipated gains failed to materialise. The party was not a significant player in the election and suffered from being led by Davies, an alcoholic who was hospitalised at the time the election was called and who played no significant role in the campaign. Sinn Féin, for the first time since 1918, secured seats, winning Mid-Ulster and Fermanagh & South Tyrone, but with both Members making clear they would not be taking their seats, though their stance was academic, both being barred by virtue of being in prison, serving long sentences for felony.

Other than the incumbent party, the main victor in the election was a sense of indifference. According to the *Daily Express*, people were more interested in the romance between Princess Margaret and Peter Townsend than they were in the election. Despite being fought on a fresh electoral register, turnout was down compared with 1951 – just under 77 per cent compared with just over 82 per cent in 1951. The election ensured the continuation of a Tory government, faced by a Labour opposition.

Labour's defeat was ascribed by some observers to Bevan's role. According to the *Sunday Dispatch*, 'Apart from their own impressive record as a government, the Conservative Party's greatest asset was undoubtedly Mr Aneurin Bevan.' Even Labour-inclined publications recognised the impact of 'the confusion of civil warfare' within Labour's ranks. Labour's divisions did not help the party, but the Conservatives would likely have won anyway given the state of the economy. There was nothing to disturb electors in believing that it was safe and, given the splits in the opposition, probably wisest to stick with what they had. The Conservatives had done nothing to lose the election and Labour nothing significant to win it. It was largely a case of going through the motions of an election where people expected the result from the outset, and nothing happened to upset that expectation. The best assessment was probably that of Churchill, when quizzed by his doctor, Lord Moran, during the campaign. Churchill had expressed a wish that the campaign would soon be over. 'You find it tiring?' queried Moran. 'No,' Churchill replied, 'boring.'

Philip Norton (Lord Norton of Louth) is professor of government at the University of Hull and a Conservative peer. His latest book, *The 1922 Committee: Power Behind the Scenes*, was published in 2023.

34

1959

IAIN DALE

Dissolution: 18 September 1959
Polling day: 8 October 1959
Seats contested: 630
Total electorate / Voted / Turnout: 35,397,304 / 27,862,652 / 78.7 per cent
Candidates (total 1,536): Conservative (including UUP) – 625; Labour (including NI Labour) – 621; Liberal – 216; Plaid Cymru – 20; Communist – 18; Sinn Féin – 12; SNP – 5
Prime Minister on polling day: Harold Macmillan
Main party leaders: Conservative – Harold Macmillan; Labour – Hugh Gaitskell; Liberal – Jo Grimond; Communist – John Gollan; Plaid Cymru – Gwynfor Evans; Sinn Féin – Paddy McLogan; UUP – Basil Brooke; NI Labour – Tom Boyd

Party performance:

Party	Votes	Percentage share	Seats
Conservative (including UUP)	13,750,875 (445,013)	49.4 (77.2)	365 (12)
Labour (including NI Labour)	12,216,172 (44,370)	43.8 (7.7)	258 (0)
Liberal	1,640,760	5.9	6
Sinn Féin	63,415	11	0
Communist	30,896	0.1	0
Plaid Cymru	77,571	0.3	0
SNP	21,738	0.1	0

Result: Conservative majority of 100 seats

Britain at the end of the 1950s was a place full of dichotomies. On the face of it, prosperity had returned after years of austerity. The white goods revolution had begun. In many ways, most people in Britain really had 'never had it so good', as Prime Minister Harold Macmillan so memorably put it on 20 July 1957.

And yet, prosperity masked some underlying issues in both the economy and British society. Although the country had recovered from effective bankruptcy after the Second World War, it was still living off past glories and had yet to find its place in the world. The humiliation of the Suez Crisis put the whole concept of the 'special relationship' with the US in question, while a new breed of politicians on the centre-right saw that a closer relationship with European powers was the way forward. Germany was about to undergo its *Wirtschaftswunder*, while the British economy was also living on past glories and proving resistant to modernisation and reform. And on top of all that, decolonisation meant that Britain's place in the world order was also called into question. It was no longer a superpower, yet still acted like one. Its ruling classes clung to the traditions of the Victorian and Edwardian eras, which they were largely born into.

Prime Minister Harold Macmillan was a classic example of the genre, but he was not alone. By contrast, there was a new generation of more modern-looking politicians leading the Labour Party. Unlike the ruling Conservative Party, Labour, at least on the surface, looked like a party ready to confront the challenges posed by the modern world. The electorate, however, was far from convinced.

All general elections are a contrast between the wish to 'stick with nurse for fear of worse', or the desire for change. And that's what the 1959 general election boiled down to.

On the face of it, the Conservatives should have feared a devastating defeat, but Britain at heart was, and to a large extent still is, conservative with a small 'c'.

The Conservatives had been in power since 1951 and by the autumn of 1959 had served for eight years. The last time that had happened was at the turn of the century, when Lord Salisbury won the 1895 election, and the Conservatives remained in power until the catastrophic defeat to the Liberals in 1906. Labour had enjoyed a six-year term from 1945 to 1951, when Clement Attlee led a truly radical government. But Attlee didn't stand down from the leadership of his party until after the 1955 defeat to the Tories, at the time led by the popular Sir Anthony Eden, who had taken over a few weeks before from Sir Winston Churchill. Eden, and subsequently Macmillan, were known to the electorate in a way the new Labour leader Hugh Gaitskell was not, even though he had served as Chancellor of the Exchequer in the final year of Attlee's government.

The key single event of the 1955–59 parliament was the Suez Crisis of late 1956, which eventually led to the resignation of Sir Anthony Eden as Prime Minister, ostensibly due to ill health.

It is difficult to overstate the humiliation that the Suez conflict brought onto Britain. And it was under the reign of a Prime Minister who was known for his experience and expertise in foreign policy. Cooking up a madcap scheme to take back the Suez Canal from the clutches of the Egyptian leader, Colonel Nasser, it was a joint operation between Britain and France with the assistance of the Israelis, yet the Americans were blindsided. President Eisenhower was furious at the snub and made clear he was wholly opposed to the actions of Britain and France and would do nothing to help them. The military action failed and if there was one issue which symbolised the fall of Britain from superpower to humiliation, it was Suez. Clarissa Eden said she felt as if the Suez was flowing through her living room. In the end, Anthony Eden's political career drowned in the murk of the Suez, and mentally he never really recovered from it.

When Eden resigned on 9 January 1957, he had been Prime Minister for only twenty months. In those days, there were no leadership elections. A leader would emerge after party bigwigs took soundings from MPs, peers and the voluntary party. The process was led by Lord 'Bobbety' Salisbury. He asked each Cabinet minister 'Is it Hawold or Wab?' Was it to be Chancellor Harold Macmillan or the Lord Privy Seal and Eden's de facto deputy, R. A. Butler? Butler was the favourite, and fully expected to triumph, but as in so many Conservative leadership contests, the favourite did not win. On 10 January 1957, Harold Macmillan became Her Majesty Queen Elizabeth II's third Prime Minister. He wasted no time in forming his government, moving R. A. Butler to the Home Office, appointing Lord (Peter) Thorneycroft Chancellor of the Exchequer and retaining Selwyn Lloyd as Foreign Secretary.

Since losing power in 1951, the Labour Party had undergone a series of internal convulsions, most of which concerned the former Health Secretary and Welsh firebrand Aneurin Bevan. He launched attack after attack on Clement Attlee and in turn Hugh Gaitskell, which resulted in the Parliamentary Labour Party voting narrowly to withdraw the whip from him. In December 1955, Attlee finally resigned as Labour leader. The veteran Herbert Morrison joined Gaitskell and Bevan in the fight but was to come a poor third with forty votes. In those days, only MPs voted for the leader and 157 voted for Gaitskell, and seventy for Bevan.

In the 1950s, the Liberal Party drifted further into irrelevance. Clement Davies had taken over from Sir Archibald Sinclair as party leader when the latter lost his seat in 1945. It was only ever meant to be temporary, yet he remained in the job for eleven years until the young thruster, and far more charismatic, Jo Grimond succeeded him unopposed in 1956. At that point, the party held only six seats, yet retained a loyal core vote, despite not having the financial wherewithal to put up a candidate in every seat. In the 1955 election, it stood only 110 candidates, gaining 722,000 votes, a measly 2.7 per cent of the total. When Jo Grimond took over, the only way was up. It was seven years before Grimond could promise his party to lead them 'towards the sound of gunfire', but he lost little time in starting to rebuild the party from the bottom up. In the short term, there were few signs of the green shoots of success appearing. In 1959, although the party doubled the number of seats it fought (216), and it more than doubled its vote and vote share (1.6 million and 5.9 per cent), it failed to add to its total of six MPs.

Harold Macmillan's six years in government are perhaps defined by four events and issues – the 'never had it so good' quotation, the 'little local difficulty' reshuffle in 1958, the 1960 'Winds of Change' speech and finally the 'night of the long knives' reshuffle in 1962.

Peter Thorneycroft, as a close ally, had been appointed Chancellor of the Exchequer by Macmillan after being a vocal supporter of him being appointed leader, and therefore Prime Minister. Yet less than a year later, he resigned from the post, along with junior Treasury ministers Nigel Birch and Enoch Powell. They thought Macmillan wasn't concerned enough about the rise in public spending, and failed to persuade him to adopt spending cuts. Politically, it was a devastating blow to the authority of the relatively new Prime Minister, but he managed to brush it off as 'a little local difficulty'.

Given the humiliation of Suez, Macmillan and the party elders realised they had to immediately start planning to revive the image of the Conservative Party. This couldn't just be done in an election campaign. Charles Hill was brought into the Cabinet as Minister for Information with the task of improving the party's and the government's public relations. The head of publicity at Conservative Central Office, Paul Schofield, abandoned the party's previous strategy of communicating its policies via pamphlets and instead developed a new policy of using national newspapers to achieve the same aim but reach more people. The campaign was implemented by the PR and advertising agency Colman, Prentis & Varley. From now on, all parties would hire the services of such agencies at each subsequent election.

The party started a major initiative of opinion research to find out what the electorate's priorities were, and to adapt their campaigns and PR approach accordingly. With the advent of Gallup polls, they were also able to measure success or failure more easily. Huge amounts of money were raised from party donors to fund a large-scale newspaper advertising campaign. In the twenty-seven months before the 1959 election, the party spent half a million pounds on advertising campaigns (£5.1 million in today's money). Such sums had never been spent before. Conservative chairman Oliver Poole justified it thus: 'It is not enough just to tell the truth. It is essential to see that the majority of the electorate have a chance of reading it.'

The campaign was predominantly aimed at voters the Tories thought they could convert – housewives, prosperous working-class voters and the optimistic young. They shamelessly played on Macmillan's 'you've never had it so good' quote to release a poster with the slogan: 'You're having it good. Have it better. Vote Conservative'. In January 1959, a new poster campaign was launched, which ran right up to polling day, culminating with posters carrying the main election slogan: 'Life's Better with the Conservatives – Don't Let Labour Ruin it'.

Initially, Labour had no answer to the Tories' PR campaign. They made no effort to counter it, instead just issuing the odd worthy policy pamphlet. There were no newspaper adverts. It therefore shouldn't have come as any surprise that by 1959, 25 per cent of voters told Gallup they didn't know what Labour stood for, up from 14 per cent in 1951. The party's PR seemed to be aimed at those who were already going to vote for it, rather than the voters it needed to persuade. In the period that the Conservatives spent £500,000 on newspaper advertising, Labour spent only £100,000. Their campaigns were ineffectual, too small and lacking in focus. They refused to hire a professional advertising agency and suffered the consequences. One of their posters depicted Hugh Gaitskell with the slogan 'The Man with a Plan'.

Gaitskell was always on a loser in some ways. Macmillan enjoyed all the advantages of being in office. It took some time for him to become the popular figure we remember him as, but once he did, he never looked back. A Gallup poll showed that in August 1959, only 10 per cent of voters had no opinion of Macmillan. The figure for Gaitskell was 30 per cent. The Prime Minister had an approval rating of 67 per cent, while the opposition leader's was twenty-one points behind on 46 per cent. The public liked Macmillan's relaxed and reassuring style, and his regular trips abroad impressed the voters back home. He was also, somewhat surprisingly, a big hit on the new medium of television.

By the beginning of September 1959, election fever was threatening to run out of control. On the 6th, the Prime Minister flew to Balmoral to ask the Queen to dissolve Parliament, and upon his return to London, he announced the election would take place on 8 October.

Few commentators expected anything other than a third Conservative victory, although Labour was in surprisingly good heart, given they trailed the Tories by between 4 and 7 per cent in the polls. The one result no one expected was a Conservative landslide.

On the day Macmillan called the election, Hugh Gaitskell and Aneurin Bevan were on a visit to Moscow. Rather counterintuitively, this proved to be a good thing, as they were able to portray themselves on an equal level with the Prime Minister in reporting on their meetings with the Soviet leader, Nikita Khrushchev. It also enabled the two of them to demonstrate party unity, following their clashes in the past. Indeed, Labour hit the ground running and dominated the early and middle parts of the election campaign, before eventually the Conservatives found a way to fight back.

The day after returning from Moscow, Gaitskell made a fiery speech to the TUC conference in Blackpool. Richard Crossman was appointed to run the campaign and the party quickly issued a controversial pamphlet titled 'The Tory Swindle', which galvanised party members as well as its core voters.

The Conservatives launched their manifesto, 'The Next Five Years', very early in the campaign on 11 September. It had two main messages – continued prosperity with the Conservatives and respected leadership in international affairs. Suez seemed a very long time ago.

It took a further week for Labour to publish their manifesto, 'Britain Belongs to You'.

When Parliament was finally dissolved on 18 September, little had happened to alter the general view that the Tories would prevail, even if Labour had had the better of the campaign so far.

In all, 1,536 candidates were nominated to fight the 630 seats. Labour fought all seats on the mainland. The Conservatives gave the Liberals a free run in four seats and the Liberals fought 216 seats, nearly doubling their total from 1955. The SNP fought five seats in Scotland while Plaid Cymru put up candidates in twenty of the thirty Welsh seats. The political carcass of Sir Oswald Mosley was reincarnated in North Kensington, where he tried to take advantage of the Notting Hill riots. He failed, garnering only 2,871 votes.

Labour's morning press conferences were well executed and garnered far more press coverage. Indeed, one survey reckoned they attracted ten times more column inches than their rather more staid counterparts. Their television election broadcasts were also more impactful, overseen by the young Labour MP Anthony Wedgwood Benn. The first Conservative broadcast was filmed in the drawing room of a country house, with five Cabinet ministers congratulating each other on how well each of them were doing in their respective jobs. It did not go down well. By contrast, Labour's opening election broadcast appeared to take place in a modern news studio, with an opening shot of Wedgwood Benn from behind, sitting in an office chair. As the music stopped, he spun round, faced the camera, and appeared less like a partisan politician, more like a news anchor. He said they were broadcasting from Labour's election operations room. In fact, it was a BBC TV studio. The broadcast featured younger, more appealing Labour political figures, and the twelve broadcasts (each more than twenty-five minutes long) in the series all presented an air of newness and vitality. Polls over the ensuing days showed a narrowing of the Tory lead.

Labour was buoyant, yet the Conservatives appeared remarkably unflustered and continued with their low activity campaign. It was as if, as Willie Whitelaw said two decades later, they were content to go round the country 'stirring up apathy'.

However, the Conservative leadership was not inactive. Harold Macmillan embarked on a sixteen-day national tour, making seventy-four speeches, more than twice as many as Eden in 1955, and ten times more than a 21st-century Prime Minister would make. By contrast, Gaitskell made fifty-three speeches over thirteen days. Speeches by politicians were still reported in a way that they are not today.

As the final ten days of the campaign approached, the 'low temperature' strategy adopted by the Conservatives was clearly not working. Even the cautious Hugh Gaitskell was wondering if he might pull off an unlikely victory: 'The only thing that worries me is overconfidence. I am getting to that stage.' Various newspapers took the Tories to task for their lacklustre approach to the campaign and urged them to up their collective game. Almost immediately, the tone of their morning press conferences changed, with the Jack Russell-like qualities of Lord Hailsham and party chairman Oliver Poole coming to the fore. Hailsham urged his colleagues to take off their coats and 'wade into the fight ... Let there be plenty of hard hitting above the belt ... For goodness' sake, do not let us be driven onto the defensive.' The gloves were off.

It was then that Labour made two tactical mistakes, which allowed the Conservatives to take the initiative. On 28 September, nine days before polling day, Hugh Gaitskell promised not to raise income tax. He did it in order to head off a possible Tory attack on Labour, but it spectacularly backfired and Harold Macmillan made the most of it, saying such a pledge was 'a very queer one for a professional economist and an ex-Chancellor of the Exchequer'. He said the pledge would deceive no one. Three days later, the gaffe was compounded by a leaflet handed to journalists at the daily Labour press conference which stated Labour would remove purchase tax from Labour goods. This caused much scratching of heads not only in the press but in the Labour Party itself. No one could explain why this hadn't been mentioned in the press conference, let alone been discussed by the campaign committee, which up until that point had ensured the campaign had been gaffe free. The Tories made hay launching wave after wave of attacks, with Lord Hailsham at the forefront, saying Labour were 'trying to bribe the electorate with their own money'. R. A. Butler alleged that Labour's new motto was 'a bribe a day keeps the Tories away'.

This was undoubtedly the turning point of the campaign, as evidenced by the opinion polls, which in the week before polling day showed a rising Tory lead. The Conservatives were also aided by announcements of a fall in unemployment to under 2 per cent, that output was 8 per cent higher than a year earlier and that gold and dollar reserves were at their highest level in eight years. Labour's only response was to say the figures should have been better. Labour's campaign was then further undermined by an unofficial strike by oxygen workers, which brought large parts of the motor industry to a standstill.

In the last few days of the campaign, the Conservatives altered their approach to their election broadcasts and brought in professionals to make them. It made a difference and added to the sense of momentum in the Conservative campaign. Party workers were motivated to canvas that extra house, to deliver leaflets in one more street. In the end, all the traditional campaigning methods were far more important. And the fact was that the Conservatives had a better organisation than Labour and were able to triumph in the ground war, even if the air war had been largely lost.

As campaigning concluded on the eve of poll, most Conservatives believed they were heading for victory with a reduced majority. Only one MP publicly predicted an increased majority, and that was Iain Macleod.

Polling day proved to be bright and sunny. The stock market had shot upwards during the course of the day. Polls closed at 9 p.m. Then 391 constituencies immediately started counting the votes, with the rest delaying their counts until the morning.

The BBC election night show went on air just after polls closed, presented by Richard Dimbleby, with Cliff Michelmore, David Butler, Robert McKenzie and Alan Whicker. At 10 p.m., the first result was declared in the Essex seat of Billericay, which the Conservatives held comfortably with an increased majority over Labour, in a seat Labour had hoped to gain. In the second seat to declare, the Conservatives held Cheltenham, also with an increased majority. In both seats, the Liberal vote increased substantially. The picture was muddied slightly by two results from Salford which showed swings to Labour. But the dye was cast with the announcement at 10.30 p.m. that the Conservatives had gained their first seat of the night in Holborn and St Pancras South. By 1 a.m., the writing was on the wall and Hugh Gaitskell conceded defeat.

Both the Conservative and Labour parties saw a small decline in vote share compared to 1955, largely due to the doubling of the number of Liberal candidates and the Liberal vote. The Conservatives received 49.4 per cent and Labour 43.8 per cent. The Conservatives made twenty-eight gains, ten of which came in the Midlands and nine in

London. Compared to 1955, the Labour vote among women went up but went down among men. The Conservatives made big gains among young voters, but the over-65s and poorer voters swung to Labour.

Given that this was a third Conservative election victory, and all predictions led to a clear result, it is something of a mystery that turnout increased from 76.8 per cent in 1955 to 78.7 per cent. Or is it? Without doubt, this can be described as the first TV election. Although TV viewing was on the increase in 1955, television ownership had not reached saturation point. TV broadcasts played a part in the election, but not a decisive one. By 1959, 85 per cent of the population were capable of receiving television pictures. In addition, commercial television started broadcasting in the autumn of 1955. By 1959, television news provided by the BBC and ITN rivalled that of BBC Radio in its impact.

On the face of it, after eight years in government, it was remarkable that in this third electoral victory there was a swing to the Tories. This was not a one-off. There were long-term demographic shifts in the electorate at play. Rising prosperity had reduced working-class loyalties to the Labour Party. There was evidence that the Conservatives did well in new towns and in the sprawling new council estates that had been built throughout the decade.

Among MPs elected for the first time at this election were future party leaders Margaret Thatcher and Jeremy Thorpe.

The 1959 general election was not a landmark one. It did not mark the end of an era, nor the beginning of a new one, yet it can legitimately be described as the first general election in which television played a major part.

The result heralded a new five-year mandate for the Conservative Party. It was certainly a personal victory for Harold Macmillan and a vindication of the process which led to him being chosen to succeed Sir Anthony Eden. But it was the only election Macmillan was destined to fight, as he resigned as Prime Minister during the 1963 party conference due to apparent failing health. In the general election a year later, the new leader Sir Alec Douglas-Home came within a whisker of winning an unprecedented fourth term in office. If Harold Macmillan had still been Prime Minister, could he have pulled it off? It's one of the most fascinating counterfactuals of modern political history.

Iain Dale is an award-winning broadcaster with LBC Radio and presents their evening show. He co-presents the *For the Many* podcast with Jacqui Smith. He has written or edited more than fifty books including *Kings and Queens*, *The Presidents*, *The Prime Ministers*, *On This Day in Politics* and *Why Can't We All Just Get Along*. Signed copies of all his books can be ordered from www.politicos.co.uk. He is on all social media platforms @iaindale. He lives in Tunbridge Wells.

1964

NICK THOMAS-SYMONDS

Dissolution: 25 September 1964
Polling day: 15 October 1964
Seats contested: 630
Total electorate / Voted / Turnout: 35,894,054 / 27,657,148 / 77.1 per cent
Candidates (total 1,757): Conservative (including UUP) – 630; Labour (including NI Labour) – 628; Liberal – 365; Communist – 36; Plaid Cymru – 23; SNP – 15; Independent Republican – 12
Prime Minister on polling day: Alec Douglas-Home
Main party leaders: Conservative – Alec Douglas-Home; Labour – Harold Wilson; Liberal – Jo Grimond; Communist – John Gollan; SNP – Arthur Donaldson; Plaid Cymru – Gwynfor Evans; UUP – Terence O'Neill; NI Labour – Tom Boyd

Party performance:

Party	Votes	Percentage share	Seats
Labour (including NI Labour)	12,205,808 (102,759)	44.1 (16.1)	317 (0)
Conservative (including UUP)	12,002,642 (401,897)	43.4 (63.2)	304 (12)
Liberal	3,099,283	11.2	9
Independent Republican	101,628	15.9	0
Plaid Cymru	69,507	0.3	0
SNP	64,044	0.2	0
Communist	46,442	0.2	0

Result: Labour majority of four seats

The general election of Thursday 15 October 1964 will always be associated with Labour leader Harold Wilson, who won a narrow overall majority of four seats. His subsequent appointment as Prime Minister on the Saturday was an important moment in Britain's post-war history. He arrived at Buckingham Palace for an audience with the Queen with his father Herbert, his wife Mary, his sons Robin and Giles and his loyal political secretary Marcia Williams, as the first post-war Prime Minister not to have been privately educated. In reaching the highest political office in the land as a grammar school-boy, Wilson showed that, despite the odds being stacked against people from his sort of background, the premiership was not restricted to an elite. He epitomised the – slow – changes in British society from the 'old school tie' networks of the 1950s to a more meritocratic age.

His Labour Party had secured 44.1 per cent of the vote and 317 seats; the Conservatives 43.4 per cent of the vote and 304 seats; and the Liberals' 11.2 per cent share yielded only nine seats. On election night itself, estimates of Labour's prospects varied. In the first hour of counting, there was only a small swing away from the Conservatives at Wolverhampton, and the opposition party failed to win Billericay, prompting a pessimistic assessment about the overall outcome, before the gaining of Battersea South steadied Labour nerves. Overnight, 430 seats were counted, and Labour looked on course for a majority as high as thirty, but, as the remainder of the seats were counted on the Saturday, Labour failed to make expected gains, and it was mid-afternoon before the all-important 315th seat was won that guaranteed an overall majority: Brecon and Radnor. Thirteen years of Conservative rule were over.

That the result was so close should not diminish Wilson's achievement. In the previous general election, held on 8 October 1959, the Conservatives had secured a landslide victory with an overall majority of 100 seats. Wilson had a lot of ground to make up in a very short space of time. Replacing a majority Conservative government with a majority Labour government after a single parliament was a huge challenge. Wilson knew he had to generate a sense of momentum.

After his election as party leader by Labour MPs in February 1963 at the age of forty-six, following the sudden death of Hugh Gaitskell, Wilson set about projecting an image of dynamism and vigour.

In a speech that came to define modernity on 1 October 1963 in Scarborough, Wilson told his party conference that Labour was redefining its socialism in the context of the scientific advances that were taking place. In his signature phrase, he spoke of the Britain that was going to be 'forged in the white heat of this revolution'. Wilson's vision was of computer processes becoming faster and faster, machine tools becoming more efficient and humans no longer being required to construct motor cars. If ministers chose to let events take their course, it would produce profits for a few people, and unemployment for those workers no longer required. Instead, Wilson, argued, the country needed an active Labour government than would plan the economy, save jobs and allow people to use technology to improve their lives and raise living standards.

While Wilson established himself in the minds of the public, the Conservatives were in decline. The party had been in power since 1951 and, early in 1961, started to face economic problems, making the 'time for a change' argument a powerful one. Output was rising very slowly, and a balance of payments deficit put sterling under speculative pressure. In July, the Chancellor, Selwyn Lloyd, was forced to increase the bank rate from 5 per cent to 7 per cent, raise taxes, cut public expenditure and, controversially, introduce a pay pause. This wage freeze was deeply unpopular; the Minister of Labour, John Hare, had to change to a more flexible 'guiding light' approach on 29 January 1962, the day railway workers on the London underground staged a one-day strike, following protests in other sectors.

This announcement was, however, to no avail as the Conservatives' popularity plummeted. With Labour eyeing a general election victory, the Liberals also mounted a revival under Jo Grimond, party leader since 1956. Most famously, in March 1962, the third party captured the safe Conservative seat of Orpington; then, in the North-East Leicester by-election on 12 July, the Conservatives finished in third place. The Prime Minister, Harold Macmillan, responded by sacking

Selwyn Lloyd and six other Cabinet ministers in what became known as British politics' own 'night of the long knives'. Jeremy Thorpe, Liberal MP and future party leader, remarked: 'Greater love hath no man than this, that he lay down his friends for his life.' Later, Wilson quipped that the Prime Minister had sacked 'half his Cabinet – the wrong half, as it turned out'. For all this, the Liberal surge did not impress Wilson. When he was shadow Foreign Secretary, he told the 1962 party conference that Labour 'is a moral crusade or it is nothing. That is why we have rejected timorous and defeatist proposals for a Lib-Lab alliance.'

The pressure increased on Macmillan. His application for Britain to join the European Economic Community, as it then was, had been blocked by French President Charles de Gaulle in January 1963. Then, one of the twentieth-century's great scandals rocked his government. John Profumo, the Secretary of State for War, had been having an affair with model Christine Keeler, who was, at the same time, having a relationship with Yevgeny Ivanov, senior naval attaché at the Soviet embassy. Not only was this a glaring national security risk but Profumo also had to admit that he had misled the House of Commons when, in March, he had denied any impropriety. He resigned in early June. On 10 October, on the eve of the Conservative Party conference, Macmillan himself resigned.

The new Prime Minister was Alec Douglas-Home, who had to disclaim his hereditary peerage before winning election to the House of Commons at the Kinross and Western Perthshire by-election on 7 November, meaning that there was a short period when he held the office of Prime Minister but was a member of neither House of Parliament. In setting out a vision for the future, Wilson now had an opponent that he could paint as part of the past. Thus, the Labour leader condemned Home's succession as having been arranged by an 'aristocratic cabal' and said it showed that Britain's forward democratic progress was being halted by the 14th Earl of Home. Home responded with a characteristic calmness that he was dealing with the fourteenth Mr Wilson. He offered 'straight talk' and said the Labour leader was a 'slick salesman of synthetic science'.

Home stabilised the government and the polls tightened. The Chancellor, Reginald Maudling, was trying to revive the economy with a 'dash for growth', adopting an annual target of 4 per cent, cutting taxes, including on the purchase of motor cars, and increasing spending. But time was running out in the five-year term of the parliament. After deciding against an election in May 1964, Home acted at the end of the summer. On 14 September, the Prime Minister visited the Queen at Balmoral to seek a dissolution on 25 September, with the general election date set for twenty days afterwards.

By the time Home was in Scotland, the Labour campaign was already in full swing. On 11 September, Labour had launched its manifesto, 'Let's Go with Labour for the New Britain', promising 'mobilising the resources of technology under a national plan' thereby 'reversing the decline of the thirteen wasted years'. The next day, Wilson addressed a rally at the Empire Pool, Wembley, arguing for a 'dynamic, expanding, confident and, above all, purposive New Britain'.

On 18 September, the Conservatives launched their manifesto, 'Prosperity with a Purpose'. It was low-key, arguing that 'only by trusting the individual with freedom and responsibility shall we gain the vitality to keep our country great'. Wilson, seizing the moment, stole headlines as he offered Home a television debate on the cost of what both parties were proposing. The Prime Minister was never likely to accept, but it showed that Wilson was growing in confidence. Speaking in Cardiff on 27 September, referring to the Conservative failure to provide sustained growth since 1951 and their erratic economic performance between mini-boom and stagnation, Wilson turned to the BBC hit comedy series *Steptoe and Son*. Home and Selwyn Lloyd were derided as 'Stop-Go and Son'.

The ride to victory was not, however, an entirely smooth one. On Wednesday 30 September, the national opinion poll in the *Daily Mail* showed a 2.9 per cent Tory lead. Wilson was rattled. Referring to an unofficial strike at the component firm Hardy Spicer, Wilson said at a press conference that a case could be made for an inquiry into the Conservatives fomenting strikes at election time. The Labour leader was ridiculed for making such a suggestion.

Nonetheless, he bounced back quickly. That same day, the balance of payments figures for the second quarter of 1964 were published, showing a £73 million deficit. Speaking at Norwich in the evening, Wilson likened Macmillan to John Bloom, the entrepreneur whose aggressive attempts to compete in cutting prices in household durables during the 'Washing Machine Wars' of 1962–64 had ended in voluntary liquidation.

Wilson was to have a further rocky moment, as the Conservatives speculated on his relationship with his political secretary Marcia Williams. On 6 October, Lord Hailsham, in a speech at Plymouth, was heckled about Profumo, and shot back: 'If you can tell me there are no adulterers on the front bench of the Labour Party, you can talk to me about Profumo.' The news soon reached Wilson, who was speaking in Birmingham that night for Labour candidates Roy Hattersley and Brian Walden. Harold was with both Marcia and Mary, and the allegation upset them all. The next day, Wilson chose not to respond himself and asked Clement Attlee, aged eighty-one but very active in the campaign, to comment. The last Labour Prime Minister responded magisterially to Hailsham: 'It is time he grew up.'

Things started looking up. That same day, 7 October, the stock market had its worst day in a couple of years and the bookmakers made Labour the strong favourites to win the election. The following day, when Home spoke at the Bull Ring in Birmingham, his words were drowned out by hecklers. As the campaign entered its final phase on Sunday 11 October, the ferocity of the Conservative attack on the prospect of a Labour government showed how likely such an outcome was. The Conservatives sought to exploit historic Labour weaknesses. Firstly, it was divisions on defence and the independent nuclear deterrent, an issue on which the Conservative manifesto had raised doubts: 'Nuclear abdication is the only policy on which [Labour] can unite.' Secondly, it was the economy. Lord Blakenham thundered: 'The return of a Labour government would reduce the safety of Britain and its status in international affairs. The return of a Labour government would spell financial crisis and economic disaster for this country, as it did on every other occasion when the Labour party has been entrusted with power.'

The Liberals were being squeezed by the two main parties, and relied on their morning press conferences, chaired by Frank Byers, to secure attention. When the manifesto 'Think for Yourself – Vote Liberal' was launched on 15 September, Byers had talked of achieving a 'decisive position' in the House of Commons. As the campaign continued, he talked up their chances, claiming that they would secure 3 million votes, and perhaps even 3.5 million. In the event, it was just over 3 million, though they were only fighting 365 seats. The final television appeal, on 10 October from Grimond, said the election was 'boring a great many people. They are fed up with the endless bickering between the Tory and Labour parties.' People, Byers said, should vote for Liberal candidates: 'People who will speak for you and not merely for the party machines.'

Wilson continued to focus on attacking the Conservatives and Labour's positive vision for the future. On 12 October, with Attlee appearing first, Wilson made his own final television appeal to the electorate, to 'make this a country which cares, and in which the prosperity of the nation is shared by every family'. He said:

> If you want to see Britain moving ahead and getting ahead, if you want to sweep away outmoded ideas, the old-boy network that has condemned so many of our ablest young people to frustration, then you feel with us the sense of challenge, of excitement and adventure. For if the past belongs to the Tories the future belongs to us, all of us.

Home's final television appeal praised the Conservative record: 'There is today work for the members of the family at a good wage, and the standard of living has been rising year by year.' Once again, he raised doubts about Labour's commitment to an independent nuclear deterrent.

In the final days, Home toured Essex before returning to his constituency. Wilson remained close to his own constituency in Huyton, focusing on Liverpool, where his eve-of-poll speech was at St George's Hall, after which he and Mary went back to the Adelphi Hotel. Marcia Williams's brother, Tony Field, drove Wilson, Mary and his press officer John Harris to his count where Wilson won a huge vote of 42,213 and a majority of 19,273. After little more than a couple of hours' sleep back at the hotel, Wilson, with Mary, his father Herbert, Marcia Williams, Harris and John Allen, a researcher, boarded the train from Liverpool to London. Wilson, in what was to become his trademark Gannex macintosh, ate breakfast with HP sauce, which was to be become so associated with him, it was known as 'Wilson's gravy'.

The Labour leader was in buoyant mood, with the only negative in the election results being shadow Foreign Secretary Patrick Gordon Walker losing his seat at Smethwick to a vile, racist campaign by the Conservative candidate, Peter Griffiths. The small west Midlands town became a focus of national attention as Griffiths whipped up hatred. Stickers appeared with the slogan 'If you want a n****r neighbour vote Liberal or Labour.' They did not bear Griffiths's name, but he did not disown them either, saying they were a 'manifestation of popular feeling'. Wilson lost no time in condemning Griffiths.

The campaign itself did not lead to problems for the newly elected Labour government, though the single-figure majority meant another election was expected long before the end of the five-year parliament. Rather, it was the legacy of Maudling's attempt to win the election for the Conservatives that was to have lasting consequences. With the Conservative Chancellor having cut taxes in the Budget of April 1963, then refusing to raise them in his Budget a year later, despite balance of payments issues, Wilson was left with a bleak economic inheritance. A Treasury memorandum prepared for the incoming government confirming that Britain was facing a deficit of £800 million on its overseas payments for 1964. How to address this, and the question of devaluation of the currency, was to dominate Wilson's next six years in office as Prime Minister.

Rt Hon. Nick Thomas-Symonds MP is a member of the shadow Cabinet, a fellow of the Royal Historical Society and an acclaimed political biographer. His most recent book is *Harold Wilson: The Winner*, published by Weidenfeld & Nicolson.

36

1966

PETER KELLNER

Dissolution: 10 March 1966
Polling day: 31 March 1966
Seats contested: 630
Total electorate / Voted / Turnout: 35,957,245 / 27,264,747 / 75.8 per cent
Candidates (total 1,707): Conservative (including UUP) – 629; Labour (including NI Labour) – 622; Liberal – 311; Communist – 57; SNP – 23; Plaid Cymru – 20; Independent Republican – 5; Republican Labour – 1
Prime Minister on polling day: Harold Wilson
Main party leaders: Labour – Harold Wilson; Conservative – Edward Heath; Liberal – Jo Grimond; Communist – John Gollan; SNP – Arthur Donaldson; Plaid Cymru – Gwynfor Evans; Republican Labour – Gerry Fitt; UUP – Terence O'Neill; NI Labour – Tom Boyd

Party performance:

Party	Votes	Percentage share	Seats
Labour (including NI Labour)	13,096,629 (72,613)	48 (12.2)	364 (0)
Conservative (including UUP)	11,418,455 (368,629)	41.9 (61.8)	253 (11)
Liberal	2,327,457	8.5	12
SNP	128,474	0.5	0
Independent Republican	62,782	10.5	0
Communist	62,092	0.2	0
Plaid Cymru	61,071	0.2	0
Republican Labour	26,292	4.4	1

Result: Labour majority of ninety-eight seats

In 1966, Labour fought a general election for the fourth time as the incumbent government. For the first time, it gained seats and secured a more emphatic victory. This was no great surprise on the day. The final polls all pointed to a landslide. In fact, the party's margin of victory fell slightly short of the predictions; but it was still enough to give Harold Wilson a majority of ninety-eight and, unlike in 1964, a clear mandate for a full parliament.

Yet if the outcome looked like a foregone conclusion, it followed almost eighteen months of Labour rule during which any victory, let alone a large one, looked far from certain.

At the start of the 1964–66 parliament, speculation was rife as to whether Labour's four-seat majority would quickly force Wilson into a further election. His plight was made worse in January 1965 when his majority was halved. Patrick Gordon Walker had been appointed Foreign Secretary despite losing his seat in the 1964 election – he had been the victim of racist campaigning in Smethwick, his west Midlands constituency. Determined to stand up to racism, Wilson nevertheless appointed Gordon Walker to the post he had shadowed in opposition. But this could only be a stop-gap decision. The 73-year-old Reginald Sorensen was persuaded to retire as MP for the safe Labour seat of Leyton. It turned out to be not safe enough: Gordon Walker was defeated by 205 votes. Now he had no alternative but to resign as Foreign Secretary.

His defeat reflected in part the phenomenon seen in other by-elections over the years – voters resent being asked to back a party that had provoked a contest for narrowly partisan reasons rather than, say, because the previous MP had died. But it also came at a time when the new government had emerged from the calm lagoon of its brief honeymoon with the electorate and entered rocky seas.

The dominant issue was the economy. A decision taken in the first few hours of the 1964 victory had repercussions that would last years. On the evening of 16 October, Wilson and his most senior ministers were briefed on the large balance of payments deficit and the pressure this placed on sterling. In those days, well before floating exchange rates, devaluations could help to improve a country's trade balance. But they were dramatic decisions that no government wanted to take. And as the previous devaluation, in 1949, took place when Clement Attlee was Prime Minister, the last thing Wilson wanted was for Labour to be branded as the devaluation party. Instead, ten days later, James Callaghan, the Chancellor, imposed a 15 per cent imports surcharge. Other measures that autumn included higher income tax and dearer petrol, alongside the introduction of a capital gains tax, a rise in interest rates and – when these turned out not to be enough – an emergency loan from foreign central banks to protect sterling.

Labour could, and did, argue that all these things were necessary to clean up the mess it had inherited from the Conservatives. Most voters accepted that. But Labour's poll rating started to slip; and the Leyton by-election happened to coincide with a rise in inflation.

For the moment, however, Labour still enjoyed the advantage of facing an opposition Conservative Party that was nursing the wounds of its 1964 defeat, and still being led by Sir Alec Douglas-Home, a wealthy, upper-class former hereditary peer who had given up his title to succeed Harold Macmillan as Prime Minister in 1963. Home was not the most obvious standard bearer for a party that badly needed to shed its image of being elitist and out of touch.

Rumblings in mid-1965 culminated in Home resigning. On 27 July, Conservative MPs elected Edward Heath as his successor. (This was the first time when the leader was elected, rather than 'emerging' through a private process of consultation by the party's elder statesmen.) A product of a grammar school rather than public school – five of his six predecessors as Conservative leader had been to Eton or Harrow – Heath could present himself as the face of a new, modern Tory Party. He and Wilson were born the same year (1916) and had reached Oxford without the benefits of an expensive education. Both reflected the principle that merit should outrank privilege.

The Conservatives overtook Labour in the polls, and Wilson's position looked precarious. Some weeks earlier, he had watered down a bill to renationalise the steel industry. Two Labour MPs refused to back it, putting Labour's majority in jeopardy. At the same time, left-wing Labour MPs were agitating against Wilson's refusal to oppose America's war in Vietnam. The possibility of Wilson being forced into an election within weeks was widely mooted. Not for the first time, and certainly not for the last, Wilson demonstrated his tactical skills by holding his party together, despite the noises off. He carried on, brushing aside a proposal by Jo Grimond, the Liberal leader, to take his ten MPs into a coalition with Labour, which would have given Wilson a majority of twenty-two.

By the autumn of 1965, the government was back in calmer waters. The most dramatic event in those months worked to Wilson's domestic advantage. Ian Smith, the Prime Minister of Rhodesia, a self-governing colony in which white people, who had the vote, were outnumbered by twenty-to-one by black people, who did not, declared independence unilaterally on 11 November. This gave Wilson the chance to display his progressive credentials as the principled, anti-racist leader who took on Smith. The UK persuaded the United Nations to impose tough economic sanctions, in the hope that Smith's rebellion would collapse 'in weeks not months'. In fact, it lasted fifteen years as Rhodesia managed to evade sanctions, especially oil. But in the months leading up to the 1966 election, Wilson stood firm as the leader who carried the banner for justice and democracy. This was one cause on which the various factions of his party could unite – while the Conservatives were divided between those who, like Heath, were hostile to Smith and those more sympathetic to him. In one Commons vote, fifty Conservative MPs defied Heath to vote against oil sanctions.

In the same week as Smith launched his rebellion there was another event, far less prominent at the time but which turned out to start the clock ticking for the 1966 election. Harry Solomons, the Labour MP for Hull North, collapsed during an all-night sitting in the House of Commons; he died in Westminster Hospital on his sixty-third birthday. He had gained the seat in 1964 with a majority of just 1,181. The Conservatives needed a swing of just over 1 per cent to regain it and wipe out Labour's slender majority.

To increase Labour's chances of holding the seat, Wilson instructed Barbara Castle, the Transport Secretary, to approve the building of a 1.3-mile bridge across the Humber estuary. This had long been wanted by voters in Hull, but successive ministers had long resisted the plan on the grounds that its immense cost would outweigh its real but limited social and economic benefits. (It would cut the road journey between Hull and Grimsby by fifty miles; but not that many vehicles were likely to take advantage of this.) However, the particular circumstances of the by-election meant that the political benefits to Labour could be decisive.

Political bribes do not always work. This one did. Ahead of the by-election, on 27 January 1966, press reports indicated that the Tories would win. Instead, Kevin McNamara held the seat for Labour, increasing its majority five-fold, to 5,351. The result not only sustained Labour's narrow Commons majority; together with subsequent national polls putting Labour around 10 per cent ahead across Britain, and Gallup reporting a steady 60 per cent-plus satisfied with his personal performance as Prime Minister, the evidence gave Wilson the confidence to call a general election. On 28 February, he announced that it would be held on 31 March.

As Labour entered the campaign with the same leader as it had just eighteen months earlier, and with the big national issues much the same, its manifesto reprised many of the themes as in 1964. Wilson's general, steady-as-we-go message was summed up in its slogan 'You *know* LABOUR government works'. At his party's manifesto launch, he deliberately avoided drama, telling journalists: 'There are no surprises in this document.' The last thing he wanted was any kind of controversy that would threaten his lead in the polls. New policies, such as a promise to 'create a National Freight Authority to co-ordinate the movement of freight by road and rail' did little to set pulses racing. Even the weather conspired to help the mood of contentment: it was mild and mainly dry throughout the campaign.

With the benefit of hindsight, perhaps the most significant change from 1964 was Wilson's attitude to Europe. Five years earlier, Hugh Gaitskell, his predecessor as party leader, had opposed Harold

Macmillan's application to join the Common Market. Labour's 1964 manifesto appeared to confirm this position: 'Though we shall seek to achieve closer links with our European neighbours, the Labour Party is convinced that the first responsibility of a British Government is still to the Commonwealth.'

In contrast, the 1966 manifesto noted Britain's membership of EFTA – European Free Trade Association – outside the Common Market and regretted that 'Western Europe [is] sharply divided into two conflicting groups'. It went on: 'Labour believes that Britain, in consultation with her EFTA partners, should be ready to enter the European Economic Community, provided essential British and Commonwealth interests are safeguarded.'

A pedantic philosopher, or perhaps agile barrister, might say the two manifestos were completely consistent. That is, in 1964 Labour did not rule out an application to join the Common Market, while in 1966 it insisted on preserving the interests of the Commonwealth. But the shift in tone was unmistakeable. In 1964, there had been no talk of joining the Common Market; in 1966, the idea was firmly embraced.

The Conservatives were in a different position from Labour. Not only did they have a new leader; following their defeat in 1964, it was plain that they needed to modernise their image and their appeal to the electorate. In fact, a broad-ranging policy review had started soon after the party returned to opposition; and the man that Home chose to lead it was Heath, his successor as party leader nine months later. One of Heath's first acts after taking over from Home was to oversee the final stages of the review, which was presented to the party's annual conference in October 1965. It set out new policies in four main areas:

- Tax reform: It proposed cutting income and company taxes and increasing indirect taxes; and transferring part of the cost of social services to employers.
- Europe: In 1964, the Conservatives had largely left the issue alone, following the veto of France's President de Gaulle on Macmillan's

application. Now the party proposed a new application to join the Common Market 'at the first favourable opportunity'.
- Trade unions: Workplace relations had evolved largely outside the law, which meant that union–employer agreements could not be enforced through the courts. The policy review proposed establishing industrial courts to do just that.
- The welfare state: The review wanted a major overhaul of the post-war system designed by William Beveridge and enacted by the post-war Labour government. It proposed an extension of means testing, so that help could be concentrated on the poorest families, and the spread of occupational pensions to all workers, so that 'the present State graduated pension would become a residual State scheme for those relatively few who would not otherwise be covered'.

Two 1964 policies that the review dropped were an incomes policy and national planning. All in all, the review was designed to be radical but also to return the Conservative Party to a more market-oriented, and also firmly pro-European, approach to economic policy. Some of the review's thinking can be detected in the 1966 manifesto, but its more controversial measures were omitted. It offered 'an entirely new social security strategy' but said nothing about shifting any of the cost to employers. It promised 'major reforms of both management and unions' but no industrial courts. It proposed 'wider ownership ... of pension rights' but not of diminishing the role of state pensions. Only the firm commitment to joining the Common Market remained.

Elements of Heath's policy review were included in the 1966 manifesto but would be more completely embraced by him in 1970 when he became Prime Minister.

Whereas Labour sought to calm voters down, the Conservatives tried to stir them up. Its manifesto was entitled 'Action Not Words', a phrase that was incorporated into all their posters and leaflets.

An innovation that took root immediately was the Conservatives' use of private polls. Both main parties had commissioned private polls in the late 1950s and early '60s, but not consistently. After the 1964 election, Tommy Thompson, a special adviser to the Conservatives on election tactics, argued for a big expansion of private polling. Heath's arrival as party leader made this happen. Instead of continuing to use National Opinion Polls (NOP) to do the surveys, Humphrey Taylor, the NOP executive who had worked on the Conservatives' account, set up his own company (initially Cozreledit Ltd, later Opinion Research Centre) to conduct polls for the party far more extensively. As well as normal quantitative surveys, Taylor was an early British adopter of focus groups, in which small groups were questioned at length to dig deeper into the conventional polling numbers. Early findings confirmed Heath's fears – that the party was seen as out of date, out of touch and run by and for the upper classes. Heath had the ammunition to secure support for modernising the party's image. During the election campaign, Taylor briefed the party daily. Without having an alternative universe, containing a 'control' Conservative Party that did no polling, we cannot be sure what difference the private polls made; but they may have helped to save the party from an even more crushing defeat.

In contrast, Labour, which had used polls erratically in previous years, did very little before the 1966 election.

The election campaigns were overseen by Len Williams, Labour's general secretary since 1962, and Edward du Cann, chairman of the Conservative Party since January 1965. Neither campaign created much excitement – which suited Labour well, while the Conservatives, which needed to stir up the electorate if it was to overcome Labour's big lead, fell victim to its caution in converting the bold ideas from its policy review into weaker manifesto commitments. The most obvious sign that the party was under new management was that its 1966 manifesto was less than half the length of its 1964 manifesto. Its punchier style, though welcomed by jaded journalists, somehow failed to make much impact on the wider electorate.

As a result, the most notable moments of the campaign (at least, those that received the most media attention) had little to do with policy or Britain's future. The first story of the campaign was initiated by Heath on the day the election was announced. He challenged

Wilson to a television debate – just as Wilson had challenged Home in 1964. Home, not wanting to surrender the advantage of prime ministerial incumbency, said no. This time Wilson was the incumbent, equally unwilling to concede equal status to his opponent. Rather than simply say no, Wilson suggested a three-way debate, including Grimond – knowing that Heath would reject this. Finally, Wilson adopted the technique familiar to all politicians caught in a corner. He turned from substance to process. If Heath was so keen on a television debate, he should have raised the issue far earlier and through the 'usual channels' of the party whips. The argument never quite ended but soon ran out of steam.

As in 1964, thirteen party election broadcasts were allocated, five each to Labour and the Conservatives, three to the Liberals. Each lasted ten to fifteen minutes. The 5–5–3 formula was also employed to guide the time given to coverage of each party in news and other programmes. Heath and Wilson used their final broadcasts, in election week, to speak from behind a desk directly to camera. (Grimond would have done the same, but for the death of his son, which inevitably curtailed his own campaigning.) In an age when people could view programmes on only three TV channels, and only at the time they were broadcast, audiences were large. More than one-third of Britain's adult population watched these final election broadcasts.

The daily structure of the campaign followed precedent: press conferences each morning in London (Conservative and Labour headquarters were close by, both in Smith Square), with speeches by the party leaders in different parts of Britain most evenings. Wilson sought, with some success, to say something new and significant that could be shown live on the BBC's main evening news (with the producers briefed in advance what he would say). There is little evidence that this swayed voters, but nor is it likely to have done any harm.

Heath and Wilson differed in their approach to the morning press conferences. As the challenger, and also the face of a new, more meritocratic Conservative Party, Heath led most of the Conservative Party conferences. Wilson, seeking to portray himself as a national leader above petty party point-scoring, left the daily conferences to senior colleagues, such as George Brown (deputy leader), Callaghan (Chancellor) and Denis Healey (Defence Secretary). Only in the last few days did Wilson lead Labour's press conferences himself.

The Liberals stood out in using the campaign, and the daily press conferences, to present serious and specific policies day by day, ranging from elected regional councils to cutting defence spending and reform of the voting system to a strong pro-European stance (which had been Liberal policy long before Labour or the Conservatives). Given that there was no chance of the Liberals forming a government, and little chance of them joining a coalition, their worthy think-tank approach to solving Britain's problems attracted little attention.

Nor did the economy provide the drama that anyone seeking excitement might want. For the moment, the decisions taken immediately after the 1964 election seemed to be paying off. Neither inflation nor unemployment gave much cause for concern. *The Times* generated a flurry of excitement on 10 March when it published an editorial hostile to Labour, giving twenty-seven reasons 'why the £ is weak'. Heath picked it up at the day's morning press conference, saying he would put the economy at the heart of his campaign. Two days later, the trade figures came to Wilson's rescue. They reported record exports and a sharply lower trade deficit. Sterling stayed stable. Collapse of stout (Conservative) party.

The nearest the campaign came to a serious and sustained controversy erupted out of the blue. On 9 March, a worker at the British Motor Corporation's factory in Oxford complained that local trade union officials had put him and seven workmates 'on trial' in the works canteen for refusing to join an unofficial strike. A noose, which shop stewards said had been there for months, was hovering above their heads. Reports of this led to other stories of intimidation, to the intense discomfort of the Labour Party because of its links to the unions. Heath, seeking to broaden the attack to Labour's wider dependence on union funding, said these incidents were 'only the tip of the iceberg'; he promised that a Tory government 'would end intimidation'. Ray Gunter, the Minister of Labour, set up an inquiry into the whole affair, and the national leaders of the unions attempted to bring their local officials to heel. In time, the issue died down. It had been an uncomfortable start to the campaign for Labour, although the polls suggested that it made little or no difference to the party's support.

With rival policies making little news, journalists looked elsewhere for events that might interest voters. Two of the most prominent stories some days after the 'noose' episode served to underline the cautious, lightweight character of the whole campaign.

On 18 March, Heath attempted a joke at Wilson's expense. A giant panda had been sent to Moscow for mating. Mocking Wilson's enjoyment of meeting television stars, Heath said: 'In a month's time we will be reading that Mr Wilson is having tea at No. 10 with a pregnant panda.' As 'a months' time' would be almost three weeks after polling day, journalists observed with relish that Heath seemed to be conceding defeat.

On 22 March, nine days before polling day, Wilson's more effective sense of humour served him well when he was hit in the eye by a stink bomb at a meeting in Slough. His impromptu response ensured front-page coverage in the next day's papers: 'With an aim like that, the boy ought to be in the England eleven.'

At the end of the campaign, the polls, which had moved little throughout the campaign, predicted that Labour would secure 50–54 per cent of the vote, well ahead of the Conservatives' 37–42 per cent. Labour duly won its handsome majority, though, with 48.8 per cent of the vote (up 4 per cent on 1964) and the Conservatives on 41.4 per cent (down 1.5 per cent), the victory margin of 7.4 per cent was less than any of the polls had forecast. Compared with 1964, there was a 2.7 per cent swing from Conservative to Labour. (These figures relate to Great Britain and exclude Northern Ireland, with its separate party system.) The Liberal vote fell by 2.7 points to 8.6 per cent, but the party's twelve new MPs (up three on 1964; the twelve included David Steel, who had won his seat in a by-election a year earlier) was its highest tally since 1945.

Statistically, most seats swung in line with the national average. This meant that the election night was one of the less dramatic. Clear swings to Labour occurred in all the early seats. When Labour recorded its first gain of the night – Exeter, shortly before 11 p.m. – the contest was essentially over: Wilson had secured the clear majority he wanted. As always, however, there were notable individual results. Five senior ministers from the 1951–54 administrations lost their seats: Peter Thorneycroft (Monmouth), Sir Martin Redmayne (Rushcliffe), Christopher Soames (Bedford), Henry Brooke (Hampstead) and Julian Amery (Preston).

One notable victor was Gerry Fitt, who won West Belfast as Republican Labour. He broke the Unionist monopoly of MPs from the province and was the first Nationalist MP to win a seat since 1955. In later years, as 'the Troubles' intensified, he would be a prominent voice at Westminster on behalf of the Catholic community.

Another significant result was Smethwick. As we have seen, the Conservatives had won the seat against the national trend in 1964, following a local, unofficial racist campaign against Labour. This time Heath and du Cann said they would not tolerate any candidate employing racist tactics. Peter Griffiths, the Tory victor in 1964, steered well clear of the issue. The outcome was a victory for Andrew Faulds, the new Labour candidate and a well-known actor, on a 7.6 per cent swing, one of the largest of the night.

Despite their heavy Conservative defeat, Heath remained party leader and went on to fight Wilson again in 1970. It was, however, Grimond's third and last election as leader of the Liberals. Though only fifty-three, he retired nine months later.

In the aftermath of the election, the senior ministers all retained their jobs: Callaghan (Chancellor of the Exchequer), Michael Stewart (Foreign Secretary), Roy Jenkins (Home Secretary) and George Brown (First Secretary of State). If Wilson thought he could sustain his triumph through the new parliament on the back of a reviving economy, he was soon disillusioned. The decision taken in October 1964 on his first evening as Prime Minister, to defend the value of the pound, came back to haunt him. Three months after his big victory he was engulfed by an economic crisis; the following year, he was forced to devalue the pound after all. The morning after the 1966 election was the moment of Wilson's greatest authority. As he basked in the glory of electoral success, he showed no sign of realising how soon his second electoral honeymoon would be over.

Peter Kellner is a former chairman and president of YouGov, and was an election and polling analyst from 1970 to 2019 for the BBC, *Channel 4 News*, the *Sunday Times*, the *New Statesman*, *The Independent*, *The Observer* and the *Evening Standard*.

37

1970

MICHAEL CRICK

Dissolution: 29 May 1970
Polling day: 18 June 1970
Seats contested: 630
Total electorate / Voted / Turnout: 39,342,013 / 28,305,534 / 72 per cent
Candidates (total 1,837): Conservative (including UUP) – 628; Labour (including NI Labour) – 625; Liberal – 332; Communist – 58; SNP – 65; Plaid Cymru – 36; Unity – 5; Protestant Unionist – 2; Republican Labour – 1
Prime Minister on polling day: Harold Wilson
Main party leaders: Conservative – Edward Heath; Labour – Harold Wilson; Liberal – Jeremy Thorpe; Communist – John Gollan; SNP – William Wolfe; Plaid Cymru – Gwynfor Evans; Protestant Unionist – Ian Paisley; Republican Labour – Gerry Fitt; UUP – James Chichester-Clark; NI Labour – Vivian Simpson

Party performance:

Party	Votes	Percentage share	Seats
Conservative (including UUP)	13,145,123 (422,041)	46.4 (54.2)	330 (8)
Labour (including NI Labour)	12,208,758 (98,194)	43.1 (12.6)	288 (0)
Liberal	2,117,035	7.5	6
SNP	306,802	1.1	1
Plaid Cymru	175,016	0.6	0
Unity	140,930	18.1	2
Communist	37,970	0.1	0

| Protestant Unionist | 35,303 | 4.5 | 1 |
| Republican Labour | 30,649 | 3.9 | 1 |

Result: Conservative majority of thirty seats

The general election of 1970 was the first in which I took a close interest and remember vividly. I was twelve at the time, and on polling day, 18 June 1970, my parents wouldn't let me stay up to watch the results, so I went to bed at 10 p.m. with my small crackly transistor radio and earpiece under the covers. After just a couple of declarations around 11 p.m. – from Guildford, and then Cheltenham – I decided to go to sleep. The outcome was blindingly clear – and a shock.

Britain had experienced the most surprising election result of modern times. For a Marplan poll the day before polling had given Labour a seemingly unassailable lead of 8.7 per cent. During the early months of 1970, Wilson and his party seemed to have clawed their way back after the difficult years of 1967 to 1969 when Labour plunged to historic depths of unpopularity for any political party in Britain.

Only four years before, in March 1966, Harold Wilson had returned to power with a landslide majority of ninety-seven. Four months later, England won the World Cup at Wembley with a 4–2 win over West Germany (some people erroneously think the England victory preceded Labour's triumph). Yet even by the summer of 1966, the pressure on sterling, which had dominated the 1964–66 parliament, had resumed with a run on the pound exacerbated by a six-week strike by seamen, who wanted shorter hours and a wage rise which would have breached the government's 3.5 per cent pay limit. When the dispute brought much of British shipping to a standstill, Wilson announced a 'state of emergency' and denounced left-wing activists in the seamen's union – among them the future deputy Labour leader John Prescott – as a 'tightly-knit group of politically motivated men'.

Wilson and his chancellor Jim Callaghan defended the pound for another sixteen months, helped by the deflationary 'July measures' of 1966, which were designed to avoid devaluation even though debates in Cabinet showed that most ministers favoured reducing the value of sterling. The measures included £500 million of spending cuts, a six-month wage freeze and the highly contentious Selective Employment Tax on service sector jobs.

In November 1967, the inevitable happened. Sterling was finally reduced by about 14 per cent against the US currency, from a rate of $2.80 to $2.40. Wilson famously went on television to try to assure people that devaluation wouldn't make them worse off. 'That doesn't mean', he said, 'that the pound here in Britain – in your pocket, or purse, or in your bank – has been devalued.' His words were met with disbelief, if not derision, since devaluation inevitably fuelled inflation by making imported goods more expensive, and people suffered from the further austerity measures subsequently introduced by Labour's new Chancellor Roy Jenkins, who swapped jobs with Jim Callaghan. The latter went to the Home Office after three years resisting devaluation, though the case for devaluing was not just about stemming the almost relentless runs on the pound but also correcting structural flaws in the UK economy.

Another major feature of the 1966–70 parliament was the rise of immigration as a political issue. Since the late 1940s, successive governments had encouraged migrants to come to Britain to meet growing labour shortages, especially in the NHS. First came the Windrush generation from the Caribbean, then subsequently immigrants from west Africa, and people from India, and East and West Pakistan, as well as Asians who'd originally settled in Kenya but suffered serious discrimination. Labour passed two Race Relations Acts – in 1965 and 1968 – to outlaw both racial discrimination and the promotion of racial hatred.

But in April 1968, three days before Labour's second Race Relations Bill was due for its second reading in the Commons, the shadow Conservative Defence Secretary Enoch Powell – a leadership contender in 1965 – delivered in Birmingham what has gone down as perhaps the most notorious address in modern British history: his 'Rivers of Blood' speech (though Powell never actually uttered that phrase). He warned of future violence over immigration, and race riots similar to those which had recently taken place in America. Powell sparked particular controversy by quoting an anonymous constituent who had told him: 'In this country in fifteen or twenty years' time, the black man will have the whip hand over the white man.'

'I am filled with foreboding,' Powell said. 'Like the Roman, I seem to see the River Tiber foaming with much blood.' Powell also cited a letter he'd received about an elderly pensioner living in Wolverhampton: 'She is becoming afraid to go out,' Powell read from the letter. 'Windows are broken. She finds excreta pushed through her letterbox. When she goes to the shops, she is followed by children, charming wide-grinning piccaninnies.'

The Conservative leader Edward Heath sacked Powell the next day, telling him he thought the speech was 'racialist' – and Powell never sat on the front bench again. Polls suggested, however, that the British public strongly supported Powell's views, and that single speech made him a leading political figure overnight. Heath was forced to modify his own position on immigration and declared five months later that the number of immigrants entering Britain should be 'severely curtailed'. The Wolverhampton MP, who subsequently came out against joining the Common Market, would remain a difficult enemy for the rest of Heath's leadership and would play a key role in the 1970 election (as well as the two elections of 1974). The Conservatives moved to the right in other ways, too. When education spokesman Sir Edward Boyle, a supporter of comprehensive schools, left politics to become a university vice-chancellor in 1969, Heath replaced him with the significantly more right-wing Margaret Thatcher.

During 1967, starting with the Rhondda West seat, which they lost to Plaid Cymru, Labour was defeated in five by-elections in twelve months – a record for one calendar year achieved by no government before or since, except by Labour again in 1968. During the whole 1966–70 parliament, Labour would lose an astonishing fifteen seats in by-elections – twelve to the Tories and one each to Plaid, the SNP and the Liberals – more than twice as many as any government lost in any parliament from 1945 to 2019.

In the April 1967 elections to the Greater London Council, the Conservatives won eighty-two seats and Labour just eighteen. And the humiliation of devaluation and the subsequent austerity measures only worsened Labour's electoral plight. From February to July 1968, the monthly Gallup polls gave the Conservatives an average lead of 22.5 per cent. In the local elections of 1968, the Conservatives won twenty-eight of the thirty-two London boroughs, including Lambeth (where the 24-year-old John Major won a safe Labour ward). Also that year, Labour failed to win a single ward in Birmingham or Leicester.

Around the world, 1968 was a year of revolt, of course, with the Prague Spring; weeks of student protests in Paris; and the assassinations of Robert Kennedy and Martin Luther King in America; while London saw extraordinary, feverish talk of a coup against Harold Wilson. The newspaper baron Cecil King, chairman of IPC, the group which published the Labour-supporting *Daily Mirror*, met the former defence chief Lord Mountbatten and sought his support for overthrowing Wilson and replacing his government with a temporary, non-parliamentary regime headed by Mountbatten himself. When Mountbatten declined, King instructed the *Mirror* to publish a front-page editorial calling on Wilson to be removed by extra-parliamentary action. More realistically, within Labour ranks, the new Chancellor Roy Jenkins, who had a big following among MPs, was tipped as a possible successor, but he showed no inclination to strike.

Yet surprisingly, despite the Conservatives leading the polls for most of the 1966–70 parliament, Edward Heath was almost always less popular than Harold Wilson with the public. On BBC *Panorama* in October 1967, the celebrated interviewer Robin Day bluntly asked him: 'How low does your personal rating among your own supporters have to go before you consider yourself a liability to the party you lead?' The public thought Heath was distant, dry, wooden, tetchy and colourless.

But that lack of colour suddenly improved a few days after Christmas 1969, when Heath captained his yacht *Morning Cloud* to victory in one of the world's great yachting events – the Sydney to Hobart race in Australia. Four weeks later, Heath took his shadow Cabinet to the Selsdon Park Hotel near Croydon for a three-day gathering to thrash out new ideas. The result was a strikingly right-wing programme of free market policies, including spending cuts, tax reductions, union restrictions and other measures that would later form the basis of Thatcherism. Harold Wilson quickly denounced Heath as 'Selsdon Man', hoping to paint him as a neanderthal bent on destroying the state, though the jibe may have backfired. Suddenly, Heath and his party had a clearer identity with the public. Although the right-wing Selsdon Man image can't have been one that the 'one-nation' politician Heath would have enjoyed, he was now seen as a tougher leader who was determined to cut immigration, strengthen the police and confront the unions.

Where Heath lacked colour, the Liberal leader arguably had too much of it. In January 1967, when their respected leader Jo Grimond stood down after ten years, the twelve Liberal MPs elected the 36-year-old Jeremy Thorpe, a dandyish, charismatic Etonian who'd been a barrister and a TV reporter and was known for his clever mimicry.

The years from 1966 to 1969 were a period of almost continuous economic crisis, austerity and industrial strife. The number of days lost to strikes rose year by year, and trades unions increasingly resisted Labour's incomes policies designed to limit pay rises. Barbara Castle, the left-winger appointed as Employment Secretary in 1968, tried to introduce – with Wilson's backing – a radical programme of industrial relations changes to curb trade union power, as initially set out in her famous White Paper 'In Place of Strife'. Castle's plans included proper strike ballots, penal sanctions and cooling-off periods for conciliation. But Castle and Wilson were opposed by the powerful combination of the unions themselves, the Labour Party national executive and members of the Cabinet led by the Home Secretary Jim Callaghan. Ninety-five Labour MPs were reportedly ready to back a leadership challenge to Wilson. He dismissed the rumours with characteristic wit. 'I know what's going on,' he said. 'I'm going on.'

By the summer of 1969, as the Chief Whip Bob Mellish warned

he couldn't get the Industrial Relations Bill through the Commons, Castle and Wilson had to back down and the bill was ditched. The TUC general council agreed a 'solemn and binding' declaration of intent – known as Solomon Binding – to do more to avoid strikes in future. It was purely a face-saving exercise.

Jim Callaghan then won himself back into favour with Wilson with his handling of the sudden outbreak of violence in Northern Ireland that summer, when the civil rights movement demonstrated for fairer treatment for the Catholic minority, especially in housing and jobs. In response, Protestant Loyalists attacked Nationalist districts, burning down houses and businesses, while members of the Royal Ulster Constabulary opened fire on civil rights demonstrators. In August 1969, British soldiers were deployed in Belfast and Derry to try to restore order, and they were initially welcomed by the Catholic population. As paramilitary groups such as the Irish Republican Army and the Loyalist Ulster Volunteer Force exploited the situation, the toll of sixteen deaths in 1969 would soon rise to several hundred every year, and the Troubles would last almost three decades.

Suddenly, however, from the start of 1970, Labour's ratings began to pick up, fuelled almost certainly by a growing economy, increased exports and an extraordinary rise in wage rates. Harold Wilson later claimed he pretty much decided the date of the election on the eve of the 1970 Budget, 13 April, even though the Conservatives were still narrowly ahead in the polls. A week later, however, as Wilson arrived in Glasgow from an overnight rail sleeper, a copy of the *Scottish Daily Express* was thrust into his hands with the headline: 'Good Morning, Mr Wilson'. It showed the first substantial Labour lead by any of the four major polling firms in two and a half years.

In the May 1970 local elections, Labour made a substantial recovery, and a Gallup poll a few days later giving Labour a 7 per cent lead really put the Tories on the defensive. 'We always do our best with our backs against the wall,' said former Prime Minister Sir Alec Douglas-Home, who was now shadow Foreign Secretary. 'And all I can say is that it's a damned great wall we're up against now.' Barbara Castle noted in her diary that the polls had 'started the bandwagon really rolling for a June Election. There are still some doubters – including me ... But a tide of emotion is rising which is very unsettling.'

On Thursday 14 May, Castle attended Harold Wilson's inner Cabinet, and all ten or so of the senior ministers present endorsed his plans to hold a general election five weeks later, on Thursday 18 June, as he had decided a month before. The Social Services Secretary Richard Crossman said it was a good sign that in one poll 65 per cent of the public expected Labour to win. The Chief Whip Bob Mellish reported that Labour MPs were solidly in favour, too. 'Everyone agreed?' Wilson asked his inner Cabinet colleagues. Nobody dissented. 'Right: then no one will be able to claim the virtue of hindsight.' When the rest of the Cabinet arrived for their regular meeting a few minutes later, they were told nothing about the decision and told to say that no discussion on an election date had even taken place.

Harold Wilson told the Queen of his plans at his weekly audience that night but didn't formally ask her for a dissolution until the following Monday, which meant a campaign of thirty-one days. Barbara Castle still harboured doubts and felt Labour was badly unprepared. 'I am appalled at our lack of good material with "bite" as we go into the campaign,' she wrote. 'I've never felt less well equipped for an election but the others (Harold apart) seem so lackadaisical.'

The election of 1970 was a rematch of 1966, and the Wilson v. Heath contest was probably Britain's most presidential election so far. Harold Wilson, often seen puffing away at his pipe, tried to present himself as the calm, reliable Prime Minister who had finally got a grip on the nation's economic woes. Richard Crossman, who had famously been keeping a diary about his time in Cabinet since 1964, wrote that Wilson had:

> evolved a new technique of being televised and photographed with party workers and this has brilliantly contrasted him with Heath. Harold is the easy-going, nice fellow, while Heath is making boring, serious speeches ...
>
> [Wilson] has dispensed with practically all policy and there is no party manifesto because there are no serious commitments at all. In that sense we are fighting a Stanley Baldwin, 'Trust my Harold', election.

Labour's campaign was summed up by the title of its manifesto, 'Now Britain's Strong, Let's Make It Great to Live In'. Rather than deliver long evening speeches, Wilson would make short addresses to crowds on the street, sometimes from an upstairs window. He'd get laughs with clever references to TV personalities such as Robin Day, *Doctor Who* or soap opera characters, and the spring climate was ideal. 'Fairly hot, with cloudless skies but freshened by a slight breeze,' Crossman wrote. 'Perfect electioneering weather, perfect complacency weather, weather which suits Harold Wilson's propaganda of "Trust Harold".' And this was the election campaign where Wilson effectively introduced the 'walkabout' to British politics. The Technology Minister Tony Benn suggested in his diary that the idea was inspired by the Queen's recent tour to New Zealand and Australia, when royal aides decided she should 'jazz' things up by getting out of her car to meet the crowds and chat face to face. Wilson was invariably accompanied by his wife Mary, perhaps to emphasise that Heath was a bachelor.

While Wilson preferred to travel the country by train, Heath went by plane, even for relatively short journeys, which made him look more distant and aloof. Jeremy Thorpe, who spent much of his time defending his narrow majority in North Devon, made most of his limited forays round the country by helicopter – perhaps the first British politician to do so.

To improve Edward Heath's image, his handlers arranged for him to be photographed on *Morning Cloud* with an attractive young woman, only for the event to backfire when it was discovered that the woman worked in public relations, and the yacht then ran aground. The Conservatives tried to contrast Heath with Wilson, by presenting him as honest, sincere and principled, free of gimmicks or opportunism. Labour were 'men of straw', Heath said. 'They bend to every wind. Like cushions, they merely bear the imprint of the last person to sit on them.'

Few of Heath's colleagues were enthusiastic about their leader, but they kept their reservations to themselves, with the odd exception. 'Heath's image is bloody awful,' one senior local Tory told the Nuffield election study. 'He should have been told to get married – he's got the personality of a blancmange.'

Heath eventually adopted the walkabout himself and was seen kissing pretty girls and arguing with roadside workmen. At the end of the second week, the shadow Chancellor Iain Macleod urged a more aggressive campaign on the economy. Heath duly obliged: 'I say to the British people, "For Heaven's sake, wake up and face the real issues."'

The economy dominated hostilities, and the authors of the Nuffield study, *The British General Election of 1970*, David Butler and Michael Pinto-Duschinsky, reckoned that the campaign fell into three distinct phases. First, on rising prices after the Retail Price Index, the main inflation measure, had risen by a shocking 2.1 per cent in April. Heath chased the so-called housewives' vote and Conservative election posters and TV broadcasts featured shopping baskets of ever-more expensive groceries, as the Tories warned of a three shilling (15p) loaf and minimum of a shilling (5p) for bus fares and phone calls. Conservative broadcasts also showed scissors cutting away at a pound note to symbolise the pound's rapidly decreasing value.

The second phase was on wage inflation and the possibility of a wage freeze; and the third phase, over the final ten days, dwelt on the state of the economy in general, the trade figures and whether Labour's apparent economic recovery might be short-lived.

Immigration featured heavily as an issue, too, once Enoch Powell entered the fray with the publication of his constituency election address on 28 May. 'It was immediately seen as an alternative manifesto,' says Powell's biographer Simon Heffer. Not only did he want the 'halt of immigration' but also 'voluntary repatriation' of immigrants. Powell set out other differences with his party leadership, too, notably on joining the Common Market, and on the wider question of state control in general, where he advocated lower taxes, less spending and the reversal of nationalisation.

Tony Benn then generated further headlines when he compared Powell's intervention on immigration with the Nazis: 'The flag hoisted at Wolverhampton', Benn said, 'is beginning to look like the one that fluttered over Dachau and Belsen.' And if the Tories were elected, Benn suggested, Powell's policies would be forced upon a weak Heath. The Conservatives responded by urging Harold Wilson to dismiss Benn in the way that Heath had himself sacked Powell in 1968. 'Harold is furious about it,' Benn wrote in his diary, 'and has left a message for me to keep off the racial question.'

'So now we have two extremes,' wrote Richard Crossman in his diary, 'with Powell and Benn somehow cancelling each other out.' Remarkably, the issue of immigration, Enoch Powell and the responses to him would account for 20 per cent of the election output of BBC and ITV news bulletins during the whole campaign, and Powell got more coverage across the media than the entire Liberal Party. Arguably, in no other modern British election has any individual apart from a party leader achieved such prominence.

Opinion polls featured during the 1970 campaign as never before, with at least one published almost every day. Polls had become a prestige operation for newspapers, and for the first time they were regularly fed to hungry broadcasters the night before as a form of promotion for the papers which commissioned them. The press frequently led their front pages with poll results; as did broadcast bulletins, though with few of the caveats about sample size and margin of error which are required today.

And, until the final week, the polls were almost unanimous in giving Labour a growing lead, suggesting perhaps another landslide. 'The only poll that matters is the one on polling day,' Edward Heath constantly responded, and unlike his colleagues, he seemed genuinely confident of winning. His party chairman Anthony Barber was giving Heath regular reports from the constituencies that the picture on the ground was much more promising, especially in marginal seats.

Labour had cut the voting age from twenty-one to eighteen, and Britain became the first country in the world to let people vote at such a young age, a move which was expected to favour Labour. In practice, only about 70 per cent of this age group were actually registered in time. Another change was to give students the choice of voting from home, or the constituency where they were studying.

Making polling stations close an hour later – at 10 p.m. – was also expected to help the governing party.

With less than a week to go, on Saturday 13 June, one poll gave Labour a lead of 12.5 per cent. Yet Barbara Castle wrote in her diary:

> I wish there weren't another five days before the election! I don't believe those poll figures and although Heath is making such a pathetic showing personally and is getting such a bad press, I have a haunting feeling there is a silent majority sitting behind its lace curtains, waiting to come out and vote Tory.

The next day, England lost 3–2 to West Germany in the quarter finals of the 1970 World Cup, after holding a 2–0 lead until the sixty-eighth minute. England's world-class goalkeeper Gordon Banks had suffered severe food poisoning, so had been replaced just before kick-off by Peter Bonetti who would then be blamed for at least one of the German goals. One Labour MP would later speak of the 'damned germ in Gordon Banks's tummy that punctured the mood of euphoria'.

On the Monday, news came that the balance of payments – the all-important economic indicator in those days – showed a £31 million deficit for the month of May. It didn't seem to matter that £18.5 million of the deficit was due to two jumbo jets bought from America. The figures (which were later found to be exaggerated) sowed doubts in voters' minds given that the turnaround in the trade figures since 1964 was meant to be the dazzling jewel of Labour's economic record.

'This was the first real breakthrough by Heath,' Tony Benn wrote that day. 'Now Heath is saying, "The economy is in a terrible state and only we can put it right," and "We will tackle prices. The housewife should vote for herself." These twin themes are the ones that are beginning to get through.' Fellow Cabinet diarist Barbara Castle later agreed: 'However freak this figure might be, it seemed to confirm Ted Heath's dour warnings that an economic crisis lay ahead, and the uncertain mood of voters began to crystallise into hostility.'

The future Cabinet minister Kenneth Baker says the trade figures were decisive and recalls how early that Monday afternoon – three days before polling – he and fellow candidates had been summoned to a great rally on Hounslow Heath. 'It was a scorching hot day and we were in our shirt-sleeves to welcome Ted, who arrived standing in an open-topped Land Rover. He was a man transformed.'

Edward Heath pressed home his sudden advantage and warned that Labour would be forced into another four years of austerity, further wage restraint and possibly a second devaluation.

Enoch Powell then returned to making headlines over immigration by warning that the process of brainwashing had gone 'perilously far' when political parties 'dared not discuss a subject, which, for millions of electors, transcended all others in importance'. Powell accused the civil service of deliberately understating the true migration figures, but crucially, he urged followers who were thinking of abstaining to vote Conservative. 'This election is not about me, not about Enoch Powell,' he said, 'it is about you and your future and your children's future and your country's future.'

Richard Crossman remained optimistic that Labour would win but feared Powell might have

> rallied the Tories' chances and in the last days of the campaign injected just that note which could cause some of our supporters to abstain. The British public don't deeply care about this election and, if Powell manages to crystallise their feelings or help them to decide whether to vote or not, it could make a gigantic difference.

On polling day, Edward Heath confined himself to his constituency – Bexley in south-east London – where he'd had a narrow lead over Labour in 1966 but now faced an added complication from a Eurosceptic opponent who'd changed his name to Edward Heath by deed poll, presumably to sow confusion and take votes away from the Tory leader. Fortunately for the 'real' Heath, 1970 was the first election where candidates were allowed a party label of up to six words on the ballot paper, so he was able to call himself 'Leader of the Conservative

Party'. To make sure, the future Foreign Secretary Douglas Hurd was one of several Heath aides who spent much of election day patrolling up and down outside polling stations holding placards which reminded Bexley Tory supporters to 'put your X against the BOTTOM name on the ballot paper'.

Heath also faced another irritant on polling day, with an unexpected visit from Lord (Peter) Carrington, an ally who led the Conservatives in the Upper House. According to Heath's memoirs, Carrington bluntly 'told me that should we lose, I would be expected immediately to stand down. This advice was well-meant, but quite unnecessary.'

For days, in fact, if not weeks, Heath's senior colleagues had been discussing what to do if, as they expected, the party suffered a third successive defeat, and how they could stop an inevitable Powell bandwagon. The Chief Whip Willie Whitelaw, and shadow Home Secretary Reginald Maudling agreed to visit Alec Douglas-Home at his ancestral home in the Scottish borders on the Friday, with a view perhaps to Home becoming caretaker leader. The gathering was never needed.

The shock to come was initially glimpsed on election night with another innovation in 1970: the first ever 'exit' poll in Britain, conducted solely in the seat of Gravesend in Kent, the findings of which were broadcast just after the start of the BBC TV results programme. David Butler and his team at Nuffield College had worked out that in demographic terms, Gravesend was the 'most ordinary constituency in England', typical of the country in almost every measure. As they left the polling stations, hundreds of Gravesend voters were asked how they'd voted. The exit poll result was a Conservative win by 46.4 per cent to 45.4 per cent – which suggested a national swing of 4.4 per cent, just beyond the 4.35 per cent swing needed for an outright Tory victory. People rightly treated the Gravesend poll with scepticism at the time, but it proved a remarkably good forecast.

The BBC broadcast the first real result just before 11 p.m., from Guildford, as the future Cabinet minister David Howell was re-elected with an even bigger swing than the Gravesend exit poll – 5.3 per cent. 'All of a sudden,' Tony Benn wrote, 'we realised we had lost the election. There was no question about it ... In a fraction of a second, one went from a pretty confident belief in victory to absolute certainty of defeat. It was quite a remarkable experience.'

Harold Wilson and his political secretary Marcia Williams were watching TV at the Adelphi Hotel in Liverpool, close to his seat in Huyton. 'When the Guildford result came in,' Williams later wrote, 'I looked at Harold Wilson and he looked at me. Nothing was said, but both of us knew what had happened ... Wilson was impassive, though obviously downcast; he sat alone on an enormous sofa, looking isolated and enigmatic.'

The Cheltenham declaration, a couple of minutes later, saw an even bigger swing – 6 per cent. 'This means another Tory government,' announced the re-elected MP Douglas Dodds-Parker.

'This is sensational,' the BBC analyst Bob McKenzie told presenter Cliff Michelmore. 'The Conservatives have broken through 4.35 per cent ... The whole thing becomes very exciting indeed, Cliff.'

Subsequent results confirmed the pro-Tory trend, and just after 11.40 p.m., Enoch Powell was returned in Wolverhampton South West, where he doubled his majority. As the clock approached midnight, and Powell supporters bathed in the fountains in Trafalgar Square, the BBC now predicted a Conservative majority of ninety – almost as high as Labour's in 1966. Just after midnight, came a symbolic moment when a graphic artist was seen painting extra blue numbers on the Conservative side of the BBC Swingometer while Bob McKenzie carried on speaking – so unprepared had the corporation been for a Tory success.

But through the night, it become clear the BBC had now overreacted the other way, and they gradually revised down their forecasts of a handsome Tory victory.

A buoyant Heath returned to central London in the early hours of Friday, thanked party workers at Central Office and then went home to bed and gave orders not to be disturbed. As arranged, Heath's housekeeper woke him with a cup of tea around noon. Had anything happened while he was asleep? Heath asked. 'Yes,' she replied, 'a man called Nixon keeps telephoning and demanding to speak to you. He's rung at least three times.'

The US President eventually got through to the new Prime Minister minutes later, around the same time that Harold Wilson finally conceded defeat, though the Conservatives didn't achieve their decisive 316th seat – just over half the House of Commons – until around 2 p.m. Heath eventually achieved a tally of 330, with Labour on 288, a Tory majority of thirty over the other parties and a 3.3 per cent margin in votes. No one in the shadow Cabinet had expected success, except Heath himself: 'I dare say that some senior members of the party panicked at times,' he said, 'but I always remained confident.' In the end, Enoch Powell may actually have been an asset to Heath, with his speeches on immigration and his late call to vote Conservative.

The Liberal team was halved to just six MPs, with only two of them in England. Among other casualties were the Labour deputy leader George Brown, who said he'd 'lend' his Derbyshire seat to his Tory opponent but soon took a peerage instead; the Arts Minister Jennie Lee, who was the widow of Nye Bevan; and two colourful Labour mavericks, Robert Maxwell and Woodrow Wyatt.

Among MPs elected for the first time were the future Chancellor Ken Clarke; future Labour leaders Neil Kinnock and John Smith; seamen's union militant John Prescott; the left-wing miner Dennis Skinner; and the Ulster Protestant firebrand Ian Paisley.

The election of 1970 was the last of eight successive elections since 1945 when both major parties had got more than 40 per cent of the vote, something which has only occurred once since (in 2017). It also remains the only election since the war where a decisive majority for one party was replaced by a clear lead for the other.

'The opinion polls have a lot of explaining to do,' said Harold Wilson as he lost, and he was right. Before polling day, only one survey favoured the Conservatives with any lead (ORC by 2 per cent on 31 May), while one poll – NOP on 12 June – gave Labour a whopping lead of 12.5 per cent. Then, on the day of voting, having detected a significant number of switchers from Labour, a new ORC poll also gave Ted Heath a lead of just 1 per cent. The extraordinary polling failures have never been properly explained, though it was probably a mixture of structural weaknesses and a very late swing to the Tories.

Both major parties would vent their anger against the pollsters, and against the media for placing so much emphasis on the polls and assuming a Labour victory. Douglas Hurd said later that he felt no 'sense of triumph' against Labour: 'My strongest feeling was satisfaction that the experts, the know-alls, and the trend-setters had been confounded.' Afterwards, *The Guardian* led apologies by the media to the Conservatives and their leader: 'Mr Heath's victory is his own. It is a triumph over the opinion polls, over a sceptical press and doubting colleagues, and over Mr Wilson. It is a personal success achieved by perseverance and determination when the tide seemed against him.'

On the evening of Friday 19 June, having been to Buckingham Palace, Edward Heath stood outside No. 10. 'This government will be at the service of all the people, the whole nation,' he promised. 'Our purpose is not to divide but to unite and where there are differences to bring reconciliation, to create one nation.'

Heath's Cabinet contained no surprises, with the main posts going to Iain Macleod as Chancellor; Sir Alec Douglas-Home as Foreign Secretary (the post he held from 1960 to 1963); and Reginald Maudling as Home Secretary. But tragically, Macleod died of a heart attack only a month after taking office and was replaced at the Treasury by the less substantial Anthony Barber. In its three-and-a-half-year existence, the Heath Cabinet proved remarkably stable in terms of personnel, with relatively few reshuffles compared with other ministries.

Stability was not a notable feature, however, of the Heath government as a whole. Its most notable achievement was to take Britain into the Common Market on 1 January 1973, after Heath needed sixty-nine Labour rebels to get the legislation through the Commons. Overall, though, the Heath years were marked by yet more economic crises and industrial unrest. Unemployment rose above 1 million in 1972 for the first time since the 1930s, while inflation reached almost 10 per cent between 1971 and 1973 (and much higher thereafter). The Heath government declared states of emergency five times – all in response to major strikes, including the historic miners' disputes of 1971–72 and 1973–74 – compared with just seven states of emergency over the previous fifty years of the Emergency Powers Act. The Heath years also experienced the most deadly period in the Northern Ireland Troubles, with a record 480 deaths in 1972 and around a thousand during the whole time Heath was in Downing Street. Ministers introduced internment without trial for suspected terrorists, suspended Stormont and imposed direct rule from London; yet in 1973, they also reached the Sunningdale Agreement for power-sharing between the main Northern Ireland parties, though, ultimately, it failed.

Remarkably, despite the huge political, economic and industrial disruption of the early 1970s, all three main party leaders – Edward Heath, Harold Wilson and Jeremy Thorpe – would not only survive the 1970 election but also last long enough to fight two more elections against each other.

Michael Crick spent thirty-five years as a TV correspondent, with *Channel 4 News*, *Panorama* and *Newsnight*. His books include biographies of Jeffrey Archer, David Butler and Nigel Farage. His Twitter account @tomorrowsMPs follows parliamentary selections.

38

1974 (FEBRUARY)

LEWIS BASTON

Dissolution: 8 February 1974
Polling day: 28 February 1974
Seats contested: 635
Total electorate / Voted / Turnout: 39,753,863 / 31,321,982 / 78.8 per cent
Candidates (total 2,135): Conservative – 623; Labour – 623; Liberal – 517; SNP – 70; National Front – 54; Plaid Cymru – 36; SDLP – 12; Pro-Assembly Unionist – 7; UUP – 7; Vanguard – 3; DUP – 2
Prime Minister on polling day: Edward Heath
Main party leaders: Conservative – Edward Heath; Labour – Harold Wilson; Liberal – Jeremy Thorpe; National Front – John Tyndall; SNP – William Wolfe; Plaid Cymru – Gwynfor Evans; UUP – Harry West; SDLP – Gerry Fitt; Pro-Assembly Unionist – Brian Faulkner; Vanguard – William Craig; DUP – Ian Paisley

Party performance:

Party	Votes	Percentage share	Seats
Conservative	11,872,180	37.9	297
Labour	11,645,616	37.2	301
Liberal	6,059,519	19.3	14
SNP	633,180	2	7
UUP	232,103	32.3	7
Plaid Cymru	171,374	0.5	2
SDLP	160,437	22.4	1
Pro-Assembly Unionist	94,301	13.1	0

National Front	76,865	0.2	0
Vanguard	75,944	10.6	3
DUP	58,656	8.2	1

Result: Hung parliament, Labour forms a minority government

The general election of February 1974 was one of the most bizarre in British history. It was called as a result of a miscalculation, fought at cross-purposes and produced a surprising and incoherent outcome. There is no such thing as a deadlocked election in the British constitution: government always goes on until it is defeated in Parliament, but February 1974 came closest because of the narrow margin and the unviability of any options for coalition; it made another election inevitable within a year.

The votes cast in February 1974 were a break with the past. It was the moment when the national two-party system was replaced by three-party electoral politics in England, and the moment when nationalism (and anti-Westminster Unionism) became forces to be reckoned with in the other three nations of the UK. As well as being strange, February 1974 had some of the longest-lasting consequences of any election.

After its surprising electoral triumph in June 1970, the Heath government ruled over a turbulent period of British life. Despite not making it to four years, the parliament elected in 1970 had a long-term influence on history. Heath's government accomplished the accession of the UK to the European Community in January 1973. During its term of office, the crisis in Northern Ireland worsened dramatically – 1972 was the worst single year of the Troubles and still in 1974 there were daily bombings and shootings. Northern Irish devolution was suspended in 1972 for the first time since 1921, and a replacement set of institutions were agreed in 1973 and took office in 1974. The Heath government also faced economic and industrial relations crises; the latter aggravated by the 1971 Industrial Relations Act which was opposed by the trade unions. Strikes took place across industry, in the docks, power stations, the railways and the coal mines. In 1972, unemployment climbed above 1 million for the first time since the war, and there were serious worries about social peace. The government introduced a prices and incomes policy, regulating rises in both, and dramatically reflated the economy with tax cuts and spending in the 1972 Budget. The outcome was a boom in output in 1973 but rising inflationary pressure. Into this unstable environment came the shock of the oil crisis in October 1973 and renewed industrial unrest in the coalfields.

The Heath government, after a few months of honeymoon in summer 1970, was never very popular, although it did not plumb the depths in polling that its predecessor had done in 1968–69. The Conservatives usually ran about ten points behind Labour. They suffered one by-election loss to Labour, Bromsgrove, early in the parliament, but from 1972 onwards, there was a run of Liberal successes – Rochdale from Labour, then Sutton & Cheam, Isle of Ely, Ripon and Berwick-upon-Tweed from the Conservatives. The rise of the Liberals eroded Labour's position in the polls, but when it subsided in late 1973, the Conservatives gained most and closed the polling gap with Labour.

While it was an unusually troubled government, the early 1970s were not an auspicious period for the main opposition either. Labour was divided on the urgent question of Europe into at least three camps – one group of pro-European social democrats who wished to see Heath's bid succeed, a larger group of anti-Marketeers, many from the left and the unions, and Harold Wilson attempting, without much dignity, to navigate a course through the middle. Roy Jenkins resigned as deputy leader in April 1972 and one of his supporters, Dick Taverne, resigned his Lincoln seat in Parliament and won spectacular re-election as a pro-European 'Democratic Labour' candidate in a March 1973 by-election.

Adding to Labour's divisions was a leftward trend in reaction to the 1970 defeat and Labour's perceived shortcomings in government in 1964–70. The grass roots of the party became more radical, and the tenor of Labour politics became more confrontational because of the industrial relations background. Some former ministers, notably

Tony Benn, came to endorse the left critique of the Wilson government. The party's policy-making took a sharp shift to the left, culminating in 'Labour's Programme 1973' which formed the basis of the 1974 manifesto.

In principle, Heath had a free hand in calling the election when he chose. His parliamentary majority was still in place, though dented by by-elections and the breach with the Ulster Unionists, and he was unchallenged as leader of party and government. The parliament could still run until summer 1975 if he wished, and Heath had the power to call it earlier if he saw the opportunity. However, Heath did not experience the onset of the February 1974 election as a free choice; he felt pushed into it by the political and economic forces that were buffeting his government.

There were two converging problems for the government as it contemplated the situation in late 1973. Like few other governments – the ones elected in 2005 and 2019 might compare – the Heath government had needed to change course drastically. It came to power promising to stay out of regulating wages and prices but had imposed just such a policy in November 1972. Now, with the oil shock hitting, the expansionary policies of easy credit and tax cuts that stimulated the 1973 Barber boom were going to have to come to an end; times would be tough, particularly if inflation was going to be controlled. To go for a third fundamental strategy in four years, involving hard times in what could be an election period, looked like a stretch too far.

The more immediate problem was industrial relations in the coalfields and the threat the miners posed to the third phase of the prices and incomes policy; the government wanted the miners to settle within the policy's limits or else the counter-inflation strategy would be discredited, and it was bruised from the miners' victory in the dispute in 1972. The miners' position was strong; with oil prices having shot up, coal was all the more important in Britain's energy policy.

The National Union of Mineworkers (NUM) executive voted for an overtime ban on 8 November, the day after the publication of the third phase of the incomes policy, and on 13 November the government declared a state of emergency (the fifth under Heath).

It was renewed a month later in a crisis statement in which Heath announced that the use of electricity would be restricted and industry would be put on a three-day week starting in the New Year. The mood verged on the apocalyptic in some City, establishment and Conservative circles. Cecil King's diary records that in December 1973, Geoffrey Rippon, Heath's Environment Secretary, 'looked on the future with the utmost misgivings. He thought we were on the same course as the Weimar Government, with runaway inflation and ultra-high unemployment at the end.'

The first murmurs of a crisis election came shortly after the state of emergency, floated by Cabinet ministers – James Prior and Lord Carrington – who were keener on the idea than the Prime Minister. The idea of an election as a way of dealing with the situation had taken hold as the crisis deepened and the Conservatives recovered in the polls. The Cabinet agreed that an election was, if not desirable, inevitable. The drift towards this position was exacerbated by 'groupthink' and tiredness after three and a half years of crises and the looming prospect of more and worse.

As political scientist Dennis Kavanagh wrote twenty years later: 'The election still appears to have been called because the government wanted to be seen to be doing something.' A fresher and more cynical government could have navigated out of the fix they were in. Heath's government found, after the election had been called, that the Pay Board offered some wiggle room after all. The need to pay off the miners could be bundled up with a post-OPEC 'National Plan for Energy' or the like – lots of overtime in the short term and higher pay down the line. The TUC's 21 January offer to police the third phase to stop other workers from using the miners' settlement as an argument in their negotiations might have been flimsy, but a government could have taken it up – and blamed the unions if it turned out later that it did not work. However, the Heath government was not nimble enough to sell such an outcome to its backbenchers, who were restive over the succession of policy U-turns since 1972 and keen to avoid another cave-in to the miners, whom they suspected of a political rather than industrial agenda.

The initial plan had been to hold a snap election on 7 February, but this fell victim to Heath's determination to try to give negotiations with the miners and the TUC a chance, and his reluctance to fight a crudely divisive anti-union campaign. He knew that even if the Tories won, they would still have to deal with the trade unions after the election. The decision was a disappointment to the right of the party: new Plymouth Sutton candidate Alan Clark told his diary that the 'prospect of election on anti-union platform [is very] good for Sutton prospects. Now total reversal, Heath lost his nerve at the last moment that afternoon, morale shattered.' In retrospect, Nigel Lawson, principal author of the manifesto, and many other Conservatives felt that they would have won on 7 February; it was a mistake to let the NUM have their ballot before the national one. Had an election campaign been underway, people may have regarded the strike (affirmed by a ballot vote of 81 per cent on 4 February) as an interference in the electoral process. As it was, the government's response to the miners' ballot was to call the election for 28 February.

Heath announced the dissolution of Parliament in a broadcast on the evening of Thursday 7 February:

> The issue before you is a simple one: As a country we face grave problems at home and abroad. Do you want a strong government which has clear authority for the future to take the decisions which will be needed? Do you want Parliament and the elected government to continue to fight strenuously against inflation? Or do you want them to abandon the struggle against rising prices under pressure from one particular powerful group of workers? ... It's time for your voice to be heard – the voice of the moderate and reasonable people of Britain: the voice of the majority.

Heath's reference to the power of Parliament as opposed to a group of workers was boiled down in the campaign to the question 'Who Governs?' There were three unhelpful answers to this question, which blunted its effectiveness as a campaign slogan. One was that to ask the question at all was a bad sign, suggesting that the government was not governing effectively and therefore not deserving of another term of office. Another was to ask what a Conservative government could accomplish with a renewed mandate that it could not with a majority in a parliament that had nearly a year and a half still to run. Another again was whether a Conservative government could really avoid giving the miners more money, given the global energy crisis.

Even at this moment, the message was confused. The emergency measures were softened for the election campaign, with television broadcasting permitted again after 10.30 p.m., and the miners' pay claim was referred to the Pay Board under its procedure to assess relativities with other workers. Having called the election, Heath considered it improper to use crisis measures as part of partisan conflict. Sceptics wondered whether the energy crisis and the mining dispute really necessitated an election, and the sense of urgency was much diminished.

The parties' campaign machinery worked smoothly, partly because the possibility of an election being called for 7 February had concentrated minds. February 1974 was the first campaign fought from both sides with the help of private polling. Labour had contracted Bob Worcester of MORI to do their polling, which steered Wilson's own campaign. There was mutual mistrust and disregard between Wilson's entourage and Transport House, and at times two parallel campaigns. Worcester's advice led to Wilson emphasising the bread-and-butter issues of prices and getting people back to work, and trying to appeal to working-class women and the 9 per cent of the electorate who had supported Labour in polling in 1972 but drifted away during 1973.

The public campaign was fought using techniques that were, for the most part, familiar. Television news coverage and televised interviews with leading figures became more important as targets for the parties and drivers of the momentum of the campaign but this trend had been setting in since at least 1959; 1974 developed, rather than invented, the campaign as televised spectacle. In keeping with the more serious tone – and the dull weather – there were fewer 'walkabouts' by the party leaders than in 1970. The traditional mass meeting was in decline but far from dead. Heath was not a great orator and at least at the start of the campaign, Wilson was not hitting the heights he had known in the past. Both leaders used repetitive stump speeches with paragraphs inserted on the issue of the day with a view to television coverage.

The 1974 campaign took place in a lull between the idiosyncratic stunts of the press barons and the ferocious Tory tabloids of the 1980s; the press was partisan, and mostly pro-Conservative, but the noise machine was operating at a lower gear. Even the *Mail* and the *Telegraph* reported campaign events like the 'Great Pit Pay Blunder' and the economic news in ways that cannot have helped the Conservative campaign, and the defection of Enoch Powell confused right-wing loyalties. As the campaign wore on, even the Conservative newspapers started to emphasise inflation rather than Heath's who governs as the main issue. In the final days of the campaign, the Wilson team managed to keep the lid on a *Daily Mail* story about Wilson's political secretary Marcia Williams (it became the 'slag heaps affair' about land development after the election).

Jeremy Thorpe's Liberal campaign was unusual. He stayed close to his North Devon constituency, appearing on a television link to the press conferences in London. There were two principal reasons for his caution. One was that he had won only narrowly in 1970 and boundary changes had added thousands of electors from the abolished Torrington seat; on a notional basis, he was fighting a seat with a Conservative majority. The other reason was the presence of Norman Scott, with whom he had a dalliance in the early 1960s. Thorpe feared that Scott's allegations about their relationship and Thorpe's behaviour were circulating in the seat and he wanted to be in position to squash them. His Conservative opponent Tim Keigwin was aware of the Scott affair; Thorpe's solicitor took a prominent seat at his meetings. However, Conservative Central Office had advised Keigwin firmly that he was to ignore the Scott allegations, and he duly did during the campaign – alluding darkly in his concession speech at the count to the 'truth' that would come out.

Thorpe's remoteness made him look above the fray in this confrontational election and helped with the Liberals' moderate image nationwide; but the Liberals' problem in this election was that their vote was high but too widely spread to win many constituencies. Perhaps a more energetic Thorpe campaign would have helped more in their target seats.

The other unusual personal campaign was conducted by Enoch Powell who, at the start of the campaign, chose not to stand as a Conservative candidate in the election and dismissed Heath's who governs appeal as 'fraudulent'. Powell was embittered by his sacking by Heath in 1968 and the lack of gratitude for his campaign speeches in 1970. Europe was his main concern; Labour's promise that their renegotiation would be put to a referendum (or election) was enough for him to regard them as the better option. Heckled at a rally with a cry of 'Judas', Powell electrifyingly responded: 'Judas was paid! I made a sacrifice!' Via the journalist Andrew Alexander, he kept Labour informed about his interventions in the campaign, which were timed to damage Heath and the Tories.

The campaign in Scotland was more distinct from the campaign at the main parties' headquarters in London than in previous elections, although this was a transitional stage on the way to the autonomous campaigns that took place in future elections. The SNP, as well as the Liberals, had been gaining in 1973 and Margo MacDonald won a by-election triumph in Glasgow Govan at Labour's expense in November 1973. In the same month, the Kilbrandon Commission, established after the earlier SNP surge, recommended devolution (a call that, at least in February, the Conservatives regarded with more sympathy than Labour). The imminent arrival of North Sea oil took on even greater importance with the world energy crisis. 'Do you want to be a rich Scot or a poor Briton?' asked the SNP. They had already planned a publicity campaign on the theme of 'It's Scotland's Oil' for February 1974 before the election was declared.

The election in Northern Ireland took place along entirely different lines from that in Great Britain, as the issues and the party system diverged sharply. The dominant issue was the government of the province, which had only just been devolved again after a period of direct rule from Westminster between the abolition of Stormont in March 1972 and power-sharing in January 1974. The executive that took power then was a coalition between the Ulster Unionists of Prime Minister Brian Faulkner, the constitutional Nationalist SDLP and the cross-community Alliance. Under the December 1973 Sunningdale agreement, the northern government participated in an all-island Council of Ireland. The hegemony of the Ulster Unionist Party (UUP) had been fraying in 1970 but its unity had shattered. Faulkner was forced to resign as UUP leader. These developments also ruptured the alliance between Unionism and the British Conservatives. Unionism was split in the 1974 election between supporters of Faulkner and his opponents, who formed the United Ulster Unionist Council (UUUC) electoral alliance between Ian Paisley's DUP, William Craig's Vanguard and the anti-Sunningdale majority of the UUP. Supporters of the Sunningdale accord were divided between pro-Faulkner Unionists, Alliance and his governing partners in the constitutional Nationalist SDLP. There were also Republican candidates who opposed Sunningdale. The Northern Ireland election took place in violent conditions. Thirteen people were killed in the province during the election campaign; twelve bombs exploded in Belfast on polling day including one lethal attack on the Red Star Bar.

The year 1974 was extremely eventful in the politics of many countries – as well as the UK, there was a change in leadership in the United States, France and West Germany during the year. However, February was relatively quiet, with few 'noises off' disturbing the domestic political argument of the British election campaign. The short campaign, only twenty-one days long, and the close and unexpected result mean that the events of the campaign seem important in retrospect because they might have changed the result had they been handled slightly differently. Despite the confrontational background, the February 1974 election was not particularly bitter; there was no disguising that the situation was serious and that seemed to damp down the rhetorical excesses and electioneering stunts that had influenced the last few campaigns. It also reflected the campaign strategies of the three parties, which all stressed national unity and getting back to normal as themes. For the Conservatives, William Whitelaw told Hugo Young:

> I was anxious to see the election run without bitterness. We had to avoid it at all costs. But, of course, to run a Who Runs Britain election while restoring normality to everyday life was difficult to say the least. There was a real conflict here. I shrank from it, as did Ted. For the country it was a good thing we did. But it was not good for the party, probably. We were very high-minded.

The Conservatives faced a dilemma about what sort of campaign to fight. Edward Heath and his close allies believed that the February 1974 election was an opportunity to move the national conversation on, to reflect the changed world situation and the considerable change in the Conservatives' approach since 1970. To Heath, a Conservative vote was a vote to support the incomes policy and the ambition for social consensus, and to give the government a renewed mandate to deal with the inflationary problems created by the oil crisis. The alternative course was a direct attack on the trade unions, and a 'Red Scare' campaign against communists in the unions and the left within the Labour Party, as represented by its radical 1974 manifesto. The campaign the Tories fought was an uneasy mixture of the two approaches, with Heath trying to take the high road but some of the campaign output – particularly a notoriously abrasive party election broadcast featuring Chancellor Anthony Barber – took the low road.

The first week of the campaign went roughly according to plan for the Tories. The debate was on their favoured ground of industrial relations and who governs, and the week was punctuated by the party manifestos, which were ready as a result of the speculation since December about a crisis election. Labour were first out of the blocks with their manifesto published on 8 February. It was largely a repeat of an existing policy document with a new preface, 'Let Us Work Together', and it promised nationalisation of leading companies, a state-led investment bank and 'a fundamental and irreversible shift of power and wealth in favour of working people and their families'.

Labour would start an immediate renegotiation of the terms of entry into Europe and consult the electorate on the new terms. There would be price controls and wage restraint would be voluntary, the product of a 'social contract' with the TUC.

The Conservative manifesto, 'Firm Action for a Fair Britain', was published on 10 February. It warned people to 'expect a pause in the rise in our living standards' but was not without promises, such as a twice-yearly review of pensions and benefits and the sale of council houses. The Industrial Relations Act would be amended, but on the other hand there would be regulation of union elections and reduction in social security benefits paid to strikers' families. The Liberal manifesto, 'You can Change the Face of Britain', came out on 13 February promising greater equality, partnership in industry and devolution of power.

The second week of the campaign produced a queasy sense in Conservative Central Office that things were not going according to plan. They had anticipated stepping away from who governs for a bit, but the news from the Retail Price Index figures published on 15 February was unhelpful, showing a sharp rise in food prices – up 20 per cent over the year. This was fuel for Labour's campaign, which focused on the cost of living: Wilson called on electors to 'Get rid of Mr Rising Price'. A Labour poster showed a packet of sausages with 'Usual Price 17p, Tory Price 26p' and the message 'We can't afford another Tory government ... Only Labour can get us out of this mess.' A series of financial statements from large banks showed them making large profits despite the poor economic prospects. During the second week, the parties and the media realised that the Liberals were not being squeezed – they were rising in the polls. In the third and final week, the Conservative strategy of returning to who governs was stymied by a series of unfortunate events, none of them huge in themselves but all of them costing the Tories momentum.

On 21 February, the Pay Board briefed the media about different ways of calculating miners' pay. There were defensible ways of doing so that showed the miners were not being paid as generously as other comparable workers. The attempt to explain a complex issue resulted in claims that the government had picked a fight with the miners based on wrong numbers, which ministers initially had trouble countering. The affair became known as 'Figgures's figures' after Sir Frank Figgures who chaired the Pay Board. If this were not bad enough for Heath, there was a twin blow on 25 February. Trade figures showed a £383 million deficit for January, the largest on record and twelve times more than the figures that had embarrassed Labour in June 1970. Then, in the evening, Enoch Powell gave a speech advising people to vote Labour, because the basis of the election was fraudulent and Labour would hold a referendum or election on the European issue. The next day, Powell revealed that he had voted Labour by post, and off-the-record comments by Campbell Adamson, director-general of the CBI, calling for the repeal of Heath's Industrial Relations Act were publicised. Public attention had drifted away from the territory of who governs during the campaign; 40 per cent thought industrial relations was an important issue in the first week, which dropped to 24 per cent at the end.

Even with all of these mishaps, the Conservatives were generally expected to win the election. They had led in all but one opinion poll throughout the campaign. Harold Wilson's morale was low and he made elaborate contingency plans for escaping from the media on election night should the results be bad, which – because of general muddle – ended up being implemented even though the results went the other way.

The weather on polling day was foul, particularly in the evening. Fighting Blackburn, Barbara Castle mourned: 'At 6 p.m. on polling day, a bitter wind turned into the worst snow-storm I can remember at any election. Even with cars to take people to the poll it wasn't fit to ask a dog to turn out in.' Labour memories went back to the rainstorms of 1964 that may have cost a working majority but took heart that more of the working-class vote than usual came early because of the three-day week.

As in 1970, election night was surprising. The Conservatives were widely expected to win even at the close of poll, with the betting odds being 2/5 on the Tories and 9/4 against Labour. Labour drew cautious encouragement from the exit polls that had been conducted in a handful of marginal constituencies, which showed an improvement in their position. Uncertainty was heightened because of new constituency boundaries, for a House whose overall size had increased from 630 to 635 MPs. The first constituency declaration, at Guildford, was a Conservative hold despite a Liberal surge into second place, which took slightly more from Labour than the Tories. Some strong Labour results followed and for a time it seemed that Labour were winning outright, but this was not sustained and the result was the first hung parliament since the one elected in May 1929. Labour had a narrow lead in seats, 301 to 297, but the Conservatives were slightly ahead in votes. Labour's best swings were in the large urban centres in England, and there was a patch of exceptionally large swing around Enoch Powell's heartland of Wolverhampton and the Black Country which accounted for four or five gains, enough for the plurality over the Tories. The share of the vote for both major parties plunged, like Holmes and Moriarty at the Reichenbach Falls – the Tories went from 46.4 per cent in 1970 to 37.9 per cent in 1974, which was the sharpest drop since 1945. But Labour's vote was seriously down as well, from 43 per cent to 37.2 per cent.

The Liberals won fourteen seats, their best total since 1935 but a poor reward for their 19.3 per cent share of the vote – just over 6 million votes which at the time was the largest raw number of votes the party had ever had. Liberal voters were spread too evenly, resulting in a lot of respectable second places to the Conservatives across the south of England but few MPs elected. They fell short of the take-off point that had seemed within reach in the last week of the campaign. The SNP won seven seats on 21.9 per cent of the Scottish vote; they inflicted the only Cabinet casualty of the election by unseating Scottish Secretary Gordon Campbell in Moray and Nairn. In Northern Ireland, the anti-agreement Unionist alliance won eleven of the twelve seats. Plaid Cymru won two in Wales, and two ex-Labour mavericks were returned as Independents – Dick Taverne and Eddie Milne in Lincoln and Blyth, respectively. Among the new MPs elected for the first time were Nigel Lawson, Douglas Hurd, Malcolm Rifkind and

Robin Cook; bowing out were two old rogues, Tom Driberg and Ernie Marples. Turnout was high, reflecting the fresh register and public interest in this close, crisis election: at 78.8 per cent it was the highest since 1951, a record it retains to this day.

The February 1974 election was a major break from the past which started a new era in electoral politics. It heralded the end of the dominance of the two major parties, in votes if less dramatically in seats. What had been losing shares of the vote in the post-war period, like Labour's 43 per cent in 1970, would be enough to produce big majorities in elections from 1974 onwards. The two-party system was never the same again, even if there were short-lived revivals in 1979 and 2017. Thorpe's Liberals broke the mould in February 1974. The last election at which a significant number of constituencies had Liberal votes of more than 20 per cent in competition with the Tories and Labour had been 1929. The two-party system crumbled in other respects; the SNP's haul of seven seats and the anti-agreement Unionist landslide in Northern Ireland produced lasting changes in party alignments, while Plaid Cymru's gains in Wales changed the environment more modestly.

The low winning share of the vote was one aspect of the weak relationship between seats and votes in February 1974. The most glaring was the poor reward for the Liberals from their 19.3 per cent of the vote – a mere fourteen seats (2.2 per cent of the Commons). The Liberals tried to use their leverage to open the way to electoral reform, but the limit to Heath's offer was a reference to a Royal Commission on the electoral system. The Conservatives had reason to be aggrieved as well, in that Labour had won more seats with a smaller share of the vote, thanks to a fortunate distribution of swing. The worst losers of all were the pro-agreement parties in Northern Ireland, whose 40.6 per cent of the vote won them one seat out of twelve.

The election results had serious consequences in Northern Ireland. The victory of the anti-agreement Unionists undermined the legitimacy of the power-sharing executive; they wanted, but Heath refused to offer, a new Assembly election. The Labour government was less committed to Brian Faulkner and the Sunningdale agreement than

Heath, and was intimidated by the workers' mobilisation in the May 1974 Loyalist general strike in the province. Devolution and Sunningdale were scrapped and direct rule resumed. It took until 1998 for a Northern Ireland executive to be re-established.

The Queen arrived from Australia at Heathrow early in the morning of 1 March, ready to take her part in the process of changing or reaffirming the government, but there was nothing to do on the day. As was his constitutional right, Prime Minister Heath stayed in Downing Street over the weekend to seek support from the Liberals and others. The parliamentary arithmetic was complicated, in that a pact with the Liberals was not sufficient for a majority and the Tories would need support from somewhere else – either the SNP or the seven UUP MPs elected under the UUUC banner. Jeremy Thorpe was keen to see what the Conservatives might have to offer, in terms of policy concessions and Cabinet positions.

The Conservatives had their doubts about Thorpe in the light of the *sub rosa* scandals about his private life, although at this stage of the story, no dogs had yet been harmed. But the fundamental reason why no deal was agreed was that the Liberal MPs, most of whom had won their seats from the Conservatives, were hostile to putting them back in power and did not fully trust Thorpe in the negotiations. Labour, with the advantage of having a handful more seats, sat tight, insisting that they would not engage in coalition talks but form a minority government if called upon. The financial markets had a very unsettled day.

His attempts to woo the Liberals and split the Ulster Unionist bloc having failed, Heath resigned on Monday 4 March, and Harold Wilson was summoned to Buckingham Palace that day to form a minority government.

Victory, even as half-hearted a victory as February 1974, was a surprising mixed blessing for Labour. Harold Wilson was, briefly, transformed back into the ebullient figure who had dominated politics in the 1960s, although age and illness were soon to catch up with him. Barbara Castle, appointed Health and Social Services Secretary, confided to her diary: 'Looking back over this curious election I realize what an ambivalent state of mind I have been in. I never expected us to win, but equally I did not think that Heath would get away with his contrived scenario.' The government that took office was not short of talent and experience in dealing with troubled times. Denis Healey as Chancellor, Jim Callaghan as Foreign Secretary and Roy Jenkins returning to the Home Office were as formidable a top team as any new government has boasted. Michael Foot, a backbench rebel in 1964–70, joined the government as Employment Secretary, handling the tricky industrial relations situation, and then kept it going for three years as Leader of the House of Commons without a majority. But there was a lot working against the Labour government. They had a weak parliamentary position and a feeble mandate to overcome the frightening economic and social problems they inherited. The Labour Party was deeply divided and the compromises of government would inevitably be seen as betrayal, particularly given the radical content of the manifesto. Tony Benn, as Secretary for Trade and Industry, saw himself as the guardian of the manifesto commitments on public ownership. Edmund Dell, who joined Healey's Treasury team in 1974, wrote later that 'there is no comparable example of such intellectual and political incoherence in a party coming into office in the twentieth-century history of the United Kingdom'.

The government's immediate priorities were to get the miners back to work and restore a sense of normality, and in this they proved successful. The atmosphere was calmer than during the repeated crises of the Heath government; the three-day week period was the last state of emergency to be declared to this day. The government's other concern was that the short-term outlook was dominated by the knowledge that Britain would be back at the polls before long and Labour would be aiming for an overall majority.

The election result, despite the narrow margin, was experienced by the Conservatives as a shattering defeat. They had felt confident in the justice of their cause and the importance of who governs and were surprised and disappointed that they had not prevailed, particularly against an opposition led by Wilson, whom they held in personal contempt. Politicians are usually pious about the wisdom of the electorate, but February 1974 is an exception. Edward Heath always felt that the electorate got this one wrong. 'It was the day he lost faith in democracy,' according to Peter Batey, who was his private secretary in the early 1980s. The idea that the government had been 'brought down by the miners' aided by the electorate's irresolution shaped the strategy and temperament of the Conservative government that took office in 1979. The defeat of 1974 would be avenged; the result in 1979 inspired confidence that this time the electorate would stick with it.

However, the February 1974 results themselves do not really bear the weight of such interpretations. The election took place in a climate that had taken longer to develop than the crisis of 1973–74, in which government was remote and technocratic but curiously ineffective. People were starting to ask the question about whether Britain was 'governable' at all because of the disappointing results from successive governments, and the power that was held by industry and the trade unions. The Liberal and Nationalist votes were the clearest signs of this alienation. But so too was the Labour win. The contest between Heath and Wilson pitted a remote, grand Prime Minister – more of a French President – with high-minded ideals and a long-term vision against an opposition leader who was skilled at making himself a relatable, everyman figure, and was held in residual affection by much of the electorate. Heath tried to tell the electors what the election was about – who governs, and the future of Britain in the world after the oil shock. But the electors had their own ideas about what the election was about, and Wilson was astute enough to address them. It is all very well contrasting a high-minded national appeal against the low politics of the price of sausages, but if the electorate is thinking first about the cost of living, they will go – if perhaps narrowly – with the party that talks about it.

Lewis Baston is an author on politics, elections and history and one-time archivist of the papers of Dr David Butler. He is the biographer of Reginald Maudling and his book *Borderlines*, about national boundaries and European history, is published in June 2024.

39

1974 (OCTOBER)

MICHAEL MCMANUS

Dissolution: 20 September 1974
Polling day: 10 October 1974
Seats contested: 635
Total electorate / Voted / Turnout: 40,072,970 / 29,189,104 / 72.8 per cent
Candidates (total 2,252): Labour – 623; Conservative – 622; Liberal – 619; National Front – 90; SNP – 71; Plaid Cymru – 36; SDLP – 9; UUP – 7; Alliance – 5; Vanguard – 3; DUP – 2
Prime Minister on polling day: Harold Wilson
Main party leaders: Labour – Harold Wilson; Conservative – Edward Heath; Liberal – Jeremy Thorpe; SNP – William Wolfe; UUP – Harry West; Plaid Cymru – Gwynfor Evans; SDLP – Gerry Fitt; National Front – John Kingsley Read; Vanguard – William Craig; DUP – Ian Paisley; Alliance – Oliver Napier

Party performance:

Party	Votes	Percentage share	Seats
Labour	11,457,079	39.2	319
Conservative	10,462,565	35.8	277
Liberal	5,346,704	18.3	13
SNP	839,617	2.9	11
UUP	256,053	36.5	6
Plaid Cymru	166,321	0.6	3
SDLP	154,193	22.4	1

National Front	113,843	0.4	0
Vanguard	92,622	13.1	3
DUP	59,451	8.5	1
Alliance	44,644	6.4	0

Result: Labour majority of three seats

As autumn 1974 approached, voters were less than excited at the prospect of a fourth successive election in which Harold Wilson's Labour Party would take on Ted Heath's Conservatives. Not since Gladstone and Disraeli faced off in the 1870s had party politics been so indissolubly associated with two distinctive and polarising figures. To develop any understanding of the political events of 1974 and their fall-out, it is hugely helpful, so far as possible, to understand these two extraordinary personalities. We voters often console ourselves with the belief that, beneath the public disagreements and locking of horns, surprising friendships can exist, across party lines. Not in this instance.

Wilson was the archetypally astute party manager, outwardly affable, a paradoxically patrician socialist, fluent and confident on television, generally sure of himself, academically rather brilliant and possessed of a rare gift to get under the skin of his opponents. He was the living embodiment of the old saying that 'socialism ... is whatever a Labour government does'. In contrast, Heath, born a few months later than Wilson, the son of a builder from Broadstairs, the first ever working-class leader of his party, struggled to project warmth or induce affection in others, somehow appearing both stubborn and yet also oddly irresolute, a soldier-turned-politician whose troops grew restless.

Heath resented Wilson. He was jealous of his opponent's easy facility for communication. In company, he often compared his own working-class background to Wilson's distinctly lower middle-class upbringing, and he would even claim that Wilson never genuinely smoked the pipe that crowned his patrician image (he did). Weary of all the reverential talk about his opponent's notable academic attainments, he once even asked his private office to obtain both sets of finals results. The comparison was starkly in Wilson's favour and Heath scrawled 'NFA' across the submission – no further action.

In contrast, Wilson didn't hate Heath. Even worse, he felt a slight pity for him, which incensed Heath even more. Wilson and Heath's Balliol contemporary Denis Healey both knew where the chinks were in Heath's armour – and they exploited that to the full. In later years, Heath mellowed considerably, showing a genuine and touching devotion to Mary Wilson, Harold's widow, but in the crucible of 1970s Britain, this was all-out war and October 1974 was going to be Waterloo for (at least) one of these perennial sparring partners.

We should not be deluded by the famous 'U-turns' in the second half of Heath's premiership into believing he lacked principle. He strongly believed Britain needed to modernise, improve productivity and slough off the last post-imperial delusions that persisted even after the debacle at Suez. He saw UK membership of the then European Economic Community (EEC) as the key to much of that; and he devoted himself to delivering membership, inevitably to the exclusion of other important claims upon his time. As he himself was never slow to point out, he had in fact successfully negotiated entry in the early 1960s – arguments of substance having been exhausted, all that remained to President de Gaulle was that bluntest of instruments, a petulant veto – and in 1970 he was determined not to allow that humiliation to happen again.

For Wilson, in contrast, the European question was mainly a nuisance, further incensing passions in the ecumenical and unruly coalition that was the Labour movement, generally across left-right lines, with most of his fellow centrists sharing his own ambivalence. He made a half-hearted application for membership in 1967, but everyone knew the French veto still stood and the EEC remained, so far as Wilson was concerned, someone else's problem – a matter on which Heath could happily be left to expend his political capital, while Wilson attended to matters closer to home.

Heath was also a 'one-nation' man to his core, a patriot and, at heart, an idealist. He admired the sense of shared purpose that he experienced in the army during the Second World War and despaired at the nation's failure to rediscover that unity in peacetime. He found '*Punch and Judy* politics' – at which Wilson excelled – both distasteful and entirely counter-productive, and dreamed of the day when 'men and women of goodwill' (a phrase that found its way into the October manifesto) would come together, bridging boundaries of party and class, status and background, to work together for the common good. The fatal flaw was that he unquestioningly saw himself as the indispensable head of any such initiative for saving the nation, whereas almost everyone else believed him to be a hopelessly divisive figure.

The February election had felt like a historic moment, despite the ambiguous outcome. Heath himself never used the phrase 'Who Governs?', but it did neatly characterise the election. The surge in votes for smaller parties – up from around 10 per cent in 1970 to 25 per cent in February 1974 – demonstrated the widespread uncertainty among voters about what the answer to that conundrum should be.

Many who took part in the election also sensed a shift away from Heath and the Tories in the final week, possibly in response to a Pay Board report that suggested the entire basis of the election was spurious. Certainly, there was no great love for either main party, nor for their two leaders. One of my earliest memories is of the great excitement in my home town of Southport when the Liberal Assembly came to us in the summer of 1973. My mother and I saw the excited crowds around Jeremy Thorpe as he performed his party trick of leaping over a barrier. She – a lifelong Tory – even confided to me that she intended to vote Liberal.

Turnout in February had been unusually high – 78 per cent, as compared with 72 per cent in 1970. As they girded up for another contest, the party leaderships knew turnout was likely to fall back in an election fought in the same year, with the same faces, on the same electoral registers and, in essence, on the same questions of national importance. The exhausted party machines would have to work flat out to deliver the voters. Labour was ahead issue by issue, but a decisive response to the question 'Who Governs?' seemed as elusive as ever.

Ted Heath was (and remains, at the time of writing) the only post-war politician to turn a working majority for one party into a working majority for another party, in a single election. The more common pattern – as in 1950 and 1951, 1964 and 1966, then 2010 and 2015 – is for this to take two goes. Heath's triumph of 1970, however, had been followed by some of the toughest peacetime years the nation has endured. The question was, could Wilson repeat his trick of 1966, riding the historic tide and following up a narrow defeat of the Tories with a subsequent Labour landslide? Often, general elections are not only about who wins, or even whether anyone wins. For party organisations, the scale of a defeat matters at least as much as the fact of defeat. In summer 1974, few, if any, Tories expected to win, but there was determination to minimise the scale of the defeat: a narrow defeat would keep the 'gene pool' of the parliamentary party large enough to populate an effective frontbench team and provide the basis for a rapid return to office.

The campaign for the October 1974 election began as soon as votes had been counted in February. Although Labour had won more seats, the Conservatives won more votes and Heath felt fully entitled to do his utmost to remain in office. He had lost the Ulster Unionists, however, and discussions with the Liberals felt almost embarrassingly pointless. After a gruelling and futile weekend of talks, the Heath Cabinet met for the last time and Her Majesty the Queen invited Harold Wilson to form a government. No one expected it to last longer than a few months and Wilson was clear from the outset that, if he lost even a single vote on the Queen's Speech, the sovereign would then be obligated to grant him a dissolution and an immediate second election – an election he (and everyone else) expected Labour to win comfortably.

Although shocked and disappointed, the Tories accepted their defeat with stoicism. Commendably, Heath never blamed anyone else for the decision to go to the country in February 1974. There were inevitably murmurings against him, but no one seriously argued the party could afford to indulge in a leadership campaign when another general election could happen at any time. There was simply no time for a proper postmortem – and there was also no doubt in Heath's mind that it was both his right and also his responsibility, to carry on as leader, through the seemingly inevitable election later in the year.

Without hesitation, Heath therefore reconstructed his front bench and went to battle. The most obviously important portfolio – the economy – went to his loyal adjutant Robert Carr, whose qualifications for the job were far from obvious. Arguably the second most important appointment was to lead on the environment and housing – rapidly identified as the one crucial area of policy where the Tories might be able to win back decisive votes, with eye-catching policies on home ownership, the mortgage rate and domestic rates. To this vital role, he appointed Margaret Thatcher, enjoining her to set up a high-level policy group at once, charged with fundamentally shifting the political conversation.

The first minority government since 1929 wasted little time in setting out its stall. In the Queen's Speech on 12 March, Her Majesty announced: 'I have been able to end the state of emergency, occasioned by the coal mining dispute, which had existed since 13 November 1973 and which I had renewed by proclamation on 6 March 1974 before the dispute was settled.' One of Wilson's first priorities had already been achieved. Another major focus was on the Heath government's over-complicated (and largely unintelligible) Industrial Relations Act of 1971. Before the February election, the general secretary of the TUC, Vic Feather, had told Heath that, if he lost power, 'the whole thing will be wiped out in the first week' and, as soon as he was appointed as Employment Secretary, Michael Foot declared the Act would be abolished by means of a single-clause bill, 'faster than any legislative measure in history'. This too was in the Queen's Speech.

Other measures unveiled included food subsidies (for staples) and 'a fundamental renegotiation of the terms of entry to the European Economic Community ... After these negotiations have been completed, the results will be put to the British people.' Several senior ministers, mainly on the left of the party, were still utterly unreconciled to EEC membership, believing it fettered Parliament and prevented the introduction of the socialist policies for which they yearned (a perfect mirror image of the Powellite argument). On the other side were the likes of Shirley Williams and Roy Jenkins, both of whom had rebelled in the historic EEC vote in Parliament on 28 October 1971, to support accession.

The new Foreign Secretary, James Callaghan, well knew there was no willingness to renegotiate the treaties among other member states, which recognised this to be a purely administrative exercise. Domestically, however, it suited Callaghan to portray it as something 'fundamental' – and our European colleagues had the good grace not to demur publicly. If the intention was to bind wounds and unite Labour for the 1980s, however, this process was doomed from the outset.

The first big decision for the Tories in opposition was whether to try to vote down any aspect of the Labour programme. Their bluff was easily called: everyone knew they feared a 'snap' election, which Labour would surely win at a canter; and so, on 18 March, Willie Whitelaw declined to divide the House on an opposition amendment to the Queen's Speech, not because he feared he would lose but because he feared he might win, precipitating precisely such a poll. It was a painful moment but, for the party, a necessary one.

Having, in effect, secured the confidence of Parliament and established that no secure anti-Labour majority was going to emerge, Wilson got on with the business of governing and setting out a clear position Labour could take in an election campaign. Ministers and civil servants fleshed out the party manifesto from February – no doubt extremely helpful as the party's next manifesto was being sketched out. Labour's principal means of addressing the industrial turmoil dogging the nation was a 'Social Contract' with the trade unions, an idea first floated by Tony Benn, which had been forced into service early when the February election was called.

The key to this was the Trade Union and Labour Relations Bill, which would not only repeal the 1971 Act but also create new privileges for the unions. Ministers tabled an extra clause to its Finance Bill, too, to refund money to unions which had been fined for not registering under the 1971 Act. When that was defeated in the Commons on 19 June, by 308 votes to 299 votes, Labour MPs voted solidly in favour and Tories and Liberals against, but the minority party votes were scattered, in an early indication of the knife-edge theatre that would play out in the hung parliament of the late 1970s. It was also an early warning of what would happen to the Trade Union and Labour Relations Bill, which was duly emasculated, first by the Lords and then by MPs, ending up as a simple repeal measure. Wilson and his business managers did a remarkable job in steering through some significant legislation – thirty-eight Acts in total in just five months – but there were also eighteen Commons defeats, most of them on matters of importance.

Throughout his tenure – inside and outside Downing Street – management of a fissiparous party was Wilson's greatest challenge and the principal drain upon his energies but also his opportunity to demonstrate his unique skills. While the Conservatives could put on a show of unity, everyone knew Labour was divided – inevitably a grave danger to the party's prospects. In July 1974, Roy Jenkins made a clarion call to centrism, overtly warning Labour against ignoring 'the great body of moderate, rather uncommitted opinion' and suggesting the party could and would not win outright 'upon the basis of ignoring middle opinion and telling everyone who does not agree with you to go to Hell'. Wilson made no comment.

The party's left were equally bloody minded and, when a number of left-wing ministers, including Eric Heffer, publicly criticised the government's decision to go ahead with supplying warships to the Chilean dictatorship, again, no action was taken against them. Events also seemed to militate against Labour. Power-sharing in Northern Ireland collapsed after a Protestant strike, so direct rule was reimposed; then the party was hit by a series of scandals, including the imprisonment of major party figures in the north-east. Labour, nonetheless, retained its lead in the opinion polls. Why?

The simplest answer is that, throughout this interregnum, the Labour government cunningly manipulated the economy to its own advantage, at the price of knowingly stoking up medium- and long-term inflation. Denis Healey managed to squeeze in two Budgets – a broadly neutral one on 24 March (income tax cuts were reversed and the reach of VAT extended) then a blatantly vote-buying one on 22 July – all creating a fleeting sense that real wages were rising sharply, greatly helped by the elaborate and inherently inflationary pay-board structure Labour had inherited from Heath. This was all profoundly dangerous for the Tories. They weren't going to win by citing economic theory: what they needed was popular policies.

Conservative number-crunchers estimated that around 1 million Tory voters from 1970 had defected to the Liberals in February, dwarfing the net 100,000 switching from Labour to the Tories. Over 40 per cent of Tory MPs now had a Liberal in second place, so, as Wilson pondered how to stem the SNP tide in his party's traditional heartlands, turning back the Liberal tide in England was a natural priority in Heath's mind. After his rejection at the hands of the electorate, things grew no easier for him personally, with the loss at sea in September of his boat *Morning Cloud*, resulting in the deaths of two crew members, one of whom, teenager Christopher Chadd, was Heath's godson and the son of his wartime commanding officer.

After the historic defeats of 1945 and 1964, the Conservative Party had launched full-scale reviews of its policies and its organisation. Although Heath had led the review of 1964–65 amid the dying embers of the Home leadership, in the summer of 1974, he had no interest in, or enthusiasm for, the exercise. He did, however, authorise Keith Joseph and Margaret Thatcher to set up the Centre for Policy Studies – a fateful decision indeed. Joseph had coveted the post of shadow Chancellor, but when that went to Robert Carr, he remained in the shadow Cabinet but without a portfolio. Now fully persuaded of the merits of monetarist economics, Joseph set about building an entirely new Tory philosophy. His principal ally among senior Tories was, of course, Margaret Thatcher.

Mrs Thatcher had been understandably disappointed to lose office as Education Secretary but relieved to be spared the indignity of shadowing it. She set about her new task shadowing environment and housing with characteristic assiduity and vim. She well knew her party's hopes of avoiding a debacle might rest on her, not an opportunity she was inclined to spurn. The problem was, Mrs Thatcher had been a firm believer in 'Selsdon Man' – the principles and policies that Heath put before the nation in 1970. She had gone along with EEC membership and Heath's economic and industrial U-turns in 1972, but she had also promised herself that she would never do the like again.

Now she was being charged with finding ways to buy votes by making extravagant promises to use taxpayers' money to reshape housing policy, effectively a continuation of the post-U-turn Heathite policies she was increasingly inclined to repudiate. Despite any misgivings, however, she did what she was asked to do, consoling herself with the thought that it would all serve the cause of increased home ownership – and she soon felt able to proclaim:

> For the first time in a long time, if you have not got a house, you can look forward to getting one ... I don't think we can honestly say we did get housing right last time we were in government, but this time we are determined that things shall be better.

Another immediate matter Mrs Thatcher had to address was widespread anger and pain in the country about extravagant increases in domestic rates, which seemed unsustainable. She suggested that teachers' salaries should be paid from central funds for a year and came under considerable pressure to pledge to abolish the rates altogether, but there wasn't time to come up with anything election-proof (interestingly, in light of what came to pass in the late 1980s, she indicated a preference for a system of finance that 'reflected the ability of people to pay', while eschewing a local income tax). In the Commons, she was rarely a match for Tony Crosland, but in the country, she was having an impact and developing a profile.

She cannily took full advantage of the publicity she was generating. In early June, the *Sunday Express* asked: 'Do you fall off your chair laughing at the thought of Mrs Thatcher becoming Tory leader?' The piece set out her credentials, as the 'one Opposition spokesman who carries real conviction in attack ... once dismissed as cold and imperious, [she] has impressed by the kindliness she shows to backbenchers'.

In my play *Maggie & Ted*, this episode is played out dramatically:

TED We must pledge to bring down the mortgage rate. Do something to help first-time buyers. I'll give the brief to Margaret.

TED'S PS Thatcher?

TED Yes. She's good with figures.

TED'S PS She's certainly loyal. The press even call her 'Mrs Heath'.

TED Ha! What will they think of next?

TED'S PS But she's never been in the front line before.

TED It's time she tried it.

TED [TO MAGGIE] We need policies that are specific and firm.

MAGGIE Ted, this is music to my ears.

TED We must do something for homeowners. Especially first-time buyers.

MAGGIE I agree. Too many people are trapped in social housing.

TED Could we offer to top up the deposits they've saved up?

MAGGIE I'll look into that.

TED And promise to do something about the mortgage rate?

MAGGIE Hmmm. I'll see what's possible.

MAGGIE'S PS [TO MAGGIE] This is madness – precisely the kind of intervention in the market to which you're vehemently opposed—

MAGGIE I know, but—

MAGGIE'S PS [TO MAGGIE] But?

MAGGIE But we're not going to win, so I shall never have to enact it – and this may help to minimise our defeat. And I should receive the credit.

TED Why don't we pledge to keep the mortgage rate below 10 per cent? Create some certainty.

MAGGIE The mortgage rate capped at *9.5 per cent*. It's the best I can offer.

TED By when?

MAGGIE Hmmm. By Christmas.

NEWSPAPER HEADLINE It's Santa Thatcher!

MAGGIE'S PS Labour were furious.

TONY CROSLAND It's Margaret's midsummer madness. I'm not

prepared to try and outbid Mrs Thatcher with irresponsible promises. This is the politics of bread and circuses.
MAGGIE [TO HER PS] I shall commit myself 100 per cent to this until the election is over. *Then* everything must change.

When the election was indeed called, for Thursday 10 October, after nearly a year of constant election-related activity, no one was surprised. The shortest parliament since 1681 had come to an end. The pollsters, desperate to redeem themselves after hopeless predictions in June 1970 and February 1974, were pretty consistently unanimous in suggesting Labour could hope for no more than a slender majority. It rang true and chimed with the parties' private soundings. The stability and certainty the nation supposedly craved was unlikely to be forthcoming. Wilson asked for a mandate to continue the good work he had already begun, while Heath sought to strike a note markedly different from the normal partisanship of politics. Within weeks of the February election, a number of Heath's closest advisers were recommending he should promote an appeal based on a concept of national unity. He had gradually become fully seduced by the transitory allure of this proposition. The seeds of Heath's downfall were being sown. Back to *Maggie & Ted*:

TED We need to reach out beyond the Conservative Party. Bring together all the men of goodwill.
MAGGIE [TO HER PS] What on Earth is he playing at? He's conceding before a shot has been fired. He never discussed any of this with us.
MAGGIE'S PS It is party policy now.
MAGGIE I don't care. I'm not putting any coalition nonsense into my election address to the voters of Finchley.
TED [TO MAGGIE] When you go on *Any Questions?* tomorrow night, it's essential that you support my call for a government of all the talents.
MAGGIE [ON *ANY QUESTIONS?*] I could never sit in a government with left-wingers such as Michael Foot or Mr Wedgwood Benn. Let me

be clear. Totally clear. *My* policies are firm, unshakeable promises. They are *not* negotiable.

The 'national unity' call never took flight. With a characteristic lack of self-awareness, Heath never realised he himself was perceived as the biggest single barrier to any kind of durable cross-party arrangement: he was arguably the most divisive figure of all. Many within his own party privately felt that, if only he would offer to make the 'supreme sacrifice' – offering to stand aside as leader in the event of another indecisive result – then the plan might work. Otherwise it was a dead rubber. As party chairman, Willie Whitelaw decisively crushed all disloyal talk and no one of note publicly challenged Heath's position; nor, to the best of my knowledge, did anyone approach him privately about it.

Towards the end of the campaign, there were rumours Heath would explicitly say that, if elected with a majority, he would then invite non-Tories to participate in government – and also, crucially, that he would be willing to stand down if that proved to be the necessary precondition for such an arrangement. He reacted testily to such talk: 'I am the leader of the Conservative Party.' The fact remained, however, that by this stage no one really knew what they were being asked to vote for, by Heath or by his party. If it was intended to be a 'new politics', it was poorly articulated.

The old bruiser Denis Healey brutally likened Heath to a wallflower standing in the corner of a ballroom wearing a placard proclaiming, 'I'll dance with any man in the House.' And Wilson decried 'a desperate attempt by desperate men to get back into power by any means ... Coalition would mean Con policies, Con leadership by a Con party for a Con trick.' While not especially fair, this attack was effective.

It was only in his final pre-poll message to Tory candidates that Heath first used the hitherto taboo 'C-word': 'I have no doubt that the real hope of the British people in this situation is that a national coalition government, involving all the parties, should be formed, and the party differences could be put aside until the crisis is mastered.' If he believed any of the other parties would concur to such an arrangement with him at its head, he was sadly deluded.

In stark contrast, in an eve-of-poll article in a national newspaper, Mrs Thatcher employed a tone and idiom the nation would come to know well: 'A Socialist state can come about by voting Labour or Liberal. It would be irreversible. The fight for freedom is one that knows no final victory. It has to be renewed daily by the actions and spirit of man.' Her eyes were evidently now set firmly beyond the imminent election, upon a different prize. A battle for the heart and soul of the party was about to be joined; and she would be no bit player.

In the event, there was a fairly even swing across the nation of just 2.2 per cent from Conservative to Labour. Labour did least well in Tory marginals and the result gave them a net gain of just eighteen seats – and a notional majority of three. The lingering independents, including former Labour MP Dick Taverne, the hero of Lincoln, were wiped out; and the Scottish and Welsh Nationalists made more, modest, gains. 'Of course the national outcome was a disappointment,' wrote Heath in his memoirs two decades later, 'but I was well prepared for it.' This had been, by all accounts, a dull campaign: the politics had mostly played out already and there was little, if anything, to excite by way of revelation or rhetoric. At the end of campaigning, a weary Harold Wilson even suggested that future campaigns should be cut in duration by a whole week.

As Wilson contemplated five more years in office, Heath blithely assumed he could carry on as leader, but the parliamentary Conservative Party had other ideas. There would be two immediate, obvious challengers – Keith Joseph and Edward du Cann, chairman of the backbench 1922 Committee. Scarcely a week after the October election, however, Joseph effectively ruled himself out with an unfortunate speech, in which he appeared to suggest that poor people had too many children; and du Cann then chose discretion over valour and stood aside. Faced with Heath's truculent refusal to submit to re-election, Colditz escapee Airey Neave and his ever-growing band of malcontents had to look elsewhere for a runner and rider, who was willing to challenge Heath directly and strike the mortal blow. They did not have to look for long.

In a post-election reshuffle, Heath rewarded Margaret Thatcher for her sterling campaign performance with the economic brief she craved, still not as shadow Chancellor but as Robert Carr's deputy, with a specific brief to challenge Labour's spending plans in the Commons. Heath either didn't know Mrs Thatcher was at the end of her tether with him and his works, or else he chose to ignore the fact. Just as Heath had fatefully done in 1964, she seized her economic role with extraordinary zeal and energy, setting about Denis Healey with a startling and rather beguiling absence of fear. What Heath certainly failed to appreciate was that he had now committed what, in the eyes of the Tory Party, has always been (and always will be) the greatest sin of all: he was a loser. Uniquely in the history of his party, he had lost three elections. Failure now clung to him and it was not a patina in whose baleful glow anyone else wished to dwell.

Just months before, Mrs Thatcher had been generally considered – not least by Heath himself – to be a loyal lieutenant, a competent second-tier performer with an annoying manner but a good eye for detail, who had overcome some stormy and less-than-impressive early months as a Cabinet minister to become a safe pair of hands. On that basis, it must have seemed perfectly natural for Heath to entrust to her a portfolio that seemed vitally important for a forthcoming election. It can never have occurred to him that he was helping to build the reputation of someone who would one day challenge him, then brutally displace him and, ultimately, eclipse him in the eyes of history.

A final excerpt from *Maggie & Ted* sets the scene for the sequence of events that would profoundly change our national narrative:

MAGGIE One of our lot has to stand and, if no one else will, then I will. Denis, I think I shall run for leader.
DENIS THATCHER Leader of what, dear?
MAGGIE The party, of course.
DENIS THATCHER You must be out of your mind. Heath will murder you.
MAGGIE I'd like to see him try. Denis, don't suck your teeth like that. You will support me?
DENIS THATCHER Naturally. Don't I always?

The policy U-turns of 1972 and the two ambiguous, ambivalent election results of 1974 had left Britain with the look of a seriously sick patient, desperately in need of medical intervention but still stubbornly unwilling to take its medicine. As Margaret Thatcher put it in her memoirs: 'There were many wishful thinkers who thought [economic collapse] might result in the Conservative party returning to power with a "doctor's mandate" – and Ted had no doubt of his own medical credentials.' Little did he know it but 'Doctor Heath' would soon be struck off. After five more years of crisis and drift, in May 1979, the patient would indeed be reconciled to its condition and reluctantly agree to radical and painful treatment. A very different chapter in our national history would then be written, by our first female Prime Minister.

Michael McManus is the author of *Edward Heath: A Singular Life* (Elliott & Thompson, 2016). His play *Party Games* tours the UK in 2024 and his award-nominated *Maggie & Ted* has its first full staging in 2025.

40

1979

SIMON HEFFER

Dissolution: 7 April 1979
Polling day: 3 May 1979
Seats contested: 635
Total electorate / Voted / Turnout: 41,095,649 / 31,221,362 / 76 per cent
Candidates (total 2,576): Labour – 623; Conservative – 622; Liberal – 577; National Front – 303; SNP – 71; Plaid Cymru – 36; Alliance – 12; UUP – 11; SDLP – 9; DUP – 5
Prime Minister on polling day: James Callaghan
Main party leaders: Labour – James Callaghan; Conservative – Margaret Thatcher; Liberal – David Steel; National Front – John Tyndall; SNP – William Wolfe; Plaid Cymru – Gwynfor Evans; UUP – Harry West; SDLP – Gerry Fitt; Alliance – Oliver Napier; DUP – Ian Paisley

Party performance:

Party	Votes	Percentage share	Seats
Conservative	13,697,923	43.9	339
Labour	11,532,218	36.9	269
Liberal	4,313,804	13.8	11
SNP	504,259	1.6	2
National Front	191,719	0.6	0
UUP	254,578	36.6	5
Plaid Cymru	132,544	0.4	2
SDLP	126,325	18.2	1
Alliance	82,892	11.9	0
DUP	70,795	10.2	3

Result: Conservative majority of forty-three seats

The four and a half years since Labour's paper-thin election victory in October 1974 were among the most turbulent in peacetime in the twentieth century. Within weeks of the Conservatives' defeat, the party, its MPs deeply disenchanted by the record and conduct of Edward Heath, had put pressure on him through the 1922 Committee to review the rules for electing a party leader and to stand for re-election. Heath was deeply opposed to being treated in that fashion; but if he wished to survive, he had no choice but to submit. He believed that with Enoch Powell out of the party and Keith Joseph having announced his intention not to seek the leadership, his internal opponents would not find a candidate capable of taking him on and winning. Until the point when she defeated him in the first ballot on 4 February 1975, he never believed Margaret Thatcher capable of being that person. She became leader a week later, defeating William Whitelaw by 146 votes to seventy-nine; one of the new rules was to enable candidates who had not stood in the first ballot to enter the second.

Joseph had stood aside because of a speech he made shortly after the October 1974 election about the prolific growth of the underclass, lampooned as 'pills for proles', which suggested (unfairly) that he lacked compassion for the less fortunate. He put himself behind Mrs Thatcher, with whom he had co-founded the Centre for Policy Studies. As soon as she became leader, she sought to unite her party by making Whitelaw her deputy. It was a crucial move: not only did Whitelaw, for whom regard in the party was immense, work assiduously to persuade those sceptical about the new leader that she should be supported; but as time went on, Mrs Thatcher leant increasingly on him for advice. The Conservatives had never deposed a leader in the way Heath had been removed, and the old saw about loyalty being the party's secret weapon came into play: many grass-roots members were shocked that the leader had not been allowed to go at a time of his own choosing, and required persuading otherwise. Whitelaw, assisted by Heath's truculent and at times infantile behaviour as a seriously bad loser, did much to change that initial perception. Joseph's role in her shadow Cabinet was to take charge of policy, and under his influence – and that of the Institute of Economic Affairs and, at one remove, the long-espoused monetarism of Powell – the Conservative Party began a steady progress towards what, a decade later, would be known as Thatcherism. Monetarism, in Powell's orthodoxy, was about control of the money supply in order to control inflation: something that was in the government's hands, and its hands alone. A policy document, 'The Right Approach', was published in October 1976 at the height of the Labour government's economic humiliation and prostration before the International Monetary Fund as Britain teetered on the verge of bankruptcy. It began to pave the way from the Heath years to a future that owed more to Gladstonian Liberalism, or to Powellism, than to any conventional garment from the Conservative wardrobe.

For the Labour government, victory proved to be but the beginning of a chronic struggle. It had inherited the legacy of the massive expansion of the money supply under the Heath administration in 1972–73, and by November 1975, inflation had reached 26.9 per cent. Denis Healey, the Chancellor, raised the top rate of income tax from 75 per cent to 83 per cent in his Budget in the spring of 1975, and he also raised the rate on investment income to 98 per cent. He had hoped the higher taxes would be sufficient to cover the cost of keeping his party's election promises to improve welfare provision; but Labour's spending plans would continue to advance beyond the ability to pay for them, especially as it became wedded to a programme of subsidies to cushion the effects of inflation. Although by early 1976, the country was slowly coming out of recession, inward investment slumped because of a loss of confidence in Britain's economic performance and because of penal taxation. Aside from economic turbulence, the government had had to keep its promise to hold a referendum on continued membership of the European Economic Community; the victory for those who wished to stay in, by two-thirds to a third, divided the Cabinet and the government and laid the foundations for the split in the Labour Party that would occur at the time of the birth of the Social Democratic Party in 1981. Also, the Irish Republican Army continued a relentless campaign of terror both in Ulster and on the British mainland.

The political world was stunned in March 1976 when, out of the blue and less than a week after his sixtieth birthday, Harold Wilson resigned as Prime Minister. He was succeeded by James Callaghan, the Foreign Secretary, who with the considerable support of the union movement defeated five other candidates to win the leadership. Callaghan embarked upon a premiership of relentless difficulty. After a brief period of political stability, the pound began to sink to a record low against the dollar, and in September 1976 the government was forced to ask the International Monetary Fund to rescue Britain's economy. The terms it set signalled the beginning of the end of the Labour government: it forced a real cut in public spending, which outraged the unions on which Callaghan had come to depend for his position. Labour's majority of three was quickly eroded by by-elections, forcing Callaghan to conclude a confidence and supply arrangement with the Liberal Party in March 1977. The Liberals had been led by David Steel since July 1976, following the resignation of Jeremy Thorpe who was awaiting criminal charges for the attempted murder of Norman Scott, his former lover. The party was in a state of near collapse and although Steel improved morale and organisation, the shadow of Thorpe would hang over the party until the election and eliminate the prospects of winning more seats.

Labour acquired a reputation during its period in government for developing an extremist faction at its grass roots, who wanted a more hard-core form of socialism – with further nationalisations (including of the banks), the abolition of private education, grammar schools and private healthcare, and nuclear disarmament. In several cases, the hard left – which found supporters in high places in the form of ministers such as Michael Foot and Tony Benn – infiltrated and took over the executives of constituency parties and proceeded to harry sitting MPs whom they considered insufficiently ideologically sound. One who fought a long battle with such people was Reg Prentice, whose Newham North-East party in east London had been taken over by

Trotskyists in the Militant Tendency. Prentice, who until 1975 had been Secretary of State for Education and from then until 1976 was Minister of State for Overseas Development, was deselected as the constituency's candidate. The party's national executive committee endorsed the deselection and ignored an appeal by Prentice at the 1976 party conference to reverse their decision – partly because the NEC had itself moved sharply to the left but also because of a reluctance to provoke Prentice's persecutors by being seen to interfere with local democracy. The following spring, Prentice defected from the Labour Party to the Conservatives, for whom he would successfully fight the Daventry seat in 1979: he was the most high-profile MP thus far to have left the party, but he would not be the last as it moved inexorably leftwards.

Labour had concluded what came to be known as the 'Social Contract' – of supposedly reasonably pitched pay deals in return for industrial peace – with the unions. However, this fell apart as the money ceased to be available to fund inflation-busting pay rises for an army of employees in the public sector, including the nationalised industries. Nor was it helped by unions being increasingly incapable of controlling unofficial strikes by the more militant of their brethren. The breakdown in relations between the government and the unions led to what became known as the Winter of Discontent in 1978–79, when a series of strikes paralysed local government and the public services.

The Lib-Lab pact had ended in August 1978, and the government depended on Ulster MPs and members of Nationalist parties for its majority in the Commons. Callaghan had been expected to call an election for early October 1978, but he used his party conference to say he would not do so: he sought to send the message by quoting a music-hall song which includes 'There was I, waiting at the church', with its pay-off 'Can't get away / To marry you today / My wife won't let me'. It was misinterpreted, and so he made a party political broadcast confirming there would be no election. Although the published polls put Labour, despite its record of failure, neck and neck with the Conservatives in November 1978, trailing them by just 1 per cent, at forty-two points to forty-three, Callaghan had had private polling data that looked worse for his party. He wrote in his memoirs that he was haunted by the 1959 election, when morale in the party had appeared high; but it lost heavily because many Tory voters had not forgotten Labour's part in the Suez debacle, which they considered unpatriotic. Callaghan feared that below the surface there was still deep distrust of the party over the 1976 IMF episode. He hoped the next phase of a prices and incomes policy would cause the economy to improve by the spring of 1979, thus restoring confidence in Labour's economic management. He decided the best day to go would be 5 April 1979, just over a week before Easter, though circumstances would push even that back. The delay turned out to be a fatal error.

Labour's pay policy was supposed to limit increases to 5 per cent. When it conceded a rise of 14 per cent to tanker drivers, the tsunami of union outrage and unofficial strikes gathered pace: everybody wanted well over 5 per cent, and throughout January and February 1979, one dispute after another broke out, mostly in the public sector. This winter of industrial strife seriously aggrieved the general public and showed that the Labour Party had lost any hope of controlling the actions of the unions. Its chances of victory at the election that had to come that year seemed to dwindle further. Gallup reported on 12 February that Labour was twenty points behind in the polls. In December 1978, Callaghan's personal approval ratings slipped below Mrs Thatcher's and only overtook her again during the campaign; sadly for him, his party never caught up.

Callaghan did not need to go to the country until October 1979, but the Winter of Discontent caused the government's standing in the opinion polls to slump. Callaghan did not help his party by disputing, in an interview on his return from the Guadeloupe summit in January 1979, the suggestion that a country with large number of workers on strike, the effects of which included the dead being unburied in parts of the country and piles of highly insanitary refuse piling up because of strikes by dustmen, was not perceived to be in 'chaos'. 'I don't think that other people in the world would share that view,' he said. *The Sun*'s headline the next day ridiculed him with:

'Crisis? What Crisis?' He never uttered the phrase, but it has immortalised him and symbolises why Labour lost in 1979. It inaugurated a ferocious campaign by most of Fleet Street (though not *The Times*, which missed reporting and commenting on the most important election campaign since the war because it was closed during a strike that lasted a year) against a government whose moral defeat was already obvious.

Mrs Thatcher made a dramatic, and in retrospect decisive, intervention in the campaign on 17 January 1979, as the industrial chaos became contagious and, to make matters worse, the thermometer fell and snow swept in from the east. That evening she made a party political broadcast, but she began, somewhat disingenuously, by saying:

> I don't propose to use the time to make party political points ... the crisis that our country faces is too serious for that. And it is our country, the whole nation, that faces this crisis, not just one party or even one government. This is no time to put party before country.

Demonstrating her determination to prove that she, unlike Callaghan, was in tune with the people, she said that things said to her in shopping centres and factories 'make me wonder what has happened to our sense of common nationhood and even of common humanity'. She branded strikes 'a weapon of first resort ... directed even at the sick and the disabled'. She attacked picketing 'that threatens to bring the country to its knees' and blamed Labour legislation for allowing a situation in which 'almost any determined group can strangle the country'. She continued: 'Some of our towns and cities, especially in the north and Midlands, [are] looking as though they are under siege ... export orders are locked in and food rots at the docks ... What we face is a threat to our whole way of life.' Mischievously, she said she understood why Labour could not control these forces – 'Without the unions there would be no Labour Party. Without union money there would be no Labour funds.' She urged Callaghan, out of patriotism, to agree to measures to end secondary picketing, to enforce democracy within unions and to create no-strike agreements in vital services – very much the industrial policy she would operate after her victory.

Her peroration was devastating. 'In a democracy, we choose, each one of us, what sort of society we want to live in. What sort of country do you want?' She concluded:

> We must first stop tearing ourselves apart ... There are wreckers among us who don't believe this. But the vast majority of us, and that includes the vast majority of trade unionists, do believe it ... We have to learn again to be one nation, or one day we shall be no nation.

That last phrase was borrowed from Powell. She had issued a fundamental challenge to Labour: govern in the interests of the country, or don't govern at all. It would quickly become clear that neither Callaghan nor any of his colleagues could begin to answer this assault on their record, but had to rely on stoking up fear of a radical brand of Conservatism if they were to avoid defeat when the election came.

Then Labour suffered another failure. On 1 March 1979, a referendum was held in Scotland to seek approval to enforce the provisions of the 1978 Scotland Act, which would allow devolution. A comparable poll was held in Wales. Although a simple majority of those Scots who voted narrowly supported devolution, the Act could be implemented only if those in favour constituted 40 per cent of the electorate; at barely 33 per cent it did not, and it was construed as a further defeat for the Labour government. The SNP, which had helped shore Labour up since the end of the Lib-Lab pact, now withdrew their support, and the party's majority was on a knife-edge. In Wales, the prospect of devolution was rejected even more strongly, by four votes to one. The Conservatives went in for the kill, bringing a vote of confidence, and on 28 March Labour lost, by 310 votes to 311. It was the first such defeat since Ramsay MacDonald's first Labour administration had been thrown out in October 1924. The key switch of support was that by Gerry Fitt, the leader of the Social Democratic and Labour Party in Northern Ireland, who abstained in the vote rather than back the government. His reasoning was that Labour's policy had been to further integration of Northern Ireland with the United Kingdom rather than pursue power-sharing, and he could not in conscience keep Labour in office. With the loss of the vote of confidence, there was no means to avoid an election. It was called for 3 May. Parliament was dissolved on 7 April and when nominations closed 2,576 candidates were contesting 635 seats.

Given the immediate background to the election, most in the Labour Party expected to lose it. Most in the Conservative Party expected to win, for the same reason: but there was tension within the party because of ideological battles that were barely beneath the surface. Since her election to the leadership four years earlier, Mrs Thatcher had taken trouble to include some of Heath's most fervent partisans in her shadow Cabinet, despite Heath himself being irredeemably hostile to her and her policies, and losing some of his own friends as a consequence. The Conservative manifesto was remarkably cautious compared with what would happen in the eleven and a half years of the Thatcher administration, and many in her shadow Cabinet, not least some of the veterans of the Heath Cabinet such as Sir Ian Gilmour, James Prior and Peter Walker, felt that a Conservative victory would leave room for debate about exactly in which direction a government led by Mrs Thatcher would take.

In the months before the election, Mrs Thatcher, her confidence increasing with experience of leadership, took an ever higher profile. She had undertaken extensive overseas tours, presenting herself as a Prime Minister-in-waiting; and in January 1976, long before reaching the election that would put her into power, she had attacked the Soviet Union in a speech, accusing it of being 'bent on world domination' and urging Britain to wake up to the threat to its way of life. Soviet commentators awarded her the sobriquet the 'Iron Lady' for expressing her opposition to communism and her determination to ensure her system prevailed over theirs. Labour had had little answer to her combativeness and her deep convictions, and after Callaghan had made his misjudgement of timing in October 1978, she abused him and his party as 'chickens'. However, a fissure was opening up in her party, for all its momentum. A group of MPs and shadow ministers who adhered to the philosophy espoused by Harold Macmillan and then adopted by Heath – which can be summed up as managing decline by means of an appeasement of organised labour through personal welfarism and corporate subsidy – began to express, in private, their discomfort at the monetarist policies of Mrs Thatcher that sought to ensure there was no decline to manage. Her internal opponents referred to themselves as 'one-nation Tories', after the pamphlet written by a group of high-profile new MPs following the 1950 election: it was a misleading title, since the intellectual powerhouse of that group, Enoch Powell, was effectively the man who taught Mrs Thatcher about monetarism. Mrs Thatcher and her allies referred to them as 'wets'. During the campaign itself, with so much at stake, they did not break ranks: that would come before too long.

On 30 March, two days after the vote of confidence, the *Daily Mirror* published a letter sent by Matthew Parris, who worked in the Conservative Research Department and dealt with Mrs Thatcher's correspondence from the public, that took a harsh tone towards a woman from Kent unhappy with her council house. 'You are lucky to have been given something, which the rest of us are paying for out of our taxes,' the letter had said. Parris had not referred this to Mrs Thatcher, who apologised profusely. Labour seized on the letter, made 3 million copies of the story and sent it to every council house in every marginal seat in Britain.

However, if that was a bad enough start to the campaign for the Conservatives, matters immediately became infinitely worse. Later that day, Airey Neave, one of Mrs Thatcher's closest confidants, the manager of her 1975 leadership campaign and thereafter the shadow Northern Ireland Secretary, was murdered by a car bomb planted in the Commons' underground car park by the Irish National Liberation Army. It blew up as he drove up the ramp out of Parliament. Neave, who had escaped from Colditz in 1942, had with Thatcher's support intended to step up the fight against terrorism in Northern Ireland. His death was, effectively, the first significant event of the campaign; and while deplored by the Labour Party, it hardened hearts on the Conservative side – notably Mrs Thatcher's – not just about how Irish republican terrorism should be handled but also about the sheer importance of winning the election.

The Conservatives' successful campaign was managed by Gordon Reece, who was Mrs Thatcher's publicity director. He had been a producer for ITN but had set up his own video company by the time of Heath's downfall and – having met Mrs Thatcher during earlier election campaigns – offered his services to her leadership team in early 1975. By 1979, he had altered her entire public persona. A voice that had seemed abrasive was modified by the same voice coach that Laurence Olivier had used and was lowered in register. Reece controlled who interviewed her to try to keep her away from people who might bring out her belligerence: that would have to wait until after she became Prime Minister. He knew how much she valued her Iron Lady image, but he also reasoned – apparently correctly – that her essential femininity would win supporters too: so he took pains to release images of her as a wife and mother, doing the washing up and being handy about the house. After all, half the electorate were women like her, and for the first time they were being offered a potential Prime Minister with whom they could more easily identify, which Reece hoped would break Labour's stranglehold on the working-class female vote. He prevailed in this strategy, but it was harder than it might have seemed: Mrs Thatcher had succeeded in an overwhelmingly masculine world only by adopting certain masculine traits, and she did not always find it easy to suppress them.

The election came to be remembered for the spectacularly successful, and memorable, innovatory American-style advertising campaign run by Saatchi and Saatchi on behalf of the Conservative Party. Reece had decided to hire them not least because of their reputation for creativity and aggression. Billboard campaigns had featured in elections for decades, but Saatchi's became famed for the level of slickness, wit and indeed cynicism that it revealed and was supplemented by film and television advertisements.

In a pre-digital age when billboard advertising was a crucial medium, Saatchis designed a poster with a long, snaking dole queue that simply read 'Labour Isn't Working'. It first ran in the autumn of

1978, in the expectation of Callaghan's calling an election, and was inspired by unemployment having, to the Labour government's immense embarrassment, gone over 1.5 million, the highest level since before the Second World War. At the bottom of the poster was the slogan 'Britain's better off with the Conservatives'. The poster caused immediate controversy because those depicted in it were not genuine unemployed people – though such a queue at an employment exchange would have been easy enough to find – but twenty members of the Hendon Young Conservatives, several photographs of whom were put together to create the overall image. Denis Healey described the advertising campaign as 'selling politics like soap powder'. Saatchis, and the Conservative Party, couldn't have cared less.

Once the election was called, the poster was refreshed with the slogan 'Labour Still Isn't Working'. If there was a turning point in the campaign, it was the relaunch of this penetrating advertisement, which helped cast Labour as the underdog, established the agenda on which they would have no choice but to fight, and as such left them increasingly helpless throughout a campaign in which the Conservatives concentrated on the outgoing administration's utter incompetence and the ruination it had brought upon the country – chaos that was at the front of everyone's memories, and an echo of the 17 January party political broadcast.

Lord Thorneycroft, the Conservative Party chairman, felt the poster won the election for his party. He was probably right: the impact, in the context of Labour having pledged in 1974 to reduce unemployment, was profound. It was almost certainly as significant that the poster reminded the electorate of all the other promises that had not been kept, including the failure of the Social Contract and Labour's ability to control the unions. The poster was a key part of the Conservative strategy of indicating Labour's inability to govern and to keep the main promises it made to the electorate. Given the importance of voters being able to trust the party to which they gave their support, this was a crucial message.

Mrs Thatcher and her team knew that there would be no second chance for her to become Prime Minister. Reece sought maximum exposure of her as leader while allowing her near journalists' questions as rarely as was feasible: the campaign was designed explicitly for the media, but it engaged the public as the means to give the media interesting things to broadcast, project and write about. Accompanied by her husband Denis, and on board her battle bus – another slick development in campaigning that other parties would quickly imitate – she toured the country, especially marginal seats, to undertake walkabouts and, inevitably, to create appealing photo opportunities. One of the most notable was of her cradling a calf – Maggie the Charolais – at a cattle farm in Suffolk. She defended vigorously what appeared to be a publicity stunt as being part of a visit to learn about what farmers needed, and not just a photo opportunity. There were also trips to factories and workshops, with her always attired in the right clothing and protective gear, and to supermarkets, where like any 1970s housewife she was seen with her shopping basket. Callaghan had decided to have a five-week campaign (in which he kept a lower profile, not least because he was still concerned with important affairs of state) and not the minimum three weeks because he believed Mrs Thatcher had presentational weaknesses that would turn against her, and the longer the exposure she had the worse she would implode. Again, and even though his personal popularity overtook hers, it was an alarming misjudgement.

For the first time in an election campaign, the Conservatives took slots in cinema advertising breaks (the party was far better funded by big business than the trade union-backed Labour Party) and ran advertisements showing Britain as decaying, depressed, dismal and beset by inflation and dole queues. Although, as the campaign went on, the novelty of the advertisements wore off, and some were accused of being too clever by half – always a cardinal sin in the Conservative Party – Labour, campaigning very much in a fashion that would have been familiar to Attlee in 1935 or 1945, could find nothing to match it.

When Labour launched its campaign, it became apparent that there were no new big ideas, or indeed any new ideas at all. As in previous elections, it relied on proclaiming its support for full employment and for a strong National Health Service; promises that seemed hollow in the context of the rise in joblessness during the preceding years and the cuts to the public services enforced by the IMF's order for reduced spending. When the party's manifesto, 'The Labour Way is the Better Way', appeared on 5 April, it outlined five priorities: the control of inflation, a new industrial relations strategy (one had been provisionally discussed and settled with the unions, despite the Winter of Discontent) and a renewed promise to create jobs. The fourth and fifth priorities appeared exceptionally optimistic: to 'enlarge people's freedom' and to use the country's influence to strengthen world peace and reduce world poverty. How exactly these remarkable feats would be carried out by a party committed to state control, excruciatingly high taxation and whose international standing had sunk during the preceding years would never become clear.

Its only means of taking on the Conservatives, after the debacle over which Labour had presided in the preceding months, was by trying to provoke the fear that the country would be even worse off if Mrs Thatcher were given power. Callaghan and Healey argued that the proposed tax cuts for higher earners would drive up prices and leave the poor worse off. The Labour manifesto said that the Conservatives 'are ready to gamble the people's future on a return to the nineteenth-century free market – despite its pitiless social consequences'. It was a remarkably ahistorical point: the creation of free trade in 1846 after the repeal of the Corn Laws had initiated twenty-seven consecutive years of economic growth, the Factories Acts had improved working conditions, massive slum clearances had begun in the 1870s, a new middle class was established, education became more widely available and Britain had never been so prosperous nor, since Tudor times, had there been such social mobility. To threaten a return to such a dynamic system was typical of Labour's cack-handed approach to its campaign. Such claims helped erode an already shattered credibility, which was what would underpin their defeat. They promised reductions in taxation for the lower paid, only to meet private polling evidence that the electorate trusted the Conservatives far more on taxes than it did the Labour Party.

The Conservatives focused on marginal seats, and especially on voters who had previously supported Labour but had cause to feel let down by them. They also chose to target first-time voters whose first years of political consciousness had been a nation beset by strikes, under-investment and near bankruptcy. They chose two main points of attack: the control of inflation and the bringing to heel of the trade unions after their period as over-mighty subjects. Both resonated with the electorate, but especially the second, given the privations and inconveniences so many voters had endured during the Winter of Discontent – and for which they found Callaghan, at the time, loath to take any responsibility. And there were other key aspects of the Tory manifesto that chimed with the public mood, too: the party's belief in parliamentary democracy and the rule of law was another means of attacking the trade unions' belief that they could behave largely as they wished; the manifesto also promised 'to restore incentives so that hard work pays', to create new jobs in the private sector and to reward success by ending an expropriatory tax system for the higher earners. However, at Reece's insistence, no specific promises on taxation were made and no commitments given. The post-election restructuring of taxation that would include a near-doubling of VAT in order to cut the rates of income tax was not made clear even to Sir Geoffrey Howe, the putative Chancellor.

The Conservatives also emphasised their belief in the family, not least by reorientating a welfare system that in Mrs Thatcher's view had come to cushion people who preferred not to work, or preferred not to take responsibility for their families, and instead focusing the state's largesse on those who through age, infirmity or other unavoidable obstacles could not help themselves. That was the stick: the carrot was encouraging home ownership through what became known as the 'right to buy' and promising to improve the education system.

Mrs Thatcher launched her party's campaign in Cardiff, the city that housed Callaghan's constituency, and appealed directly to Labour's voters to switch to support her, on the grounds that Labour was an extreme party. Given her convictions about free market economics, her views about a traditional party were undoubtedly sincere: and she had been briefed about the growing factionalism within the party. It would become more 'extreme' yet. Her personal sights were set on the aspirational skilled working class, and as a grammar-school girl herself (albeit one who had been to Oxford and was married to a rich businessman), she had an implicit understanding of their way of life and ambitions.

Shortly after the election was called, the former Labour MP Brian Walden, who presented the Sunday political programme *Weekend World*, suggested to Callaghan that he and Mrs Thatcher take part in two televised debates that Walden would chair; this would have been the first time such a thing had happened in Britain. The Liberal Party expressed outrage that David Steel, as their leader, had not been invited. The party was feeling vulnerable as it was tarred with the brush of having shored up an increasingly unpopular government for two of its last three years, and because of the publicity surrounding the charging the previous November of its ex-leader, Jeremy Thorpe, with the attempted murder of Norman Scott: the trial was scheduled to begin on the Tuesday after the election. In the event, it was agreed to include in the televised debates Steel, and Callaghan was happy to take part, but Mrs Thatcher, on Reece's strong advice, declined the offer, arguing that the election was about choosing a government, not a President. In fact, Reece was sure Callaghan would come over as more reasonable than she would in such a discussion.

Early in the campaign, Callaghan made a party election broadcast that foretold, accurately, the result of a Conservative victory: 'The question you will have to consider,' he warned the country, 'is whether we risk tearing everything up by the roots.' History has come to recognise that the watershed nature of the 1979 election was precisely because the Conservatives were determined – however vaguely the prospective transformation was detailed in the manifesto – to break the consensus between the government, the management class and the working class that had pertained since 1945. Callaghan saw the possibility of the breach with this precedent more clearly than most and in that, at least, he was proved right. He would warn, later in the campaign, that the Conservatives would not contemplate using public money to shore up failing businesses to preserve jobs, and therefore unemployment would mount. That prediction, too, was correct: the Thatcher administration would see no merit in throwing good money after bad.

As the campaign went on, the Conservatives' lead in the polls narrowed from the hefty 20 per cent at the depths of the Winter of Discontent; and by the week before polling day, Mrs Thatcher's personal standing was below that of her party. On 27 April, the Conservative opinion poll lead was just 3 per cent; a *Daily Mail* poll not published until 30 April, but taken a week earlier and perhaps suppressed, showed the lead at just 0.7 per cent. But Labour could still not claw back an overall advantage. The apparent hopelessness of the predicament was summed up by the *Private Eye* cover just before the election: it was a picture of Callaghan and his two small granddaughters coming out of a church, with one girl observing: 'I didn't know Grandpa believed in God.' The other says, 'Once every five years he does.'

In an age before digital media, and with only three television channels, national and big regional newspapers exerted great influence on the outcome of the campaign. Only *The Guardian* and the *Daily Mirror* overtly supported the Labour Party; the rest of the mainstream national press backed the Conservatives. *The Sun* had a particularly powerful impact: it had a substantial working-class readership, and one highly susceptible to the promises made by the Conservatives to extend economic enfranchisement, not least through the opportunity to buy council houses. Callaghan had understood the old industrial working class; but there was little grasp in his party of the aspirations of those living in more prosperous areas, especially in and around Greater London. *The Sun* drove this new message home not least by recruiting a group of former Labour ministers, including the ex-deputy leader Lord George-Brown, Lord Chalfont, Alf Robens, Richard Marsh and Reg Prentice, to write in their editorial columns about the importance of supporting the Conservatives. On polling day, *The Sun*'s headline was 'Vote Tory This Time: It's the Only Way to Stop the Rot'. After the Parris letter, the *Daily Mail* facilitated the only other major gaffe of the campaign. It interviewed Sir Harold Wilson, who conceded that his wife might well vote for the Conservatives because they were led by a woman. Privately, Wilson's former aide Lady Falkender had indicated that she wanted to help Mrs Thatcher win.

Towards the end, there were moments of panic in Central Office – some prompted by polls, others by a rare poor performance at the daily press conference by the leader (an institution that Reece had wished to abandon, but she had refused), but also by dissatisfaction with Howe as a charisma-free spokesman on economic affairs. However, Callaghan told his closest aide, Bernard Donoughue, a week before polling day that there was a sea change in the air, and the people wanted Mrs Thatcher. He was right. When the results were all counted by the afternoon of 4 May, it transpired that the Conservatives had won 43.9 per cent of the vote, had seventy seats more than Labour and a majority over all other parties of forty-three. Their election also secured the appointment of the first female Prime Minister in British history. Ironically, this happened after a contest that had included the election of a total of just nineteen female MPs, compared with twenty-seven in October 1974. The swing to the Conservatives of 5.2 per cent was the highest between the parties since the Attlee landslide of 1945. The Labour Party was driven back to its industrial heartland; the Conservatives, buoyed by the promise to allow council tenants to buy their houses at a discount, won from Labour new towns such as Basildon and Stevenage, where Shirley Williams lost her seat. One legacy of the election was the move towards what came to be known as a 'north-south divide', with Labour predominating in the former and the Conservatives in the more populous latter.

Mrs Thatcher went to see Queen Elizabeth II on the afternoon of 4 May 1979 and on the steps of 10 Downing Street directly afterwards quoted some words attributed to St Francis of Assisi: 'Where there is discord, may we bring harmony. Where there is error, may we bring truth. Where there is doubt, may we bring faith. And where there is despair, may we bring hope.' Her key allies in government, Parliament and, perhaps most important, Fleet Street then began the fight against her internal enemies to fulfil her free market, socially conservative and unashamedly nationalist vision of Britain. The administration embarked on a ferociously energetic programme, her ministers mostly following her example of industry. As she also said outside Downing Street, 'in the words of Airey Neave, whom we had hoped to bring here with us, "There is now work to be done."'

Labour retained Callaghan as leader until the autumn of 1980; but with their defeat came a fierce internal debate in the party, with an increasingly prevalent view that the party had lost because it had not been socialist enough. This was the heyday of Michael Foot and Tony Benn, and it was Foot who succeeded Callaghan when the former Prime Minister finally resigned. The view that the party needed to be more socialist prevailed, resulting in a manifesto in 1983 that Gerald Kaufman described as 'the longest suicide note in history' and a far more crushing defeat than suffered in 1979. The two minor parties in Great Britain that had contributed to the shoring up of the Callaghan administration – the Liberals and the Scottish National Party – also saw their support fall. For the SNP, the outcome was near catastrophic: it lost nine of the seats it held at the time the election was called, being left with only two, the same number as Plaid Cymru. Where they were concerned, Callaghan had, for once, the last laugh. When MPs from those parties refused to back Labour in the vote of confidence, he observed: 'It is the first time in recorded history that turkeys have been known to vote for an early Christmas.'

Oddly enough, one of the key points of interest once Mrs Thatcher had won was whether she would offer her predecessor, Heath, a place in her administration. She was keen to unite the party: but his behaviour towards her since 1975 had been so brusque, rude and offensive that the notion of the two of them sitting around the same Cabinet table again was impossible, especially with Heath in a subordinate position. She offered him the Washington embassy – an amusing gesture for a woman credited with little or no sense of humour, given Heath's incipient anti-Americanism and desire to be involved with European politics – and he, unsurprisingly, turned it down, as he did the prospect of becoming secretary-general of NATO.

Her Cabinet appointments were mostly predictable, following on in many cases from the shadow portfolios her colleagues had held.

In the key jobs, Howe became Chancellor, Lord Carrington Foreign Secretary – despite criticism that, as a peer, he could not answer to the House of Commons – and the conspicuously loyal Whitelaw, who showed the sort of abundant grace Heath lacked, went to the Home Office. Mrs Thatcher was keen to show continuity with the party's past, even if her policy programme indicated a departure from the minimal ideology of Conservatism in the preceding decades. Lord Hailsham, a veteran of the Macmillan and Heath years, returned as Lord Chancellor; and Lord Soames, who had also served under Macmillan and was, perhaps more to the point, Sir Winston Churchill's son-in-law, became Leader of the House of Lords.

Many of her other Cabinet colleagues were not merely veterans of the Heath years but retained a degree of personal loyalty to her predecessor and to his ideas: Sir Ian Gilmour (Lord Privy Seal), Peter Walker (Minister of Agriculture), Norman St John-Stevas (Leader of the Commons), James Prior (Employment Secretary) and Michael Heseltine (Environment Secretary) all fell into that category. All in some degree would cause her trouble. Other than Keith Joseph, who became Industry Secretary with the crucial brief to prepare the nationalised industries for privatisation by bringing in management from the private sector, the only Powellite or monetarist ministers (the term Thatcherite had yet fully to come into usage) were John Biffen, the Chief Secretary to the Treasury, Angus Maude, the Paymaster General, and John Nott, the Trade Secretary. The balance would change, though not unduly radically, before the 1983 election.

It rapidly became clear – after Howe's first Budget and the government's determination both that the country should no longer live beyond its means and that elected government, and not unelected trade unions, should control the country's destiny – that the United Kingdom had witnessed not merely a change of leadership but a change of epoch.

Simon Heffer is professor of modern British history at the University of Buckingham and a columnist for the *Daily* and *Sunday Telegraph*. His most recent book is *Sing As We Go: Britain Between the Wars* (Hutchinson Heinemann, 2023).

41

1983

PETER SNOW

Dissolution: 13 May 1983
Polling day: 9 June 1983
Seats contested: 650
Total electorate / Voted / Turnout: 42,192,999 / 30,671,137 / 72.7 per cent
Candidates (total 2,578): SDP–Liberal Alliance – 636; Conservative – 633; Labour – 633; SNP – 72; Plaid Cymru – 38; SDLP – 17; UUP – 16; DUP – 14; Sinn Féin – 14; Alliance – 12
Prime Minister on polling day: Margaret Thatcher
Main Party leaders: Conservative – Margaret Thatcher; Labour – Michael Foot; SDP–Liberal Alliance – Roy Jenkins and David Steel; SNP – Gordon Wilson; UUP – James Molyneaux; SDLP – John Hume; Plaid Cymru – Dafydd Wigley; DUP – Ian Paisley; Sinn Féin – Ruairí Ó Brádaigh; Alliance – Oliver Napier

Party performance:

Party	Votes	Percentage share	Seats
Conservative	13,012,316	42.4	397
Labour	8,456,934	27.6	209
SDP–Liberal Alliance	7,794,770	25.4	23
SNP	331,975	1.1	2
UUP	259,952	34	11
DUP	152,749	20	3
SDLP	137,012	17.9	1

Plaid Cymru	125,309	0.4	2
Sinn Féin	102,701	13.4	1
Alliance	61,275	8	0

Result: Conservative majority of 144 seats

Few elections have followed a period of such fracture in the country's political fabric as the election of 1983. The only constant was the towering personality and jarring self-belief of Margaret Thatcher – traits that for a time threatened to destroy her and her government but ended in her winning the largest majority in forty years.

The spectacular Conservative win in the early summer of 1983 was the last of a series of startling shocks. The three main political parties had spent the early years of Mrs Thatcher's first Conservative government on a rollercoaster of volatile public opinion that settled down only in the aftermath of the Falklands War. For a time, it appeared that a political revolution was taking place. The Labour Party plunged into a disastrous internal civil war prompted by a sharp shift to the left. Its election of the unpopular socialist Michael Foot as its leader was part of an upheaval that led to the desertion of a 'gang' of more moderate Labour celebrities. For a midterm moment, a brand-new centrist party, Alliance – a star-studded bandwagon of social democrats and liberals – looked to be attracting a majority of voters. The country appeared on the brink of a unique electoral breakthrough. But on 2 April 1982, Argentina invaded the Falklands. Thatcher's victory in the South Atlantic made her impregnable at the election she called only twelve months later. Her own leadership and her party, which had earlier sunk in the polls to a catastrophic low, dramatically recovered and emerged with the largest majority of seats since the Second World War.

They were four turbulent years in the world of politics. After her 1979 triumph as the first woman to win the premiership, the honeymoon was short-lived. Her fierce monetary grip soon shattered the surge of popular support that had swept her to power and lost her the admiration of some of her own Cabinet. In order to cure Britain's severe economic malaise, she was determined, unashamedly, to shift the country to the right, to squeeze inflation, to shake out unproductive jobs and weaken the grip of the trade unions on the economy. 'The two great problems of the British economy', she said, 'are the monopoly nationalised industries and the monopoly trade unions.' The result was soaring unemployment. It beat all recent records, rising to a record of over 11 per cent in four years. She cut income tax but doubled the more regressive value added tax. She also moved fast to cut public spending.

Within two years, her own rating in the public opinion polls was hitting records for unpopularity. Few Prime Ministers have been as heartily loathed as Mrs Thatcher was at that time. Newspapers and broadcasting were full of distressing stories of deprivation and broken businesses. Moreover, her forthright and single-minded dominance of her colleagues soon alienated some of the more old-fashioned and more liberally inclined Tories. Her employment secretary James Prior said he 'found it very difficult to stomach'. She always thought she knew best and boasted: 'Deep in their instincts, people find what I am saying and doing right.' The word 'consensus' was not in her vocabulary. She once told Sir Anthony Parsons, one of her leading diplomats, 'I regard people who believe in consensus politics as quislings and traitors.'

The year of 1981 was a critical one. Britain's growth was down by 5.5 per cent, and 2.7 million were jobless. Yet the Prime Minister ignored calls from 364 leading economists and even from some so-called 'wets' within her own Cabinet to ease her economic clampdown. The spring Budget saw a further tightening, income tax thresholds frozen, beer and cigarettes up. A number of Conservatives walked out of the Commons during the Budget speech. Mrs Thatcher was convinced that this tough line was necessary, though as she walked into the Commons to hear the Budget speech, she confided to her economic adviser Alan Walters: 'You know, Alan, they may want to get rid of me for this. At least I shall have gone knowing I did the right thing.' The certitude with which she conducted herself and the direction of her policies brought some of her Cabinet ministers close to staging a coup against her. It fizzled out, and James Prior and Ian Gilmour, her Lord Privy Seal, later regretted they didn't resign at the time.

But the Conservative government's leadership and policy problems were a pale shadow of the commotion taking place on the opposition benches. After its defeat in 1979, following five years of uninspired government, Labour descended into a convulsive internal dispute about policy and party democracy. Membership had declined and the driving enthusiasm for party reform came mainly from the left. The battle, which reached visceral intensity, arose from the clamorous demands of activists at the party conference to curb the power of its members of Parliament. The party was soon torn three ways by rows between politicians like Denis Healey on the moderate right, the so-called soft left under the new leader Michael Foot and the hard left under Tony Benn. The outcome made most Labour supporters bewildered and steered the party sharply to the left. The increasingly powerful Labour Party conference voted for nuclear disarmament, nationalisation and withdrawal from the European Economic Community. By the middle of 1981, Labour's support had followed the Tory plunge to a near all-time low.

The collapse of the two main parties left a gaping hole in the centre – an opportunity seized by four Labour moderates, who famously abandoned the party disgusted by its swerve to the left. The retiring European Commission president and former Labour deputy leader Roy Jenkins, who had earlier called for a new 'radical centre party', inspired Labour stalwarts Shirley Williams, William Rodgers and David Owen to join him in creating the Social Democratic Party. They agreed an 'Alliance' with David Steel's Liberal Party and within a year, twenty-nine Labour MPs and one Conservative joined the rebels. By-election wins for Jenkins and Williams and a surge in the Alliance's poll rating appeared to promise a breakthrough in the centre.

Towards the end of 1981, most workers were paying a higher proportion of earnings in tax and national insurance than in 1979. Thatcher's popularity as PM was down to 23 per cent... as unpopular as any premier since polling had started. But rather than react to this and to the mutterings in her party and even in her Cabinet by softening her stance, Thatcher doubled down. She sacked or demoted 'wets' in her Cabinet and pressed on. She relished the nickname Tina ('There is no alternative') that had followed her defiant speech a year earlier in which she had said, 'You turn if you want to… the lady's not for turning.'

There was, even so, a strong current within the Tory Party and across the electorate which admired her chutzpah and the ferocity of her dealings with the EEC. Cartoonists had her waving her handbag like a cudgel, demanding and winning a reduction in Britain's financial contribution. As she approached her third year in power, there were signs that the economy was past its worst. But these were small shoots in a pretty barren field. In the Budget debate in 1982, Michael Foot was able to point his finger at Britain's 'unemployment catastrophe'. And in a useful boost to the new centre party, Roy Jenkins triumphed in a by-election in Glasgow Hillhead, a seat the Tories had held since 1918. Gallup showed the Tories below 20 per cent in the polls in March 1982.

But a week after Hillhead, on 2 April, Argentina invaded the Falklands. There followed two months of nail-biting tension as Thatcher sent a task force 8,000 miles south, defiantly sweeping aside all attempts to persuade her to compromise. Defeat would have seen the collapse of her government. Kenneth Clarke was one of the few ministers who dared ask her if 'we weren't taking a terrible risk? She strode over to me and jabbed me firmly in the chest saying, "Politics is about taking risks you know, my dear boy."' Her determined pursuit of a perilously risky military solution and her utter joy when the Union flag was raised again at Port Stanley's Government House left Thatcher bathed in political glory. Some urged an early election she was perfectly entitled to call, though she still had two more years to run.

The Falklands immensely enhanced Thatcher's international reputation. She had long been dubbed the Iron Lady and she made it her business to show she would play her part in working to win the Cold War against the Soviet Union. In the autumn of 1982, she visited the Berlin Wall for the first time. Her eyes filled with tears as she said,

'It's even worse than I imagined.' She went on to predict, 'One day, liberty will dawn on the other side of it.' Three years in No. 10 meant she had now been in power longer than all her international counterparts – President Reagan in the USA, Helmut Kohl in Germany and François Mitterrand in France – all only recently elected. When she risked spending a day or two in the middle of her campaign in 1983 flying to Williamsburg in the USA for a summit, she was greeted with a kiss by President Reagan, who told her he hoped she would be re-elected.

Remarkably, an early election victory was not what many Conservatives – even Thatcher – expected. The economic prospects, though brighter, still looked uncertain – unemployment by the end of 1982 was near 11 per cent. Embarrassingly, proposals for a very radical right-wing shift in government policy were leaked from a paper by the Central Policy Review Staff. It suggested that state funding for higher education should be abolished and the NHS replaced by private health insurance. The ideas were rapidly shelved. But in her memoirs, Mrs Thatcher admitted 'we were to be plagued by talk of secret proposals and hidden manifestos up to polling day. It was the greatest nonsense.'

There was talk of an election in October 1982 and not just in order to cash in on the Falklands. There were other things swinging Thatcher's way such as her Environment Secretary Michael Heseltine's popular sale of council houses and a few more signs of an uptick in the economy. But an October election would have looked highly opportunistic coming twenty months before it had to be called. Thatcher had little hesitation in deciding against going that early. Besides, it would have interrupted the Boundary Commission report which was likely to give the Tories around thirty extra seats. Another political hazard in the aftermath of the Falklands was the work of the Franks Committee that was examining whether government complacency had helped lead to the war that cost 255 British lives. Thatcher was mighty relieved in January 1983 when Franks absolved the government of any blame. That was one more worry out of the way, and as the days got warmer, election fever was in all the headlines.

To most political pundits, the Tories would have a spring election in the bag, but Thatcher was still reluctant about calling it a year earlier than she had to. She told Ferdinand Mount, her lead election planner, 'If we lose it, we lose it all.' And Cecil Parkinson, the Tory Party chairman, recalled, 'She knew this was a massive decision and that she alone was responsible.' Her preference was to hold on until October 1983. The Conservatives also had wary eyes on the Lib–SDP Alliance. Simon Hughes had won a spectacular victory in the Bermondsey by-election in February '83. It looked as if this might be followed by an Alliance victory in the normally safe Labour seat of Darlington. The Tory fear was that defeat in such a stronghold could prompt the Labour Party to strip the leadership from Michael Foot, whose extreme views the Tories counted on to win Thatcher the election. When Labour won the Darlington by-election, Conservative Central Office heaved a sigh of relief.

The opposition, for its part, was alarmed at the prospect of a spring election. Denis Healey, Labour's deputy leader, had a go at Thatcher in the Commons, accusing her of being ready to 'cut and run'. She shot back that Healey was obviously 'frit' – afraid of a Labour defeat.

Favourable local election results on 5 May edged Thatcher a little closer to naming the day, but even a get together of her top team at Chequers three days later wasn't enough to persuade her to commit. She confessed she still had 'some lingering doubts: I needed some convincing'. She even offered the excuse that the Queen was too busy to see her. One of her ministers deftly snuck off, telephoned the palace and returned to tell the PM that the Queen was very ready to see her anytime. She still refused saying, 'It's always best to sleep on these things.' This was too much for her husband Denis. Ferdinand Mount tells us that Denis was blunt: 'You can't do that, Margaret. They've all gone back to town saying it's going to be the 9th. You can't go back on that now.' So she gave in: 9 June it was.

The month-long campaign saw the Conservatives steadily on top, revelling in Thatcher's self-assured command. Labour was a near disaster, flailing in the polls on leadership and policy; the Alliance was fighting for second place but making disappointing progress with only a brief surge in the last week. The opening poll ratings showed the Conservatives with around 45 per cent support, Labour in the low thirties and the Alliance on around 20 per cent. On average, the Tories enjoyed a poll lead of around 15 per cent over Labour. A Harris poll put them 21 per cent ahead.

The Conservative manifesto was prepared by Ferdinand Mount and Adam Ridley under the overall command of Geoffrey Howe, the Chancellor of the Exchequer. It was unadventurous. Its main promises were to abolish the Greater London Council, to give trade union members the right to secret ballots and to add British Airways and Rolls-Royce to British Telecom as candidates for privatisation. There was little sign of the right-wing dreams of the party's more strident members. Thatcher later wrote it was 'not an exciting document', she was 'somewhat disappointed' by it and 'perhaps Geoffrey Howe was too safe a pair of hands'. She wished she'd taken a stronger role in drawing up the manifesto. 'I decided', she wrote in her memoirs, 'to oversee the preparation of the [next] 1987 manifesto myself.' All the same, she admitted it was probably wise to issue a 'tame' manifesto in order to concentrate on 'exposing Labour's wildness'. She made up for the document's blandness with her own pronouncement that the election was 'a chance to banish from our land the dark divisive clouds of Marxist socialism'.

The Tories' campaign strategy was to make a meal of Labour's manifesto: unilateral nuclear disarmament, the end of the council house sales, industries nationalised and withdrawal from the European Community. Labour's own Gerald Kaufman described it as the 'longest suicide note in history'. Thatcher saw it as a gift. She quoted delightedly from it throughout the campaign. She was exuberant at the press conference that launched her campaign and, typically, took the lead even when one of her ministers was speaking. She freely interrupted the always soft-spoken Geoffrey Howe and when the unfortunate Foreign Secretary Francis Pym talked of having further conversations with Argentina, she broke in saying, 'No! I'm sorry,' indicating that she thought the press might believe Britain was ready to make concessions. Pym also infuriated Mrs Thatcher by telling a

BBC audience that 'landslides on the whole don't produce successful governments', which was taken to mean he didn't want a large Conservative majority. Pym was not to last long in office after the election.

Coverage of Thatcher's daily press conferences was on the whole favourable. She was blatantly arrogant in her self-confident delivery and utterly in command of the detail. After the morning conferences, the Prime Minister was flown off deep into the country – not so much to make speeches as to be seen in carefully choreographed press photographs. But she couldn't resist mixing with people and responding to hecklers. After one election rally, she reported in her memoirs with typical self-satisfaction that someone noticed a cinema sign behind her advertising a film called *The Missionary*.

On a visit to a garden in Cornwall, a *Daily Mail* photographer asked Thatcher to pick a handful of grass off a newly mown lawn. The following day's caption read 'Let them eat grass'. She remarked wryly that 'it doesn't do to be too co-operative'.

The Tories had summoned the former producer Gordon Reece from the United States to advise on how to handle television appearances during the campaign. He suggested that Thatcher should engage in debates with Michael Foot and separately with the Alliance leaders. 'I rejected the idea,' she later wrote, 'I disliked the way that elections were turned into media circuses.'

All the party leaders had to face TV interviews and Mrs Thatcher found the BBC's Sir Robin Day the 'most aggressive': she certainly didn't win him over by continually calling him 'Mr Day'. He had no hard feelings and graciously described her campaign interviews as 'overpowering and virtually unstoppable'.

There were some Conservative organisers who feared that 'too much Thatcher' and her shrill voice might put voters off, but by the end of the campaign such worries had vanished and she was featured freely in Tory advertising. The Conservative advertising campaign was managed efficiently by Saatchi and Saatchi under the eagle eye of the Tory chairman and Thatcher favourite Cecil Parkinson. Two major upsets occurred when the Tories decided to give comedian Kenny

Everett star billing at their Wembley youth rally four days before polling day. He provoked a chorus of public opprobrium by urging his audience to 'bomb Russia' and to 'kick Michael Foot's stick away'. A large part of the young Tory audience howled its approval, but the wider public were unimpressed.

The other awkward moment came in a BBC *Nationwide* television programme when the Prime Minister was confronted by a Mrs Diana Gould who asked why she had felt it necessary to sink the Argentine cruiser *Belgrano*. It was a classic case of an ordinary member of the public challenging a political leader without a trace of the deference of a professional broadcaster. It was electrifying stuff. The *Belgrano* was 'sailing AWAY from the Falklands', said Mrs Gould. 'But it was NOT sailing away from the Falklands,' said Mrs T. Mrs Gould was having none of it. She continued to insist that the *Belgrano* was sailing away from the Falklands – which it was. Thatcher was careful not to repeat her assertion that it wasn't sailing away, and the atmosphere became heated. 'That's not good enough, Mrs Thatcher,' said Mrs Gould. 'Would you please let me answer' shot back the Prime Minister. Afterwards, Denis Thatcher and their daughter Carol aimed their fury at the BBC. Mrs Thacher said she found 'the whole episode distasteful'.

Anything Mrs Thatcher lost in the carefully balanced coverage of the television companies during the campaign she gained from the newspapers. The most strident support came from *The Sun* which, a year earlier, had glorified her order to torpedo the *Belgrano* with the headline 'GOTCHA!' Only the *Daily* and *Sunday Mirror* firmly supported Labour. On the whole, the newspapers were more partisan than ever to the Conservatives. On polling day, the *Daily Express* front-page headline was 'Now is the Hour. Maggie is the Man'. The Alliance's rather thin newspaper coverage was offset by the much fairer distribution of television news stories and party political broadcasts.

Labour's campaign came badly unstuck. Michael Foot was far less sure-footed than Thatcher. He was pictured on the campaign leaning on his walking stick with his dog called Dizzy (named after Disraeli, the Conservative Victorian premier he'd written about). His policy presentation was as shambling as his personal demeanour. He attacked the Tories on joblessness and the economy but suffered from his party's weakness on defence and nationalisation. He looked out of date with a strange attack on Tory grandee Lord Hailsham for supporting appeasement when, back in 1938 as Quintin Hogg, he fought and won the so-called 'Munich' by-election. Hailsham quickly countered with: 'The old boy has plainly lost his marbles. Poor old, dear old Worzel Gummidge.' The comparison with the energetic Thatcher was a no-brainer for the Tories' advertising campaign, although one ageist portrayal of 69-year-old Mr Foot was halted by Mrs Thatcher before publication. It pictured him with the slogan 'Under the Tories all pensioners are better off'.

Labour's problem was that for all the wretchedness of unemployment and public worries about the economy, the National Health Service and pensions, memories of the Falklands victory remained strong and Thatcher's image as a leader who looked as if she knew exactly where she was going scored highly. Labour misfired when it tried to attack her on the Falklands. The party's deputy leader Denis Healey accused her of 'glorifying in slaughter'. At a lunch shortly afterwards, Tory chairman Cecil Parkinson refused to sit down at the same table as Healey, who later apologised for the remark. Prominent Labour left-winger Neil Kinnock responded to a heckler who said Thatcher had 'guts' with the words it was 'a pity that people had to leave theirs on the ground at Goose Green in order to prove it'. That did not go down well. Worse, Labour's stand on defence policy was shattered by the former Labour Prime Minister James Callaghan sternly debunking the party's commitment to scrapping Britain's nuclear weapons. Even some of Foot's own shadow Cabinet ministers piled in expressing disquiet. Denis Healey said it was 'a matter of common sense not to abandon Polaris'. And try as Labour leaders did to wrong foot her on rumours of Tory plans to privatise the National Health Service, Thatcher shot back: 'I have no more intention of dismantling the NHS than I have of dismantling Britain's defences.'

Labour had plenty of other upsets during the campaign. Denis Healey visited a factory in Huddersfield which was later revealed to have supplied parts for Argentine warships. Neil Kinnock almost lost his voice by the end of the campaign, having to shout at meetings where the organisers failed to provide microphones. He later attacked the party's running of the campaign as 'incompetent. It was insane – there's no other word for it.'

If Conservative Central Office was delighted by disarray in the Labour Party, its view of the Alliance was quite the reverse. The centre parties, it was feared, could attract the support of less committed Conservative voters. But this worry soon faded. The Alliance began the campaign with around 20 per cent support and although that rose to nearer 25 per cent by the end of the campaign, it failed to recapture the popular enthusiasm of the heady days of 1981. There was confusion about the Alliance leadership. Early polling disenchantment at Roy Jenkins being mooted as its Prime Minister-designate led to what almost looked like an attempted coup by Liberal leader David Steel. He called a meeting at his home in Scotland at which he hoped to secure Jenkins's concession that he, Steel, should be the overall leader. Jenkins said no. The Alliance failed to promise the hoped-for breakthrough and appeared to confirm Jenkins's own rather foolishly stated concern that they might look as if they were 'playing a fuddled fiddle in the muddled middle'. The Alliance campaigner who shone most was David Owen, who not only held his seat in the election but also replaced Jenkins as leader shortly afterwards. One mortifying revelation for the Alliance was that the polls indicated a quarter of Conservative voters and a third of Labour's would have been ready to vote Alliance if they'd thought it had a chance of winning.

In the BBC studio on election night, as results began to come in, I was the commentator watching for the seats that would give us the trigger for our first forecast of the overall outcome. One or two early results gave some hope to the opposition: the Liberal–SDP Alliance vote in Torbay and Guildford was up a little, though the Tories hung on to the seats. And then Paddy Ashdown won Yeovil for the Alliance. But it wasn't long before the Tory gain at Nuneaton signalled the disaster in store for Labour. We were soon predicting a handsome Tory victory. In the end, the Conservatives romped home with a majority of 144, a hundred higher than they had won in 1979. It may have been its largest majority in seats (the largest of any party) since the war, but the share of the vote – at 42.4 per cent – was the lowest winning share since 1922. This was because the opposition was so conclusively, though disproportionately, split.

Michael Foot's party ended with 209 seats, down sixty. It was Labour's worst since 1935, and its 27.6 per cent share of the vote, the lowest since 1918, only just scraped in ahead of the Alliance on 25.4 per cent. The map of the country showed a sharp dividing line between a Labour north and Conservative south. Labour held only four seats in the south outside London. Labour's performance, which saw only four in ten trade unionists vote for the party, had some commentators predicting the total collapse of the party. Tony Benn lost his seat, and two notable Labour deserters to the SDP, Bill Rodgers and Shirley Williams, lost theirs. Only David Owen and Roy Jenkins kept their seats. Of the other twenty-six Labour MPs who had deserted to the SDP, only three won.

The centre parties were quick to point to what they saw as the rank unfairness of the electoral system. The Liberal–SDP Alliance came in third with its 25.4 per cent share of the vote but only twenty-three MPs, under 4 per cent of the seats. Labour won 33 per cent of the seats with 27.6 per cent of the votes. If the seats had been distributed in strict proportion to the share of the vote, the Tories would have won 120 fewer seats, Labour twenty fewer and the Alliance would have won 140 more. The Conservatives would have won 275 (not 397). Labour would have won 179 (not 209).

Opinion polls had a high profile during the campaign with publication almost daily and constant comment on party policies and leadership. But few people said the polls affected their vote. For the first time, all the parties spent large sums on private polling. The final 'on-the-day' opinion polls – unlike in some of the elections before and after – predicted the result with an accuracy of as much as plus or minus 1 per cent.

Late on election night a triumphant Mrs Thatcher appeared at a window in Conservative Central Office with Cecil Parkinson at her side. Thatcherism had decisively won a second term. Although she had a thumping majority in the new House, Thatcher felt she had not yet launched a real crusade to change the country. Her campaign had promised 'more of the same', but she believed a lot more was needed. There was, she later said in her memoirs, 'a revolution but too few revolutionaries'. Francis Pym was sacked. In an effort to shake things up, she shifted the Chancellor of the Exchequer Geoffrey Howe to the Foreign Office and replaced him with the more radical Nigel Lawson. Her new government was to startle the world with the reforms that followed. Margaret Thacher had set the Tories on a path of dominance that was to last a decade and a half.

Peter Snow is a broadcaster and historian. He presented *Newsnight* for seventeen years and wielded the Swingometer on BBC election programmes. He is author of ten books, the most recent being *Kings and Queens: The Real Lives of the English Monarchs*.

42

1987

SIMON BURNS

Dissolution: 18 May 1987
Polling day: 11 June 1987
Seats contested: 650
Total electorate / Voted / Turnout: 43,180,753 / 32,529,578 / 75.3 per cent
Candidates (total 2,325): Conservative – 633; Labour – 633; SDP–Liberal Alliance – 633; Green – 133; SNP – 72; Plaid Cymru – 38; Alliance – 16; Sinn Féin – 14; SDLP – 13; UUP – 12; DUP – 4
Prime Minister on polling day: Margaret Thatcher
Main party leaders: Conservative – Margaret Thatcher; Labour – Neil Kinnock; SDP–Liberal Alliance – David Owen and David Steel; SNP – Gordon Wilson; UUP – James Molyneaux; SDLP – John Hume; Plaid Cymru – Dafydd Elis-Thomas; DUP – Ian Paisley; Sinn Féin – Gerry Adams; Alliance – John Alderdice

Party performance:

Party	Votes	Percentage share	Seats
Conservative	13,760,583	42.2	376
Labour	10,029,807	30.8	229
SDP–Liberal Alliance	7,341,633	22.6	22
SNP	416,473	1.3	3
UUP	276,230	38	9
SDLP	154,067	21.2	3
Plaid Cymru	123,599	0.4	3

Green	89,753	0.3	0
DUP	85,642	11.8	3
Sinn Féin	83,389	11.5	1
Alliance	72,671	10	0

Result: Conservative majority of 102 seats

The result of the 1987 general election which returned Margaret Thatcher for a record-breaking third term was by no means inevitable. The ease with which she had won the 1983 election, aided by her handling of the Falklands War, the weakness of the Labour Party which never appeared as a plausible alternative government and a split opposition between the Labour Party and the SDP–Lib Alliance were not as potent factors as they had been in 1983.

After 1983, the Labour Party appeared to have learnt some of the lessons of its debacle by replacing their leader with the more charismatic Neil Kinnock, who ruthlessly sought to marginalise the left wing of the party even if he did not ditch some of the more unpopular policies like unilateral nuclear disarmament. The SDP–Liberal Alliance had been buoyed by the 26 per cent of the vote that they had received in 1983 and were misguidedly confident that they could build upon that at the next election – especially among middle-class Tory voters who were alienated by Thatcher's increasing stridency – and were encouraged by the fact that for two out of every three Conservative MPs, the Alliance was their main challenger.

For the Tories, the 1983–87 government had been a rollercoaster. It is true that they were the main beneficiaries of major social changes. Thanks to Margaret Thatcher, there was a significant move towards home ownership (up from 52 per cent in 1979 to 66 per cent in 1987 and the number of council house tenants dropped from 45 per cent to 27 per cent) and as a result of the privatisation of many nationalised industries, far more people owned shares, often for the first time in their lives. Each of these trends encouraged pro-Conservative tendencies in some voters and despite there still being widespread areas of deprivation and poverty, the country overall was becoming more middle class. However, the record of the government was not a stunning success. Although the economy was beginning to recover, the recovery was sluggish and painful and unemployment remained stubbornly high. Mrs Thatcher's style of government also came in for criticism in certain quarters, as highlighted by the Westland affair in early 1986 when she lost two Cabinet ministers and came very near to losing her own job.

The foundations for the Tory re-election campaign were laid in the autumn of 1985 when Mrs Thatcher appointed her close ally and political soulmate, Norman Tebbit, as party chairman. He swiftly reorganised the structures of party HQ in readiness for a general election at any time in the next three years. Surprisingly, the relationship between Thatcher and Tebbit was not harmonious and communications were poor, which led to disastrous consequences in the middle of the general election when it came.

The 1986 Conservative Party conference was the launching pad for the Conservative fightback and recovery under the slogan 'The Next Move Forward' to neutralise the notion that after eight years it was time for a change. In practical terms, there were targeted increases in spending on the NHS and education, two areas where the Conservatives were seen to be weak, and above inflation pay increases for nurses and teachers.

During early 1987, considerable work was carried out as to what the themes of any election campaign should be. Norman Tebbit was determined that the overall theme should be to attack Labour and to a lesser extent the SDP–Liberal Alliance. While not disagreeing with attacking the opposition parties, Mrs Thatcher believed the main emphasis should be on highlighting the government's successes and what they would do with another term in office. Eventually, a compromise for the two approaches was reached. Mrs Thatcher always believed that elections should be held in the fifth year of a government and so realistically the earliest she would call an election would be in June 1987. Momentum started building for an election early in the New Year. As a result of the successful party conference in October 1986 and the split opposition, the opinion polls had begun to show consistent Conservative leads which increased the pressure for an election in the summer. The good local election results in early May, which showed the Conservatives making modest gains over their excellent performance four years earlier, sealed the decision and the election was called for 11 June.

For the Labour Party, there was a mountain to climb if they were to win as they had 147 fewer seats than the Conservatives. It is true that Neil Kinnock was a far better leader than Michael Foot had been, but he was a poor performer in the House of Commons and his verbosity earned him the unflattering sobriquet of the 'Welsh windbag'. His campaign to rid Labour of Militant and the far left did help to persuade people that he was serious in attacking extremism within the Labour Party but did not convince them that the Labour Party was less extremist or divided. He was far more successful, with the help of Peter Mandelson and Patricia Hewitt, in transforming the communications and messaging of the party. This paid dividends in that people liked Kinnock's personality but he lagged far behind Thatcher in questions relating to leadership, such as strength of personality, decisiveness and gaining respect for the country abroad. To counteract this, the party decided to run a presidential-like campaign during the election, focusing heavily on Kinnock. When drawing up the manifesto, there were significant public disputes on a range of policies, but the most damaging one was Kinnock's strong commitment to unilateral disarmament, which Thatcher ruthlessly exploited, arguing that he could not be trusted with Britain's safety and defence.

Superficially, the SDP–Lib Alliance were in a good position in the lead up to the election but beneath the surface there were a number of irreconcilable tensions. The Liberals were a far more radical party than the SDP and suffered under the misapprehension that they could potentially win the election, while David Owen of the SDP never believed that was possible but the best they could hope for was a hung parliament with the Alliance holding the balance of power and acting as kingmakers. However, the most damaging split between the two parties was over defence policy and Britain's nuclear deterrent. A joint Defence Commission proposed that Trident should be abandoned and no decision would be taken at that stage as to whether Polaris should be replaced. David Owen completely rejected this and came out in support of Britain keeping its nuclear deterrent and replacing Polaris. There was a fudged compromise, but to make matters worse, the SDP conference accepted this but the Liberal Assembly threw it out. The tension over defence policy remained throughout the campaign, which I well remember because I was the Conservative candidate in Chelmsford, defending a majority of only 378 against the Liberals. Chelmsford at the time was a major employer in defence-related industries, having five defence-related companies and the issue of defence came up time and time again to the detriment of the Liberals.

As the campaign got underway, the Labour Party initially captured the initiative with a highly emotive and effective party election broadcast (PEB) that became known as 'Kinnock: The Movie', which has stood the test of time and is still considered the best PEB that has ever been made. Directed by Hugh Hudson, who was responsible for the Oscar-winning film *Chariots of Fire*, the PEB focused on Neil Kinnock at his most passionate and caring, by splicing excerpts from two of his most famous speeches. The first was his speech to the 1985 Labour Party conference when he vigorously attacked the threat of Militant Tendency to the Labour Party, which exemplified his courage and determined leadership. The second was his speech at the beginning of the 1987 general election campaign, when he tackled the problems of economic and social inequalities and asked the famous question 'why am I the first Kinnock...?'

Unlike most PEBs, which are instantly forgotten, this one was an instant success which led to an immediate nineteen-point rise in Kinnock's personal ratings. Labour took the unprecedented step of showing it again later in the campaign.

Despite the success of the PEB and the fillip it gave to peoples' perception of Kinnock, it did not have a lasting effect on the campaign itself because three issues dominated the election from start to finish – defence, the 'loony left' and economic competence. All three were detrimental to Labour and, try as they may, they never managed to move the agenda away from these damaging issues.

Throughout the campaign, Labour was on the back foot on defence. It was not simply that Kinnock's commitment to unilateralism at a time of heightened tensions with the Soviet Union was unpopular but that the Labour Party was not able to paper over the divisions within the party, especially the commitment to multilateral disarmament favoured by senior figures like Denis Healey and James Callaghan. The Tories relentlessly plugged away at the issue to great effect. They produced a stunning advertisement of a soldier with his hands in the air signifying surrender and the caption 'Labour's policy on Arms', which encapsulated the problems Labour had with the policy and were aided by Ronald Reagan and the Americans on the sidelines who made no secret of their concern of what a Labour government would do. By the end of the campaign, Labour was perceived as soft on defence.

The Tories also unceasingly attacked Labour on the problem of the 'loony left', citing example after example of their antics, especially in London, which alienated middle-of-the-road voters who saw the party as unfit to govern.

On the central issue of the economy, the Tories cleverly turned the issue away from a debate on their record to who was the most competent in managing the economy in the future. Their most effective propaganda was to cost the commitments made by Labour on future spending, claiming that Labour had made commitments worth £35 billion in extra spending, which would lead to income tax at 58 per cent or VAT at 50 per cent to fund. In the last week of the campaign, the Tories were helped by conflicting claims by senior Labour figures about the impact their commitments would have on taxpayers. Bryan Gould and Roy Hattersley had promised that no one earning £500 a week or less would be affected, but later Neil Kinnock admitted that there would be some losers in this group, which led the pro-Tory tabloid press to have a field day of calling the Labour Party liars and accusing them of misleading the electorate.

The Tories were not free from their own gaffes, though they were mostly on side issues in the campaign. Mrs Thatcher scored an own goal when she announced she used private health facilities because she wanted to go into hospital on the day she wanted with the doctor she wanted. She also caused confusion when she seemingly suggested that there could be an element of fee paying in state education, but this controversy was swiftly closed down when she reiterated that state education would remain free.

The most damaging problem for the Tories became known as 'Wobbly Thursday'. The background to this wobble was that for some time, Mrs Thatcher had been concerned about the way Conservative Central Office had been planning the campaign and their management of it. She had been using Lord Young as a conduit to her advertising agency, Saatchis, to beef up the impact of their advertising campaign. She was also nervous and plagued by toothache and worried about the professionalism of the Labour campaign. This all came to a head a week before polling day when a *Newsnight* poll of marginal seats suggested the country was heading for a hung parliament and that the *Telegraph* was planning to release a poll the next day that allegedly showed the Tory lead narrowing to 4 per cent. Mrs Thatcher insisted the party's advertising was strengthened to highlight the government's successes, but when Norman Tebbit saw the proofs of the new adverts, he was dismissive of them. Following a blazing row between Tebbit and Young, a compromise was arrived at and Mrs Thatcher began to appear more on television programmes and beefed up her speeches to stress more of the government's successes in the last week of the campaign. The crisis evaporated when the next set of polls showed a Tory lead of 10 per cent, but it had been an unsettling two days for the Tories.

Opinion polls played a far more intrusive role in this election compared to previous ones. In the month leading up to polling day, there were seventy-three nationwide polls and eighteen devoted to marginal seats. Their results were widely reported in the national press and often became news stories in themselves, especially with the Tory-leaning tabloid press which used the results to bash the Labour Party in particular. This was made easier because every national poll throughout the campaign showed the Tories in the lead, helped by the fact that the opposition was split between Labour and the Alliance.

The national press were significantly in favour of the Tories winning the election with seven out of the eleven national daily newspapers endorsing them. Their circulation was significantly higher than that of the newspapers that endorsed Labour or did not make an endorsement. All of the papers except the *Mirror* gave more coverage to Labour than the Tories and the tabloids – *The Sun*, *Express* and *Mail* – concentrated on vitriolic attacks on Labour, while the *Mirror* concentrated its efforts on attacking the Tories. The quality papers were more balanced in their news with the exception of the *Telegraph*, which spent much of its column inches highlighting Labour failings.

By the day before polling day, all the polls showed a healthy Tory lead of between 7 per cent and 12 per cent. The final result exceeded expectations with the Tories winning with an overall majority of 102, on a turnout of 75.3 per cent which was 2.6 per cent higher than in 1983. The national swing to Labour was 1.2 per cent. In the south, the Tories gained overall four seats. In the west Midlands, they gained one and lost one. They lost four seats in the east Midlands, four in Wales and eleven in Scotland. Labour gained one seat in the south, seven in the north of England. In Scotland, Labour got fifty out of seventy-two seats and the Scottish Nationalists lost two seats to Labour but gained three from the Tories. Plaid Cymru gained an extra seat in Wales. The Alliance ended up with twenty-two seats – a loss of one from their 1983 result. They lost three of their five by-election wins. Apart from Roy Jenkins, the most high-profile loss was Enoch Powell in Northern Ireland.

Although the Tories won the general election with a convincing majority, it was widely considered that Labour fought the best campaign despite their poor result. With hindsight, the Tory election campaign has received widespread criticism. Tory-supporting newspapers criticised the party for its lack of vigour, while the quality papers felt there was a lack of proper discussion of the issues. Everyone agreed, though, that this was a media-oriented election with the parties concentrating on getting their messages and images across. It was the election where the photo opportunity came into its own and policy statements and initiatives were tailored to meet television deadlines.

The importance of television to the parties to get their messages across (and this was in the days before 24-hour news cycles) made the election more presidential, as shown by the media's concentration on the party leaders.

It is fair to say, as the *Telegraph* did, that the Tory campaign was 'lacklustre', but the fact remains that however professional and media friendly the Labour campaign was, the Tories were more disciplined in sticking to their key attack areas of defence, the 'loony left' and taxation and that is what delivered them a historic victory.

It was historic because Mrs Thatcher was the first Prime Minister since Lord Liverpool in the 1820s to win three elections in a row and the overall majority of 102 was the second largest since 1945. It may not have been a landmark election like 1945 or 1979, but Mrs Thatcher could certainly take satisfaction in the fact that it was a historic, if dull, election victory for which she deserves the credit.

Sir Simon Burns was the Conservative MP for Chelmsford for thirty years from 1987 to 2017 and in that time he was twice a Health Minister and a Transport Minister.

43

1992

PETER RIDDELL

Dissolution: 16 March 1992
Polling day: 9 April 1992
Seats contested: 651
Total electorate / Voted / Turnout: 43,275,316 / 33,614,074 / 77.7 per cent
Candidates (total 2,949): Conservative – 645; Labour – 634; Liberal Democrats – 632; Green – 253; SNP – 72; Plaid Cymru – 38; Alliance – 16; Sinn Féin – 14; SDLP – 13; UUP – 13; DUP – 7
Prime Minister on polling day: John Major
Main party leaders: Conservative – John Major; Labour – Neil Kinnock; Liberal Democrats – Paddy Ashdown; SNP – Alex Salmond; Green – Jean Lambert and Richard Lawson; UUP – James Molyneaux; SDLP – John Hume; Plaid Cymru – Dafydd Wigley; Sinn Féin – Gerry Adams; DUP – Ian Paisley; Alliance – John Alderdice

Party performance:

Party	Votes	Percentage share	Seats
Conservative	14,093,007	41.9	336
Labour	11,560,484	34.4	271
Liberal Democrats	5,999,606	17.8	20
SNP	629,564	1.9	3
UUP	271,049	34.5	9
SDLP	184,445	23.5	4
Green	170,047	0.5	0

Plaid Cymru	156,796	0.5	4
DUP	103,039	13.1	3
Sinn Féin	78,291	10	0
Alliance	68,665	8.7	0

Result: Conservative majority of twenty-one seats

As a political journalist covering the 1992 general election, my most vivid memory was a few days before polling when I was in a very cramped car with a member of the shadow Cabinet and I suggested that he might soon be travelling in more comfort as a minister. 'Don't be daft, Peter, Labour isn't going to win the election.' That rare, even private, acknowledgement of another Labour defeat came from the ever-realistic Tony Blair.

Even at that late stage in the campaign, the widespread media and political expectation was still that the most likely outcome was Labour as the largest single party even if in a hung parliament. So, for many, and not just the pollsters, the result was unexpected. For the first time in 170 years, a party was re-elected for a fourth time with a clear majority. While any sense of Conservative triumph proved to be short-lived, the result of five more years in office, if not really in power, entrenched the policy changes summed up in the term Thatcherism and forced Labour eventually into a further far-reaching review of its own approach.

The campaign was marked by battles over rival tax plans, the 'war of Jennifer's ear', John Major's soap box and Neil Kinnock's triumphalism at the Sheffield rally, all much remarked on at the time but probably none in themselves decisive, compared with voters' views about Major's character as a leader and about whether Labour could be trusted in office.

When the election was called on 11 March, Major was widely seen as facing an uphill task after a tumultuous five years for his party and the country. The key event was the ousting of Margaret Thatcher in November 1990. That did not come out of the blue but was the result of growing divisions within her government and among

Tory MPs – over her approach to Europe and over the introduction of the poll tax or community charge which provoked riots and was unpopular with many. The early part of the parliament saw further stages in the development of the Thatcher programme with electricity and coal privatisation. The economy was also booming with strong growth and soaring house prices, further fuelled by tax-cutting Budgets. But interest rates started rising sharply in the second half of 1988 and the outlook worsened over the following two years as the economy moved into recession, while high interest and mortgage rates, and then falling house prices, particularly hit the many new homeowners created in that decade.

The post-1987 period was marked by a series of disasters and terrorist attacks which claimed large numbers of lives: the great tree-destroying storm in southern England and the King's Cross fire in 1987; the Piper Alpha oil rig explosion, the Clapham rail crash and the Pan Am bombing at Lockerbie in 1988; and the M1 air crash and the Hillsborough football crowd disaster in 1989. Then, in Thatcher's final year, there were the poll tax riots in April 1990 and the assassination of Ian Gow, her close friend and ally, at the end of July.

The latter period of Thatcher's premiership was a time of far-reaching international events with the crumbling of the Berlin Wall in November 1989 and the overthrow of communist regimes in the previous Soviet satellite countries in eastern Europe signalling the end of the Cold War. However, by opposing the seemingly inexorable move towards German unification, Thatcher isolated herself from the administration of George Bush, who had succeeded as President in January 1989 and who was never as personally close to her as Ronald Reagan, his predecessor. Relations quickly became more harmonious, however, after August 1990 when Saddam Hussein's Iraq invaded Kuwait and Thatcher became the staunchest ally of the USA in resisting and promising to reverse the aggression.

Thatcher herself moved to what came to be called a more Eurosceptic position, notably in her Bruges speech of September 1988. Her central theme was: 'We have not rolled back the frontiers of the state in Britain to see them reimposed at a European level with a European superstate exercising a new dominance from Brussels.' After her earlier support for the European single market, the speech was a turning point in the Conservative Party debate over Europe. Thatcher was increasingly in conflict over linking sterling with other European countries in the Exchange Rate Mechanism (ERM) of the European Monetary System with Nigel Lawson and Sir Geoffrey Howe, two of the key architects of Thatcherism. After a confrontation ahead of the Madrid summit in June 1989, Howe was shifted out of the Foreign Office to be Deputy Prime Minister while Lawson resigned that October over the role of Sir Alan Walters, Thatcher's personal economic adviser. That was followed by a leadership challenge by a maverick backbencher Sir Anthony Meyer. Thatcher easily saw him off by 314 votes to twenty-four with thirty-one abstentions, but this level of opposition boded badly for a later challenge.

Thatcher's position steadily worsened during 1990 as her government became more unpopular and she became more isolated from many of her colleagues. She was forced to accept sterling's entry into the ERM in October 1990. Howe resigned at the beginning of November in exasperation over Thatcher's approach to Europe and her imperious leadership style. His surprisingly forceful resignation speech – evoking a 'tragic conflict of loyalties' – made a fresh contest inevitable. Michael Heseltine was a divisive figure, but not only did he succeed in narrowly denying Thatcher the super-majority she required under the Conservatives' election rules – winning 152 votes to her 204 – but the size of his vote persuaded many, including in Thatcher's own Cabinet, that she had to go. Thatcher then strongly backed John Major, mainly to stop Heseltine and in the belief that he was a continuity candidate. As it turned out, Major was a very different type of Prime Minister, though he did preserve key parts of Thatcher's legacy on trade union legislation and privatisation (which he took forward in some areas).

Major won comfortably with 185 votes against 131 for Heseltine and fifty-six for Douglas Hurd. He was little known outside Westminster, having been in the Cabinet for only two and a half years. He turned this into an advantage as the fresh face, the Brixton boy who came from a poor background and had never been to university. He brought back Heseltine and appointed Chris Patten, never a Thatcherite, as party chairman. Patten knew Conservative Central Office well from the past and made a number of changes, including rehiring Saatchis to handle advertising and appointing Shaun Woodward as head of communications.

Major was naturally a consensus figure and talked of making Britain 'a country at ease with itself'. He distanced himself from his predecessor, notably by abolishing the poll tax/community charge and replacing it with the new property-related council tax. A keynote, though often misunderstood, policy was the Citizen's Charter, which sought to increase the public's rights over the delivery of public services. Major signalled a different approach in foreign affairs by saying he wanted to keep Britain 'at the very heart of Europe', leading to stirrings among the Eurosceptic Tories, including Thatcher. But he achieved a diplomatic success in December 1991 by securing two opt-outs on any future European currency and social policy from the Maastricht Treaty and this helped to reduce internal party dissent ahead of the election.

The appointment of the little-known Major after the global superstar Thatcher at a time when military action was likely in the Gulf puzzled foreign leaders who had not appreciated the decline in her internal political position. But Major quickly established good relations with Bush and European leaders like Helmut Kohl and impressed with his calm leadership during the brief Gulf War of early 1991 and his decisive response to the plight of the Kurds in northern Iraq. Combined with his more emollient domestic style, this led to a marked, though not sustained, improvement in the Conservatives' poll ratings in early 1991. Major also enjoyed positive personal ratings in contrast to Thatcher's negative ones, and was more highly rated than Neil Kinnock, Labour leader since 1983.

The arrival of Major posed big challenges for the opposition parties which had been running against Thatcher for so long that they had to rethink their approaches. Their familiar enemy had gone, but could they adjust? Both main opposition parties had themselves been through big changes. After the 1987 defeat, Kinnock and his allies – notably the increasingly prominent Gordon Brown and Tony Blair – accepted that the modernisation of Labour had to be taken a lot further. First, Kinnock and deputy leader Roy Hattersley easily saw off challenges to their positions by the hard-left Tony Benn and Eric Heffer as well as shifting the party's position on Europe and nuclear defence. The party enjoyed a run of electoral success both at elections to the European Parliament and in winning four by-elections from the Conservatives during the parliament, though losing one to the Scottish Nationalists. Kinnock ran the party with a small group around him, including, initially, Peter Mandelson before he became a parliamentary candidate, Charles Clarke as chief of staff, Patricia Hewitt on the media side, with Philip Gould as polling and campaigning strategist.

The Liberal Democrats, initially called the Social and Liberal Democrats, emerged in 1988 from the long-standing Liberal Party and remnants of the former Social Democratic Party. The latter split following the 1987 election between supporters of David Owen and the majority who favoured a merger. David Steel stepped down as Liberal leader and Paddy Ashdown became head of the new party. Initially, its support was in low single figures, being totally eclipsed by the Greens as the mid-term protest vote in the 1989 elections to the European Parliament. Their respective vote shares were 6 per cent and 15 per cent. Ashdown's energy and shrewdness – as well as the Conservatives' growing unpopularity – led to a steady improvement in the Liberal Democrats' ratings, up from low single figures to the mid-teens and higher by 1990–91, as well as victories in three by-elections in that period.

While the economic situation appeared to favour the opposition parties, Major was an elusive target. He believed he needed time to establish himself. He ruled out both a spring 'khaki' election following the end of the short Gulf War – which he believed would be false and cynical – and also one in early summer following poor local election results in May and a by-election loss in Monmouth. He then rejected the autumn of 1991 in the hope/belief that there would be better economic news in the New Year. This left the spring of 1992 as the only option and the parties duly started long campaigns at the start of the year, highlighting what would become familiar themes – by Labour about the state of the NHS and schools and by the Conservatives against Labour's alleged tax bombshell of £1,000 more that people would pay. More significant was the absence of any sign of economic recovery while Labour remained ahead in the polls. This period culminated in the 10 March Budget when Norman Lamont produced a surprise of a new 20p band for the first £2,000 of taxable income. Labour denounced the plan but was in a dilemma about how to respond, underlining some of the tensions between Kinnock and John Smith, the shadow Chancellor, on tax and spending issues. The shadow, alternative budget on 16 March, after the election had been called, proposed increasing taxes for the wealthiest and helping the poor, but the details left room for eventual Conservative attacks that a large number of people would be adversely affected.

The party manifestos had few surprises since so many of the themes had been well trailed. The Conservatives – under the title 'The Best Future for Britain' – promised the sale of British Coal and certain parts of British Rail, an Urban Regeneration Agency and a Millennium Fund for arts and Britain's heritage. Under the title 'It's Time to Get Britain Working Again', Labour underlined its now pro-European stance, its abandonment of unilateralism and its acceptance of most of the Conservatives' trade union laws, while promising a sweeping package of constitutional reform, including a Scottish Parliament with tax-raising powers, a Bill of Rights and a Freedom of Information Act – plus a national minimum wage. The Liberal Democrats also stressed constitutional reform and promised 1p on the basic rate of income tax to pay for more education spending. What was striking, however, was how small a part the details in the manifestos played in the campaign. Revealingly, in view of what happened only a few weeks after the election, the issue of Europe and the Maastricht Treaty were barely mentioned.

The election was called just after the Budget and the dissolution of Parliament saw the departure from the Commons of many of the leading figures of the Thatcher era and before – Thatcher herself, as well as Howe, Lawson, Norman Tebbit, Cecil Parkinson, Nicholas Ridley, Ian Gilmour, John Moore, George Younger, John Wakeham (who became Leader of the Lords) and Alan Clark (who returned five years later). On the Labour side, the list included Denis Healey, Michael Foot and Merlyn Rees; while former SDP leader David Owen also stepped down, along with outgoing Commons Speaker Bernard Weatherill. Edward Heath remained almost alone as a relic of the earlier battles.

The campaigns themselves now appear rather dated, continuing the long-established pattern of the previous two decades. Press conferences were held first thing in the morning each weekday, and often on Saturdays, around Westminster with the party leaders turning up for the vast majority of them, answering questions from a wide range of journalists. And the leaders went in battle buses around the country. The leaders' activities and voter images of the campaign were dominated by the television news coverage which was moving more in the direction of comment than reporting. Kinnock's request for a televised debate was brushed aside by Major before the campaign started. There were rows – notably the Jennifer's ear controversy over a Labour election broadcast featuring delays to NHS treatment for an ear condition for a young girl in Kent. The consequent recriminations about who leaked what dominated media coverage for a few days but did not do either of the big parties any good. The most talked-about Conservative election broadcast – dubbed 'The Journey' and made by film director John Schlesinger – featured Major in the back of a car going round his old haunts in Brixton, drawing comparisons with a similarly personal Hugh Hudson film about Kinnock in 1987. Major was himself embarrassed about the film. The other much-discussed event was Labour's Sheffield rally which – modelled on President François Mitterrand's ones in France – was depicted as prematurely triumphalist after a few crass unprime ministerial words by a hyped-up Kinnock before what was otherwise a strong speech.

None of this seemed to have much effect – the polls and expectations on seats changed little during the campaign, though there was increased talk about a hung parliament. There were complaints from the Thatcherite old guard that the Conservative campaign was lacklustre and was not bold enough, but similar mid-campaign complaints occurred in 1987. Ashdown argued that his party would insist on a commitment to electoral reform and Kinnock appeared to flirt with at least discussions on PR. In retrospect, this speculation unquestionably helped the Conservatives not least by spurring Major into a strong counter-attack in the last phase of the campaign – 'the United Kingdom is in danger. Wake up, my fellow countrymen. Wake up before it is too late.' This was effective not because the public was necessarily interested in the constitutional debate about devolution or the electoral system but because it showed a determined, strong Major.

Admittedly, in the final few days, some Labour leaders, including Kinnock, began to have doubts, mainly privately in the case of Blair noted earlier. But a hung parliament remained the expected outcome and was even indicated by the exit polls at 10 p.m. when voting ended. The civil service had been preparing for a possible change, even tactlessly asking Norma Major whether she had arranged a removal van. It was only when the first results came in – a smaller than needed swing in Sunderland South and then the Conservatives holding Basildon – that it became clear that Labour would fail, yet again. The Conservatives won 336 seats, thirty-nine down on 1987 – with losses including party chairman Patten in Bath and of promising junior ministers Lynda Chalker (who retained her ministerial post but went to the Lords), Francis Maude and John Maples. But the party regained all its by-election losses since 1987 and emerged with an overall majority of twenty-one. In some respects, this was a meagre return since the Conservatives won the highest number of votes achieved by any party at 14.1 million, and, on 41.9 per cent, were comfortably ahead of Labour on 34.4 per cent. The answer partly lies in differential turnout. Overall turnout rose by 2.4 points compared with 1987 to 77.7 per cent, the highest level since February 1974, another closely fought election. But the rise in turnout was higher in Conservative safe seats than in Labour-held seats. Labour's steady post-1983 recovery continued, as the party won 271 seats, compared with 229 in 1987. The Liberal Democrats gained 18 per cent of the vote, compared with 22 per cent for the two pre-merger parties in 1987, but they won only twenty seats, down from twenty-two. But as the party fell back in some Labour target areas, they gained ground in the south-west. There was little overall change in Scotland, though; after losing half their seats in 1987, the Conservatives' total rose by one to eleven. The Scottish Nationalists increased their share of the vote from 14 per cent to over 21 per cent, but still had only three MPs. In Wales, Labour made small gains in both vote share and numbers of MPs, at the expense of the Conservatives and the Liberal Democrats.

The new intake of Conservative MPs included many who would play an important part in the coming decades, though only one future party leader – Iain Duncan Smith. He was one of a new group of strongly Eurosceptic Conservative MPs, also including Bernard Jenkin and John Whittingdale, all from outer London or Essex. Other new MPs including Liam Fox, Eric Pickles, Angela Browning, Cheryl Gillan and Edward Garnier as well as two figures best known outside politics in Olympic gold medallist Sebastian Coe and entertainer Gyles Brandreth. The Labour new intake included many of the key figures of the New Labour era, such as Tessa Jowell, Alan Milburn, Estelle Morris, John Denham and John Hutton, all of whom won seats from the Conservatives, as well as Peter Mandelson, Geoff Hoon and Stephen Byers, and a whole host of future junior ministers. One of the few Liberal Democrat new entrants was Paul Tyler, who returned to the Commons after an interval of seventeen and a half years, having served briefly between February and October 1974.

Major carried out a limited Cabinet reshuffle, though not the one he wanted. His original intention had been to make Patten Chancellor of the Exchequer, but after losing his seat the latter rejected the options of an arranged by-election or going to the Lords and, instead, became the final governor of Hong Kong. He would have been a valuable ally for Major in the turbulent 1992–97 parliament. Instead, Lamont remained for an unsettled further thirteen months as Chancellor. Some long-serving ministers – Kenneth Baker (having turned down the Welsh Office), Tom King, Peter Brooke (temporarily before his return that autumn after David Mellor's departure) and David Waddington. In came Gillian Shephard, John Patten, Virginia Bottomley and, more controversially, Michael Portillo on his meteor-like rise.

Neil Kinnock immediately announced his intention to resign after eight and a half years as leader and two general elections which had taken Labour from the depths of 1983 to within touching distance of office, a long way but not enough. John Smith beat Bryan Gould by a nine-to-one margin in July. He appointed Brown – who had declined himself to stand against his old Scottish friend – as shadow Chancellor and Blair as shadow Home Secretary. The start of the 1992 parliament also saw the election of Betty Boothroyd as the first female Speaker of the House of Commons, an early marker of what was to become a big change in the gender balance among MPs in the following decade – though she never saw it in those terms.

The outcome, against expectations, led to lots of soul-searching. Did the campaign make a difference? After all, a small further swing to Labour would have denied the Conservatives an overall majority and might have put Kinnock in No. 10. Perhaps Major's final combativeness over the future of the UK may have solidified support, while doubts lingered over Labour's economic plans. Smith's shadow budget had too many loose ends, giving ammunition to Conservative claims that Labour could not be trusted on tax and the economy. Paradoxically, some voters may have been reluctant to vote Labour when the economic outlook was uncertain in 1992, though they felt it safer to do so five years later when the economy was strong. Labour was divided in its analysis between those like Tony Benn who urged more socialism and what became known as the modernisers such as Blair, Brown and Mandelson who believed more changes were needed to reassure voters, drawing parallels with Bill Clinton's campaign in the 1992 US presidential election. Smith was instinctively cautious, especially when the government hit severe political problems later that year.

Labour also blamed a strongly Conservative-supporting press, notably after *The Sun*, then still selling 3.5 million copies a day, and with a readership of just under 10 million, gleefully proclaimed 'It's *The Sun* Wot Won It' after the election. This followed its memorable but cruel polling day front page showing Kinnock's head inside a light bulb and saying, 'If Kinnock wins today will the last person to leave Britain turn out the lights'. The tabloids were highly partisan but then they always had been – and their circulations had generally fallen since 1987. Nevertheless, the Conservative-supporting press accounted for 70 per cent of total circulation of national dailies, against 27 per cent for Labour (including, for once, the *Financial Times* which favoured Labour in a hung parliament). And *The Sun* had more electorally volatile Labour and uncommitted voters among its readers than the *Express* and the *Mail*, according to the analysis in the Nuffield study of the election. The New Labour leadership as it emerged after 1994 certainly believed in the influence of the tabloids since they eagerly and successfully courted the Murdoch press. The broadcasters – then still dominated by the BBC and ITN, rather than the newcomer Sky – remained the main source of election news in 1992, and the main stories were the economy, the NHS, the polls and the prospects/dangers of a hung parliament.

A central question is over the errors in the opinion polls. There was probably a late, and only partially appreciated, swing back to the Conservatives in the last few days, but that still did not show the real position and throughout the campaign the polls got the level of support for the two main parties wrong. The final poll of polls published on election day pointed to a 0.9 point Labour lead when the Conservatives won by a 7.6 point margin. This mattered not only in affecting the expectations of voters and financial markets but also in influencing the parties' own approaches, persuading some, but not all, Labour strategists that they were better placed than they were, while Conservative leaders at best thought they might scrape in as the largest single party. These findings affected media coverage and the Conservatives were treated throughout as underdogs, and Labour as a potential government, not necessarily to their advantage. This was not just one or two rogue polls, as always occurs in an election. Only ten out of fifty of the polls published during the campaign put the Conservatives ahead, and then only by a tiny margin. The polling industry was immediately involved in bruising post-mortems into what had gone so spectacularly wrong. These suggested a variety of reasons to do with the representativeness of those interviewed compared to those who voted and differential turnout. Late swing was reckoned to account for about only a quarter of the error. Despite inevitably hostile headlines about the pollsters, their influence continued. The pollsters refined their methods and, as always, their work was closely followed by the parties and the media.

The 1992 general election did not appear decisive at the time, in part because the post-election honeymoon proved so short as the Conservative Party at Westminster plunged within weeks into fratricidal warfare over Europe following the Danish rejection of the Maastricht Treaty in early June and then sterling was forced out of the ERM in mid-September. Yet Major and the Conservatives remained in office for another five years, entrenching and in part extending their earlier achievements. As Major concluded in his memoirs written at the end of the decade:

> Above all our victory in 1992 killed socialism in Britain. It also made the world safe for Tony Blair. Our win meant that between 1992 and 1997 Labour had to change. No longer is Britain trapped in the old two-party tango, with one government neatly undoing everything its predecessor has created.

Sir Peter Riddell is a journalist and author. Previously, he worked for the *Financial Times*, served as the British government's Commissioner for Public Appointments and was the director of the Institute for Government.

1997

JOHN CURTICE

Dissolution: 8 April 1997
Polling day: 1 May 1997
Seats contested: 659
Total electorate / Voted / Turnout: 43,846,152 / 31,286,284 / 71.4 per cent
Candidates (total 3,724): Conservative – 648; Labour – 639; Liberal Democrats – 639; Referendum – 547; Green – 89; SNP – 72; Plaid Cymru – 40; SDLP – 18; Alliance – 17; Sinn Féin – 17; UUP – 16; DUP – 9
Prime Minister on polling day: John Major
Main party leaders: Conservative – John Major; Labour – Tony Blair; Liberal Democrats – Paddy Ashdown; Referendum – James Goldsmith; UKIP – Alan Sked; SNP – Alex Salmond; UUP – David Trimble; SDLP – John Hume; Plaid Cymru – Dafydd Wigley; Sinn Féin – Gerry Adams; DUP – Ian Paisley; Alliance – John Alderdice

Party performance:

Party	Votes	Percentage share	Seats
Labour	13,518,167	43.2	419
Conservative	9,600,943	30.7	165
Liberal Democrats	5,242,947	16.8	46
Referendum	811,849	2.6	0
SNP	621,550	2	6
UUP	258,439	32.7	10
SDLP	190,844	24.1	3

Plaid Cymru	161,030	0.5	4
Sinn Féin	126,921	16.1	2
DUP	107,348	13.6	2
UKIP	105,722	0.3	0
Alliance	62,972	8	0

Result: Labour majority of 179 seats

The 1997 election resulted in a landslide for the Labour Party. It was an outcome that, despite the message of the polls, many had doubted could possibly happen. Yet, in truth, the fate of the Conservative government had effectively been sealed long before the election campaign began. As a result, the campaign itself had more the air of a performative ritual than a fierce combat. Nevertheless, election night proved to be highly dramatic and has since become part of Britain's political folk memory.

The outcome of the previous election in April 1992 was deeply disappointing for Labour. The polls had suggested the election was likely to produce a hung parliament in which Labour would probably be the largest party and thus able to bring an end to thirteen years of Conservative rule. Yet, in the event, the Conservatives won comfortably in terms of votes, leading Labour by as much as eight points, although this translated into a narrow majority of only twenty-one in terms of seats. Speculation ensued that perhaps Britain's post-war system of alternating single-party government was being replaced by a Japanese-style system of predominantly right-of-centre one-party rule.

Yet within months, John Major's Conservative government was in deep trouble. Two years previously, in October 1990, Major, then Chancellor, had finally persuaded a reluctant Prime Minister, Margaret Thatcher, that sterling should join the European Exchange Rate Mechanism. Under this mechanism, the values of European currencies were pegged to each other, with a view to laying the foundations for European Monetary Union. However, sterling entered the mechanism at a value of DM2.95, a relatively high valuation but one that had the attraction that it might help reduce an inflation rate that was running as high as 10 per cent. On Wednesday 16 September 1992, traders began to sell the pound in high volumes, and despite two hikes in the Bank of England base rate that eventually saw it reach the dizzying height of 15 per cent, it proved impossible to maintain the value of the pound. By that evening the Chancellor, Norman Lamont, was forced to announce that sterling was being withdrawn from the Exchange Rate Mechanism.

This was, in effect, a forced devaluation of the pound. Previous Labour governments had presided over devaluation crises in 1948 and 1967, while another Labour government was obliged in 1976 to seek a loan facility from the International Monetary Fund – in return for significant cuts in public expenditure. In each case, the government had found itself unable to defend both the symbolism and the substance of Britain's sovereignty against overseas pressures, and as a result its reputation for economic competence was badly damaged. Now it was a Conservative government that found itself in that position – but the consequence was much the same. In the weeks running up to what became known as 'Black Wednesday', the Conservatives had been averaging 41 per cent in the polls, enough to put them a point ahead of Labour. By October, they were down to 34 per cent, and eleven points behind their principal opponents. They were behind in the polls throughout the remainder of the parliament.

Meanwhile, the issue of the Exchange Rate Mechanism had a particular resonance for the Conservatives. Whether the UK should join any future European single currency was divisive within the party. A growing mood of Euroscepticism was reflected in the opposition of many Conservative MPs to joining the proposed European single currency. Their doubts were fuelled further by the fate of the pound on Black Wednesday. Yet at the same time, two of the senior members of the government, the Deputy Prime Minister, Michael Heseltine, and the (from 1993) Chancellor, Ken Clarke, were ardent Europhiles who did not want joining the euro to be ruled out. Major was to have to spend much of the next five years trying to keep his party together on an issue on which it was deeply divided.

Matters first came to a head when the government sought to secure approval of the legislation needed to implement the Maastricht Treaty. This treaty marked the latest stage in the process of European integration, not least through making provision for the establishment of the common currency. Although in the negotiations that had led up to the treaty, Major had secured an opt-out for the UK from the single currency, together with one for the treaty's 'social chapter' provisions that tightened regulation of the labour market, the legislation was subjected to significant delaying tactics by Eurosceptic Conservative MPs. It was eventually passed only after the insertion of a requirement to hold a separate parliamentary vote on the opt-out from the social chapter. When that vote was held in July 1993, the government lost, and it was forced to put down a confidence vote on the issue in order to get its will.

Then the following year, the government had to pursue legislation that would increase the financial contribution the UK made to the EU. Despite making the issue a matter of confidence, eight Conservative MPs abstained, resulting in them having the Conservative whip withdrawn. However, this had the effect of turning the government, whose original small majority had already been eroded through by-election losses, into a minority administration. Eventually, the rebels had the whip restored without any promise about their future behaviour. The episode simply served to undermine the authority of John Major's government.

Meanwhile, the Eurosceptic mood within much of the Conservative Party – and, indeed, the wider public – was further fuelled by the European Union's decision to ban the export of British beef following the UK government's admission in March 1996 that the consumption of beef from cows suffering from bovine spongiform encephalopathy (BSE), a serious brain disease, was the cause of a similar condition, a variant of Creutzfeldt-Jakob disease, in humans. As a result, a food that was not only economically important to the UK but also an icon of British culture became the subject of a trade dispute between the UK and the EU.

Shortly thereafter, in April 1996, Major announced that the government would not join the single currency – by now scheduled by the EU to start in January 1999 – without first holding a referendum on the subject. The move, designed to try to keep the peace within his party, was strongly reminiscent of Labour's decision in the 1970s to resolve its internal disagreements on Europe by promising the referendum on membership that was eventually held in 1975. Aware of the relative unpopularity of the single currency, a few months later Labour adopted the same stance on the issue.

Yet for all the political angst to which Black Wednesday gave rise, economically it heralded the beginning of one of the most successful periods in post-war British economic history. Economic growth averaged 3 per cent a year, unemployment eventually fell, yet inflation held steady at around 2 per cent to 3 per cent. It seemed that the UK had finally broken the 'stop-go' cycle that during the post-war period had repeatedly seen economic growth constrained in order to curb inflation. It was to the eternal frustration of ministers that, in the wake of Black Wednesday, voters appeared reluctant to give them any credit for this achievement.

Europe was not the only source of the government's troubles. Also important was what came to be known as 'sleaze'. In an attempt to turn his party's fortunes around, at the 1993 Conservative conference John Major gave what came to be dubbed his 'Back to Basics' speech. Acknowledging a pace of social change that some found uncomfortable, Major made a nostalgic appeal for the need to uphold traditional values of 'neighbourliness, decency, courtesy', a stance that came to be interpreted as an indication of the importance of family. It was to prove a bear trap for the Conservative Party when, the following year, some Conservative MPs were accused of taking cash for asking questions in the House of Commons, while others were reported to have engaged in sexual activity that was not consistent with their marriage vows. In short, the opposition were able to paint a picture of a party tainted by financial and sexual impropriety that appeared at odds with the traditional values that Major had been espousing. All in all, these allegations of 'sleaze', to which the Prime Minister attempted to respond by creating the Committee on Standards in Public Life, resulted in the resignation of eight ministers, though it was the Prime

Minister's good fortune that the affair that he had had with the well-known Conservative MP Edwina Currie did not come to light until after the 1997 election.

The divisions within the party on Europe and the party's dire position in the polls eventually persuaded Major to face down his critics – and to call a leadership election himself rather than face the risk of having one imposed on him, as had happened to Margaret Thatcher. On 22 June 1995, Major resigned as party leader and a ballot of MPs was held on 4 July. Only one challenger emerged, John Redwood, who resigned as Secretary of State for Wales in order to stand against the Prime Minister on a strongly Eurosceptic and right-wing platform. Under the rules for the election, if he was to avoid a second ballot in which new challengers could enter the race, the Prime Minister needed to win the support of over half of all Tory MPs and defeat his opponent by a margin of fifteen percentage points. Major passed that threshold comfortably, winning the backing of 56 per cent of MPs, while Redwood was supported by just 27 per cent. That result ensured the issue of the Tory leadership was settled until the election.

Labour's despondency about losing the 1992 election did not last long. Black Wednesday put paid to that. Meanwhile, the party now had a new leader, the Scots MP John Smith, who had first made his name in piloting the devolution legislation through the House of Commons in the 1970s. An Edinburgh lawyer, Smith offered a more urbane style than his predecessor, Neil Kinnock, a Welshman famous for his passionate rhetoric. Though some in the party felt the new leader did not take seriously enough the need for Labour to take further steps to improve its image and processes, Smith did win a key vote at the 1993 party conference on the introduction of one member, one vote in the selection of parliamentary candidates and in the trade union section of the electoral college that elected the party leader. The reform was designed to reduce the influence within the party of the trade unions' block vote. Smith also instigated the creation of Labour's National Policy Forum that served to reduce the role of party conference – and thus of both party activists and trade unions – in the party's policy-making process.

However, John Smith's sudden death from a heart attack in May 1994 required the party to find a new leader. There were two potentially leading candidates: Tony Blair, the shadow Home Secretary, whose charismatic style had already given him a high public profile, and Gordon Brown, the party's shadow Chancellor, who had deep roots in the party and especially in his native Scotland. The two men had long shared a similar view of the need for the party to reform, a cause that might suffer if both of them stood. At what became an apocryphal dinner at the Granita restaurant in Islington, it was reportedly agreed that, as seemingly the more popular of the two, Blair should put himself forward in the leadership contest but that he would then stand down in favour of Brown after serving two terms as Prime Minister.

Before the leadership election could be concluded, however, elections to the European Parliament were due to take place. The outcome of the ballot, held on 9 June, confirmed the message of the polls that the standing of the parties was now very different from what it had been two years before. Labour won as much as 44 per cent of the vote, while the Conservatives trailed on 28 per cent. Thus, when Tony Blair was declared the party's new leader with 57 per cent of the vote under the revised rules that had been pushed through by John Smith the previous year, he was inheriting a party that was seemingly already well set for victory at the next general election.

Nevertheless, Blair vigorously set about reforming his party with the aim of making it more electable. Central to this strategy was a belief that the party needed to move to the 'centre ground' ideologically in order to appeal to middle-class and aspirant working-class voters who, thanks to long-term change in the occupational structure, now constituted a majority of the electorate. His initial move was to indicate in his first party conference speech as leader that he wanted his party to rewrite Clause IV of its constitution. This clause committed Labour to 'the common ownership of the means of production, distribution and exchange' – that is, to an economy in which many key industries are nationalised. Symbolically, Blair's proposal represented a significant shift away from a socialist perspective. Moreover, it did so at a time when much of the existing structure of nationalised industries had recently been dismantled by the Conservative government, with many of the shares sold to individual investors. In short, Labour was now being invited to accept that government should not normally be involved in commercial activity.

Inevitably, the proposal met with vociferous opposition within the party, but at a special conference in April 1995, the party voted by three to one in favour of a change to a clause that said that Labour is a 'democratic socialist party' that believes in 'a community in which power, wealth and opportunity are in the hands of the many, not the few', a vision that was at least as consistent with the 'share-owning democracy' that Mrs Thatcher had espoused as it was a system of nationalised industries. Thereafter, the party changed a number of other key policy stances, and in so doing brought it closer to the position of the current government. It accepted the principle of 'welfare for work', under which receipt of benefits for those of working age was linked with stronger requirements to search or train for work. Much of the Conservative legislation on industrial relations was to be retained. Above all, the party was determined not to present their opponents with the opportunity to suggest that Labour would put up people's taxes, a tactic that Labour reckoned had cost it dear in 1992 when the Tories warned of 'Labour's Tax Bombshell'. Few spending pledges were offered, while the party committed itself to no increases in income tax rates and, for the first two years of a Labour government, to keeping to the tax and spending plans of the current government. As a result, even the pledge to create a devolved Scottish Parliament that would have the power to vary income tax was to be made conditional on the outcome of a referendum in which there would be a separate vote on whether it should have that tax power.

This ideological and policy repositioning was reflected in the party's campaigning. The party was rebranded 'New Labour', a deliberate attempt to convey the message that it had moved on from its difficult days in office between 1974 and 1979 and the divisions that had plagued it in the 1980s. 'New Labour, New Britain' was its battle cry. The party attempted to popularise its policy stances and address the increased scepticism about politics occasioned by the 'sleaze' revelations by creating a pledge card that contained five specific pledges as to what a Labour government would achieve. Meanwhile, the links with the trade unions were loosened not only in the party's procedures but also as a source of finance. The party increased its individual (fee-paying) membership by 150,000 between 1992 and 1996, while its attempts to woo business included not only assuaging their political fears but also seeking their financial contributions.

The Conservatives tried to counteract Labour's repositioning. In 1996, the party unveiled a controversial poster campaign in which Labour's slogan was rewritten as 'New Labour, New Danger' accompanied by a picture of a smiling Tony Blair with red eyes against a black background. What came to be known as the 'Demon Eyes' campaign was certainly one of the most striking in British post-war campaigning, but it was, in truth, an implicit acknowledgement that Labour had changed the way in which it was being viewed and discussed – and it had little impact on Labour's standing and Tony Blair's personal popularity in the polls. Meanwhile, having attacked Labour's alleged tax plans so vociferously in 1992, the Conservatives now found themselves on the defensive for the decisions they had subsequently made. In particular, the 1993 Budget froze income tax allowances, imposed VAT on domestic fuel and reduced mortgage interest relief. Reductions in the basic rate of income tax in 1995 and again in 1996 were not enough to take the sting out of Labour's charge that the Conservatives had presided over twenty-two tax increases since the 1992 general election. According to Ipsos, Labour were narrowly ahead of the Conservatives in the run-up to the election as the best party on taxation.

Labour's repositioning on tax did, however, open up some potential space for the Liberal Democrats. The party had fought the 1992 election on a proposal to increase the basic rate of income tax by a penny in the pound, which, together with an extra 5p on a packet of cigarettes, was designed to fund extra spending on education. The policy was retained and now gave the party a distinctive edge. That said, the advent of New Labour meant that Tony Blair's party was ideologically in much the same space as that occupied by the Social Democrat Party (SDP), formed in 1981 as a result of a split in the Labour Party and one of the two predecessor parties to the Liberal Democrats. The Liberal Democrats struggled to retain their support in the wake of Labour's rebranding as New Labour. Prior to the election of Tony Blair as Labour leader, the Liberal Democrats were averaging 20 per cent in the polls, while the party won 17 per cent of the vote and two seats – their first ever – in the May 1994 European elections. But just a year later, the party's support was down to 15 per cent, and by the time the general election came into view at the beginning of 1997, it was running at just 13 per cent.

Yet the collapse in Conservative support also opened up opportunities for the Liberal Democrats. Most of the seats they had a chance of gaining were currently held by John Major's party. Indeed, the Liberal Democrats gained four seats from the Conservatives in by-elections during the parliament, three of them before the change of Labour leader. Although first signalled within a month of the 1992 election – that is, well before the collapse in Conservative support – the decision of the party leader, Paddy Ashdown, to present his party as anti-Conservative rather than as 'equidistant' between the two main parties proved to be well timed. Meanwhile, there was some speculation that Tony Blair would seek to form a coalition with the Liberal Democrats should Labour have little or no majority after the next election. Certainly, concern in Labour's ranks that, as in the 1970s, the party would not have a big enough majority to pursue successfully what was potentially a divisive programme of constitutional reform led in the months leading up to the election to talks between the two parties, headed by Robin Cook for Labour and Robert Maclennan for the Liberal Democrats, that resulted in a joint commitment to pursue a programme of constitutional reform, including Scottish and Welsh devolution, a mayor for London and a commission on electoral reform.

Despite a healthy economy, the introduction of tax cuts and attacks on New Labour, the Conservatives struggled in the run-up to the election to make much of an impression on Labour's lead in the polls. By the beginning of 1997, the party stood on average at 31 per cent. Although that represented something of an improvement on the nadir in its fortunes during the parliament – it was down to 25 per cent at the beginning 1995 – the party was still trailing Labour by as much as twenty points. There was little the Prime Minister could do other than to play a long game. The last Thursday on which an election could be held was 22 May, but with local elections due to take place in England three weeks earlier, Major eventually opted to hold a dual poll on that date. The announcement to that effect was made on 17 March, thereby paving the way for a six-week campaign rather than one of three or four weeks as had become the norm. If a long parliament had failed to turn things around for the Conservatives, perhaps the opportunity to turn the heat on Labour in a long campaign would enable them to do so.

One key feature of the election was that it was to be fought on new parliamentary boundaries. In giving the party an overall majority of just twenty-one despite enjoying as much as an eight-point lead over their principal opponents, the electoral system had been relatively unkind to the Conservatives in 1992. One key reason was that the average electorate in constituencies won by Labour was nearly 10,000 less than the average electorate in seats won by the Conservatives, a gap that had widened since the boundaries were last redrawn before the 1983 election because Britain's population was moving out of (mainly Labour) urban conurbations into more suburban and more rural (and thus more Conservative) locations. One of the government's first actions on winning the 1992 election was to speed up the process of redrawing parliamentary constituencies in order to ensure that what could otherwise be a lengthy process was completed before the next election. That, the party hoped, would at least ensure that it did not have to fight the next election with one hand behind its back.

In practice, however, the review was not as favourable to the Conservatives as they had hoped. According to estimates of what the outcome of the 1992 election would have been if the new boundaries had been in place, the Conservatives would still have secured only a majority of twenty-seven, just six more than they actually achieved.

In part, this was because the review did not fully eliminate the difference between the average electorate in Conservative and Labour seats – not least because constituencies in predominantly Labour Scotland and Wales were still smaller than those in England. But it was also because Labour was more effective at putting forward proposals to the Boundary Commissions that resulted in a more efficient geographical distribution of its vote. Not only were the Conservatives well behind Labour in the polls; but they faced the prospect of needing to be as much as five points ahead just to secure an overall majority of one.

Meanwhile, it looked like the party's task would not be made any easier by the Referendum Party, formed in 1994 by the multi-millionaire Sir James Goldsmith, which campaigned against the UK's membership of what it regarded was now a 'federal Europe' and backed holding a referendum on the UK's membership of the European Union. Its presence thus rubbed the sore of the Conservative Party's internal divisions on Europe. Sir James's party eventually contested 547 of the 641 seats in Great Britain, the largest fourth-party slate in post-war British politics. The only seats the party did not contest were those held by avowedly Eurosceptic Conservative or Labour MPs. It provided a more substantial challenge than that provided by the UK Independence Party (UKIP), which had been founded in 1993 by the historian Dr Alan Sked, and which in its first general election eventually contested 194 seats, most of them constituencies that were also contested by the Referendum Party, thereby fracturing what the polls suggested was only a relatively low level of support for any kind of Eurosceptic party.

Any hopes that John Major might have had that a long campaign would be to his advantage soon withered. One consequence of his decision to prorogue Parliament early was that it stopped the publication of a report by Sir Gordon Downey, the Parliamentary Commissioner for Standards, an office that had also been created in the wake of the concern about sleaze, on various allegations involving Conservative MPs. In particular, this included Sir Gordon's investigation into claims that Tim Smith and Neil Hamilton had taken money from a lobbyist to ask parliamentary questions on behalf of Mohamed

Al-Fayed, the owner of Harrods department store. The opposition felt able to claim there was a deliberate cover-up and the suspicion that there might be gave journalists a reason to pursue the story. Eventually, some of Sir Gordon's unpublished evidence appeared in *The Guardian* on 21 March. But while its publication persuaded Smith to withdraw from his Beaconsfield seat, Hamilton was still endorsed by his local Conservative association as the candidate for his local constituency, Tatton.

'Tory sleaze' thus came to dominate the beginning of the election campaign. The issue further made the headlines when the Labour Party persuaded its candidate in Tatton (a safe Tory seat) to offer to stand down if a cross-party agreement could be forged to back a single 'anti-sleaze' candidate. On 30 March, Martin Bell, a well-known BBC war correspondent, put himself forward as an independent candidate and was soon endorsed by both Labour and the Liberal Democrats. He then proceeded to have a much-publicised encounter with Hamilton and his wife. Meanwhile, on 27 March, *The Sun* published allegations of an affair involving Piers Merchant, the Conservative MP for Beckenham, though eventually Merchant survived. Only when John Major tackled the issue head-on at a press conference on 1 April did the story began to die down – but in the meantime, the public had been reminded of one of the key issues on which the government had persistently been on the defensive during the 1992–97 parliament.

Yet just as sleaze began to disappear from the headlines, so Tory divisions on Europe came to dominate the media agenda once again. The government's official stance on joining the single currency was to 'negotiate and then decide', a stance designed to keep the party's Eurosceptics and Europhiles on side. But apart from criticism of this stance from the Referendum Party and UKIP, the press were aware of the Conservative Party's divisions and began to peruse the statements about monetary union in the addresses of individual Conservative candidates. Not only did many a backbencher indicate that they were opposed to monetary union but so also did some junior ministers. Of 385 addresses obtained by the *Daily Telegraph*, nearly half (190) indicated opposition to a common currency. The issue eventually forced John Major into his most dramatic intervention in the campaign when he pleaded with his party, 'Don't bind my hands when I am negotiating on behalf of the British people.'

Between them, sleaze and the European Union, together with speculation about the parties' strategies and prospects, dominated the front-page headlines and the lead stories on the television news. In contrast, taxation and the economy largely took a back seat. In short, the agenda of the election campaign was far from helpful to the Conservatives. Not that Labour did not come under some pressure where its determination to be seen as fiscally responsible rather than profligate potentially gave rise to internal tensions. At its 1996 party conference, Labour's transport spokesperson, Andrew Smith, had indicated opposition to the privatisation of the National Air Traffic Services (NATS) by declaring, 'Our air is not for sale.' However, the promise to keep to the Conservatives' spending plans implied reliance on the funds that were due to be raised by NATS's privatisation in the next parliament. An acknowledgement of that fact by the shadow Chancellor, Gordon Brown, was followed by pressure, including not least on Smith, to indicate when the policy was changed.

Meanwhile, it was also thought that Blair was less keen than many of his colleagues on his party's proposals for devolution in Scotland and Wales. There had been considerable disquiet within the Labour Party and elsewhere at Blair's announcement in June 1996 that the proposed parliament in Scotland and assembly in Wales would be established only after referendums had been held – it had been the failure to secure sufficient public support for devolution in the two countries in referendums held in 1979 that had eventually scuppered the plans put forward by the government of Jim Callaghan and subsequently led to that government's downfall. As we noted earlier, the Labour leader was particularly keen to avoid the impression that devolution would occasion an increase in taxes in Scotland. However, Blair's suggestion in an interview with *The Scotsman* that the financial powers of the proposed parliament were akin to those of an English parish council resulted in criticism not only from the Conservatives, who opposed devolution, but also from the Liberal Democrats and the Scottish National Party, both of whom were keen to see the parliament established.

Since the late 1950s, television had become the principal mechanism through which voters learnt about what was being said and promised in an election campaign. Yet, in contrast to the United States and elsewhere, no British election had as yet been graced by a televised debate between the main party leaders. All the parties were wary of the impact such a debate could have on the structure of the campaign. They were keen to promote their own messages rather than dance to the tune of the media. Meanwhile, Prime Ministers were often reluctant to add authority to an event in which opposition leaders would be treated as their equal, while the party that was ahead in the polls was often reluctant to take the risk of participating in such an uncontrolled event, and there was always the thorny question of whether and on what terms the Liberal Democrats and the nationalist parties in Scotland and Wales should participate. On the other hand, the television channels were themselves keen that one or more debates should be held, ideally with one for each of the two main terrestrial broadcasters, the BBC and ITV.

However, with his party badly behind in the polls, the opportunity to debate with Blair was potentially not unattractive to Major. Meanwhile, Labour had sufficient confidence in their own standard bearer to challenge the Prime Minister to take part in a debate. Indeed, discussions had already taken place between the parties and the media in the months leading up to the election, and they continued in earnest when John Major announced on 16 March that he was willing to take part in a debate. However, in the event, the talks came to nothing. Although near agreement had seemingly been reached on two debates, one on the BBC, one on ITV, in which some of the time would be a head-to-head between Major and Blair while the remainder would also provide space for Paddy Ashdown, in the event, disagreement about the details of Ashdown's involvement together with Labour's decision to impose a deadline on reaching a final agreement saw the talks fail. Almost inevitably, there were suggestions that perhaps, as the prospect neared, both the Conservatives and Labour got cold feet about the idea.

Unlike the broadcast media, the press were, of course, not required to be impartial in their coverage of the campaign. Indeed, the support given to the Conservatives in election campaigns by a predominantly pro-Conservative press was the source of much angst and criticism within Labour's ranks. That outlook was only reinforced when, in the wake of the Conservatives' surprise success in 1992, *The Sun* had declared that it was '*The Sun* Wot Won It' for John Major. However, this was a very different election. After being heavily courted by Labour, this time *The Sun*, aware of the party's current popularity among its own readers, changed sides and endorsed Labour. Meanwhile, traditionally Conservative papers like the *Daily Mail* and the *Daily Express* were heavily Eurosceptic in outlook and thus were lukewarm about John Major's government, while *The Times* did not endorse a Conservative victory but stayed on the fence. With the *Daily Mirror* still firmly backing Labour, the overall readership of Labour-supporting papers was double that of Conservative-backing ones – the first time Labour had enjoyed such an advantage. This was an election in which newspapers were following their readers rather than vice versa.

Not only was the newspaper landscape very different, but so also were some of the mechanisms by which the parties attempted to secure more favourable coverage. True, the structure of the typical campaign morning was what had by now become a familiar one. Journalists trudged across SW1, first to attend a Liberal Democrat press conference at 8 a.m., then, after a quick exit, a Labour one at 8.30 a.m. and, finally, the Conservatives at 9.15 a.m. or 9.30 a.m. These press conferences were regarded by the parties as their opportunity to send out the message they hoped would dominate the news agenda, at least until the lunchtime bulletins, though on occasion the subject on which they focused was changed as a result of developments during the campaign. However, the press conferences were now more than just a public exchange of views. Also of importance were the unattributable briefings from 'spin doctors' who provided off-the-record assistance (favourable to their party) in interpreting what had been said on stage. The party leaders' press officers, Sheila Gunn for the Conservatives and Alastair Campbell for Labour, were key figures in their respective campaign teams.

Meanwhile, the advent of rolling 24-hour news – Sky News, founded in 1989, was now becoming a significant presence in the media landscape while the BBC's Radio 5 started its round-the-clock programming of news and sport in 1994 – was beginning to increase the speed of the news cycle. This made it important for the parties to rebut their opponents' negative claims quickly before they secured widespread publicity. During the 1992–97 parliament, Labour had invested in Excalibur Electronic Filing Software, which enabled its researchers quickly to compile the facts needed to rebut Conservative accusations. Rebuttal was something at which the Conservative Research Department had always been relatively adept, but the adoption of new technology enabled Labour to develop an edge in an election where negative campaigning was again much in evidence.

Technological change also enabled the centre of each party's campaign to communicate the messages it wanted to convey, including rebuttals, more quickly to its candidates, spokespersons and the press. Fax machines were by now ubiquitous, while email was becoming more common and could be used to convey internal messages to candidates as well as press releases to the press. Meanwhile, the use of pagers to convey messages could now be supplemented by greater use of mobile phones, especially following the advent of SMS messaging shortly after the 1992 election and the emergence of the smart phone in 1994. The speed and intensity of the information war between the party machines, as well as the opportunity to centralise party campaigns, reached new heights. Labour, in particular, was keen to take the opportunity afforded by new technology to avoid its candidates unwittingly going 'off message' and disrupting the party's carefully planned messaging.

The 1992–97 parliament had also witnessed a growing use of personal computers. Not only did they enable constituency parties to develop and print their leaflets; but they could also be used to create databanks of voters, their demographics and known political history

– and thus send direct mail or even videos tailored to their particular interests and concerns. They were also used to support canvassing, an activity that was increasingly being undertaken by phone, including from centralised phone banks. The 1992–97 parliament also witnessed the advent of the first party websites, though as yet access to the internet for the general population was still relatively limited. The websites were primarily used to post material such as policy pronouncements and press releases that were also made available elsewhere.

One traditional ritual of British election campaigns – the party election broadcasts that gave the parties free airtime but which were accompanied by a ban on paid political advertising – appeared once again during the campaign. The Conservatives and Labour were given five broadcasts, the Liberal Democrats four, while, as at previous elections, any party that fielded fifty candidates was entitled to one. Separate arrangements were made for the nationalist parties in Scotland and Wales. However, a gradually diversifying media landscape was beginning to take its toll on the audience figures. Most of the broadcasts either featured the leader or were heavily laced with negative campaigning. Only one broadcast, a Labour video that featured a bulldog as a symbol of patriotism, secured much in the way of wider publicity.

The 1992 election had proven to be something of a disaster for the opinion polls. On average, those whose interviewing concluded within forty-eight hours of the election had suggested that Labour was a point ahead of the Conservatives, well adrift of the eight-point lead that emerged from the ballot boxes. It was the polls' worst attempt at anticipating the outcome of an election since 1970. A lengthy inquiry by the Market Research Society pointed to deficiencies in sampling plus a relative reluctance among Conservative voters to declare their voting intentions. Changes in methods and reporting ensued.

Hitherto, all polling had been conducted face to face with interviewers given a 'quota' of different kinds of people (in terms of their age, sex and social background) that they were required to interview and a location where their interviews should be obtained. Otherwise interviewers had discretion about whom they contacted. After 1992,

ICM, and subsequently Gallup, switched to conducting their polls by phone with the numbers called selected by random digit dialling. Most companies also attempted to adjust the results of their polls for the apparent impact of differential refusal or aimed to improve the quality of their quota sampling. Nevertheless, their performance in 1992 helped explain some of the scepticism about the large Labour lead now being reported by the polls, and certainly resulted in less prominence being given to their results in the media.

Thanks to the rules on impartiality, the Liberal Democrats, typically, receive more coverage from the broadcasters during an election campaign than during peacetime – and they often register an increase in their support during the campaign. The 1997 election certainly proved to be a case in point. When the election was announced, the Liberal Democrats were on average down at just 12 per cent in the polls, while Labour was way ahead on 55 per cent, twenty-six points ahead of the Conservatives on 29 per cent. By the time polling day arrived, the Liberal Democrats had moved up to 16 per cent, while the Conservatives had done no more than edge up to 30 per cent. Labour, though still dominant on 48 per cent, had proven unable to retain all the gains it had made after 1994 at the expense of the Liberal Democrats. Labour's task in the campaign had been to hang on to as much as possible of the large volume of support it seemingly already had, and while it largely fended off the threat from the Conservatives, it was rather less successful at beating off the challenge from Paddy Ashdown's party.

Published at 10 p.m. when the polls closed, two exit polls, one commissioned by the BBC and one by ITV, pointed to much the same outcome. Based on an exercise conducted solely in marginal seats, MORI for ITV suggested that Labour would secure an overall majority of 159. Meanwhile, on the basis of a poll conducted by NOP, the BBC initially simply said that Labour was heading for a 'landslide', though it subsequently revealed that, in line with the final opinion polls, it was expecting Labour, on 47 per cent, to be eighteen points ahead of the Conservatives, while the Liberal Democrats were expected to win 18 per cent. In short, as the first ballot boxes were being opened shortly after the close of the polls at 10 p.m., all the evidence pointed unequivocally to Tony Blair replacing John Major as Prime Minister, backed by a majority of a size that many had thought impossible for Labour to achieve.

It was not long before it was clear that this expectation would be fulfilled. By 11 p.m., the race to be the first constituency to declare had been won by Sunderland South. Although a safe Labour seat, the 11 per cent swing from Conservative to Labour it reported would, if replicated elsewhere, deliver a large Labour majority. Ninety minutes later, Gisela Stuart secured the first Labour gain of the night on a 10 per cent swing in Birmingham Edgbaston, a seat the party had never previously won. Meanwhile, just before 1 a.m., Basildon, where the Conservatives' success in defending the seat in 1992 had been the first key sign that the polls were wrong, was captured by Labour's Angela Smith on a 15 per cent swing. By now, there was no doubt that Labour would win, and win well.

But the high drama of the night came a little later, as Tory notable after Tory notable lost their seats. First, the former Cabinet minister David Mellor, once dubbed the 'Minister for Fun' but who had resigned shortly after the 1992 election in the wake of a 'kiss and tell' story about an extra-marital affair, lost his seat in Putney. Shortly thereafter, the first current Cabinet minister fell – the Secretary of State for Scotland, Michael Forsyth, lost his Stirling seat in what was to prove an unprecedented whitewash for the Conservatives north of the border. And then just after 3 a.m., the charismatic and Eurosceptic Secretary of State for Defence, Michael Portillo, lost his Enfield Southgate seat on as much as a 17.5 per cent swing, a result that was greeted with an ashen face by his Cabinet colleague Gillian Shephard. Portillo's spectacular defeat came to symbolise the story of the election, and indeed a book about election night was entitled *Were you still up for Portillo?* Shortly after Portillo's defeat was announced, Labour reached the magic total of 330 seats required for an overall majority. By the end of the night, as many as seven current Cabinet ministers had lost their seats, beating the previous record of five at the 1945 election.

1997 – JOHN CURTICE

Many Labour activists and senior MPs certainly were up when, at 5.30 a.m., an early May dawn greeted Tony Blair as he addressed a rally outside the Royal Festival Hall that had spent the night celebrating to the tune of Labour's campaign theme song, 'Things Can Only Get Better'. 'A new dawn has broken, has it not?' quipped Tony Blair. He went on: 'We have been elected as New Labour, and we will govern as New Labour.' He promised 'a new era of politics' from what he said was now the 'the party of all the people'. Even with victory now achieved, he was still keen to put clear distance between the Labour Party he now led and the 'Old Labour' of the past.

Later that morning, John Major announced he was standing down as Conservative leader and in accordance with the ritual of how power is transferred in Britain, travelled to Buckingham Palace to hand in his resignation as Prime Minister. Later that day, he used his new freedom to watch Surrey play cricket at the Oval. After also visiting Buckingham Palace in order to be invited by the Queen to form a new government, Blair was greeted in Downing Street by a large and enthusiastic crowd of well-wishers, all of them waving the Union flag. They cheered Blair as he vacated his official car and opted to walk up Downing Street to the door of No. 10, shaking hands with the crowd along the way. It looked like a deliberate change of style designed to herald what Blair promised would be a different kind of government.

Once the final straggle of results had been counted on Friday morning, it emerged that Labour had secured an overall majority of 179. With 419 seats, the party had more MPs than it had ever won before. The Liberal Democrats, too, had a good election, winning forty-six seats, the highest third-party tally since 1929. Meanwhile, the Conservatives, with 165 seats only narrowly kept their tally above the all-time low of 157 seats to which the party sank in 1906. Indeed, it was often argued that, much like 1906 and also 1945, the outcome heralded a new political epoch.

Yet, although the 10.3 per cent swing from Conservative to Labour since 1992 represented the biggest swing since 1945, in terms of votes Labour's success was not as spectacular as that anticipated by the polls. The party won 44 per cent of the vote (in Great Britain), rather less than the 48 per cent anticipated by the final polls. Meanwhile, at twelve points, the lead over the Conservatives was notably short of the eighteen-point lead in the final polls, an overestimate that, in a closer election, would have secured much more attention from critics of an industry that had apparently not fully resolved the difficulties it had encountered in 1992. Indeed, despite Labour's record tally of seats, the party's share of the vote was well down on the 49 per cent the party secured in 1945, while it did no more than replicate what the party had achieved in the 1994 European election shortly before Blair became Labour leader.

The explanation for the landslide in terms of seats lies in the geography of how people voted. First, the decline in Conservative support since 1992 was more marked in seats where the party had previously been strong. This was almost an arithmetical inevitability in the wake of what was as much as an eleven-point decline in its support across the country as a whole, but it meant that the swing against the party was greater in those seats it was trying to defend. Second, voters demonstrated an unprecedented level of willingness to vote tactically for whichever opposition party, Labour or the Liberal Democrats, seemed best able to defeat the Conservatives locally. One estimate suggested that this pattern cost the Conservatives between twenty-five and thirty-five seats and – together with the fact that the Liberal Democrats were better placed to win Conservative rather than Labour seats – played a key role in the Liberal Democrats' ability to win a record high tally of seats, even though the party's share of the overall vote was less than that of the Liberal–SDP Alliance in 1983 (26 per cent) or 1987 (23 per cent). The Liberal Democrats' success in concentrating their vote enabled them to overcome partially at least the barrier to converting votes into seats that the single-member plurality electoral system had hitherto created for the party.

In truth, there was a simple message coming from the ballot boxes. Most voters wanted a change of government, and some were sufficiently indifferent between Labour and the Liberal Democrats that they were willing to use their vote in what seemed the most effective way of achieving that outcome. It was a mood that had seemingly set in early during the 1992–97 parliament, while thereafter the divisions and sleaze allegations that surrounded the Conservatives militated against its ability to rehabilitate itself with the electorate despite a healthy economy and tax cuts. New Labour seized the opportunity it was afforded, and indeed generated a degree of enthusiasm about the prospect of a change of government, but this was an election in which, above all, voters wanted 'to throw the rascals out'.

John Curtice is a professor of politics at Strathclyde University and a senior research fellow at the National Centre for Social Research and the UK in a Changing Europe network.

45

2001

ALIA MIDDLETON

Dissolution: 11 May 2001
Polling day: 7 June 2001
Seats contested: 659
Total electorate / Voted / Turnout: 44,403,238 / 26,367,383 / 59.4 per cent
Candidates (total 3,319): Conservative – 643; Labour – 640; Liberal Democrats – 639; UKIP – 428; Green – 145; SNP – 72; Plaid Cymru – 40; SNP – 33; SDLP – 18; Sinn Féin – 18; UUP – 17; DUP – 14
Prime Minister on polling day: Tony Blair
Main party leaders: Labour – Tony Blair; Conservative – William Hague; Liberal Democrats – Charles Kennedy; SNP – John Swinney; UKIP – Jeffrey Titford; UUP – David Trimble; Plaid Cymru – Ieuan Wyn Jones; DUP – Ian Paisley; Sinn Féin – Gerry Adams; SDLP – John Hume; Green – Margaret Wright and Mike Woodin

Party performance:

Party	Votes	Percentage share	Seats
Labour	10,724,953	40.7	412
Conservative	8,357,615	31.6	166
Liberal Democrats	4,814,321	18.3	52
SNP	464,314	1.8	5
UKIP	390,563	1.5	0
UUP	216,839	26.8	6
Plaid Cymru	195,893	0.7	4

DUP	181,999	22.5	5
Sinn Féin	175,933	21.7	4
SDLP	169,865	21	3
Green	166,477	0.6	0

Result: Labour majority of 167 seats

After the 1997 general election, with Labour in a seemingly unassailable position, buoyed by positive economic results and – at first – continued high poll ratings, it appeared that, whenever the next election might occur, the party would have an uncomplicated contest to retain power. The Conservatives, by contrast, were at the same level of support ahead of the 2001 election as they had been ahead of the 1997 election, while support for the Liberal Democrats remained consistent. In this environment, it seemed that a Labour victory was all but a foregone conclusion. Yet for a while in September and October 2000, Labour's prospects looked far bleaker.

An original election date of 8 May 2001 had been preferred by Blair and his team for some time, coming shortly after a Budget where they expected positive economic news; however, there had been some nervousness after Labour took a dramatic dip in the polls in September and October 2000. This was due to protests and blockades over rising petrol and diesel prices, which led to widespread disruption of supplies. Polls showed that the public thought the government had handled the crisis badly. However, with threats to essential services and declining public enthusiasm, by November, the government's polling began to recover – and plans for a May election were underway. By the turn of 2001, key personnel were in place, posters approved and policy announcements planned for the upcoming Labour campaign. Likewise, by this point, Hague had taken to spending considerably more time in party HQ than his predecessors; a sophisticated targeting of potential voters was planned. However, February saw the emergence of foot-and-mouth disease; the first outbreak in the United Kingdom since 1967. More than 6 million cows and sheep were culled, public rights of way halted and key events postponed. In total, the outbreak cost the taxpayer £3 billion.

Speculation continued in the media regarding a May election, but a lack of public appetite, plus issues regarding potential cross-contamination in rural polling stations – as well as a degree of reticence by Blair in calling an election before the outbreak was under control – led to both the local elections and the general election moving to 7 June 2001. The postponement also meant that the public would be less likely to be confronted with images of the outbreak during the campaign, and it would provide Labour's incumbent candidates in fifteen rural marginal seats with a more favourable context in which to fight the election.

Since the 1997 general election, there had been key changes in the leadership of both the Conservative Party and the Liberal Democrats. John Major resigned on 2 May 1997 after almost seven years leading the party. Six candidates announced their intention to succeed him: his opponent from the 1995 leadership contest John Redwood, former Home Secretary Michael Howard, former Health Secretary Stephen Dorrell, long-standing Cabinet minister and former Chancellor Ken Clarke, former Cabinet minister under both Thatcher and Major, Peter Lilley, and William Hague, Welsh Secretary for the last two years of the Major government, who had been an MP for only eight years – the least experienced of all. Dorrell withdrew before the first ballot, declaring his support for Clarke. In the first ballot of MPs, Howard was eliminated, Lilley withdrew, while Clarke came out on top. Clarke won by just two votes in the second ballot a week later, when Redwood was eliminated. Despite attempts to inveigle Michael Heseltine into the leadership contest, and a pact between Redwood and Clarke, in the final ballot on 19 June, Hague triumphed, with ninety votes to Clarke's seventy-two, arguably due to his comparatively Eurosceptic position versus Clarke. This was the last Conservative leadership election before a rule change a year later enabled party members to have the final say. Hague was just thirty-six.

Despite being faced with a Herculean task in turning around a party decimated to the extent the Conservatives had been in 1997, there were some positive hints regarding Hague's leadership, particularly with the party's doubling of the number of their seats at the

European Parliament elections in 1999 from eighteen to thirty-six, pushing Labour into second place. For the Liberal Democrats, Paddy Ashdown, who had led the party since 1988, resigned somewhat unexpectedly in 1999. He said at the time that he had achieved all that he wished, although there was speculation that he was hoping to take over as secretary-general of NATO. Victorious after four rounds of voting was Charles Kennedy, first elected to Parliament in 1983, becoming the 23-year-old Baby of the House. Kennedy, for the first time, introduced a shadow Cabinet to the party and adopted a genial, relaxed leadership persona, enhanced by his appearance on TV panel shows. For Labour, with the resignation of Peter Mandelson, Gordon Brown was now overseeing the campaign alongside Douglas Alexander. Alastair Campbell was also based in Millbank to keep channels of communication open. As far as possible, the successful 1997 campaign and campaign team were replicated.

The election was formally announced by Blair on a visit to St Saviour's and St Olave's School in Southwark, rather than the more traditional lectern outside No. 10 Downing Street. Despite being greeted by protesters as he arrived, Blair toured the school, before listening to the choir and giving a speech in which he asked for a mandate for new and radical change. He was pictured prayerbook in hand, framed by a stained-glass window, and the juxtaposition of the school environment with a partisan call to arms was met with criticism from his own party, other parties, the media and the hosting headmistress.

William Hague, meanwhile, launched his campaign from a soapbox in the centre of Watford; a constituency lost by the Conservatives in 1997 after holding it for eighteen years, promising to give British people back their country. Charles Kennedy hopped onto a plane, despite his fear of flying, to begin a whistle-stop tour, including visiting eleven cities in three days. Yet despite the leaders' expressed desire to meet and engage with the public, the press noted that such meetings were highly orchestrated and the leaders remained remote.

The day of 16 May was one in the campaign that Labour may have wished to forget. Jack Straw, the then Home Secretary, was addressing the annual Police Federation conference in Brighton, speaking on

Labour's achievements in tackling crime. His speech was met with laughter, heckling and – in a sobering reflection of Tony Blair's experience the previous year in front of the Women's Institute – slow hand-clapping. Straw appeared flustered and left the stage, his mood dampened, although he later claimed to be used to 'rumbustious debate'. Shortly afterwards, Tony Blair arrived at the Queen Elizabeth Hospital in Birmingham, to tour the facilities and meet staff and patients, accompanied by a throng of journalists and cameras. Before he crossed the threshold, he was confronted by Sharon Storer – a member of the public who passionately expressed the poor treatment her partner was receiving in the hospital. He had been forced to wait in A&E overnight despite his vulnerability as the unit treating his cancer had no beds. Storer also upbraided Blair on the lack of investment in facilities and staff, leading to poor care. After a two-minute tirade, Storer pushed past a somewhat taken-aback Blair, who later spoke to journalists about the investments promised for the health service. That evening, blissfully unaware of the difficult day on the Labour campaign, Deputy Prime Minister John Prescott arrived in Rhyl aboard the Prescott Express bus, ready to address activists in the village hall. As he crossed the road, accompanied by journalists, he was confronted by a group of protesters angry about the planned fox-hunting ban as well as the low level of rural wages. Amid the booing, one protester, Craig Evans, threw an egg at close-range, hitting Prescott on the side of the face. The Deputy Prime Minister proceeded to punch Evans in the face, before grappling with him. As Prescott was rushed away into the village hall, and other protesters continued to shout at him, the Labour candidate Chris Ruane, the seat's MP since 1997, told the protesters they had embarrassed themselves. Prescott later made a statement but did not apologise for the punch. Despite fears from Blair and Labour HQ about how the incident would be received, there seemed to be no negative repercussions; indeed, quite the opposite. The press leapt on it, with front pages featuring 'the Prescott Punch' and 'Two Jabs' (a play on Prescott's nickname of Two Jags). He had got away with it.

Hague had been selected as Conservative leader partly on the basis of his comparative Eurosceptic approach, with the Conservatives voting to oppose monetary union in the next two parliaments in 1998 and standing on this basis in the European parliamentary elections the following year. Partly due to their success at these elections, Europe – and specifically not joining the euro – became a key theme of the Conservatives' campaign. Under Conservative policy proposals, Britain would be 'in Europe, not run by Europe'. This was a policy area in which the party had an opportunity to clearly articulate a policy that was demonstrably different not only from the cautious approach of Major but from the more positive positioning of Labour and the Liberal Democrats. Hague further emphasised this in his speech of March 2001, where he likened Britain to a 'foreign land' if Labour were allowed to continue governing. The Conservatives were also trying to pick the party up from the ashes of 1997, and Europe was seen as an issue that core Conservative voters valued; the first step on the way to rebuilding the vote.

Former Prime Minister Margaret Thatcher made a campaign appearance on 22 May in Plymouth to deliver a speech, which was less gung-ho support for William Hague and more of a concerted effort to undermine the New Labour record. At times, she went off-script, declaring that she would never join the euro, rather than the next parliament timeframe agreed in the party. Thatcher's speech also caused further issues within the Conservative camp over Europe, with some MPs agreeing with her total opposition to the euro. Longer-lasting was the cultural reference at the start of her speech, where she equated her appearance in Plymouth with the recent cinema release of *The Mummy Returns* – an advert for which she had been driven past. This gave rise to considerable glee among political cartoonists but also demonstrated just how difficult it was for Hague to escape from her shadow.

With less than a week to go before polling day, Hague launched a countdown 'to save the pound' (including a countdown clock), proposing that the result of the election being a de facto referendum on Europe. Yet, despite the media reporting regularly on the party's policies towards Europe, it did not resonate with voters, who showed themselves to be more concerned with health and education. A late shift by the party towards these issues was too little too late. Labour, on the other hand, pressed ahead with Brown's five tests of economic readiness and also committed to a referendum prior to monetary union.

A controversial statement emerged from an anonymous Conservative in the *Financial Times* on 14 May 2001; they stated that the party would make £20 billion of tax cuts if they were elected, rather than the £8 billion publicly claimed by the party in their manifesto. It emerged that the source was Oliver Letwin, shadow Chief Secretary to the Treasury, who subsequently went into hiding. Labour humorously released a wanted poster for him. On Letwin's re-emergence, although he confirmed he had indeed been the source of the story, he disputed the figures discussed. Yet the strength of the economy was one of the major assets of the Labour campaign.

The election of 2001 was still very much one fought via party election broadcasts and posters. One of the most famous being the superimposition of Thatcher's hair onto Hague's head above a message trying to dispel voter apathy. The Conservatives retaliated, playing on the expected Labour victory, by placing Blair's head in a bubble and inviting voters to burst it by voting Conservative. Conservative party election broadcasts were markedly negative in their attacks on Labour, with one using actors to portray criminals released by Labour, the party having moved away from Saatchi. Labour had also changed their advertising agency to TBWA, which had never worked for a political party before, resulting in election broadcasts that veered from positive stories about their time in office to mock-horror movies about the Conservatives. The Liberal Democrats offered a feel-good broadcast about Kennedy and his life.

The campaign also saw the creeping emergence of digital campaigning, although it was often experimental, rarely widely adopted and limited in its reach. Email proved to be a useful way to disseminate messages from party HQ to local candidates, and party websites were relaunched to adapt to technological advancements including targeted messaging, with resources specifically for journalists and party members, as well as carrying the latest news and the manifestos. Candidate websites also became more widespread, with facilities where voters could directly email the candidates. Tactical voting websites also began to appear. However, the potential of sending out mass emails to voters was complicated as parties needed voters to have explicitly consented to further communication from signing up to a newsletter before they were put on a mailing list. With the spread of mobile phone usage, parties were still reluctant to exploit this as a campaigning medium, but Labour did send out a limited number of text messages in the week leading up to polling day.

As in 1997, Labour were particularly adept at embedding the media into their campaign, with daily press conferences, often attended by Blair, and leaking of exclusives to friendly newspapers. Similarly, the Liberal Democrats also held regular press conferences. However, Hague held comparatively fewer, arguing instead that it was more important to be travelling around the country. The press landscape in 2001 was even more favourable to New Labour than it had been in 1997; the so-called Tory press had been replaced by the 'Tony press'. While the *Daily Mail* and *Daily Telegraph* continued to endorse the Conservatives (Margaret Thatcher wrote several bylines for the *Telegraph* during the campaign), *The Sun*, the *Daily Express*, *The Times*, *The Guardian*, the *Mirror* and *The Independent* all endorsed Labour – *The Times* and the *Daily Express* switching to Labour for the first time. However, this did not bring with it ringing praise for Blair; rather a general acceptance that a Labour victory would be the most likely outcome. Although the campaign was seen as a lengthy prelude to a foregone conclusion, the papers still reported at an equivalent level to 1997 on the policies and individuals. However, there were days when the election was not the front-page story, and the volume of stories marginally decreased in some as the campaign progressed. The *Daily Mail* dialled down its reporting on the contest, with no front-page feature on polling day itself. Yet there was a disparity between what polling suggested the voters valued (health and education) with what the press were reporting (Europe and the economy). Perhaps unsurprisingly given its newsworthiness, the 'Prescott punch' also proved to be one of the most popular lead stories during the campaign, including the dredging up of some images of Prescott boxing in his navy days, but this was also a sign of the media seizing on anything out of the ordinary that would liven up the coverage.

During the campaign itself, there was remarkably little movement in the polls. While Labour support did experience a slight decline, from just over 50 per cent to 45 per cent in the polls immediately before polling day, the Conservative level of support remained remarkably consistent – albeit low. Hague remained bullish throughout much of the campaign, though, arguing that there was plenty of time and that polls were often wrong. However, the Conservatives' own pollsters began predicting on 31 May that the Conservatives would lose, which subdued the rest of the party's campaign. Reportedly, some of the shadow Cabinet had bets on a Labour victory. By contrast, the campaign itself was a great boon in shaping positive public responses to Charles Kennedy, who was seen as an affable and effective communicator, liable to make humorous observations regarding his opponents and pop up at photo opportunities around the country. Honor Blackman, a former Bond girl, described Kennedy as 'sexier than Sean Connery' on one memorable campaign visit. As such, the Liberal Democrats saw an overall rise in support over the campaign, and a specific rise in Kennedy's popularity. Labour consistently retained a lead across different policy areas, as well as Blair's leadership versus Hague's.

By the early hours of 8 June, it became clear that Labour were once again victorious. Once again, it was a landslide; perhaps unsurprising, given the inability of Hague's Conservatives to have any cut through in the polls. Blair had, in his speech announcing the date of the general election, requested a mandate to support his planned improvements to health and education, and the 2001 general election provided it, alongside a majority of 167. Labour, although losing eight seats, also gained two, making a net loss of just six seats. The Conservatives gained a single seat overall while the Liberal Democrats gained six. Notably, Richard Taylor, a local GP standing independently on a platform of supporting Kidderminster Hospital, won

Wyre Forest from Labour. Voting for the SNP fell in 2001, with the party losing Galloway and Upper Nithsdale to the Conservatives. It is worth noting that this election saw the entry of two future Prime Ministers – David Cameron and Boris Johnson – to Parliament.

The morning after polling day, William Hague stood outside Conservative Central Office and resigned as leader of the Conservative Party, stating that 'no man is indispensable' and that the party were yet to convince the public that they were a plausible alternative government. Yet Hague remained in Parliament and serving a generally well-respected turn as David Cameron's first Foreign Secretary between 2010 and 2014, before retiring from Westminster at the 2015 general election. His successor in his seat, Richmond (Yorks), was future Prime Minister Rishi Sunak.

More concerning was the historically low turnout of 59.4 per cent – this was twelve percentage points down on 1997 and the lowest since 1918. This was largely blamed on the sense of inevitability that had accompanied another Labour victory from the start of the campaign, and – apart from the events of 16 May – a largely unremarkable campaign. For some, despite disillusionment with Labour's time in government so far, the Conservatives still did not represent a plausible governing alternative. Whatever the cause, the Conservatives, Labour and the Liberal Democrats all received fewer votes than they had in 1997.

Alia Middleton is a senior lecturer at the University of Surrey. Her research interests include political leadership and campaigning strategies, and her publications include *Communicating and Strategising Leadership in British Elections* (Palgrave Macmillan).

46

2005

ROBERT FORD

Dissolution: 11 April 2005
Polling day: 5 May 2005
Seats contested: 646
Total electorate / Voted / Turnout: 44,245,939 / 27,148,975 / 61.4 per cent
Candidates (total 3,554): Conservative – 630; Labour – 627; Liberal Democrats – 626; UKIP – 496; Green – 182; BNP – 119; SNP – 59; Plaid Cymru – 40; DUP – 18; SDLP – 18; Sinn Féin – 18; UUP – 18
Prime Minister on polling day: Tony Blair
Main party leaders: Labour – Tony Blair; Conservative – Michael Howard; Liberal Democrats – Charles Kennedy; UKIP – Roger Knapman; BNP – Nick Griffin; SNP – Alex Salmond; Green – Caroline Lucas and Keith Taylor; Plaid Cymru – Ieuan Wyn Jones; DUP – Ian Paisley; Sinn Féin – Gerry Adams; SDLP – Mark Durkan; UUP – David Trimble

Party performance:

Party	Votes	Percentage share	Seats
Labour	9,552,436	35.2	355
Conservative	8,784,915	32.4	198
Liberal Democrats	5,985,454	22	62
UKIP	605,973	2.2	0
SNP	412,267	1.5	6
Green	257,758	1	0

DUP	241,856	33.7	9
BNP	192,745	0.7	0
Plaid Cymru	174,838	0.6	3
Sinn Féin	174,530	24.3	5
UUP	127,414	17.8	1
SDLP	125,626	17.5	3

Result: Labour majority of sixty-six seats

Everything changed for Tony Blair at 9.03 a.m. Eastern Standard Time on 11 September 2001, when United Airlines Flight 175 collided with the South Tower of the World Trade Center in Manhattan. Blair and his colleagues had secured an unprecedented second landslide election win just months earlier. Both elections had been fought and won through a relentless focus on the domestic centre ground. The agenda Blair had set out for his second term was on the same terrain – deepening and broadening reforms meant to unleash economic growth and improve public services. All that now changed. The United States responded to the worst terror attacks in its history with an aggressive new foreign policy – the 'war on terror' – invading and occupying Afghanistan and Iraq in swift succession. Tony Blair sought to position himself as President George W. Bush's closest ally and therefore committed Britain as a major player in both wars. This was not a comfortable position for his party or the public. Blair's decision to join the American invasion of Iraq on flimsy evidence, and without United Nations support, divided his party and polarised the public. Blair won parliamentary backing for his war but paid a heavy price. His hitherto exceptional approval ratings collapsed in the wake of the war and never recovered. A leader with an unmatched gift for reading and articulating the public mood now fell to earth. Blair had carried his party to two landslide wins. To win a third term, his party would have to carry him.

Two wars in one term meant both the election and the parliament preceding it were unusually dominated by foreign policy. The Labour Prime Minister's unlikely personal alliance with a right-wing

Republican President isolated him at home and abroad – Blair was the only European social democratic leader to back both of America's wars of 'regime change'. Thousands of British troops were dispatched to support the invasion and occupation of Afghanistan in late 2001 and of Iraq in 2003. Both wars were fought and won quickly, prompting dreams of liberal democracies growing from the barrels of western guns. These dreams did not last. Both occupations unleashed chaos, corruption and communal violence, and local populations soon turned against the invaders. Lethal attacks by insurgents on civilians and British troops became a bloody staple of British evening news programmes throughout the parliament.

As chaos reigned in Baghdad and Basra, one question dominated debate in Westminster: did Prime Minister Blair lie in making the case to invade Iraq? Most of the public and much of the Labour Party had been wary about backing a second American invasion in two years, this time of a country whose links to the 9/11 terror attacks were tenuous at best. A case, therefore, needed to be made. Blair put all of his formidable persuasive talents into building the case for war, claiming Iraq's dictator Saddam Hussein had weapons of mass destruction (WMDs) which he was willing to use against Britain. Neither UN weapons inspectors nor the invading armies found any functional WMDs. But had Blair known this before the war began? In making the case for war to a sceptical party and public, had he crossed the line into exaggeration and deceit?

Things came to a head in August 2003 when BBC journalist Andrew Gilligan reported that Blair had 'sexed up' the dossier of evidence presented to MPs on the case for war. The source for this allegation was a previously obscure weapons expert, Dr David Kelly, who was wholly unprepared for the media maelstrom that followed. When Dr Kelly committed suicide just days after appearing before a parliamentary select committee, the pressure for a broader investigation became impossible for the government to resist. In the end, there were two independent inquiries, by Lords Hutton and Butler. Neither report satisfied the government or its opponents or succeeded in putting questions over the case for war to rest. Iraq was seldom out of the news as election day approached and was coming to be seen as an avoidable disaster produced by the worst pathologies of an untrustworthy government: an obsession with controlling communication and a tendency to misrepresentation, exaggeration and 'spin'.

The Iraq controversies did lasting damage to Blair's authority as leader and his standing with the public, ending an unprecedented nine-year run of exceptional approval ratings. The leader whose popularity had set him apart from all colleagues and rivals for nearly a decade went into the 2005 campaign as a more typical political figure – liked and disliked in equal measure. But he and his party still had two big cards to play. Labour were widely seen as competent stewards of a strong economy and of public services starting to see the benefits of sustained investment. And the Conservatives were still seen as dysfunctional and distrusted despite eight years in opposition.

The Conservatives' second term in opposition to Blair started poorly and got worse from there. William Hague resigned as leader immediately following the landslide defeat of June 2001, and the ensuing leadership unexpectedly returned obscure right-wing backbencher Iain Duncan Smith as the party's new leader. Duncan Smith, a favourite son of the rebellious Eurosceptics dubbed 'bastards' by the Conservatives' last Prime Minister John Major, was not an obvious choice for a party seeking to reassure voters who saw it as extreme and out of touch. The more popular and emollient former Chancellor Ken Clarke was favoured by MPs in the first round of the contest, but he was then brushed aside in the final vote by party members seemingly keener on a leader who reflected their views than one in touch with the broader public.

The problems with this choice were soon obvious. 'IDS', as he was known, was a flop from the outset, with dismal poll numbers and little support from his parliamentary colleagues, the traditional Tory press or even Conservative Central Office – seen by the leader's office as sympathetic to third-placed candidate Michael Portillo. An attempted clear-out on 14 February 2003 was immediately dubbed the 'St Valentine's Day Massacre'. One of those departing was 31-year-old Director of Strategy Dominic Cummings, recruited from the anti-euro campaign, who had angered his leader by saying publicly that 'the only thing less popular than the euro is the Conservative Party'.

IDS, a neo-Conservative, backed the Iraq War from the start, despite more unease among Conservatives than is now remembered. Fifteen Conservative MPs voted against the war in the crucial March 2003 Commons vote, and three former Conservative Foreign secretaries – Lords Howe and Hurd and Malcolm Rifkind – spoke out against it. Conservative support for the Iraq War was perhaps IDS's most significant legacy, leaving his successor unable to mobilise growing public discontent in the election campaign.

Duncan Smith did make some efforts at renewing his party's appeal – he had a deep and sincere interest in poverty and social justice and sought to get his party to take up such issues. His newly appointed party chair Theresa May warned party members in autumn 2002 that major changes were needed to make the party ready for government: 'Our base is too narrow and so, occasionally, are our sympathies. You know what some people call us: the nasty party.' But IDS was hobbled by unpopularity and a lack of personal authority. His attempt to turn a bland public persona to his advantage by telling the 2002 Conservative conference to 'never underestimate the determination of a quiet man' fell flat, and when a year later he announced that 'the quiet man is turning up the volume', his colleagues decided it was time to change the record. Duncan Smith was out within two months.

The experience of the 2001 leadership contest was not one Conservative MPs were eager to repeat and thus, to avoid the risk of a second unpopular hardliner being foisted on them by party members, they now united rapidly around a single candidate, former Home Secretary Michael Howard. Howard's elevation as leader was ratified by the Conservative Party board without a members' vote, setting a precedent which would later be used by Theresa May and Rishi Sunak to avoid potentially awkward consultation of the party grass roots.

Howard had the gravitas and experience IDS lacked – a formidable frontbench debater with a decade of ministerial and Cabinet experience. He also had a compelling personal story to tell. The child of a Romanian refugee father and a Welsh mother who had risen far, he talked in an early speech of his 'British dream' of a fair and tolerant nation where people from humble origins were given a chance to follow his example and work their way to the top. But hopes for renewal were soon dashed. Howard retreated to the Conservative comfort zones of tax cuts and privatisation, issues which appealed to the party's shrunken core vote but fell flat with everyone else. Howard also resisted pressure to turn against the Iraq War, and his half-hearted efforts to criticise Blair's approach to the conflict didn't work – attacked as opportunism at home, while damaging relations with Republican allies in the United States. The Conservatives continued to flatline in the polls and came fourth in a by-election in Hartlepool in September 2004, dubbed by the *Telegraph* 'the worst by-election performance by an official opposition in modern history'.

The Conservatives' limp line on Iraq left the field open to Charles Kennedy's Liberal Democrats. The third party had opposed the war from the outset, and in the latter half of the parliament they reaped the benefits, winning two big by-election victories in Brent East (September 2003) and Leicester South (July 2004), and advancing strongly in local elections, seizing cities such as Liverpool, Sheffield and Newcastle from Labour. The Lib Dems were a rising force – their cohort of MPs had more than doubled from twenty-two to fifty-two between 1992 and 2001 despite no increase in their overall vote share thanks to ruthless targeting and tactical voting. Now their popular standing was on the rise, too – polls put them above 20 per cent, their best performance since the merger of the SDP and the Liberals in 1988. While Kennedy, the party's affable leader since 1999, was criticised for a laid-back attitude and a lack of attention to detail, he had kept a diverse and fractious party united, and his strong stance against Iraq looked likely to pay off.

Scotland's third party by Commons seats – the SNP – also sought to revitalise its appeal, by restoring Alex Salmond, leader from 1990 to 2000, to lead the party again in 2004. The choice attracted little attention at the time, yet within three years Salmond would be leading the first SNP devolved government, the beginning of a wave of change which would crest with an historic independence referendum in 2014, and the collapse of the Labour Party in Scotland a year later.

The timing of the 2005 election was a surprise to nobody. Though the Prime Minister could theoretically go to the voters as late as June 2006, Blair was widely expected to bank Labour's fragile poll lead early. An early May 2005 election was the obvious choice, helping Labour councillors by coinciding with local elections, and coming exactly eight years after the first New Labour landslide of 1997. Parliament rose for its Easter recess on 24 March 2005 and the Prime Minister was widely expected to announce dissolution immediately upon its return on 4 April. Events abroad intervened. Pope John Paul II died on 2 April, leading Blair to delay his announcement out of respect for the long-serving pontiff. He went to the palace at 11 a.m. on Tuesday 5 April and then an hour later gave a statement outside Downing Street framing the contest to come: 'It is a big choice ... The challenge is ... to accelerate the changes, to widen the opportunities ... and above all else to take that hard-won economic stability ... and entrench it.'

The campaign began with near-universal expectations that Labour would win a historically unprecedented third Commons majority. This consensus was in some respects surprising: the government's poll lead was narrow, the Prime Minister was much diminished and the opposition had found its feet again under a new leader. In part, this reflected Labour's huge lead in Commons seats and the absence of any evidence of a sustained Conservative revival in polling or in by-elections: Labour had gone a remarkable eight years in office without losing a single by-election contest to their main opponents. But it was also a tribute to the remarkable spell cast by Blair and New Labour that, despite a fragile government poll lead and clear signs of voter unhappiness, hardly anyone in the parties or the press seriously contemplated an opposition win or even a hung parliament.

No one inside Labour had any doubt as to the coming result, though the Prime Minister and the Chancellor had different goals for the campaign. Blair hoped to repair his reputation and win a mandate for the agenda of radical domestic reforms which had been derailed by four years of foreign entanglements. His longtime partner and rival Gordon Brown sought to use the campaign to promote his own credentials as the Chancellor presiding over prosperity and record investment in public services, setting out a platform for what he hoped would be a rapid post-election transition of power.

The Conservative leadership, relieved to have steadied their ship under Howard, had modest goals for the campaign ahead. They hoped for a hung parliament, while accepting that even depriving Labour of a majority would most likely not prevent another term in opposition. The Liberal Democrats had positioned themselves to the left of Labour on domestic issues, while opposing the Iraq War. They had high hopes of a historic breakthrough, hoping to gain at least seventy seats by advancing on two fronts, mobilising disillusioned left-wingers and Muslim voters to take seats from Labour while consolidating anti-Tory votes among moderate suburban voters turned off by a divided and doctrinaire opposition to take seats from the opposition in the south of England. The third party hoped that their advance could leave them in the kingmaker position in an evenly divided hung parliament – though few had any doubts as to which king they would crown if given the chance. There were also rumblings on the right – the UK Independence Party had capitalised on a celebrity recruit, daytime television star Robert Kilroy-Silk, to boost their profile and surge to third place in the 2004 European Parliament elections. Though Kilroy-Silk had parted ways with UKIP in 2005 and was now running against them, the fledgling Eurosceptic movement was hoping to capitalise on rising concern about immigration and general discontent with politics.

Labour's early pre-election planning was disrupted by a deep rift between Blair and Brown over the coming transfer of power in Downing Street. Brown wanted a concrete, early date. Blair did not want to be tied down, knowing power would drain from him as soon as a departure date became known. Uncertainty over Brown's role in the coming campaign paralysed preparations – until Blair and

Brown could agree terms, no one below them could move forward. New Labour campaign veterans Alastair Campbell and Philip Gould were convinced Brown was essential to a successful campaign and worked to rebuild relations between the two sulking principals. By late spring, an unusual double-headed campaign was agreed, fronted by the Prime Minister and Chancellor together and organised by a team featuring both men's closest aides. This was a team of familiar faces, featuring Campbell and Gould, senior campaign aides since Blair's elevation as leader in 1994, along with Alan Milburn, Douglas Alexander, Ed Miliband and Ed Balls – all established veterans of New Labour campaigns.

Public and private polling showed a marked shift in the public mood over the course of the parliament. Attention had shifted away from the economy and public services and towards a host of social and security issues – terrorism, crime, Iraq and particularly immigration, which was barely mentioned in 2001 but was the most named priority in the 2005 British Election Study polling of the campaign. Labour's campaign had three goals – neutralise potential weaknesses on the security agenda; emphasise Labour's economic record and investment in public services; and underline the risks of voting Conservative.

The opposition, unable to mobilise discontent on foreign policy, spied opportunities in the new domestic policy agenda. Conservative Central Office recruited a new campaign director in October 2004 – the Australian Lynton Crosby, who was widely admired as the architect of four successive election victories for John Howard and the Liberal Party in his home country and would be a major force in Conservative Party election campaigns for more than a decade to come. Crosby, whose campaigns for the Liberals had featured aggressive, controversial messaging on immigration, saw the shift in public opinion as an opportunity to mobilise similar sentiments in Britain. Michael Howard recruited two rising young MPs – David Cameron and George Osborne – to work alongside Crosby developing policy and messaging. The elevation of an ambitious pair of young modernisers determined to make their party electable again inevitably led to comparisons with Blair and Brown in the early 1990s – a parallel which did Cameron and Osborne's profile and prospects no harm at all.

Having settled their differences, at least temporarily, Blair and Brown worked in close harmony to hit Labour's campaign objectives. Blair took the lead on neutralising Labour's weak points, addressing his failings on Iraq and other issues through a 'masochism strategy' of TV appearances where he took hostile questions from interviewers and audience members. Blair also volunteered for a different kind of masochism by appearing on popular entertainment shows such as *This Morning* and *Ant & Dec's Saturday Night Takeaway*, fielding questions from primary school children: 'My dad says you're mad. Are you mad?'

Brown's agenda was lower risk and higher brow, leading the campaign to sell Labour's track record and plans. Campaign set-pieces featured Blair and Brown sharing ice cream and trading jokes and, lest the electorate miss the point, it was hammered home in a five-minute party election broadcast produced by celebrity director Anthony Minghella, with Blair and Brown reflecting on their relationship like an ageing married couple:

BROWN   We came into Parliament twenty-two years ago … Shared an office for three years …
BLAIR   The question is how you sustain it …
BROWN   Growth, the key to everything we're doing …
BLAIR   Whatever the tensions are from time to time, it's a partnership that's worked.

Labour's approach wasn't subtle, but it was effective, as both leaders agreed with their strategists about the goals of the campaign and their dual role in it. The Conservatives struggled to match this discipline. Lynton Crosby and other campaign strategists favoured a leader-focused campaign, but Michael Howard was resistant to campaigning on his personal story and family background, preferring policy-focused campaigning over what he dismissed as 'personality politics'. The Conservatives had more success with their issue messaging, striking a chord in particular on immigration, with a characteristically controversial Crosby slogan – 'It's not racist to impose limits on immigration' – garnering much criticism but also ensuring plenty of public attention for the Conservatives' 'Australian-style points-based system', which would impose quotas on immigration while favouring those with high skills or in high-demand jobs.

As the Conservatives' immigration campaign gained traction, Labour responded. First, they stole the most popular element of the Tory plan by promising their own 'Australian-style points-based system'. Then Blair hit back at the controversial Conservative campaign ads with a powerful speech at Dover confronting opposition claims head on:

> I never want this to be an issue that divides our country, that sets communities against each other. We are a tolerant, decent nation. That tolerance should not be abused. But neither should it be turned on its head ...
>
> Let me make clear my objection to the Tory campaign on this issue. Their campaign is based on the statement that it isn't racist to talk about immigration. I know of no senior politician who has ever said it was. So why do they put it like that? ...
>
> It is an attempt deliberately to exploit people's fears, to suggest that, for reasons of political correctness, those in power don't dare deal with the issue ... that we are blindly ignoring them or telling them that to raise the issue is racist, when actually the opposite is true.

While the speech did not fully defuse the issue, which continued to rank high up the list of voters' concerns right through to polling day, it threw the spotlight back onto the Conservatives. The opposition faced growing criticism over the tone and language used, and the apparent hypocrisy of Howard, the child of refugees, mobilising hostility to asylum seekers. The issue most likely lifted the Conservatives somewhat, but it also gave a boost to parties further right, with UKIP and the BNP both securing record vote shares on the back of uncompromising anti-immigration campaigns.

There were relatively few gaffes or missteps in the short campaign, a testament to disciplined campaign teams. The Conservatives weathered a minor crisis just before the election was called, when after-dinner remarks by party vice-chairman Howard Flight were leaked. Flight suggested that in a Conservative government, cuts to public spending would go 'much further' than the £35 billion publicly announced. He was immediately dismissed by Michael Howard, but the comments lingered, adding weight to Labour's claim that the Conservatives could not be trusted on public services.

A second leak late in the campaign threatened to disrupt Labour's hitherto successful efforts to limit the impact of Iraq. On 23 April, *Channel 4 News* revealed the contents of the Attorney General's legal advice to the Cabinet on the legality of going to war in Iraq without a UN resolution. Days of hostile headlines followed, focused on the Prime Minister's untrustworthiness: 'Tories taunt liar Blair', 'Blair lied and lied again', 'Our sons died for Iraq lies'. Michael Howard eagerly took up the charge, accusing Blair of taking Britain to war on a lie in election posters and a TV interview. The Conservatives were, however, hamstrung by their own support for Iraq which made these attacks look like opportunism. The main beneficiaries were the Liberal Democrats, who ran heavily on the Iraq issue in the final days of the campaign, calling for the election to be a 'referendum on the war', which perhaps helped to drive a late rise in their polling numbers.

The duelling headlines and interviews seen in the wake of the legal advice leak underlined how this was a campaign still fought primarily through traditional print and broadcast media. Though the reach of the internet was rapidly growing, and all parties and candidates had campaign websites, Facebook was barely a year old in 2005, and Twitter would not be founded for another year. The news cycles were still dominated by the traditional rhythms of evening news roundups and early edition print deadlines; the manic pace of 24-hour news cycles and the swirling unpredictability of social media-driven campaigning were still to come. With print still powerful, endorsements from big titles carried weight. Blair's remarkable success in winning over traditionally right-leaning titles continued in his final campaign – the mass-market *Sun* and the more upmarket *Times*, both large titles owned by Rupert Murdoch, endorsed a third Labour term, as did the *Financial Times*, the house paper of the business class, and (despite its reservations over Iraq) *The Guardian*, the house paper of the chattering class. Even the *Daily Mail*, usually the Conservatives' most loyal tabloid ally, could not bring itself to issue a full-throated endorsement of the opposition, instead calling limply for 'Not a Labour victory'.

Broadcast – particularly television – played perhaps the largest role in communicating the campaign to voters. Though the fragmentation of media markets was well underway, the traditional channels could still pull in large audiences, particularly for the big news bulletins. Tight regulation of broadcast news coverage limits parties' abilities to use it to their advantage, though in this election, as others, it likely benefited the Liberal Democrats and smaller parties, which received a great deal more attention than they receive at other times. Interviews on TV and radio tend to make the biggest impact when they go wrong. This, however, was a disciplined campaign fought by talented veterans. There were few surprises on air and no major gaffes by the principals.

As polling day approached, Labour strategists could afford to breathe a little easier. The main goals of their campaign had been achieved – thorny issues had been addressed, if not neutralised; Labour's record had been burnished and heavily touted; and doubts about the Conservatives had been reinforced. Labour's modest lead in the polls barely budged through the whole campaign, while the Conservatives' standing had steadily declined. Two concerns remained. First, while a large surge for the Liberal Democrats was unlikely to deny the government a third victory, it could weaken Labour's Commons position. Second, anxieties about complacency and disaffection were widespread in the Labour team after the historic slump in turnout in 2001. If traditionally loyal Labour voters stayed home en masse again in 2005, while the Conservatives delivered their base to the polls, then a third majority could be in jeopardy.

These fears did not materialise. The outcome on polling day was the one universally expected all the way through the campaign:

another large Labour majority. Labour support fell by more than five points to just over 35 per cent, but this still left them well ahead of the Conservatives, who barely advanced for the second election in a row and finished on 32 per cent. The Liberal Democrats were up substantially to 22 per cent, their best showing since the merged party was created but not enough to threaten the big party duopoly in many seats. The party made eleven gains and finished on sixty-two seats – a best-ever total but well below activists' hopes.

The 2005 election result was historic in one respect – the role of the electoral system. Labour won 55 per cent of the seats with 35 per cent of the vote. No party since the advent of the universal franchise had won an overall majority with such a low vote share, and no party has done it since. Just over one in three of those who participated (and far fewer of those eligible to vote) backed a third Labour term in 2005, yet the party was able to continue governing with a comfortable Commons majority. Labour received a dual blessing from their opponents – the Liberal Democrats' vote was too thinly spread to win seats, while the Conservatives' vote was too concentrated in seats already held by the opposition. The cumulative impact of these effects was a huge bias to Labour. The Conservatives actually won the popular vote in England – edging Labour out 35.7 to 35.5 – yet the English seat count was 286–194, a 92-seat Labour advantage. This huge assist from first past the post left Labour looking much stronger, and the Conservatives much weaker, than the underlying vote share figures suggested. But the electoral system is a fickle mistress. In 2017, Labour would win ninety seats fewer than in 2005, despite a vote share five points higher. Triumph on 35 per cent turned to disaster on 40 per cent – such are the vagaries of first past the post.

While the rules of the contest may have played a larger than usual role, this mattered little for the political implications of the outcome. Labour were weakened but still dominant, the Conservatives had once again failed to revive, the Liberal Democrats had grown but were still politically impotent. All of that would soon change. The 2005 campaign was the last hurrah for a New Labour political and electoral machine which dominated British politics for fifteen years.

The Labour Party's most successful election winner would depart Downing Street within two years. Gordon Brown's reputation as the 'Iron Chancellor' presiding over economic growth, sound finances and improving public services would be dashed to pieces soon after by the 2008–09 global financial crisis. New Labour's advance into deep blue Middle England would wither away in the wake of recession, while later on the bill for a decade neglecting traditional Labour heartlands in Scotland and the post-industrial English towns of the Midlands and north would eventually come due.

Many seeds of the whirlwinds to come were sown in 2005. The war in Iraq damaged Labour with its core supporters, deepening feelings of neglect and distrust which would lead many Labour activists, and two Labour leaders, to define themselves in opposition to Blair and all his works. Lynton Crosby's 2005 campaign – focused on a strong leader, divisive messages and hot-button issues – would provide the template for four successful Conservative campaigns to come. And the blueprint for both Nigel Farage's UKIP insurgency and Dominic Cummings's Vote Leave campaign can be seen in the polarising populist Conservative 2005 drive on immigration. Low turnout, rising distrust of the government and continued suspicion of the Conservatives were also all early indicators of deeper pressures building. A growing hostility to politics in general was already evident in 2005, with more and more voters losing faith in politics altogether and turning against institutions seen as corrupt, venal and dysfunctional. These forces would erupt soon enough, sweeping away the political landscape on which the 2005 election was fought and won.

Robert Ford is a professor of political science at the University of Manchester and the author of *The British General Election of 2019* (with Tim Bale, Will Jennings and Paula Surridge), *Brexitland* (with Maria Sobolewska) and *Sex, Lies and Politics* (co-edited with Philip Cowley).

47

2010

ADAM BOULTON

Dissolution: 12 April 2010
Polling day: 6 May 2010
Seats contested: 650
Total electorate / Voted / Turnout: 45,597,461 / 29,687,604 / 65.1 per cent
Candidates (total 4,150): Conservative – 631; Labour – 631; Liberal Democrats – 631; UKIP – 558; BNP – 338; Green – 335; SNP – 59; Plaid Cymru – 40; Alliance – 18; SDLP – 18; Sinn Féin – 17; DUP – 16
Prime Minister on polling day: Gordon Brown
Main party leaders: Conservative – David Cameron; Labour – Gordon Brown; Liberal Democrats – Nick Clegg; Green – Caroline Lucas; UKIP – Malcolm Pearson; BNP – Nick Griffin; SNP – Alex Salmond; Plaid Cymru – Ieuan Wyn Jones; DUP – Peter Robinson; Sinn Féin – Gerry Adams; SDLP – Margaret Ritchie; Ulster Conservatives and Unionists – Reg Empey; Alliance – David Ford

Party performance:

Party	Votes	Percentage share	Seats
Conservative	10,703,754	36.1	306
Labour	8,609,527	29	258
Liberal Democrats	6,836,824	23	57
UKIP	919,546	3.1	0
BNP	564,331	1.9	0
SNP	491,386	1.7	6

Green	285,616	0.9	1
Sinn Féin	171,942	25.5	5
DUP	168,216	25	8
Plaid Cymru	165,394	0.6	3
SDLP	110,970	16.5	3
Ulster Conservatives and Unionists	102,361	15.2	0
Alliance	42,762	6.3	1

Result: Hung parliament, Conservatives and Liberal Democrats form a coalition government

> *'I want to make a big, open and comprehensive offer to the Liberal Democrats.'*
> DAVID CAMERON, 7 MAY 2010

The general election of 2010 was a change election. It ended thirteen years of Labour government under Tony Blair, who had won three successive elections, and Gordon Brown who took over the premiership in 2007. The Conservative leader David Cameron eventually became Prime Minister.

But 2010 brought in bigger changes than that. For only the second time since the Second World War, the election resulted in a hung parliament with no party able to command a majority in the House of Commons. For the first time since 1945, the UK ended up under a formal coalition government, with both Tories and Liberal Democrats taking ministerial office. Nick Clegg, the Lib Dem leader, was appointed Deputy Prime Minister and there were five other Liberal Democrat Cabinet ministers.

The election extended beyond the results into an unprecedented five days of private negotiations, involving all the main parties, before a government was formed. Together, the Conservatives and Liberal Democrats had the support of 59.1 per cent of the popular vote. By the standards of what was to follow in the early twenty-first century, the coalition government would be remarkably stable and last for a full five-year term.

This campaign was also the only one in Great Britain, before or since, to be dominated by three properly conducted televised leaders' debates. None of the three men who would find themselves debating – neither Brown, Cameron nor Clegg – had previous experience of leading their parties through an election. Cameron claimed subsequently that the debates 'sucked the life out of the campaign'. But independent research found that the electorate, and especially younger voters, considered themselves better informed and more engaged as a result of the debates.

There was no surprise when the election was called. After a full, five-year term of parliament, a general election was due, if not overdue. Gordon Brown had run down the clock. He had taken over the premiership from Tony Blair, without a contest for the Labour leadership, three years previously.

Many felt he had already missed his best chance of winning an election in his own right. He prepared the Labour Party for a snap general election capitalising on his honeymoon period in the autumn of 2007. All was set, but then he dithered and called off what became known as 'the election that never was'. That weekend, the *News of the World* published a survey suggesting Labour's prospects were less good than expected in key marginal seats. Brown denied this was a factor in his decision, but the label 'Bottler Brown' stuck.

By April 2010, Brown had little alternative but to go to Buckingham Palace to request a dissolution of Parliament. Polling day was set for Thursday 6 May, the same date as the local council elections, five years and a day after the last general election on 5 May 2005. Brown decided not to wait until the very last possible date, which would have been a month later. (In the event, the Conservatives did best at council level as well with 35 per cent, to Labour's 27 per cent and the Liberal Democrats' 26 per cent. One small consolation for the opposition parties was that their respective vote shares were up 1 per cent on the last equivalent elections and the Conservatives were down 4 per cent. The Conservatives' net loss of 121 seats was the first time they had lost councillors in a local election since 1996.)

Making his announcement in Downing Street on his return from his audience with the Queen, Brown declared: 'I come from an ordinary family in an ordinary town.' This was a clear sign that Labour expected this election campaign to be more presidential than ever, focused on the personalities of the party leaders. Labour's hope was that Brown's relative ordinariness would appeal to voters more than the privileged backgrounds of his privately educated rivals.

Gordon Brown was a 'son of the manse', the Scottish equivalent of the son of a preacher man. His father was a minister in the Church of Scotland. He and his brothers went to local schools in Kirkcaldy. He had two exceptional formative experiences during his school days. A sporting injury playing rugby permanently damaged his eyesight. That did not stop his excelling academically. Placed in an experimental fast stream at Kirkcaldy High School, he was accepted to study at the University of Edinburgh at the age of sixteen. He graduated in 1972 with a first-class degree in history.

The two main UK-wide opposition parties had been through a period of unrest during the long New Labour years. David Cameron was the fourth party leader since the defeated John Major resigned in 1997. William Hague and then Iain Duncan Smith had taken the party to the right without electoral success. The veteran Michael Howard took over unopposed after 'IDS' lost a confidence vote of his own MPs. Howard immediately set about grooming the next generation of leadership. Howard was thought to prefer the younger George Osborne, but Osborne demurred in favour of his brasher, slightly older, 'chum', David Cameron. Following the Conservatives' third general election defeat in a row in 2005, Cameron stood on a modernising platform and beat the older David Davis by a margin of two to one. The new leader was thirty-nine. Both Cameron and Osborne expressed admiration for Blair's achievements modernising his party. Cameron described himself as the 'heir to Blair', Osborne privately referred to Blair as 'the Master'.

The Liberal Democrats had a record number of MPs, sixty-two, in the 2005 parliament and numerous party leaders. Their long-serving and charismatic leader Charles Kennedy was forced out in March 2006, as his struggle with alcoholism became increasingly public.

(Kennedy would die of alcohol-related illness in 2015 at home in the Scottish Highlands, aged fifty-five, having lost his seat in the SNP sweep of 2015.)

Another Scottish MP, Sir Menzies 'Ming' Campbell, subsequently Baron Campbell of Pittenweem, took over in March 2006 at the age of sixty-five. He struggled to establish his authority inside his party or with the voters. He resigned in October 2007 when Vince Cable, another 65-year-old veteran, became acting leader of the Liberal Democrats. A new generation came into power in the party at the end of the year when forty-year-old Nick Clegg narrowly beat Chris Huhne in a bitterly fought contest.

David Cameron's father was a stockbroker and investment adviser. There had been Tory MPs in his mother's family since at least Victorian times. Cameron went to Heatherdown Prep School followed by Eton. Both schools were also attended by British royal princes. He gained a first in PPE at Brasenose College, Oxford.

Nick Clegg came from a cosmopolitan background. His father was a banker, his mother was Dutch. He is multilingual, speaking English, Dutch, German, French and Spanish (the native tongue of his wife). He went to the elite Westminster School and took a 2:1 in social anthropology at Robinson College, Cambridge.

Unlike Brown, both Cameron and Clegg had disciplinary brushes involving drink and drugs during their schooldays. Differences of class, age and experience separated the incumbent Prime Minister from his two main rivals. At the time of the 2010 election, Clegg had been an MP, for Sheffield Hallam, since 2005 and leader of the Liberal Democrats for less than two years. Cameron was elected to Parliament for Witney in 2001 and had been party leader since 2005. Both were forty-three years old. Brown was fifty-nine. He'd been an MP continuously since 1983, first for Dunfermline East and then, after constituency boundary reorganisation, for Kirkcaldy and Cowdenbeath. He was Chancellor of the Exchequer throughout Tony Blair's ten years in power.

Where the opposition parties could run on promises of generational change, Gordon Brown had, inevitably, to defend the record of the

New Labour government which he and the frenemy he called 'Tony' had both led.

Blair and Brown were elected to Parliament on the same day. Initially, Brown was clearly the senior partner in the rise of New Labour. He and his supporters were never quite reconciled to Blair eclipsing Brown when John Smith died in May 1994. Brown stood down voluntarily in Blair's favour in that contest but remained convinced that the two had made a 'deal' that Blair would hand over power at some point. In the autumn of 2006, threatened waves of resignations by ministers supporting Brown forced Blair to commit to depart within twelve months. In his first speech as Prime Minister on 27 June 2007, Brown sought to draw a clear line: 'This will be a new government with new priorities.' Within barely three minutes, he managed to mention 'change' eight times, ending with: 'Now let the work of change begin.'

Senior Blairites attempted to challenge Brown on two occasions during his premiership. In June 2009, as polls closed in European and local elections in which Labour did badly, the Work and Pensions Secretary James Purnell resigned and urged Brown to step down. Ed Miliband persuaded his brother David, the Foreign Secretary, not to join the revolt which could have proved fatal. In January 2010, former Cabinet ministers Patricia Hewitt and Geoff Hoon called for a secret ballot to resolve the leadership question, unsuccessfully.

Neither Blair's truncated third term following Labour's victory on 5 May 2005 nor Brown's subsequent two years were a happy period for the UK, at home or abroad.

Bloodshed was out of control in the Middle East and came to London in terrorist attacks. Exposure of MPs' expense claims created a scandal which lastingly eroded public trust and respect for politicians. By the time of the election, three Labour MPs were facing criminal prosecution over expenses and would be subsequently imprisoned.

After nearly a decade of growth and public sector investment under Blair, the economy soured. From August 2007 through to the end of 2008, there was a rolling financial crisis in the UK, the US and

Europe. In America, major institutions, including Lehman Brothers and Bear Stearns, collapsed. In the so-called credit crunch, the UK government was forced to use taxpayers' money to bail out Northern Rock, Bradford & Bingley, Lloyds TSB, HBOS and Royal Bank of Scotland.

In August 2008, much to Brown's annoyance, his Chancellor Alistair Darling warned correctly that 'the economic times we are facing ... are arguably the worst they have been for sixty years'. The tax rises and spending constraints Darling announced in his Budgets inaugurated what was to be a decade of 'austerity' in the UK.

Gordon Brown convened a meeting of the G20 in London in late 2008 commenting clumsily 'we saved the world', when he meant to say that steps had been agreed to avoid the collapse of global financial system.

George W. Bush and Tony Blair had been re-elected after the military invasions of Iraq and Afghanistan in response to the 9/11 attacks on America by al-Qaeda in 2001. In part, this was because insurrection broke out slowly at first in those occupied nations. By 2010, civil war was flaring in both countries alongside attacks on allied forces. In Iraq, the bombing of the golden dome shrine in early 2006 inflamed tensions between Sunnis and Shias and accelerated the rise of al-Qaeda in Iraq. The US response was the 'surge' of troops which lasted into the new decade. In an attempt to move on, Prime Minister Gordon Brown set up an inquiry, headed by Sir John Chilcot, into Britain's role in the Iraq invasion. In the months before the election, both Blair and Brown appeared before the committee; Brown later writing to correct his oral evidence on defence spending. The inquiry's deliberations hung over the campaign.

The 2010 election was more heavily polled than ever before. In large part, this was because of the rise of online polling companies. YouGov alone was responsible for nearly half the ninety polls in the month-long period. At the start of the campaign, competing organisations gave a broadly similar picture of the state of the parties. The Conservatives were between 7 per cent and 10 per cent ahead of Labour, with the Liberal Democrats a further 10 per cent behind.

There were significant movements during the campaign, notably around the Liberal Democrats. Ultimately, these starting prices in the polls were not so different from the actual results in Great Britain: Conservatives 36.1 per cent (+3.7 on 2005), Labour 29 per cent (-6.2), Liberal Democrats 23 per cent (+1).

David Cameron needed the biggest swing since 1945 to gain the 116 seats required for a Conservative parliamentary majority. This seemed unlikely, according to the opinion polls. There was intense speculation in Whitehall and Westminster in the months prior to the election that it would deliver a 'hung parliament' with no party in command of an overall majority.

The Cabinet Secretary Gus O'Donnell took decisive action to make sure that the civil service, the media and the public were briefed on the constitutional implications of that eventuality. As the political editor of Sky News, a national broadcaster, I was invited to and attended numerous briefings – in the Cabinet Office, at the Institute for Government and elsewhere – on what would happen if there was no decisive winner.

These briefings amounted to three essential points. Firstly, there would be no uncertainty about who was in charge of the government. Secondly, Gordon Brown would continue as Prime Minister until negotiations between the parties agreed on the formation of the new government. Thirdly, Her Majesty the Queen would not get involved. She would not summon individuals to ask them to form a government. She would wait for the politicians to put forward their candidate. This last point was repeatedly stressed by her principal private secretary Christopher Geidt. Both O'Donnell and Geidt subsequently became members of the House of Lords, as holders of their offices usually do. In as much as it exists as an entity, 'the establishment' laid the groundwork for a coalition after the election.

The prospect of a close result increased the chances that the three potential Prime Ministers might agree to debate each other during the campaign. A frontrunner would have been unwilling to cede an equal platform to their rivals. The challengers, Cameron and Clegg, were up for it and Brown had little to lose.

Britain's main terrestrial broadcasters, the BBC and ITV, had repeatedly failed to get election debates to take place. In part, this was because they bid against each other with competing proposals. The BBC was reluctant to press political parties hard for fear of violating political impartiality but wished to keep editorial control of any format. For ratings and revenue reasons, ITV wanted a show exclusively on its channel. These divisions were exploited by reluctant campaigns, especially since debate negotiations threatened to be a distraction to the campaign, which was usually underway when they were proposed.

By 2010, Sky News, the rolling 24-hour news channel launched in 1989 by Rupert Murdoch, was established as a significant third force in British TV news. I was Sky's founding political editor, only leaving the channel in 2021. John Ryley, the head of Sky News, and I decided to take a fresh and proactive approach to bring about debates. On 2 September 2009, Sky News launched a sustained media campaign for leaders' debates, backed by other News Group outlets including *The Times* and *The Sun*. Ryley used an op-ed in *The Times* to announce: 'Today, I have written to Gordon Brown, David Cameron and Nick Clegg, informing them that Sky will be hosting a live debate between them during the election campaign.'

This was the most dedicated attempt yet and it had significant differences to previous efforts. Firstly, we opened the discussion away from any election campaign – the election was not expected until well into the following year. Secondly, from the outset, Sky News proposed that any debates should be a public service not 'owned' by any channel, free live to all other broadcasters and, if possible, set up in collaboration with them. Finally, as spelt out in *The Times*' headline, 'Who'll Show Up for the TV Showdown?', Sky News made clear that it was prepared to 'empty chair' any leader who declined to take part, provided that the other two would debate. Recent changes to electoral law made this a credible threat, especially when made by a rolling news channel rather than a terrestrial broadcaster, jealous of its prime time.

An ITV spokesman dismissed Sky's proposal as 'childish' and 'a marketing stunt'. The BBC withdrew Sky's invitation to a pre-election broadcasters' meeting it planned to convene. But they gradually accepted that Sky News was sincere in wishing to collaborate rather than compete.

As expected, Cameron and Clegg quickly agreed to take part. The pressure was on Brown, leading to an ugly confrontation when I interviewed him on the floor of the Labour Party conference in late September. Unfortunately, this took place the morning after *The Sun* newspaper, totally independently of Sky, had switched its endorsement from Labour to the Conservatives. I pressed Brown to take part in the debates. 'You sound like a political propagandist yourself,' he retorted, before storming off without detaching his microphone, all in full view of print reporters taking notes. The front-page splash of the *Evening Standard* dubbed it 'Meltdown'.

Had circumstances been otherwise, Labour sources suggest that Brown was preparing to use his leader's speech at conference to agree to debate. In any case, three weeks later, No. 10 announced that he would take part, subject to negotiations and agreement on the rules with the other parties and the broadcasters.

It took from October until mid-February to reach full agreement on the broadcasters' proposal for three debates, chaired by each of ITV, Sky and BBC but under the same rules. Senior executives represented each broadcaster: Sue Inglish and Ric Bailey for the BBC, Chris Birkett and Jon Levy for Sky and Michael Jermey and Jonathan Munro for ITV. Gordon Brown was represented by two of his special advisers, David Muir and Justin Forsyth. David Cameron fielded his media chief Andy Coulson, former editor of the *News of the World*, and Michael Salter. Jonny Oates, another broadcast professional, negotiated for Clegg.

The teams met regularly on the neutral ground of either RIBA, near BBC Broadcasting House, or the Mother's Union, which was close to both Parliament and the broadcasters' shared Westminster HQ at 4 Millbank. In spite of a four-week hiatus when Brown's team held the debates to ransom over his demands, on 2 March the broadcasters were able to announce that three debates, each a week apart, would take place during the campaign, with dates to be confirmed once Brown went to the palace to call the election. The broadcasters drew lots for the order in which they would host the debates and for the lead topic between home affairs, foreign affairs and the economy.

As Sky News intended, this historic agreement had been reached without entangling the issue of debates in the fevered final weeks of electioneering. As a curtain-raiser, and consolation for a channel which withdrew from the main negotiations, Channel 4 staged *Ask the Chancellors*, a ground-breaking debate between finance spokespeople moderated by Krishnan Guru-Murthy on 29 March.

The eve of the campaign was marked by an exchange of posters which had a retro feel about them, just as those running the campaigns were retreads. The Conservatives retained the Saatchi brothers, considered Svengalis of Mrs Thatcher's victories, through their new business M&C Saatchi. Labour went with the brothers' old firm, Saatchi and Saatchi. Brown also patched up his differences to recall Blair's old henchmen Peter Mandelson and Alastair Campbell to his campaign team.

The Labour poster mocked up Cameron as Gene Hunt, the macho detective from the BBC's hit time-travelling drama *Ashes to Ashes*, with the slogan 'Don't let him take Britain back to the 1980s'. Within hours, the Conservatives responded with their version of a Hunt catchphrase: 'Fire up the Quattro [his model of car]. It's time for change.' The Liberal Democrats produced a pastiche of old Conservative posters: 'Tory VAT Bombshell'.

The first ten days of the campaign were dominated by bickering over economic policy. George Osborne, Cameron's closest ally and future Chancellor, had the best of it, promising a reduction in the planned national insurance increase and a married couple's tax break worth £150 a year for 4 million families.

A Populus poll for *The Times* reported that two in five voters – and 50 per cent of women – did not feel any party was making a convincing case.

On 12 April, Labour launched its manifesto, 'A Future Fair for All', at a shiny new hospital wing in Birmingham. The large format pamphlet's cover design, chosen by Mandelson, featured a 1930s Soviet-style drawing of a family staring into bright sunshine. David Cameron presented his A5 retro hardback text-book style, 'Invitation to Join the Government of Britain' in the then derelict Battersea Power Station. The main theme was handing power back to people to regenerate the country through volunteering. His 'Big Society' idea did not catch on during the campaign or after it.

The Liberal Democrats went to the former City HQ of Bloomberg. The Liberal Democrats' paperback 'Change That Works for You: Building a Fairer Britain' may have contained the most consequential pledge: to 'scrap unfair university tuition fees for all students taking their first degree'. But it was largely overlooked in the commentary at the time.

The three main parties all produced chunky manifestos in 2010, running to more than 30,000 words for Labour, 27,000 for the Conservatives and 20,000 for the Lib Dems. But the campaign did not revolve around what was said in them.

The election came alive on Thursday 15 April with the first leaders' debate themed on home affairs and moderated by Alastair Stewart at ITV's Granada studios in Manchester. Anticipation was all the greater due to the fear it would not be able to take place because of the disruption to air traffic over western Europe caused by the eruption of Eyjafjallajökull, a volcano in Iceland.

The debates did not disappoint. An audience of 9.6 million people tuned into ITV to watch ninety minutes of live, uninterrupted politics on television, with reruns and clips readily available on TV, radio and online around the world. Followed by 4.2 million live for the Sky News debate in Bristol (the record audience for the channel) and 8.4 million for BBC One in Birmingham.

The first question raised immigration, the only issue to feature in all three debates. Neither Cameron nor Brown performed well. Unlike Clegg, Cameron struggled to connect with the audience and was mocked afterwards for his use of pre-cooked anecdotes. The leaders agreed that Brown, because of his eyesight, would always occupy the podium on the right of the screen, but he was still uncomfortable, his statistics and prepared quips fell flat. Worse, wary of upsetting centrist voters, both of Clegg's rivals said 'I agree with Nick' several times. The Liberal Democrats picked this up as a catchphrase. In reliable surveys, Clegg was judged to have 'won'. The Liberal Democrats surged in opinion polls. 'Cleggmania' was born.

Much of the rest of the campaign was given over to what to do about the Liberal Democrats and their leader, appropriately enough because that also became the issue once the results were in. Both Labour and the Conservatives privately adjusted their list of target seats away from the Liberal Democrats.

The second debate, which I moderated at the Arnolfini arts centre on Bristol's historic harbourside, was the most intensively produced in the scrupulously non-partisan style of debates organised by the US commission. The rules and Ofcom had stipulated that the selection of the audience and the formulation of their questions was not the responsibility of the broadcaster. We spent hours sifting through the questions which were submitted. We wanted to avoid repeats, so we did not return to the topic of Iraq which had already been discussed in Manchester. Reportedly, this omission surprised the debaters, as did a question we included about the Pope's forthcoming visit to Britain.

By now, the Conservative press was in full cry to damage Clegg. 'Vote Lib, get Lab' Trevor Kavanagh opined in *The Sun*. The *Mail on Sunday* began its profile: 'His wife is Spanish, his mother Dutch, his father half-Russian and his spin doctor German.' Conservative HQ was spreading anti-Clegg stories 'however dirty it was'. On the morning of the second debate, the *Daily Telegraph* and *Daily Mail* both made fresh allegations against Clegg. When none of the leaders raised the attacks in a round about integrity and leadership, I raised it with them in general terms when bringing in Clegg. Such relevant topical follow-ups by the moderator were explicitly permitted in the agreed rules, but I was the only moderator to do so. The Liberal Democrats did not make an official complaint. There were several hundred complaints to Ofcom, which the regulator subsequently did not uphold, offering the ruling that I had acted within the relevant guidelines.

The exchanges in Bristol were the most substantive. There was disagreement with Clegg on immigration, Trident and MPs' expenses. Cameron challenged Brown to withdraw leaflets which he said contained 'lies, pure and simple lies'. Clegg held his own, but exit polls showed the leaders coming out closer than they had been the previous week.

By now, campaign discussion was focused on the hung parliament, which Labour and the Conservatives were urging voters to avoid. Clegg repeatedly refused to say which way he would jump. But on Sunday 25 April, he gave Andrew Marr an indication of his thinking. He said he would not support Gordon Brown staying as Prime Minister, if the vagaries of the first-past-the-post system, which his party opposed, gave Labour the largest number of MPs, while coming third in share of the popular vote. 'You can't have Gordon Brown squatting in No. 10 just because of the irrational idiosyncrasies of our electoral system.'

Television had been steadily gaining ground and it was the dominant medium of the 2010 election. Traditional forms of campaigning were in decline and new digital media had not yet reached maturity. This was why Sky News considered proper debates were so essential.

Billboards and party election broadcasts were dwindling into insignificance, as audiences fragmented and the costs soared. Nor was it the 'Web 2.0 election' or the 'Mumsnet election', predicted by Brown's pollster Deborah Mattinson, who would later advise Sir Keir Starmer. Twitter had launched since the last election in 2007 and WhatsApp was less than a year old. Neither were yet the essential media of communication they have become.

There was a growing reluctance by both main parties to hold daily news conferences. When two Labour frontbenchers were asked to give a briefing on Saturday afternoon, a note was photographed passed between them in which Yvette Cooper called it 'second division' and Liam Byrne agreed it was 'like being allowed to play in the sand pit'.

The party leaders still purported to do whistle-stop battle bus tours – Labour charged £14,000 for a seat on theirs, and the Liberal Democrats had two buses emblazoned with the face of Clegg and Vince

Cable – an indication of pre-campaign nerves about the young leader. In truth, these outings had become photo opportunities in target seats. The leader was on the ground briefly and met very few people. 'The crowd' often consisted of local activists and people who had got off the bus with him.

Nevertheless on the eve of the final debate, a walkabout by Gordon Brown in Rochdale went so disastrously wrong that it almost turned that debate into a non-event. The Labour leader's team had asked for him to wear a radio microphone so he could be filmed meeting ordinary voters for the television pool being fed to the broadcasters. Sky News was on duty that day and complied.

Brown was introduced to Gillian Duffy, a 65-year-old grandmother out shopping, who said she was 'ashamed of saying I'm Labour' because of her worries about immigration. The two appeared to part on good terms. Brown, who is notoriously un-media savvy, got into his car still wearing his live microphone. He was heard berating his aide Justin Forsyth: 'That was a disaster. Should never have put me with that woman. Whose idea was that? ... She's just this sort of bigoted woman who said she used to be a Labour voter. Ridiculous.'

Bigotgate immediately went viral. Brown repeatedly apologised and tore up his schedule to do so again in person to Mrs Duffy. She said she would not be voting Labour this time. Brown had his gaffe played back to him live on the *Jeremy Vine Show* on Radio 2 while a camera recorded his reaction. He slumped in his chair and put his head in his hands. A US network animated the footage to show Brown's 'political soul leaving his body'.

The last debate the following day paled in comparison. The BBC's designated moderator, the second-generation broadcasting grandee David Dimbleby, had in any case made it clear that he preferred the bear-pit format of his regular *Question Time* show. The BBC was the only organisation to place its moderator at a podium equal with the debaters. After the debate, Dimbleby went on to present a live episode of *Question Time*, also from the Birmingham University campus.

In the final days before polling, the leaders continued their tours. All three spoke separately to a Citizens UK event in Methodist

Central Hall. Brown, in particular, seemed to blossom in the religious vibe. By now, some senior Labour figures were openly advocating tactical voting to stop the Tories.

On polling day, Cameron's team met at the home of his aide Steve Hilton, who would go on to be an anchor on the Fox News Channel in America. The consensus was that the Conservatives would be the largest party in a hung parliament. The Brown camp was gloomy.

The main news event that day was a potentially fatal air accident involving Nigel Farage, who was breaking protocol by standing for UKIP, the anti-EU independence party, in Buckinghamshire against the Speaker of the Commons, John Bercow. A UKIP banner being towed got entangled in the two-seater plane he was travelling in and it crashed. Farage was hospitalised with injuries.

For the first time, the BBC, ITV and Sky collaborated to produce an exit poll as soon as voting ended at 10 p.m. This pointed to a hung parliament and turned out to be surprisingly accurate. The broadcasters announced Conservatives 307 seats (one more than the final result), Labour 255 (three fewer) and Liberal Democrats fifty-nine (two more).

The Conservatives ended up the largest party but nineteen seats short of an overall majority. In spite of Cleggmania, the Liberal Democrats had lost some seats. Combined, Labour and the Liberal Democrats had 315 MPs, still short of majority.

In the early hours of the day after, 7 May, Cameron used his constituency acceptance speech in West Oxfordshire to claim that 'the Labour government has lost its mandate to govern our country'. In Scotland, Brown was still more noncommittal, pledging only to play his part forming 'a strong and stable government'. A few hours later, at his home in Sheffield, Clegg admitted: 'We simply haven't achieved what we'd hoped.'

UK elections are usually decisive overnight. Instead, an unprecedented five days of negotiations ensued to decide who would govern Britain.

Whoever ended up in No. 10, it was already a change election and new era at Westminster. More than a third of the Commons would now be made up of first-time MPs. In total, 147 sitting MPs had stood down before the election and a further fifty-seven were defeated – the majority of them Labour. Departed New Labour stars included Charles Clarke, Stephen Byers, Patricia Hewitt and Geoff Hoon.

Among the newly elected who would become prominent were the Conservatives Liz Truss, Amber Rudd, Matt Hancock, Rory Stewart, Penny Mordaunt, Zac Goldsmith and Priti Patel. Ian Paisley Jr replaced his father for the DUP. Caroline Lucas became the Green Party's first ever MP, in Brighton Pavilion. Labour's Rachel Reeves was elected. Keir Starmer and Rishi Sunak would not become MPs for another five years.

Devolutionary politics barely stirred in the 2010 election. In line with other results outside England, the SNP still had six MPs out of fifty-nine in Scotland: no change.

Less than twenty-four hours after polls closed, plunging the UK into political uncertainty, the Conservative leader seized the initiative. Speaking in the St Stephen's Club – a pastiche of No. 10 also with St James's Park as a backdrop – David Cameron proposed an idea tossed around that morning with George Osborne, Steve Hilton, Michael Gove and Ed Llewellyn, a friend of Nick Clegg. Cameron proposed a coalition with the Liberal Democrats, although he did not use that word then.

'I want to make a big, open and comprehensive offer to the Liberal Democrats,' he explained, 'I want us to work together in tackling our country's big and urgent problems: the debt crisis, our deep social problems and our broken political system.'

Formal negotiations between the parties began that evening in the Cabinet Office building, made available by the well-prepared Cabinet Secretary Sir Gus O'Donnell. The Conservatives had formed their team during the campaign: Oliver Letwin, William Hague, George Osborne and Ed Llewellyn. Three MPs and the diplomat who became Cameron's chief of staff. The Liberal Democrat negotiators became known only as they made their way into 70 Whitehall. Four MPs: Danny Alexander, Chris Huhne, David Laws and Andrew Stunell.

Talks between the two sides continued on the record, as well as consultative meetings with each party's councils and MPs. There were also private conversations between the leaders.

It was a most exciting career highlight to find myself reporting live politics on a rolling news channel. Liberal Democrat and Conservative parliamentarians made their cases, for and against coalition, on air.

Labour retreated into a huddle, Brown demanding a news blackout across the weekend into Monday as he clung on in Downing Street. He did not hold a meeting of the Cabinet or the parliamentary party, relying instead on a group of largely unelected advisers, some of whom were sleeping in Downing Street: Alastair Campbell, Peter Mandelson and Andrew Adonis.

Off the record, senior Labour MPs were telling reporters that the game was up. Labour could not form a stable government able to command Parliament, even in a 'rainbow' coalition with smaller parties such as the Greens and the Nationalists.

On Monday afternoon, Brown at last called a Cabinet meeting. But before it could meet, he made a confused announcement that he planned to form a government with the Liberal Democrats but would resign as Prime Minister in four months' time.

At 5.30 p.m., the spin doctor Alastair Campbell – who had no official position, elected or unelected, in the Labour government – appeared before the cameras to speak for Brown. A vicious live spat ensued between the two of us over whether Labour had 'effectively lost' the election or could form a stable government. Campbell attacked my professional integrity. The row trended on Twitter. Campbell subsequently attempted to get me disciplined with unsuccessful complaints to Sky and Ofcom. On a daily basis for years afterwards, passers-by would stop to congratulate me.

The next day, Gordon Brown's time ran out. He continued to have frequent contact with Clegg, making increasingly desperate policy offers, while in the Cabinet Office the two teams had not yet inked a coalition agreement. Finally, just after 7 p.m., Brown cut short yet another phone conversation with Clegg: 'Nick, Nick, Nick, Nick … I know the country's mood. They will not tolerate me waiting another night. You are a good man and you have made a decision. I have made mine. It is final. I am going to the palace. Goodbye.'

Minutes later, Brown left Downing Street for the last time as Prime Minister, holding hands with his wife Sarah and their young sons Fraser and John. Around the corner in the Cabinet Office meeting, the coalition talks broke up for the last time. 'Very positive', commented a tight-lipped Hague; 'good atmosphere', Alexander agreed. Hague was franker back home, telling his wife Ffion: 'I think I may have killed the Liberal Democrats.' Five years later at the 2015 general election, the Conservatives' 'decapitation strategy' against their erstwhile coalition partners led to the Liberal Democrats losing forty-nine of their fifty-seven seats including those of Vince Cable, Ed Davey and 2010 negotiator Danny Alexander.

The next day, Wednesday 10 May, David Cameron and the new Deputy Prime Minister Nick Clegg appeared side by side in the sunshine of the Downing Street garden for a light-hearted news conference. A new detailed manifesto, 'Coalition Programme for Government', was published, laying down red lines for what the new partners would or would not do with each other, including a referendum on voting reform but not on EU membership.

Policy was co-ordinated by regular meetings of the 'quad', with Cameron and Clegg joined by Danny Alexander and George Osborne. There were five Liberal Democrats in the new Cabinet, with similar representation in the lower ranks of government.

One of the new ministers, David Laws, revealed the letter left behind for him in the Treasury by his Labour predecessor Liam Byrne: 'Dear Chief Secretary, I'm afraid there is no money. Kind regards – and good luck! Liam.'

The coalition government of 2010–15 will be remembered for the austerity imposed in the wake of the banking crisis. To date, it also is the last stable full-term government the UK has enjoyed.

Adam Boulton is a broadcaster and veteran political journalist. Having worked with Sky News in 1989 to found the channel's respected politics team, he continued as its political editor until 2014 when he became editor-at-large. Following his departure from Sky News at the end of 2021, he now presents Times Radio's flagship Sunday morning programme and is a weekly columnist for Sky News online and Reaction Life. He has written extensively on British politics, including the books *Tony's Ten Years: Memories of the Blair Administration* (2008) and *Hung Together: The 2010 Election and the Coalition Government* with Joey Jones (2010), both published by Simon & Schuster.

48

2015

PHILIP COWLEY

Dissolution: 30 March 2015
Polling day: 7 May 2015
Seats contested: 650
Total electorate / Voted / Turnout: 46,354,197 / 30,697,525 / 66.2 per cent
Candidates (total 3,971): Conservative – 647; Labour – 631; Liberal Democrats – 631; UKIP – 624; Green – 573; SNP – 59; Plaid Cymru – 40; Alliance – 18; SDLP – 18; Sinn Féin – 18; DUP – 16; UUP – 15
Prime Minister on polling day: David Cameron
Main party leaders: Conservative – David Cameron; Labour – Ed Miliband; Liberal Democrats – Nick Clegg; UKIP – Nigel Farage; Green – Natalie Bennett; SNP – Nicola Sturgeon; Plaid Cymru – Leanne Wood; DUP – Peter Robinson; Sinn Féin – Gerry Adams; UUP – Mike Nesbitt; SDLP – Alasdair McDonnell; Alliance – David Ford

Party performance:

Party	Votes	Percentage share	Seats
Conservative	11,299,609	36.8	330
Labour	9,347,273	30.4	232
UKIP	3,881,099	12.6	1
Liberal Democrats	2,415,916	7.9	8
SNP	1,454,436	4.7	56
Green	1,111,603	3.8	1
DUP	184,260	25.7	8

Plaid Cymru	181,704	0.6	3
Sinn Féin	176,232	24.5	4
UUP	114,935	16	2
SDLP	99,809	13.9	3
Alliance	61,556	8.6	0

Result: Conservative majority of twelve seats

The potential significance of the 2015 election was clear almost as soon as the ballot boxes were opened. On page thirty of the Conservative Party manifesto was a pledge to offer 'a straight in-out referendum on our membership of the European Union'. That referendum, held just over a year later, led to Britain leaving the EU, overturning what had been a central plank of British government policy for more than a generation. The 2015 general election can therefore stake a claim as one of the more consequential of the post-war era.

It was also one of the more surprising results. A Conservative majority was not widely expected. The opinion polls had been deadlocked for months and much of the election commentary focused on the various deals or pacts that would be required to form a government after what appeared to be an inevitable hung parliament. On polling day, the odds on a Conservative majority were 11/1; you could get 1/25 on a hung parliament.

While the majority of twelve achieved by David Cameron was a slim one, and with a share of the national vote that many previous Prime Ministers would have scoffed at, it was still the first majority Conservative government elected for twenty-three years – and Cameron was the first incumbent Tory Prime Minister to increase his party's vote share in sixty years. After five years of coalition – and much talk of how the era of single-party government was over – the Conservatives were back in power alone.

The 2015 contest was also noteworthy for its many subplots, which transformed British electoral geography:

- the collapse of the Liberal Democrats, who had been the Conservatives' coalition partners for the previous five years and who fell from fifty-seven seats to just eight, undoing decades of work building the third force in British politics.
- the rise, if in electoral terms still the failure, of the UK Independence Party (UKIP), who in votes achieved the best result for an 'other' party in modern British politics but who ended up with just a single seat.
- and perhaps most spectacular of all, the rise of the Scottish National Party (SNP), taking fifty-six of the fifty-nine seats in Scotland, up by fifty.

For the first time since the rise of the Labour Party, Britain's third party was no longer the Liberals or its successor party – and for the first time since 1832, a different party topped the poll in each part of the United Kingdom.

One reason why the result came as such a shock was that opinion polls that had been more numerous than in any previous contest proved to be deeply flawed; the 2015 contest joined 1970 and 1992 as one the pollsters would sooner forget. The contest also saw developments in campaign techniques, especially the rise of targeted campaigning online, and it brought about notable changes in the composition of the Commons. The 2015 election returned more female and ethnic minority MPs than in any previous parliament, and more gay and lesbian MPs than in any parliament in the world.

Little of this had been predictable at the start of the parliament. The Conservative–Lib Dem administration formed in 2010 was the first peacetime coalition government at Westminster since 1931. David Cameron was Prime Minister; Nick Clegg, the Lib Dem leader, served as Deputy Prime Minister. Key decisions were taken by the 'quad' – in essence, an inner Cabinet – consisting of two Conservatives (Cameron and Chancellor George Osborne) and two Lib Dems (Clegg and Chief Secretary to the Treasury Danny Alexander). Relationships at the top of the coalition were relatively harmonious, but tensions were ever-present elsewhere and there were plenty of observers – and some participants – who wondered if the government would last the full five years of the parliament.

The parties signed up to a 'Programme of Government', superseding their manifestos. Some 75 per cent of Lib Dem manifesto commitments made it into this coalition agreement, compared to only 60 per cent of those of the Conservatives, but there was an important qualitative element: the Lib Dems made politically damaging concessions on spending cuts and on university tuition fees, two issues that would come to define the parliament.

The legacy of the 2008 financial crash shaped the formation of the coalition and dominated its life. The Queen's Speech of 2010 stated that the government's first priority was 'to reduce the deficit and restore economic growth'. With only a few exceptions, departments across Whitehall faced big reductions; local government was particularly badly hit.

A key Lib Dem goal was to try to demonstrate that hung parliaments and coalitions did not inevitably lead to weak government. They attempted to do this by 'owning' the entire coalition, good and bad. The first significant test of this position came over tuition fees, which the Lib Dem manifesto had promised to phase out and where Lib Dem MPs had signed a pledge to vote against any increase in fees. When the issue came to a vote in the Commons, the policy passed, but with the Lib Dems splitting three ways. It is sometimes claimed that the party's stance over fees was what damaged the Lib Dems electorally, but while it was totemic – an example of the party's supposed betrayal by entering government with the Conservatives – they were already polling poorly before this. It was going into coalition with the Conservatives that damaged the Lib Dems' standing with the electorate. Within months of the coalition forming, Lib Dem support had virtually halved, then dropped yet further at the end of 2010, following the tuition fees vote, before trending gently downwards for the rest of the parliament.

The issue of Europe proved equally difficult for the Conservatives. In his first party speech as party leader in 2006, Cameron had said that the party should 'stop banging on about it'. He favoured British membership, even if – like many Prime Ministers – the more dealings he had with the EU, the more sceptical about it he became. His scepticism, however, was nothing compared to that of his backbench MPs, who kept up unremitting pressure on the government. The party began the parliament ruling out a referendum on EU membership, but by January 2013, the Prime Minister had given in and he agreed that one would be held by 2017 at the latest.

Conservative nerves on the issue were heightened by the growing success of UKIP, under Nigel Farage, which called for Britain to leave the EU altogether, and which saw their opinion poll rating grow throughout the parliament. UKIP made gains in local elections, won two by-elections with Conservative defectors and topped the 2014 European elections, the first time a party other than Labour or the Conservatives had done so in any nationwide election for over 100 years. The referendum pledge was seen as a way of seeing off UKIP, enabling the Conservatives to argue that only a vote for them would deliver a vote on the subject.

Yet while the Conservatives suffered in the polls, their position was never catastrophic. Conversely, while Labour led in the polls for most of the parliament, and while they made gains in local elections, their performance was never impressive enough to convince people – including many of those inside the party – that they were on course for a general election victory.

Ed Miliband had been elected Labour leader in 2010, narrowly beating his brother, David, in the final round of voting. The idea that he had betrayed his brother – 'stabbed him in the back' – or that the party had chosen the 'wrong brother' would surface throughout the parliament and into the election campaign. Reactions to Miliband in focus groups – as well as to Labour canvassers and candidates – were often disheartening. An unflattering photo of him eating a bacon sandwich at a campaign event was widely circulated. Owen Jones in *The Guardian* noted that the photo was used to portray Miliband as a 'sad pathetic geeky loser who cannot even eat a bacon sandwich with any dignity'. That photo was to be used by *The Sun* as their front-page photo the day before the election.

Miliband tried to present himself as a break from his immediate predecessors – 'the era of New Labour is over', he declared – but the party never overcame the perceptions of the last Labour government's economic record and the effectiveness of a highly negative Conservative narrative about it. Labour were not helped by a note, written in 2010 by the outgoing Chief Secretary to the Treasury to his successor, which read 'I'm afraid there is no money'. Supposed to be private, it was soon made public, and a copy of the letter was waved around vigorously by David Cameron when on the stump, as proof of Labour's financial recklessness. Even by 2015, a YouGov poll found by 38 per cent to 32 per cent that voters were still blaming Labour 'for the current spending cuts'.

The parliament saw two referenda. The first, in May 2011, on electoral reform, saw an overwhelming victory for the status quo. It was a significant setback for the Lib Dems, who had hoped that the next election would be fought under a different electoral system, and was the first sign that what had had the potential to be a constitutionally radical government would end up a damp squib; Lords reform would later also be blocked, brought down by Conservative backbench MPs. One of the few constitutional innovations that survived was the Fixed-term Parliaments Act, which set the date of the next election. This had long been Lib Dem policy, but its implementation had a further purpose: to prevent the Conservatives dumping their coalition partners at a moment's notice. The original intention had been for the length of a parliament under the Act to be set at four years, but during the coalition negotiations, George Osborne had suggested five. The 2015 election was the only one to go the full distance, before the law was scrapped in 2022.

The second referendum came in late-2014, in Scotland. The unionist parties coalesced in a 'Better Together' campaign, emerging victorious. But the referendum proved polarising and the fall-out dominated the remaining months of the parliament. Some in the SNP had worried that a defeat would see the party fall in on itself, as it had after the referendum in 1979. Yet by early 2015, polling made it clear that there had been a sea change in Scottish public opinion; and by April 2015 onwards, the SNP led in every poll by at least twenty percentage points. While the UK-wide polls were to prove distinctly unreliable, the Scottish ones turned out to be a much more accurate predictor of what was to come. Suddenly, every seat in Scotland was up for grabs. An SNP surge on this scale reduced the chances of Labour securing an overall majority, making it more likely that they would be reliant on other parties to govern, something that was to become a major theme in the election campaign.

By the end of the parliament, relations between the two coalition partners were becoming ever more strained, with the Lib Dems in particular increasingly trying to differentiate themselves in the eyes of the electorate. According to opinion polls, most voters wanted a return to single-party government, but according to those same polls, there was little chance of that happening. Labour support had declined from late 2013 and the two parties were closely matched in the last twelve months of the parliament, at around 33 per cent each. Even before the formal campaigns began, both Labour and the Conservatives had prepared their negotiating teams, ready for the inevitable hung parliament.

Because the election date was known well in advance, the campaign had been underway long before the dissolution of Parliament on 30 March, with the rhetorical battlelines well established. According to the Conservatives, a Labour government 'propped up' or 'held to ransom' by the SNP would be a risk to the economic recovery and the maintenance of the UK. In turn, Labour warned that the Conservative programme of steep spending cuts would return Britain to the 1930s and destroy the NHS. The Conservatives forecast 'chaos' under Labour and the latter warned voters of 'cuts'. It was 'the long-term economic plan' and 'competence versus chaos' on one side, and 'a millionaires' tax cut' and a 'hundred hours to save the NHS' on the other.

The Liberal Democrats attacked both parties and offered themselves as a head for Labour and heart for the Conservatives, but it was an indictment of the failure of their broader strategy that after spending five years trying to demonstrate the benefits of coalition, the supposed dangers of a hung parliament became such a major issue in the 2015 campaign.

The campaign itself was not especially exciting. There were relatively few incidents; not much of significance happened; the polls barely moved. Indeed, at the time, the extent to which nothing seemed to be making any difference caused consternation in the Conservative camp. Some key issues were largely neglected, including foreign policy, Europe (ironically, given what was to come), reform of public services and, despite the increased presence of the Greens whose support had grown before the election, climate change. No party made clear where the inevitable cuts in spending programmes would be made. Anyone expecting a Socratic dialogue about great matters of state would have been disappointed, but then they would be disappointed by most election campaigns.

Yet the 2015 campaign is still noteworthy. For one thing, it provided yet more evidence for Nye Bevan's dictum that in every election the Conservatives needed a bogeyman ('If you haven't got a programme, a bogeyman will do'). Their focus on the SNP was unrelenting. More than 60 per cent of the press releases put out by the Conservatives during the campaign mentioned the SNP in some form. In late January 2015, the Conservatives released an image of Miliband and Alex Salmond together captioned: 'Your worst nightmare… just got worse.' After Miliband visited Northern Ireland a few days later, Gerry Adams, the president of Sinn Féin, was added to the picture: 'Your worst nightmare… just got even worse.' (It was a sign of how fevered possible post-election speculation was getting that the idea of the abstentionist Sinn Féin taking their seats at Westminster was even being discussed.) On 9 March, the Conservatives released a poster featuring Alex Salmond looking down at a tiny Ed Miliband in his pocket, which they deployed in and around marginal constituencies in England and Wales. When Labour launched their campaign, Conservative activists turned up in Alex Salmond masks.

The irony was that Salmond was no longer SNP leader or First Minister, having stood down after the referendum result. Yet his successor, Nicola Sturgeon, was not yet well known enough south of the border for the campaign tactic to work. But once the campaign raised her profile, the Conservatives got themselves a bogeywoman; to coincide with the debates, the Conservatives released a revised version of their Miliband-in-pocket post, this time with Sturgeon in place of Salmond, and from then on Conservative activists picketing Labour events turned up in Sturgeon masks.

Party leaders continued to be the most prominent voices for their parties' messages – not helped by the disappearance of morning press conferences, which had previously necessitated at least some sharing of the limelight. The top five politicians to feature in the media were the leaders of the Conservatives, Labour, Lib Dems, SNP and UKIP, in that order. David Cameron was featured in the media almost four times as often as the second most featured Conservative politician, George Osborne, while Ed Miliband featured almost six times as often as the second most prominent Labour politician, shadow Chancellor Ed Balls. The disparity was even starker for the smaller parties. For the most part, the leaders' campaigns were heavily stage-managed, often appearing before preselected and politically supportive or otherwise safe audiences for televised events. Sturgeon was an exception to this, but the three main leaders played it exceptionally safe.

The 2015 election campaign also saw a noticeable decline in the use of campaign posters. Many poster 'launches' were merely media events to generate publicity, with the poster being unveiled on a moveable board (and then used online) but never hitting a paid poster site.

Even the Conservatives, who continued to use some posters, spent around one-sixth of what they had spent in 2010 on them.

The introduction of leaders' debates in the preceding election had then been thought to have set a precedent. But although there were some debates in 2015, head-to-head contests between the main party leaders did not take place, largely because the Conservatives refused to participate. The prolonged and painful nature of the negotiations preceding the debates and their eventual formats were testimony to how British politics was mutating beyond the three 'main' parties, but they also had the effect of blunting their edge.

The only TV debate in which David Cameron and Ed Miliband appeared on stage together came on 2 April, along with five other leaders, including two, Nicola Sturgeon and Leanne Wood for Plaid Cymru, who were not even candidates in the election; it lasted two hours, involving just four questions. In addition, there was also a 'challengers' debate – consisting of just the opposition parties; a special edition of *Question Time*, with Cameron, Miliband and Clegg all appearing one after the other; and a Sky/Channel 4 programme in which Cameron and Miliband both faced a studio audience as well as questions from Jeremy Paxman. None of these had the same cut through as five years before. In 2010, the debates had been the major staging posts of the campaign; that was not true in 2015.

The 2015 campaign also saw a clear advance in the use of digital campaign tools. 'Everyone claimed that 2010 was the first digital election in British political history,' wrote those in charge of the digital team for the Conservatives. 'Well we worked on it, and trust us – it really wasn't. None of the parties had a clue how to use digital effectively. But 2015 was different.' Or, as one of Labour's digital team noted: 'This was the first digital campaign with firepower. We could cut through.' The debate over whether digital campaigning worked was essentially over: all the parties did it and they all thought it was effective.

The rise of digital campaigning allowed the parties to make broadcast adverts more like US campaign ads, much shorter than traditional party election broadcasts and often more negative. These were posted on YouTube or on the party's own website, but the main mechanism for their delivery to voters was through social media such as Twitter or Facebook, increasingly subverting the traditional ban on television advertising. The parties also put considerable efforts into targeting online material to swing voters in marginal constituencies. The digital campaign was as much part of the electoral ground war as it was the air war.

By contrast, the party election broadcasts were unimaginative and relatively cheaply produced. The majority ran to a maximum of three minutes and were a fairly predictable mix of voiceover and footage.

One of the few to run longer was 'Ed Miliband: A Portrait', which ran for five minutes and was an attempt to do for Miliband what had been done for Kinnock in 1987 or Blair in 1997. It did not succeed.

Yet, for all that, the main mechanism of direct contact between the parties and the voters remained the leaflet or letter, pushed through someone's letterbox, by a party activist or supporter (or, in some cases, by commercial delivery companies), and the main indirect mechanism remained the press and broadcast media. Although the combined circulation of the newspapers was the lowest it had been in any election since 1945, they still mattered, both directly and in the way they helped determine the broadcast agenda. While social media grew up as a partial counterpoint, it was still only a partial one. After the election, many Labour politicians worried that all it had done was create an echo chamber, in which those on the left convinced themselves that they were virtuous and that no sane person would vote for the Conservatives.

The overseas influence on British elections was again evident in personnel. The Conservatives imported Jim Messina for ground war strategy and Bill Knapp for debate preparations as well as Lynton Crosby and Mark Textor from Australia. Labour also called on veterans of the Obama election, including Stan Greenberg, the pollster, David Axelrod on messaging and the Brit Matthew McGregor, based in New York, for digital work. The Liberal Democrats turned to Ryan Coetzee, a South African strategist.

Gaffes or incidents during the campaign itself were relatively trivial. There were a handful of candidates who were found to have said some unpleasant things online and were defenestrated accordingly. There was a poster unveiled by the Conservatives in early 2015 ('Let's stay on the road to a stronger economy'), only for the road in question to turn out to be in Germany. Launching the Green campaign, the party leader Natalie Bennett was interviewed by Nick Ferrari on LBC Radio and had what was widely described as a car-crash interview. 'To be fair to Ms Bennett,' wrote the *Daily Telegraph*'s sketch writer, 'Ferrari did ask her a lot of tough questions, such as what her policies were and how she would fund them.'

Ed Miliband had a couple of slip-ups during televised debates – a weird 'hell, yeah' when asked if he was tough enough and a poorly phrased answer on the economy. David Cameron slipped up during a speech on multiculturalism in which he appeared to confuse Aston Villa – a football team which he had always said he supported – with West Ham United, an error that to his critics revealed him as the sort of person who would say anything to get elected.

Labour's final head-in-hands moment was more carefully planned and literally more monumental: an 8ft 6in. limestone tablet inscribed with Labour's six policy pledges, unveiled in a car park in Hastings, and indicating, according to Ed Miliband, how serious Labour was about keeping them: 'These six pledges are now carved in stone, and they are carved in stone because they won't be abandoned after the general election.' It quickly became known as the 'Ed stone' and was much ridiculed ('the heaviest suicide note in history').

Yet all of this was fairly trivial. Nothing seemed to move the dial. Some Labour politicians had feared that Ed Miliband would crumble on the campaign trail, while the head of the Conservative campaign Lynton Crosby kept promising that there would be a crossover point in the polling, when the Conservatives would emerge clearly in the lead. Neither materialised. With the parties still deadlocked, George Osborne spent polling day sending Nick Clegg text messages calling for another coalition.

The exit poll, broadcast simultaneously at 10 p.m. on the BBC, ITV and Sky News, therefore came as a shock. It predicted the Conservatives to win 316 seats, Labour 239, with the Lib Dems down to just ten and the SNP taking an almost clean sweep in Scotland with fifty-eight of the fifty-nine constituencies. Although still shy of an outright Conservative majority, it was near enough to see how the Conservatives could stay in power, propped up by the DUP. As in 2010, there was some initial scepticism about the forecast, but it proved to be very accurate, if anything slightly underestimating the scale of Conservative success.

For Labour, the result was a disaster. They had begun election night thinking they had a realistic chance of entering government.

They ended it more than six percentage points behind the Conservatives, trailing by just shy of 100 seats. Electoral casualties included the shadow Foreign Secretary, Douglas Alexander, who lost to the SNP (as did the leader of Scottish Labour, Jim Murphy), and Ed Balls, defeated by the Conservatives.

At the beginning of the parliament, the Lib Dem hope had been that after initial unpopularity, their poll ratings would pick up again, as people became impressed by the success of the coalition. When that never materialised, they instead banked on the local reputations of their MPs. Privately, the party had been still hopeful of holding at least twenty seats, with an upper target of thirty, enough to keep them viable. They ended up with eight, one of whom was Nick Clegg who held on, narrowly, in Sheffield Hallam.

Replacing them in the Commons as the third party came the SNP. Some fifty seats changed hands in Scotland, on swings of up to 39.3 per cent. The SNP won more seats in that one night than they had in the party's entire history previously and they came within under 5,000 votes of taking every seat in Scotland. Labour, the Lib Dems and the Conservatives were left with one lone Scottish MP each. 'The tectonic plates of Scottish politics shifted,' declared Sturgeon.

UKIP managed under just 4 million votes – more than the SNP and Lib Dems combined – but no party had ever piled up so many votes for so little return. They won Clacton, taken in a by-election in 2014, but they failed to hold on to their other by-election victory and fell short in all their target seats, most significantly in Thanet South where Nigel Farage came second. The Greens, too, managed their highest ever vote haul but won no seats beyond holding Brighton Pavilion. Party leader Natalie Bennett came third in Holborn and St Pancras.

For all the drama and the talk of the election being close, the turnout increased by a mere 1 per cent to 66 per cent. Turnouts that would have seemed shockingly low a generation before now seemed to be the norm in British elections.

Within a day, Ed Miliband, Nick Clegg and Nigel Farage had all announced their resignations as party leaders, even if a few days later

Farage was to withdraw his. Clegg was later quoted as saying 'live by the sword, die by the sword – I just didn't realise there'd be so many swords'. David Cameron was to describe the result as 'the sweetest victory of all', yet less than a year later he would also resign, brought down by the referendum his manifesto had promised. At one point, campaigning in Leeds, he had mistakenly described the election as 'career-defining', before quickly correcting himself to 'country-defining' – but both turned out to be right.

In a tweet towards the end of the campaign, he had claimed that 'Britain faces a simple and inescapable choice – stability and strong Government with me, or chaos with Ed Miliband'. It was not quite how things turned out.

All elections are followed by 'what ifs'. Some members of Miliband's team, including Miliband himself, reflected after polling day that if the polls had been more accurate and reported a clear Conservative lead, the campaign would have been very different. The broadcasters and the press would not have been relentlessly discussing the consequences of a Labour–SNP accommodation but would have provided greater scrutiny of the policies a majority Conservative government would implement.

There may be some truth in this, but even if the polls had been completely accurate, they would only have been reporting a projected Conservative majority of twelve, a slim enough majority that the margin of error alone could have reduced the government to minority status. There would presumably still have been considerable speculation about the possibility of a hung parliament, and the role that the SNP might play in it.

There is, anyway, some debate about how crucial the role of the SNP was in that victory. The British Election Study claimed to have found no evidence in its survey that the rise of the SNP played a role in influencing voters in England and Wales. Yet the key party strategists for Labour, the Conservatives and the Liberal Democrats have no doubt that this had a major influence on the result of the election south of the border. And other surveys did pick up some effect. The TUC's post-election survey, for example, found that the fear that a

Labour government would be 'bossed around by Nicola Sturgeon and the Scottish nationalists' was the third biggest doubt voters had about voting Labour; it was the second biggest doubt for those who had only considered voting Labour. During the campaign, polling by the Conservatives had discovered that focusing on the threat of a hung parliament was a good way to undermine local support for Lib Dem incumbent MPs; the seats the Lib Dems lost to Labour or to the SNP had mostly been expected, but what destroyed them were the twenty-seven seats they lost to the Conservatives, more than they lost to Labour and the SNP combined and including many they had considered safe.

Yet here too, however, we need to be careful. If there was an SNP effect, it operated in multiple ways. At its most indirect, it dominated the media agenda and prevented Labour from getting its message across. Second, while for some people in England and Wales the fear of the SNP in government may have been sufficiently strong on its own, for others it will just have reinforced existing doubts about Labour and Ed Miliband. Labour's own internal report into the election noted that 'SNP threat messaging had a strong impact with middle-class families in England', but it went on: 'This line of messaging also played into concerns around Labour's leadership.'

Regardless, the *belief* that fear of the SNP played a key role in the election result entered political discourse in the UK; the idea that the 'Coalition of Chaos' was an electoral trump card soon became widely accepted.

And then there is perhaps the most significant 'what if' of all. What if the result had not been a Conservative majority? What then for the referendum pledge and Brexit? It is often claimed that David Cameron made the pledge only because he assumed there would be no Conservative majority – and he would therefore not need to implement it. It existed, some of his critics say, merely as an electoral ploy, to be bargained away in the expected post-election negotiations. But then he won a majority he never expected and was forced to carry it out. Britain left the EU, this argument goes, because of something David Cameron never intended to do.

Yet although this is frequently claimed, it seems implausible. In his memoirs, Cameron dismisses it entirely, claiming that the referendum pledge was an absolute red line for him in any post-election negotiations, not least for the rather obvious reason that there would have been a peasants' revolt among Conservative MPs and members had he attempted to resile from it. This is exactly how senior Lib Dems understood his position at the time. In other words, it seems more likely that the referendum would have happened under any form of Conservative government returned in 2015 – majority, minority or a Conservative-led coalition.

Perhaps a more interesting counter-factual is what would have happened if the Conservatives had lost the election. There would have been no immediate referendum, for sure, but the issue would not have gone away. Cameron would have stepped down as party leader shortly afterwards; on polling day, he had already rehearsed a resignation speech. Given the centre of gravity in the Conservative Party, it seems highly likely that most (if not all?) candidates for the leadership would have supported a referendum, either out of conviction or calculation. It seems very difficult to imagine anyone emerging victorious from such a contest without taking such a position. Unless we assume that an Ed Miliband premiership would have ushered in an extremely long period of centre-left government, during which the British grew to love the EU, it therefore seems likely that there would have been a referendum whenever the Conservatives next entered government. It was probably coming, regardless.

Philip Cowley is a professor of politics at Queen Mary University of London.

49

2017

STEPHEN PARKINSON

Dissolution: 3 May 2017
Polling day: 8 June 2017
Seats contested: 650
Total electorate / Voted / Turnout: 46,836,533 / 32,204,184 / 68.8 per cent
Candidates (total 3,304): Conservative – 638; Labour – 631; Liberal Democrats – 629; Green – 467; UKIP – 378; SNP – 59; Plaid Cymru – 40; Alliance – 18; Sinn Féin – 18; UUP – 14
Prime Minister on polling day: Theresa May
Main party leaders: Conservative – Theresa May; Labour – Jeremy Corbyn; Liberal Democrats – Tim Farron; Green – Caroline Lucas and Jonathan Bartley; UKIP – Paul Nuttall; SNP – Nicola Sturgeon; Plaid Cymru – Leanne Wood; DUP – Arlene Foster; Sinn Féin – Gerry Adams; SDLP – Colum Eastwood; UUP – Robin Swann; Alliance – Naomi Long

Party performance:

Party	Votes	Percentage share	Seats
Conservative	13,636,684	42.3	317
Labour	12,877,918	40	262
Liberal Democrats	2,371,861	7.4	12
SNP	977,568	3	35
UKIP	594,068	1.8	0
Green	525,665	1.6	1

DUP	292,316	36	10
Sinn Féin	238,915	29.4	7
Plaid Cymru	164,466	0.5	4
SDLP	95,419	11.7	0
UUP	83,280	10.3	0
Alliance	64,553	7.9	0

Result: Hung parliament with the Conservatives governing through a confidence and supply agreement with the DUP

The 2017 general election began, for me, with a telephone call in St James's Park on Tuesday 18 April. I was walking through the spring sunlight back to Downing Street after a pleasant Easter weekend when I got a call from Ross, one of the private secretaries to the Prime Minister's joint chiefs of staff Nick Timothy and Fiona Hill. 'Nick would like to see you as soon as you're in,' he said. The sunlight seemed to fade; I have never been much of a morning person, but I was starting the new term with good intentions, and it was still early. I hastened my pace and made for the back gate of Downing Street, ready to find out whatever I was in trouble for now.

When I got in, I reported to the 'bollocking room' – the office adjoining the Cabinet Room which Nick and Fi used as a meeting room, so named for the dressings-down we had received there from their Cameron-era predecessor Ed Llewellyn when we were special advisers at the Home Office. (It was also the original home of the No. 10 political office, which I would be delighted to restore – after some wrangling – later that year.)

Sitting around the rickety table were John Godfrey, head of the Downing Street Policy Unit, and Chris Brannigan, director of government relations. Nick walked in with a grin on his face. 'What are you doing on 8 June?' he asked. We looked back at him blankly. 'You'll be voting in a general election.'

A number of thoughts ran through my head. I was surprised, of course: although the suggestion of an early election had been raised occasionally, it was always in hushed or furtive tones and hastily dismissed. The news smarted too – as the Prime Minister's political secretary, I was responsible for relations with Conservative Central Office and the voluntary party. Despite this, and my involvement in two recent by-elections in Copeland and Stoke-on-Trent Central, I had not been asked for a view. I would like to say that I raised concerns about the preparedness of our campaign machinery, but the decision had clearly been taken – and I took some solace that I was finding out before most of the Cabinet. I did, however, highlight one hurdle which immediately struck me: the party was waiting to hear whether criminal charges would be brought against it for a number of alleged spending breaches at the 2015 general election, relating to the 'battle bus' which had ferried activists to a slew of marginal constituencies, and to its campaign in South Thanet. I was right to be anxious: the Crown Prosecution Service announced its decisions on both cases during the ensuing campaign. On 10 May, it said that no charges would be brought in relation to the battle bus, but on 2 June – just six days before polling day – it announced that it would press charges against three people, including Craig Mackinlay, who was standing again in South Thanet. (In the event, he won the seat with an increased majority, and went on to be cleared of any wrongdoing.) This brief warning aside, I took the news in the spirit with which it had been imparted and had a brief chat with Nick about seeking a constituency to contest myself. One way or another, I did not expect to be returning to Downing Street after the election.

My (unsuccessful) attempt to get selected as a candidate occupied much of the first two weeks of the campaign: I had my heart set on Saffron Walden, where Sir Alan Haselhurst was retiring after forty years, and which had previously been represented by my political hero, Rab Butler. I spent a frantic fortnight trying to meet as many members of the local association as possible and reading back issues of the *Saffron Walden Reporter* in the local library. Whether this helped or hindered my case I do not know: at the selection meeting in the town hall on 2 May, I lost by a dozen votes to Kemi Badenoch, who gave the sort of passionate and stirring speech for which she has now become more widely known, in a three-way contest with Laura

Farris, whom I was also delighted to see become an MP two years later.

When I sloped back to Conservative Central Office from my unsuccessful escapade in Essex, I found it a hive of activity. Rather than trying to fight my way into what was already a tight and confusing campaign structure, I opted to spend the campaign in Tynemouth, where my friend and former Vote Leave colleague Nick Varley was standing. Historically one of the more dependably Conservative seats in the north-east, the constituency had been Labour since 1997. The constituency of my birth, and still home to much of my family, I had wondered about throwing my hat in the ring here, dizzied by the early polls and the prospect of seats which looked in play. I had great fun campaigning for Nick, who won more votes for Tynemouth Tories than they had scored at any election for a quarter of a century – yet saw Labour win with their biggest majority ever. This perplexing picture proved to be one which was repeated across the country.

There was, of course, not supposed to have been an election in 2017. Launching her campaign to become leader of the Conservative Party on 30 June 2016, Theresa May had been very clear that 'there should be no general election until 2020' – a response both to the anxieties of Tory MPs and to the widespread desire for political stability which followed the divisive referendum on the UK's membership of the European Union. It was a commitment that she and the team around her repeated throughout her first eight months in office. While Nick and Fi discussed the notion of an early election in the garden of No. 10 in December 2016, no plans were made at this stage. The poll ratings were good – a Tory lead of fifteen points at Christmas extended to as much as twenty-one by Easter – but people remained wary of going to the country sooner than expected. On 6 March, the former Tory leader Lord Hague of Richmond used his column in the *Daily Telegraph* to lay out the arguments for an early election. Pointing to the challenges of negotiating the UK's exit from the European Union, as well as the renewed calls for a second independence referendum in Scotland, Lord Hague said an early poll 'would strengthen the Government's hand at home and abroad', offering the prospect of 'a large and decisive majority in the Commons and a new full term ahead of them'. A few MPs now expressed a similar view. The Conservative victory in Copeland (the first time a governing party had gained a by-election in my lifetime) showed that we could win in seats we had not won since the 1930s. And the memory of Gordon Brown bottling his chance to call an election in 2007 hung heavy in our memories.

Theresa May's own thinking was, as ever, much less cynical, motivated by what would be the best timing in relation to the Brexit negotiations. A general election fixed for May 2020 would hang over the crunch point in these discussions and could be exploited by Brussels. A likely transition period could also stretch beyond the end of the parliament, meaning the process would not be complete before another election was held. The French presidential election offered a narrow window of opportunity between the triggering of Article 50 and negotiations beginning in June. Our negotiators supported seizing it. But it was not a decision the Prime Minister took with relish – in her speech to the nation announcing it, she mentioned twice that she had come to her conclusion reluctantly.

The number of people she consulted while reaching that reluctant conclusion was very small. The most important was her husband, Philip, with whom she mulled it over during a five-day walking holiday in Snowdonia the week before Easter. On her return, the party chairman, Sir Patrick McLoughlin, was asked to come to the Prime Minister's constituency home in Sonning, Berkshire, on 12 April. He came straight from a lunchtime meeting of the Privy Council at Windsor, where he had been struck by a perspicacious remark from the Duke of Edinburgh that the Prime Minister should be able to request a general election whenever she wanted. Sir Patrick did not inform his driver of their post-prandial destination until they set off, so as not to arouse wider suspicion. Arriving early, he reminded May over a cup of tea that Margaret Thatcher had said that deciding when to call an election was one of the most difficult choices facing a Prime Minister. 'Tell me about it,' came her reply.

The Prime Minister spoke to the Queen on Easter Monday, 17 April, to notify Her Majesty of her intentions. She did not call to request a dissolution of Parliament, since the royal prerogative to do so had been constrained by the Fixed-term Parliaments Act of 2011 (a piece of legislation which did not succeed in fixing the terms of two of the three parliaments during which it was in operation, and which has now sensibly been repealed). A second new law – the Electoral Registration and Administration Act of 2013 – had recently extended the electoral timetable from seventeen to twenty-five days. Together, these slowed things down considerably. As well as the usual parliamentary wash-up, time had to be set aside for a short bill making provision for an early election in the event that the Commons did not approve its dissolution by the requisite two-thirds majority (as would be the case two years later). With the Lords in recess until 24 April, Parliament was not prorogued until 27 April or dissolved until 3 May – the longest gap since 1970. After some confusion with the local returning officer, a motion also had to be passed superseding the writ which had been moved for a by-election in Manchester Gorton following the death of the Father of the House, Sir Gerald Kaufman. All of this combined to produce a gap of more than seven weeks from announcement to polling day – and the longest campaign in modern history (since general elections began to be held on a single day, in 1918). It may have come as a surprise, but this was certainly not a 'snap' election.

The election had also come as a surprise to the Prime Minister's own party, meaning the Conservatives had no head start on their opponents. Hundreds of candidates had to be selected, holidays cancelled, leaflets printed and campaign teams assembled. In many parts of the country, campaigning was already underway for local elections across Great Britain – the first time these had taken place during a general election campaign since 1955. They offered a tantalising glimpse of what might have been. Across the country, the Conservatives gained more than 560 councillors and eleven councils, with Labour losing 382 councillors and seven local authorities. In England, the Tories won Derbyshire and Lancashire county councils and took control of Northumberland for the first time since the 1960s. (They missed an overall majority on the drawing of straws after a tied vote and two recounts in South Blyth.) There were sensational victories in the mayoral elections in new combined authorities, with the former managing director of John Lewis, Andy Street, winning the West Midlands with 50.4 per cent of the vote in the second round, and thirty-year-old solicitor Ben Houchen winning in Tees Valley with 51.1 per cent. In Scotland, the Conservatives more than doubled their tally of councillors and displaced Labour as the second largest party. In Wales, Labour lost more than a hundred councillors to Plaid Cymru and the Welsh Conservatives, who gained seventy-nine councillors and won control of Monmouthshire.

These were heartening results for the Conservatives – but also a wake-up call to those who did not want to see a large Tory majority in Westminster. That was the widely expected outcome of the election – 'May heads for election landslide', proclaimed *The Times* on the first day of the campaign, while *The Sun* predicted 'Blue murder' – but the pitch to achieve it was not well framed.

In her speech outside No. 10 on 18 April, the Prime Minister told the nation: 'At this moment of enormous national significance there should be unity here in Westminster, but instead there is division. The country is coming together, but Westminster is not.'

She was right to warn that 'division in Westminster will risk our ability to make a success of Brexit and it will cause damaging uncertainty and instability to the country'. But at this juncture, the threat was not as apparent as it would become. On 1 February, the House of Commons had voted by a majority of 384 to give the Prime Minister the statutory authority to trigger Article 50 of the Lisbon Treaty, formally notifying the EU of the United Kingdom's intention to leave. And although the House of Lords had made two amendments to the bill providing for it, these had been easily overturned in the Commons. For all the sound and fury in Westminster, Brexit did not seem to be under threat.

Among those who voted for the bill enabling Article 50 to be triggered were Heidi Allen, Sam Gyimah, Phillip Lee, Antoinette Sandbach, Anna Soubry and Sarah Wollaston – all of whom would go on to leave the Conservative Party because of their opposition to Brexit – and Labour MPs including Yvette Cooper, Hilary Benn and Dame Margaret Beckett who would employ novel procedures to thwart the government in the next parliament. (Most dismally, Dame Margaret argued that allegations of bullying by John Bercow – which subsequently led to his lifetime ban from the Palace of Westminster – should be overlooked in favour of embarking on what she called a 'huge constitutional experiment in which there may be a key role for the Speaker', suggesting that his importance to that experiment 'trumps bad behaviour'.) All of these MPs, bar Allen and Benn, represented seats which had voted Leave. Before the election, they were largely muted in their opposition, perhaps conscious that they were at odds with their electorates. One of the consequences of the 2017 election was to embolden them (as well as Leave-supporting MPs in Remain-voting constituencies, such as Steve Baker and Sir John Redwood) to be more outspoken once re-elected. Yvette Cooper, for instance, promised the electors of Normanton, Pontefract & Castleford in her election leaflets that she would 'not vote to block Brexit'. They took her at face value and returned her to Parliament with her highest ever share of the vote. Twenty-one months later, she helped to seize control of the order paper from the government and passed a bill seeking an extension to Article 50.

As well as the inapparent threat to Brexit, there was another confusing element in the Prime Minister's pitch for a larger majority. Was she offering change or continuity? It was a confusion which went to the heart of the Conservative campaign strategy – laid bare, but left unresolved, at an 'awayday' held at Chequers on 16 February. Ostensibly to discuss the strategy leading towards a 2020 general election, it gathered together senior Downing Street staff – Nick and Fi, Alex Dawson, Chris Wilkins and me – with trusted electoral strategists and campaigners: Sir Lynton Crosby and Stephen, Lord Gilbert of Panteg. As director of strategy, Chris presented a memorandum outlining a bold pitch to present the new administration as a departure from the Cameron government, recognising that the referendum result had exposed a widespread desire for change. Sir Lynton, architect of the 2015 election triumph, argued powerfully that the Prime

Minister needed to present herself as a tried and tested leader in a time of uncertainty. Each had polling data to back up their arguments. As the matter did not need to be settled there and then, it was left unresolved as we went downstairs for lunch. Like the slightly curious chicken lasagne we were served, it would come back to haunt us before long.

The 'change' pitch can be found in an unused text for the speech announcing the election, drafted by Wilkins and cited in Philip Cowley and Dennis Kavanagh's Nuffield study of the election. In that version, Theresa May would have framed the election as follows:

> As I have often said, the referendum was not just a vote to leave the EU, but an instruction to change the way the country works – and the people for whom it works – for ever.
>
> It was a call from all those who have been let down, ignored and left behind for too long, to change Britain into a country that works for everyone, not just the privileged few.
>
> And to respond to that cry for change, we need an ambitious programme of economic and social reform on a par with the great eras of progress our country has experienced before.

Instead, the speech May delivered made five references to a phrase which would become a wearyingly familiar refrain: 'strong and stable leadership in the national interest'. As Cowley and Kavanagh record, 'this distinction – between the Prime Minister representing change or stability – was fundamental, yet it remained largely unresolved and was to run like a fault line throughout the entire Conservative campaign'.

While Labour had made some rudimentary plans for a possible snap election, the secrecy with which the election had been decided meant the Conservatives were not ready for their own campaign. This accentuated the temptation simply to dust off the plans which had worked so well for David Cameron two years earlier (in some cases, visit options and briefing documents simply involved taking old files and writing over them). But with such different styles, the old campaign garments did not suit the new leader. Rather than stump speeches to crowds of placard-waving activists, a more traditional campaign, with daily press conferences featuring the Prime Minister and an array of her Cabinet colleagues sitting at a table taking questions might have been a better format.

The shape of the campaign was one of the few instances of Nick and Fi ceding control to others during their time as chiefs of staff; while they have come in for much criticism for their uncompromising approach, perhaps things would have been different if they had held it more tightly. But neither had run an election campaign before, and they were glad to have persuaded both Sir Lynton and Lord Gilbert to return to the fray. Unlike in 2015, however, neither of the men had been given the chance to lay the groundwork, nor been granted the clear authority to make final decisions. Whereas Sir Lynton had been at the helm in Central Office for eighteen months before the 2015 election, he was on holiday in Fiji for his wife's sixtieth birthday when the 2017 campaign began (he did not arrive until 25 April), and his business partner Mark Textor played a more active role.

With no campaign grid and a confused decision-making chain, the Tory campaign was drawn up day by day – the location of the manifesto launch was not decided until late the day before, for instance. But it was the content of that manifesto, not the late decision to unveil it in Halifax, which caused consternation. Nick Timothy, who wrote it (along with Paymaster General Ben Gummer, the only Cabinet-level casualty of the election), explained in *The Spectator* diary one week after the poll that it had been a conscious exercise in electoral candour: 'One of the criticisms is that, instead of offering voters giveaways and bribes, we spelt out where cuts would fall. While I accept that the manifesto might have been too ambitious, I worry that the implication of this argument is that politicians should not be straight with the electorate.'

The manifesto spelt out a change in the up-rating of pensions: maintaining the 'triple lock' – by which they would rise in line with earnings, inflation, or 2.5 per cent, whichever was highest – until 2020, but thereafter moving to a 'double lock', based on earnings and inflation alone. Although either earnings or inflation have always been above 2.5 per cent in the years since then, it attracted some criticism on the doorstep, as did the proposal to limit the Winter Fuel Payment to the most needy pensioners.

The policy which attracted the greatest level of concern, however, was social care – an area where Nick Timothy accepts 'we did get it wrong; it did worry people'. Although it took just one of the manifesto's eighty-six pages to set out, the policy was a complex one to explain on the doorstep – and the secrecy surrounding the manifesto's contents meant neither leaflets nor guidance for activists had been prepared. The shorthand depiction of it as a 'dementia tax' – in use by lunchtime on the day it was announced – meanwhile, was pithy and effective.

Historians and political scientists have long debated how much difference manifestos make to election campaigns; 2017 will surely be cited as evidence that they do. But it seems to me that it was not so much individual policy proposals as the overall picture they painted which moved the dial. As outlined above, the Conservative campaign began by trying to straddle competing propositions of change and continuity: the manifesto was the moment these strategies collided. The 2015 and 2017 Tory manifestos, for instance, made the same commitment to a free vote on the Hunting Act (in fact, the 2017 manifesto used more neutral wording, promising 'the opportunity to decide the future of' the Act, rather than 'the opportunity to repeal' it) – but the issue was more prominent in the later campaign. Some have ascribed this to the greater influence of social media, but I think it was because of differing expectations: many electors expected David Cameron – an Old Etonian with a rural upbringing – to be in favour of hunting; they did not expect Theresa May – of whom they were still forming an opinion – to say the same. Her manifesto promised change, but parts of it sounded like the 'same old Tories'. It was one of a number of reasons to give them pause for thought.

Labour's manifesto, by contrast, was greeted with fresh interest – and the leaking of a full draft of it on the evening of 10 May gave the opposition two chances to lead the news with their policy ideas. The

Tories' decision not to publish a costings document alongside their manifesto meant they could not attack Labour for their sums, which even by their own admission did not add up.

The Conservative manifesto was launched on Thursday 18 May; a YouGov poll for the *Sunday Times* on 21 May had the Tory lead down to single figures, which chimed with the negative feedback reported by party activists on the doorsteps that weekend. A particular anxiety was the lack of cap on social care costs. The manifesto talked of a 'floor' but no 'ceiling'. This was hastily added and announced by the Prime Minister in a speech in Wrexham on Monday 22 May, where she maintained that 'nothing has changed', betraying her irritation under fire from journalists. She has herself described this as 'the most obvious, and arguably defining, mistake' she made during the campaign. 'Obviously something had changed. I knew what I meant – that the fundamental policy had not changed – but it was a fatal error on my part.'

This was the day that postal ballots began to land on voters' doormats – more than a fifth of all votes in the election would be cast that way. That evening would pause the campaign for far grimmer reasons. At the end of an Ariana Grande concert at the Manchester Arena that evening, an Islamist terrorist blew himself up, killing twenty-two people, the youngest of them eight years old, and injuring around 500 more. It was the worst terrorist attack in the United Kingdom since 2005.

The main parties agreed to suspend campaigning for three days – though UKIP went ahead with their manifesto launch. The Prime Minister and her closest aides returned to Downing Street and led the government response to the atrocity. For a few days, electioneering – and party politics – seemed to stop. There was some criticism of the Prime Minister for chairing a meeting in the Cabinet Office briefing room rather than attending a vigil in Manchester, but the Home Secretary attended to represent the government.

That was not a substitute which worked when it came to the televised debate which took place on 31 May. Again, May accepts that this was a mistake: 'I should have done the TV debates,' she has since written:

I had always thought that preparing for those debates took up too much campaign time and did not add much to the overall arguments. I now realise that they have come to be an accepted part of campaigns that may not change the view of many voters but do shape the media's approach to the party leaders.

This was only the third election in which TV debates featured: 2010 had seen the Labour and Tory campaigns derailed by 'Cleggmania', and 2015 dominated by squabbles over format. Initially, Jeremy Corbyn took the same view as May – but decided on the day of the debate to take part after all. Amber Rudd acquitted herself admirably in the seven-way debate – particularly given the death of her father just two days before. May and Corbyn took part in a *Question Time* special on 2 June, when Corbyn was grilled about his views on the IRA and the nuclear deterrent – but the damage had been done. A participant in a focus group held by Lord Ashcroft summed up the views of many about the Prime Minister's earlier absence: 'She called the snap election and now she can't be bothered turning up to it.'

The following night, terrorists struck for a second time. Late in the evening of Saturday 3 June, three Islamist extremists drove a van at high speed into pedestrians on London Bridge, then stabbed people trying to flee through Borough Market, wearing fake suicide belts to heighten the panic. Eight people were killed and another forty-eight injured.

Less than five days before polling day, this presented all the parties with a difficult decision about the right way to respond: terrorism could not be allowed to prevent the country going to the polls with a fully contested election. This time, it was agreed that there would be only a pause in national campaigning, while local activists could continue to deliver leaflets.

Even that agreement lasted less than twenty-four hours. The evening after the attack, Corbyn delivered a speech in Carlisle, attacking May's record as Home Secretary and cuts to police numbers. Many in government thought that politicising the terrorist attack was contemptible – but linking security to austerity was an effective way of flipping what had been expected to be a difficult topic for Labour. (It was not until his failure to condemn Russia for the Salisbury poisonings in 2018 that many voters hardened their views on the threat Corbyn posed to national security.) Somehow the Conservatives, led by the longest-serving Home Secretary for sixty-five years, were on the back foot.

The Conservatives were certainly on the back foot when it came to the ground campaign. While the Tory campaign machine was left cowed after a police investigation and a series of scandals involving its 2015 'battle bus', the groundswell which had propelled Jeremy Corbyn to the leadership of the Labour Party – and then defended him against a leadership challenge in the summer of 2016 – meant that Labour candidates could draw on the well-organised and energetic campaigners of Momentum. Gavin Barwell, who lost his marginal seat of Croydon Central despite a well-organised local campaign, says his 200-strong team of supporters on polling day were outnumbered by more than three to one. (Registered as a non-party campaigner, meaning its expenditure could be counted separately from Labour's, Momentum was subsequently fined £16,700 by the Electoral Commission, which concluded that it had committed a number of offences.)

I began polling day with a 'dawn raid' of leaflets in Tynemouth and helped to 'get out the vote' until an early evening train back to London. I had planned to be in Conservative Central Office for the exit poll, but delays on the East Coast Main Line meant I pulled into King's Cross just in time to watch it on my mobile telephone from the platform. I went home and watched the rest of the coverage from my kitchen table, nursing a single bottle of beer. I went into Central Office just before 7 a.m. – where the party's excellent treasurer (and soon-to-be chief executive), Sir Mick Davis, was already stepping into the breach with great calm and good sense – then on to No. 10, where I stayed until the Prime Minister's last day in office 775 days later.

In general elections, all that matters is how many seats you win. Theresa May's Conservatives gained twenty but lost thirty-three – and, with it, our majority in Parliament. That crushing disappointment masked a number of frustrating successes. Our vote held firm throughout the campaign – only dropping 0.5 points from start to finish. More than 2.3 million more people voted Conservative than at the previous election – the largest increase for a governing party since 1832. We secured the highest Tory vote share since 1983, gained twelve new MPs in Scotland (six of them coming from third place) and our highest vote share in Wales for a century. In many ways, the story of the election was the hoovering-up of other votes by Labour, who achieved their biggest polling shift during a campaign since 1945. The Conservatives did not see it coming because we were sending our activists to targeted households based on a model developed by Jim Messina, an American Democrat who had brought success to David Cameron's 2015 campaign (but less to his campaign in the 2016 EU referendum). Again, Theresa May should have trusted her instincts and insisted on the campaigning style she prefers – knocking on everyone's door and trusting campaigners who know the mood of their local area.

With an effective Labour squeeze, the Liberal Democrats lost a record 375 deposits – 60 per cent of all the candidates they fielded – and were wiped out entirely in Wales. Their former leader and Deputy Prime Minister, Sir Nick Clegg, lost his seat – as did the former SNP leader and First Minister, Alex Salmond. All of this amounted to a vote share for the two main parties of 82.5 per cent across the UK – the highest since 1970 (and all the more remarkable a statistic given the SNP's dominance in Scotland).

How did Labour confound expectations to do so well? In part, because Jeremy Corbyn was not viewed as a particular threat – many people did not think he could win but did want to clip the wings of a Conservative Party which looked like it had called an election to seize a landslide, then had failed to persuade the electorate that it deserved it. Above all, this was not a Brexit election. Despite the Prime Minister's opening speech, the mandate of the referendum was not perceived to be at risk – and she had little of substance to add about how she would deliver it before negotiations began. Quite understandably, many electors assumed their 2016 decision would be honoured. Some

4 million Leave voters did not turn out in the election twelve months later – an absence which the pollster Peter Kellner estimates cost the Conservatives thirty seats. For those who did cast a vote, their focus shifted to other topics – austerity, tuition fees, social care, the NHS and other issues raised during the long election campaign. Rather than repeating themselves, most voters prefer to cast their minds forward when given the opportunity – echoing the American pop star whose name will forever be sadly linked to the 2017 election when she sang 'Thank U, Next'.

Theresa May's speech at the Conservative Party conference four months after the election was overshadowed by things which were – and weren't – supposed to be onstage with her. But its opening passage began with an acknowledgement of the shortcomings of her campaign and an apology for them:

> We did not get the victory we wanted because our national campaign fell short.
>
> It was too scripted. Too presidential. And it allowed the Labour Party to paint us as the voice of continuity, when the public wanted to hear a message of change.
>
> I hold my hands up for that. I take responsibility. I led the campaign. And I am sorry.

She had come close – she was eight seats short of a majority, and there were ten where the Conservative candidate had lost by a majority of less than 1 per cent. Just fifty-one people voting differently in the four seats the Tories lost by under thirty votes would have given her a majority. The party chairman, Sir Patrick McLoughlin, thinks a campaign just one week shorter would have done the same.

So was Theresa May wrong to call the 2017 election? She was not the first Prime Minister to call an election sooner than needed and to fall short: Harold Wilson and Ted Heath had done so in 1970 and 1974 – and both ended up out of Downing Street as a result. There had been no dissent to the proposition at the Cabinet meeting May held on 18 April. There would have had to have been an election before the Brexit process was complete – and given the margins by which the government went on to lose key votes during it, its lack of majority seems rather by the by. Some argued valiantly that the election had established some broad parameters – securing a mandate to leave the single market and customs union, in a way the referendum had not explicitly done. But the Prime Minister found herself in a precarious position and marooned in a hung parliament which was keener to rule things out than to reach a compromise. By 2019, she led the only party which was committed to leaving the European Union on the basis of a deal – a shocking narrowing of the options offered to the British public (and the logic for fielding Conservative candidates in the European elections held, to widespread frustration, that summer).

While the 2017 election made Theresa May's central mission as Prime Minister – to deliver Brexit – harder, the Tories' good results in Scotland helped to see off calls for a second independence referendum. She won her party its highest ever vote share among skilled working-class (C2) voters – doing slightly better among them than with middle-class voters, in fact. A changing Conservative vote delivered victories in Walsall North, Stoke-on-Trent South and North East Derbyshire for the first time in generations – and in Mansfield for the first time ever. The tectonic plates were still shifting a year later in the 2018 local elections, when the Conservative vote held up, and the party gained control of a number of councils. But, of course, it was not until after the impasse of 2019 – when the existential threat to Brexit was evident, the instruction to get it done had to be restated and the dangers posed by Jeremy Corbyn all too sadly demonstrated – that the dramatic rupture was achieved. We had been on to something.

Stephen Parkinson, Lord Parkinson of Whitley Bay, served as special adviser to Theresa May as Home Secretary (2012–15) and as political secretary to her as Prime Minister (2016–19). He is chairman of the Conservative History Group.

50

2019

TIM BALE

Dissolution: 6 November 2019
Polling day: 12 December 2019
Seats contested: 650
Total electorate / Voted / Turnout: 47,568,611 / 32,014,110 / 67.3 per cent
Candidates (total 3,220): Conservative – 635; Labour – 631; Liberal Democrats – 611; Green – 494; Brexit – 275; SNP – 59; UKIP – 44; Plaid Cymru – 36; Alliance – 18; DUP – 17; SDLP – 15; Sinn Féin – 15
Prime Minister on polling day: Boris Johnson
Main party leaders: Conservative – Boris Johnson; Labour – Jeremy Corbyn; Liberal Democrats – Jo Swinson; Green – Siân Berry; Brexit Party – Nigel Farage; SNP – Nicola Sturgeon; Plaid Cymru – Adam Price; DUP – Arlene Foster; Sinn Féin – Mary Lou McDonald; SDLP – Colum Eastwood; Alliance – Naomi Long

Party performance:

Party	Votes	Percentage share	Seats
Conservative	13,966,454	43.6	365
Labour	10,269,051	32.1	202
Liberal Democrats	3,696,419	11.6	11
SNP	1,242,380	3.9	48
Green	835,597	2.6	1
Brexit Party	644,257	2	0
DUP	244,128	30.6	8

Sinn Féin	181,853	22.8	7
Plaid Cymru	153,265	0.5	4
Alliance	134,115	16.8	1
SDLP	118,737	14.9	2

Result: Conservative majority of eighty seats

The countdown to the 2019 general election effectively began as soon as ballots were counted in 2017. Rather than increasing the unexpected (but uncomfortably narrow) majority won by David Cameron two years before, Theresa May had somehow managed to throw it away. The Conservatives would now have to govern as a minority, dependent for confidence and supply on Northern Ireland's Democratic Unionist Party. Although few Tory MPs said it publicly – at least to begin with – that meant May was living on borrowed time, highly unlikely to lead them into the next election unless by some miracle she could negotiate a Withdrawal Agreement with the European Union that would satisfy the party's Brexit ultras, especially those MPs belonging to the self-styled European Research Group (ERG). Since May had no intention of 'reaching across the aisle' to obtain opposition support for a deal which would, to all intents and purposes, see the UK remain in a customs union with the EU for the foreseeable future, the ERG was now able to block any arrangement that, in their view, did not constitute a truly 'clean break' from Brussels – which for some of the most hardline members of the group actually meant a 'no-deal Brexit'.

Realising that May (who had unwittingly encouraged such thinking by earlier warning the EU that 'no deal is better than a bad deal') was never going to be able to satisfy them on that score, Boris Johnson seized his chance to resign as Foreign Secretary in the summer of 2018, the better to mount a campaign to replace her as leader. That campaign – waged through the pages of the Tory-supporting press, through broadcast media interviews and via high-profile appearances at the party conference that autumn – eventually came to fruition a year later. Having survived a confidence vote triggered by her Brexit ultras, May was unable to come even close to securing a majority for her Withdrawal Agreement, and, after leading the party to its heaviest defeat in a national contest for well over a century (winning just 9 per cent in the European Parliament elections held on 23 May), she stepped down. Desperate to find someone, anyone, who might stand a chance of pulling the party out of its nosedive, Conservative MPs set aside the serious reservations many of them had about Johnson and voted him into the final two candidates put before its grass-roots members. Numbering just 159,000 (or just 0.3 per cent of the electorate as a whole), they duly awarded him the leadership – and therefore the premiership – by a convincing two-thirds to one-third victory over Jeremy Hunt.

From that moment on, Johnson and his advisers (principally Vote Leave mastermind Dominic Cummings and the party's Australian campaign manager Isaac Levido) worked towards engineering an early election, doing everything they could to show that Johnson was determined to get the UK out of the EU come what may and that he was only prevented from doing so by a 'Remainer Parliament' supposedly hell-bent on stopping Brexit. The fact that Johnson was prepared to (as it turned out, unlawfully) prorogue Parliament and expel (in some cases permanently) twenty-one of his own MPs from the parliamentary Conservative Party only served to show, they hoped, that he meant business.

The calling of the general election of 2019 was far from straightforward. Under the Fixed-term Parliaments Act (FTPA), an early election required two-thirds of MPs to vote for a resolution that would permit one or else a vote of no confidence in the government, which (unless superseded by a vote of confidence in the meantime) would trigger a contest fourteen days after its passage. Prime Minister Boris Johnson had tried and failed on two occasions to meet the first criteria thanks to the determination of the majority of MPs to rule out any possibility of a no-deal Brexit. When, however, the government announced on 17 October that it had at last managed to negotiate a Withdrawal Agreement with the European Union (which then agreed an extension of the date on which the UK was supposed to leave that effectively took no-deal off the table), their objections finally fell away.

Labour MPs had, of course, to pretend that they couldn't wait for a general election to get rid of a Tory government. In private, however, they were less than enthusiastic. True, in 2017, the party had managed to narrow the Conservatives' poll lead to almost nothing over the course of the campaign. But Johnson was a far more impressive campaigner than Theresa May, while the shine had long come off Jeremy Corbyn, especially in the wake of accusations of antisemitism and his handling of the Salisbury nerve-agent attack in March 2018. Moreover, Labour MPs were well aware that many of their own constituents were either pro-Brexit or just wanted the whole thing over with. However, they were essentially bounced into agreeing to an early contest by the Liberal Democrats and the Scottish National Party (SNP), both parties apparently hoping that an election, as well as seeing Remain voters flocking to them rather than to the more equivocal Labour Party, might offer them one last chance to actually stop Brexit.

So it was that Parliament passed the Early Parliamentary General Election Act of 2019, which circumvented the FTPA and required only a simple majority, over the course of just two days. The contest was set for 12 December (the first to take place in that month since 1923), the assumption on the Tory side being that, should they win it, they would be able to use their majority to obtain parliamentary approval for Johnson's Withdrawal Agreement in short order, allowing the UK to formally leave the EU by 31 January. There was no dissension within the Cabinet about the decision, nor the date: not only did ministers support leaving; they also agreed with Conservative strategists that (in marked contrast to 2017) the party would now have no difficulty in persuading voters of the need for a contest, the purpose of which could be easily communicated to a frustrated electorate – namely, in the words of their new mantra, to 'Get Brexit Done'.

The Conservatives were well aware that they had made a mess of the 2017 campaign. Theresa May was hardly the ideal politician to front a presidential pitch to the electorate, but she wasn't the only problem back then. The party's pre-election research had suggested that the election might not be the slam-dunk to which its headline polling lead seemed to point – in part because voters weren't persuaded that a contest was really necessary. Then there was a manifesto, drafted to provide a mandate for potentially unpopular policies on the assumption that victory was basically in the bag. And, finally, there was confusion at the very heart of the campaign as to who was ultimately in charge, while the party, both at CCHQ and in constituencies up and down the country, was caught as much by surprise as the rest of the nation by May's announcement. What constituency canvassing had been done (and in some seats the Tories were hoping to win, there was none) was badly out of date, increasing dependence on 'big data' assembled centrally that proved an unreliable guide as to where the voters the party needed to mobilise were located. The party's IT wasn't as good as it should have been, which didn't help communication with local associations, many of which had already fallen out with CCHQ over its heavy-handed attempts to steer candidate selection. In the constituencies, local campaign organisers weren't necessarily in place or, if they were, not yet firmly bedded in. Some fairly basic campaign materials (including paper) were in short supply. And even if digital could make up for that, the party seemed to have lost its edge over Labour on social media.

The 2019 Conservative campaign was all about avoiding a recurrence of these problems. First and foremost, it was clear from the summer onward that, especially once the election was called, Cummings would step back, leaving Levido completely in charge of the party's campaign, with Michael Brooks working on opinion research and members of the consultancy firm Hanbury coming in to help with data analytics. This, and the fact that many organisers were already in place, meant that constituency targeting, as well as voter identification and contact, were significantly improved. The party also recruited New Zealand firm Topham Guerin to handle their digital campaign, which was much edgier and more fleet-footed and savvy as a result, directing resources towards buying myriad creative ads on platforms like YouTube and Google rather than towards Twitter and (the still admittedly important) Facebook. Candidate selection still caused some friction but was generally handled rather more sensitively this time round, while most of the party's IT problems had been ironed out. All in all, then, the Tories were more than ready to fight a campaign – one in which voters' worries about public services would be assuaged by making it clear that getting Brexit done would allow the government to focus, for instance, on building hospitals and recruiting more nurses and police officers. And this time around, they felt confident that their leader, as long as he could be kept on message, possessed the sheer force of personality and the stamina required to sell that message to the public over and over again.

Labour had also been gearing up for an early general election since the summer, fully expecting that Johnson would do his damnedest to engineer one while Labour's support among both Leave voters (who were flocking to the Tories) and Remain voters (many of whom seemed to be toying with the idea of voting Lib Dem) was falling. However, all was not well at Labour's Southside London HQ. Some of the big-ego staffers and advisers were barely talking to each other, and a hopelessly conflict-avoidant leader, Jeremy Corbyn, proved no more capable of knocking heads together than deciding whether it would be best (as some advised) to focus on shoring up support among Remainers or whether (as others were insisting) the emphasis should be on winning back Leave voters. As a result, the clear structure and management so crucial to successful campaigns just wasn't there, with Southside and LOTO (the Leader of the Opposition's office) not only failing to co-operate but often actively working to undermine each other. And this time it was Labour running into IT problems and failing to get its act together on constituency organisers in order to ensure that the latter were in place (if they were there at all) at the right time. The grass-roots pro-Corbyn movement, Momentum, still had a fair few members and at least some residual strength left; but there was no serious attempt to integrate it into the party's official effort, most of which, in the end, boiled down to trying to persuade voters to ignore Brexit and focus instead on what Labour would do to restore public services and, in particular, the NHS.

The Lib Dems weren't anywhere near as factionalised as Labour, but they were not without their problems. The relationship of their leader, Jo Swinson, with the party's HQ wasn't as smooth as it might have been and she therefore tended to rely on her inner circle. There were also tensions over a couple of key decisions made in the early autumn, when the party had benefited from widespread voter disillusionment with both Labour and the Conservatives. The first was to place Swinson herself front and centre of the campaign in spite of signs that voter opinion about her was mixed and a slide in the opinion polls that made a mockery of her claim that she could be Prime Minister. The second was to campaign not just on the attention-grabbing 'Bollocks to Brexit' message the party had been pushing for months but actually on revoking Article 50 – the UK's notification to the EU of its intention to leave. That commitment alienated even some Remainers, primarily on the grounds that it would be undemocratic to use Parliament, rather than another referendum, to undermine the decision voters came to in 2016. That may well have undone whatever good the party's move to forge a 'Unite to Remain' pact with the Greens and Plaid Cymru did – one that ended up covering sixty seats and which allowed forty-three Lib Dem candidates to stand without facing rivals from those parties. Worse, the party's polling in the summer had led it to decide that more constituencies were in play than was in fact the case, meaning that, ultimately, there was less focus and fewer resources put into those that (on a good day anyway) might actually have been up for grabs.

Although most of the attention during the early part of the campaign was focused on the Conservatives, Labour and the Liberal Democrats (and, north of the border, the Scottish National Party), one big question remained: now that it looked as if Brexit was finally going to happen for real, what was Nigel Farage and his Brexit Party (which had finished top in the summer's European Parliament election after winning nearly a third of the vote) going to do? The answer came in the second week of November, when Farage, who could see voters were deserting his party in droves for the Conservatives, declared he would not be standing candidates in Tory-held seats. This was a boon to the government, not so much because it otherwise feared losing some of those seats (it didn't) but because it sent a clear message that if a voter wanted out of the EU, then the high-priest of Brexit was – however much he might deny it – effectively telling them to vote Conservative. The downside was that, by continuing to stand candidates in constituencies which CCHQ was hoping to snatch from Labour, the Brexit Party might siphon off votes that a Tory candidate may well need to get them over the line in a tight race.

Johnson, however, had rather more immediate concerns – most obviously the criticism he was getting for not rushing up to the north of England to oversee the response to serious flooding, but also the news that waits in NHS accident and emergency departments were now the worst on record at a time when Labour was promising to inject a cool £26 billion into the system. On the other hand, CCHQ seemed to be doing a good job by rolling that promise into a whole bunch of what it asserted were multiple unfunded Labour giveaways to the tune of £1.2 trillion. Moreover, as Johnson made clear in the UK's first ever Conservative versus Labour head-to-head televised leaders' debate on 18 November, his re-election would see neither austerity nor profligacy: instead, more would be spent on public services post-Brexit, but it would be done wisely.

Johnson had agreed to the event so as to avoid being lambasted, as Theresa May had been, as being too scared to take part – probably the right decision because he emerged from it pretty much unscathed, with pollsters and journalists writing it up as a 'bore draw' with no obvious winner, while more excitement and controversy was generated by CCHQ temporarily rebranding itself as 'factcheckuk' for the evening than by the back and forth between the two leaders. Corbyn didn't, in truth, perform too badly, particularly as he hadn't taken as much time to practise as his team had wanted. But it was far from the kind of breakthrough that they'd hoped for and he had provoked only laughter from the studio audience when he claimed he'd made his position on Brexit (seen as the most important issue according to polls) clear. Nor, of course, did the debate compensate for the fact that the lack of communication within the Labour camp meant that a number of Corbyn's colleagues who appeared in other television shows were all too often finding themselves asked about announcements (some of them involving gigantic sums of money) to which they hadn't until that moment been privy.

The hope in the Labour camp was that any confusion would soon be cleared up by the release of the party's manifesto – and that the launch of the document would go better than it had for the Lib Dems. Their leader, Jo Swinson, had encountered a fair degree of scepticism about the idea that its costly promises on childcare and schools (among other things) could be paid for by the 'Remain bonus' that would come about as the result of the UK deciding to stay in the EU after all. Since Corbyn was promising only a referendum on a renegotiated deal, that particular magic money tree wasn't available to him when he launched Labour's offering in Birmingham. That didn't, however, prevent the party from presenting a document stuffed full of pledges on social, industrial and environmental policy that added up to hundreds of billions, most of which could supposedly be paid for by raising taxes on corporates and wealthy individuals. Sadly for Labour, polling suggested that, while the public liked the sound of some of the 'free stuff' the party was promising, they were highly dubious about where the money was going to come from to pay for it. The Conservative manifesto, launched a few days later, was relatively unexciting, even dull – quite deliberately so: the absolute priority of those writing (and 'bomb-proofing') it was to avoid a repeat of 2017 when a promise on social care (quickly branded 'the dementia tax' by the party's opponents) had helped to derail the Tory campaign. As a consequence, its pledges on the NHS, policing and even potholes totalled only around £3 billion – a figure that usefully provided maximum contrast with a supposedly spendthrift Labour opposition.

A couple of days before the Tory launch, Johnson had taken part in and essentially survived a BBC *Question Time* with Corbyn, the

SNP's Nicola Sturgeon and Jo Swinson. In fact, it was the latter who got the roughest ride, with the audience laying into her for her role in the 2010–15 coalition, for her pretensions to being Prime Minister and most of all for her promise to revoke Article 50. The Lib Dem leader didn't fare much better either during a grilling by the BBC's veteran inquisitor Andrew Neil. But it was Jeremy Corbyn's interview that was the real car crash, with Neil taking him to task (and, according to many observers, the cleaners) over spending, Brexit and his failure to apologise over antisemitism. Even worse for Labour, they were denied the pleasure of seeing the Prime Minister being given the same treatment, Johnson (perhaps wisely) deciding that the criticism he would get for pulling out of the interview was unlikely to be anything like as risky as turning up and doing it. Johnson (along with Nigel Farage) also declined to appear on a Channel 4 leaders' debate on climate change, leading to a row after the broadcaster refused to allow Cabinet minister Michael Gove to deputise, preferring instead to 'empty chair' the two missing leaders with ice sculptures.

An attempt by the opposition to change the narrative back to the NHS by producing leaked documents from US–UK trade talks that supposedly proved that, under Johnson, the NHS was 'on the table and … up for sale' admittedly did gain some traction, with polls beginning to show that Labour had at the very least bottomed out as voters began to focus more on the state of the health service. But it came too late to have any effect on the opinion poll that many commentators were really waiting for – a YouGov survey with a sample large enough to allow it to extrapolate its results (via a statistical technique called 'multiple regression with post-stratification', better known by its initials – MRP) to all the constituencies in Britain, so as to provide a snapshot of which party looked most likely to win where. And predictably enough, it made worrying reading for Labour, which, if the results were the same on polling day, was set to lose fifty-one seats while the Conservatives gained forty-two (many of them in Labour's so-called Red Wall in the north and the Midlands), giving them a majority of sixty-eight.

Both the 2016 EU referendum and the 2017 general election

campaigns had been interrupted by terrorist attacks, so it was shocking but not entirely surprising when, as November drew to a close, two young people were fatally stabbed in London Bridge by an Islamist terrorist who was then shot dead by police. In contrast to 2017, it was decided not to pause campaigning – a decision that saw Labour almost immediately try, as it had done fairly successfully two years previously, to link the attacks to cuts in policing and the security services. This time, however, the Tories wasted no time in hitting back by pointing to a decision by the last Labour government to extend early release to a wide range of prisoners – a policy that the Conservatives now promised to overturn when it came to anyone jailed for a terrorist offence. It wasn't pretty; but it was, it seemed, effective.

For CCHQ, then, yet another ghost of 2017 had been laid to rest. That did not necessarily mean, however, a smooth glide path to victory. After all, they still had a visit to London for the NATO summit by Donald Trump to worry about. In the event, they needn't have. For once, the President behaved himself: there was no off-colour banter and certainly no undermining of Johnson in the way that Trump had, on a previous visit, undermined Theresa May. More than that, he helpfully declared that the US wouldn't want the NHS even if it were handed to it on a silver platter. Possibly even more helpfully, he cancelled his final press conference so he could get home earlier than planned. As for the summit itself, it threw up no issues for the government, reflecting the fact that, not unusually in the UK, foreign and military affairs played little or no part in the election as a whole.

But even as Trump flew back to Washington, the Conservatives still couldn't breathe a final sigh of relief: the final Friday night of the campaign brought with it a second head-to-head televised debate with Corbyn; something could still go wrong. In the event, however, it didn't. Corbyn was as underprepared as he was for the first such event, having refused to alter his punishing (but ultimately unproductive) schedule of constituency visits to make time to rehearse, while Johnson stayed doggedly on message, matching each and every mention of the NHS and austerity by the Labour leader with an appeal to 'Get Brexit Done', so as to allow the government to increase investment in the country's public services. Perhaps not surprisingly, then, overnight polling suggested, once again, that viewers had seen little to choose between the two men – not, incidentally, something that could be said about voters: Johnson's personal ratings in the polls were consistently negative and got more so as the campaign continued, but they were nowhere near as bad as Corbyn's or, indeed (by the end of the campaign anyway), Swinson's.

Although it did little to shift the dial, one thing that final head-to-head debate did do, of course, was to emphasise to voters (at least in England if not in Scotland, Wales and Northern Ireland) that, ultimately, their choice of government came down to either the Conservatives or Labour – a stark reality that was always likely to see their smaller competitors struggle. And, with election day fast approaching, opinion polls were making this more and more obvious. The Liberal Democrats, for instance, were haemorrhaging support – mainly as a result of Remain voters holding their noses and either moving back to Labour or sticking with the Tories. Meanwhile, the air was going out of the Brexit Party's balloon as the bulk of those Leave voters who had loaned their vote to Nigel Farage in the summer were now falling in behind Boris Johnson, some of them perhaps swayed by the embarrassing announcement just a week before polling day by four of Farage's MEPs that they were resigning from his party and recommending people vote Conservative. Their decision, predictably enough, was greeted with approval in the country's Tory/Brexit-supporting newspapers, whose combined circulation far outweighed that of the Remain/Labour press and which did a bang-up job throughout the campaign of recycling CCHQ press releases and launching the kind of poisonous personal attacks on Corbyn that might have proved counterproductive had they come direct (as, to a greater extent, they had in 2017) from Conservative spokespeople.

Meanwhile, the party's decision to take a more creative approach to digital campaigning seemed to be bearing fruit. Topham Guerin's YouTube ad based on the film *Love Actually* was not only widely praised but widely watched, its reach probably amplified by (ultimately unfounded) allegations from Labour supporters that it had ripped off a similar clip by Labour candidate Rosena Allin-Khan. Within a few hours of its release, the Tory version had clocked up over half a million views on Twitter, and getting on for that on Facebook, picking up millions more from its broadcast on television and hundreds of thousands (possibly even millions) of pounds' worth of free advertising when it was picked up by the newspapers and their websites the next day. Moreover, by beginning with a shot of a (mixed-race) couple sitting on their sofa watching another Conservative advert, it may also have contributed to the 3.5 million views achieved by that earlier ad, too, although those numbers were also boosted by the small fortune CCHQ spent to get it onto the top banner of YouTube's homepage.

Much the same had already been done for a shorter YouTube ad ('Stop the Chaos. Get Brexit Done. Vote Conservative'), allowing it, too, to garner some 3 million views. Its evidently low production values were perfectly deliberate – and in some ways the point, the aim being to get people talking about it in order to extend its reach. The same could be said for CCHQ's 'lo-fi' 'Boriswave'. Apparently inspired by a craze for 'vaporwave' (chilled-out and repurposed electronica), lasting a whole seventy-one minutes and posted, once again, on YouTube, it put segments of Johnson's speeches together with a music track and footage of Johnson checking his notes while sat on a train, with the whole thing captioned 'beats to relax/get brexit done to'. CCHQ also did a fair bit of 'shitposting' – producing intentionally lame and superficially poorly executed ads and memes pushing the Get Brexit Done message with the aim of provoking the kind of millennial mockery that would, it was hoped, see them go viral.

True, Facebook metrics suggested that Labour content once again achieved more shares and views than its Conservative equivalent, particularly where the original source was Corbyn's rather than the party's page. But the Tories did significantly better on Google, where they had concentrated far more of their spend, and could argue (with some justification, perhaps) that, whereas Labour's product was shared among a narrower band of devoted followers, its output reached a wider, 'swing voter' audience. Ultimately, of course, it remains very difficult to judge whether buying, sharing and viewing social media – indeed any media – translates into additional support at the ballot box, not least because survey research suggests many voters either distrust or discount it. Parties, however, will continue to invest more and more resources in digital campaigning for fear that, if they don't, their opponents will steal a march on them as more traditional forms supposedly fall by the wayside.

The final week of the campaign for the Tories was essentially about Johnson hammering home the idea that a vote for them would end the 'dither and delay' over Brexit, all the while pretending, lest they be tempted to stay at home after reading polls that suggested the election was in the bag, that the contest was actually much closer than it looked. It was also about avoiding issues that didn't play so well for the party – which was why Johnson, when asked by Sky News political correspondent Joe Pike to look at some photos on his phone of a four-year-old forced to lie on the floor in A&E, panicked and popped Pike's mobile into his own pocket. Labour, however, couldn't be entirely happy with how things played out, since Johnson's bizarre reaction (as well as a wholly false claim that a protester outside the hospital had later that day thrown a punch at Health Secretary Matt Hancock's aide) threatened to overshadow the substance of the story. And, in any case, they were having to deal with the charge – one reignited during an event hosted by shadow Chancellor John McDonnell – that the party's policy on Brexit was an unconvincing mess given that he (and many of his colleagues) would clearly have preferred the UK to remain in the EU rather than exit via a Withdrawal Agreement renegotiated by a putative Labour government.

Things didn't get any better for Labour the next day when rightwing website Guido Fawkes released a covert recording of Labour's shadow Health Secretary Jonathan Ashworth making it clear to a Tory friend that the party's prospects were 'dire' because voters outside the country's main cities 'can't stand Corbyn and they think Labour's blocked Brexit'. As a result, he was forced to spend most of the day trying to laugh off the call rather than pressing home the attack on the NHS. Meanwhile, the Conservatives were staging what became the iconic stunt of the campaign by getting Johnson to drive a bulldozer bearing the slogan 'GET BREXIT DONE' through a wall of Styrofoam bricks stamped with the word 'GRIDLOCK'. Even the release of YouGov's final MRP poll later that evening was in some ways music to the ears of CCHQ: rather than showing the Conservatives romping home to an easy victory (as most private and public polling was doing), it suggested that the race was tightening, helping Tory candidates to persuade voters that, if they wanted Brexit rather than Corbyn, then they really would need to get down to the polling stations on Thursday.

There was, however, one day still to go – and it didn't begin that well for Johnson, who on live television, inexplicably, decided to try to avoid a reporter's question by taking refuge with his team in a walk-in refrigerated container, a clip then shared again and again on social media. Even then, however, there was an upside for the Conservatives since the story blew up sufficiently to eclipse Nigel Farage's last media appearance of the campaign. And anyway, Corbyn was having to cope that same day with the news that fifteen former Labour MPs were urging voters not to back him because of antisemitism, extremism and the danger he supposedly posed to national security. Even better, CCHQ managed to stage yet another iconic photo op involving Johnson supposedly baking a pie to symbolise his 'oven-ready' Brexit deal. Now all they had to do was to wait and see just how big the majority that most Conservatives were privately expecting would actually turn out to be.

The release of the broadcasters' exit poll at 10 p.m. on election night made it obvious that the Conservatives had, indeed, chalked up a huge win, suggesting as it did an 86-seat majority with Labour heading for one of its worst results since the drubbing Michael Foot had received at the hands of Margaret Thatcher in 1983. Once all the votes were counted, it turned out to be pretty much on the money, overstating the Tory majority by just six seats and underestimating Labour's seat haul by eleven; the Lib Dems eventually won eleven seats rather than the thirteen the exit poll had predicted and the SNP forty-eight rather than fifty-five – all in all, a good night for the statisticians and academics involved and certainly an even better one for the Conservatives than even many of them had dared hope for.

The result was, it should be said, also a good one for the pollsters, even if YouGov's MRP seat share exercise hadn't fared quite as well as it had in 2017. The average of the final polls conducted by thirteen companies understated the Tory vote share by just 1.5 points, while overstating Labour's by a mere 0.6 points and the Lib Dems' by a minuscule 0.2 points. Polling from start to finish had, in fact, suggested that the Conservatives were maintaining a fairly consistent eleven-point lead over Labour throughout. True, Labour improved its position over the course of the campaign, starting at just below 30 per cent and finishing just above it as the Lib Dems faded from the mid- to the low twenties. But this had little impact on the Tories, who, after starting just below 40 per cent, had risen to the mid-forties, picking up voters as the Brexit Party's support halved (from 10 per cent to 5 per cent) over the course of the campaign.

The eighty-seat majority won by the Conservatives, along with the fact that the party not only gained a swathe of seats in the Red Wall but also did exceptionally well among working-class voters, led many commentators to talk about a 'realignment' of British politics. Johnson, they claimed, had leveraged Brexit and the widespread antipathy towards an apparently unpatriotic, spendthrift Labour opposition to put together a novel, powerful and long-lasting electoral coalition. Onto the Tories' traditional base of well-heeled voters in the shires and wealthier suburbs, he had grafted a group of rather less affluent, sometimes less well-educated but similarly culturally conservative voters, most of whom lived in small towns across England – the part of the UK which so dwarfs all the others in terms of population and parliamentary representation that, even if Labour had managed to rescue its position in Scotland (which anyway it didn't), practically guarantees a Tory government when it turns blue.

The fact that it did turn blue clearly owed a lot to Brexit and to Johnson's success in clawing back Leave voters from Nigel Farage's latest vehicle: after all, the overwhelming majority of the

Conservatives' gains came in seats that backed Brexit in the 2016 referendum. Indeed, had Farage stood down all his candidates rather than only those in Tory-held constituencies, Johnson's parliamentary majority would have risen to just over 100. There are, however, two important caveats to all this.

Firstly, for all the praise showered upon Johnson as the key to victory by an adoring print media, it was the Conservative Party's strategy (and its ruthless execution of that strategy) which was ultimately responsible, not Johnson himself. In reality, the Prime Minister was far from being an especially popular politician: in fact, polling clearly shows that his favourability ratings in 2019 were lower than Theresa May's had been during the 2017 campaign. Admittedly, what limited popularity he enjoyed, he enjoyed among the right people. But, more importantly in the end, he was fortunate to be fighting a Leader of the Opposition who, by 2019, was generating even more hostility from key groups of voters than he had back then. Johnson also benefited from the fact that many of those voters were well into middle and old age – indeed, age, along with education (and ethnicity), turned out to be one of the best predictors of vote choice in 2019. That meant that those voters were not only more likely to be registered to vote in the first place but also significantly more likely to make the effort to actually pop down to the polling station or to use their postal votes than their younger counterparts.

Secondly, 'getting Brexit done' was, as it were, only the half of it. It was no less crucial to the Conservatives' appeal that they were promising to do that in order to be able to move on to tackle voters' more prosaic priorities – namely, getting the economy growing faster and fixing public services, focusing in particular on those areas previously 'left behind' by London and the south-east (a policy labelled 'levelling up.'). Johnson, in putting together his post-election Cabinet, insisted that this – along with negotiating a post-Brexit trade and co-operation agreement with Brussels (eventually signed in December 2020) – was indeed his priority. Perhaps as a consequence, and as a consequence of his tendency to value personal loyalty over intrinsic merit, there were relatively few changes at the top: Priti Patel, the combative right-wing populist, remained at the Home Office while Sajid Javid, a symbol of fiscal rectitude, stayed as Chancellor (until that is, his principled refusal a few weeks later to co-operate fully with Dominic Cummings's desire to exert No. 10's control over No. 11 saw him resign, to be replaced by Rishi Sunak); Dominic Raab, another combative right-wing populist, continued as de facto Deputy Prime Minister and Foreign Secretary, and born-again Brexiteer Liz Truss remained responsible for working on the trade deals that would supposedly make leaving the EU worthwhile.

Unfortunately for Johnson, however, Covid (plus, his critics would say, the fact that he had neither the interest nor the inclination to develop a serious plan to deliver on his promises) saw to it that there was precious little progress made on any of his pledges. Meanwhile, the resignation of Jeremy Corbyn as Labour leader, and his eventual replacement by the seemingly more electable Keir Starmer, ensured that Johnson, especially after he ran into trouble over 'Partygate' and the economy faltered still further, never came close to chalking up the ten years in power that many of his admirers were freely predicting in the immediate aftermath of the election. Within just eighteen months of polling day, he was replaced as Prime Minister, first by Truss and then Sunak – the man who would presumably lead the party into the 2024 election.

As for the longer term, while it is undeniable that catering to the preferences of older, more Eurosceptic, culturally conservative and not especially well-educated voters paid off handsomely in 2019, it arguably came at a cost. To head off the threat from an authoritarian, anti-European insurgency on their right flank, the Tories had to adopt, more or less willingly, a rhetoric and, on occasion, policies pinched pretty much direct from that selfsame insurgency. In so doing, they arguably came to sound and, indeed, behave more like a populist radical right party than a traditional mainstream, centre-right outfit. This was by no means unusual: many Continental European parties hitherto assumed to be conventionally conservative (fiscally responsible, market-friendly and only moderately nationalist) have felt obliged to go the same way. But such a strategy is not without risk in the long term — not when a significant proportion of those whose economic good fortune might incline them to the Conservative Party are well-educated people with open, tolerant and relatively pro-European worldviews to match; and not in a country which, like it or not, is becoming more multicultural and more socially liberal with each passing year. That a party famous for its ability to adapt to the spirit of the age will eventually realise that presumably isn't in doubt. How long it might take to do so, however, is another matter entirely.

Tim Bale teaches politics at Queen Mary University of London. He has written several books on British and European politics, the latest of which is *The Conservative Party after Brexit: Turmoil and Transformation*. He posts on Twitter/X as @ProfTimBale and his media writing is collected at proftimbale.com.

HOW CANDIDATES CAMPAIGN IN MODERN-DAY GENERAL ELECTIONS

SOFIA COLLIGNON AND WOLFGANG RÜDIG

Electoral campaigning in Britain has seen some major changes over the past fifty years. A central element to this has been the change in the media outlets that could be used by candidates and parties. For many years, the shift of focus from personal contacts with voters via hustings, rallies and canvassing to mass media campaigns dominated the discussion of electoral politics. This was followed by the rise of technical innovations such as the use of computer programs to target voters with campaign messages via the telephone and direct mail. These techniques were often seen as part of an increasing 'professionalisation' of electoral campaigning supported by the use of political consultants. This process also appeared to be linked to an increasing centralisation of campaigning, with national parties seeking to take a greater level of control over communication to ensure that candidates remained 'on message'.

This 'professionalisation' of election campaigning appeared to reduce the role of individual candidates to being local messengers of national campaigns designed by party headquarters. However, this view was increasingly challenged. Empirical studies of local campaigning efforts demonstrated that the constituency-related campaigns of individual candidates did have a significant, if small, effect on electoral performance. The 'ground war' thus seems to matter. Beyond this, the dominance of the national party was challenged by the idea of an increase in 'personalised' campaigning in which individual candidates emphasised their own issues, for example issues of particular importance in the constituency, and campaigned to highlight their personal qualities. Some candidates might also be more or less faithful to the national campaign and even disagree with some policies of their parties in order to garner a personal vote.

A new platform for the possible conflict between election campaigns run by central party bureaucracies and personalised campaigns designed by individual candidates was created with the rise of social media. While initial analyses emphasised the new opportunities offered by social media, the practical role of online campaigning remained uncertain. A more critical view of the politics of social media emphasised its role in promoting a more divisive and uncivil political culture.

One aspect was the rise of harassment and intimidation of election candidates and elected representatives. While candidates may have experienced various forms of harassment during campaigning activities before, social media allows a variety of threats to be made against politicians by anonymous users. Certainly by the late 2010s, harassment and intimidation of candidates had become a major issue with potential effects on how candidates behaved during their campaigns. How have these developments manifested themselves in Britain?

While there is limited evidence on the character of election campaigns from the perspective of election candidates over recent decades, a series of surveys of candidates standing in UK general elections since 2010 allows us to analyse the changing nature of campaigning over the past four general elections. The surveys asked all candidates who stood in these elections identical questions facilitating the comparison over time. This allows us to answer: how important are conventional modes of campaigning such as canvassing, leafleting and local hustings in comparison with online campaigning, including writing blogs and using Twitter and Facebook to communicate with voters? Has campaigning become more 'personalised', with candidates emphasising their own political positions and characteristics? Finally, what effect has the harassment of candidates had on the way in which they are campaigning?

To begin, how do candidates engage with traditional campaign activities such as canvassing, leafleting, debating with rival candidates and public speeches? And to what extent have these modes of campaigning been challenged by the rise of online politics? Traditional media, including television, radio, newspapers and direct mail, have long been the primary means of reaching a broad audience in political campaigns. New media encompasses digital and online platforms, including social media and websites, and has gained prominence in recent years. New media campaigns present some advantages as they can be more cost-effective, reaching wider audiences but also allowing microtargeting. But they also present some challenges related to the spread of misinformation and the risk of them being contained in filter bubbles where they are unlikely to persuade new voters to support the party.

Our results suggest that leafleting and canvassing remain the most important means of campaigning in the perception of candidates who stood in the 2015, 2017 and 2019 general elections. This, in particular, applies to the major parties whose candidates regard these campaign methods as the most important. They also spent the most time on them. More than 90 per cent of Conservative candidates were involved in canvassing, and more than 50 per cent of them spent more than twenty hours per week on canvassing in the last month of the campaign. Labour, Plaid Cymru and SNP candidates also consistently prioritised canvassing activities. Liberal Democrat candidates spent slightly less time on canvassing, and Green and UKIP candidates considered canvassing less important. Apart from most of their candidates not having a realistic chance of being elected, differences in resources between parties may also play a role here.

Leafleting continues to be regarded as an important activity. We can observe a slight decline since 2010 when more than 90 per cent of candidates spent time leafleting to 83 per cent in 2015, 78 per cent in 2017 and 82 per cent in 2019. This decline was particularly pronounced for the Liberal Democrats, whose share of candidates spending time on leafleting declined from 92 per cent in 2010 to 71 per cent in 2015. Conservative Party candidates spent the most time leafleting, with an average of 40 per cent devoting more than twenty hours per week to leafleting in the last month of the campaign.

Compared with canvassing and leafleting, other traditional forms of campaigning are seen as less important. Most candidates are involved in debates with their opponents, with a slight decline from 2015 to 2019 (92 per cent in 2015, 85 per cent in 2017 and 83 per cent in 2019). The 'snap election' character of the 2017 and 2019 elections may have given less time to organise debates between candidates. There are significant differences between parties in the importance given to these debates. Most Conservative candidates consider them not to be particularly important, with on average just 15 per cent of Conservatives considering them to be very important compared with 45 per cent of Green candidates. Hustings thus offer smaller parties a welcome resource to challenge the major party candidates.

Participation in public speeches and rallies appears to be in decline for most parties. In 2015, 44 per cent of candidates were not involved in speeches and rallies at all. This rose to 56 per cent in 2017 but fell slightly to 50 per cent in 2019. Only Labour candidates consider this way of campaigning to be of great significance, with 16 per cent in 2015 regarding it as very important, rising to 23 per cent in 2019.

Most candidates engage in traditional media activities like interviews and press releases. Contrary to what is suggested sometimes about the decline of traditional media campaigns, the engagement of candidates on such activities has remained constant over time. Overall, 71 per cent of candidates did interviews and press releases and considered them to be important campaign activities.

How does the rise of online campaigning compare with the use of traditional techniques? The use of Facebook and Twitter has become increasingly important. In 2020, 35 per cent of candidates used Twitter and 55 per cent used social media such as Facebook in their election campaign. By 2015, this had risen to 76 per cent and 74 per cent, respectively. In 2017 and 2019, the use stabilised at a fairly high level at 85 per cent and 87 per cent for social media use including Facebook and 76 per cent and 83 per cent for the use of Twitter. The 2017 and 2019 elections also saw a significant rise in the perception of the importance of social media: in 2019, 37 per cent of candidates considered social media very important, in 2017 it was 41 per cent but in 2015, only 24 per cent had rated social media that important. However, despite this high level of perceived importance, candidates spent relatively little time campaigning on social media. The vast majority of candidates spent less than five hours per week in the month before election day on social media.

Looking at differences between parties, the Conservatives, Labour, Plaid Cymru and the SNP have embraced social media fairly extensively, with the Lib Dems and Greens lagging a bit behind. Least enthusiastic have been UKIP candidates. Only 15 per cent of UKIP candidates had used Twitter in 2010, rising to 57 per cent in 2015.

While Facebook and Twitter thus have been frequently used, other forms of online campaigning have not made much of an impact. In 2010, a third of candidates used a blog as a campaign means. By 2015, this had risen to 40 per cent before falling back to 33 per cent in 2017 and 29 per cent in 2019. Only 6 per cent of candidates considered blogging to be a very important campaign tool.

One form of online electoral activity that has seen a relative decline is personal websites. In 2010, almost two-thirds of candidates, 64 per cent, stated that they had a webpage largely designed and maintained by their local campaign. By 2015, the share of candidates with a personal website increased slightly to 69 per cent but fell back to 62 per cent in 2017 and further to 59 per cent in 2019. Just 15 per cent considered personal websites to be very important. Other possible online tools such as instant messaging systems like WhatsApp had not made a major impact by 2019, with 64 per cent not using these systems for campaigning and just 10 per cent considering them to be very important.

The overall picture is thus that most candidates are using social media in their campaigning but spend relatively little time on it. Compared with traditional campaigning tools like canvassing and leafleting, candidates on average regard online campaigning tools to be less important.

This is also reflected in the perception of candidates of the importance of different ways of campaigning for their electoral performance. Asked to rate the effectiveness of a range of campaigning activities to maximise a party's constituency vote on a scale of one (not at all effective) to five (extremely effective) in both 2015 and 2017, candidates considered door-to-door canvassing (mean score of 3.52) and leafleting (3.37) to be most effective. This was followed by media appearances (3.04) and internet campaigning (3.01), with public meetings (2.84) and telephone canvassing (2.65) being the least important campaign means.

There are small differences between the parties. Conservatives who do the most leafleting consider this activity to be the most effective, a view shared by UKIP candidates. Labour, Lib Dem, Plaid Cymru and SNP candidates think canvassing is the most effective. The Greens think media appearances are the most important element for electoral success. Internet campaigning is rated the most highly by SNP candidates and is considered the least effective by Conservative candidates.

Have recent general elections in the UK seen a rise in personalised campaigning? One aspect of personalised campaigning is the relative focus on a candidate's own personal qualities in contrast to support of a political party. The rise of online campaigning methods could provide new opportunities to candidates to run more personalised campaigns. We asked candidates in all surveys to rate their campaign focus on a scale of zero to ten, with 'zero' indicating that the main aim was to 'attract as much attention to me as a candidate' and 'ten' meaning to 'attract as much attention as possible to my party'.

Overall, we did not find a clear change over time. For all parties, the mean score increased slightly from 5.48 in 2010 to 5.75 in 2015, 5.72 in 2017 and 5.63 in 2019. For most parties, there was a high level of stability over time. The Conservatives, Labour and the SNP had the largest number of candidates who tended to focus more on their personal qualities rather than support for the party. Green Party and UKIP candidates were the least likely to adopt a personalised campaigning focus.

Comparative research has suggested that candidate visibility is an important predictor of personalised campaigning. All three main parties would enter elections with a large number of incumbent MPs whose higher visibility might encourage them to draw more attention to their personal qualities. This effect is nicely demonstrated by a change in campaign focus of SNP candidates which was more firmly focused on supporting the party in 2010 and 2015 (5.62 and 6.27) but then moved to a greater level of personal campaigning after the 2015 SNP landslide, with means of 4.13 and 4.59 on this scale for the 2017 and 2019 elections.

The only other case of a significant change over time can be observed for the Conservatives, whose candidates in 2010 and 2015 tended to opt for a more personalised campaign (4.08 and 4.39) but then moved closer to a party focus in 2017 and 2019 (5.61 and 5.20). This might suggest a stronger tendency of Conservative candidates to draw attention to their party in the political environment following the Brexit referendum.

The issue of the security threats to and harassment and intimidation of election candidates and MPs became a major issue in the late 2010s, particularly following the murder of the MP Jo Cox in 2016. The 2017 survey for the first time asked candidates about any forms of harassment they had experienced during the campaign. Overall, 38 per cent of candidates reported some form of harassment. The same question was asked again in the 2019 candidate survey and this time 49 per cent of candidates reported harassment.

It is difficult to assess the historical development of the harassment problem before 2017 as candidates were not surveyed about this issue. However, there was a survey of security threats experienced by MPs in 2010 which suggests that the problem is not entirely new. While some of the harassment experienced by candidates in the late 2010s was not dissimilar to that of MPs in 2010, the new element was the social media factor. Most of the harassment, abuse and intimidation experienced by candidates was communicated via social media, with 29 per cent of 2017 and 44 per cent of 2019 candidates suffering in this way.

This then raises the question of whether harassment, either as a result of personal experience or in anticipation of possible inappropriate behaviour that candidates might fear they could be exposed to, has an effect on how candidates behave during an election. Do they take steps to limit the chance of being the subject of harassment, and how frequent is this behaviour? In the 2019 candidate survey, we asked candidates: 'Which, if any, of the following things have you done during the 2019 General Election campaign for reasons of personal security?' The results were as follows: 11 per cent of candidates carried a personal safety alarm to protect themselves; 12 per cent avoided going to political meetings or rallies; 18 per cent avoided canvassing voters; and 30 per cent avoided using online media, like Twitter. A further 29 per cent took a variety of other measures.

A total of 54 per cent of candidates took at least one measure to protect their personal security. Candidates of the major parties – Conservative, Labour and SNP – as well as Brexit Party candidates were the most likely to take such measures. Green Party candidates were the least likely to modify their behaviour. These results suggest very strongly that harassment, intimidation and threats to security have an important impact on election campaigns in the UK.

These effects of harassment may not be limited to behaviour in a specific election campaign but may have a more long-lasting and profound impact on political careers and the future behaviour of candidates. In a detailed analysis of 2017 and 2019 data, we tried to explore what effect harassment experienced by candidates in the 2017 general election had on their future behaviour. Were candidates who were harassed in 2017 more likely to drop out of politics? If they stood again in 2019, did they behave differently in the election campaign?

The results of our analysis showed that while candidates experiencing harassment did not necessarily drop out of politics altogether, they changed their campaigning behaviour significantly. Harassed candidates were more likely to reduce their canvassing activities in 2019, thus potentially damaging their electoral chances. As women and younger candidates were more likely to be harassed than men and older candidates, harassment imposes further obstacles for the political advancement of candidates based on their gender and age. Harassment thus has an important effect on campaigning and, indirectly, also on electoral outcomes.

The UK general elections of the 2010s involved both traditional and novel ways of campaigning. In addition to leafleting and canvassing voters, the rise of social media has broadened the spectrum of campaigning activity. The effect of social media has, however, not been as revolutionary as some observers had been expecting. Candidates still regard leafleting and particularly canvassing, making direct contact with voters, as the most effective campaigning methods. Candidates spend more time on these traditional activities than on any other campaigning means. Most candidates engage in at least one form of online campaigning, such as being active on Facebook or Twitter, but this activity has not come to dominate campaigning. It is an addition to the range of options, and most candidates engage but few think that it is of decisive importance.

Social media also was expected to increase the possibility of candidates to opt for more personalised styles of campaigning, drawing more attention to their personal qualities. The evidence here also does not support the idea of a major change of behaviour. Candidates with a high visibility, such as incumbent MPs, are more likely to engage in more personalised campaigning, but there is no apparent link to the increased use of social media.

The main impact that the rise of social media appears to have had on campaigning in the UK concerns the issues of harassment, abuse, intimidation and security threats which many candidates are exposed to. Social media is a major vehicle for such electoral violence to be disseminated to candidates. This has important effects on how candidates behave. There is evidence that candidates who experience harassment in one election are likely to change their campaigning behaviour in subsequent elections, in particular limiting their use of canvassing which is likely to have an adverse effect on their electoral chances.

Dr Sofia Collignon is a senior lecturer in comparative politics in the School of Politics and International Relations at Queen Mary University of London. Her research focuses on the experiences, careers, trajectories and motivations of election candidates. She possesses extensive expertise in the causes and consequences of gendered violence against political elites.

Dr Wolfgang Rüdig is a reader in politics in the Department of Government and Public Policy at the University of Strathclyde. His main research interest is the empirical study of political behaviour including protest, party members and election candidates.